Bayesian Modeling and Computation in Python

CHAPMAN & HALL/CRC
Texts in Statistical Science Series
Joseph K. Blitzstein, *Harvard University, USA*
Julian J. Faraway, *University of Bath, UK*
Martin Tanner, *Northwestern University, USA*
Jim Zidek, *University of British Columbia, Canada*

Recently Published Titles

A First Course in Linear Model Theory, Second Edition
Nalini Ravishanker, Zhiyi Chi, Dipak K. Dey

Foundations of Statistics for Data Scientists
With R and Python
Alan Agresti and Maria Kateri

Fundamentals of Causal Inference
With R
Babette A. Brumback

Sampling
Design and Analysis, Third Edition
Sharon L. Lohr

Theory of Statistical Inference
Anthony Almudevar

Probability, Statistics, and Data
A Fresh Approach Using R
Darrin Speegle and Brain Claire

Bayesian Modeling and Computation in Python
Osvaldo A. Martin, Ravin Kumar and Junpeng Lao

Bayes Rules!
An Introduction to Applied Bayesian Modeling
Alicia Johnson, Miles Ott and Mine Dogucu

Stochastic Processes with R
An Introduction
Olga Korosteleva

Introduction to Design and Analysis of Scientific Studies
Nathan Taback

Practical Time Series Analysis for Data Science
Wayne A. Woodward, Bivin Philip Sadler and Stephen Robertson

**For more information about this series, please visit: https://www.routledge.com/
Chapman--HallCRC-Texts-in-Statistical-Science/book-series/CHTEXSTASCI**

Bayesian Modeling and Computation in Python

Osvaldo A. Martin, Ravin Kumar and Junpeng Lao

CRC Press
Taylor & Francis Group
Boca Raton London New York

CRC Press is an imprint of the
Taylor & Francis Group, an **informa** business

A CHAPMAN & HALL BOOK

First edition published 2022
by CRC Press
6000 Broken Sound Parkway NW, Suite 300, Boca Raton, FL 33487-2742

and by CRC Press
2 Park Square, Milton Park, Abingdon, Oxon, OX14 4RN

CRC Press is an imprint of Taylor & Francis Group, LLC

ISBN: 978-0-367-89436-8 (hbk)
ISBN: 978-1-032-18029-8 (pbk)
ISBN: 978-1-003-01916-9 (ebk)

DOI: 10.1201/9781003019169

Publisher's note: This book has been prepared from camera-ready copy provided by the authors.

Typeset in CMR10
by KnowledgeWorks Global Ltd.

To Romina and Abril, and their caring love. To everyone who helped me get here.

Osvaldo Martin

To the educators, both formal and informal, who unconditionally shared their knowledge and wisdom making me who I am today. In order of appearance in my life, Tim Pegg, Mr. Michael Collins, Mrs. Sara LaFramboise Saadeh, Professor Mehrdad Haghi, Professor Winny Dong, Professor Dixon Davis, Jason Errington, Chris Lopez, John Norman, Professor Ananth Krishnamurthy, and Kurt Campbell.
Thank you

Ravin Kumar

To Yuli.

Junpeng Lao

Contents

Foreword   xiii

Preface   xv

Symbols   xxi

1 Bayesian Inference   **1**
  1.1   Bayesian Modeling   1
   1.1.1   Bayesian Models   2
   1.1.2   Bayesian Inference   3
  1.2   A DIY Sampler, Do Not Try This at Home   6
  1.3   Say Yes to Automating Inference, Say No to Automated Model Building   .   10
  1.4   A Few Options to Quantify Your Prior Information   13
   1.4.1   Conjugate Priors   15
   1.4.2   Objective Priors   18
   1.4.3   Maximum Entropy Priors   20
   1.4.4   Weakly Informative Priors and Regularization Priors   23
   1.4.5   Using Prior Predictive Distributions to Assess Priors   25
  1.5   Exercises   25

2 Exploratory Analysis of Bayesian Models   **31**
  2.1   There is Life After Inference, and Before Too!   31
  2.2   Understanding Your Assumptions   32
  2.3   Understanding Your Predictions   35
  2.4   Diagnosing Numerical Inference   40
   2.4.1   Effective Sample Size   41
   2.4.2   Potential Scale Reduction Factor $\hat{R}$ 43
   2.4.3   Monte Carlo Standard Error   43
   2.4.4   Trace Plots   45
   2.4.5   Autocorrelation Plots   46
   2.4.6   Rank Plots   46
   2.4.7   Divergences   48
   2.4.8   Sampler Parameters and Other Diagnostics   51
  2.5   Model Comparison   52
   2.5.1   Cross-validation and LOO   53
   2.5.2   Expected Log Predictive Density   56
   2.5.3   Pareto Shape Parameter, $\hat{\kappa}$ 57
   2.5.4   Interpreting p_loo When Pareto $\hat{\kappa}$ is Large   58
   2.5.5   LOO-PIT   59
   2.5.6   Model Averaging   60
  2.6   Exercises   61

3 Linear Models and Probabilistic Programming Languages   **67**

3.1   Comparing Two (or More) Groups 67

     3.1.1   Comparing Two PPLs 72

3.2   Linear Regression 77

     3.2.1   Linear Penguins 78

     3.2.2   Predictions 81

     3.2.3   Centering 83

3.3   Multiple Linear Regression 85

     3.3.1   Counterfactuals 88

3.4   Generalized Linear Models 90

     3.4.1   Logistic Regression 91

     3.4.2   Classifying Penguins 92

     3.4.3   Interpreting Log Odds 98

3.5   Picking Priors in Regression Models 100

3.6   Exercises 104

4 Extending Linear Models   **107**

4.1   Transforming Covariates 107

4.2   Varying Uncertainty 110

4.3   Interaction Effects 112

4.4   Robust Regression 114

4.5   Pooling, Multilevel Models, and Mixed Effects 119

     4.5.1   Unpooled Parameters 119

     4.5.2   Pooled Parameters 122

     4.5.3   Mixing Group and Common Parameters 125

4.6   Hierarchical Models 126

     4.6.1   Posterior Geometry Matters 131

     4.6.2   Predictions at Multiple Levels 137

     4.6.3   Priors for Multilevel Models 140

4.7   Exercises 140

5 Splines   **145**

5.1   Polynomial Regression 145

5.2   Expanding the Feature Space 146

5.3   Introducing Splines 148

5.4   Building the Design Matrix using Patsy 152

5.5   Fitting Splines in PyMC3 154

5.6   Choosing Knots and Prior for Splines 157

     5.6.1   Regularizing Prior for Splines 158

5.7   Modeling CO_2 Uptake with Splines 160

5.8   Exercises 164

6 Time Series   **169**

6.1   An Overview of Time Series Problems 169

6.2   Time Series Analysis as a Regression Problem 170

     6.2.1   Design Matrices for Time Series 175

     6.2.2   Basis Functions and Generalized Additive Model 178

6.3   Autoregressive Models 181

     6.3.1   Latent AR Process and Smoothing 187

     6.3.2   (S)AR(I)MA(X) 189

6.4   State Space Models 193

		6.4.1	Linear Gaussian State Space Models and Kalman filter	195
		6.4.2	ARIMA, Expressed as a State Space Model	198
		6.4.3	Bayesian Structural Time Series	202
	6.5	Other Time Series Models		206
	6.6	Model Criticism and Choosing Priors		206
		6.6.1	Priors for Time Series Models	207
	6.7	Exercises		208

7   Bayesian Additive Regression Trees   **213**

	7.1	Decision Trees		213
		7.1.1	Ensembles of Decision Trees	216
	7.2	The BART Model		217
	7.3	Priors for BART		217
		7.3.1	Prior Independence	218
		7.3.2	Prior for the Tree Structure $\mathcal{T}_j$	218
		7.3.3	Prior for the Leaf Values μ_{ij} and Number of Trees m	218
	7.4	Fitting Bayesian Additive Regression Trees		218
	7.5	BART Bikes		219
	7.6	Generalized BART Models		221
	7.7	Interpretability of BARTs		222
		7.7.1	Partial Dependence Plots	223
		7.7.2	Individual Conditional Expectation	225
	7.8	Variable Selection		226
	7.9	Priors for BART in PyMC3		229
	7.10	Exercises		230

8   Approximate Bayesian Computation   **233**

	8.1	Life Beyond Likelihood		233
	8.2	Approximating the Approximated Posterior		235
	8.3	Fitting a Gaussian the ABC-way		235
	8.4	Choosing the Distance Function, ϵ and the Summary Statistics		238
		8.4.1	Choosing the Distance	239
		8.4.2	Choosing ϵ	240
		8.4.3	Choosing Summary Statistics	241
	8.5	g-and-k Distribution		243
	8.6	Approximating Moving Averages		247
	8.7	Model Comparison in the ABC Context		249
		8.7.1	Marginal Likelihood and LOO	250
		8.7.2	Model Choice via Random Forest	254
		8.7.3	Model Choice for MA Model	256
	8.8	Choosing Priors for ABC		257
	8.9	Exercises		258

9   End to End Bayesian Workflows   **261**

	9.1	Workflows, Contexts, and Questions		261
		9.1.1	Applied Example: Airlines Flight Delays Problem	263
	9.2	Getting Data		264
		9.2.1	Sample Surveys	264
		9.2.2	Experimental Design	264
		9.2.3	Observational Studies	265
		9.2.4	Missing Data	265

9.2.5   Applied Example: Collecting Airline Flight Delays Data   265
9.3   Making a Model and Probably More Than One   266
9.3.1   Questions to Ask Before Building a Bayesian Model   266
9.3.2   Applied Example: Picking Flight Delay Likelihoods   267
9.4   Choosing Priors and Predictive Priors   269
9.4.1   Applied Example: Picking Priors for Flight Delays Model   270
9.5   Inference and Inference Diagnostics   271
9.5.1   Applied Example: Running Inference on Flight Delays Models   271
9.6   Posterior Plots   272
9.6.1   Applied Example: Posterior of Flight Delays Models   272
9.7   Evaluating Posterior Predictive Distributions   273
9.7.1   Applied Example: Posterior Predictive Distributions of Flight Delays   274
9.8   Model Comparison   275
9.8.1   Applied Example: Model Comparison with LOO of Flight Delays . .   275
9.9   Reward Functions and Decisions   277
9.9.1   Applied Example: Making Decisions Based on Flight Delays Modeling
Results   278
9.10   Sharing the Results With a Particular Audience   280
9.10.1   Reproducibility of Analysis Workflow   280
9.10.2   Understanding the Audience   283
9.10.3   Static Visual Aids   283
9.10.4   Reproducible Computing Environments   285
9.10.5   Applied Example: Presenting Flight Delay Conclusions   285
9.11   Experimental Example: Comparing Between Two Groups   286
9.12   Exercises   290

10 Probabilistic Programming Languages   **293**
10.1   A Systems Engineering Perspective of a PPL   293
10.1.1   Example: Rainier   294
10.2   Posterior Computation   294
10.2.1   Getting the Gradient   295
10.2.2   Example: Near Real Time Inference   297
10.3   Application Programming Interfaces   298
10.3.1   Example: Stan and Slicstan   299
10.3.2   Example: PyMC3 and PyMC4   300
10.4   PPL Driven Transformations   301
10.4.1   Log Probabilities   301
10.4.2   Random Variables and Distributions Transformations   303
10.4.3   Example: Sampling Comparison between Bounded and Unbounded
Random Variables   304
10.5   Operation Graphs and Automatic Reparameterization   305
10.6   Effect handling   309
10.6.1   Example: Effect Handling in TFP and Numpyro   309
10.7   Base Language, Code Ecosystem, Modularity and Everything Else   311
10.8   Designing a PPL   312
10.8.1   Shape Handling in PPLs   317
10.9   Takeaways for the Applied Bayesian Practitioner   320
10.10   Exercises   320

11 Appendiceal Topics **323**
  11.1 Probability Background 323
    11.1.1 Probability 324
    11.1.2 Conditional Probability 326
    11.1.3 Probability Distribution 327
    11.1.4 Discrete Random Variables and Distributions 328
    11.1.5 Continuous Random Variables and Distributions 332
    11.1.6 Joint, Conditional and Marginal Distributions 337
    11.1.7 Probability Integral Transform (PIT) 339
    11.1.8 Expectations 341
    11.1.9 Transformations 344
    11.1.10 Limits 345
    11.1.11 Markov Chains 347
  11.2 Entropy 350
  11.3 Kullback-Leibler Divergence 353
  11.4 Information Criterion 354
  11.5 LOO in Depth 356
  11.6 Jeffreys' Prior Derivation 358
    11.6.1 Jeffreys' Prior for the Binomial Likelihood in Terms of θ 358
    11.6.2 Jeffreys' Prior for the Binomial Likelihood in Terms of κ 359
    11.6.3 Jeffreys' Posterior for the Binomial Likelihood 361
  11.7 Marginal Likelihood 361
    11.7.1 The Harmonic Mean Estimator 361
    11.7.2 Marginal Likelihood and Model Comparison 362
    11.7.3 Bayes Factor vs WAIC and LOO 364
  11.8 Moving out of Flatland 366
  11.9 Inference Methods 369
    11.9.1 Grid Method 369
    11.9.2 Metropolis-Hastings 370
    11.9.3 Hamiltonian Monte Carlo 372
    11.9.4 Sequential Monte Carlo 377
    11.9.5 Variational Inference 378
  11.10 Programming References 379
    11.10.1 Which Programming Language? 380
    11.10.2 Version Control 381
    11.10.3 Dependency Management and Package Repositories 381
    11.10.4 Environment Management 381
    11.10.5 Text Editor vs Integrated Development Environment vs Notebook . 381
    11.10.6 The Specific Tools Used for this Book 382

Glossary **383**

Bibliography **387**

Index **397**

Foreword

Bayesian modeling provides an elegant approach to many data science and decision-making problems. However, it can be hard to make it work well in practice. In particular, although there are many software packages that make it easy to specify complex hierarchical models – such as Stan, PyMC3, TensorFlow Probability (TFP), and Pyro – users still need additional tools to diagnose whether the results of their computations are correct or not. They may also need advice on what to do when things do go wrong.

This book focuses on the ArviZ library, which enables users to perform exploratory analysis of Bayesian models, for example, diagnostics of posterior samples generated by any inference method. This can be used to diagnose a variety of failure modes in Bayesian inference. The book also discusses various modeling strategies (such as centering) that can be employed to eliminate many of the most common problems. Most of the examples in the book use PyMC3, although some also use TFP; a brief comparison of other probabilistic programming languages is also included.

The authors are all experts in the area of Bayesian software and are major contributors to the PyMC3, ArviZ, and TFP libraries. They also have significant experience applying Bayesian data analysis in practice, and this is reflected in the practical approach adopted in this book. Overall, I think this is a valuable addition to the literature, which should hopefully further the adoption of Bayesian methods.

Kevin P. Murphy

Preface

The name Bayesian statistics is attributed to Thomas Bayes (1702–1761), a Presbyterian minister, and amateur mathematician, who for the first time derived what we now know as Bayes' theorem, which was published (posthumously) in 1763. However, one of the first people to really develop Bayesian methods was Pierre-Simon Laplace (1749–1827), so perhaps it would be a bit more correct to talk about Laplacian Statistics. Nevertheless, we will honor Stigler's law of eponymy and also stick to tradition and keep talking about Bayesian approaches for the rest of this book. From the pioneering days of Bayes and Laplace (and many others) to the present day, a lot has happened – new ideas were developed, many of which were motivated and or being enabled by computers. The intent of this book is to provide a modern perspective on the subject, from the fundamentals in order to build a solid foundation into the application of a modern Bayesian workflow and tooling.

We write this book to help beginner Bayesian practitioners to become intermediate modelers. We do not claim this will automatically happen after you finish reading this book, but we hope the book can guide you in a fruitful direction specially if you read it thoroughly, do the exercises, apply the ideas in the book to your own problems and continue to learn from others.

Specifically stated this book targets the Bayesian practitioners who are interested in applying Bayesian models to solve data analysis problems. Often times a distinction is made between academia and industry. This book makes no such distinction, as it will be equally useful for a student in a university as it is for a machine learning engineer at a company.

It is our intent that upon completion of this book you will not only be familiar with **Bayesian Inference** but also feel comfortable performing **Exploratory Analysis of Bayesian Models**, including model comparison, diagnostics, evaluation and communication of the results. It is also our intent to teach all this from a modern and computational perspective. For us, Bayesian statistics is better understood and applied if we take a **computational** approach, this means, for example, that we care more about empirically checking how our assumptions are violated than trying to prove assumptions to be right. This also means we use many visualizations (if we do not do more is to avoid having a 1000 pages book). Other implications of the modeling approach will become clear as we progress through the pages.

Finally, as stated in the book's title, we use the Python programming language in this book. More specifically, we will mainly focus on PyMC3 [138] and TensorFlow Probability (TFP) [47], as the main probabilistic programming languages (PPLs) for model building and inference, and use ArviZ as the main library for exploratory analysis of Bayesian models [91]. We do not intend to give an exhaustive survey and comparison of all Python PPLs in this book, as there are many choices, and they rapidly evolve. We instead focus on the practical aspects of Bayesian analysis. Programming languages and libraries are merely bridges to get where we want to go.

Even though our programming language of choice for this book is Python, with few selected libraries, the statistical and modeling concepts we cover are language and library agnostic and available in many computer programming languages such as R, Julia, and

Scala among others. A motivated reader with knowledge of these languages but not Python can still benefit from reading the book, especially if they find the suitable packages that support, or code, the equivalent functionality in their language of choice to gain hands on practice. Furthermore, the authors encourage others to translate the code examples in this work to other languages or frameworks. Please get in touch if you like to do so.

Prior knowledge

As we write this book to help beginners to become intermediate practitioners, we assume prior exposure, but not mastery, of the basic ideas from Bayesian statistics such as priors, likelihoods and posteriors as well as some basic statistical concepts like random variables, probability distributions, expectations. For those of you that are a little bit rusty, we provide a whole section inside Chapter 11, Appendiceal Topics, with a refresher about basic statistical concepts. A couple of good books explaining these concepts in more depth are Understanding Advanced Statistical Methods [158] and Introduction to Probability [21]. The latter is a little bit more theoretical, but both keep application in mind.

If you have a good understanding of statistics, either by practice or formal training, but you have never being exposed to Bayesian statistics, you may still use this book as an introduction to the subject, the pace at the start (mostly the first two chapters) will be a bit rapid, and may require a couple read troughs.

We expect you to be familiar with some mathematical concepts like integrals, derivatives, and properties of logarithms. The level of writing will be the one generally taught at a technical high school or maybe the first year of college in science, technology, engineering, and mathematics careers. For those who need a refresher of such mathematical concepts we recommend the series of videos from 3Blue1Brown [1]. We will not ask you to solve many mathematical exercises instead, we will primarily ask you to use code and an interactive computing environment to understand and solve problems. Mathematical formulas throughout the text are used only when they help to provide a better understanding of Bayesian statistical modeling.

This book assumes that the reader comes with some knowledge of scientific computer programming. Using the Python language we will also use a number of specialized packages, in particular Probabilistic Programming Languages. It will help, but is not necessary, to have fit at least one model in a Probabilistic Programming language prior to reading this book. For a reference on Python, or how to setup the computation environment needed for this book, go to README.md in Github to understand how to setup a code environment

How to read this book

We will use toy models to understand important concepts without the data obscuring the main concepts and then use real datasets to approximate real practical problems such as sampling issues, reparametrization, prior/posterior calibration, etc. We encourage you to run these models in an interactive code environment while reading the book.

---

[1] https://www.youtube.com/channel/UCYO_jab_esuFRV4b17AJtAw, we recommend these videos even if you do not need a refresher.

We strongly encourage you to read and use the online documentation for the various libraries. While we do our best to keep this book self-contained, there is an extensive amount of documentation on these tools online and referring it will aid in both learning this book, as well as utilizing the tools on your own.

Chapter 1 offers a refresher or a quick introduction to the basic and central notions in Bayesian inference. The concepts from this chapter are revisited and applied in the rest of the book.

Chapter 2 offers an introduction to Exploratory Analysis of Bayesian models. Namely introduces many of the concepts that are part of the Bayesian workflow but are not inference itself. We apply and revisit the concepts from this chapter in the rest of the book.

Chapter 3 is the first chapter dedicated to a specific model architecture. It offers an introduction to Linear Regression models and establishes the basic groundwork for the next 5 chapters. Chapter 3 also fully introduces the primary probabilistic programming languages used in the book, PyMC3 and TensorFlow Probability.

Chapter 4 extends Linear Regression models and discusses more advanced topics like robust regression, hierarchical models and model reparametrization. This chapter uses PyMC3 and TensorFlow Probability.

Chapter 5 introduces basis functions and in particular splines as an extension to linear models that allows us to build more flexible models. This chapter uses PyMC3.

Chapter 6 focuses on time series models, from modeling time series as a regression to more complex model like ARIMA and linear Gaussian State Space model. This chapter uses TensorFlow Probability.

Chapter 7 offers an introduction to Bayesian additive regression trees a non-parametric model. We discuss the interpretability of this model and variable importance. This Chapter use PyMC3.

Chapter 8 brings the attention to the Approximate Bayesian Computation (ABC) framework, which is useful for problems where we do not have an explicit formulation for the likelihood. This chapter uses PyMC3.

Chapter 9 gives an overview of end-to-end Bayesian workflows. It showcases both an observational study in a business setting and an experimental study in a research setting. This chapter uses PyMC3.

Chapter 10 provides a deep dive on Probabilistic Programming Languages. Various different Probabilistic Programming languages are shown in this chapter.

Chapter 11 serves as a support when reading other chapters, as the topics inside it are loosely related to each other, and you may not want to read linearly.

Text Highlights

Text in this book will be emphasized with **bold** or *italics*. **Bold text** will highlight new concepts or emphasis of a concept. *Italic text* will indicate a colloquial or non-rigorous expression. When a specific code is mentioned they are also highlighted: `pymc3.sample`.

Code

Blocks of code in the book are marked by a shaded box with the lines numbers on the left.
And are referenced using the chapter number followed by the number of the Code Block.
For example:

Code 0.1

```
1  for i in range(3):
2      print(i**2)
```

```
0
1
4
```

Every time you see a code block look for a result. Often times it is a figure, a number, code output, or a table. Conversely most figures in the book have
an associated code block, sometimes we omit code blocks in the book to save
space, but you can still access them at the GitHub repository `https://github.com/`
`BayesianModelingandComputationInPython`. The repository also includes additional material for some exercises. The notebooks in that repository may also include additional
figures, code, or outputs not seen in the book, but that were used to develop the models
seen in the book. Also included in GitHub are instructions for how to create a standard
computation environment on whatever equipment you have.

Boxes

We use boxes to provide a quick reference for statistical, mathematical, or (Python) Programming concepts that are important for you to know. We also provide references for you
to continue learning about the topic.

Central Limit Theorem

In probability theory, the central limit theorem establishes that, in some situations,
when independent random variables are added, their properly normalized sum tends
toward a normal distribution even if the original variables themselves are not normally distributed.
Let $X_1, X_2, X_3, \ldots$ be i.i.d. with mean μ and standard deviation σ. As $n \to \infty$, we
got:

$$\sqrt{n}\left(\frac{\bar{X} - \mu}{\sigma}\right) \xrightarrow{\text{d}} \mathcal{N}(0, 1)$$

The book Introduction to Probability [21] is a good resource for learning many
theoretical aspects of probability that are useful in practice.

Code Imports

In this book we use the following conventions when importing Python packages.

Code 0.2

```
1  # Basic
2  import numpy as np
3  from scipy import stats
4  import pandas as pd
5  from patsy import bs, dmatrix
6  import matplotlib.pyplot as plt
7
8  # Exploratory Analysis of Bayesian Models
9  import arviz as az
10
11 # Probabilistic programming languages
12 import bambi as bmb
13 import pymc3 as pm
14 import tensorflow_probability as tfp
15
16 tfd = tfp.distributions
17
18 # Computational Backend
19 import theano
20 import theano.tensor as tt
21 import tensorflow as tf
```

We also use the ArviZ style `az.style.use("arviz-grayscale")`

How to interact with this book

As our audience is not a *Bayesian reader*, but a Bayesian practitioner. We will be providing the materials to practice Bayesian inference and exploratory analysis of Bayesian models. As leveraging computation and code is a core skill required for modern Bayesian practitioners, we will provide you with examples that can be played around with to build intuition over many tries. Our expectation is that the code in this book is read, executed, modified by the reader, and executed again many times. We can only show so many examples in this book, but you can make an infinite amount of examples for yourself using your computer. This way you learn not only the statistical concepts, but how to use your computer to generate value from those concepts.

Computers will also remove you from the limitations of printed text, for example lack of colors, lack of animation, and side-by-side comparisons. Modern Bayesian practitioners leverage the flexibility afforded by monitors and quick computational "double checks" and we have specifically created our examples to allow for the same level of interactivity. We have included exercises to test your learning and extra practice at the end of each chapter as well. Exercises are labeled Easy (E), Medium (M), and Hard (H). Solutions are available on request.

Acknowledgments

We are grateful to our friends and colleagues that have been kind enough to provide their time and energy to read early drafts and propose and provide useful feedback that helps us to improve the book and also helps us to fix many bugs in the book. Thank you:

Oriol Abril-Pla, Alex Andorra, Paul Anzel, Dan Becker, Tomás Capretto, Allen Downey, Christopher Fonnesbeck, Meenal Jhajharia, Will Kurt, Asael Matamoros, Kevin Murphy, and Aki Vehtari.

Symbols

Symbol	Description
$\log(x)$	Natural logarithm of x
$\mathbb{R}$	Real numbers
$\mathbb{R}^n$	n-dimensional vector space of real numbers
$\mathcal{A}, \mathcal{S}$	Sets
$x \in A$	Set membership. x is an element of the set A
$\mathbb{1}_A$	Indicator function. Returns 1 if $x \in A$ and 0 otherwise
$a \propto b$	a is proportional to b
$a \stackrel{\propto}{\sim} b$	a is approximately proportional to b
$a \approx b$	a is approximately equal to b
a, c, α, γ	Scalars are lowercase
$\mathbf{x}, \mathbf{y}$	Vectors are bold lowercase, thus we write a column vector as $\mathbf{x} = [x_1, \ldots, x_n]^T$
$\mathbf{X}, \mathbf{Y}$	Matrices are bold uppercase
X, Y	Random variables are specified as upper case Roman letters
x, y	Outcomes from random variables are generally specified as lower case roman letters
$\boldsymbol{X}, \boldsymbol{Y}$	Random vectors are in uppercase slanted bold font, $\boldsymbol{X} = [X_1, \ldots, X_n]^T$
$\boldsymbol{\theta}$	Greek lowercase characters are generally used for model parameters. Notice, that as we are Bayesians parameters are generally considered random variables
$\hat{\theta}$	Point estimate of $\boldsymbol{\theta}$
$\mathbb{E}_X[X]$	Expectation of X with respect to X, most often than not this is abbreviated as $\mathbb{E}[X]$
$\mathbb{V}_X[X]$	Variance of X with respect to X, most often than not this is abbreviated as $\mathbb{V}[X]$
$X \sim p$	Random variable X is distributed as p
$p(\cdot)$	Probability density or probability mass function
$p(y \mid \boldsymbol{x})$	Probability (density) of y given $\boldsymbol{x}$. This is the short form for $p(Y = y \mid \boldsymbol{X} = \boldsymbol{x})$
$f(x)$	An arbitrary function of x
$f(\boldsymbol{X}; \theta, \gamma)$	f is a function of $\boldsymbol{X}$ with parameters θ and γ. We use this notation to highlight that $\boldsymbol{X}$ is the data we pass to a function or model and θ and γ are parameters
$\mathcal{N}(\mu, \sigma)$	A Gaussian (or normal) distribution with mean μ and standard deviation σ
$\mathcal{HN}(\sigma)$	A Half-Gaussian (or half-normal) distribution with standard deviation σ
$\text{Beta}(\alpha, \beta)$	Beta distribution with shape parameters α, β
$\text{Expo}(\lambda)$	An Exponential distribution with rate parameter λ
$\mathcal{U}(a, b)$	A Uniform distribution with lower boundary a and upper boundary b
$\text{T}(\nu, \mu, \sigma)$	A Student's t-distribution with grade of normality ν (also known as degrees of freedom), location parameter μ (the mean when $\nu > 1$), scale parameter σ (the standard deviation as $\lim_{\nu \to \infty}$).
$\mathcal{HT}(\nu\sigma)$	A Half Student's t-distribution with and grade of normality ν (also known as degrees of freedom) and scale parameter σ
$\text{Cauchy}(\alpha, \beta)$	Cauchy distribution with location parameters α and scale parameter β

$\mathcal{H}\mathrm{C}(\beta)$	Half-Cauchy distribution with scale parameter β
$\mathrm{Laplace}(\mu, \tau)$	Laplace distribution with mean μ and scale τ
$\mathrm{Bin}(n, p)$	Binomial distribution with trials n and success p
$\mathrm{Pois}(\mu)$	Poisson distribution with mean (and variance) μ
$\mathrm{NB}(\mu, \alpha)$	Negative Binomial distribution with Poisson parameter μ and Gamma distribution parameter α
$\mathcal{G}RW(\mu, \sigma)$	Gaussian random walk distribution with innovation drift μ and innovation standard deviation σ
$\mathbb{KL}(p \parallel q)$	Kullback-Leibler divergence from p to q

1

Bayesian Inference

Modern Bayesian statistics is mostly performed using computer code. This has dramatically changed how Bayesian statistics was performed from even a few decades ago. The complexity of models we can build has increased, and the barrier of necessary mathematical and computational skills has been lowered. Additionally, the iterative modeling process has become, in many aspects, much easier to perform and more relevant than ever. The popularization of very powerful computer methods is really great but also demands an increased level of responsibility. Even if expressing statistical methods is easier than ever, statistics is a field full of subtleties that do not magically disappear by using powerful computational methods. Therefore having a good background about theoretical aspects, especially those relevant in practice, is extremely useful to effectively apply statistical methods. In this first chapter, we introduce these concepts and methods, many, which will be further explored and expanded throughout the rest of the book.

1.1 Bayesian Modeling

A conceptual model is a representation of a system, made of the composition of concepts that are used to help people know, understand, or simulate the object or process the model represents [39]. Additionally, models are human-designed representations with very specific goals in mind. As such, it is generally more convenient to talk about the adequacy of the model to a given problem than its intrinsic correctness. Models exist solely as an aid to a further goal.

When designing a new car, a car company makes a physical model to help others understand how the product will look when it is built. In this case, a sculptor with prior knowledge of cars, and a good estimate of how the model will be used, takes a supply of raw material such as clay, uses hand tools to sculpt a physical model. This physical model can help inform others about various aspects of the design, such as whether the appearance is aesthetically pleasing, or if the shape of the car is aerodynamic. It takes a combination of domain expertise and sculpting expertise to achieve a useful result. The modeling process often requires building more than one model, either to explore different options or because the models are iteratively improved and expanded as a result of the interaction with other members of the car development team. These days it is also common that in addition to a physical car model, there is a digital model built-in Computer-Aided Design software. This computer model has some advantages over a physical one. It is simpler and cheaper to use for digital for crash simulations versus testing on physical cars. It is also easier to share this model with colleagues in different offices.

These same ideas are relevant in Bayesian modeling. Building a model requires a combination of domain expertise and statistical skill to incorporate knowledge into some computable objectives and determine the usefulness of the result. Data is the raw material, and statistical distributions are the main mathematical tools to shape the statistical model. It

DOI: 10.1201/9781003019169-1

1

takes a combination of domain expertise and statistical expertise to achieve a useful result. Bayesian practitioners also build more than one model in an iterative fashion, the first of which is primarily useful for the practitioner themselves to identify gaps in their thinking, or shortcomings in their models. These first sets of models are then used to build subsequent improved and expanded models. Additionally, the use of one inference mechanism does not obviate the utility for all others, just as a physical model of a car does not obviate the utility of a digital model. In the same way, the modern Bayesian practitioner has many ways to express their ideas, generate results, and share the outputs, allowing a much wider distribution of positive outcomes for the practitioner and their peers.

1.1.1   Bayesian Models

Bayesian models, computational or otherwise, have two defining characteristics:

- Unknown quantities are described using probability distributions [1]. We call these quantities parameters [2].

- Bayes' theorem is used to update the values of the parameters conditioned on the data. We can also see this process as a reallocation of probabilities.

At a high-level we can describe the process of constructing Bayesian modeling in 3 steps.

1. Given some data and some assumptions on how this data could have been generated, we design a model by combining and transforming random variables.

2. We use Bayes' theorem to condition our models to the available data. We call this process **inference**, and as a result we obtain a posterior distribution. We hope the data reduces the uncertainty for possible parameter values, though this is not a guaranteed of any Bayesian model.

3. We criticize the model by checking whether the model makes sense according to different criteria, including the data and our expertise on the domain-knowledge. Because we generally are uncertain about the models themselves, we sometimes compare several models.

If you are familiar with other forms of modeling, you will recognize the importance of criticizing models and the necessity of performing these 3 steps iteratively. For example, we may need to retrace our steps at any given point. Perhaps we introduced a, silly, coding mistake, or after some challenges we found a way to improve the model, or we find that the data is not useful as we originally thought, and we need to collect more data or even a different kind of data.

Throughout this book we will discuss different ways to perform each of these 3 steps and we will learn about ways to expand them into a more complex **Bayesian workflow**. We consider this topic so important that we dedicated an entire Chapter 9 to revisit and rediscuss these ideas.

---

[1]If you want to be more general you can even say that everything is a probability distribution as a quantity you assume to know with arbitrary precision that can be described by a Dirac delta function.

[2]Some authors call these quantities latent variables and reserve the name parameter to identify fixed, but unknown, quantities.

1.1.2   Bayesian Inference

In colloquial terms, inference is associated with obtaining conclusions based on evidence and reasoning. Bayesian inference is a particular form of statistical inference based on combining probability distributions in order to obtain other probability distributions. Bayes' theorem provides us with a general recipe to estimate the value of the parameter $\boldsymbol{\theta}$ given that we have observed some data $\boldsymbol{Y}$:

$$
\underbrace{p(\boldsymbol{\theta} \mid \boldsymbol{Y})}_{\text{posterior}} = \frac{\overbrace{p(\boldsymbol{Y} \mid \boldsymbol{\theta})}^{\text{likelihood}} \overbrace{p(\boldsymbol{\theta})}^{\text{prior}}}{\underbrace{p(\boldsymbol{Y})}_{\text{marginal likelihood}}} \tag{1.1}
$$

The likelihood function links the observed data with the unknown parameters while the prior distribution represents the uncertainty [3] about the parameters before observing the data $\boldsymbol{Y}$. By multiplying them we obtain the posterior distribution, that is the joint distribution over all the parameters in the model (conditioned on the observed data). Figure 1.1 shows an example of an arbitrary prior, likelihood and the resulting posterior [4].

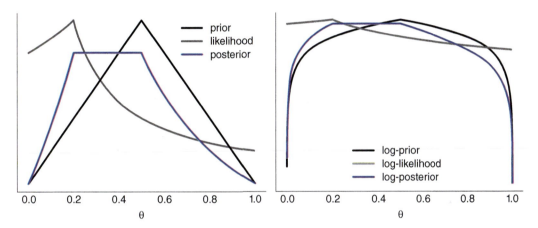

FIGURE 1.1
Left panel. A hypothetical prior indicating that the value $\theta = 0.5$ is more likely and the plausibility of the rest of the values decreases linearly and symmetrically (black). A likelihood showing that the value $\theta = 0.2$ is the one that better agrees with the hypothetical data (gray) and the resulting posterior (blue), a compromise between prior and likelihood. We have omitted the values of the y-axis to emphasize that we only care about relative values. Right panel, the same functions as in the left panel but the y-axis is in the log-scale. Notice that the information about relative values is preserved, for example, the location of the maxima and minima is the same in both panels. The log scale is preferred to perform calculations as computations are numerically more stable.

Notice that while $\boldsymbol{Y}$ is the observed data, it also is a random vector as its values depend on the results of a particular experiment [5]. In order to obtain a posterior distribution, we regard the data as fixed at the actual observed values. For this reason a common alternative notation is to use y_{obs}, instead of $\boldsymbol{Y}$.

---

[3] Alternatively you can think of this in terms of certainty or information, depending if you are a glass half empty or glass half full person.

[4] Sometimes the word *distribution* will be implicit, this commonly occurs when discussing these topics.

[5] Here we are using experiment in the broad sense of any procedure to collect or generate data.

As you can see evaluating the posterior at each specific *point* is conceptually simple, we just need to multiply a prior times a likelihood. However, that is not enough to inform us about the posterior, as we not only need the posterior probability at that specific *point*, but also in relation to the surrounding *points*. This *global* information of the posterior distribution is represented by the normalizing constant. Unfortunately, difficulties arise from the need to compute the normalizing constant $p(\boldsymbol{Y})$. This is easier to see if we write the marginal likelihood as:

$$p(\boldsymbol{Y}) = \int_{\boldsymbol{\Theta}} p(\boldsymbol{Y} \mid \boldsymbol{\theta}) p(\boldsymbol{\theta}) d\boldsymbol{\theta} \qquad (1.2)$$

where Θ means we are integrating over all the possible values of θ.

Computing integrals like this can be much harder than would first appear (see Section 11.7 and a funny XKCD comic [6]). Especially when we realize that for most problems a closed-form expression is not even available. Fortunately, there are numerical methods that can help us with this challenge if used properly. As the marginal likelihood is not generally computed, it is very common to see Bayes' theorem expressed as a proportionality:

$$\underbrace{p(\boldsymbol{\theta} \mid \boldsymbol{Y})}_{\text{posterior}} \propto \overbrace{p(\boldsymbol{Y} \mid \boldsymbol{\theta})}^{\text{likelihood}} \overbrace{p(\boldsymbol{\theta})}^{\text{prior}} \qquad (1.3)$$

A note on notation

In this book we use the same notation $p(\cdot)$ to represent different quantities, like a likelihood function and a prior probability distribution. This is a slightly abuse of notation but one we find useful. This notation provides the same epistemological status to all quantities. Additionally it reflects that even when the likelihood is not strictly a probability density function, we just do not care as we only think about the likelihood in the context of a prior and vice versa. In other words, we think of both quantities as equally necessary elements of models in order to compute a posterior distribution.

One nice feature of Bayesian statistics is that the posterior is (always) a distribution. This fact allows us to make probabilistic statements about the parameters, like the probability of a parameter τ being positive is 0.35. Or the most likely value of ϕ is 12 with a 50% chance of being between 10 and 15. Moreover, we can think of the posterior distribution as the logical consequence of combining a model with the data, and thus the probabilistic statements derived from them are guaranteed to be mathematically consistent. We just need to remember that all these nice mathematical properties are only valid in the *platonic world of ideas* where mathematical objects such as spheres, Gaussians and Markov chains exist. As we move from mathematical purity into the applied math messiness of the *real world* we must always keep in mind that our results are conditioned not only on the data but also on the models. Consequently, bad data and/or bad models could lead to nonsensical statements, even if they are mathematically consistent. We must always have a healthy quota of skepticism about our data, models, and results. To make this more explicit, we may want to express Bayes' theorem in a more nuanced way:

$$p(\boldsymbol{\theta} \mid \boldsymbol{Y}, M) \propto p(\boldsymbol{Y} \mid \boldsymbol{\theta}, M) \, p(\boldsymbol{\theta}, M) \qquad (1.4)$$

---

[6]https://xkcd.com/2117/

Emphasizing that our inferences are always dependent on the assumptions made by model M.

Having said that, once we have a posterior distribution we can use it to derive other quantities of interest. This is generally done by computing expectations, for example:

$$J = \int f(\boldsymbol{\theta}) \, p(\boldsymbol{\theta} \mid \boldsymbol{Y}) \, d\boldsymbol{\theta} \tag{1.5}$$

If f is the identity function J will turn out be the mean [7] of $\boldsymbol{\theta}$.:

$$\bar{\boldsymbol{\theta}} = \int_{\boldsymbol{\Theta}} \boldsymbol{\theta} p(\boldsymbol{\theta} \mid \boldsymbol{Y}) \, d\boldsymbol{\theta} \tag{1.6}$$

The posterior distribution is the central object in Bayesian statistics, but it is not the only one. Besides making inferences about parameter values, we may want to make inferences about data. This can be done by computing the **prior predictive distribution**:

$$p(\boldsymbol{Y}^*) = \int_{\boldsymbol{\Theta}} p(\boldsymbol{Y}^* \mid \boldsymbol{\theta}) \, p(\boldsymbol{\theta}) \, d\boldsymbol{\theta} \tag{1.7}$$

This is the expected distribution of the data according to the model (prior and likelihood). That is the data we expect, given the model, before actually seeing any observed data $\boldsymbol{Y}^*$. Notice that Equations 1.2 (marginal likelihood) and Equation 1.7 (prior predictive distribution) look really similar. The difference is in the former case, we are conditioning on our observed data Y while in the latter, we are not conditioning on the observed data. As a result the marginal likelihood is a number and the prior predictive distribution is a probability distribution.

We can use samples from the prior predictive distribution as a way to evaluate and calibrate our models using domain-knowledge. For example, we may ask questions such as "Is it OK for a model of human heights to predict that a human is -1.5 meters tall?". Even before measuring a single person, we can recognize the absurdness of this query. Later in the book we will see many concrete examples of model evaluation using prior predictive distributions in practice, and how the prior predictive distributions inform the validity, or lack thereof, in subsequent modeling choices.

> ### Bayesian models as generative models
>
> Adopting a probabilistic perspective for modeling leads to the mantra *models generate data* [158]. We consider this concept to be of central importance. Once you internalize it, all statistical models become much more clear, even non-Bayesian ones. This mantra can help to create new models; if models generate data, we can create suitable models for our data *just* by thinking of how the data could have been generated! Additionally, this mantra is not just an abstract concept. We can adopt a concrete representation in the form of the prior predictive distribution. If we revisit the 3 steps of Bayesian modeling, we can re-frame them as, write a prior predictive distribution, add data to constrain it, check if the result makes sense. Iterate if necessary.

---

[7] Technically we should talk about the expectation of a random variable. See Section 11.1.8 for details.

Another useful quantity to compute is the **posterior predictive distribution**:

$$p(\tilde{\boldsymbol{Y}} \mid \boldsymbol{Y}) = \int_{\boldsymbol{\Theta}} p(\tilde{\boldsymbol{Y}} \mid \boldsymbol{\theta}) \, p(\boldsymbol{\theta} \mid \boldsymbol{Y}) \, d\boldsymbol{\theta} \tag{1.8}$$

This is the distribution of expected, future, data $\tilde{\boldsymbol{Y}}$ according to the posterior $p(\boldsymbol{\theta} \mid \boldsymbol{Y})$, which in turn is a consequence of the model (prior and likelihood) and observed data. In more common terms, this is the data the model is expecting to see after seeing the dataset $\boldsymbol{Y}$, i.e. these are the model's predictions. From Equation 1.8, we can see that predictions are computed by integrating out (or marginalizing) over the posterior distribution of parameters. As a consequence predictions computed this way will incorporate the uncertainty about our estimates.

Bayesian posteriors in a Frequentist light

Because posteriors are derived from the model and the observed data only, we are not making statements based on non-observed, but potentially observed realizations of the underlying data-generating process. Inferring on non-observed is generally done by the so called frequentists methods. Nevertheless, if we use posterior predictive samples to check our models we are (partially) embracing the frequentist idea of thinking about non-observed but potentially observable data. We are not only comfortable with this idea, we will see many examples of this procedure in this book. We think it is one honking great idea – let us do more of these!

1.2   A DIY Sampler, Do Not Try This at Home

Closed form expressions for the integral in Equation 1.2 are not always possible and thus much of modern Bayesian inference is done using numerical methods that we call **Universal Inference Engines** (see Section 11.9) just to compensate for the fact we live in the 21st century and we still do not have flying cars. Anyway, there are many well-tested Python libraries providing such numerical methods so in general it is very unlikely that a Bayesian practitioner will need to code their own Universal Inference Engine.

As of today there are generally only two good reasons to code your own engine, you are either designing a new engine that improves on the old ones, or you are learning how the current engines work. Since we are learning in this chapter we will code one, but for the rest of the book we are going to use engines available in Python libraries.

There are many algorithms that can be used as *Universal Inference Engines*. Probably the most widely adopted and powerful is the family of Markov chain Monte Carlo methods (MCMC). At a very high level, all MCMC methods approximate the posterior distribution using samples. The samples from the posterior distribution are generated by accepting or rejecting samples from a different distribution called the proposal distribution. By following certain rules [8] and under certain assumptions, we have theoretical guarantees that we will get samples that are a good approximation of the posterior distribution. Thus, MCMC methods are also known as samplers. All these methods require to be able to evaluate the prior and likelihood at a given parameter value. That is, even when we do not know what the entire posterior looks like, we can ask for its density point-wise.

---

[8]See detailed balance at Sections 11.1.11 and 11.9.2.

One such algorithm is Metropolis-Hastings [103, 78, 135]. This is not a very modern or particularly efficient algorithm, but Metropolis-Hastings is simple to understand and also provides a foundation to understand more sophisticated and powerful methods. [9]

The Metropolis-Hasting algorithm is defined as follows:

1. Initialize the value of the parameter X at x_i

2. Use a proposal distribution [10] $q(x_{i+1} \mid x_i)$ to generate a new value x_{i+1} from the old one x_i.

3. Compute the probability of accepting the new value as:

$$p_a(x_{i+1} \mid x_i) = \min\left(1, \frac{p(x_{i+1})\, q(x_i \mid x_{i+1})}{p(x_i)\, q(x_{i+1} \mid x_i)}\right) \tag{1.9}$$

4. If $p_a > R$ where $R \sim \mathcal{U}(0,1)$, save the new value, otherwise save the old one.

5. Iterate 2 to 4 until a *sufficiently large* sample of values has been generated

The Metropolis algorithm is very general and can be used in non-Bayesian applications but for what we care in this book, $p(x_i)$ is the posterior's density evaluated at the parameter value x_i. Notice that if q is a symmetric distribution the terms $q(x_i \mid x_{i+1})$ and $q(x_{i+1} \mid x_i)$ will cancel out (conceptually it means it is equally likely are we are to go from x_{i+1} to x_i or to go from x_i to x_{i+1}), leaving just the ratio of the posterior evaluated at two points. From Equation 1.9 we can see this algorithm will always accept moving from a low probability region to a higher one and will probabilistically accept moving from a high to low probability region.

Another important remark is that the Metropolis-Hastings algorithm is not an optimization method! We do not care about finding the parameter value with the maximum probability, we want to *explore* the p distribution (the posterior). This can be seen if we take note that once at a maximum, the method can still move to a region of lower probabilities in subsequent steps.

To make things more concrete let us try to solve the Beta-Binomial model. This is probably the most common example in Bayesian statistics, and it is used to model binary, mutually-exclusive outcomes such as 0 or 1, positive or negative, head or tails, spam or ham, hotdog or not hotdog, healthy or unhealthy, etc. More often than not Beta-Binomial model is used as the first example to introduce the basics of Bayesian statistics, because it is a simple model that we can solve and compute with ease. In statistical notation we can write the Beta-Binomial models as:

$$\begin{aligned} \theta &\sim \text{Beta}(\alpha, \beta) \\ Y &\sim \text{Bin}(n = 1, p = \theta) \end{aligned} \tag{1.10}$$

In Equation 1.10 we are saying the parameter θ has $\text{Beta}(\alpha, \beta)$ as its prior distribution. And we assume the data is distributed following a Binomial distribution $\text{Bin}(n = 1, p = \theta)$, which represents our likelihood distribution. In this model the number of successes θ can represent quantities like the proportion of heads or the proportion of dying patients,

---

[9]For a more extensive discussion about inference methods you should read the Section 11.9 and references therein.

[10]This is sometimes referred to as a kernel in other Universal Inference Engines.

sometimes statistics can be a very dark place. This model has an analytical solution (see Section 1.4.1) for the details. For the sake of the example, let us assume we do not know how to compute the posterior, and thus we will implement the Metropolis-Hastings algorithm into Python code in order to get an approximate answer. We will do it with the help of SciPy statistical functions:

Code 1.1

```
1  def post(θ, Y, α=1, β=1):
2      if 0 <= θ <= 1:
3          prior = stats.beta(α, β).pdf(θ)
4          like  = stats.bernoulli(θ).pmf(Y).prod()
5          prob = like * prior
6      else:
7          prob = -np.inf
8      return prob
```

We also need data, so we will generate some random fake data for this purpose.

Code 1.2

```
1  Y = stats.bernoulli(0.7).rvs(20)
```

And finally we run our implementation of the Metropolis-Hastings algorithm:

Code 1.3

```
1  n_iters = 1000
2  can_sd = 0.05
3  α = β =  1
4  θ = 0.5
5  trace = {"θ":np.zeros(n_iters)}
6  p2 = post(θ, Y, α, β)
7
8  for iter in range(n_iters):
9      θ_can = stats.norm(θ, can_sd).rvs(1)
10     p1 = post(θ_can, Y, α, β)
11     pa = p1 / p2
12
13     if pa > stats.uniform(0, 1).rvs(1):
14         θ = θ_can
15         p2 = p1
16
17     trace["θ"][iter] = θ
```

At line 9 of Code Block 1.3 we generate a proposal distribution by sampling from a Normal distribution with standard deviation `can_sd`. At line 10 we evaluate the posterior at the new generated value θ_`can` and at line 11 we compute the probability of acceptance. At line 20 we save a value of θ in the **trace** array. Whether this value is a new one or we repeat the previous one, it will depends on the result of the comparison at line 13.

> **Ambiguous MCMC jargon**
>
> When we use Markov chain Monte Carlo Methods to do Bayesian inference, we typically refer to them as MCMC samplers. At each iteration we draw a random sample from the sampler, so naturally we refer to the output from MCMC as *samples* or *draws*. Some people make the distinction that a sample is made up by a collection of draws, other treat samples and draws as interchangeably.
>
> Since MCMC draws samples sequentially we also say we get a *chain* of draws as result, or just MCMC chain for short. Usually it is desired to draw many chains for computational and diagnostic reasons (we discuss how to do this in Chapter 2). All the output chains, whether singular or plural, are typically referred to as a trace or simple the posterior. Unfortunately spoken language is imprecise so if precision is needed the best approach is to review the code to understand exactly what is happening.

Note that the code implemented in Code Block 1.3 is not intended to be efficient, in fact there are many changes that would be present in production-grade code, like computing the probabilities on the log scale to avoid under/overflow issues (see Section 10.4.1), or precomputing the proposal and the Uniform values. This is where the purity of math needs to be adjusted to meet the reality of computers, and why building these engines is best left to experts. Similarly, the value of `can_sd`, is a parameter of the Metropolis-Hastings algorithm, not a parameter from the Bayesian model. In theory this parameter should not affect the correct behavior of the algorithm, but in practice it is very important as the efficiency of the method will certainly be affected by its value (see Section 11.9 for an in-depth discussion).

Returning to our example, now that we have our MCMC samples we want to understand *what it looks like*. A common way to inspect the results of a Bayesian inference is to plot the sampled values per iteration together with a histogram, or other visual tool, to represent distributions. For example, we can use the code in Code Block 1.4 to plot Figure 1.2 [11]:

Code 1.4

```
1  _, axes = plt.subplots(1,2, sharey=True)
2  axes[1].hist(trace["θ"], color="0.5", orientation="horizontal", density=True)
```

Generally it is also useful to compute some numerical summaries. Here we will use the Python package ArviZ [91] to compute these statistics:

Code 1.5

```
az.summary(trace, kind="stats", round_to=2))
```

	mean	sd	hdi_3%	hdi_97%
θ	0.69	0.01	0.52	0.87

ArviZ's function `summary` computes the mean, standard deviation and the highest density interval (HDI) 94% of our parameter θ. The HDI is the shortest interval containing a given probability density, 94% for this particular example [12]. Figure 1.3, generated with

---

[11]You can use ArviZ `plot_trace` function to get a similar plot. This is how we will do in the rest of the book.

[12]Notice that in principle the number of possible intervals containing a given proportion of the total density is infinite.

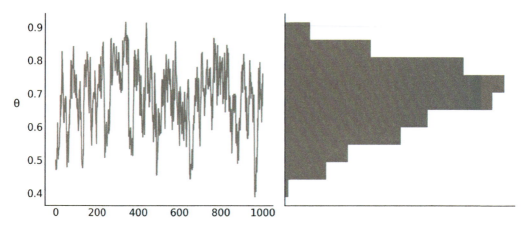

FIGURE 1.2
On the left, we have the sampled values of the parameter θ at each iteration. On the right, we have the histogram of the sampled values of θ. The histogram is rotated, to make it easier to see that both plots are closely related. The plot on the left shows the *sequence* of sampled values. This sequence is our Markov Chain. The plot on the right shows the distribution of the sampled values.

`az.plot_posterior(trace)` is a close visual equivalent of the above summary in 1.2. We can see the mean and the HDI, on top of a curve representing the entire posterior distribution. The curve is computed using a **kernel density estimator (KDE)**, which is like the smooth version of a histogram. ArviZ uses KDEs in many of its plots, and even internally for a few computations.

The HDI is a common choice in Bayesian statistics and *round* values like 50% or 95% are commonplace. But ArviZ uses 94% (or 0.94) as the default value as seen in both the summary Table 1.2 and Figure 1.3. The reason for this choice is that 94 is close to the *widely used* 95 but is different enough to serve as a friendly reminder that there is nothing special about these *round* values [101]. Ideally you should choose a value that fits your needs [92], or at least acknowledge that you are using a default.

1.3   Say Yes to Automating Inference, Say No to Automated Model Building

Instead of writing our own sampler and having to define our models using `scipy.stats` method we can leverage the aid of **Probabilistic Programming Languages** (PPL). These tools allow users to express Bayesian models using code and then perform Bayesian inference in a fairly automated fashion thanks to Universal Inference Engines. In short PPLs help practitioners focus more on model building and less on the mathematical and computational details. The availability of such tools has helped increase the popularity and usefulness of Bayesian methods in the last few decades. Unfortunately, these Universal Inference Engines methods are not really that universal, as they will not be able to efficiently solve every Bayesian model (but we still like the cool name!). Part of the job of the modern Bayesian practitioner is being able to understand and work around these limitations.

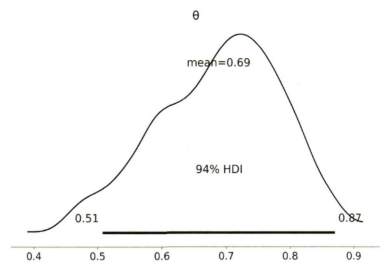

FIGURE 1.3
Posterior plot visualizing the samples generated from Code Block 1.3. The posterior distribution is represented using a KDE, the mean and the limits of the HDI 94% are represented in the figure.

In this book we will use PyMC3 [138] and TensorFlow Probability [47]. Let us write the model from Equation 1.10 using PyMC3:

Code 1.6

```
1  # Declare a model in PyMC3
2  with pm.Model() as model:
3      # Specify the prior distribution of unknown parameter
4      θ = pm.Beta("θ", alpha=1, beta=1)
5
6      # Specify the likelihood distribution and condition on the observed data
7      y_obs = pm.Binomial("y_obs", n=1, p=θ, observed=Y)
8
9      # Sample from the posterior distribution
10     idata = pm.sample(1000, return_inferencedata=True)
```

You should check by yourself that this piece of code provides essentially the same answer as our DIY sampler we used before, but with much less effort. If you are not familiar with the syntax of PyMC3, just focus on the intent of each line as shown in the code comments for now. Since we have defined our model in PyMC3 syntax we can also utilize `pm.model_to_graphviz(model)` to generate a graphical representation of the model in Code Block 1.6 (see Figure 1.4).

A Probabilistic Programming Language can not only evaluate the log-probability of the random variables to get the posterior distribution, but also simulate from various distributions as well. For example, Code Block 1.7 shows how to use PyMC3 to generate 1000 samples from the prior predictive distribution and 1000 samples from the posterior predictive distribution. Notice how for the first one, we have a function taking the **model** as argument while for the second function we have to pass both **model** and **trace**, reflecting the fact that the prior predictive distribution can be computed just from the model while the posterior predictive distribution we need a model and posterior. The generated samples

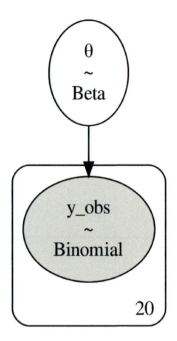

FIGURE 1.4
A graphical representation of the model defined in Equation 1.10 and Code Block 1.6. The ovals represent our prior and likelihood, whereas the 20 in this case indicates the number of observations.

from the prior and posterior predictive distributions are represented in the top and bottom panel, respectively, from Figure 1.5.

Code 1.7

```
1 pred_dists = (pm.sample_prior_predictive(1000, model)["y_obs"],
2               pm.sample_posterior_predictive(idata, 1000, model)["y_obs"])
```

Equations 1.1, 1.7, and 1.8 clearly define the posterior, the prior predictive, and the posterior predictive distributions as different mathematical objects. The two later are distributions over data and the first one is a distribution over the parameters in a model. Figure 1.5 helps us visualize this difference and also includes the prior distribution for completeness.

> **Expressing models in multiple ways**
>
> There are numerous methods to communicate the architecture of statistical models. These can be, in no particular order:
>
> - Spoken and written language
> - Conceptual diagrams: Figure 1.4.
> - Mathematical notation: Equation 1.10
> - Computer Code: Code Block 1.6
>
> For a modern Bayesian practitioner it is useful to be literate across all these mediums. They are formats you see presented in talks, scientific papers, hand sketches when discussing with colleagues, code examples on the internet, etc. With fluency across these mediums you will be better able to understand concepts presented one way, and then apply them in another way. For example, read paper and then implement a model, or hear about a technique in a talk and then be able to write a blog post on it. For you personally fluency will likely speed up your learning and increase your ability to communicate with others. Ultimately this helps achieve what general statistics community always strives for a better shared understanding of the world.

As we already mentioned, posterior predictive distributions take into account the uncertainty about our estimates. Figure 1.6 shows that the predictions using the mean are less spread than predictions from the posterior predictive distribution. This result is not only valid for the mean, we would get a similar picture if we change the mean to any other point-estimate.

1.4 A Few Options to Quantify Your Prior Information

Having to choose a prior distribution is portrayed both as a burden and as a blessing. We choose to affirm that is a necessity, if you are not choosing your priors someone else is doing it for you. Letting others decide for you is not always a bad thing. Many of these non-Bayesian methods can be very useful and efficient if applied in the correct context, and with awareness of their limitations. However, we firmly believe there is an advantage for the practitioner in knowing the model assumptions and have the flexibility to alter them. Priors are just one form of assumption.

We also understand that prior elicitation can be a source of doubts, anxiety, and even frustration for many practitioners, especially for, but not necessarily only for, newcomers. Asking what is the best-ever prior for a given problem, is a common and totally valid question. But it is difficult to give a straight satisfying answer other than, there is no such thing. At best there are some useful defaults that we can use as starting points in an iterative modeling workflow.

In this section we discuss a few general approaches for selecting prior distributions. This discussion follows more or less an *informativeness gradient* from "blank slates" which include no information, to highly informative, which put as much information as possible into the priors. As with the other sections in this chapter, this discussion is more on the

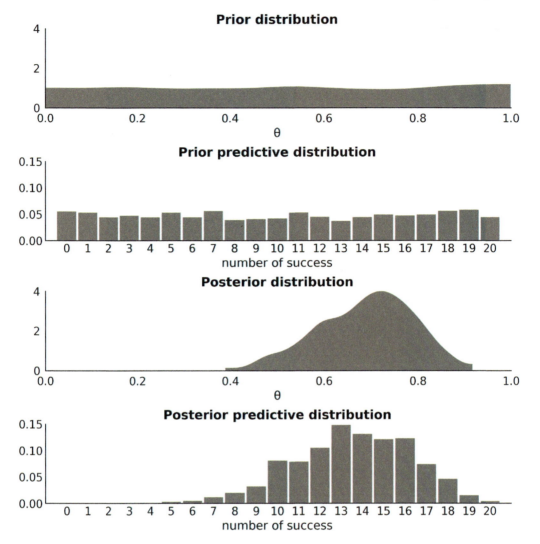

FIGURE 1.5
From top plot to bottom plot we show: (1) samples from the prior distribution of the parameter θ; (2) samples from the prior predictive distribution, where we are plotting the probability distribution of the total number of successes; (3) posterior samples of the parameter θ; (4) posterior predictive distribution of the total number of successes. The x-axis and y-axis scales are shared between the first and third plots and then between the second and fourth plots.

theoretical side. In the following chapters we will discuss how to choose priors in more practical settings.

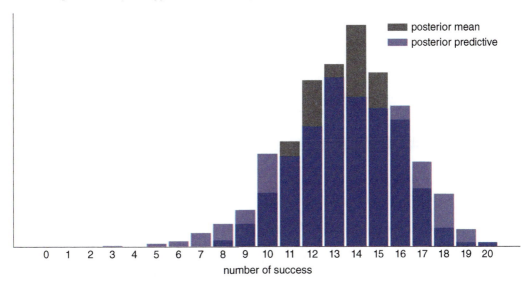

FIGURE 1.6
Predictions for the Beta-Binomial model, using the posterior mean (gray histogram) vs predictions using the entire posterior, i.e. the posterior predictive distribution (blue histogram).

1.4.1 Conjugate Priors

A prior is conjugate to a likelihood if the posterior belongs to the same family of distributions as the prior. For example, if the likelihood is Poisson and the prior Gamma, then the posterior will also be a Gamma distribution [13].

From a purely mathematical perspective, **conjugate priors** are the most convenient choice as they allow us to calculate the posterior distribution analytically with "pen and paper", no complex computation required [14]. From a modern computational perspective, conjugate priors are generally not better than alternatives, the main reason being that modern computational methods allow us to perform inference with virtually any choice of priors and not just those that are mathematically convenient. Nevertheless, conjugate priors can be useful when learning Bayesian inference and also under some situations when there is a need to use analytical expressions for the posterior (see Section 10.2.2 for an example). As is such, we will briefly discuss analytical priors using the Beta Binomial model.

As the name suggests, the conjugate prior for the binomial distribution is the Beta distribution:

$$p(\theta \mid Y) \propto \overbrace{\frac{N!}{y!(N-y)!}\theta^y(1-\theta)^{N-y}}^{\text{binomial-likelihood}} \overbrace{\frac{\Gamma(\alpha+\beta)}{\Gamma(\alpha)\Gamma(\beta)}\theta^{\alpha-1}(1-\theta)^{\beta-1}}^{\text{beta.prior}} \quad (1.11)$$

Because all the terms not depending on θ are constant we can drop them and we get:

$$p(\theta \mid Y) \propto \overbrace{\theta^y(1-\theta)^{N-y}}^{\text{binomial-likelihood}} \overbrace{\theta^{\alpha-1}(1-\theta)^{\beta-1}}^{\text{beta.prior}} \quad (1.12)$$

---

[13]For more examples check `https://en.wikipedia.org/wiki/Conjugate_prior#Table_of_conjugate_distributions`

[14]Except, the ones happening in your brain.

Reordering:

$$p(\theta \mid Y) \propto \theta^{\alpha-1+y}(1-\theta)^{\beta-1+N-y} \tag{1.13}$$

If we want to ensure that the posterior is a proper probability distribution function, we need to add a normalization constant ensuring that the integral of the PDF is 1 (see Section 11.1.5). Notice that expression 1.13 looks like the kernel of a Beta distribution, thus by adding the normalization constant of a Beta distribution we arrive to the conclusion that the posterior distribution for a Beta-Binomial model is:

$$p(\theta \mid Y) \propto \frac{\Gamma(\alpha_{post} + \beta_{post})}{\Gamma(\alpha_{post})\Gamma(\beta_{post})}\theta^{\alpha_{post}-1}(1-\theta)^{\beta_{post}-1} = \text{Beta}(\alpha_{post}, \beta_{post}) \tag{1.14}$$

where $\alpha_{post} = \alpha + y$ and $\beta_{post} = \beta + N - y$.

As the posterior of a Beta-Binomial model is a Beta distribution we can use a Beta-posterior as the prior for a future analysis. This means that we will get the same result if we update the prior one data-point at a time or if we use the entire dataset at once. For example, the first four panels of Figure 1.7 show how different priors get updated as we move from 0 to 1, 2, and 3 trials. The result is the same if we follow this succession or if we *jump* from 0 to 3 trials (or, in fact, n trials).

There are a lot of other interesting things to see from Figure 1.7. For instance, as the number of trials increases, the width of the posterior gets lower and lower, i.e. the uncertainty gets lower and lower. Panels 3 and 5 show the results for 2 trials with 1 success and 12 trials with 6 success, for these cases, the sampling proportion estimator $\hat{\theta} = \frac{y}{n}$ (black dot) is the same 0.5 for both cases (the posterior mode is also 0.5), although the width of the posteriors are concentrated in panel 5 reflecting that the number of observations is larger and thus uncertainty lower. Finally, we can see how different priors converge to the same posterior distribution as the number of observations increase. In the limit of infinite data, the posteriors (irrespective of priors used to compute those posteriors) will have all its density at $\hat{\theta} = \frac{y}{n}$.

Code 1.8

```
1  _, axes = plt.subplots(2,3, sharey=True, sharex=True)
2  axes = np.ravel(axes)
3
4  n_trials = [0, 1, 2, 3, 12, 180]
5  success = [0, 1, 1, 1, 6, 59]
6  data = zip(n_trials, success)
7
8  beta_params = [(0.5, 0.5), (1, 1), (10, 10)]
9  θ = np.linspace(0, 1, 1500)
10 for idx, (N, y) in enumerate(data):
11     s_n = ("s" if (N > 1) else "")
12     for jdx, (a_prior, b_prior) in enumerate(beta_params):
13         p_theta_given_y = stats.beta.pdf(θ, a_prior + y, b_prior + N - y)
14
15         axes[idx].plot(θ, p_theta_given_y, lw=4, color=viridish[jdx])
16         axes[idx].set_yticks([])
17         axes[idx].set_ylim(0, 12)
18         axes[idx].plot(np.divide(y, N), 0, color="k", marker="o", ms=12)
19         axes[idx].set_title(f"{N:4d} trial{s_n} {y:4d} success")
```

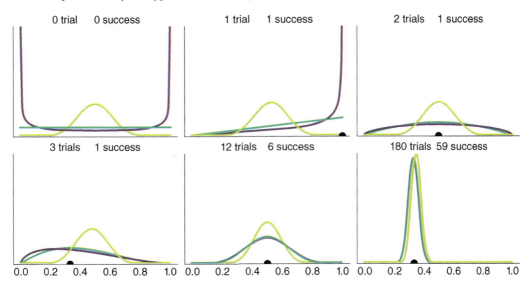

FIGURE 1.7
Successive prior updating starting from 3 different priors and increasing the number of trials (and possible the number of successes too). The black dot represents the sampling proportion estimator $\hat{\theta} = \frac{y}{n}$.

The mean of the Beta distribution is $\frac{\alpha}{\alpha+\beta}$, thus the prior mean is:

$$\mathbb{E}[\theta] = \frac{\alpha}{\alpha + \beta} \tag{1.15}$$

and the posterior mean is:

$$\mathbb{E}[\theta \mid Y] = \frac{\alpha + y}{\alpha + \beta + n} \tag{1.16}$$

We can see that if the value of n is small in relation with the values of α and β then the posterior mean will be closer to the prior mean. That is, the prior contributes more to the result than the data. If we have the opposite situation the posterior mean will be closer to the sampling proportion estimator $\hat{\theta} = \frac{y}{n}$, in fact in the limit of $n \to \infty$ the posterior mean will exactly match the sample proportion no matter which prior values we choose for α and β.

For the Beta Binomial model the posterior mode is:

$$\underset{\theta}{\mathrm{argmax}}\,[\theta \mid Y] = \frac{\alpha + y - 1}{\alpha + \beta + n - 2} \tag{1.17}$$

We can see that when the prior is Beta$(\alpha = 1, \beta = 1)$ (Uniform) the posterior mode is numerically equivalent to the sampling proportion estimator $\hat{\theta} = \frac{y}{n}$. The posterior mode is often called the **maximum a posteriori** (MAP) value. This result is not exclusive for the Beta-Binomial model. In fact the results from many non-Bayesian methods can be understood as the MAP from Bayesian methods under some particular priors [15].

Compare Equation 1.16 to the sampling proportion $\frac{y}{n}$. The Bayesian estimator is adding α to the number of successes and $\alpha + \beta$ to the number of trials. Which makes β the number

---

[15]For example, a regularized linear regression with a L2 regularization is the same as using a Gaussian prior on the coefficient.

of failures. In this sense we can think of the prior parameters as *pseudo counts* or if you want prior data. A prior Beta$(1, 1)$ is equivalent to having two trials with 1 success and 1 failure. Conceptually, the shape of the Beta distribution is controlled by parameter α and β, the observed data updates the prior so that it shifts the shape of the Beta distribution closer and more narrowly to the majority of observations. For values of $\alpha < 1$ and/or $\beta < 1$ the prior interpretations becomes a little bit weird as a literal interpretation would say that the prior Beta$(0.5, 0.5)$ corresponds to 1 trial with half failure and half success or maybe one trial with undetermined outcome. Spooky!

1.4.2 Objective Priors

In the absence of prior information, it sounds reasonable to follow the *principle of indifference* also known as the *principle of insufficient reason*. This principle basically says that if you do not have information about a problem then you do not have any reason to believe one outcome is more likely than any other. In the context of Bayesian statistics this principle has motivated the study and use of **objective priors**. These are systematic ways of generating priors that have the least possible influence on a given analysis. The champions of ascetic statistics favor objective priors as these priors eliminate the *subjectivity* from prior elicitation. Of course this does not remove other sources of subjectivity such as the choice of the likelihood, the data selection process, the choice of the problem being modeled or investigated, and a long *et cetera*.

One procedure to obtain objective priors is known as Jeffreys' prior (JP). These type of priors are often referred as *non-informative* even when priors are always informative in some way. A better description is to say that JPs have the property of being invariant under **reparametrization**, i.e. writing an expression in a different but mathematically equivalent way. Let us explain what this exactly means with an example. Suppose Alice has a binomial likelihood with unknown parameter θ, she chooses a prior and computes a posterior. Alice's friend Bob is interested on the same problem but instead of the number of success θ, Bob is interested on the **odds** of the success, i.e. κ, with $\kappa = \frac{\theta}{1-\theta}$. Bob has two choices: uses Alice's posterior over θ to compute κ [16] or choose a prior over κ to compute the posterior by himself. JPs guarantee that if both Alice and Bob use JPs then no matter which of the two choices Bob takes in order to compute the posteriors, he will get the same result. In this sense we say the results are invariant to the chosen parameterization. A corollary of this explanation could be, that unless we use JPs there is no guarantee that two (or more) parameterization of a model will necessarily lead to posteriors that are coherent.

For the one-dimensional case JP for θ is

$$p(\theta) \propto \sqrt{I(\theta)} \tag{1.18}$$

where $I(\theta)$ is the expected Fisher information:

$$I(\theta) = -\mathbb{E}_{\mathbb{Y}}\left[\frac{d^2}{d\theta^2}\log p(Y \mid \theta)\right] \tag{1.19}$$

Once the likelihood function $p(Y \mid \theta)$ has been decided by the practitioner, then the JP gets automatically determined, eliminating any discussion over prior choices, until that annoying person at the back of the conference room objects your choice of a JP in the first place.

---

[16] For example, if we have samples from the posterior, then we can plug those samples of θ into $\kappa = \frac{\theta}{1-\theta}$.

For a detailed derivation of the JPs for both Alice and Bob problem see Section 11.6. If you want to skip those details here we have the JP for Alice:

$$p(\theta) \propto \theta^{-0.5}(1-\theta)^{-0.5} \qquad (1.20)$$

This turns to be the kernel of the Beta(0.5, 0.5) distribution. Which is a u-shaped distribution as shown in the left-top panel of Figure 1.8.

For Bob the JP is:

$$p(\kappa) \propto \kappa^{-0.5}(1+\kappa)^{-1} \qquad (1.21)$$

This is a half-u-shaped distribution, defined in the $[0, \infty)$ interval, see top-right panel in Figure 1.8. Saying this is a half-u-shaped may sound a little bit weird. Actually it is not that weird when we find that this is the kernel of a close cousin of the Beta distribution, the Beta-prime distribution with parameters $\alpha = \beta = 0.5$.

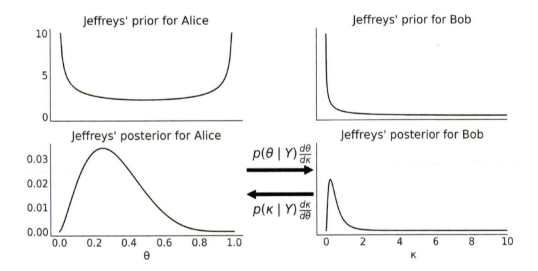

FIGURE 1.8
Top: Jeffreys' prior (unnormalized) for the binomial likelihood parameterized in term of the number of success θ (left) or in term of the odds κ (right). Bottom: Jeffreys' posteriors (unnormalized) for the binomial likelihood parameterized in term of the number of success θ (left) or in term of the odds κ (right). The arrows between the posteriors indicate that the posterior are inter-convertible by applying the change of variable rule (see Section 11.1.9 for details).

Notice that as the expectation in Equation 1.19 is with respect to $Y \mid \theta$, that is an expectation over the sample space. This means that in order to obtain a JP we need to average over all possible experimental outcomes. This is a violation of the likelihood principle [17] as the inferences about θ depends not just on the data at hand, but also on the set of potentially (but not yet) observed data.

A JP can be improper prior, meaning that it does not integrate to 1. For example, the JP for the mean of a Gaussian distribution of known variance is uniform over the entire

---

[17]https://en.wikipedia.org/wiki/Likelihood_principle

real line. Improper priors are fine as long as we verify that the combination of them with a likelihood produces a proper posterior distribution, that is one integrating to 1. Also notice that we can not draw random samples from improper priors (i.e., they are non-generative) this can invalidate many useful tools that allow us to reason about our model.

JPs are not the only way to obtain an objective prior. Another possible route is to obtain a prior by maximizing the expected Kullback-Leibler divergence (see Section 11.3) between the prior and posterior. These kind of priors are known as Bernardo reference priors. They are objective as these are the priors that *allow the data to bring* the maximal amount of information into the posterior distribution. Bernardo reference priors and Jeffreys' prior do not necessarily agree. Additionally, objective priors may not exist or be difficult to derive for complicated models.

1.4.3   Maximum Entropy Priors

Yet another way to justify a choice of priors is to pick the prior with the highest entropy. If we are totally indifferent about the plausible values then such prior turns out to be the Uniform distribution over the range on plausible values [18]. But what about when we are not completely indifferent about the plausible values a parameter can take? For example, we may know our parameter is restricted to the $[0, \infty)$ interval. Can we obtain a prior that has maximum entropy while also satisfying a given constraint? Yes we can and that is exactly the idea behind maximum entropy priors. In the literature it is common to find the word MaxEnt when people talk about the maximum entropy principle.

In order to obtain a maximum entropy prior we need to solve an optimization problem taking into account a set of constraints. Mathematically this can be done using what is known as Lagrangian multipliers. Instead of a formal proof however, we are going to use a couple code examples to gain some intuition.

Figure 1.9 shows 3 distributions obtained by entropy maximization. The purple distribution is obtained under no constraint, and we are happy to find that this is indeed the Uniform distribution as expected from the discussion about entropy in Section 11.2. If we do not know anything about the problem all events are equally likely a priori. The second distribution, in cyan, is obtained under the constraint that we know the mean value of the distribution. In this example the mean value is 1.5). Under this constraint we get an Exponential-like distribution. The last one in yellow-green was obtained under the restriction that the value 3 and 4 are known to appear with a probability of 0.8. If you check Code Block 1.9 you will see all distributions were computed under two constraints that probabilities can only take values in the interval $[0, 1]$ and that the total probability must be 1. As these are general constraints for valid probability distribution we can think of them as *intrinsic* or even *ontological* constraints. For that reason we say that the purple distribution in Figure 1.9 was obtained under no-constraint.

Code 1.9

```
1  cons = [[{"type": "eq", "fun": lambda x: np.sum(x) - 1}],
2          [{"type": "eq", "fun": lambda x: np.sum(x) - 1},
3           {"type": "eq", "fun": lambda x: 1.5 - np.sum(x * np.arange(1, 7))}],
4          [{"type": "eq", "fun": lambda x: np.sum(x) - 1},
5           {"type": "eq", "fun": lambda x: np.sum(x[[2, 3]]) - 0.8}]]
6
7  max_ent = []
8  for i, c in enumerate(cons):
```

---

[18]See Section 11.2 for more details.

```
 9     val = minimize(lambda x: -entropy(x), x0=[1/6]*6, bounds=[(0., 1.)] * 6,
10                    constraints=c)['x']
11     max_ent.append(entropy(val))
12     plt.plot(np.arange(1, 7), val, 'o--', color=viridish[i], lw=2.5)
13 plt.xlabel("$t$")
14 plt.ylabel("$p(t)$")
```

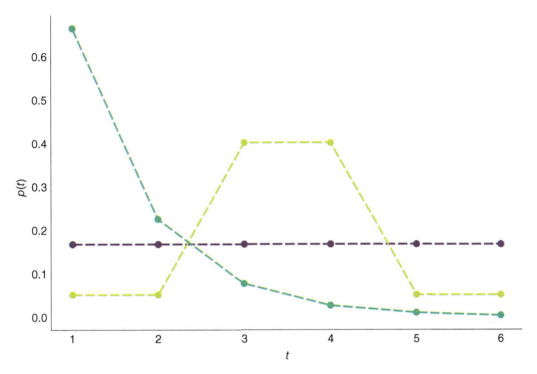

FIGURE 1.9
Discrete distributions obtained by maximizing the entropy under different constraints. We are using the function **entropy** from `scipy.stats` to estimate these distributions. Notice how adding constraints can drastically change the distribution.

We can think of the maximum entropy principle as the procedure of choosing the flattest distribution, and by extension the flattest prior distribution, under a given constraint. In Figure 1.9 the Uniform distribution is the flattest distribution, but notice that the distribution in green is also the flattest distribution once we include the restriction that the values 3 and 4 have a 80% chance of arising. Notice how the values 3 and 4 have both a probability of 0.4, even when you have infinite other ways to combine their probabilities to obtain the target value of 0.8, like 0+0.8, 0.7+0.1, 0.312+0.488 and so on. Also notice something similar is true for the values 1, 2, 5 and 6, they have a total probability of 0.2 which is evenly distributed (0.05 for each value). Now take a look at the Exponential-like curve, which certainly does not look very flat, but once again notice that other choices will be less flat and more concentrated, for example, obtaining 1 and 2 with 50% chance each (and thus zero change for the values 3 to 6), which will also have 1.5 as the expected value.

Code 1.10

```
1  ite = 100_000
2  entropies = np.zeros((3, ite))
3  for idx in range(ite):
4      rnds = np.zeros(6)
5      total = 0
6      x_ = np.random.choice(np.arange(1, 7), size=6, replace=False)
7      for i in x_[:-1]:
8          rnd = np.random.uniform(0, 1-total)
9          rnds[i-1] = rnd
10         total = rnds.sum()
11     rnds[-1] = 1 - rnds[:-1].sum()
12     H = entropy(rnds)
13     entropies[0, idx] = H
14     if abs(1.5 - np.sum(rnds * x_)) < 0.01:
15         entropies[1, idx] = H
16     prob_34 = sum(rnds[np.argwhere((x_ == 3) | (x_ == 4)).ravel()])
17     if abs(0.8 - prob_34) < 0.01:
18         entropies[2, idx] = H
```

Figure 1.10 shows the distribution of entropies computed for randomly generated samples under the exact same conditions as the 3 distributions in Figure 1.9. The dotted vertical line represents the entropy of the curves in Figure 1.10. While this is not a proof, this experiment seems to suggest that there is no distribution with higher entropy than the distributions in Figure 1.10, which is in total agreement with what the theory tells us.

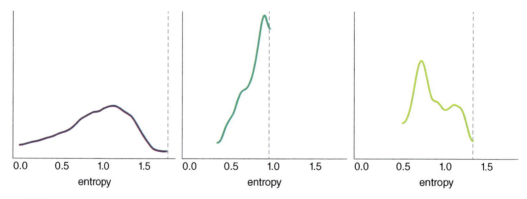

FIGURE 1.10

The distribution of entropy for a set of randomly generated distributions. The dotted vertical line indicates the value for the distributions with maximum entropy, computed with Code Block 1.9. We can see that none of the randomly generated distributions have an entropy larger that the distributions with maximum entropy, while this is no formal proof, this is certainly reassuring.

The distributions with the largest entropy under the following constraints are [19]:

- No constraints: Uniform (continuous or discrete, according to the type of variable)

- A positive mean, with support $[0, \infty)$: Exponential

- An absolute value mean, with support $(-\infty, \infty)$: Laplace (also known as double Exponential)

- A given mean and variance, with support $(-\infty, \infty)$: Normal distribution

- A given mean and variance, with support $[-\pi, \pi]$: Von Mises

- Only two unordered outcomes and a constant mean: Binomial, or the Poisson if we have rare events (the Poisson can be seen as a special case of the binomial)

It is interesting to note that many of the generalized linear models like the ones described in Chapter 3 are traditionally defined using maximum entropy distributions, given the constraints of the models. Similar to objective priors, MaxEnt prior may not exist or are difficult to derive.

1.4.4   Weakly Informative Priors and Regularization Priors

In previous sections we used general procedures to generate vague, non-informative priors designed to not put *too much* information into our analysis. These procedures to generate priors also provide a "somehow" automated way of generating priors. These two features may sound appealing, and in fact they are for a large number of Bayesian practitioners and theorists.

But in this book we will not rely too much on these kinds of priors. We believe prior elicitation (as other modeling decisions) should be context dependent, meaning that details from specific problems and even idiosyncrasies of a given scientific field could inform our choice of priors. While MaxEnt priors can incorporate some of these restrictions it is possible to move a little bit closer to the informative end of the informativeness prior spectrum. We can do this with so called weakly informative priors.

What constitutes a weakly informative priors is usually not mathematically well defined as JPs or MaxEnt are. Instead they are more *empirical* and *model-driven*, that is they are defined through a combination of relevant domain expertise and the model itself. For many problems, we often have information about the values a parameter can take. This information can be derived from the physical meaning of the parameter. We know heights have to be positive. We may even know the plausible range a parameter can take from previous experiments or observations. We may have strong reasons to justify a value should be close to zero or above some predefined lower-bound. We can use this information to weakly inform our analysis while keeping a good dose of ignorance to us from *to pushing too much*.

Using the Beta-Binomial example again, Figure 1.11 shows four alternative priors. Two of them are the JP and maximum entropy prior from previous sections. One is what could called a weakly informative prior that gives preference to a value of $\theta = 0.5$ while still being broad or relatively vague about other values. The last is an informative prior, narrowly centered around $\theta = 0.8$ [20]. Using informative priors is a valid option if we have good-quality

---

[19]Wikipedia has a longer list at `https://en.wikipedia.org/wiki/Maximum_entropy_probability_distribution#Other_examples`

[20]Even when the definition of such priors will require more context than the one provided, we still think the example conveys a useful intuition, that will be refined as we progress through this book.

information from theory, previous experiments, observational data, etc. As informative priors are very strong priors conveying a lot of information they generally require a stronger justification than other priors. As Carl Sagan used to say "Extraordinary claims require extraordinary evidence" [45]. It is important to remember that informativeness of the prior depends on model and model context. An uninformative prior in one context can become highly informative in another [63]. For instance if modeling the mean height of adult humans in meters, a prior of $\mathcal{N}(2,1)$ can be considered uninformative, but if estimating the height of giraffes that same prior becomes highly informative as in reality giraffe heights differ greatly than human heights.

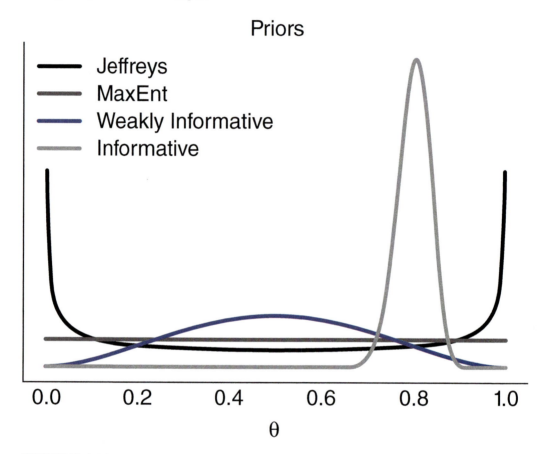

FIGURE 1.11
Prior informativeness spectrum: While Jeffreys and MaxEnt priors are uniquely defined for a binomial likelihood, weakly informative and informative priors are not and instead depend on previous information and practitioner's modeling decisions.

Because weakly-informative priors work to keep the posterior distribution within certain reasonable bounds, they are also known as regularizing priors. Regularization is a procedure of adding information with the aim of solving an ill-posed problem or to reduce the chance of overfitting and priors offer a principled way of performing regularization.

In this book, more often than not, we will use weakly-informative priors. Sometimes the prior will be used in a model without too much justification, simply because the focus of the example may be related to other aspects of the Bayesian modeling workflow. But we will also show some examples of using prior predictive checks to help us calibrate our priors.

> **Overfitting**
>
> Overfitting occurs when a model generates predictions very close to the limited dataset used to fit it, but it fails to fit additional data and/or predict future observations reasonably well. That is it fails to generalize its predictions to a wider set of possible observations. The counterpart of overfitting is underfitting, which is when a model fails to adequately capture the underlying structure of the data. We will discuss more about there topics in Sections 2.5 and 11.4.

1.4.5 Using Prior Predictive Distributions to Assess Priors

When evaluating the choice of priors, the prior predictive distribution shown in Section 1.3 is a handy tool. By sampling from the prior predictive distribution, the computer does the work of translating choices made in the parameter space into samples in the observed variable space. Thinking in terms of observed values is generally easier than thinking in terms of the model's parameters which makes model evaluation easier. Following a Beta Binomial model, instead of judging whether a particular value of θ is plausible, prior predictive distributions allow us to judge whether a particular number of successes is plausible. This becomes even more useful for complex models where parameters get transformed through many mathematical operations or multiple priors interact with each other. Lastly, computing the prior predictive could help us ensure our model has been properly written and is able to run in our probabilistic programming language and can even help us to debug our model. In the following chapters, we will see more concrete examples of how to reason about prior predictive samples and use them to choose reasonable priors.

1.5 Exercises

Problems are labeled Easy (E), Medium (M), and Hard (H).

1E1. As we discussed, models are artificial representations used to help define and understand an object or process. However, no model is able to perfectly replicate what it represents and thus is deficient in some way. In this book we focus on a particular type of models, statistical models. What are other types of models you can think of? How do they aid understanding of the thing that is being modeled? How are they deficient?

1E2. Match each of these verbal descriptions to their corresponding mathematical expression:

(a) The probability of a parameter given the observed data

(b) The distribution of parameters before seeing any data

(c) The plausibility of the observed data given a parameter value

(d) The probability of an unseen observation given the observed data

(e) The probability of an unseen observation before seeing any data

1E3. From the following expressions, which one corresponds to the sentence, The probability of being sunny given that it is July 9th of 1816?

    (a) $p(\text{sunny})$

    (b) $p(\text{sunny} \mid \text{July})$

    (c) $p(\text{sunny} \mid \text{July 9th of 1816})$

    (d) $p(\text{July 9th of 1816} \mid sunny)$

    (e) $p(\text{sunny}, \text{July 9th of 1816})/p(\text{July 9th of 1816})$

1E4. Show that the probability of choosing a human at random and picking the Pope is not the same as the probability of the Pope being human. In the animated series Futurama, the (Space) Pope is a reptile. How does this change your previous calculations?

1E5. Sketch what the distribution of possible observed values could be for the following cases:

    (a) The number of people visiting your local cafe assuming Poisson distribution

    (b) The weight of adult dogs in kilograms assuming a Uniform distribution

    (c) The weight of adult elephants in kilograms assuming Normal distribution

    (d) The weight of adult humans in pounds assuming skew Normal distribution

1E6. For each example in the previous exercise, use SciPy to specify the distribution in Python. Pick parameters that you believe are reasonable, take a random sample of size 1000, and plot the resulting distribution. Does this distribution look reasonable given your domain knowledge? If not adjust the parameters and repeat the process until they seem reasonable.

1E7. Compare priors Beta(0.5, 0.5), Beta(1, 1), Beta(1, 4). How do the priors differ in terms of shape?

1E8. Rerun Code block 1.8 but using two Beta-priors of your choice. Hint: you may what to try priors with $\alpha \neq \beta$ like Beta(2, 5).

1E9. Try to come up with new constraints in order to obtain new Max-Ent distributions (Code Block 1.9)

1E10. In Code Block 1.3, change the value of `can_sd` and run the Metropolis-Hastings sampler. Try values like 0.001 and 1.

    (a) Compute the mean, SD, and HDI and compare the values with those in the book (computed using `can_sd=0.05`). How different are the estimates?

    (b) Use the function `az.plot_posterior`.

1E11. You need to estimate the weights of blue whales, humans, and mice. You assume they are normally distributed, and you set the same prior $\mathcal{HN}(200\text{kg})$ for the variance.

What type of prior is this for adult blue whales? Strongly informative, weakly informative, or non-informative? What about for mice and for humans? How does informativeness of the prior correspond to our real world intuitions about these animals?

1E12. Use the following function to explore different combinations of priors (change the parameters a and b) and data (change heads and trials). Summarize your observations.

Code 1.11

```
1  def posterior_grid(grid=10, a=1, b=1, heads=6, trials=9):
2      grid = np.linspace(0, 1, grid)
3      prior = stats.beta(a, b).pdf(grid)
4      likelihood = stats.binom.pmf(heads, trials, grid)
5      posterior = likelihood * prior
6      posterior /= posterior.sum()
7      _, ax = plt.subplots(1, 3, sharex=True, figsize=(16, 4))
8      ax[0].set_title(f"heads = {heads}\ntrials = {trials}")
9      for i, (e, e_n) in enumerate(zip(
10             [prior, likelihood, posterior],
11             ["prior", "likelihood", "posterior"])):
12         ax[i].set_yticks([])
13         ax[i].plot(grid, e, "o-", label=e_n)
14         ax[i].legend(fontsize=14)
15
16
17 interact(posterior_grid,
18     grid=ipyw.IntSlider(min=2, max=100, step=1, value=15),
19     a=ipyw.FloatSlider(min=1, max=7, step=1, value=1),
20     b=ipyw.FloatSlider(min=1, max=7, step=1, value=1),
21     heads=ipyw.IntSlider(min=0, max=20, step=1, value=6),
22     trials=ipyw.IntSlider(min=0, max=20, step=1, value=9))
```

1E13. Between the prior, prior predictive, posterior, and posterior predictive distributions which distribution would help answer each of these questions. Some items may have multiple answers.

(a) How do we think is the distribution of parameters values before seeing any data?

(b) What observed values do we think we could see before seeing any data?

(c) After estimating parameters using a model what do we predict we will observe next?

(d) What parameter values explain the observed data after conditioning on that data?

(e) Which can be used to calculate numerical summaries, such as the mean, of the parameters?

(f) Which can can be used to to visualize a Highest Density Interval?

1M14. Equation 1.1 contains the marginal likelihood in the denominator, which is difficult to calculate. In Equation 1.3 we show that knowing the posterior up to a proportional constant is sufficient for inference. Show why the marginal likelihood is not needed for the Metropolis-Hasting method to work. Hint: this is a pen and paper exercise, try by expanding Equation 1.9.

1M15. In the following definition of a probabilistic model, identify the prior, the likelihood, and the posterior:

$$Y \sim \mathcal{N}(\mu, \sigma)$$
$$\mu \sim \mathcal{N}(0, 1)$$
$$\sigma \sim \mathcal{HN}(1)$$

1M16. In the previous model, how many parameters will the posterior have? Compare your answer with that from the model in the coin-flipping problem in Equation 1.10.

1M17. Suppose that we have two coins; when we toss the first coin, half of the time it lands tails and half of the time on heads. The other coin is a loaded coin that always lands on heads. If we choose one of the coins at random and observe a head, what is the probability that this coin is the loaded one?

1M18. Modify Code Block 1.2 to generate random samples from a Poisson distribution with parameters of your choosing. Then modify Code Blocks 1.1 and 1.3 to generate MCMC samples estimating your chosen parameters. Test how the number of samples, MCMC iterations, and initial starting point affect convergence to your true chosen parameter.

1M19. Assume we are building a model to estimate the mean and standard deviation of adult human heights in centimeters. Build a model that will make these estimation. Start with Code Block 1.6 and change the likelihood and priors as needed. After doing so then

(a) Sample from the prior predictive. Generate a visualization and numerical summary of the prior predictive distribution

(b) Using the outputs from (a) to justify your choices of priors and likelihoods

1M20. From domain knowledge you have that a given parameter can not be negative, and has a mean that is roughly between 3 and 10 units, and a standard deviation of around 2. Determine two prior distribution that satisfy these constraints using Python. This may require trial and error by drawing samples and verifying these criteria have been met using both plots and numerical summaries.

1M21. A store is visited by n customers on a given day. The number of customers that make a purchase Y is distributed as $\text{Bin}(n, \theta)$, where θ is the probability that a customer makes a purchase. Assume we know θ and the prior for n is $\text{Pois}(4.5)$.

(a) Use PyMC3 to compute the posterior distribution of n for all combinations of $Y \in 0, 5, 10$ and $\theta \in 0.2, 0.5$. Use `az.plot_posterior` to plot the results in a single plot.

(b) Summarize the effect of Y and θ on the posterior

1H22. Modify Code Block 1.2 to generate samples from a Normal Distribution, noting your choice of parameters for the mean and standard deviation. Then modify Code Blocks 1.1 and 1.3 to sample from a Normal model and see if you can recover your chosen parameters.

1H23. Make a model that estimates the proportion of the number of sunny versus cloudy days in your area. Use the past 5 days of data from your personal observations. Think through the data collection process. How hard is it to remember the past 5 days. What if needed the past 30 days of data? Past year? Justify your choice of priors. Obtain a posterior distribution that estimates the proportion of sunny versus cloudy days. Generate predictions for the next 10 days of weather. Communicate your answer using both numerical summaries and visualizations.

1H24. You planted 12 seedlings and 3 germinate. Let us call θ the probability that a seedling germinates. Assuming Beta$(1, 1)$ prior distribution for θ.

(a) Use pen and paper to compute the posterior mean and standard deviation. Verify your calculations using SciPy.

(b) Use SciPy to compute the equal-tailed and highest density 94% posterior intervals.

(c) Use SciPy to compute the posterior predictive probability that at least one seedling will germinate if you plant another 12 seedlings.

After obtaining your results with SciPy repeat this exercise using PyMC3 and ArviZ

2

Exploratory Analysis of Bayesian Models

As we saw in Chapter 1, Bayesian inference is about conditioning models to the available data and obtaining posterior distributions. We can do this using pen and paper, computers, or other devices [1]. Additionally we can include, as part of the inference process, the computation of other quantities like the prior and posterior predictive distributions. However, Bayesian modeling is wider than inference. While it would be nice if Bayesian modeling was as simple as specifying model and calculating a posterior, it is typically not. The reality is that other equally important tasks are needed for successful Bayesian data analysis. In this chapter we will discuss some of these tasks including, checking model assumptions, diagnosing inference results and model comparison.

2.1   There is Life After Inference, and Before Too!

A successful Bayesian modeling approach requires performing additional tasks beyond inference [2]. Such as:

- Diagnosing the quality of the inference results obtained using numerical methods.

- Model criticism, including evaluations of both model assumptions and model predictions.

- Comparison of models, including model selection or model averaging.

- Preparation of the results for a particular audience.

These tasks require both numerical and visual summaries to help practitioners analyze their models. We collectively call these tasks **Exploratory Analysis of Bayesian Models**. The name is taken from the statistical approach known as Exploratory Data Analysis (EDA) [150]. This approach to data analysis aims at summarizing the main characteristics of a data set, often with visual methods. In the words of Persi Diaconis [46]:

Exploratory data analysis (EDA) seeks to reveal structure, or simple descriptions, in data. We look at numbers or graphs and try to find patterns. We pursue leads suggested by background information, imagination, patterns perceived, and experience with other data analyses.

EDA is generally performed before, or even instead of, an inferential step. We, as many others before us [57, 64], think that many of the ideas from EDA can be used, reinterpreted and expanded into a robust Bayesian modeling approach. In this book we will mainly use the Python library ArviZ [3] [91] to help us perform exploratory analysis of Bayesian models.

---

[1]https://www.countbayesie.com/blog/2015/2/18/bayes-theorem-with-lego

[2]We are omitting tasks related to obtaining the data in the first place, but experimental design can be as critical if not more than other aspects in the statistical analysis, see Chapter 10.

[3]https://arviz-devs.github.io/arviz/

DOI: 10.1201/9781003019169-2

In a real life setting, Bayesian inference and exploratory analysis of Bayesian models get tangled into an iterative workflow, that includes silly coding mistakes, computational problems, doubts about the adequacy of models, doubts about our current understanding of the data, nonlinear model building, model checking, etc. Trying to emulate this intricate workflow in a book is challenging. Thus throughout these pages we may omit some or even all the exploratory analysis steps or maybe leave them as exercises. This is not because they are not necessary or not important. On the contrary during writing this book we have performed many iterations "behind the scenes". However, we omit them in certain areas so focus on other relevant aspects such as model details, computational features, or fundamental mathematics.

2.2   Understanding Your Assumptions

As we discussed in Section 1.4, "what is the best-ever prior?" is a tempting question to ask. However, it is difficult to give a straight satisfying answer other than: "it depends". We can certainly find default priors for a given model or family of models that will yield good results for a wide range of datasets. But we can also find ways to outperform them for particular problems if we can generate more informative priors for those specific problems. Good default priors can serve as good priors for quick/default analysis and also as good placeholder for better priors if we can invest the time and effort to move into an iterative, exploratory Bayesian modelling workflow.

One problem when choosing priors is that it may be difficult to understand their effect as they propagate down the model into the data. The choices we made in the parameter space may induce something unexpected in the observable data space. A very helpful tool to better understand our assumptions is the prior predictive distribution, which we presented in Section 1.1.2 and Equation 1.7. In practice we can compute a prior predictive distribution by sampling from the model, but without conditioning on the observed data. By sampling from the prior predictive distribution, the computer does the work of translating choices we made in the parameter space into the observed data space. Using these samples to evaluate priors is known as **prior predictive checks**.

Let us assume we want to build a model of football (or soccer for the people in USA). Specifically we are interested in the probability of scoring goals from the penalty point. After thinking for a while we decide to use a geometric model [4]. Following the sketch in Figure 2.1 and a little bit of trigonometry we come up with the following formula for the probability of scoring a goal:

$$p\left(|\alpha| < \tan^{-1}\left(\frac{L}{x}\right)\right) = 2\Phi\left(\frac{\tan^{-1}\left(\frac{L}{x}\right)}{\sigma}\right) - 1 \qquad (2.1)$$

The intuition behind Equation 2.1 is that we are assuming the probability of scoring a goal is given by the absolute value of the angle α being less than a threshold $\tan^{-1}\left(\frac{L}{x}\right)$. Furthermore we are assuming that the player is trying to kick the ball straight, i.e at a zero angle, but then there are other factors that result in a trajectory with a deviation σ.

---

[4]This example has been adapted from `https://mc-stan.org/users/documentation/case-studies/golf.html` and `https://docs.pymc.io/notebooks/putting_workflow.html`

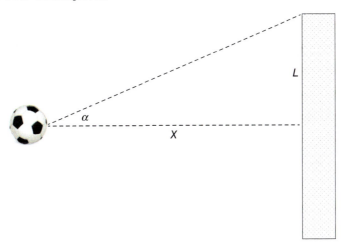

FIGURE 2.1
Sketch of a penalty shot. The dashed lines represent the angle α within which the ball must be kicked to score a goal. x represents the reglementary distance for a penalty shot (11 meters) and L half the length of a reglementary goal mouth (3.66 meters).

The only unknown quantity in Equation 2.1 is σ. We can get the values of L and x from the rules of football. As good Bayesians, when we do not know a quantity, we assign a prior to it and then try to build a Bayesian model, for example, we could write:

$$\sigma = \mathcal{HN}(\sigma_\sigma)$$

$$\text{p\_goal} = 2\Phi\left(\frac{\tan^{-1}\left(\frac{L}{x}\right)}{\sigma}\right) - 1 \tag{2.2}$$

$$Y = \text{Bin}(n = 1, p = \text{p\_goal})$$

At this point we are not entirely certain how well our model encodes our domain knowledge about football, so we decide to first sample from the prior predictive to gain some intuition. Figure 2.2 shows the results for three priors (encoded as three values of σ_σ, 5, 20, and 60 degrees). The gray circular area represents the set of angles that should lead to scoring a goal assuming that the player kicks the ball completely straight and no other factors come in play like wind, friction, etc. We can see that our model assumes that it is possible to score goals even if the player kicks the ball with a greater angle than the gray area. Interestingly enough for large values of σ_σ the model thinks that kicking in the opposite direction is not that bad idea.

At this point we have a few alternatives: we can rethink our model to incorporate further geometric insights. Alternatively we can use a prior that reduces the chance of nonsensical results even if we do not exclude them completely, or we can just fit the data and see if the data is informative enough to estimate a posterior that excludes nonsensical values. Figure 2.3 shows another example of what we may consider unexpected [5]. The example shows how for a logistic regression [6] with binary predictors and priors $\mathcal{N}(0,1)$ on the regression coefficients. As we increase the number of predictors, the mean of the prior predictive distributions shifts from being more concentrated around 0.5 (first panel) to Uniform (middle) to favor extreme, 0 or 1, values (last panel). This example shows us that as the number of predictors increase, the induced prior predictive distribution puts

---
[5]The example has been adapted from [64].
[6]See Chapter 3 for details of the logistic regression model.

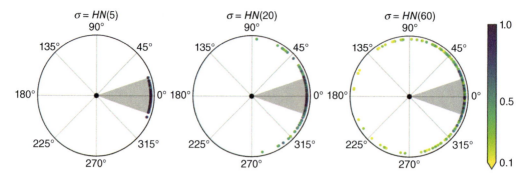

FIGURE 2.2
Prior predictive checks for the model in Equation 2.2. Each subplot corresponds to a different value of the prior for σ. The black dot at the center of each circular plot represents the penalty point. The dots at the edges represent shots, the position is the value of the angle α (see Figure 2.1), and the color represents the probability of scoring a goal.

more mass on extreme values. Thus we need a *stronger regularizing prior* (e.g., Laplace distribution) in order to keep the model away from those extreme values.

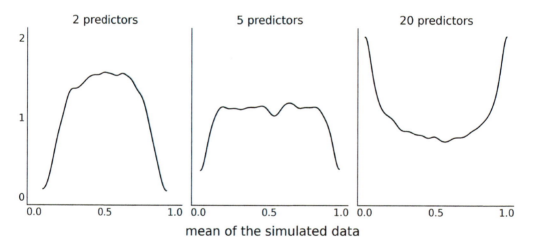

FIGURE 2.3
Prior predictive distribution for a logistic regression models with 2, 5, or 15 binary predictors and with 100 data points. The KDE represents the distributions of the mean of the simulated data over 10000 simulations. Even when the prior for each coefficient, $\mathcal{N}(0,1)$, is the same for all 3 panels, increasing the numbers of the predictor is effectively equivalent to using a prior favoring extreme values.

Both previous examples show that priors can not be understood in isolation, we need to put them in the context of a particular model. As thinking in terms of observed values is generally easier than thinking in terms of the model's parameters, prior predictive distributions can help make model evaluation easier. This becomes even more useful for complex models where parameters get transformed through many mathematical operations, or multiple priors interact with each other. Additionally, prior predictive distributions can be used to present results or discuss models in a more intuitive way to a wide audience. A domain expert may not be familiar with statistical notation or code and thus using those devices may not lead to a productive discussion, but if you show them the implications of one or more models, you provide them more material to discuss. This can provide valuable insight both for your domain partner and yourself. And again computing the prior predictive has other advantages, such as helping us debug models, ensuring they are properly written and able to run in our computational environment.

2.3 Understanding Your Predictions

As we can use synthetic data, that is generated data, from the prior predictive distribution to help us inspect our model, we can perform a similar analysis with the posterior predictive distribution, introduced in Section 1.1.2 and Equation 1.8. This procedure is generally referred as **posterior predictive checks**. The basic idea is to evaluate how close the synthetic observations are to the actual observations. Ideally the way we assess closeness should be problem-dependent, but we can also use some general rules. We may even want to use more than one metric in order to assess different ways our models (mis)match the data.

Figure 2.4 shows a very simple example for a binomial model and data. On the left panel we are comparing the number of observed successes in our data (blue line) with the number of predicted successes over 1000 samples from the posterior predictive distribution. On the right panel is an alternative way of representing the results, this time showing the proportion of success and failures in our data (blue line) against 1000 samples from the posterior distribution. As we can see the model is doing a very good job at capturing the mean value in this case, even when the model recognizes there is a lot of uncertainty. We should not be surprised that the model is doing a good job at capturing the mean. The reason is that we are directly modeling the mean of the binomial distribution. In the next chapters we will see examples when posterior predictive checks provide less obvious and thus more valuable information about our model's fit to the data.

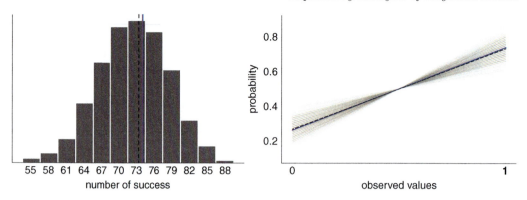

FIGURE 2.4

Posterior predictive check for a Beta-Binomial model. On the left panel we have the number of predicted success (gray histogram), the dashed black line represents the mean predicted success. The blue line is the mean computed from the data. On the right panel we have the same information but represented in an alternative way. Instead of the number of success we are plotting the probability of getting 0's or 1's. We are using a line to represent that the probability of $p(y = 0) = 1 - p(y = 1)$. the dashed black line is the mean predicted probability, and the blue line is the mean computed from the data.

Posterior predictive checks are not restricted to plots. We can also perform numerical tests [59]. One way of doing this is by computing:

$$p_B = p(T_{sim} \leq T_{obs} \mid \tilde{Y}) \tag{2.3}$$

where p_B is a Bayesian p-value and is defined as the probability the simulated test statistic T_{sim} is less or equal than the observed statistic T_{obs}. The statistic T is basically any metric we may want to use to assess our models fit to the data. Following the binomial example we can choose T_{obs} as the observed success rate and then compare it against the posterior predictive distribution T_{sim}. The ideal value of $p_B = 0.5$ means that we compute a T_{sim} statistic that half the time is below and half the time above the observed statistics T_{obs}, which is the expected outcome for a good fit.

Because we love plots, we can also create plots with Bayesian p-values. The first panel of Figure 2.5 shows the distribution of Bayesian p-values in black solid line, the dashed line represents the expected distribution for a dataset of the same size. We can obtain such a plot with ArviZ `az.plot_bpv(., kind="p_value")`. The second panel is conceptually similar, the twist is that we evaluate how many of the simulations are below (or above) the observed data "per observation". For a well-calibrated model, all observations should be equally well predicted, that is the expected number of predictions above or below should be the same. Thus we should get a Uniform distribution. As for any finite dataset, even a perfectly calibrated model will show deviations from a Uniform distribution, we plot a band where we expected to see 94% of the Uniform-like curves.

Bayesian p-values

We call p_B Bayesian p-values as the quantity in Equation 2.3 is essentially the definition of a p-value, and we say they are Bayesian because, instead of using the distribution of the statistic T under the null hypothesis as the sampling distribution we are using the posterior predictive distribution. Notice that we are not conditioning on any null hypothesis. Neither are we using any predefined threshold to declare statistical significance or to perform hypothesis testing.

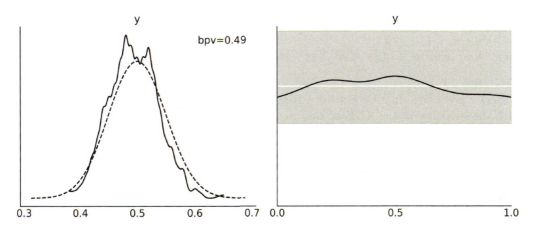

FIGURE 2.5
Posterior predictive distribution for a Beta-Binomial model. In the first panel, the curve with the solid line is the KDE of the proportion of predicted values that are less or equal than the observed data. The dashed lines represent the expected distribution for a dataset of the same size as the observed data. On the second panel, the black line is a KDE for the proportion of predicted values that are less or equal than the observed computed per observation instead of over each simulation as in the first panel. The white line represents the ideal case, a standard Uniform distribution, and the gray band deviations of that Uniform distribution that we expect to see for a dataset of the same size.

As we said before we can choose from many T statistics to summarize observations and predictions. Figure 2.6 shows two examples, in the first panel T is the mean and in the second one T is the standard deviation. The curves are KDEs representing the distribution of the T statistics from the posterior predictive distribution and the dot is the value for the observed data.

Before continue reading you should take a moment to carefully inspect Figure 2.7 and try to understand why the plots look like they do. In this figure we have a series of simple examples to help us gain intuition about how to interpret posterior predictive checks plots[7]. In all these examples the observed data (in blue) follows a Gaussian distribution.

1. On the first row, the model predicts observations that are systematically shifted to higher values with respect to the observed data.

2. On the second row, the model is making predictions that are more spread than the observed data.

---

[7]Posterior predictive checks are a very general idea. These figures do not try to show the only available choices, just some of the options offered by ArviZ.

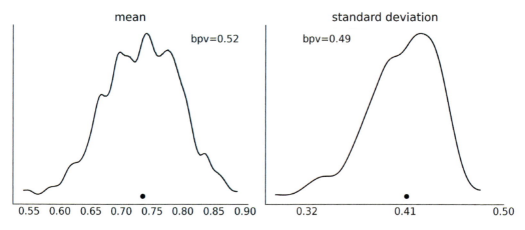

FIGURE 2.6
Posterior predictive distribution for a Beta-Binomial model. In the first panel, the curve with the solid line is the KDE of the proportion of simulations of predicted values with mean values less or equal than the observed data. On the second panel, the same but for the standard deviation. The black dot represented the mean (first panel) or standard deviation (second panel) computed from the observed data.

3. On the third row we have the opposite scenario, the model is not generating enough predictions at the tails.

4. On the last row shows a model making predictions following a mixture of Gaussians.

We are now going to pay special attention to the third column from Figure 2.7. Plots in this column are very useful but at the same time they can be confusing at first. From top to bottom, you can read them as:

1. The model is missing observations on the left tail (and making more on the right).

2. The model is making less predictions at the middle (and more at the tails).

3. The model is making less predictions for both tails.

4. The model is making more or less well-calibrated predictions, but I am a skeptical person so I should run another posterior predictive check to confirm.

If this way of reading the plots still sounds confusing to you, we could try from a different perspective that is totally equivalent, but it may be more intuitive, as long as you remember that you can change the model, not the observations [8]. From top to bottom, you can read them as:

1. There are more observations on the left

2. There are more observations on the middle

3. There are more observations at the tails.

4. Observations seem well distributed (at least within the expected boundaries), but you should not trust me. I am just a platonic model in a platonic world.

---

[8]Unless you realize you need to collect data again, but that is another story.

We hope Figure 2.7 and the accompanying discussion provide you with enough intuition to better perform model checking in real scenarios.

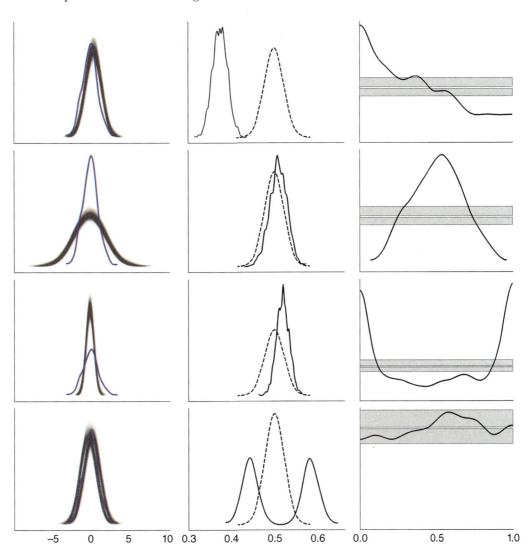

FIGURE 2.7
Posterior predictive checks for a set of simple hypothetical models. On the first column, the blue solid line represents the observed data and the light-gray ones predictions from an hypothetical model. On the second column, the solid line is the KDE of the proportion of predicted values that are less or equal than the observed data. The dashed lines represent the expected distribution for a dataset of the same size as the observed data. On the third panel, the KDE is for the proportion of predicted values that are less or equal than the observed computed per each observation. The white lines represent the expected Uniform distribution and the gray band the expected deviations from uniformity for a dataset of the same size as the one used. This figure was made using the ArviZ's functions `az.plot_ppc(.)`, `az.plot_bpv(., kind="p_values")` and `az.plot_bpv(., kind="u_values")`.

Posterior predictive checks, either using plots or numerical summaries, or even a combination of both, is a very flexible idea. This concept is general enough to let the practitioner use their imagination to come up with different ways to explore, evaluate, and better understand model through their predictions and how well a model (or models) work for a particular problem.

2.4 Diagnosing Numerical Inference

Using numerical methods to approximate the posterior distribution allows us to solve Bayesian models that could be tedious to solve with pen and paper or that could be mathematically intractable. Unfortunately, they do not always work as expected. For that reason we must always evaluate if the results they offer are of any use. We can do that using a collection of numerical and visual diagnostic tools. In this section we will discuss the most common and useful diagnostics tools for Markov chain Monte Carlo methods.

To help us understand these diagnostic tools, we are going to create three *synthetic posteriors*. The first one is a sample from a Beta$(2, 5)$. We generate it using SciPy, and we call it `good_chains`. This is an example of a "good" sample because we are generating independent and identically distributed (iid) draws and ideally this is what we want in order to approximate the posterior. The second one is called `bad_chains0` and represents a poor sample from the posterior. We generate it by sorting `good_chains` and then adding a small Gaussian error. `bad_chains0` is a poor sample for two reasons:

- The values are not independent. On the contrary they are highly autocorrelated, meaning that given any number at any position in the sequence we can compute the values coming before and after with high precision.

- The values are not identically distributed, as we are reshaping a previously flattened and sorted array into a 2D array, representing two chains.

The third *synthetic posterior* called `bad_chains1` is generated from `good_chains`, and we are turning it into a representation of a poor sample from the posterior, by randomly introducing portions where consecutive samples are highly correlated to each other. `bad_chains1` represents a very common scenario, a sampler can resolve a region of the parameter space very well, but one or more regions are difficult to sample.

Code 2.1

```
1  good_chains = stats.beta.rvs(2, 5,size=(2, 2000))
2  bad_chains0 = np.random.normal(np.sort(good_chains, axis=None), 0.05,
3                                 size=4000).reshape(2, -1)
4
5  bad_chains1 = good_chains.copy()
6  for i in np.random.randint(1900, size=4):
7      bad_chains1[i%2:,i:i+100] = np.random.beta(i, 950, size=100)
8
9  chains = {"good_chains":good_chains,
10           "bad_chains0":bad_chains0,
11           "bad_chains1":bad_chains1}
```

Notice that the 3 synthetic posteriors are samples from a scalar (single parameter) posterior distribution. This is enough for our current discussion as all the diagnostics we will see are computed per parameter in the model.

2.4.1 Effective Sample Size

When using MCMC sampling methods, it is reasonable to wonder if a particular sample is large enough to confidently compute the quantities of interest, like a mean or an HDI. This is something we can not directly answer just by looking at the number of samples, the reason is that samples from MCMC methods will have some degree of **autocorrelation**, thus the actual *amount of information* contained in that sample will be less than the one we would get from an iid sample of the same size. We say a series of values are autocorrelated when we can observe a similarity between them as a function of the time lag between them. For example, if today the sunset was at 6:03 am, you know tomorrow the sunset will be about the same time. In fact the closer you are to the equator the longer you will be able to predict the time for future sunsets given the value of today. That is, the autocorrelation is larger at the equator than closer to the poles [9].

We can think of the effective sample size (ESS) as an estimator that takes autocorrelation into account and provides the number of draws we would have if our sample was actually iid. This interpretation is appealing, but we have to be careful about not over-interpreting it as we will see next.

Using ArviZ we can compute the effective sample size for the mean with `az.ess()`

Code 2.2

```
az.ess(chains)
```

```
<xarray.Dataset>
Dimensions:      ()
Data variables:
    good_chains   float64 4.389e+03
    bad_chains0   float64 2.436
    bad_chains1   float64 111.1
```

We can see that even when the count of actual samples in our synthetic posteriors is 4000, `bad_chains0` has efficiency equivalent to an iid sample of size ≈ 2. This is certainly a low number indicating a problem with the sampler. Given the method used by ArviZ to compute the ESS and how we created `bad_chains0`, this result is totally expected. `bad_chains0` is a bimodal distribution with each chain stuck in each mode. For such cases the ESS will be approximately equal to the number of modes the MCMC chains explored. For `bad_chains1` we also get a low number ≈ 111 and only ESS for `good_chains` is close to the actual number of samples.

> **On the effectiveness of effective samples**
>
> If you rerun the generation of these synthetic posteriors, using a different random seed, you will see that the effective sample size you get will be different each time. This is expected as the samples will not be exactly the same, they are after all samples. For `good_chains`, on average, the value of effective sample size will be lower than the number of samples. But notice that ESS could be in fact larger! When using the NUTS sampler (see Section 11.9) values of ESS larger than the total number of samples can happen for parameters which posterior distributions are close to Gaussian and which are almost independent of other parameters in the model.

---

[9]Try `https://www.timeanddate.com/sun/ecuador/quito`

Convergence of Markov chains is not uniform across the parameter space [155], intuitively it is easier to get a good approximation from the bulk of a distribution than from the tails, simply because the tails are dominated by rare events. The default value returned by `az.ess()` is `bulk-ESS` which mainly assesses how well the *center* of the distribution was resolved. If you also want to report posterior intervals or you are interested in rare events, you should check the value of `tail-ESS`, which corresponds to the minimum ESS at the percentiles 5 and 95. If you are interested in specific quantiles, you can ask ArviZ for those specific values using `az.ess(., method='quantile')`.

As the ESS values vary across the parameter space, we may find it useful to visualize this variation in a single plot. We have at least two ways to do it. Plotting the ESS for specifics quantiles `az.plot_ess(., kind="quantiles"` or for small intervals defined between two quantiles `az.plot_ess(., kind="local")` as shown in Figure 2.8.

Code 2.3

```
1  _, axes = plt.subplots(2, 3, sharey=True, sharex=True)
2  az.plot_ess(chains, kind="local", ax=axes[0]);
3  az.plot_ess(chains, kind="quantile", ax=axes[1]);
```

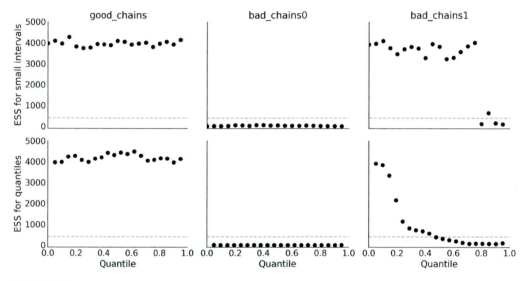

FIGURE 2.8

Top: Local ESS of small interval probability estimates. Bottom: Quantile ESS estimates. The dashed lines represent the minimum suggested value of 400 at which we would consider the effective sample size to be sufficient. Ideally, we want the local and quantile ESS to be high across all regions of the parameter space.

As a general rule of thumb we recommend a value of ESS greater than 400, otherwise, the estimation of the ESS itself and the estimation of other quantities, like $\hat{R}$ that we will see next, will be basically unreliable [155]. Finally, we said that the ESS provides the number of draws we would have if our sample was actually iid. Nevertheless, we have to be careful with this interpretation as the actual value of ESS will not be the same for different regions of the parameter space. Taking that detail into account, the intuition still seems useful.

2.4.2   Potential Scale Reduction Factor $\hat{R}$

Under very general conditions Markov chain Monte Carlo methods have theoretical guarantees that they will get the right answer irrespective of the starting point. Unfortunately, the fine print says that the guarantees are valid only for infinite samples. Thus in practice we need ways to estimate convergence for finite samples. One pervasive idea is to run more than one chain, starting from very different points and then check the resulting chains to see if they *look similar* to each other. This intuitive notion can be formalized into a numerical diagnostic known as $\hat{R}$. There are many versions of this estimator, as it has been refined over the years [155]. Originally the $\hat{R}$ diagnostic was interpreted as the overestimation of variance due to MCMC finite sampling. Meaning that if you continue sampling infinitely you should get a reduction of the variance of your estimation by a $\hat{R}$ factor. And hence the name "potential scale reduction factor", with the target value of 1 meaning that increasing the number of samples will not reduce the variance of the estimation further. Nevertheless, in practice it is better to just think of it as a diagnostic tool without trying to over-interpret it.

The $\hat{R}$ for the parameter θ is computed as the standard deviation of all the samples of θ, that is including all chains together, divided by the root mean square of the separated within-chain standard deviations. The actual computation is a little bit more involved but the overall idea remains true [155]. Ideally we should get a value of 1, as the variance between chains should be the same as the variance within-chain. From a practical point of view values of $\hat{R} \lesssim 1.01$ are considered safe.

Using ArviZ we can compute the $\hat{R}$ diagnostics with the `az.rhat()` function

Code 2.4

```
az.rhat(chains)
```

```
<xarray.Dataset>
Dimensions:      ()
Data variables:
    good_chains  float64 1.000
    bad_chains0  float64 2.408
    bad_chains1  float64 1.033
```

From this result we can see that $\hat{R}$ correctly identifies `good_chains` as a good sample and `bad_chains0` and `bad_chains1` as samples with different degree of problems. While `bad_chains0` is a total disaster, `bad_chains1` seems to be closer to reaching the *ok-chain status*, but still off.

2.4.3   Monte Carlo Standard Error

When using MCMC methods we introduce an additional layer of uncertainty as we are approximating the posterior with a finite number of samples. We can estimate the amount of error introduced using the Monte Carlo standard error (MCSE), which is based on Markov chain central limit theorem (see Section 11.1.11). The MCSE takes into account that the samples are not truly independent of each other and are in fact computed from the ESS [155]. While the values of ESS and $\hat{R}$ are independent of the scale of the parameters, interpreting whether MCSE is small enough requires domain expertise. If we want to report the value of an estimated parameter to the second decimal, we need to be sure the MCSE is below the second decimal otherwise, we will be, wrongly, reporting a higher precision than we really have. We should check the MCSE only once we are sure ESS is high enough and $\hat{R}$ is low enough; otherwise, MCSE is of no use.

Using ArviZ we can compute the MCSE with the function `az.mcse()`

Code 2.5

```
az.mcse(chains)
```

```
<xarray.Dataset>
Dimensions:       ()
Data variables:
    good_chains   float64 0.002381
    bad_chains0   float64 0.1077
    bad_chains1   float64 0.01781
```

As with the ESS the MCSE varies across the parameter space and then we may also want to evaluate it for different regions, like specific quantiles. Additionally, we may also want to visualize several values at once as in Figure 2.9.

Code 2.6

```
az.plot_mcse(chains)
```

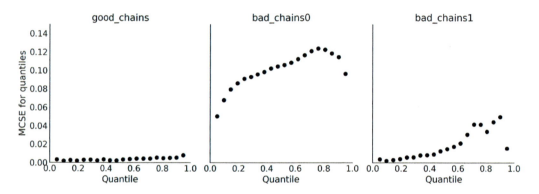

FIGURE 2.9
Local MCSE for quantiles. Subplots y-axis share the same scale to ease comparison between them. Ideally, we want the MCSE to be small across all regions of the parameter space. Note how the MCSE values for `good_chains` is relatively low across all values compared to MCSE of both bad chains.

Finally, the ESS, $\hat{R}$, and MCSE can all be computed with a single call to the `az.summary(.)` function.

Code 2.7

```
az.summary(chains, kind="diagnostics")
```

	mcse_mean	mcse_sd	ess_bulk	ess_tail	r_hat
good_chains	0.002	0.002	4389.0	3966.0	1.00
bad_chains0	0.108	0.088	2.0	11.0	2.41
bad_chains1	0.018	0.013	111.0	105.0	1.03

The first column is the Monte Carlo standard error for the mean or (expectation), the second one is the Monte Carlo standard error for the standard deviation [10]. Then we have the bulk and tail effective sample size and finally the $\hat{R}$ diagnostic.

2.4.4 Trace Plots

Trace plots are probably the most popular plots in Bayesian literature. They are often the first plot we make after inference, to visually check *what we got*. A trace plot is made by drawing the sampled values at each iteration step. From these plots we should be able to see if different chains converge to the same distribution, we can get a *sense* of the degree of autocorrelation, etc. In ArviZ by calling the function `az.plot_trace(.)` we get a trace plot on the right plus a representation of the distribution of the sample values, using a KDE for continuous variables and a histogram for discrete ones on the left.

Code 2.8

```
az.plot_trace(chains)
```

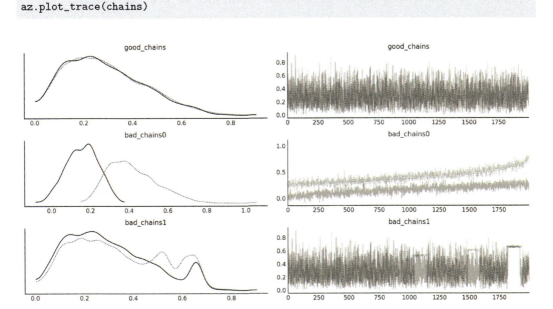

FIGURE 2.10
On the left column, we see one KDE per chain. On the right, column we see the values of the sampled values per chain per step. Note the differences in the KDE and trace plots between each of the example chains, particularly the *fuzzy caterpillar* appearance in `good_chains` versus the irregularities in the other two.

Figure 2.10 shows the trace plots for `chains`. From it, we can see that the draws in `good_chains` belong to the same distribution as there are only small (random) differences between both chains. When we see the draws ordered by iteration (i.e. the trace itself) we can see that chains look rather *noisy* with no apparent trend or pattern, it is also difficult to distinguish one chain from the other. This is in clear contrast to what we get for `bad_chains0`. For this sample we clearly see two different distributions with only some overlap. This is easy to see both from the KDE and from the trace. The chains are exploring two different regions of the parameter space. The situation for `bad_chains1` is a little bit more subtle. The KDE shows distributions that seem to be similar to those from `good_chains`

---

[10]Do not confuse with the standard deviation of the MCSE for the mean.

the differences between the two chains are more clear. Do we have 2 or 3 peaks? The distributions do not seem to agree, maybe we just have one mode and the extra peaks are artifacts! Peaks generally look suspicious unless we have reasons to believe in multi-modal distributions arising, for example, from sub-populations in our data. The trace also seems to be somehow similar to the one from `good_chains`, but a more careful inspection reveals the presence of long regions of monotonicity (the lines parallel to the x-axis). This is a clear indication that the sampler is getting stuck in some regions of the parameter space, maybe because we have a multimodal posterior with barrier between modes of very low probability or perhaps because we have some regions of the parameter space with a curvature that is too different from the rest.

2.4.5   Autocorrelation Plots

As we saw when we discussed the effective sample size, autocorrelation decreases the actual amount of information contained in a sample and thus something we want to keep at a minimum. We can directly inspect the autocorrelation with `az.plot_autocorr`.

Code 2.9

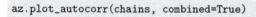

```
az.plot_autocorr(chains, combined=True)
```

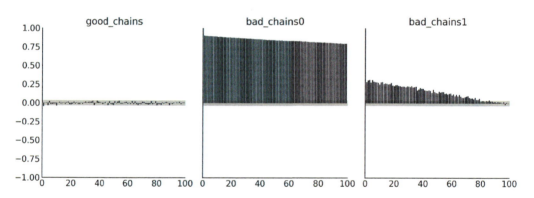

FIGURE 2.11
Bar plot of the autocorrelation function over a 100 steps window. The height of the bars for `good_chains` is close to zero (and mostly inside the gray band) for the entire plot, which indicates very low autocorrelation. The tall bars in `bad_chains0` and `bad_chains1` indicate large values of autocorrelation, which is undesirable. The gray band represents the 95% confidence interval.

What we see in Figure 2.11 is at least qualitatively expected after seeing the results from `az.ess`. `good_chains` shows essentially zero autocorrelation, `bad_chains0` is highly correlated and `bad_chains1` is not that bad, but autocorrelation is still noticeable and is long-range, i.e. it does not drop quickly.

2.4.6   Rank Plots

Rank plots are another visual diagnostic we can use to compare the sampling behavior both within and between chains. Rank plots, simply put, are histograms of the ranked samples. The ranks are computed by first combining all chains but then plotting the results separately for each chain. If all of the chains are targeting the same distribution, we expect the ranks to have a Uniform distribution. Additionally if rank plots of all chains look similar, this indicates good mixing of the chains [155].

Code 2.10

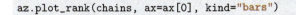

```
az.plot_rank(chains, ax=ax[0], kind="bars")
```

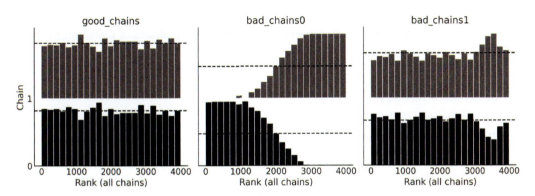

FIGURE 2.12
Rank plots using the `bar` representation. In particular, compare the height of the bar to the dashed line representing a Uniform distribution. Ideally, the bars should follow a Uniform distribution.

One alternative to the "bars" representation is vertical lines, shortened to "vlines".

Code 2.11

```
az.plot_rank(chains, kind="vlines")
```

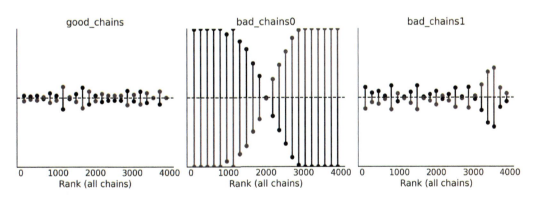

FIGURE 2.13
Rank plots using the `vline` representation. The shorter the vertical lines the better. vertical lines above the dashed line indicate an excess sampled values for a particular rank, vertical lines below indicate a lack of sampled values.

We can see in Figures 2.12 and 2.13 that for `good_chains` the ranks are very close to Uniform and that both chains look similar to each other with not distinctive pattern. This is in clear contrast with the results for `bad_chains0` where the chains depart from uniformity, and they are exploring two separate sets of value, with some overlap over the middle ranks.

Notice how this is consistent to the way we created `bad_chains0` and also with what we saw in its trace plot. `bad_chains1` is somehow Uniform but with a few large deviations here and there, reflecting that the problems are more *local* than those from `bad_chains0`.

Rank plots can be more sensitive than trace plots, and thus we recommend them over the latter. We can obtain them using `az.plot_trace(., kind="rank_bars")` or `az.plot_trace(., kind="rank_vlines")`. These functions not only plot the ranks but also the marginal distributions of the posterior. This kind of plot can be useful to quickly get a sense of what the posterior *looks like*, which in many cases can help us to spot problems with sampling or model definition, especially during the early phases of modeling when we are most likely not sure about what we really want to do and as a result, we need to explore many different alternatives. As we progress and the model or models start to make more sense we can then check that the ESS, $\hat{R}$, and MCSE are okay and if not okay know that our model needs further refinements.

2.4.7   Divergences

So far we have been diagnosing how well a sampler works by studying the generated samples. Another way to perform a diagnostic is by monitoring the behavior of the inner workings of the sampling method. One prominent example of such diagnostics is the concept of divergences present in some **Hamiltonian Monte Carlo** (HMC) methods [11]. Divergences, or more correctly divergent transitions, are a powerful and sensitive way of diagnosing samples and works as complement to the diagnostics we saw in the previous sections.

Let us discuss divergences in the context of a very simple model, we will find more realistic examples later through the book. Our model consists of a parameter $\theta 2$ following a Uniform distribution in the interval $[-\theta 1, \theta 1]$, and $\theta 1$ is sampled from a normal distribution. When $\theta 1$ is large $\theta 2$ will follow a Uniform distribution spanning a wide range, and when $\theta 1$ approaches zero, the width of $\theta 2$ will also approach zero. Using PyMC3 we can write this model as:

Code 2.12

```
1  with pm.Model() as model_0:
2      θ1 = pm.Normal("θ1", 0, 1, testval=0.1)
3      θ2 = pm.Uniform("θ2", -θ1, θ1)
4      idata_0 = pm.sample(return_inferencedata=True)
```

> ### The ArviZ InferenceData format
>
> `az.InferenceData` is a specialized data format designed for MCMC Bayesian users. It is based on xarray [82], a flexible N dimensional array package. The main purpose of the InferenceData object is to provide a convenient way to store and manipulate the information generated during a Bayesian workflow, including samples from distributions like the posterior, prior, posterior predictive, prior predictive and other information and diagnostics generated during sampling. InferenceData objects keeps all this information organized using a concept called groups.
>
> In this book we extensively utilize `az.InferenceData`. We use it to store Bayesian inference results, calculate diagnostics, generate plots, and read and write from disk. Refer to the ArviZ documentation for a full technical specification and API.

---

[11] Most useful and commonly used sampling methods for Bayesian inference are variants of HMC, including for example, the default method for continuous variables in PyMC3. For more details of this method, see Section 11.9.3).

Notice how the model in Code Block 2.12 is not conditioned on any observations, which means `model_0` specified a posterior distribution parameterized by two unknowns ($\theta 1$ and $\theta 2$). You may have also noticed that we have included the argument `testval=0.1`. We do this to instruct PyMC3 to start sampling from a particular value (0.1 in this example), instead of from its default. The default value is $\theta 1 = 0$ and for that value the probability density function of $\theta 2$ is a Dirac delta [12], which will produce an error. Using `testval=0.1` only affects how the sampling is initialized.

In Figure 2.14 we can see vertical bars at the bottom of the KDEs for `model0`. Each one of these bars represents a divergence, indicating that something went wrong during sampling. We can see something similar using other plots, like with `az.plot_pair(., divergences=True)` as shown in Figure 2.15, here the divergences are the blue dots, which are everywhere!

Something is definitely problematic with `model0`. Upon inspection of the model definition in Code Block 2.12 we may realize that we defined it in a weird way. $\theta 1$ is a Normal distribution centered at 0, and thus we should expect half of the values to be negative, but for negative values $\theta 2$ will be defined in the interval $[\theta 1, -\theta 1]$, which is at least a little bit weird. So, let us try to **reparameterize** the model, i.e. express the model in a different but mathematically equivalent way. For example, we can do:

Code 2.13

```
1  with pm.Model() as model_1:
2      θ1 = pm.HalfNormal("θ1", 1 / (1-2/np.pi)**0.5)
3      θ2 = pm.Uniform("θ2", -θ1, θ1)
4      idata_1 = pm.sample(return_inferencedata=True)
```

Now $\theta 1$ will always provide reasonable values we can feed into the definition of $\theta 2$. Notice that we have defined the standard deviation of $\theta 1$ as $\frac{1}{\sqrt{(1-\frac{2}{\pi})}}$ instead of just 1. This is because the standard deviation of the half-normal is $\sigma \sqrt{(1 - \frac{2}{\pi})}$ where σ is the scale parameter of the half-normal. In other words, σ is the standard deviation of the *unfolded* Normal, not the Half-normal distribution.

Anyway, let us see how these reparameterized models do with respect to divergences. Figure 2.14 and Figure 2.15 show that the number of divergences has been reduced dramatically for `model1`, but we still can see a few of them. One easy option we can try to reduce divergences is increasing the value of `target_accept` as shown in Code Block 2.14, by default this value is 0.8 and the maximum valid value is 1 (see Section 11.9.3 for details).

Code 2.14

```
1  with pm.Model() as model_1bis:
2      θ1 = pm.HalfNormal("θ1", 1 / (1-2/np.pi)**0.5)
3      θ2 = pm.Uniform("θ2", -θ1, θ1)
4      idata_1bis = pm.sample(target_accept=.95, return_inferencedata=True)
```

`model1bis` in Figure 2.14 and 2.15 is the same as `model1` but with we have changed the default value of one of the sampling parameters `pm.sample(., target_accept=0.95)`. We can see that finally we have removed all the divergences. This is already good news, but in order to trust these samples, we still need to check the value of $\hat{R}$ and ESS as explained in previous sections.

---

[12] A function which is zero everywhere and infinite at zero.

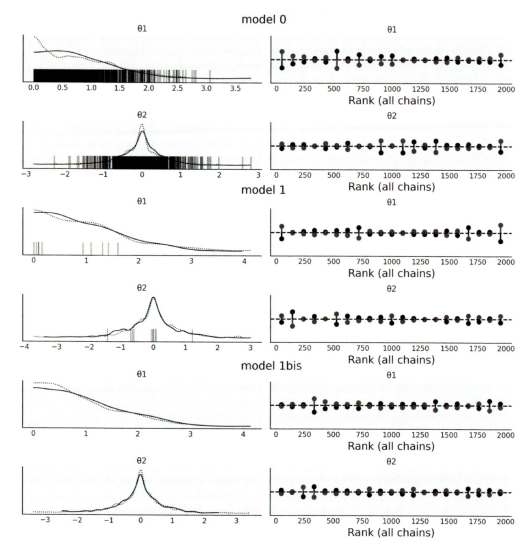

FIGURE 2.14
KDEs and rank plots for Model 0 Code 2.12, Model 1 2.13 and Model 1_bis, which is the same as Model 1 2.13 but with `pm.sample(., target_accept=0.95)`. The black vertical bars represent divergences.

Reparameterization

Reparameterization can be useful to turn a difficult to sample posterior geometry into an easier one. This could help to remove divergences, but it can also help even if no divergences are present. For example, we can use it to speed up sampling or increase the number of effective samples, without having to increase the computational cost. Additionally, reparameterization can also help to better interpret or communicate models and their results (see Alice and Bob example in Section 1.4.1).

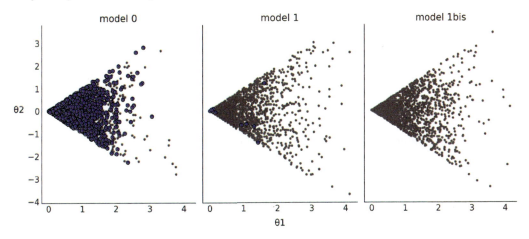

FIGURE 2.15
Scatter plot of the posterior samples from Model 0 from Code 2.12, Model 1 from Code
Block 2.13, and Model 1_bis, which is the same as Model 1 in Code Block 2.13 but with
`pm.sample(., target_accept=0.95)`. The blue dots represent divergences.

2.4.8   Sampler Parameters and Other Diagnostics

Most sampler methods have hyperparameters that affect the sampler performance. While
most PPLs try to use sensible defaults, in practice, they will not work for every possible combination of data and models. As we saw in the previous sections, divergences can
sometimes be removed by increasing the parameter `target_accept`, for example, if the divergences originated from numerical imprecision. There are other sampler parameters that
can also help with sampling issues, for example, we may want to increase the number of
iterations used to tune MCMC samplers. In PyMC3 we have `pm.sample(.,tune=1000)`
by default. During the tuning phase sampler parameters get automatically adjusted. Some
models are more complex and require more interactions for the sampler to learn better
parameters. Thus increasing the turning steps can help to increase the ESS or lower the $\hat{R}$.
Increasing the number of draws can also help with convergence but in general other routes
are more productive. If a model is failing to converge with a few thousands of draws, it will
generally still fail with 10 times more draws or the slight improvement will not justify the
extra computational cost. Reparameterization, improved model structure, more informative
priors, or even changing the model will most often be much more effective [13] We want to
note that in the early stages of modeling we could use a relatively low number of draws to
test that the model runs, that we have actually written the intended model, that we broadly
get reasonable results. For this initial check around 200 or 300 is typically sufficient., Then
we can increase the number of draws to a few thousand, maybe around 2000 or 4000, when
we are more confident about the model.

In addition to the diagnostics shown in this chapter, additional diagnostics exist, such as
parallel plots, and separation plots. All these diagnostics are useful and have their place but
for the brevity of this text we have omitted them from this section. To see others we suggest
visiting the ArviZ documentation and plot gallery which contains many more examples.

---

[13]For a sampler like Sequential Monte Carlo, increasing the number of draws also increases the number
of particles, and thus it could actually provide better convergence. See Section 11.9.4.

2.5   Model Comparison

Usually we want to build models that are not too simple that they miss valuable information in our data nor too complex that they fit the noise in the data. Finding this *sweet spot* is a complex task. Partially because there is not a single criteria to define an optimal solution, partly because such optimal solution may not exist, and partly because in practice we need to choose from a limited set of models evaluated over a finite dataset.

Nevertheless, we can still try to find good general strategies. One useful solution is to compute the generalization error, also known as out-of-sample predictive accuracy. This is an estimate of how well a model behaves at predicting data not used to fit it. Ideally, any measure of predictive accuracy should take into account the details of the problem we are trying to solve, including the benefits and costs associated with the model's predictions. That is, we should apply a decision theoretic approach. However, we can also rely on general devices that are applicable to a wide range of models and problems. Such devices are sometimes referred to as scoring rules, as they help us to score and rank models. From the many possible scoring rules it has been shown that the logarithmic scoring rule has very nice theoretical properties [67], and thus is widely used. Under a Bayesian setting the log scoring rule can be computed as.

$$\text{ELPD} = \sum_{i=1}^{n} \int p_t(\tilde{y}_i) \, \log p(\tilde{y}_i \mid y_i) \, d\tilde{y}_i \qquad (2.4)$$

where $p_t(\tilde{y}_i)$ is distribution of the true data-generating process for $\tilde{y}_i$ and $p(\tilde{y}_i \mid y_i)$ is the posterior predictive distribution. The quantity defined in Equation 2.4 is known as the **expected log pointwise predictive density** (ELPD). Expected because we are integrating over the true data-generating process i.e over all the possible datasets that could be generated from that process, and pointwise because we perform the computations per observation (y_i), over the n observations. For simplicity we use the term density for both continuous and discrete models [14].

For real problems we do not know $p_t(\tilde{y}_i)$ and thus the ELPD as defined in Equation 2.4 is of no immediate use, in practice we can instead compute:

$$\sum_{i=1}^{n} \log \int p(y_i \mid \boldsymbol{\theta}) \, p(\boldsymbol{\theta} \mid y) d\boldsymbol{\theta} \qquad (2.5)$$

The quantity defined by Equation 2.5 (or that quantity multiplied by some constant) is usually known as the deviance, and it is use in both Bayesians and non-Bayesians contexts [15]. When the likelihood is Gaussian, then Equation 2.5 will be proportional to the quadratic mean error.

To compute Equation 2.5 we used the same data used to fit the model and thus we will, on average, overestimate the ELPD (Equation 2.4) which will lead us to choose models prone to overfitting. Fortunately, there are a few ways to produce better estimations of the ELPD. One of them is cross-validation as we will see in the next section.

---

[14]Strictly speaking we should use probabilities for discrete models, but that distinction rapidly becomes annoying in practice.

[15]In non-Bayesians contexts $\boldsymbol{\theta}$ is a point estimate obtained, for example, by maximizing the likelihood.

2.5.1 Cross-validation and LOO

Cross-validation (CV) is a method of estimating out-of-sample predictive accuracy. This method requires re-fitting a model many times, each time excluding a different portion of the data. The excluded portion is then used to measure the accuracy of the model. This process is repeated many times and the estimated accuracy of the model will be the average over all runs. Then the entire dataset is used to fit the model one more time and this is the model used for further analysis and/or predictions. We can see CV as a way to simulate or approximate out-of-sample statistics, while still using all the data.

Leave-one-out cross-validation (LOO-CV) is a particular type of cross-validation when the data excluded is a single data-point. The ELPD computed using LOO-CV is $\text{ELPD}_{\text{LOO-CV}}$:

$$\text{ELPD}_{\text{LOO-CV}} = \sum_{i=1}^{n} \log \int p(y_i \mid \boldsymbol{\theta}) \, p(\boldsymbol{\theta} \mid y_{-i}) d\boldsymbol{\theta} \qquad (2.6)$$

Computing Equation 2.6 can easily become too costly as in practice we do not know $\boldsymbol{\theta}$ and thus we need to compute n posteriors, i.e. as many values of $\boldsymbol{\theta}_{-i}$ as observations we have in our dataset. Fortunately, we can approximate $\text{ELPD}_{\text{LOO-CV}}$ from a single fit to the data by using a method known as Pareto smoothed importance sampling leave-one-out cross validation PSIS-LOO-CV (see Section 11.5 for details). For brevity, and for consistency with ArviZ, in this book we call this method LOO. It is important to remember we are are talking about PSIS-LOO-CV and unless we state it otherwise when we refer to ELPD we are talking about the ELPD as estimated by this method.

ArviZ provides many LOO-related functions, using them is very simple but understanding the results may require a little bit of care. Thus, to illustrate how to interpret the output of these functions we are going to use 3 simple models. The models are defined in Code Block 2.15.

Code 2.15

```
1   y_obs = np.random.normal(0, 1, size=100)
2   idatas_cmp = {}
3
4   # Generate data from Skewnormal likelihood model
5   # with fixed mean and skewness and random standard deviation
6   with pm.Model() as mA:
7       σ = pm.HalfNormal("σ", 1)
8       y = pm.SkewNormal("y", 0, σ, alpha=1, observed=y_obs)
9       idataA = pm.sample(return_inferencedata=True)
10
11  # add_groups modifies an existing az.InferenceData
12  idataA.add_groups({"posterior_predictive":
13                  {"y":pm.sample_posterior_predictive(idataA)["y"][None,:]}})
14  idatas_cmp["mA"] = idataA
15
16  # Generate data from Normal likelihood model
17  # with fixed mean with random standard deviation
18  with pm.Model() as mB:
19      σ = pm.HalfNormal("σ", 1)
20      y = pm.Normal("y", 0, σ, observed=y_obs)
21      idataB = pm.sample(return_inferencedata=True)
22
23  idataB.add_groups({"posterior_predictive":
```

```
24                          {"y":pm.sample_posterior_predictive(idataB)["y"][None,:]}})
25  idatas_cmp["mB"] = idataB
26
27  # Generate data from Normal likelihood model
28  # with random mean and random standard deviation
29  with pm.Model() as mC:
30      μ = pm.Normal("μ", 0, 1)
31      σ = pm.HalfNormal("σ", 1)
32      y = pm.Normal("y", μ, σ, observed=y_obs)
33      idataC = pm.sample(return_inferencedata=True)
34
35  idataC.add_groups({"posterior_predictive":
36                          {"y":pm.sample_posterior_predictive(idataC)["y"][None,:]}})
37  idatas_cmp["mC"] = idataC
```

To compute LOO we just need samples from the posterior [16]. Then we can call `az.loo(.)`, which allows us to compute LOO for a single model. In practice it is common to compute LOO for two or more models, and thus a commonly used function is `az.compare(.)`. Table 2.1 was generated using `az.compare(idatas_cmp)`.

	rank	loo	p_loo	d_loo	weight	se	dse	warning	loo_scale
mB	0	-137.87	0.96	0.00	1.0	7.06	0.00	False	log
mC	1	-138.61	2.03	0.74	0.0	7.05	0.85	False	log
mA	2	-168.06	1.35	30.19	0.0	10.32	6.54	False	log

TABLE 2.1

Summary of model comparison as computed by `az.compare(.)`. The compared models `mA`, `mB`, and `mC` are ranked from lowest to highest ELPD values (loo column).

There are many columns in Table 2.1 so let us detail their meaning one by one:

1. The first column is the index which lists the names of the models taken from the keys of the dictionary passed to `az.compare(.)`.

2. `rank`: The ranking on the models starting from 0 (the model with the highest predictive accuracy) to the number of models.

3. `loo`: The list of ELPD values. The DataFrame is always sorted from best ELPD to worst.

4. `p_loo`: The list values for the penalization term. We can roughly think of this value as the estimated effective number of parameters (but do not take that too seriously). This value can be lower than the actual number of parameters in model that *has more structure* like hierarchical models or can be much higher than the actual number when the model has very weak predictive capability and may indicate a severe model misspecification.

5. `d_loo`: The list of relative differences between the value of LOO for the top-ranked model and the value of LOO for each model. For this reason we will always get a value of 0 for the first model.

---

[16]We are also computing samples from the posterior predictive distribution to use them to compute LOO-PIT.

6. `weight`: The weights assigned to each model. These weights can be loosely interpreted as the probability of each model (among the compared models) given the data. See Section 2.5.6 for details.

7. `se`: The standard error for the ELPD computations.

8. `dse`: The standard errors of the difference between two values of the ELPD. `dse` is not necessarily the same as the `se` because the uncertainty about the ELPD can be correlated between models. The value of `dse` is always 0 for the top-ranked model.

9. `warning`: If `True` this is a warning that the LOO approximation may not be reliable (see 2.5.3 for details).

10. `loo_scale`: The scale of the reported values. The default is the log scale. Other options are deviance, this is the log-score multiplied by -2 (this will reverse the order: a lower ELPD will be better). And negative-log, this is the log-score multiplied by -1, as with the deviance scale, a lower value is better.

We can also represent part of the information in Table 2.1 graphically in Figure 2.16. Models are also ranked from higher predictive accuracy to lower. The open dots represent the values of `loo`, the black dots are the predictive accuracy without the `p_loo` penalization term. The black segments represent the standard error for the LOO computations `se`. The grey segments, centered at the triangles, represent the standard errors of the difference `dse` between the values of LOO for each model and the best ranked model. We can see that `mB` $\approx$ `mC` > `mA`.

From Table 2.1 and Figure 2.16 we can see that model `mA` is ranked as the lowest one and clearly separated from the other two. We will now discuss the other two as their differences are more subtle. `mB` is the one with the highest predictive accuracy, but the difference is negligible when compared with `mC`. As a rule of thumb a difference of LOO (`d_loo`) below 4 is considered small. The difference between these two models is that for `mB` the mean is fixed at 0 and for `mC` the mean has a prior distribution. LOO penalizes the addition of this prior, indicated by the value of `p_loo` which is larger for `mC` than `mB`, and the distance between the black dot (unpenalized ELPD) and open dot (ELPD$_{\text{LOO-CV}}$) is larger for `mC` than `mB`. We can also see that `dse` between these two models is much lower than their respective `se`, indicating their predictions are highly correlated.

Given the small difference between `mB` and `mC`, it is expected that under a slightly different dataset the rank of these model could swap, with `mC` becoming the highest ranked model. Also the values of the weights are expected to change (see Section 2.5.6). We can easily check this is true by changing the random seed and refitting the model a few times.

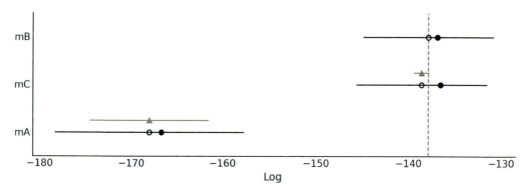

FIGURE 2.16

Model comparison using LOO. The open dots represent the values of `loo`, the black dots are the predictive accuracy without the `p_loo` penalization term. The black segments represent the standard error for the LOO computations `se`. The grey segments, centered at the triangles, represent the standard errors of the difference `dse` between the values of LOO for each model and the best ranked model.

2.5.2   Expected Log Predictive Density

In the previous section we computed a value of the ELPD for each model. Since this is a *global* comparison it reduces a model, and data, to a single number. But from Equation 2.5 and 2.6 we can see that LOO is computed as a sum of point-wise values, one for each observation. Thus we can also perform *local* comparisons. We can think of the individual values of the ELPD as an indicator of how difficult it is for the model to predict a particular observation.

To compare models based on the per-observation ELPD, ArviZ offers the `az.plot_elpd(.)` function. Figure 2.17 shows the comparison between models `mA`, `mB` and `mC` in a pairwise fashion. Positive values indicate that observations are better resolved by the first model than by the second. For example, if we observed the first plot (`mA`- `mB`), observation 49 and 72 are better resolved by model `mA` than model `mB`, and the opposite happens for observations 75 and 95. We can see that the first two plots `mA`- `mB` and `mA`- `mC` are very similar, the reason is that model `mB` and model `mC` are in fact very similar to each other. Figure 2.19 shows that observations 34, 49, 72, 75 and 82 are in fact the five most *extreme* observations.

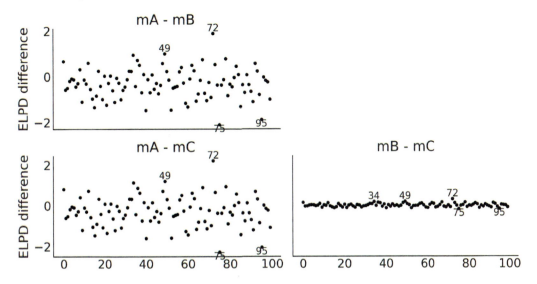

FIGURE 2.17
Pointwise ELPD differences. Annotated points correspond to observations with an ELPD difference 2 times the standard deviation of the computed ELPD differences. Differences are small in all 3 examples, especially between `mB` and `mC`. Positive values indicate that observations are better resolved for the first model than the second.

2.5.3 Pareto Shape Parameter, $\hat{\kappa}$

As we already mentioned we use LOO to approximate $\text{ELPD}_{\text{LOO-CV}}$. This approximation involves the computation of a Pareto distribution (see details in Section 11.5), the main purpose is to obtain a more robust estimation, the side-effect of this computation is that the $\hat{\kappa}$ parameter of such Pareto distribution can be used to detect highly influential observations, i.e. observations that have a large effect on the predictive distribution when they are left out. In general, higher values of $\hat{\kappa}$ can indicate problems with the data or model, especially when $\hat{\kappa} > 0.7$ [154, 57]. When this is the case the recommendations are[152]:

- Use the matching moment method [113] [17]. With some additional computations, it is possible to transform the MCMC draws from the posterior distribution to obtain more reliable importance sampling estimates.

- Perform exact leave-one-out cross validation for the problematic observations or use k-fold cross-validation.

- Use a model that is more robust to anomalous observations.

When we get at least one value of $\hat{\kappa} > 0.7$ we will get a warning when calling `az.loo(.)` or `az.compare(.)`. The `warning` column in Table 2.1 has only `False` values because all the computed values of $\hat{\kappa}$ are < 0.7 which we can check by ourselves from Figure 2.18. We have annotated the observations with $\hat{\kappa} > 0.09$ values in Figure 2.18, 0.09 is just an arbitrary number we picked, you can try with other cutoff value if you want. Comparing Figure 2.17 against Figure 2.18 we can see that the highest values of $\hat{\kappa}$ are not necessarily the ones with the highest values of ELPD or vice versa.

---

[17]At time of writing this book the method has not been yet implemented in ArviZ, but it may be already available by the time you are reading this.

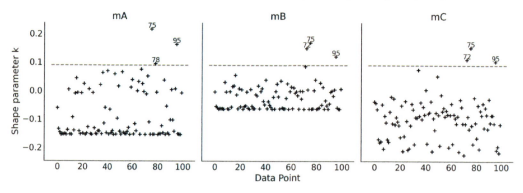

FIGURE 2.18

$\hat{\kappa}$ values. Annotated points correspond to observations with $\hat{\kappa} > 0.09$, a totally arbitrary threshold.

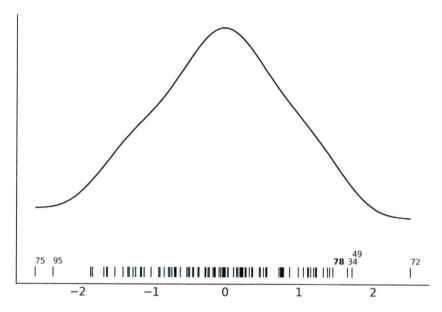

FIGURE 2.19

Kernel density estimate of the observations fitted with mA, mB and mC. The black lines represent the values of each observation. The annotated observations are the same one highlighted in Figure 2.17 except for the observation 78, annotated in boldface, which is only highlighted in Figure 2.18.

2.5.4 Interpreting p_loo When Pareto $\hat{\kappa}$ is Large

As previously said p_loo can be loosely interpreted as the estimated effective number of parameters in a model. Nevertheless, for models with large values of $\hat{\kappa}$ we can obtain some additional additional information. If $\hat{\kappa} > 0.7$ then comparing p_loo to the number of parameters p can provides us with some additional information [152]:

- If $p\_loo << p$, then the model is likely to be misspecified. You usually also see problems in the posterior predictive checks that the posterior predictive samples match the observations poorly.

- If $p\_loo < p$ and p is relatively large compared to the number of observations (e.g., $p > \frac{N}{5}$, where N is the total number of observations), it is usually an indication that the model is too flexible or the priors are too uninformative. Thus it becomes difficult to predict the left out observation.

- If $p\_loo > p$, then the model is also likely to be badly misspecified. If the number of parameters is $p << N$, then posterior predictive checks are also likely to already reveal some problem [18]. However, if p is relatively large compared to the number of observations, say $p > \frac{N}{5}$, it is possible you do not see problems in the posterior predictive checks.

A few heuristics for fixing model misspecification you may try are: adding more structure to the model, for example, adding nonlinear components; using a different likelihood, for example, using an overdispersed likelihood like a NegativeBinomial instead of a Poisson distribution, or using mixture likelihood.

2.5.5 LOO-PIT

As we just saw in Sections 2.5.2 and 2.5.3 model comparison, and LOO in particular, can be used for purposes other than declaring a model is *better* than another model. We can compare models as a way to better understand them. As the complexity of a model increases it becomes more difficult to understand it just by looking at its mathematical definition or the code we use to implement it. Thus, comparing models using LOO or other tools like posterior predictive checks, can help us to better understand them.

One criticism of posterior predictive checks is that we are using the data twice, once to fit the model and once to criticize it. The LOO-PIT plot offers an answer to this concern. The main idea is that we can use LOO as a fast and reliable approximation to cross-validation in order to avoid using the data twice. The "PIT part", stands for Probability Integral Transform[19], which is transformation in 1D where we can get a $\mathcal{U}(0,1)$ distribution from any continuous random variable if we transform that random variable using its own CDF (for details see Section 11.5). In LOO-PIT we do not know the true CDF, but we approximate it with the empirical CDF. Putting aside these mathematical details for a moment, the take-home-message is that for a well calibrated model we should expect an approximately Uniform distribution. If you are experiencing a Déjà vu, do not worry you do not have extrasensory powers nor is this a glitch in the matrix. This may sound familiar because this is in fact the very same idea we discussed in Section 2.3 with the function `az.plot_bpv(idata, kind="u_value")`.

LOO-PIT is obtained by comparing the observed data y to posterior predicted data $\tilde{y}$. The comparison is done point-wise. We have:

$$p_i = P(\tilde{y}_i \leq y_i \mid y_{-i}) \tag{2.7}$$

Intuitively, LOO-PIT is computing the probability that the posterior predicted data $\tilde{y}_i$ has lower value than the observed data y_i, when we remove the i observation. Thus the difference between `az.plot_bpv(idata, kind="u_value")` and LOO-PIT is that with the latter we are approximately avoiding using the data twice, but the overall interpretation of the plots is the same.

Figure 2.20 shows the LOO-PIT for models mA, mB and mC. We can observe that from the perspective of model mA there is more observed data than expected for low values and

---

[18]See the case study `https://avehtari.github.io/modelselection/roaches.html` for an example.

[19]A deeper give into Probability Integral Transform can be found in Section 11.1.7

less data for high values, i.e. the model is biased. On the contrary, models mB and mC seem to be very well calibrated.

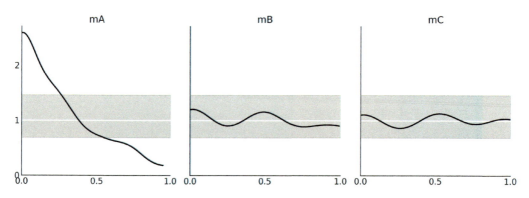

FIGURE 2.20
The black lines are a KDE of LOO-PIT, i.e. the proportion of predicted values that are less or equal than the observed data, computed per each observation. The white lines represent the expected Uniform distribution and the gray band the expected deviation for a dataset of the same size as the one used.

2.5.6   Model Averaging

Model averaging can be justified as being Bayesian about model uncertainty as we are Bayesian about parameter uncertainty. If we can not absolutely be sure that *a* model is *the* model (and generally we can not), then we should somehow take that uncertainty into account for our analysis. One way of taking into account model uncertainty is by performing a weighted average of all the considered models, giving more weight to the models that seem to explain or predict the data better.

A *natural* way to weight Bayesian models is by their marginal likelihoods, this is known as Bayesian Model Averaging [79]. While this is theoretically appealing, it is problematic in practice (see Section 11.7 for details). An alternative is to use the values of LOO to estimate weights for each model. We can do this by using the following formula:

$$w_i = \frac{e^{-\Delta_i}}{\sum_j^k e^{-\Delta_j}} \tag{2.8}$$

where Δ_i is the difference between the i value of LOO and the highest one, assuming we are using the log- scale, which is the default in ArviZ.

This approach is called pseudo Bayesian model averaging, or Akaike-like [20] weighting and is an heuristic way to compute the relative probability of each model (given a fixed set of models) from LOO[21]. See how the denominator is just a normalization term ensuring that the weights sum up to one. The solution offered by Equation 2.8 for computing weights is a very nice and simple approach. One major caveat is that it does not take into account the uncertainty in the computation of the values of LOO. We could compute the standard error assuming a Gaussian approximation and modify Equation 2.8 accordingly. Or we can do something more robust, like using Bayesian Bootstrapping.

---

[20]The Akaike information criterion (AIC) is an estimator of the generalization error, it is commonly used in frequentists statistics, but their assumptions are generally not adequate enough for general use with Bayesians models.
[21]This formula also works for WAIC [22] and other information criteria

Yet another option for model averaging is stacking of predictive distributions [163]. The main idea is to combine several models in a meta-model in such a way that we minimize the divergence between the meta-model and the *true* generating model. When using a logarithmic scoring rule this is equivalently to compute:

$$\max_{n} \frac{1}{n} \sum_{i=1}^{n} log \sum_{j=1}^{k} w_j p(y_i \mid y_{-i}, M_j) \tag{2.9}$$

where n is the number of data points and k the number of models. To enforce a solution we constrain w to be $w_j \geq 0$ and $\sum_{j=1}^{k} w_j = 1$. The quantity $p(y_i \mid y_{-i}, M_j)$ is the leave-one-out predictive distribution for the M_j model. As we already said computing it can bee too costly and thus in practice we can use LOO to approximate it.

Stacking has more interesting properties than pseudo Bayesian model averaging. We can see this from their definitions, Equation 2.8 is just a normalization of weights that have been computed for each model independently of the rest of the models. Instead in Equation 2.9 the weights are computed by maximizing the combined log-score, i.e. even when the models have been fitted independently as in pseudo Bayesian model averaging, the computation of the weights take into account all models together. This helps to explain why model mB gets a weight of 1 and mC a weight of 0 (see Table 2.1), even if they are very similar models. Why are the weights not around 0.5 for each one of them? The reason is that according to the stacking procedure once mB is included in our set of compared models, mC does not provide new information. In other words including it will be redundant.

The function `pm.sample_posterior_predictive_w(.)` accepts a list of traces and a list of weights allowing us to easily generate weighted posterior predictive samples. The weights can be taken from anywhere, but using the weights computed with `az.compare(., method="stacking")`, makes a lot of sense.

2.6 Exercises

2E1. Using your own words, what are the main differences between prior predictive checks and posterior predictive checks? How are these empirical evaluations related to Equations 1.7 and 1.8.

2E2. Using your own words explain: ESS, $\hat{R}$ and MCSE. Focus your explanation on what these quantities are measuring and what potential issue with MCMC they are identifying.

2E3. ArviZ includes precomputed InferenceData objects for a few models. We are going to load an InferenceData object generated from a classical example in Bayesian statistic, the eight schools model [137]. The InferenceData object includes prior samples, prior predictive samples and posterior samples. We can load the InferenceData object using the command `az.load_arviz_data("centered_eight")`. Use ArviZ to:

    (a) List all the groups available on the InferenceData object.

    (b) Identify the number of chains and the total number of posterior samples.

    (c) Plot the posterior.

    (d) Plot the posterior predictive distribution.

    (e) Calculate the estimated mean of the parameters, and the Highest Density Intervals.

If necessary check the ArviZ documentation to help you do these tasks `https://arviz-devs.github.io/arviz/`

2E4. Load `az.load_arviz_data("non_centered_eight")`, which is a reparametrized version of the "centered_eight" model in the previous exercise. Use ArviZ to assess the MCMC sampling convergence for both models by using:

   (a) Autocorrelation plots

   (b) Rank plots.

   (c) $\hat{R}$ values.

   Focus on the plots for the mu and tau parameters. What do these three different diagnostics show? Compare these to the InferenceData results loaded from `az.load_arviz_data("centered_eight")`. Do all three diagnostics tend to agree on which model is preferred? Which one of the models has better convergence diagnostics?

2E5. InferenceData object can store statistics related to the sampling algorithm. You will find them in the `sample_stats` group, including divergences (`diverging`):

   (a) Count the number of divergences for "centered_eight" and "non_centered_eight" models.

   (b) Use `az.plot_parallel` to identify where the divergences tend to concentrate in the parameter space.

2E6. In the GitHub repository we have included an InferenceData object with a Poisson model and one with a NegativeBinomial, both models are fitted to the same dataset. Use `az.load_arviz_data(.)` to load them, and then use ArviZ functions to answer the following questions:

   (a) Which model provides a better fit to the data? Use the functions `az.compare(.)` and `az.plot_compare(.)`

   (b) Explain why one model provides a better fit than the other. Use `az.plot_ppc(.)` and `az.plot_loo_pit(.)`

   (c) Compare both models in terms of their pointwise ELPD values. Identify the 5 observations with the largest (absolute) difference. Which model is predicting them better? For which model p_loo is closer to the actual number of parameters? Could you explain why? Hint: the Poisson model has a single parameter that controls both the variance and mean. Instead, the NegativeBinomial has two parameters.

   (d) Diagnose LOO using the $\hat{\kappa}$ values. Is there any reason to be concerned about the accuracy of LOO for this particular case?

2E7. Reproduce Figure 2.7, but using `az.plot_loo(ecdf=True)` in place of `az.plot_bpv(.)`. Interpret the results. Hint: when using the option `ecdf=True`, instead of the LOO-PIT KDE you will get a plot of the difference between the LOO-PIT Empirical Cumulative Distribution Function (ECDF) and the Uniform CDF. The ideal plot will be one with a difference of zero.

2E8. In your own words explain why MCMC posterior estimation techniques need convergence diagnostics. In particular contrast these to the conjugate methods described in Section 1.4.1 which do not need those diagnostics. What is different about the two inference methods?

2E9. Visit the ArviZ plot gallery at `https://arviz-devs.github.io/arviz/examples/index.html`. What diagnoses can you find there that are not covered in this chapter? From the documentation what is this diagnostic assessing?

2E10. List some plots and numerical quantities that are useful at each step during the Bayesian workflow (shown visually in Section 9.1). Explain how they work and what they are assessing. Feel free to use anything you have seen in this chapter or in the ArviZ documentation.

(a) Prior selection.

(b) MCMC sampling.

(c) Posterior predictions.

2M11. We want to model a football league with N teams. As usual, we start with a simpler version of the model in mind, just a single team. We assume the scores are Poisson distributed according to a scoring rate μ. We choose the prior Gamma$(0.5, 0.00001)$ because this is sometimes recommend as an "objective" prior.

Code 2.16

```
1 with pm.Model() as model:
2     μ = pm.Gamma("μ", 0.5, 0.00001)
3     score = pm.Poisson("score", μ)
4     trace = pm.sample_prior_predictive()
```

(a) Generate and plot the prior predictive distribution. How reasonable it looks to you?

(b) Use your knowledge of sports in order to refine the prior choice.

(c) Instead of soccer you now want to model basketball. Could you come with a reasonable prior for that instance? Define the prior in a model and generate a prior predictive distribution to validate your intuition.

Hint: You can parameterize the Gamma distribution using the rate and shape parameters as in Code Block 2.16 or alternatively using the mean and standard deviation

2M12. In Code Block 1.3 from Chapter 1, change the value of `can_sd` and run the Metropolis sampler. Try values like 0.2 and 1.

(a) Use ArviZ to compare the sampled values using diagnostics such as the autocorrelation plot, trace plot and the ESS. Explain the observed differences.

(b) Modify Code Block 1.3 so you get more than one independent chain. Use ArviZ to compute rank plots and $\hat{R}$.

2M13. Generate a random sample using `np.random.binomial(n=1, p=0.5, size=200)` and fit it using a Beta-Binomial model.

Use `pm.sample(., step=pm.Metropolis())` (Metropolis-Hastings sampler) and `pm.sample(.)` (the standard sampler). Compare the results in terms of the ESS, $\hat{R}$, autocorrelation, trace plots and rank plots. Reading the PyMC3 logging statements what sampler is autoassigned? What is your conclusion about this sampler performance compared to Metropolis-Hastings?

2M14. Generate your own example of a synthetic posterior with convergence issues, let us call it `bad_chains3`.

(a) Explain why the synthetic posterior you generated is "bad". What about it would we not want to see in an actual modeling scenario?

(b) Run the same diagnostics we run in the book for `bad_chains0` and `bad_chains1`. Compare your results with those in the book and explain the differences and similarities.

(c) Did the results of the diagnostics from the previous point made you reconsider why `bad_chains3` is a "bad chain"?

2H15. Generate a random sample using `np.random.binomial(n=1, p=0.5, size=200)` and fit it using a Beta-Binomial model.

(a) Check that LOO-PIT is approximately Uniform.

(b) Tweak the prior to make the model a bad fit and get a LOO-PIT that is low for values closer to zero and high for values closer to one. Justify your prior choice.

(c) Tweak the prior to make the model a bad fit and get a LOO-PIT that is high for values closer to zero and low for values closer to one. Justify your prior choice.

(d) Tweak the prior to make the model a bad fit and get a LOO-PIT that is high for values close to 0.5 and low for values closer to zero and one. Could you do it? Explain why.

2H16. Use PyMC3 to write a model with Normal likelihood. Use the following random samples as data and the following priors for the mean. Fix the standard deviation parameter in the likelihood at 1.

(a) A random sample of size 200 from a $\mathcal{N}(0, 1)$ and prior distribution $\mathcal{N}(0, 20)$

(b) A random sample of size 2 from a $\mathcal{N}(0, 1)$ and prior distribution $\mathcal{N}(0, 20)$

(c) A random sample of size 200 from a $\mathcal{N}(0, 1)$ and prior distribution $\mathcal{N}(201)$

(d) A random sample of size 200 from a $\mathcal{U}(0, 1)$ and prior distribution $\mathcal{N}(10, 20)$

(e) A random sample of size 200 from a $\mathcal{HN}(0, 1)$ and a prior distribution $\mathcal{N}(10, 20)$

Assess convergence by running the same diagnostics we run in the book for `bad_chains0` and `bad_chains1`. Compare your results with those in the book and explain the differences and similarities.

2H17. Each of the four sections in this chapter, prior predictive checks, posterior predictive checks, numerical inference diagnostics, and model comparison, detail a specific step in the Bayesian workflow. In your own words explain what the purpose of each step is, and conversely what is lacking if the step is omitted. What does each tell us about our statistical models?

3

Linear Models and Probabilistic Programming Languages

With the advent of Probabilistic Programming Languages, modern Bayesian modeling can be as simple as coding a model and "pressing a button". However, effective model building and analysis usually takes more work. As we progress through this book we will be building many different types of models but in this chapter we will start with the humble linear model. Linear models are a broad class of models where the expected value of a given observation is the linear combination of the associated predictors. A strong understanding of how to fit and interpret linear models is a strong foundation for the models that will follow. This will also help us to consolidate the fundamentals of Bayesian inference (Chapter 1) and exploratory analysis of Bayesian models (Chapter 2) and apply them with different PPLs. This chapter introduces the two PPLs we will use for the majority of this book, PyMC3, which you have briefly seen, as well as TensorFlow Probability (TFP). While we are building models in these two PPLs, focusing on how the same underlying statistical ideas are mapped to implementation in each PPL. We will first fit an intercept only model, that is a model with no covariates, and then we will add extra complexity by adding one or more covariates, and extend to generalized linear models. By the end of this chapter you will be more comfortable with linear models, more familiar with many of the steps in a Bayesian workflow, and more comfortable conducting Bayesian workflows with PyMC3, TFP and ArviZ.

3.1 Comparing Two (or More) Groups

If you are looking for something to compare it is hard to beat penguins. After all, what is not to like about these cute flightless birds? Our first question may be "What is the average mass of each penguin species?", or may be "How different are those averages?", or in statistics parlance "What is the dispersion of the average?" Luckily Kristen Gorman also likes studying penguins, so much so that she visited 3 Antarctic islands and collected data about Adelie, Gentoo and Chinstrap species, which is compiled into the Palmer Penguins dataset[81]. The observations consist of physical characteristics of the penguin mass, flipper length, and sex, as well as geographic characteristics such as the island they reside on.

We start by loading the data and filtering out any rows where data is missing in Code Block 3.1. This is called a complete case analysis where, as the name suggests, we only use the rows where all observations are present. While it is possible to handle the missing values in another way, either through data imputation, or imputation during modeling, we will opt to take the simplest approach for this chapter.

DOI: 10.1201/9781003019169-3

species	mean (grams)	std	count
Adelie	3706	459	146
Chinstrap	3733	384	68
Gentoo	5092	501	119

TABLE 3.1
Empirical mean and standard deviation of penguin mass. The count column indicates the observed number of penguins per species.

Code 3.1

```
1  penguins = pd.read_csv("../data/penguins.csv")
2  # Subset to the columns needed
3  missing_data = penguins.isnull()[
4      ["bill_length_mm", "flipper_length_mm", "sex", "body_mass_g"]
5  ].any(axis=1)
6  # Drop rows with any missing data
7  penguins = penguins.loc[~missing_data]
```

We can then calculate the empirical mean of the mass `body_mass_g` in Code Block 3.2 with just a little bit of code, the results of which are in Table 3.1

Code 3.2

```
1  summary_stats = (penguins.loc[:, ["species", "body_mass_g"]]
2                   .groupby("species")
3                   .agg(["mean", "std", "count"]))
```

Now we have point estimates for both the mean and the dispersion, but we do not know the uncertainty of those statistics. One way to get estimates of uncertainty is by using Bayesian methods. In order to do so we need to conjecture a relationship of observations to parameters as example:

$$\overbrace{p(\mu, \sigma \mid Y)}^{Posterior} \propto \overbrace{\mathcal{N}(Y \mid \mu, \sigma)}^{Likelihood} \overbrace{\underbrace{\mathcal{N}(4000, 3000)}_{\mu} \underbrace{\mathcal{H}\text{T}(100, 2000)}_{\sigma}}^{Prior} \tag{3.1}$$

Equation 3.1 is a restatement of Equation 1.3 where each parameter is explicitly listed. Since we have no specific reason to choose an informative prior, we will use wide priors for both μ and σ. In this case, the priors are chosen based on the empirical mean and standard deviation of the observed data. And lastly instead of estimating the mass of all species we will first start with the mass of the Adelie penguin species. A Gaussian is a reasonable choice of likelihood for penguin mass and biological mass in general, so we will go with it. Let us translate Equation 3.1 into a computational model.

Code 3.3

```
1  adelie_mask = (penguins["species"] == "Adelie")
2  adelie_mass_obs = penguins.loc[adelie_mask, "body_mass_g"].values
3
4  with pm.Model() as model_adelie_penguin_mass:
5      σ = pm.HalfStudentT("σ", 100, 2000)
6      μ = pm.Normal("μ", 4000, 3000)
7      mass = pm.Normal("mass", mu=μ, sigma=σ, observed=adelie_mass_obs)
8
9      prior = pm.sample_prior_predictive(samples=5000)
10     trace = pm.sample(chains=4)
11     inf_data_adelie_penguin_mass = az.from_pymc3(prior=prior, trace=trace)
```

Before computing the posterior we are going to check the prior. In particular we are first checking that sampling from our model is computationally feasible and that our choice of priors is reasonable based on our domain knowledge. We plot the samples from the prior in Figure 3.1. Since we can get a plot at all we know our model has no "obvious" computational issues, such as shape problems or mispecified random variables or likelihoods. From the prior samples themselves it is evident we are not overly constraining the possible penguin masses, we may in fact be under constraining the prior as the prior for the mean of the mass includes negative values. However, since this is a simple model and we have a decent number of observations we will just note this aberration and move onto estimating the posterior distribution.

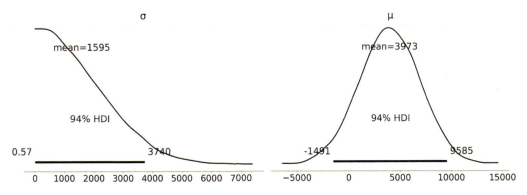

FIGURE 3.1
Prior samples generated in Code Block 3.3. The distribution estimates of both the mean and standard deviation for the mass distribution cover a wide range of possibilities.

After sampling from our model, we can create Figure 3.2 which includes 4 subplots, the two on the right are the rank plots and the left the KDE of each parameter, one line for each chain. We also can reference the numerical diagnostics in Table 3.2 to confirm our belief that the chains converged. Using the intuition we built in Chapter 2 we can judge that these fits are acceptable and we will continue with our analysis.

Comfortable with the fit we plot a posterior plot in Figure 3.3 that combines all the chains. Compare the point estimates from Table 3.1 of the mean and standard deviation with our Bayesian estimates as shown in Figure 3.3.

	mean	sd	hdi_3%	hdi_97%	mcse_mean	mcse_sd	ess_bulk	ess_tail	r_hat
μ	3707	38	3632	3772	0.6	0.4	3677.0	2754.0	1.0
σ	463	27	401	511	0.5	0.3	3553.0	2226.0	1.0

TABLE 3.2
Bayesian estimates of the mean (μ) and standard deviation (σ) of Adelie penguin mass. For both parameters the posteriors mean, standard deviation (sd) and HDI are reported. We also include the diagnostics (`mcse`, `ess` and `r_hat`) to verify there were no issues during sampling.

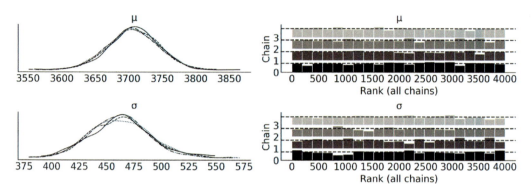

FIGURE 3.2
KDE and rank plot of the posterior of the Bayesian model in Code Block 3.3 of Adelie penguin mass. This plot serves as a visual diagnostic of the sampling to help judge if there were any issues during sampling across the multiple sampling chains.

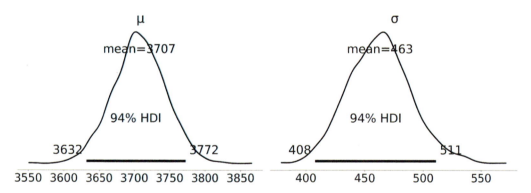

FIGURE 3.3
Posterior plot of the posterior of the Bayesian model in Code Block 3.3 of Adelie penguins mass. The vertical lines are the empirical mean and standard deviation.

With the Bayesian estimate however, we also get the distribution of plausible parameters. Using the tabular summary in Table 3.2 from the same posterior distribution in Figure 3.2 values of the mean from 3632 to 3772 grams are quite plausible. Note that the standard deviation of the marginal posterior distribution varies quite a bit as well. And remember the posterior distribution is not the distribution of an individual penguin mass but rather possible parameters of a Gaussian distribution that we assume describes penguin mass. If we wanted the estimated distribution of individual penguin mass we would need to generate a posterior predictive distribution. In this case it will be the same Gaussian distribution conditioned on the posterior of μ and σ.

Now that we have characterized the Adelie penguin's mass, we can do the same for the other species. We could do so by writing two more models but instead let us just run one model with 3 separated groups, one per species.

Code 3.4

```
1  # pd.categorical makes it easy to index species below
2  all_species = pd.Categorical(penguins["species"])
3
4  with pm.Model() as model_penguin_mass_all_species:
5      # Note the addition of the shape parameter
6      σ = pm.HalfStudentT("σ", 100, 2000, shape=3)
7      μ = pm.Normal("μ", 4000, 3000, shape=3)
8      mass = pm.Normal("mass",
9                       mu=μ[all_species.codes],
10                      sigma=σ[all_species.codes],
11                      observed=penguins["body_mass_g"])
12
13     trace = pm.sample()
14     inf_data_model_penguin_mass_all_species = az.from_pymc3(
15         trace=trace,
16         coords={"μ_dim_0": all_species.categories,
17                 "σ_dim_0": all_species.categories})
```

We use the optional shape argument in each parameter and add an index in our likelihood indicating to PyMC3 that we want to condition the posterior estimate for each species individually. In programming language design small tricks that make expressing ideas more seamless are called **syntactic sugar**, and probabilistic programming developers include these as well. Probabilistic Programming Languages strive to allow expressing models with ease and with less errors.

After we run the model we once again inspect the KDE and rank plots, see Figure 3.4. Compared to Figure 3.2 you will see 4 additional plots, 2 each for the additional parameters added. Take a moment to compare the estimate of the mean with the summary mean shows for each species in Table 3.1. To better visualize the differences between the distributions for each species, we plot the posterior again in a forest plot using Code Block 3.5. Figure 3.5 makes it easier to compare our estimates across species and note that the Gentoo penguins seem to have more mass than Adelie or Chinstrap penguins.

Code 3.5

```
az.plot_forest(inf_data_model_penguin_mass_all_species, var_names=["μ"])
```

Figure 3.5 makes it easier to compare our estimates and easily note that the Gentoo penguins have more mass than Adelie or Chinstrap penguins. Let us also look at the standard deviation in Figure 3.6. The 94% highest density interval of the posterior is reporting uncertainty in the order of 100 grams.

Code 3.6

```
az.plot_forest(inf_data_model_penguin_mass_all_species, var_names=["σ"])
```

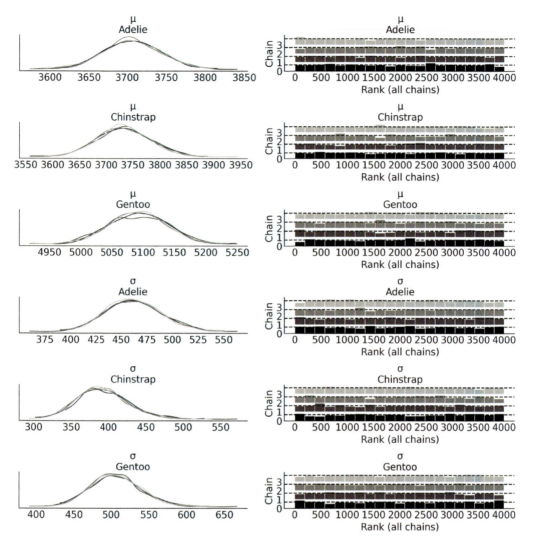

FIGURE 3.4
KDE and rank plot for posterior estimates of parameters of masses for each species of penguins from the `penguins_masses` model. Note how each species has its own pair of estimates for each parameter.

3.1.1 Comparing Two PPLs

Before expanding on the statistical and modeling ideas further, we will take a moment to talk about the probabilistic programming languages and introduce another PPL we will be using in this book, TensorFlow Probability (TFP). We will do so by translating the PyMC3 intercept only model in Code Block 3.4 into TFP.

It may seem unnecessary to learn different PPLs. However, there are specific reasons we chose to use two PPLs instead of one in this book. Seeing the same workflow in different PPLs will give you a more thorough understanding of computational Bayesian modeling, help you separate computational details from statistical ideas, and make you a stronger modeler overall. Moreover, different PPLs have different strength and focus. PyMC3 is a

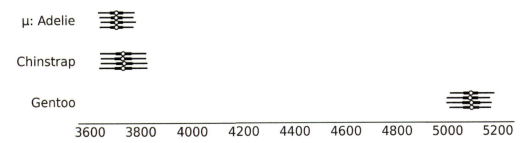

FIGURE 3.5

Forest plot of the mean of mass of each species group in `model_penguin_mass_all_species`. Each line represents one chain in the sampler, the dot is a point estimate, in this case the mean, the thin line is the interquartile range from 25% to 75% of the posterior and the thick line is the 94% Highest Density Interval.

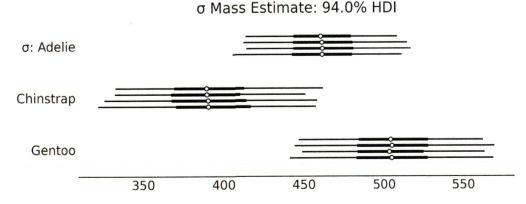

FIGURE 3.6

Forest plot of the standard deviations of the mass for each species group in `model_penguin_mass_all_species`. This plot depicts our estimation of the dispersion of penguin mass, so for example, given a mean estimate of the Gentoo penguin distribution, the associated standard deviation is plausibly anywhere between 450 grams to 550 grams.

higher level PPL that makes it easier to express models with less code, whereas TFP provides a lower level PPL for compostable modeling and inference. Another is that not all PPLs are able to express all models as easily as each other. For instance Time Series models (Chapter 6) are more easily defined in TFP whereas Bayesian Additive Regression Trees are more easily expressed in PyMC3 (Chapter 7). Through this exposure to multiple languages you will come out with a stronger understanding of both the fundamental elements of Bayesian modeling and how they are implemented computationally.

Probabilistic Programming Languages (emphasis on language) are composed of primitives. The primitives in a programming language are the simplest elements available to construct more complex programs. You can think of primitives are like words in natural languages which can form more complex structures, like sentences. And as different languages use different words, different PPLs use different primitives. These primitives are mainly used to express models, perform inference, or express other parts of the workflow. In PyMC3, model building related primitives are contained under the namespace pm. For example, in Code Block 3.3 we see pm.HalfStudentT(.), and pm.Normal(.), which represent a random variable. The **with** pm.Model() **as** . statement evokes a Python context manager, which PyMC3 uses to build the model model_adelie_penguin_mass by collecting the random variables within the context manager. We then use pm.sample_prior_predictive(.) and pm.sample(.) to obtain samples from the prior predictive distribution and from the posterior distribution, respectively.

Similarly, TFP provides primitives for user to specify distributions and model in tfp.distributions, running MCMC (tfp.mcmc), and more. For example, to construct a Bayesian model, TensorFlow provides multiple primitives under the name tfd.JointDistribution [122] API. In this chapter and the remaining of the book we mostly use tfd.JointDistributionCoroutine, but there are other variants of tfd.JointDistribution which may better suit your use case[1]. Since basic data import and summary statistics stays the same as Code Block 3.1 and 3.2 we can focus on the model building and inference. model_penguin_mass_all_species expressed in TFP which is shown in Code Block 3.7 below

Code 3.7

```
1  import tensorflow as tf
2  import tensorflow_probability as tfp
3
4  tfd = tfp.distributions
5  root = tfd.JointDistributionCoroutine.Root
6
7  species_idx = tf.constant(all_species.codes, tf.int32)
8  body_mass_g = tf.constant(penguins["body_mass_g"], tf.float32)
9
10 @tfd.JointDistributionCoroutine
11 def jd_penguin_mass_all_species():
12     σ = yield root(tfd.Sample(
13             tfd.HalfStudentT(df=100, loc=0, scale=2000),
14             sample_shape=3,
15             name="sigma"))
16     μ = yield root(tfd.Sample(
17             tfd.Normal(loc=4000, scale=3000),
18             sample_shape=3,
19             name="mu"))
20     mass = yield tfd.Independent(
21         tfd.Normal(loc=tf.gather(μ, species_idx, axis=-1),
22                 scale=tf.gather(σ, species_idx, axis=-1)),
23         reinterpreted_batch_ndims=1,
24         name="mass")
```

Since this is our first encounter with a Bayesian model written in TFP, let us spend a few paragraphs to detail the API. The primitives are distribution classes in tfp.distributions, which we assign a shorter alias tfd = tfp.distributions. tfd contains commonly used distributions like tfd.Normal(.). We also used tfd.Sample, which returns multiple independent copies of the base distribution (conceptually we achieve the similar goal as using the

---

[1]You can find more information in the TensorFlow tutorials and documentations. For example, https://www.tensorflow.org/probability/examples/JointDistributionAutoBatched_A_Gentle_Tutorial and https://www.tensorflow.org/probability/examples/Modeling_with_JointDistribution.

syntactic sugar `shape=(.)` in PyMC3). `tfd.Independent` is used to indicate that the distribution contains multiple copies that we would like to sum over some axis when computing the log-likelihood, which specified by the `reinterpreted_batch_ndims` function argument. Usually we wrap the distributions associated with the observation with `tfd.Independent`[2]. You can read a bit more about shape handling in TFP and PPL in Section 10.8.1.

An interesting signature of a `tfd.JointDistributionCoroutine` model is, as the name suggests, the usage of Coroutine in Python. Without getting into too much detail about Generators and Coroutines, here a **yield** statement of a distribution gives you some random variable inside of your model function. You can view y = **yield** Normal(.) as the way to express $y \sim Normal(.)$. Also, we need to identify the random variables without dependencies as root nodes by wrapping them with `tfd.JointDistributionCoroutine.Root`. The model is written as a Python function with no input argument and no return value. Lastly, it is convenient to put *@tfd.JointDistributionCoroutine* on top of the Python function as a decorator to get the model (i.e., a `tfd.JointDistribution`) directly.

The resulting `jd_penguin_mass_all_species` is the intercept only regression model from 3.4 restated in TFP. It has similar methods like other `tfd.Distribution`, which we can utilize in our Bayesian workflow. For example, to draw prior and prior predictive samples, we can call the `.sample(.)` method, which returns a custom nested Python structure similar to a `namedtuple`. In Code Block 3.8 we draw 1000 prior and prior predictive samples.

Code 3.8

```
prior_predictive_samples = jd_penguin_mass_all_species.sample(1000)
```

The `.sample(.)` method of a `tfd.JointDistribution` can also draw conditional samples, which is the mechanism we will make use of to draw posterior predictive samples. You can run Code Block 3.9 and inspect the output to see how random samples change if you condition some random variables in the model to some specific values. Overall, we invoke the *forward* generative process when calling `.sample(.)`.

Code 3.9

```
1  jd_penguin_mass_all_species.sample(sigma=tf.constant([.1, .2, .3]))
2  jd_penguin_mass_all_species.sample(mu=tf.constant([.1, .2, .3]))
```

Once we condition the generative model `jd_penguin_mass_all_species` to the observed penguin body mass, we can get the posterior distribution. From the computational perspective, we want to generate a function that returns the posterior log-probability (up to some constant) evaluated at the input. This could be done by creating a Python function closure or using the `.experimental_pin` method, as shown in Code Block 3.10:

Code 3.10

```
1  target_density_function = lambda *x: jd_penguin_mass_all_species.log_prob(
2      *x, mass=body_mass_g)
3
```

---

[2]`tfd.Sample` and `tfd.Independent` are distribution constructors that takes other distributions as input and return a new distribution. There are other meta distribution but with different purposes like `tfd.Mixture`, `tfd.TransformedDistribution`, and `tfd.JointDistribution`. A more comprehensive introduction to `tfp.distributions` can be found in https://www.tensorflow.org/probability/examples/TensorFlow_Distributions_Tutorial

```
4  jd_penguin_mass_observed = jd_penguin_mass_all_species.experimental_pin(
5      mass=body_mass_g)
6  target_density_function = jd_penguin_mass_observed.unnormalized_log_prob
```

Inference is done using `target_density_function`, for example, we can find the maximum of the function which gives the **maximum a posteriori probability** (MAP) estimate. We can also use methods in `tfp.mcmc` [94] to sample from the posterior. Or more conveniently, using a standard sampling routine similar to what is currently used in PyMC3 [3] as shown in Code Block 3.11:

Code 3.11

```
1  run_mcmc = tf.function(
2      tfp.experimental.mcmc.windowed_adaptive_nuts,
3      autograph=False, jit_compile=True)
4  mcmc_samples, sampler_stats = run_mcmc(
5      1000, jd_penguin_mass_all_species, n_chains=4, num_adaptation_steps=1000,
6      mass=body_mass_g)
7
8  inf_data_model_penguin_mass_all_species2 = az.from_dict(
9      posterior={
10         # TFP mcmc returns (num_samples, num_chains, ...), we swap
11         # the first and second axis below for each RV so the shape
12         # is what ArviZ expected.
13         k:np.swapaxes(v, 1, 0)
14         for k, v in mcmc_samples._asdict().items()},
15     sample_stats={
16         k:np.swapaxes(sampler_stats[k], 1, 0)
17         for k in ["target_log_prob", "diverging", "accept_ratio", "n_steps"]}
18 )
```

In Code Block 3.11 we ran 4 MCMC chains, each with 1000 posterior samples after 1000 adaptation steps. Internally it invokes the `experimental_pin` method by conditioning the model (pass into the function as an argument) with the observed (additional keyword argument `mass=body_mass_g` at the end). Lines 8-18 parse the sampling result into an ArviZ InferenceData, which we can now run diagnostics and exploratory analysis of Bayesian models in ArviZ. We can additionally add prior and posterior predictive samples and data log-likelihood to `inf_data_model_penguin_mass_all_species2` in a transparent way in Code Block 3.12 below. Note that we make use of the `sample_distributions` method of a `tfd.JointDistribution` that draws samples *and* generates a distribution conditioned on the posterior samples.

Code 3.12

```
1  prior_predictive_samples = jd_penguin_mass_all_species.sample([1, 1000])
2  dist, samples = jd_penguin_mass_all_species.sample_distributions(
3      value=mcmc_samples)
4  ppc_samples = samples[-1]
5  ppc_distribution = dist[-1].distribution
6  data_log_likelihood = ppc_distribution.log_prob(body_mass_g)
7
```

---

[3]https://mc-stan.org/docs/2_23/reference-manual/hmc-algorithm-parameters.html#automatic-parameter-tuning

```
8  # Be careful not to run this code twice during REPL workflow.
9  inf_data_model_penguin_mass_all_species2.add_groups(
10     prior=prior_predictive_samples[:-1]._asdict(),
11     prior_predictive={"mass": prior_predictive_samples[-1]},
12     posterior_predictive={"mass": np.swapaxes(ppc_samples, 1, 0)},
13     log_likelihood={"mass": np.swapaxes(data_log_likelihood, 1, 0)},
14     observed_data={"mass": body_mass_g}
15 )
```

This concludes our whirlwind tour of TensorFlow Probability. Like any language you likely will not gain fluency in your initial exposure. But by comparing the two models you should now have a better sense of what concepts are *Bayesian centric* and what concepts are *PPL centric*. For the remainder of this chapter and the next we will switch between PyMC3 and TFP to continue helping you identify this difference and see more worked examples. We include exercises to translate Code Block examples from one to the other to aid your practice journey in becoming a PPL polyglot.

3.2   Linear Regression

In the previous section we modeled the distribution of penguin mass by setting prior distributions over the mean and standard deviation of a Gaussian distribution. Importantly we assumed that the mass did not vary with other features in the data. However, we would expect that other observed data points could provide information about expected penguins mass. Intuitively if we see two penguins, one with long flippers and one with short flippers, we would expect the larger penguin, the one with long flippers, to have more mass even if we did not have a scale on hand to measure their mass precisely. One of the simplest ways to estimate this relationship of observed flipper length on estimated mass is to fit a linear regression model, where the mean is *conditionally* modeled as a linear combination of other variables

$$\begin{aligned} \mu &= \beta_0 + \beta_1 X_1 + \cdots + \beta_m X_m \\ Y &\sim \mathcal{N}(\mu, \sigma) \end{aligned} \tag{3.2}$$

where the coefficients, also referred to as covariates, are represented by the parameter β_i. For example, β_0 is the intercept of the linear model. X_i is referred to predictors or independent variables, and Y is usually referred to as target, output, response, or dependent variable. It is important to notice that both $\boldsymbol{X}$ and Y are observed data and that they are paired $\{y_j, x_j\}$. That is, if we change the order of Y without changing X we will destroy some of the information in our data.

We call this a linear regression because the parameters (not the covariates) enter the model in a linear fashion. Also for models with a single covariate, we can think of this model as fitting a line to the (X, y) data, and for higher dimensions a plane or more generally a hyperplane.

Alternatively we can express Equation 3.2 using matrix notation:

$$\mu = \mathbf{X}\boldsymbol{\beta} \tag{3.3}$$

where we are taking the matrix-vector product between the coefficient column vector β and the matrix of covariates $\mathbf{X}$.

An alternative expression you might have seen in other (non-Bayesian) occasions is to rewrite Equation 3.2 as noisy observation of some linear prediction:

$$Y = \mathbf{X}\boldsymbol{\beta} + \epsilon, \ \epsilon \sim \mathcal{N}(0, \sigma) \tag{3.4}$$

The formulation in Equation 3.4 separates the deterministic part (linear prediction) and the stochastic part (noise) of linear regression. However, we prefer Equation 3.2 as it shows the generative process more clearly.

Design Matrix

The matrix $\mathbf{X}$ in Equation 3.3 is known as design matrix and is a matrix of values of explanatory variables of a given set of objects, plus an additional column of ones to represent the intercept. Each row represents an unique observation (e.g., a penguin), with the successive columns corresponding to the variables (like flipper length) and their specific values for that object.

A design matrix is not limited to continuous covariates. For discrete covariates that represent categorical predictors (i.e., there are only a few categories), a common way to turn those into a design matrix is called dummy coding or one-hot coding. For example, in our intercept per penguin model (Code Block 3.5), instead of `mu = `μ`[species.codes]` we can use `pandas.get_dummies` to parse the categorical information into a design matrix `mu = pd.get_dummies(penguins["species"]) @ `μ`.` where `@` is a Python operator for performing matrix multiplication. There are also few other functions to perform one hot encoding in Python, for example, `sklearn.preprocessing.OneHotEncoder`, as this is a very common data manipulation technique.

Alternatively, categorical predictors could be encoded such that the resulting column and associated coefficient representing linear contrast. For example, different design matrix encoding of two categorical predictors are associated with Type I, II and III sums of squares in null-hypothesis testing setting for ANOVA.

If we plot Equation 3.2 in "three dimensions" we get Figure 3.7, which shows how the estimated parameters of the likelihood distribution can change based on other observed data x. While in this one illustration, and in this chapter, we are using a linear relationship to model the relationship between x and Y, and a Gaussian distribution as a likelihood, in other model architectures, we may opt for different choices as we will see in Chapter 4.

3.2.1 Linear Penguins

If we recall our penguins we were interested using additional data to better estimate the mean mass of a group of penguins. Using linear regression we write the model in Code Block 3.13, which includes two new parameters β_0 and β_1 typically called the intercept and slope.

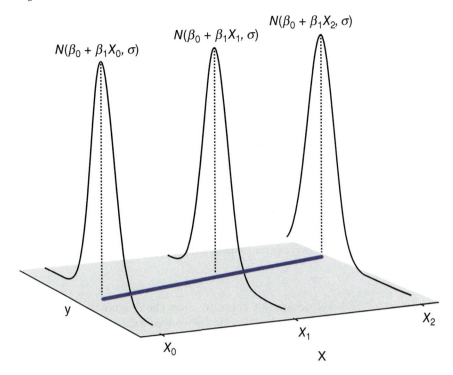

FIGURE 3.7
A linear regression with the Gaussian likelihood function evaluated at 3 points. Note this plot only shows one possible Gaussian distribution at each value of x, where after fitting a Bayesian model we will end up with a distribution of Gaussian, whose parameters may follow a distribution other than Gaussian.

For this example we set wide priors of $\mathcal{N}(0, 4000)$ to focus on the model, which also is the same as saying we assume no domain expertise. We subsequently run our sampler, which has now estimated three parameters σ, β_1 and β_0.

Code 3.13

```
1   adelie_flipper_length_obs = penguins.loc[adelie_mask, "flipper_length_mm"]
2
3   with pm.Model() as model_adelie_flipper_regression:
4       # pm.Data allows us to change the underlying value in a later code block
5       adelie_flipper_length = pm.Data("adelie_flipper_length",
6                                        adelie_flipper_length_obs)
7       σ = pm.HalfStudentT("σ", 100, 2000)
8       β_0 = pm.Normal("β_0", 0, 4000)
9       β_1 = pm.Normal("β_1", 0, 4000)
10      μ = pm.Deterministic("μ", β_0 + β_1 * adelie_flipper_length)
11
12      mass = pm.Normal("mass", mu=μ, sigma=σ, observed = adelie_mass_obs)
13
14      inf_data_adelie_flipper_regression = pm.sample(return_inferencedata=True)
```

To save space in the book we are not going to show the diagnostics each time but you should neither trust us or your sampler blindly. Instead you should run the diagnostics to verify you have a reliable posterior approximation.

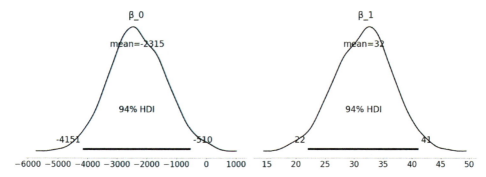

FIGURE 3.8
Estimates of the parameter value distributions of our linear regression coefficient from `model_adelie_flipper_regression`.

After our sampler finishes running we can plot Figure 3.8 which shows a full posterior plot we can use to inspect β_0 and β_1. The coefficient β_1 expresses that for every millimeter change of Adelie flipper length we can nominally expect a change of 32 grams of mass, although anywhere between 22 grams to 41 grams could reasonably occur as well. Additionally, from Figure 3.8 we can note how the 94% highest density interval does not cross 0 grams. This supports our assumption that there is a relationship between mass and flipper length. This observation is quite useful for interpreting how flipper length and mass correlate. However, we should be careful about not over-interpreting the coefficients or thinking a linear model necessarily implies a causal link. For example, if we perform a flipper extension surgery to a penguin this will not necessarily translate into a gain in mass, it could actually be the opposite due to stress or impediments of this penguin to get food. The opposite relation is not necessarily true either, providing more food to a penguin could help her to have a larger flipper, but it could also make it just a fatter penguin. Now focusing on β_0 however, what does it represent? From our posterior estimate we can state that if we saw an Adelie penguin with a 0 mm flipper length we would expect the mass of this impossible penguin to somewhere between -4213 and -546 grams. According to our model this statement is true, but negative mass does not make sense. This is not necessarily an issue, there is no rule that every parameter in a model needs to be interpretable, nor that the model provide reasonable prediction at every parameter value. At this point in our journey the purpose of this particular model was to estimate the relationship between flipper length and penguin mass and with our posterior estimates, we have succeeded with that goal.

Models: A balance between math and reality

In our penguin example it would not make sense if penguin mass was below 0 (or even close to it), even though the model allowed it. Because we fit the model using values for the masses that are far from 0, we should not be surprised that the model fails if we want to extrapolate conclusions for values close to 0 or below it. A model does not necessarily have to provide sensible predictions for all possible values, it just needs to provide sensible predictions for the purposes that we are building it for.

We started on this section surmising that incorporating a covariate would lead to better predictions of penguin mass. We can verify this is the case by comparing the posterior estimates of σ from our fixed mean model and with our linearly varying mean model in Figure 3.9, our estimate of the likelihood's standard deviation has dropped from a mean of around ≈ 460 grams to ≈ 380 grams.

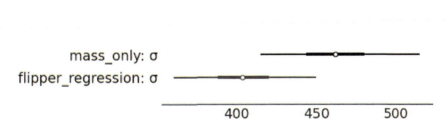

FIGURE 3.9
By using the covariate of flipper length when estimating penguin mass the magnitude of the estimated error is reduced from a mean of slightly over 460 grams to around 380 grams. This intuitively makes sense as if we are given information about a quantity we are estimating, we can leverage that information to make better estimates.

3.2.2 Predictions

In the Section 3.2.1 we estimated a linear relationship between flipper length and mass. Another use of regression is to leverage that relationship in order to make predictions. In our case given the flipper length of a penguin, can we predict its mass? In fact we can. We will use our results from `model_adelie_flipper_regression` to do so. Because in Bayesian statistics we are dealing with distributions we do not end up with a single predicted value but instead a distribution of possible values. That is the posterior predictive distribution as defined in Equation 1.8. In practice, more often than not, we will not compute our

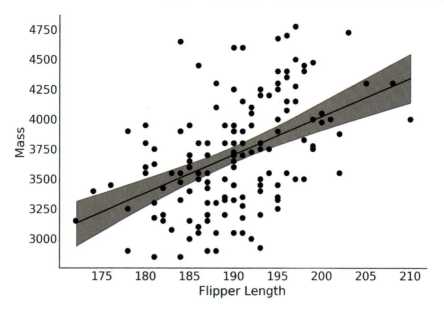

FIGURE 3.10
Observed Adelie data of flipper length vs mass as scatter plot, and mean estimate of the
likelihood as black line, and 94% HDI of the mean as gray interval. Note how our mean
estimate varies as flipper varies.

predictions analytically but we will use a PPL to estimate them using our posterior samples.
For example, if we had a penguin of average flipper length and wanted to predict the likely
mass using PyMC3 we would write Code Block 3.14:

Code 3.14

```
1  with model_adelie_flipper_regression:
2      # Change the underlying value to the mean observed flipper length
3      # for our posterior predictive samples
4      pm.set_data({"adelie_flipper_length": [adelie_flipper_length_obs.mean()]})
5      posterior_predictions = pm.sample_posterior_predictive(
6          inf_data_adelie_flipper_regression.posterior, var_names=["mass", "μ"])
```

In the first line of Code Block 3.14 we fix the value of our flipper length to the average observed flipper length. Then using the regression model `model_adelie_flipper_regression`,
we can generate posterior predictive samples of the mass at that fixed value. In Figure 3.11
we plot the posterior predictive distribution of the mass for penguins of average flipper
length, along the posterior of the mean.

In short not only can we use our model in Code Block 3.13 to estimate the relationship
between flipper length and mass, we also can obtain an estimate of the penguin mass at
any arbitrary flipper length. In other words we can use the estimated β_1 and β_0 coefficients
to make predictions of the mass of unseen penguins of any flipper length using posterior
predictive distributions.

As such, the posterior predictive distribution is an especially powerful tool in a Bayesian
context as it let us predict not just the most likely value, but a distribution of plausible
values incorporating the uncertainty about our estimates, as seen from Equation 1.8.

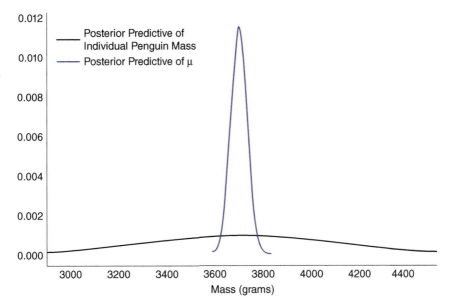

FIGURE 3.11
The posterior distribution of the mean, μ, evaluated at the mean flipper length in blue and the posterior predictive distribution evaluated at the mean flipper length in black. The black curve is wider as it describes the distribution of the predicted data (for a given flipper length), while the blue curve represents the distribution of just the mean of the predicted data.

3.2.3 Centering

Our model in Code Block 3.13 worked well for estimating the correlation between flipper length and penguin mass, and in predicting the mass of penguins at a given flipper length. Unfortunately with the data and the model provided our estimate of β_0 was not particularly useful. However, we can use a transformation to make β_0 more interpretable. In this case we will opt for a centering transformation, which takes a set a value and centers its mean value at zero as shown in Code Block 3.15.

Code 3.15

```
1  adelie_flipper_length_c = (adelie_flipper_length_obs -
2                             adelie_flipper_length_obs.mean())
```

With our now centered covariate let us fit our model again, this time using TFP.

Code 3.16

```
1  def gen_adelie_flipper_model(adelie_flipper_length):
2      adelie_flipper_length = tf.constant(adelie_flipper_length, tf.float32)
3
4      @tfd.JointDistributionCoroutine
5      def jd_adelie_flipper_regression():
6          σ = yield root(
7              tfd.HalfStudentT(df=100, loc=0, scale=2000, name="sigma"))
```

```
8            β_1 = yield root(tfd.Normal(loc=0, scale=4000, name="beta_1"))
9            β_0 = yield root(tfd.Normal(loc=0, scale=4000, name="beta_0"))
10           μ = β_0[..., None] + β_1[..., None] * adelie_flipper_length
11           mass = yield tfd.Independent(
12               tfd.Normal(loc=μ, scale=σ[..., None]),
13               reinterpreted_batch_ndims=1,
14               name="mass")
15
16       return jd_adelie_flipper_regression
17
18   # If use non-centered predictor, this will give the same model as
19   # model_adelie_flipper_regression
20   jd_adelie_flipper_regression = gen_adelie_flipper_model(
21       adelie_flipper_length_c)
22
23   mcmc_samples, sampler_stats = run_mcmc(
24       1000, jd_adelie_flipper_regression, n_chains=4, num_adaptation_steps=1000,
25       mass=tf.constant(adelie_mass_obs, tf.float32))
26
27   inf_data_adelie_flipper_length_c = az.from_dict(
28       posterior={
29           k:np.swapaxes(v, 1, 0)
30           for k, v in mcmc_samples._asdict().items()},
31       sample_stats={
32           k:np.swapaxes(sampler_stats[k], 1, 0)
33           for k in ["target_log_prob", "diverging", "accept_ratio", "n_steps"]}
34   )
```

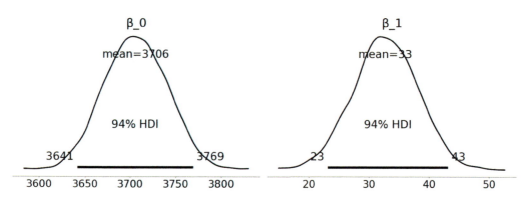

FIGURE 3.12
Estimates of coefficients from Code Block 3.16. Notice that the distribution of *beta_1* is the same as in 3.8, but the distribution of *beta_0* has shifted. Because we centered the observations around the mean of flipper length *beta_0* now represents the mass distribution of the average flipper penguin.

The mathematical model we defined in Code Block 3.16 is identical to the PyMC3 model `model_adelie_flipper_regression` from Code Block 3.13, with sole difference being the centering of the predictor. PPL wise however, the structure of TFP necessitates the addition of `tensor_x[..., None]` in various lines to extend a batch of scalars so that they are broadcastable with a batch of vectors. Specifically **None** appends a new axis, which could also be done using `np.newaxis` or `tf.newaxis`. We also wrap the model in a function so we can easily condition on different predictors. In this case we use the centered flipper length, but could also use the non-centered predictor which will yield similar results to our previous model.

When we plot our coefficients again, β_1 is the same as our PyMC3 model but the distribution of β_0 has changed. Since we have centered our input data on its mean, the distribution of β_0 is the same as our prediction for the group mean with the non-centered dataset. By centering the data we now can directly interpret β_0 as the distribution of mean masses for Adelie penguins with a mean flipper length. The idea of transforming the input variables can also be performed at arbitrary values of choice. For example, we could subtract out the minimum flipper length and fit our model. In this transformation this would change the interpretation β_0 to the distribution of means for the smallest observed flipper length. For a greater discussion of transformations in linear regression we recommend Applied Regression Analysis and Generalized Linear Models [53].

3.3   Multiple Linear Regression

In many species there is a dimorphism, or difference, between different sexes. The study of sexual dimorphism in penguins actually was the motivating factor for collecting the Palmer Penguin dataset [71]. To study penguin dimorphism more closely let us add a second covariate, this time sex, encoding it as a categorical variable and seeing if we can estimate a penguins mass more precisely.

Code 3.17

```
1  # Binary encoding of the categorical predictor
2  sex_obs = penguins.loc[adelie_mask ,"sex"].replace({"male":0, "female":1})
3
4  with pm.Model() as model_penguin_mass_categorical:
5      σ = pm.HalfStudentT("σ", 100, 2000)
6      β_0 = pm.Normal("β_0", 0, 3000)
7      β_1 = pm.Normal("β_1", 0, 3000)
8      β_2 = pm.Normal("β_2", 0, 3000)
9
10     μ = pm.Deterministic(
11         "μ", β_0 + β_1 * adelie_flipper_length_obs + β_2 * sex_obs)
12
13     mass = pm.Normal("mass", mu=μ, sigma=σ, observed=adelie_mass_obs)
14
15     inf_data_penguin_mass_categorical = pm.sample(
16         target_accept=.9, return_inferencedata=True)
```

You will notice a new parameter, β_2 contributing to the value of μ. As sex is a categorical predictor (in this example just female or male), we encode it as 1 and 0, respectively. For the model this means that the value of μ, for females, is a sum over 3 terms while for males is a sum of two terms (as the β_2 term will zero out).

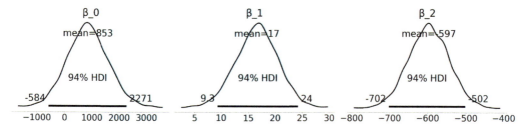

FIGURE 3.13

Estimate of coefficient for sex covariate, β_2 in model. As male is encoded as 0, and female is encoded as 1, this indicates the additional mass we would expect between a male and female Adelie penguin with the same flipper length.

Syntactic Linear Sugar

Linear models are so widely used that specialized syntax, methods, and libraries have been written just for regression. One such library is Bambi (BAyesian Model-Building Interface[30]). Bambi is a Python package for fitting generalized linear hierarchical models using a formula-based syntax, similar to what one might find in R packages, like lme4 [7], nlme [121], rstanarm [56] or brms [28]). Bambi uses PyMC3 underneath and provides a higher level API. To write the same model, if disregarding the priors[a] as the one in Code Block 3.17 in Bambi we would write:

Code 3.18

```
1  import bambi as bmb
2  model = bmb.Model("body_mass_g ~ flipper_length_mm + sex",
3                      penguins[adelie_mask])
4  trace = model.fit()
```

The priors are automatically assigned if not provided, as is the case in the code example above. Internally, Bambi stores virtually all objects generated by PyMC3, making it easy for users to retrieve, inspect, and modify those objects. Additionally Bambi returns an `az.InferenceData` object which can be directly used with ArviZ.

---

[a]If wanted exactly the same model we could specify the priors in Bambi, not shown here. For our purposes however, the models are "close enough".

Since we have encoded male as 0 this posterior from `model_penguin_mass_categorical` estimates the difference in mass compared to a female Adelie penguin *with the same flipper length*. This last part is quite important, by adding a second covariate we now have a multiple linear regression and we must use more caution when interpreting the coefficients. In this case, the coefficients provides the relationship of a covariate into the response variable, **if** all other covariates are held constant [4].

We again can compare the standard deviations across our three models in Figure 3.15 to see if we have reduced uncertainty in our estimate and once again the additional information has helped to improve the estimate. In this case our estimate of σ has dropped a mean of 462 grams in our no covariate model defined in Code Block 3.3 to a mean value 298 grams

---

[4]You can also parse the design matrix differently so that covariates represents the contrast between 2 categories within a column.

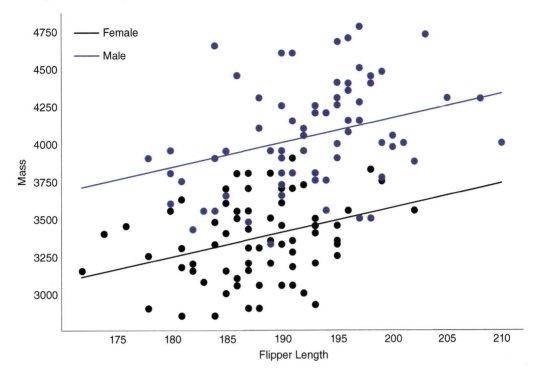

FIGURE 3.14

Multiple regression for flipper length versus mass with male and female Adelie penguins coded as a categorical covariate. Note how the difference mass between male and female penguins is constant at every flipper length. This difference is equivalent to the magnitude of the β_2 coefficient.

from the linear model defined in Code Block 3.17 that includes flipper length and sex as a covariates. This reduction in uncertainty suggests that sex does indeed provide information for estimating a penguin's mass.

Code 3.19

```
1  az.plot_forest([inf_data_adelie_penguin_mass,
2        inf_data_adelie_flipper_regression,
3        inf_data_penguin_mass_categorical],
4        var_names=["σ"], combined=True)
```

> **More covariates is not always better**
>
> All model fitting algorithms will find a signal, even if it is random noise. This phenomenon is called overfitting and it describes a condition where the algorithm can quite handily map covariates to outcomes in seen cases, but fails to generalize to new observations. In linear regressions we can show this by generating 100 random covariates, and fitting them to a random simulated dataset [101]. Even though there is no relation, we would be led to believe our linear model is doing quite well.

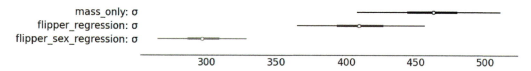

FIGURE 3.15

By incorporating sex as a covariate in `model_penguin_mass_categorical` the estimated distribution of σ from this model is centered around 300 grams, which lower value than estimated by our fixed mean model and our single covariate model. This figure is generated from Code Block 3.19.

3.3.1   Counterfactuals

In Code Block 3.14 we made a prediction using parameters fitted in a model with a single covariate and our target, and changing that covariate, flipper length, to get an estimate of mass at that fixed flipper length. In multiple regression, we can do something similar, where we take our regression, hold all covariates constant except one, and see how that change to that one covariate changes our expected outcome. This analysis is called a counterfactual analysis. Let us extend the multiple regression from the previous section (Code Block 3.17), this time including bill length, and run a counterfactual analysis in TFP. The model building and inference is shown in Code Block 3.20.

Code 3.20

```
def gen_jd_flipper_bill_sex(flipper_length, sex, bill_length, dtype=tf.float32):
    flipper_length, sex, bill_length = tf.nest.map_structure(
        lambda x: tf.constant(x, dtype),
        (flipper_length, sex, bill_length)
    )

    @tfd.JointDistributionCoroutine
    def jd_flipper_bill_sex():
        σ = yield root(
            tfd.HalfStudentT(df=100, loc=0, scale=2000, name="sigma"))
        β_0 = yield root(tfd.Normal(loc=0, scale=3000, name="beta_0"))
        β_1 = yield root(tfd.Normal(loc=0, scale=3000, name="beta_1"))
        β_2 = yield root(tfd.Normal(loc=0, scale=3000, name="beta_2"))
        β_3 = yield root(tfd.Normal(loc=0, scale=3000, name="beta_3"))
        μ = (β_0[..., None]
             + β_1[..., None] * flipper_length
             + β_2[..., None] * sex
             + β_3[..., None] * bill_length
             )
        mass = yield tfd.Independent(
            tfd.Normal(loc=μ, scale=σ[..., None]),
            reinterpreted_batch_ndims=1,
            name="mass")

    return jd_flipper_bill_sex

bill_length_obs = penguins.loc[adelie_mask, "bill_length_mm"]
```

```
28  jd_flipper_bill_sex = gen_jd_flipper_bill_sex(
29      adelie_flipper_length_obs, sex_obs, bill_length_obs)
30
31  mcmc_samples, sampler_stats = run_mcmc(
32      1000, jd_flipper_bill_sex, n_chains=4, num_adaptation_steps=1000,
33      mass=tf.constant(adelie_mass_obs, tf.float32))
```

In this model you will note the addition of another coefficient `beta_3` to correspond to the addition of bill length as a covariate. After inference, we can simulate the mass of penguins with different fictional flipper lengths, while holding the sex constant at male, and the bill length at the observed mean of the dataset. This is done in Code Block 3.21 with the result shown in Figure 3.16. Again since we wrap the model generation in a Python function (a functional programming style approach), it is easy to condition on new predictors, which useful for counterfactual analyses.

Code 3.21

```
1   mean_flipper_length = penguins.loc[adelie_mask, "flipper_length_mm"].mean()
2   # Counterfactual dimensions is set to 21 to allow us to get the mean exactly
3   counterfactual_flipper_lengths = np.linspace(
4       mean_flipper_length-20, mean_flipper_length+20, 21)
5   sex_male_indicator = np.zeros_like(counterfactual_flipper_lengths)
6   mean_bill_length = np.ones_like(
7       counterfactual_flipper_lengths) * bill_length_obs.mean()
8
9   jd_flipper_bill_sex_counterfactual = gen_jd_flipper_bill_sex(
10      counterfactual_flipper_lengths, sex_male_indicator, mean_bill_length)
11  ppc_samples = jd_flipper_bill_sex_counterfactual.sample(value=mcmc_samples)
12  estimated_mass = ppc_samples[-1].numpy().reshape(-1, 21)
```

Following McElreath[101] Figure 3.16 is called a counterfactual plot. As the word counterfactual implies, we are evaluating a situation counter to the observed data, or facts. In other words, we are evaluating situations that have not happened. The simplest use of a counterfactual plot is to adjust a covariate and explore the result, exactly like we just did. This is great, as it enables us to explore *what-if* scenarios, that could be beyond our reach otherwise [5]. However, we must be cautious when interpreting this trickery. The first trap is that counterfactual values may be impossible, for example, no penguin may ever exist with a flipper length larger than 1500mm but the model will happily give us estimates for this fictional penguin. The second is more insidious, we assumed that we could vary each covariate independently, but in reality this may not be possible. For example, as a penguin's flipper length increases, its bill length may as well. Counterfactuals are powerful in that they allow us to explore outcomes that have not happened, or that we at least did not observe happen. But they can easily generate estimates for situations that will *never* happen. It is the model that will not discern between the two, so you as a modeler must.

---

[5]Maybe because collecting more data is expensive or difficult or even impossible

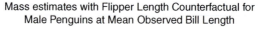

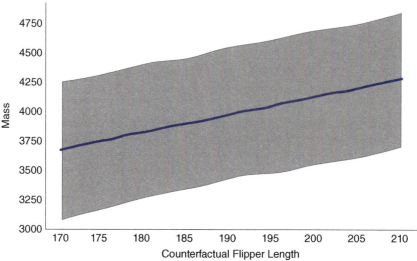

FIGURE 3.16
Estimated counterfactual mass values for Adelie penguins from Code Block 3.21 where flipper length is varied holding all other covariates constant.

Correlation vs Causality

When interpreting linear regressions it is tempting to say "An increase in X **causes and increase in** Y". This is not necessarily the case, in fact causal statements can not be made from a (linear) regression alone. Mathematically a linear model links two (or more variables) together but this link does not need to be causal. For example, increasing the amount of water we provide to a plant can certainly (and causally) increase the plant's growth (at least within some range), but nothing prevents us from inverting this relationship in a model and use the growth of plants to estimate the amount of rain, even when plant growth do not cause rain [a]. The statistical sub-field of Causal Inference is concerned with the tools and procedures necessary to make causal statements either in the context of randomized experiments or observational studies (see Chapter 7 for a brief discussion)

---

[a]Unless we are talking about large systems like rain forests, where the presence of plants actually have an impact in the weather. Nature can be hard to grasp with simple statements.

3.4 Generalized Linear Models

All linear models discussed so far assumed the distribution of observations are conditionally Gaussian which works well in many scenarios. However, we may want to use other distributions. For example, to model things that are restricted to some interval, a number in the interval $[0, 1]$ like probabilities, or natural numbers $\{1, 2, 3, \dots\}$ like counting events. To do this we will take our linear function, $\mathbf{X}\beta$, and modify it using an inverse link function [6] ϕ as shown in Equation 3.5.

$$\mu = \phi(\mathbf{X}\beta)$$
$$Y \sim \Psi(\mu, \theta) \tag{3.5}$$

where Ψ is some distribution parameterized by μ and θ indicating the data likelihood.

The specific purpose of the inverse link function is to map outputs from the range of real numbers $(-\infty, \infty)$ to a parameter range of the restricted interval. In other words the inverse link function is the specific "trick" we need to take our linear models and generalize them to many more model architectures. We are still dealing a linear model here in the sense that the expectation of the distribution that generates the observation still follows a linear function of the parameter and the covariates but now we can generalize the use and application of these models to many more scenarios [7].

3.4.1 Logistic Regression

One of the most common generalized linear model is the logistic regression. It is particularly useful in modeling data where there are only two possible outcomes, we observed either one thing or another thing. The probability of a head or tails outcome in a coin flip is the usual textbook example. More "real world" examples includes the chance of a defect in manufacturing, a negative or positive cancer test, or the failure of a rocket launch[43]. In a logistic regression the inverse link function is called, unsurprisingly, the logistic function, which maps $(-\infty, \infty)$ to the $(0, 1)$ interval. This is handy because now we can map linear functions to the range we would expect for a parameter that estimates probability values, that must be in the range 0 and 1 by definition.

$$p = \frac{1}{1 + e^{-\mathbf{X}\beta}} \tag{3.6}$$

With logistic regression we are able to use linear models to estimate probabilities of an event. Sometimes, instead we want to classify, or to predict, a specific class given some data. In order to do so we want to turn the continuous prediction in the interval $(-\infty, \infty)$ to one between 0 and 1. We can do this with a decision boundary to make a prediction in the set

---

[6]Traditionally people apply functions like ϕ to the left side of Equation 3.5, and call them link functions. We instead prefer to apply them to the right-hand side and then to avoid confusion we use term inverse link function.

[7]Usually in the traditional Generalized Linear Models Literature, the likelihood of the observation need to be from the Exponential family, but being Bayesian we are actually not restricted by that and can use any likelihood that can be parameterized by the expected value.

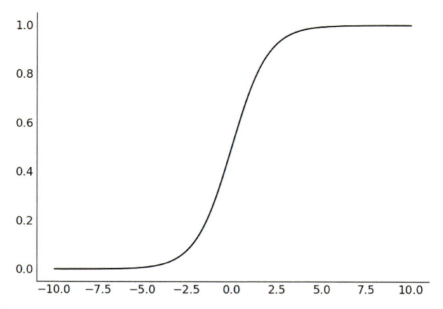

FIGURE 3.17
A plot of a sample logistic function. Note the response has been "squished" into the interval (0,1).

0, 1. Let us assume we want our decision boundary set at a probability of 0.5. For a model with an intercept and one covariate we have:

$$0.5 = logistic(\beta_0 + \beta_1 * x)$$
$$logit(0.5) = \beta_0 + \beta_1 * x$$
$$0 = \beta_0 + \beta_1 * x \tag{3.7}$$
$$x = -\frac{\beta_0}{\beta_1}$$

Note that *logit* is the inverse of *logistic*. That is, once a logistic model is fitted we can use the coefficients β_0 and β_1 to easily compute the value of x for which the probability of the class is greater than 0.5.

3.4.2 Classifying Penguins

In the previous sections we used the sex, and bill length of a penguin to estimate the mass of a penguin. Lets now alter the question, if we were given the mass, sex, and bill length of a penguin can we predict the species? Let us use two species Adelie and Chinstrap to make this a binary task. Like last time we use a simple model first with just one covariate, bill length. We write this logistic model in Code Block 3.22

Code 3.22

```
1  species_filter = penguins["species"].isin(["Adelie", "Chinstrap"])
2  bill_length_obs = penguins.loc[species_filter, "bill_length_mm"].values
```

	mean	sd	hdi_3%	hdi_97%
β_0	-46.052	7.073	-58.932	-34.123
β_1	1.045	0.162	0.776	1.347

TABLE 3.3

Logistic regression coefficients of fit estimated from `model_logistic_penguins_bill_length`. The HDI range for β_1 which does not cross zero suggests that bill length provide an identifying the difference between species.

```
3  species = pd.Categorical(penguins.loc[species_filter, "species"])
4
5  with pm.Model() as model_logistic_penguins_bill_length:
6      β_0 = pm.Normal("β_0", mu=0, sigma=10)
7      β_1 = pm.Normal("β_1", mu=0, sigma=10)
8
9      μ = β_0 + pm.math.dot(bill_length_obs, β_1)
10
11     # Application of our sigmoid  link function
12     θ = pm.Deterministic("θ", pm.math.sigmoid(μ))
13
14     # Useful for plotting the decision boundary later
15     bd = pm.Deterministic("bd", -β_0/β_1)
16
17     # Note the change in likelihood
18     yl = pm.Bernoulli("yl", p=θ, observed=species.codes)
19
20     prior_predictive_logistic_penguins_bill_length = pm.sample_prior_predictive()
21     trace_logistic_penguins_bill_length = pm.sample(5000, chains=2)
22     inf_data_logistic_penguins_bill_length = az.from_pymc3(
23         prior=prior_predictive_logistic_penguins_bill_length,
24         trace=trace_logistic_penguins_bill_length)
```

In generalized linear models, the mapping from parameter prior to response can sometimes be more challenging to understand. We can utilize prior predictive samples to help us visualize the expected observations. In our classifying penguins example we find it reasonable to equally expect a Gentoo penguin, as we would an Adelie penguin, at all bill lengths, prior to seeing any data. We can double-check our modeling intention has been represented correctly by our priors and model using the prior predictive distribution. The classes are roughly even in Figure 3.18 prior to seeing data which is what we would expect.

After fitting the parameters in our model we can inspect the coefficients using `az.summary(.)` function (see Table 3.3). While we can read the coefficients they are not as directly interpretable as in a linear regression. We can tell there is some relationship with bill length and species given the positive β_1 coefficient whose HDI does not cross zero. We can interpret the decision boundary fairly directly seeing that around 44 mm in bill length is the nominal cutoff for one species to another. Plotting the regression output in Figure 3.19 is much more intuitive. Here we see the now familiar logistic curve move from 0 on the left to 1 on the right as the classes change, and a decision boundary where one would expect it given the data.

Let us try something different, we still want to classify penguins but this time using mass as a covariate. Code Block 3.23 shows a model for that purpose.

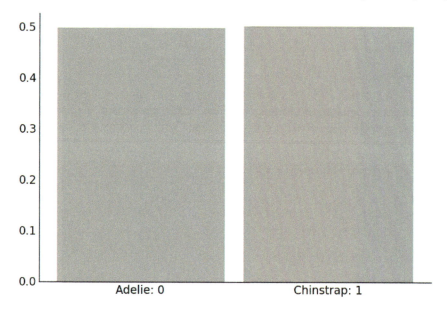

FIGURE 3.18
5000 prior predictive samples of class prediction from the `model_logistic_penguins_bill_length`. This likelihood is discrete, more specifically binary, as opposed to the continuous distribution of mass that was being estimated in earlier models.

	mean	sd	hdi_3%	hdi_97%
β_0	-1.131	1.317	-3.654	1.268
β_1	0.000	0.000	-0.000	0.001

TABLE 3.4
Logistic regression coefficients of fit estimated from `model_logistic_penguins_mass`. The value of 0 for β_1 suggests that mass does not provide much value in identifying the difference between species.

Code 3.23

```
1  mass_obs = penguins.loc[species_filter, "body_mass_g"].values
2
3  with pm.Model() as model_logistic_penguins_mass:
4      β_0 = pm.Normal("β_0", mu=0, sigma=10)
5      β_1 = pm.Normal("β_1", mu=0, sigma=10)
6
7      μ = β_0 + pm.math.dot(mass_obs, β_1)
8      θ = pm.Deterministic("θ", pm.math.sigmoid(μ))
9      bd = pm.Deterministic("bd", -β_0/β_1)
10
11     yl = pm.Bernoulli("yl", p=θ, observed=species.codes)
12
13     inf_data_logistic_penguins_mass = pm.sample(
14         5000, target_accept=.9, return_inferencedata=True)
```

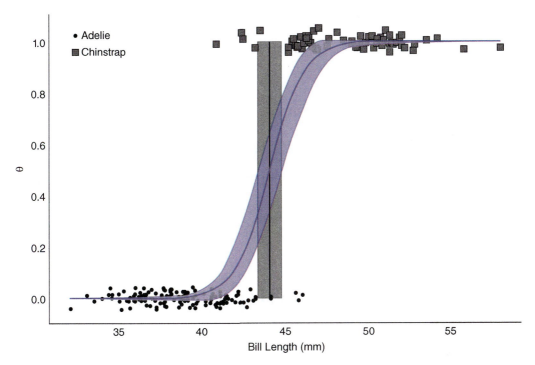

FIGURE 3.19

Fitted logistic regression, showing probability curve, observed data points and decision boundary for `model_logistic_penguins_bill_length`. Looking at just the observed data it seems there is a separation around 45mm bill length for both species, and our model similarly discerned the separation around that value.

Our tabular summary in Table 3.4 shows that β_1 is estimated to be 0 indicating there is not enough information in the mass covariate to separate the two classes. This is not necessarily a bad thing, just the model indicating to us that it does not find discernible difference in mass between these two species. This becomes quite evident once we plot the data and logistic regression fit in Figure 3.20.

We should not let this lack of relationship discourage us, effective modeling includes a dose of trial an error. This does not mean try random things and hope they work, it instead means that it is ok to use the computational tools to provide you clues to the next step.

Let us now try using both bill length and mass to create a multiple logistic regression in Code Block 3.24 and plot the decision boundary again in Figure 3.21. This time the axes of the figure are a little bit different. Instead of the probability of class on the Y-axis, we instead have mass. This way we can see the decision boundary between the dependent variables. All these visual checks have been helpful but subjective. We can quantify our fits numerically as well using diagnostics.

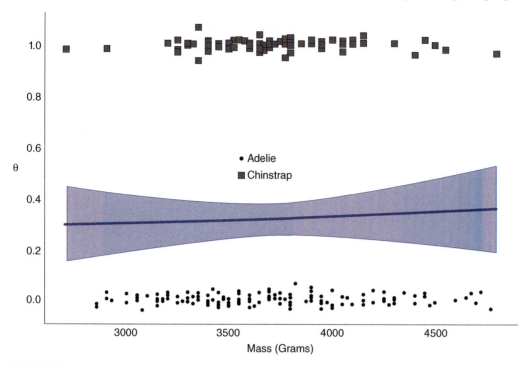

FIGURE 3.20

Plot of the observed data and logistic regression for `model_logistic_penguins_mass`. Unlike Figure 3.19 the data does not look very separable and our model did discern one as well.

Code 3.24

```
1  X = penguins.loc[species_filter, ["bill_length_mm", "body_mass_g"]]
2
3  # Add a column of 1s for the intercept
4  X.insert(0,"Intercept", value=1)
5  X = X.values
6
7  with pm.Model() as model_logistic_penguins_bill_length_mass:
8      β = pm.Normal("β", mu=0, sigma=20, shape=3)
9
10     μ = pm.math.dot(X, β)
11
12     θ = pm.Deterministic("θ", pm.math.sigmoid(μ))
13     bd = pm.Deterministic("bd", -β[0]/β[2] - β[1]/β[2] * X[:,1])
14
15     yl = pm.Bernoulli("yl", p=θ, observed=species.codes)
16
17     inf_data_logistic_penguins_bill_length_mass = pm.sample(
18         1000,
19         return_inferencedata=True)
```

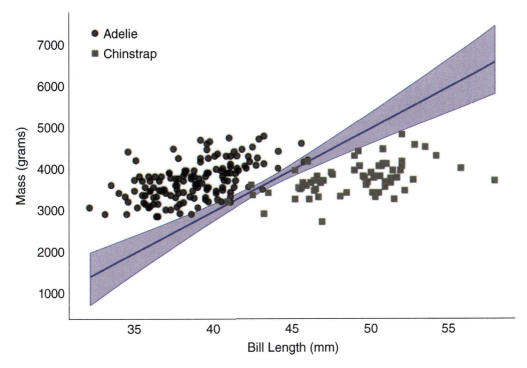

FIGURE 3.21
Decision boundary of species class plotted against bill length and mass. We can see that most of the species separability comes from bill length although mass now adds some extra information in regards to class separability as indicated by the slope of the line.

To evaluate the model fit for logistic regressions we can use a separation plot [72], as shown in Code Block 3.25 and Figure 3.22. A separation plot is a way to assess the calibration of a model with binary observed data. It shows the sorted predictions per class, the idea being that with perfect separation there would be two distinct rectangles. In our case we see that none of our models did a perfect job separating the two species, but the models that included bill length performed much better than the model that included mass only. In general, perfect calibration is not the goal of a Bayesian analysis, nevertheless separation plots (and other calibration assessment methods like LOO-PIT) can help us to compare models and reveal opportunities to improve them.

Code 3.25

```
1  models = {"bill": inf_data_logistic_penguins_bill_length,
2            "mass": inf_data_logistic_penguins_mass,
3            "mass bill": inf_data_logistic_penguins_bill_length_mass}
4
5  _, axes = plt.subplots(3, 1, figsize=(12, 4), sharey=True)
6  for (label, model), ax in zip(models.items(), axes):
7      az.plot_separation(model, "p", ax=ax, color="C4")
8      ax.set_title(label)
```

We can also use LOO to compare the three models we have just created, the one for the mass, the one for the bill length and the one including both covariates in Code Block 3.26 and Table 3.4.2. According to LOO the mass only model is the worst at separating the

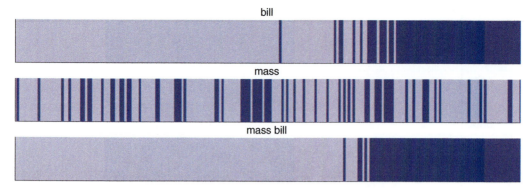

FIGURE 3.22

Separation plot of all three penguin models. The light versus dark value indicates the binary class label. In this plot its much more evident that the mass only model does a poor job separating the two species, where are the bill and mass bill models perform better at this task.

	rank	loo	p_loo	d_loo	weight	se	dse	warning	loo_scale
mass_bill	0	-11.3	1.6	0.0	1.0	3.1	0.0	True	log
bill	1	-27.0	1.7	15.6	0.0	6.2	4.9	False	log
mass	2	-135.8	2.1	124.5	0.0	5.3	5.8	False	log

species, the bill length only is the middle candidate model, and the mass and bill length model performed the best. This is unsurprising given what we have seen from the plots, and now we have a numerical confirmation as well.

Code 3.26

```
1  az.compare({"mass":inf_data_logistic_penguins_mass,
2             "bill": inf_data_logistic_penguins_bill_length,
3             "mass_bill":inf_data_logistic_penguins_bill_length_mass})
```

3.4.3   Interpreting Log Odds

In a logistic regression the slope is telling you the increase in log odds units when x is incremented one unit. Odds most simply are the ratio between the probability of occurrence and probability of no occurrence. For example, in our penguin example if we were to pick a random penguin from Adelie or Chinstrap penguinsthe probability that we pick an Adelie penguin would be 0.68 as seen in Code Block 3.27

Code 3.27

```
1  # Class counts of each penguin species
2  counts = penguins["species"].value_counts()
3  adelie_count = counts["Adelie"],
4  chinstrap_count = counts["Chinstrap"]
5  adelie_count / (adelie_count + chinstrap_count)
```

```
array([0.68224299])
```

And for the same event the odds would be

Code 3.28

```
adelie_count / chinstrap_count
```

```
array([2.14705882])
```

Odds are made up of the same components as probability but are transformed in a manner that makes interpreting the ratio of one event occurring from another more straightforward. Stated in odds, if we were to randomly sample from Adelie and Chinstrap penguins we would expect to end up with a ratio of 2.14 more Adelie penguins than Chinstrap penguins as calculated by Code Block 3.28.

Using our knowledge of odds we can define the logit. The logit is the natural log of the odds which is the fraction shown in Equation 3.8. We can rewrite the logistic regression in Equation 3.6 in an alternative form of using the logit.

$$\log\left(\frac{p}{1-p}\right) = \boldsymbol{X}\beta \tag{3.8}$$

This alternative formulation lets us interpret the coefficients of logistic regression as the change in log odds. Using this knowledge we can calculate the probability of observing Adelie to Chinstrap penguins given a change in the observed bill length as shown in Code Block 3.29. Transformations like these are both interesting mathematically, but also very practically useful when discussing statistical results, a topic we will discuss more deeply in Section 9.10.

Code 3.29

```
1  x = 45
2  β_0 = inf_data_logistic_penguins_bill_length.posterior["β_0"].mean().values
3  β_1 = inf_data_logistic_penguins_bill_length.posterior["β_1"].mean().values
4  bill_length = 45
5
6  val_1 = β_0 + β_1*bill_length
7  val_2 = β_0 + β_1*(bill_length+1)
8
9  f"(Class Probability change from 45mm Bill Length to 46mm:
10 {(special.expit(val_2) - special.expit(val_1))*100:.0f}%)"
```

```
'Class Probability change from 45mm Bill Length to 46mm: 15%'
```

3.5   Picking Priors in Regression Models

Now that we are familiar with generalized linear models let us focus on the prior and its effect on posterior estimation. We will be borrowing an example from Regression and Other Stories [58], in particular a study[63] where the relationship between the attractiveness of parents and the percentage of girl births of those parents is explored. In this study researchers estimated the attractiveness of American teenagers on a five-point scale. Eventually many of these subjects had children, of which the ratio of gender per each attractiveness category was calculated, the resulting data points of which are shown in Code Block 3.30 and plotted in Figure 3.23. In the same code block we also write a model for single variable regression. This time however, focus specifically on how priors and likelihoods should be assessed together and not independently.

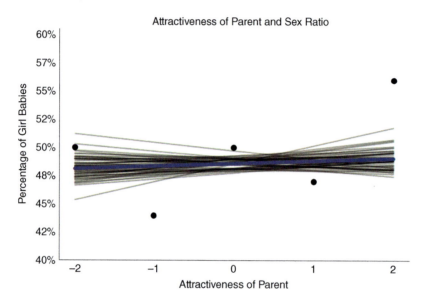

FIGURE 3.23
Data on the attractiveness of parents plotted against the gender ratio of their children.

Code 3.30

```
1  x = np.arange(-2, 3, 1)
2  y = np.asarray([50, 44, 50, 47, 56])
3
4  with pm.Model() as model_uninformative_prior_sex_ratio:
5      σ = pm.Exponential("σ", .5)
6      β_1 = pm.Normal("β_1", 0, 20)
7      β_0 = pm.Normal("β_0", 50, 20)
8
9      μ = pm.Deterministic("μ", β_0 + β_1 * x)
10
11     ratio = pm.Normal("ratio", mu=μ, sigma=σ, observed=y)
12
13     prior_predictive_uninformative_prior_sex_ratio = pm.sample_prior_predictive(
14         samples=10000
```

```
15    )
16    trace_uninformative_prior_sex_ratio = pm.sample()
17    inf_data_uninformative_prior_sex_ratio = az.from_pymc3(
18        trace=trace_uninformative_prior_sex_ratio,
19        prior=prior_predictive_uninformative_prior_sex_ratio
20    )
```

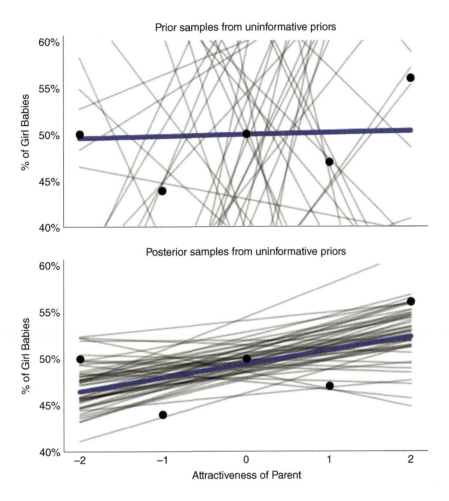

FIGURE 3.24
With vague or very wide priors the model shows that large differences in birth ratios are possible for parents rated as attractive. Some of these possible fits are as large as a 20% change which seems implausible as no other study has shown an effect this large on the sex ratio of births.

Nominally we will assume births are equally split between males and females, and that attractiveness has no effect on sex ratio. This translates to setting the mean of the prior for intercept β_0 to be 50 and the prior mean for the coefficient β_1 to be 0. We also set a wide dispersion to express our lack of knowledge about both the intercept and the effect of attractiveness on sex ratio. This is not a fully *uninformative priors*, of which we covered in Section 1.4, however, a very wide prior. Given these choices we can write our model in Code Block 3.30), run inference, and generate samples to estimate posterior distribution. From the data and model we estimate that the mean of β_1 to be 1.4, meaning the least attractive group when compared to the most attractive group the birth ratio will differ by 7.4% on average. In Figure 3.24 if we include the uncertainty, the ratio can vary by over 20% per unit of attractiveness [8] from a random sample of 50 possible "lines of fit" prior to conditioning the parameters to data.

From a mathematical lens this result is valid. But from the lens of our general knowledge and our understanding of birth sex ratio outside of this studies, these results are suspect. The "natural" sex ratio at birth has been measured to be around 105 boys per 100 girls (ranging from around 103 to 107 boys), which means the sex ratio at birth is 48.5% female, with a standard deviation of 0.5. Moreover, even factors that are more intrinsically tied to human biology do not affect birth ratios to this magnitude, weakening the notion that attractiveness, which is subjective, should have this magnitude of effect. Given this information a change of 8% between two groups would require extraordinary observations.

Let us run our model again but this time set more informative priors shown in Code Block 3.31 that are consistent with this general knowledge. Plotting our posterior samples the concentration of coefficients is smaller and the plotted posterior lines fall into bounds that more reasonable when considering possible ratios.

Code 3.31

```
1  with pm.Model() as model_informative_prior_sex_ratio:
2      σ = pm.Exponential("σ", .5)
3
4      # Note the now more informative priors
5      β_1 = pm.Normal("β_1", 0, .5)
6      β_0 = pm.Normal("β_0", 48.5, .5)
7
8      μ = pm.Deterministic("μ", β_0 + β_1 * x)
9      ratio = pm.Normal("ratio", mu=μ, sigma=σ, observed=y)
10
11     prior_predictive_informative_prior_sex_ratio = pm.sample_prior_predictive(
12         samples=10000
13     )
14     trace_informative_prior_sex_ratio = pm.sample()
15     inf_data_informative_prior_sex_ratio = az.from_pymc3(
16         trace=trace_informative_prior_sex_ratio,
17         prior=prior_predictive_informative_prior_sex_ratio)
```

This time we see that estimated effect of attractiveness on gender is negligible, there simply was not enough information to affect the posterior. As we mentioned in Section 1.4 choosing a prior is both a burden and a blessing. Regardless of which you believe it is, it is important to use this statistical tool with an explainable and principled choice.

---

[8] Estimate shown in corresponding notebook.

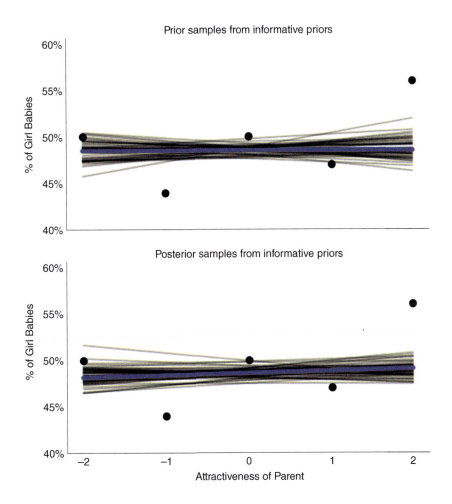

FIGURE 3.25
With priors informed from other papers and domain expertise the mean posterior hardly changes across attractiveness ratio indicating that if there is a belief there is an effect on birth ratio from the parents attractiveness more data should be collected to showcase the effect.

3.6 Exercises

3E1. Comparisons are part of everyday life. What is something you compare on a daily basis and answer the following question:

- What is the numerical quantification you use for comparison?

- How do you decide on the logical groupings for observations? For example in the penguin model we use species or sex

- What point estimate would you use to compare them?

3E2. Referring to Model 3.3 complete the following tasks.

(a) Compute the values of Monte Carlo Standard Error Mean using `az.summary`. Given the computed values which of the following reported values of μ would not be well supported as a point estimate? 3707.235, 3707.2, or 3707.

(b) Plot the ESS and MCSE per quantiles and describe the results.

(c) Resample the model using a low number of draws until you get bad values of $\hat{R}$, and ESS

(d) Report the HDI 50% numerically and using `az.plot_posterior`

3E3. In your own words explain how regression can be used to do the following:

(a) Covariate estimation

(b) Prediction

(c) Counterfactual analysis

Explain how they are different, the steps to perform each, and situations where they would be useful. Use the penguin example or come up with your own.

3E4. In Code Block 3.15 and Code Block 3.16 we centered the flipper length covariate. Refit the model, but instead of centering, subtract the minimum observed flipped length. Compare the posterior estimates of the slope and intercept parameters of the centered model. What is different, what is the same. How does the interpretation of this model change when compared to the centered model?

3E5. Translate the following primitives from PyMC3 to TFP. Assume the model name is `pymc_model`

(a) `pm.StudentT("x", 0, 10, 20)`

(b) `pm.sample(chains=2)`

Hint: write the model and inference first in PyMC3, and find the similar primitives in TFP using the code shown in this chapter.

3E6. PyMC3 and TFP use different argument names for their distribution parameterizations. For example in PyMC3 the Uniform Distribution is parameterized as `pm.Uniform.dist(lower=, upper=)` whereas in TFP it is `tfd.Uniform(low=, high=)`. Use the online documentation to identify the difference in argument names for the following distributions.

(a) Normal

(b) Poisson

(c) Beta

(d) Binomial

(e) Gumbel

3E7. A common modeling technique for parameterizing Bayesian multiple regressions is to assign a wide prior to the intercept, and assign more informative prior to the slope coefficients. Try modifying the `model_logistic_penguins_bill_length_mass` model in Code Block 3.24. Do you get better inference results? Note that there are divergence with the original parameterization.

3E8. In linear regression models we have two terms. The mean linear function and the noise term. Write down these two terms in mathematical notation, referring to the equations in this chapter for guidance. Explain in your own words what the purpose of these two parts of regression are. In particular why are they useful when there is random noise in any part of the data generating or data collection process.

3E9. Simulate the data using the formula $y = 10 + 2x + \mathcal{N}(0, 5)$ with integer covariate x generated np.linspace(-10, 20, 100). Fit a linear model of the form $b_0 + b_1 * X + \sigma$. Use a Normal distribution for the likelihood and covariate priors and a Half Student's T prior for the noise term as needed. Recover the parameters verifying your results using both a posterior plot and a forest plot.

3E10. Generate diagnostics for the model in Code Block 3.13 to verify the results shown in the chapter can be trusted. Use a combination of visual and numerical diagnostics.

3E11. Refit the model in Code Block 3.13 on Gentoo penguins and Chinstrap penguins. How are the posteriors different from each other? How are they different from the Adelie posterior estimation? What inferences can you make about the relationship between flipper length and mass for these other species of penguins? What does the change in σ tell you about the ability of flipper length to estimate mass?

3M12. Using the model in Code Block 3.21 run a counterfactual analysis for female penguin flipper length with mean flipper length and a bill length of 20mm. Plot a kernel density estimate of the posterior predictive samples.

3M13. Duplicate the flipper length covariate in Code Block 3.13 by adding a β_2 coefficient and rerun the model. What do diagnostics such as ESS and rhat indicate about this model with a duplicated coefficient?

3M14. Translate the PyMC3 model in Code Block 3.13 into Tensorflow Probability. List three of the syntax differences.

3M15. Translate the TFP model in Code Block 3.16 into PyMC3. List three of the syntax differences.

3M16. Use a logistic regression with increasing number of covariates to reproduce the prior predictive Figure 2.3. Explain why its the case that a logistic regression with many covariates generate a prior response with extreme values.

3H17. Translate the PyMC3 model in Code Block 3.24 into TFP to classify Adelie and Chinstrap penguins. Reuse the same model to classify Chinstrap and Gentoo penguins. Compare the coefficients, how do they differ?

3H18. In Code Block 3.3 our model allowed for negative values mass. Change the model so negative values are no longer possible. Run a prior predictive check to verify that your change was effective. Perform MCMC sampling and plot the posterior. Has the posterior changed from the original model? Given the results why would you choose one model over the other and why?

3H19. The Palmer Penguin dataset includes additional data for the observed penguins such as island and bill depth. Include these covariates into the linear regression model defined in Code Block 3.13 in two parts, first adding bill depth, and then adding the island covariates. Do these covariates help estimate Adelie mass more precisely? Justify your answer using the parameter estimates and model comparison tools.

3H20. Similar the exercise 2H19, see if adding bill depth or island covariates to the penguin logistic regression help classify Adelie and Gentoo penguins more precisely. Justify if the additional covariates helped using the numerical and visual tools shown in this chapter.

4

Extending Linear Models

A common trope in a sales pitch is the phrase "But wait! There is more!" In the lead up an audience is shown a product that incredibly seems to do it all, but somehow the salesperson shows off another use case for the already incredibly versatile tool. This is what we say to you about linear regression. In Chapter 3 we show a variety of ways to use and extend linear regression. But there is still a lot more we can do with linear models. From covariate transformation, varying variance, to multilevel models: each of these ideas provide extra flexibility to use linear regressions in an even wider set of circumstances.

4.1   Transforming Covariates

In Chapter 3 we saw that with a linear model and an identity link function, a unit change in x_i led to a β_i change in the expected response variable Y, at any value of X_i. Then we saw how Generalized Linear Models can be created by changing the likelihood function (e.g. from a Gaussian to Bernoulli), which in general requires a change in the link function.

Another useful modification, to the vanilla linear model, is to transform the covariates $\mathbf{X}$, in order to make the relationship between $\mathbf{X}$ and Y nonlinear. For example, we may assume that a square-root-unit change or log-unit change, etc. in x_i led to a β_i change in the expected response variable Y. We can note express mathematically by extending Equation 3.2 with an additional term, $f(.)$, which indicates an arbitrary transformation applied to each covariate (X_i):

$$
\begin{aligned}
\mu &= \beta_0 + \beta_1 f_1(X_1) + \cdots + \beta_m f_m(X_m) \\
Y &\sim \mathcal{N}(\mu, \sigma)
\end{aligned}
\tag{4.1}
$$

In most of our previous examples $f(.)$ was present but was the identity transformation. In a couple of the previous examples we centered the covariates to make the coefficient easier to interpret and the centering operation is one type of covariate transformation. However, $f(.)$ can be any arbitrary transformation. To illustrate, let us borrow an example from Bayesian Analysis with Python[100] and create a model for the length of babies. First we will load the data and plot in Code Block 4.1 and plot the age and month in Figure 4.1.

Code 4.1

```
1  babies = pd.read_csv("../data/babies.csv")
2  # Add a constant term so we can use the dot product to express the intercept
3  babies["Intercept"] = 1
```

DOI: 10.1201/9781003019169-4

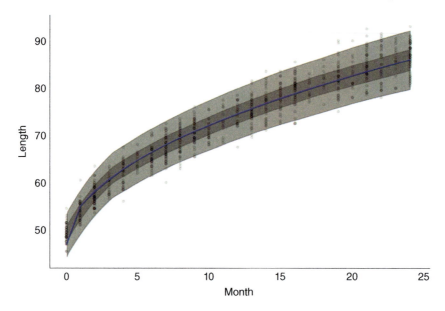

FIGURE 4.1
Scatter plot of the nonlinear correlation between a baby's age in months and observed, or measured, length.

Let us formulate a model in Code Block 4.2 which we can use to predict the length of the baby at each month of their childhood, as well as determine how quickly a child is growing per month. Note that this model formulation contains no transformations, and nothing we have not seen already in Chapter 3.

Code 4.2

```
1  with pm.Model() as model_baby_linear:
2      β = pm.Normal("β", sigma=10, shape=2)
3
4      μ = pm.Deterministic("μ", pm.math.dot(babies[["Intercept", "Month"]], β))
5      ε = pm.HalfNormal("ε", sigma=10)
6
7      length = pm.Normal("length", mu=μ, sigma=ε, observed=babies["Length"])
8
9      trace_linear = pm.sample(draws=2000, tune=4000)
10     pcc_linear = pm.sample_posterior_predictive(trace_linear)
11     inf_data_linear = az.from_pymc3(trace=trace_linear,
12                               posterior_predictive=pcc_linear)
```

`model_linear` faithfully gives us a linear growth rate as shown Figure 4.2, estimating that babies will grow at the same rate of around 1.4 cm in each month of their observed childhood. However, it likely does not come as a surprise to you that humans do not grow at the same rate their entire lives and that they tend to grow more rapidly in the earlier stages of life. In other words the relationship between age and length is nonlinear. Looking more closely at Figure 4.2 we can see some issues with the linear trend and the underlying data. The model tends to overestimate the length of babies close to 0 months of age, and over estimate length at 10 months of age, and then once again underestimate at 25 months of age. We asked for a straight line and we got a straight line even if the fit is not all that great.

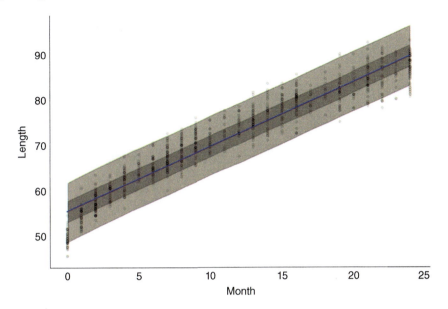

FIGURE 4.2
A linear prediction of baby length, where the mean is the blue line, the dark gray is the 50% highest density interval of the posterior predictive and the light gray is the 94% highest density interval of the posterior predictive. The highest density interval around the mean line of fit covers most of the data points despite the predictions tend to be either biased high in the early months, 0 to 3, as well as late months, 22 to 25, and biased low in the middle at months 10 to 15.

Thinking back to our model choices, we still believe that at any age, or vertical slice of the observed data, the distribution of baby lengths being Gaussian-like, but the relationship between the month and mean length is nonlinear. Specifically, we decide that the nonlinearity generally follows the shape of a square root transformation on the month covariate which we write in **model_sqrt** in Code Block 4.3.

Code 4.3

```
1  with pm.Model() as model_baby_sqrt:
2      β = pm.Normal("β", sigma=10, shape=2)
3
4      μ = pm.Deterministic("μ", β[0] + β[1] * np.sqrt(babies["Month"]))
5      σ = pm.HalfNormal("σ", sigma=10)
6
7      length = pm.Normal("length", mu=μ, sigma=σ, observed=babies["Length"])
8      inf_data_sqrt = pm.sample(draws=2000, tune=4000)
```

Plotting the fit of the means, along with bands representing the highest density interval of the expected length, yields Figure 4.3, in which the means tends to fit the curve of the observed relationship. In addition to this visual check we can also use **az.compare** to verify the ELPD value for the nonlinear model. In your own analysis you can use any transformation function you would like. As with any model the important bit is to be able to justify your choice whatever it may be, and verify your results are reasonable using visual and numerical checks.

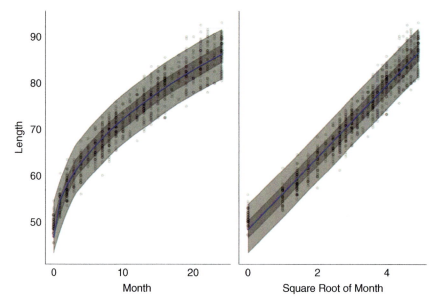

FIGURE 4.3
Linear prediction with transformed covariate. On the left the x-axes is untransformed and
on the right transformed. The linearization of the nonlinear growth rate is visible on the
transformed axes on the right.

4.2   Varying Uncertainty

Thus far we have used linear models to model the mean of Y while assuming the variance
of the residuals [1] is constant along the range of the response. However, this assumption
of fixed variance is a modeling choice that may not be adequate. To account for changing
uncertainty we can extend Equation 4.1 into:

$$
\begin{aligned}
\mu &= \beta_0 + \beta_1 f_1(X_1) + \cdots + \beta_m f_m(X_m) \\
\sigma &= \delta_0 + \delta_1 g_1(X_1) + \cdots + \delta_m g_m(X_m) \\
Y &\sim \mathcal{N}(\mu, \sigma)
\end{aligned}
\tag{4.2}
$$

This second line estimating σ is very similar to our linear term which models the mean.
We can use linear models to model parameters other than the mean/location parameter. For
a concrete example let us expand `model_sqrt` defined in Code Block 4.3. We now assume
that when children are young their lengths tend to cluster closely together, but as they age
their lengths tend to become more dispersed.

---

[1]The difference between the observed value and the estimated value of a quantity of interest is call the
residual.

Code 4.4

```
1  with pm.Model() as model_baby_vv:
2      β = pm.Normal("β", sigma=10, shape=2)
3
4      # Additional variance terms
5      δ = pm.HalfNormal("δ", sigma=10, shape=2)
6
7      μ = pm.Deterministic("μ", β[0] + β[1] * np.sqrt(babies["Month"]))
8      σ = pm.Deterministic("σ", δ[0] + δ[1] * babies["Month"])
9
10     length = pm.Normal("length", mu=μ, sigma=σ, observed=babies["Length"])
11
12     trace_baby_vv = pm.sample(2000, target_accept=.95)
13     ppc_baby_vv = pm.sample_posterior_predictive(trace_baby_vv,
14                               var_names=["length", "σ"])
15     inf_data_baby_vv = az.from_pymc3(trace=trace_baby_vv,
16                               posterior_predictive=ppc_baby_vv)
```

To model increasing dispersion of the length of as the observed children get older we changed our definition of σ from a fixed value to a value that varies as a function of age. In other words we change the model assumption from **homoscedastic**, that is having constant variance, to **heteroscedastic**, that is having varying variance. In our model, defined in Code Block 4.4 all we need to do is change the expression defining σ of our model and the PPL handle the estimation for us . The results of this model are plotted in Figure 4.4.

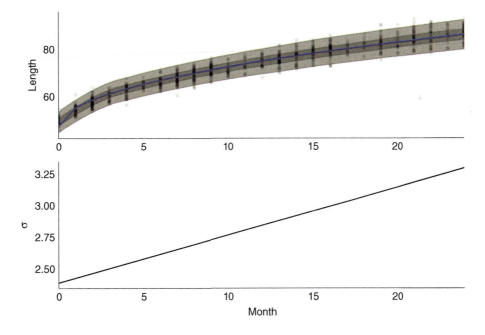

FIGURE 4.4
Two plots showing parameter fits of baby month versus length. In the top plot the expected mean prediction, represented with a blue line, is identical to Figure 4.3, however, the HDI intervals of the posterior are non-constant. The bottom graph plots the expected error estimate σ as a function of age in months. Note how the expected estimate of error increases as months increase.

4.3   Interaction Effects

In all our models thus far, we have assumed the effect of one covariate to the response variable is independent of any other covariates. This is not always the case. Consider a situation where we want to model ice cream sales for a particular town. We might say if there are many ice cream shops, more ice cream is available so we expect a large volume of ice cream purchases. But if this town in a cold climate with an average daily temperature of -5 degrees Celsius, we doubt there would be many sales of ice cream. However, in the converse scenario if the town was in a hot desert with average temperature of 30 degrees Celsius, but there are no ice cream stores, sales of ice cream would also be low. It is only when there is both hot weather *and* there are many places to buy ice cream that we expect an increased volume of sales. Modeling this kind of joint phenomena requires that we introduce an *interaction effect*, where the effect of one covariate on the output variable depends on the value of other covariates. Thus, if we assume covariates to contribute independently (as in a standard linear regression model), we will not be able to fully explain the phenomena. We can express an interaction effect as:

$$
\begin{aligned}
\mu &= \beta_0 + \beta_1 X_1 + \beta_2 X_2 + \beta_3 X_1 X_2 \\
Y &\sim \mathcal{N}(\mu, \sigma)
\end{aligned}
\tag{4.3}
$$

where β_3 is the coefficient for the interaction term $X_1 X_2$. There are other ways to introduce interactions but computing the products of original covariates is a very widely used option. Now that we have defined what an interaction effect is we can by contrast define a main effect, as the effect of one covariate on the dependent variable while ignoring all other covariates.

To illustrate let us use another example where we model the amount of tip a diner leaves as a function of the total bill in Code Block 4.5. This sounds reasonable as the amount of the tip is generally calculated as a percentage of the total bill with the exact percentage varying by different factors like the kind of place you are eating, the quality of the service, the country you are living, etc. In this example we are going to focus on the difference in tip amount from smokers versus non-smokers. In particular, we will study if there is an interaction effect between smoking and the total bill amount[2]. Just like Model 3.17 we can include smokers as an independent categorical variable in our regression.

Code 4.5

```
1  tips_df = pd.read_csv("../data/tips.csv")
2  tips = tips_df["tip"]
3  total_bill_c = (tips_df["total_bill"] - tips_df["total_bill"].mean())
4  smoker = pd.Categorical(tips_df["smoker"]).codes
5
6  with pm.Model() as model_no_interaction:
7      β = pm.Normal("β", mu=0, sigma=1, shape=3)
8      σ = pm.HalfNormal("σ", 1)
9
```

---

[2]Remember this is just a toy dataset, so the take-home message should be about modeling interactions and not about tips.

```
10      μ = (β[0] +
11           β[1] * total_bill_c +
12           β[2] * smoker)
13
14      obs = pm.Normal("obs", μ, σ, observed=tips)
15      trace_no_interaction = pm.sample(1000, tune=1000)
```

Let us also create a model where we include an interaction term in Code Block 4.6.

Code 4.6

```
1  with pm.Model() as model_interaction:
2      β = pm.Normal("β", mu=0, sigma=1, shape=4)
3      σ = pm.HalfNormal("σ", 1)
4
5      μ = (β[0]
6          + β[1] * total_bill_c
7          + β[2] * smoker
8          + β[3] * smoker * total_bill_c
9          )
10
11      obs = pm.Normal("obs", μ, σ, observed=tips)
12      trace_interaction = pm.sample(1000, tune=1000)
```

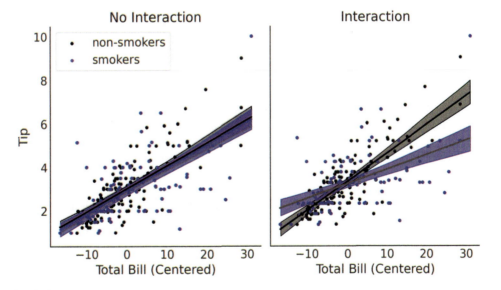

FIGURE 4.5
Plots of linear estimates from our two tips models. On the right we show the non-interaction estimate from Code Block 4.5, where the estimated lines are parallel. On the left we show our model from Code Block 4.5 that includes an interaction term between smoker or non-smoker and bill amount. In the interaction model the slopes between the groups are allowed to vary due to the added interaction term.

The difference is visible in Figure 4.5. Comparing the non-interaction model on the left and the interaction on the right, the mean fitted lines are no longer parallel, the slopes for smokers and non-smokers are different! By introducing an interaction we are building a model that is effectively splitting the data, in this example into two categories, smokers and non-smokers. You may be thinking that it is a better idea to split the data manually and fit two separate models, one for the smokers and one for the non-smokers. Well, not so fast. One of the benefits of using interactions is that we are using all the available data to fit a single model, increasing the accuracy of the estimated parameters. For example, notice that by using a single model we are assuming that σ is not affected by the variable `smoker` and thus σ is estimated from both smokers and non-smokers, helping us to get a better estimation of this parameter. Another benefit is that we get an estimate of the size effect of the interaction. If we just split the data we are implicitly assuming the interaction is exactly 0, by modeling the interaction we get an estimate about how strong the interaction is. Finally, building a model with and without interactions for the same data to make easier to compare models using LOO. If we split the data we end-up with different models evaluated on different data, instead of different models evaluated on the same data, which is a requisite for using LOO. So in summary, while the primary difference in interaction effect models is flexibility in modeling different slopes per group, there are many additional benefits that arise from modeling all the data together.

4.4   Robust Regression

Outliers, as the name suggests, are observations that lie outside of the range "reasonable expectation". Outliers are undesirable, as one, or few, of these data points could change the parameter estimation of a model significantly. There are a variety of suggested formal methods [75] of handling outliers, but in practice how outliers are handled is a choice a statistician has to make (as even the choice of a formal method is subjective). In general though there are at least two ways to address outliers. One is removing data using some predefined criteria, like 3 standard deviations or 1.5 times the interquartile range. Another strategy is choosing a model that can handle outliers and still provide useful results. In regression the latter are typically referred to as robust regression models, specifically to note these models are less sensitive to observations away from the bulk of the data. Technically speaking, robust regression are methods designed to be less affected by violations of assumptions by the underlying data-generating process. In Bayesian regression one example is changing the likelihood from a Gaussian distribution to a Student's t-distribution.

Recall that Gaussian distributions are defined by two parameters typically known as location μ and scale σ. These parameters control the mean and standard deviation of the Gaussian distribution. Student's t-distributions also have one parameter for the location and scale respectively [3]. However, there is an additional parameter, typically known as degrees of freedom ν. This parameter controls the weight of the tails of the Student's t-distribution, as shown in Figure 4.6. Comparing the 3 Student's t-distributions against each other and the Normal distribution, the key difference is the proportion of the density in the tails versus the proportion at the bulk of the distributions. When ν is small there is more mass distributed in the tails, as the value of ν increases the proportion of density concentrated towards the bulk also increases and the Student's t-distribution becomes closer and closer to the Gaussian. Practically speaking what this means is that values farther from the mean are more likely to occur when ν is small. Which provides robustness to outliers when substituting a Gaussian likelihood with a Student's t-distribution.

---

[3] Although the mean is defined only for $\nu > 1$, and the value of σ agrees with the standard deviation only when $\nu \to \infty$.

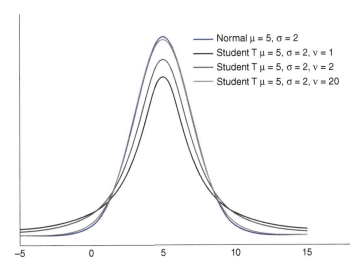

FIGURE 4.6

Normal distribution, in blue, compared to 3 Student's t-distributions with varying ν parameters. The location and scale parameters are all identical, which isolates the effect ν has on the tails of the distribution. Smaller values of ν put more density into the tails of the distribution.

This can be shown in an example. Say you own a restaurant in Argentina and you sell empanadas [4]. Over time you have collected data on the number of customers per day and the total amount of Argentine pesos your restaurant has earned, as shown in Figure 4.7. Most of the data points fall along a line, except during a couple of days where the number of empanadas sold per customer is much higher than the surrounding data points. These may be days of big celebration such as the 25th of May or 9th of July [5], where people are consuming more empanadas than usual.

Regardless of the outliers, we want to estimate the relationship between our customers and revenue. When plotting the data a linear regression seems appropriate, such as the one written in Code Block 4.7 which uses a Gaussian likelihood. After estimating the parameters we plot the mean regression in Figure 4.8 at two different scales. In the lower plot note how the fitted regression line lies above all visible data points. In Table 4.1 we also can see the individual parameter estimates, noting in particular σ which at a mean value of 574 seems high when compared to the plot of the nominal data. With a Normal likelihood the posterior distribution has to "stretch" itself over the nominal observations and the 5 outliers, which affects the estimates.

Code 4.7

```
1  with pm.Model() as model_non_robust:
2      σ = pm.HalfNormal("σ", 50)
3      β = pm.Normal("β", mu=150, sigma=20)
4
5      μ = pm.Deterministic("μ", β * empanadas["customers"])
```

---

[4]A thin dough filled with a salty or sweet preparation and baked or fried. The filling can include red or white meat, fish, vegetables, or fruit. Empanadas are common in Southern European, Latin American, and the Filipino cultures.

[5]The commemoration of the first Argentine government and the Argentine independence day respectively.

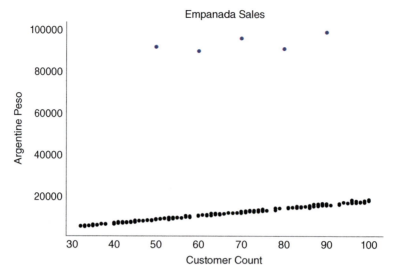

FIGURE 4.7
Simulated data of number of customers plotted against the pesos returned. The 5 dots at the top of the chart are considered outliers.

```
6
7    sales = pm.Normal("sales", mu=μ, sigma=σ, observed=empanadas["sales"])
8
9    inf_data_non_robust = pm.sample(.)
```

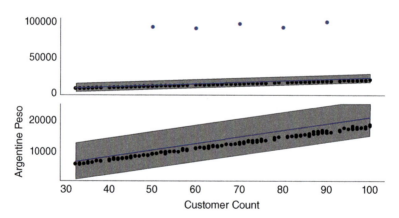

FIGURE 4.8
A plot of the data, fitted regression line, and 94% HDI of `model_non_robust` from Code Block 4.7 at two scales, the top including the outliers, and the bottom focused on the regression itself. The systemic bias is more evident in bottom plot as the mean regression line is estimated to be above the nominal data points.

We can run the same regression again but this time using the Student's t-distribution as likelihood, shown in Code Block 4.8. Note that the dataset has not changed and the outliers are still included. When inspecting the fitted regression line in Figure 4.9 we can see that the fit falls between the nominal observed data points, closer to where we would expect. Inspecting the mean parameter estimates in Table 4.2 note the addition of the

	mean	sd	hdi_3%	hdi_97%
β	207.1	2.9	201.7	212.5
σ	2951.1	25.0	2904.5	2997.7

TABLE 4.1
Estimate of parameters for `non_robust_regression`. Note how the estimate of σ is quite wide compared to the plotted data in Figure 4.8.

	mean	sd	hdi_3%	hdi_97%
β	179.6	0.3	179.1	180.1
σ	152.3	13.9	127.1	179.5
ν	1.3	0.2	1.0	1.6

TABLE 4.2
Estimate of parameters for `robust_regression`. Note how the estimate of σ is lower compared to Table 4.1 and is logically reasonable compared to the plotted data.

extra parameter ν. Furthermore we can see that the estimate of σ has fallen substantially from ≈ 2951 pesos in the non-robust regression to ≈ 152 pesos in the robust regression. The change in likelihood distribution shows that there is enough flexibility in the Student's t-distribution to reasonably model the nominal data, despite the presence of outliers.

Code 4.8

```
1  with pm.Model() as model_robust:
2      σ = pm.HalfNormal("σ", 50)
3      β = pm.Normal("β", mu=150, sigma=20)
4      ν = pm.HalfNormal("ν", 20)
5
6      μ = pm.Deterministic("μ", β * empanadas["customers"])
7
8      sales = pm.StudentT("sales", mu=μ, sigma=σ, nu=ν,
9                          observed=empanadas["sales"])
10
11     inf_data_robust = pm.sample(.)
```

In this example the "outliers" are actually part of the problem we want to model, in the sense that they are not measurement error, data entry errors etc, but observations that can actually happened under certain conditions. Hence, it is ok to treat them as outliers if we want to model the average number of empanadas on a "regular" day, but it will lead to a disaster if we use this average to make plans for the next 25th of May or 9th of July. Therefore in this example the robust linear regression model is a trick to avoid explicitly modeling the high sales day which, if needed, will be probably better modeled using mixture model or a multilevel model.

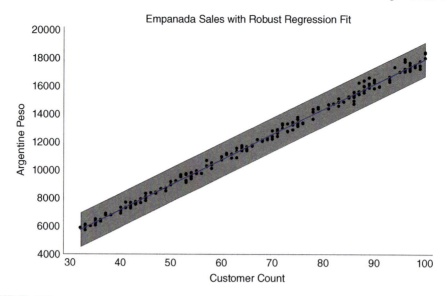

FIGURE 4.9

A plot of the data, fitted regression line of `model_robust` and 94% HDI from Code Block 4.8. The outliers are not plotted but are present in the data. The fitted line falls within the range of the nominal data points, particularly if compared to Figure 4.8.

Model adaptions for data considerations

Changing the likelihood to accommodate for robustness is just one example of a modification we can make to the model to better suit the observed data. For example, in detecting radioactive particle emission a zero count can arise because of a faulty sensor[16] (or some other measuring problem), or because there was actually no event to register. This unknown source of variation has the effect of *inflating* the count of zeros. A useful aid for this kind of problem is the class of models aptly named zero-inflated models which estimate the combined data generating process. For example, a Poisson likelihood, which will generally be a starting point for modeling counts, can be expanded into a zero-inflated Poisson likelihood. With such a likelihood we can better separate the counts generated from a Poisson process from those generated from the *excess zero generating process*.

Zero-inflated models are an example of handling a mixture of data, in which observations come from two or more groups, without knowledge of which observation belongs to which group. Actually, we can express another type of robust regression using a mixture likelihood, which assigns a latent label (outlier or not) to each data point.

In all of these situations and many more the bespoke nature of Bayesian models allows the modeler the flexibility to create a model that fits the situation, rather than having to fit a situation to a predefined model.

4.5 Pooling, Multilevel Models, and Mixed Effects

Often we have dataset that contain additional nested structures among the predictors, which gives some hierarchical way to group the data. We can also think of it as different data generation processes. We are going to use an example to illustrate this. Let us say you work at a restaurant company which sells salads. This company has a long-established business in some geographic markets and, due to customer demand, has just opened a location in a new market as well. You need to predict how many US dollars the restaurant location in this new market will earn each day for financial planning purposes. You have two datasets, 3 days of data for the sales of salads, as well as roughly a year's worth of data on pizza and sandwich sales in the same market. The (simulated) data is shown in Figure 4.10.

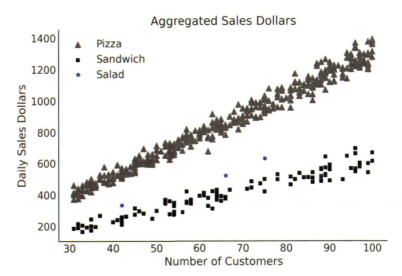

FIGURE 4.10
A simulated dataset for a real world scenario. In this case an organization has 3 data points for the daily sales of salads, but has lots of data on the sales of pizza and sandwiches.

From both expert knowledge and data, there is agreement that there are similarities between the sales of these 3 food categories. They all appeal to the same type of customer, represent the same "food category" of *quick to go* food but they are not exactly the same either. In the following sections we will discuss how to model this *similarity-yet-disimilarity* but let us start with the simpler case, all groups are unrelated to each other.

4.5.1 Unpooled Parameters

We can create a regression model where we treat each group, in this case food category, as completely separated from the others. This is identical to running a separate regression for each category, and that is why we call it unpooled regression. The only difference to run separated regression is that we are writing a single model and estimating all coefficients at the same time. The relationship between parameters and groups is visually represented in Figure 4.11 and in mathematical notation in Equation 4.4, where j is an index identifying each separated group.

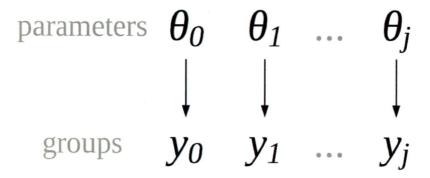

FIGURE 4.11

An unpooled model where each group of observations, $y_1, y_2, ..., y_j$ has its own set of parameters, independent from any other group.

$$
\beta_{mj} \sim \overbrace{\mathcal{N}(\mu_{\beta m}, \sigma_{\beta m})}^{\text{Group-specific}}
$$

$$
\sigma_j \sim \overbrace{\mathcal{HN}(\sigma_\sigma)}^{\text{Group-specific}}
$$

$$
\mu_j = \beta_{1j} X_1 + \cdots + \beta_{mj} X_m
$$

$$
Y \sim \mathcal{N}(\mu_j, \sigma_j)
$$

(4.4)

The parameters are labeled as *group-specific* parameters to denote there is one dedicated to each group. The unpooled PyMC3 model, and some data cleaning, is shown in Code Block 4.9 and the block representation is shown in Figure 4.12. We do not include an intercept parameter for the simple reason that if a restaurant has zero customers, total sales will also be zero, so there is neither any interest nor any need for the extra parameter.

Code 4.9

```
customers = sales_df.loc[:, "customers"].values
sales_observed = sales_df.loc[:, "sales"].values
food_category = pd.Categorical(sales_df["Food_Category"])

with pm.Model() as model_sales_unpooled:
    σ = pm.HalfNormal("σ", 20, shape=3)
    β = pm.Normal("β", mu=10, sigma=10, shape=3)

    μ = pm.Deterministic("μ", β[food_category.codes] *customers)

    sales = pm.Normal("sales", mu=μ, sigma=σ[food_category.codes],
                      observed=sales_observed)

    trace_sales_unpooled = pm.sample(target_accept=.9)
    inf_data_sales_unpooled = az.from_pymc3(
        trace=trace_sales_unpooled,
        coords={"β_dim_0":food_category.categories,
                "σ_dim_0":food_category.categories})
```

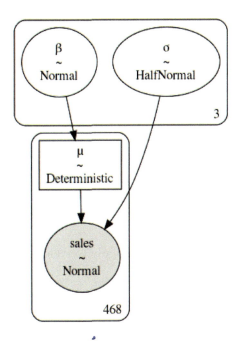

FIGURE 4.12
A diagram of `model_sales_unpooled`. Note how the box around parameters β and σ has a three in the lower right, indicating that the model estimated 3 parameters each for β and σ.

After sampling from `model_sales_unpooled` we can create forest plots of the parameter estimates as shown in Figures 4.13 and 4.14. Note how the estimate of σ for the salad food category is quite wide compared to the sandwich and pizza groups. This is what we would expect from our unpooled model when we have large amounts of data for some of the categories, but much less for others.

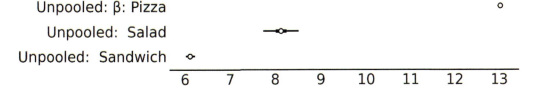

FIGURE 4.13
Forest plot of the β parameter estimates `model_sales_unpooled`. As expected the estimate of the β coefficient for the salads group is the widest as this group has the least amount of data.

The unpooled model is no different than if we have created three separated models with subsets of the data, exactly as we did in Section 3.1, where the parameters of each group were estimated separately so we can consider the unpooled model architecture syntactic sugar for modeling independent linear regressions of each group. More importantly now we can use the unpooled model and the estimated parameters from it as a baseline to compare

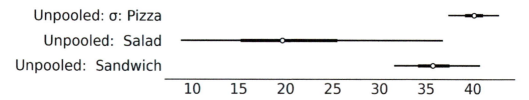

FIGURE 4.14

Forest plot of the σ parameter estimates `model_sales_unpooled`. Like Figure 4.13 the estimate of the variation of sales, σ, is largest for the salads group as there are not as many data points relative to the pizza and sandwich groups.

other models in the following sections, particularly to understand if the extra complexity is justified.

4.5.2   Pooled Parameters

If there are unpooled parameters, you might guess there are pooled parameters and you would be correct. As the name suggests pooled parameters are ones where the group distinction is ignored. Conceptually, this type of model is shown in Figure 4.15 were each group shares the same parameters and thus we also refer to them as common parameters.

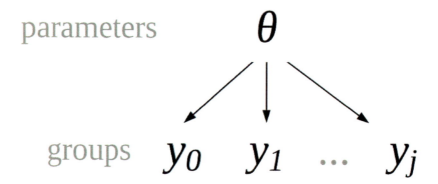

FIGURE 4.15

A pooled model where each group of observations, $y_1, y_2, ..., y_j$ shares parameters.

For our restaurant example, the model is written in Equation 4.5 and Code Block 4.10. The GraphViz representation is also shown in Figure 4.12.

$$\beta \sim \overbrace{\mathcal{N}(\mu_\beta, \sigma_\beta)}^{\text{Common}}$$

$$\sigma \sim \overbrace{\mathcal{HN}(\sigma_\sigma)}^{\text{Common}}$$ (4.5)

$$\mu = \beta_1 X_1 + \cdots + \beta_m X_m$$

$$Y \sim \mathcal{N}(\mu, \sigma)$$

Code 4.10

```
1  with pm.Model() as model_sales_pooled:
2      σ = pm.HalfNormal("σ", 20)
3      β = pm.Normal("β", mu=10, sigma=10)
4
5      μ = pm.Deterministic("μ", β * customers)
6
7      sales = pm.Normal("sales", mu=μ, sigma=σ,
8                        observed=sales_observed)
9
10     inf_data_sales_pooled = pm.sample()
```

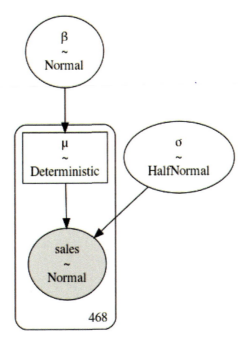

FIGURE 4.16
Diagram of `model_sales_pooled`. Unlike Figure 4.12 there is only one instance of β and σ.

The benefit of the pooled approach is that more data will be used to estimate each parameter. However, this means we cannot understand each group individually, just all food categories as a whole. Looking at Figure 4.18, our estimates β and σ are not indicative of any particular food group as the model is grouping together data with very different

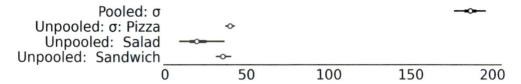

FIGURE 4.17
A comparison of the estimates of the σ parameter from `model_pooled_sales` and `model_unpooled_sales`. Note how we only get one estimate of σ that is much higher compared to the unpooled model as the single linear fit estimated must capture the variance in the pooled data.

scales. Compare the value of σ with the ones from the unpooled model in Figure 4.17. When plotting the regression in Figure 4.18 we can see that a single line, despite being informed by more data than any single group, fails to fit any one group well. This result implies that the differences in the groups are too large to ignore and thus pooling the data it is not particularly useful for our intended purpose.

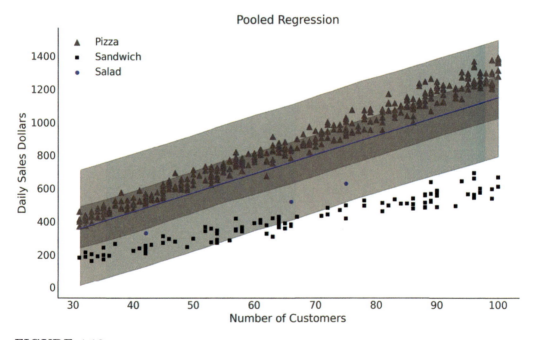

FIGURE 4.18
Linear regression `model_sales_pooled` where all the data is pooled together. Each of the parameters is estimated using all the data but we end up with poor estimates of each individual group's behavior as a 2 parameter model cannot generalize well enough to capture the nuances of each group.

4.5.3   Mixing Group and Common Parameters

In the unpooled approach we get the benefit of preserving the differences in our groups, and thus getting an estimated set of parameters for each group. In the pooled approach we get the benefit of utilizing all the data to estimate a single set of parameters, and thus more informed, albeit more generic, estimates. Fortunately we are not forced to pick just one option or the other. We can mix these two concepts in a single model shown in Equation 4.6. In this formulation we have decided to keep the estimate of β group specific, or unpooled, and to use a common, or pooled, σ. In our current example we do not have an intercept, but in a regression that included an intercept term we would have a similar choice, pool all the data into a single estimate, or leave the data separated in groups for an estimate per group.

$$
\begin{aligned}
\beta_{mj} &\sim \overbrace{\mathcal{N}(\mu_{\beta m}, \sigma_{\beta m})}^{\text{Group-specific}} \\
\sigma &\sim \overbrace{\mathcal{HN}(\sigma_\sigma)}^{\text{Common}} \\
\mu_j &= \beta_{1j} X_1 + \cdots + \beta_m X_m \\
Y &\sim \mathcal{N}(\mu_j, \sigma)
\end{aligned}
\tag{4.6}
$$

> **Random and fixed effects and why you should forget these terms**
>
> The parameters that are specific to each level and those that are common across levels get different names, including random or varying effect, or fixed or constant effect, respectively. To add to the confusion different people may assign different meanings to these terms especially when talking about fixed and random effects [60]. If we have to label these terms we suggest *common* and *group-specific* [56, 30]. However, as all these different terms are widely used we recommend that you always verify the details of the model so to avoid confusions and misunderstandings.

To reiterate in our sales model we are interested in pooling the data to estimate σ as we believe there could be identical variance of the sales of pizza, sandwiches, and salads, but we leave our estimate of β unpooled, or independent, as we know there are differences between the groups. With these ideas we can write our PyMC3 model as shown in Code Block 4.11, as well as generate a graphical diagram of the model structure shown in Figure 4.19. From the model we can plot Figure 4.20 showing the estimate of fit overlaid on the data, as well as a comparison of the σ parameter estimates from the multilevel and unpooled models in Figure 4.21. These results are encouraging, for all three categories the fits looks reasonable and for the salad group in particular it seems this model will be able to produce plausible inferences about salad sales in this new market.

Code 4.11

```
1  with pm.Model() as model_pooled_sigma_sales:
2      σ = pm.HalfNormal("σ", 20)
3      β = pm.Normal("β", mu=10, sigma=20, shape=3)
4
5      μ = pm.Deterministic("μ", β[food_category.codes] * customers)
6
7      sales = pm.Normal("sales", mu=μ, sigma=σ, observed=sales_observed)
```

```
8
9      trace_pooled_sigma_sales = pm.sample()
10     ppc_pooled_sigma_sales = pm.sample_posterior_predictive(
11         trace_pooled_sigma_sales)
12
13     inf_data_pooled_sigma_sales = az.from_pymc3(
14         trace=trace_pooled_sigma_sales,
15         posterior_predictive=ppc_pooled_sigma_sales,
16         coords={"β_dim_0":food_category.categories})
```

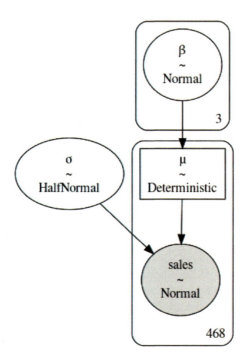

FIGURE 4.19
`model_pooled_sigma_sales` where β is unpooled, as indicated by the box with 3 in the right corner, and σ is pooled, as the lack of number indicates a single parameter estimate for all groups.

4.6 Hierarchical Models

In our data treatment thus far we have had two options for groups, pooled where there is no distinction between groups, and unpooled where there a complete distinction between groups. Recall though in our motivating restaurant example we believed the parameter σ of the 3 food categories to be similar, but not exactly the same. In Bayesian modeling we can express this idea with *hierarchical models*. In hierarchical models the parameters are *partially pooled*. The partial refers to the idea that groups that do not share one fixed parameter, but share a hyperprior distribution which describes the distribution of for the

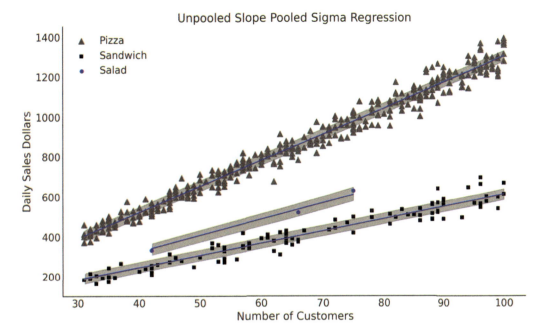

FIGURE 4.20
Linear model with 50% HDI from `model_pooled_sigma_sales`. This model is more useful for our purposes of estimating salad sales as the slopes are independently estimated for each group. Note how all the data is being used to estimate the single posterior distribution of σ.

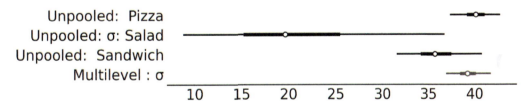

FIGURE 4.21
Comparison of σ from `model_pooled_sigma_sales` and `model_pooled_sales`. Note how the estimated of σ in the multilevel model is within the bounds of the σ estimates from the pooled model.

parameters of the prior itself. Conceptually this idea is shown in Figure 4.22. Each group gets its own parameters which are drawn from a common hyperprior distribution.

Using statistical notation we can write a hierarchical model in Equation 4.7, the computational model in Code Block 4.12, and a graphical representation in Figure 4.23.

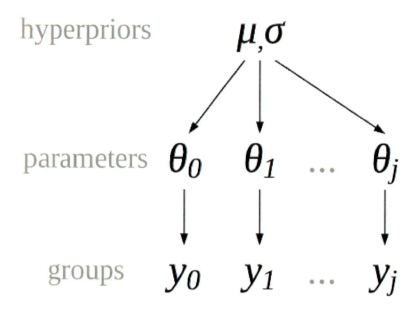

FIGURE 4.22

A partially pooled model architecture where each group of observations, $y_1, y_2, ..., y_k$ has its own set of parameters, but they are not independent as they are drawn from a common distribution.

$$\beta_{mj} \sim \mathcal{N}(\mu_{\beta m}, \sigma_{\beta m})$$

$$\sigma_h \sim \overbrace{\mathcal{HN}(\sigma)}^{\text{Hyperprior}}$$

$$\sigma_j \sim \overbrace{\mathcal{HN}(\sigma_h)}^{\substack{\text{Group-specific} \\ \text{pooled}}}$$

$$\mu_j = \beta_{1j}X_1 + \cdots + \beta_{mj}X_m$$

$$Y \sim \mathcal{N}(\mu_j, \sigma_j)$$

(4.7)

Note the addition of σ_h when compared to the multilevel model in Figure 4.19. This is our new hyperprior distributions that defines the possible parameters of individual groups. We can add the hyperprior in Code Block 4.12 as well. You may ask "could we have added a hyperprior for the β terms as well?", and the answer is quite simply yes we could have. But in this case we assume that only the variance is related, which justifying the use of partial pooling and that the slopes are completely independent. Because this is a simulated textbook example we can plainly make this statement and "get away with it", in a real life scenario more domain expertise and model comparison would be advised to justify this claim.

Code 4.12

```
1  with pm.Model() as model_hierarchical_sales:
2      σ_hyperprior = pm.HalfNormal("σ_hyperprior", 20)
3      σ = pm.HalfNormal("σ", σ_hyperprior, shape=3)
4
5      β = pm.Normal("β", mu=10, sigma=20, shape=3)
6      μ = pm.Deterministic("μ", β[food_category.codes] * customers)
7
8      sales = pm.Normal("sales", mu=μ, sigma=σ[food_category.codes],
9                        observed=sales_observed)
10
11     trace_hierarchical_sales = pm.sample(target_accept=.9)
12
13     inf_data_hierarchical_sales = az.from_pymc3(
14         trace=trace_hierarchical_sales,
15         coords={"β_dim_0":food_category.categories,
16                 "σ_dim_0":food_category.categories})
```

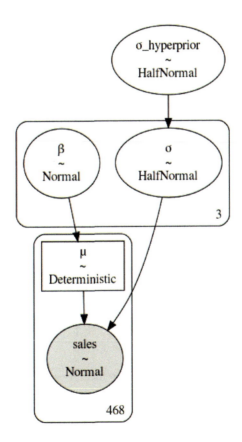

FIGURE 4.23
`model_hierarchical_sales` where $\sigma_{hyperprior}$ is the single hierarchical distribution for the three σ distributions.

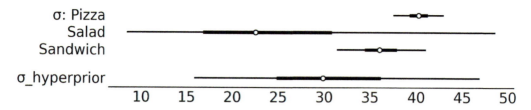

FIGURE 4.24
Forest plot of the σ parameter estimates for `model_hierarchical_sales`. Note how the hyperprior tends to represent fall within the range of the three group priors.

	mean	sd	hdi_3%	hdi_97%
σ[Pizza]	40.1	1.5	37.4	42.8
σ[Salad]	21.3	8.3	8.8	36.8
σ[Sandwich]	35.9	2.5	31.6	40.8

TABLE 4.3
Estimates of σ for each category from the unpooled sales model. Note how the estimates of each sigma are distinctly different from each other. Given that our observed data and the model which does not share information between groups this consistent with our expectations.

After fitting the hierarchical model we can inspect the σ parameter estimates in Figure 4.24. Again note the addition of $\sigma_{hyperprior}$ which is a distribution that estimates the distribution of the parameters for each of the three food categories. We can also see the effect of a hierarchical model if we compare the summary tables of the unpooled model and hierarchical models in Table 4.3. In the unpooled estimate the mean of the σ estimate for salads is 21.3, whereas in the hierarchical estimate the mean of the same parameter estimate is now 25.5, and has been "pulled" up by the means of the pizza and sandwiches category. Moreover, the estimates of the pizza and salad categories in the hierarchical category, while regressed towards the mean slightly, remain largely the same as the unpooled estimates.

	mean	sd	hdi_3%	hdi_97%
σ[Pizza]	40.3	1.5	37.5	43.0
σ[Salad]	25.5	12.4	8.4	48.7
σ[Sandwich]	36.2	2.6	31.4	41.0
$\sigma_{hyperprior}$	31.2	8.7	15.8	46.9

TABLE 4.4
Estimates of σ for each category from the hierarchical as well for the hyperprior distribution for σ which shares information across groups.

I heard you like hyperpriors so I put a hyperpriors on top of your hyperpriors

In Code Block 4.14 we placed hyperprior on group level parameter σ_j. Similarly, we can extend the model by also adding hyperprior to parameter β_{mj}. Note that since β_{mj} has a Gaussian distributed prior, we can actually choose two hyperprior - one for each hyperparameter. A natural question you might ask is can we go even further and adding hyperhyperprior to the parameters that are parameterized the hyperprior? What about hyperhyperhyperprior? While it is certainly possible to write down such models and sample from it, it is worth to take a step back and think about what hyperpriors are doing. Intuitively, they are a way for the model to "borrow" information from sub-group or sub-cluster of data to inform the estimation of other sub-group/cluster with less observation. The group with more observations will inform the posterior of the hyperparameter, which then in turn regulates the parameters for the group with less observations. In this lens, putting hyperprior on parameters that are not group specific is quite meaningless.

Hierarchical estimates are not just limited to two levels. For example, the restaurant sales model could be extended into a three-level hierarchical model where the top level represented the company level, the next level represented the geographical market (New York, Chicago, Los Angeles), and the lowest level represented an individual location. By doing so we can have a hyperprior characterizing how the whole company was doing, hyperpriors indicating how a region was doing, and priors on how each store was doing. This allows easy comparisons in mean and variation, and expands the application in many different ways based on a single model.

4.6.1 Posterior Geometry Matters

So far we have largely focused on the structure and math behind the model, and assumed our sampler would be able to provide us an "accurate" estimate of the posterior. And for relatively simple models this is largely true, the newest versions of Universal Inference Engines mostly "just work", but an important point is that they do not *always* work. Certain posterior geometries are challenging for samplers, a common example is Neal's Funnel[111] shown in Figure 4.25. As the name funnel connotes, the shape at one end is quite wide, before narrowing into a small neck. Recalling Section 1.2 samplers function by taking steps from one set of parameter values to another, and a key setting is how big of a step to take when exploring the posterior surface. In complex geometries, such as with Neal's funnel, a step size that works well in one area, fails miserably in another.

In hierarchical models the geometry is largely defined by the correlation of hyperpriors to other parameters, which can result in funnel geometry that are difficult to sample. Unfortunately this is not only a theoretical problem, but a practical one, that can sneak up relatively quickly on an unsuspecting Bayesian modeler. Luckily, there is a relatively easy tweak to models, referred to as a non-centered parameterization, that helps alleviate the issue.

Continuing with our salad example, let us say we open 6 salad restaurants and like before are interested in predicting the sales as a function of the number of customers. The synthetic dataset has been generated in Python and is shown in Figure 4.26. Since the restaurants are selling the exact same product a hierarchical model is appropriate to share

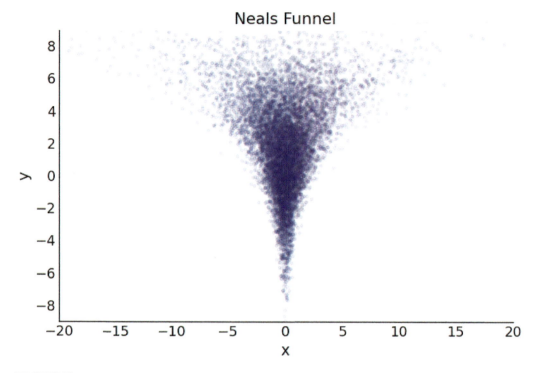

FIGURE 4.25

Correlated samples in a particular shape referred to as Neal's Funnel. At sampling at the top of the funnel where Y is around a value 6 to 8, a sampler can take wide steps of lets say 1 unit, and likely remain within a dense region of the posterior. However, if sampling near the bottom of the funnel where Y is around a value -6 to -8, a 1 unit step in almost any direction will likely result in step into a low-density region. This drastic difference in the posterior geometry shape is one reason poor posterior estimation, can occur for sampling based estimates. For HMC samplers the occurence of divergences can help diagnose these sampling issues.

information across groups. We write the centered model mathematically in Equation 4.8 and also Code Block 4.13. We will be using TFP and `tfd.JointDistributionCoroutine` in the rest of the chapter, which more easily highlights the change in parameterization. This model follows the standard hierarchical format, where a hyperprior partially pools the parameters of the slope β_m.

$$
\begin{aligned}
\beta_{\mu h} &\sim \mathcal{N} \\
\beta_{\sigma h} &\sim \mathcal{HN} \\
\beta_m &\sim \overbrace{\mathcal{N}(\beta_{\mu h}, \beta_{\sigma h})}^{\text{Centered}} \\
\sigma_h &\sim \mathcal{HN} \\
\sigma_m &\sim \mathcal{HN}(\sigma_h) \\
Y &\sim \mathcal{N}(\beta_m * X_m, \sigma_m)
\end{aligned}
\tag{4.8}
$$

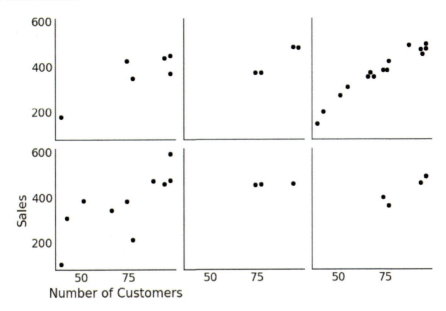

FIGURE 4.26
Observed salad sales across 6 locations. Note how some locations have very few data points relative to others.

Code 4.13

```
1  def gen_hierarchical_salad_sales(input_df, beta_prior_fn, dtype=tf.float32):
2      customers = tf.constant(
3          hierarchical_salad_df["customers"].values, dtype=dtype)
4      location_category = hierarchical_salad_df["location"].values
5      sales = tf.constant(hierarchical_salad_df["sales"].values, dtype=dtype)
6
7      @tfd.JointDistributionCoroutine
8      def model_hierarchical_salad_sales():
9          β_μ_hyperprior = yield root(tfd.Normal(0, 10, name="beta_mu"))
10         β_σ_hyperprior = yield root(tfd.HalfNormal(.1, name="beta_sigma"))
11         β = yield from beta_prior_fn(β_μ_hyperprior, β_σ_hyperprior)
12
13         σ_hyperprior = yield root(tfd.HalfNormal(30, name="sigma_prior"))
14         σ = yield tfd.Sample(tfd.HalfNormal(σ_hyperprior), 6, name="sigma")
15
16         loc = tf.gather(β, location_category, axis=-1) * customers
17         scale = tf.gather(σ, location_category, axis=-1)
18         sales = yield tfd.Independent(tfd.Normal(loc, scale),
19                                       reinterpreted_batch_ndims=1,
20                                       name="sales")
21
22     return model_hierarchical_salad_sales, sales
```

Similar to the TFP models we used in Chapter 3, the model is wrapped within a function so we can condition on an arbitrary inputs more easily. Besides the input data, gen_hierarchical_salad_sales also takes a callable beta_prior_fn which defines the prior of slope β_m. Inside the Coroutine model we use a **yield from** statement to invoke the beta_prior_fn. This description may be too abstract in words but is easier to see action in Code Block 4.14:

Code 4.14

```
1  def centered_beta_prior_fn(hyper_mu, hyper_sigma):
2      β = yield tfd.Sample(tfd.Normal(hyper_mu, hyper_sigma), 6, name="beta")
3      return β
4
5  # hierarchical_salad_df is the generated dataset as pandas.DataFrame
6  centered_model, observed = gen_hierarchical_salad_sales(
7      hierarchical_salad_df, centered_beta_prior_fn)
```

As shown above, Code Block 4.14 defined a centered parameterization of the slope β_m, which follows a Normal distribution with hyper_mu and hyper_sigma. centered_beta_prior_fn is a function that yields a tfp.distribution, similar to the way we write a tfd.JointDistributionCoroutine model. Now that we have our model, we can run inference and inspect the result in Code Block 4.15.

Code 4.15

```
1  mcmc_samples_centered, sampler_stats_centered = run_mcmc(
2      1000, centered_model, n_chains=4, num_adaptation_steps=1000,
3      sales=observed)
4
5  divergent_per_chain = np.sum(sampler_stats_centered["diverging"], axis=0)
6  print(f"""There were {divergent_per_chain} divergences after tuning per chain.""")
```

```
There were [37 31 17 37] divergences after tuning per chain.
```

We reuse the inference code previously shown in Code Block 3.11 to run our model. After running our model the first indication of issues is the divergences, the details of which we covered in Section 2.4.7. A plot of the sample space is the next diagnostic and is shown in Figure 4.27. Note how as the hyperprior $\beta_{\sigma h}$ approaches zero, the width of the posterior estimate of the β_m parameters tend to shrink. In particular note how there are no samples near zero. In other words as the value $\beta_{\sigma h}$ approaches zero, there the region in which to sample parameter β_m collapses and the sampler is not able to effectively characterize this space of the posterior.

To alleviate this issue the centered parameterization can be converted into a non-centered parameterization shown in Code Block in 4.16 and Equation 4.9. The key difference is that instead of estimating parameters of the slope β_m directly, it is instead modeled as a common term shared between all groups and a term for each group that captures the deviation from the common term. This modifies the posterior geometry in a manner that allows the sampler to more easily explore all possible values of $\beta_{\sigma h}$. The effect of this posterior geometry change is as shown in Figure 4.28, where there are multiple samples down to the 0 value on the x-axis.

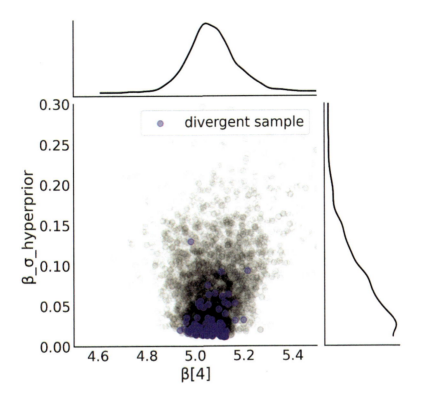

FIGURE 4.27
Scatter plot of the hyperprior and the slope of $\beta[4]$ from `centered_model` defined in Code Block 4.14. As the hyperprior approaches zero the posterior space for slope collapses results in the divergences seen in blue.

$$\begin{aligned}
\beta_{\mu h} &\sim \mathcal{N} \\
\beta_{\sigma h} &\sim \mathcal{HN} \\
\beta_{\text{m\_offset}} &\sim \mathcal{N}(0, 1) \\
\beta_m &= \overbrace{\beta_{\mu h} + \beta_{\text{m\_offset}} * \beta_{\sigma h}}^{\text{Non-centered}} \\
\sigma_h &\sim \mathcal{HN} \\
\sigma_m &\sim \mathcal{HN}(\sigma_h) \\
Y &\sim \mathcal{N}(\beta_m * X_m, \sigma_m)
\end{aligned} \tag{4.9}$$

Code 4.16

```
1  def non_centered_beta_prior_fn(hyper_mu, hyper_sigma):
2      β_offset = yield root(tfd.Sample(tfd.Normal(0, 1), 6, name="beta_offset"))
3      return β_offset * hyper_sigma[..., None] + hyper_mu[..., None]
4
```

```
5  # hierarchical_salad_df is the generated dataset as pandas.DataFrame
6  non_centered_model, observed = gen_hierarchical_salad_sales(
7      hierarchical_salad_df, non_centered_beta_prior_fn)
8
9  mcmc_samples_noncentered, sampler_stats_noncentered = run_mcmc(
10     1000, non_centered_model, n_chains=4, num_adaptation_steps=1000,
11     sales=observed)
12
13 divergent_per_chain = np.sum(sampler_stats_noncentered["diverging"], axis=0)
14 print(f"There were {divergent_per_chain} divergences after tuning per chain.")
```

```
There were [1 0 2 0] divergences after tuning per chain.
```

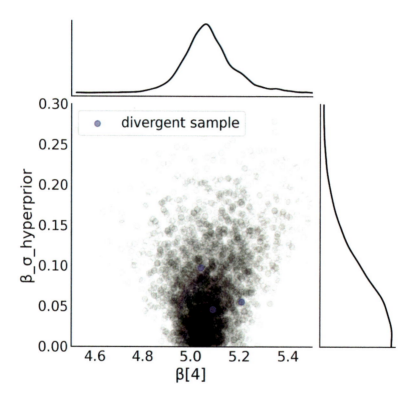

FIGURE 4.28
Scatter plot of the hyperprior and the estimated slope $\beta[4]$ of location 4 from
`non_centered_model` defined in Code Block 4.16. In the non-centered parameterization
the sampler is able to sample parameters close to zero. The divergences are lesser in number and are not concentrated in one area.

The improvement in sampling has a material effect on the estimated distribution shown
in Figure 4.29. While it may be jarring to be reminded of this fact again, samplers merely
estimate the posterior distribution, and while in many cases they do quite well, it is not
guaranteed! Be sure to pay heed to the diagnostics and investigate more deeply if warnings
arise.

It is worth noting that there is no one size fits all solution when it comes to centered or non-centered parameterization [115]. It is a complex interaction among the informativeness of the individual likelihood at group level (usually the more data you have for a specific group, the more informative the likelihood function will be), the informativeness of the group level prior, and the parameterization. A general heuristic is that if there are not a lot of observations, a non-centered parameterization is preferred. In practice however, you should try a few different combinations of centered and non-centered parameterizations, with different prior specifications. You might even find cases where you need *both* centered and non-centered parameterization in a single model. We recommend you to read Michael Betancourt's case study Hierarchical Modeling on this topic if you suspect model parameterization is causing you sampling issues [15].

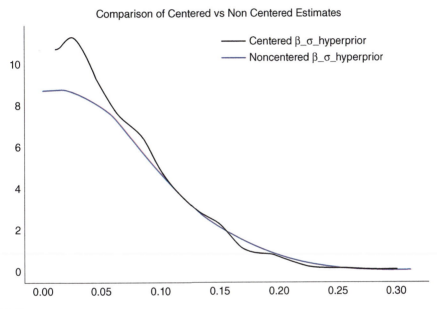

FIGURE 4.29
KDE of the distributions of $\beta_{\sigma h}$ in both centered and non-centered parameterizations. The change is due to the sampler being able to more adequately explore the possible parameter space.

4.6.2 Predictions at Multiple Levels

A subtle feature of hierarchical models is that they are able to make estimates at multiple levels. While seemingly obvious this is very useful, as it lets us use one model to answer many more questions than a single level model. In Chapter 3 we could built a model to estimate the mass of a single species or a separate model to estimate the mass of any penguin regardless of species. Using a hierarchical model we could estimate the mass of all penguins, and each penguin species, at the same time with one model. With our salad sales model we can both make estimations about an individual location and about the population a whole. We can do so by using our previous `non_centered_model` from Code Block 4.16, and write an `out_of_sample_prediction_model` as shown in Code Block 4.17. This using the fitted parameter estimates to make an out of sample prediction for the distribution of customers for 50 customers, at two locations and for the company as a whole *simultaneously*. Since our `non_centered_model` is also a TFP distribution, we can nest it into another `tfd.JointDistribution`, doing so constructed a larger Bayesian graphical model that extends our initial `non_centered_model` to include nodes for out of sample prediction. The estimates are plotted in Figure 4.30.

Code 4.17

```
1  out_of_sample_customers = 50.
2
3  @tfd.JointDistributionCoroutine
4  def out_of_sample_prediction_model():
5      model = yield root(non_centered_model)
6      β = model.beta_offset * model.beta_sigma[..., None] + model.beta_mu[..., None]
7
8      β_group = yield tfd.Normal(
9          model.beta_mu, model.beta_sigma, name="group_beta_prediction")
10     group_level_prediction = yield tfd.Normal(
11         β_group * out_of_sample_customers,
12         model.sigma_prior,
13         name="group_level_prediction")
14     for l in [2, 4]:
15         yield tfd.Normal(
16             tf.gather(β, l, axis=-1) * out_of_sample_customers,
17             tf.gather(model.sigma, l, axis=-1),
18             name=f"location_{l}_prediction")
19
20 amended_posterior = tf.nest.pack_sequence_as(
21     non_centered_model.sample(),
22     list(mcmc_samples_noncentered) + [observed],
23 )
24 ppc = out_of_sample_prediction_model.sample(var0=amended_posterior)
```

Another feature in making predictions is using hierarchical models with hyperpriors is that we can make prediction for never before seen groups. In this case, imagine we are opening another salad restaurant in a new location we can already make some predictions of how the salad sales might looks like by first sampling from the hyper prior to get the β_{i+1} and σ_{i+1} of the new location, then sample from the posterior predictive distribution to get salad sales prediction. This is demonstrated in Code Block 4.18.

Code 4.18

```
1  out_of_sample_customers2 = np.arange(50, 90)
2
3  @tfd.JointDistributionCoroutine
4  def out_of_sample_prediction_model2():
5      model = yield root(non_centered_model)
6
7      β_new_loc = yield tfd.Normal(
8          model.beta_mu, model.beta_sigma, name="beta_new_loc")
9      σ_new_loc = yield tfd.HalfNormal(model.sigma_prior, name="sigma_new_loc")
10     group_level_prediction = yield tfd.Normal(
11         β_new_loc[..., None] * out_of_sample_customers2,
12         σ_new_loc[..., None],
13         name="new_location_prediction")
14
15 ppc = out_of_sample_prediction_model2.sample(var0=amended_posterior)
```

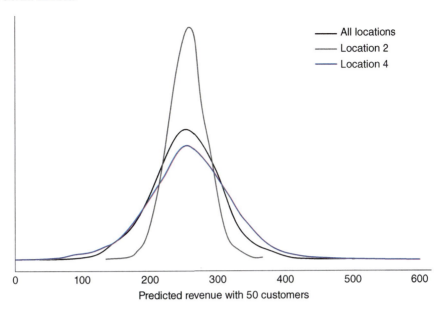

FIGURE 4.30
Posterior predictive estimates for the revenues for two of the groups and for total population estimated by model `model_hierarchical_salad_sales_non_centered`.

In addition to the mathematical benefits of hierarchical modeling, there is a benefit from a computational perspective as we only need to construct and fit a single model. This speeds up the modeling process and the subsequent model maintenance process, if the model is reused multiple times over time.

On the validity of LOO

Hierarchical models allow us to make posterior predictions even for group(s) that have never been seen before. However, how valid would the prediction be? Could we use cross-validation to assess the performance of the model? As usually in statistics the answer is *that depends*. Whether cross-validation (and methods like LOO and WAIC) is valid or not depends on the prediction task you want to perform, and also on the data generating mechanism. If we want to use LOO to assess how well the model is able to predict new observations globally, then LOO is fine. Now if we want to assess how well one entire group is predicted, then you will need to perform leave one-group-out cross validation, which is a well defined procedure. In that case however, the LOO method will most likely not be good, as we are removing many observations at a time and the importance sampling step at the core of the LOO approximation relies on the distributions with and without the point/group/etc being close to each other.

4.6.3   Priors for Multilevel Models

Prior choice is all the more important for multilevel models, because of how the prior interacts with the informativeness of the likelihood, as shown above in Section 4.6.1. Moreover, not only does the shape of prior distribution matter, we also have additional choices of how to parameterize them. This does not limit us to Gaussian priors as it applies to all distributions in the location-scale distribution family [6].

In multilevel models prior distributions not only characterize the in-group variation, but the between-group variation as well. In a sense the choice of hyperprior is defining the "variation of variation", which could make expressing and reasoning about prior information difficult. Moreover, since the effect of partial pooling is the combination of how informative the hyperprior is, the number of groups you have, and the number of observations in each group. Due to this the same hyperprior might not work if you are performing inference using the same model on similar dataset but with fewer groups.

As is such besides empirical experience (e.g., general recommendations published in articles) or general advice [7], we can also perform sensitivity studies to better inform our prior choice. For instance Lemoine [95] showed that when modeling ecology data with a model structure of

$$
\begin{aligned}
\alpha_i &\sim \mathcal{N}(\mu_\alpha, \sigma_\alpha^2) \\
\mu_i &= \alpha_i + \beta Day_i \\
Y &\sim \mathcal{N}(\mu_j, \sigma^2)
\end{aligned}
\tag{4.10}
$$

where the intercept is unpooled, Cauchy priors provide regularization at few data points, and do not obscure the posterior when the model is fitted on additional data. This is done through prior sensitivity analysis across both prior parameterizations and differing amounts of data. In your own multilevel models be sure to note multitude of ways a prior choice affects inference, and use either your domain expertise or tools such as prior predictive distributions to make an informed choice.

4.7   Exercises

4E1. What are examples of covariate-response relationships that are nonlinear in everyday life?

4E2. Assume you are studying the relationship between a covariate and an outcome and the data can be into 2 groups. You will be using a regression with a slope and intercept as your basic model structure.

$$
\begin{aligned}
\mu &= \beta_0 + \beta_1 X_1 \\
Y &\sim \mathcal{N}(\mu, \sigma)
\end{aligned}
\tag{4.11}
$$

---

[6] https://en.wikipedia.org/wiki/Locationscale_family
[7] https://github.com/stan-dev/stan/wiki/Prior-Choice-Recommendations

Also assume you now need to extend the model structure in each of the ways listed below. For each item write the mathematical equations that specify the full model.

(a) Pooled

(b) Unpooled

(c) Mixed Effect with pooled β_0

(d) Hierarchical β_0

(e) Hierarchical all parameters

(f) Hierarchical all parameters with non-centered β parameters

4E3. Use statistical notation to write a robust linear regression model for the baby dataset.

4E4. Consider the plight of a bodybuilder who needs to lift weights, do cardiovascular exercise, and eat to build a physique that earns a high score at a contest. If we were to build a model where weightlifting, cardiovascular exercise, and eating were covariates do you think these covariates are independent or do they interact? From your domain knowledge justify your answer?

4E5. An interesting property of the Student's t-distribution is that at values of $\nu = 1$ and $\nu = \infty$, the Student's t-distribution becomes identical two other distributions the Cauchy distribution and the Normal distribution. Plot the Student's t-distribution at both parameter values of ν and match each parameterization to Cauchy or Normal.

4E6. Assume we are trying to predict the heights of individuals. If given a dataset of height and one of the following covariates explain which type of regression would be appropriate between unpooled, pooled, partially pooled, and interaction. Explain why

(a) A vector of random noise

(b) Gender

(c) Familial relationship

(d) Weight

4E7. Use LOO to compare the results of `baby_model_linear` and `baby_model_sqrt`. Using LOO justify why the transformed covariate is justified as a modeling choice.

4E8. Go back to the penguin dataset. Add an interaction term to estimate penguin mass between species and flipper length. How do the predictions differ? Is this model better? Justify your reasoning in words and using LOO.

4M9. Ancombe's Quartet is a famous dataset highlighting the challenges with evaluating regressions solely on numerical summaries. The dataset is available at the GitHub repository. Perform a regression on the third case of Anscombe's quartet with both robust and non-robust regression. Plot the results.

4M10. Revisit the penguin mass model defined in 3.4. Add a hierarchical term for μ. What is the estimated mean of the hyperprior? What is the average mass for all penguins?

Compare the empirical mean to the estimated mean of the hyperprior. Do the values of the two estimates make sense to you, particularly when compared to each other? Why?

4M11. The compressive strength of concrete is dependent on the amount of water and cement used to produce it. In the GitHub repository we have provided a dataset of concrete compressive strength, as well the amount of water and cement included (kilograms per cubic meter). Create a linear model with an interaction term between water and cement. What is different about the inputs of this interaction model versus the smoker model we saw earlier? Plot the concrete compressive strength as function of concrete at various fixed values of water.

4M12. Rerun the pizza regression but this time do it with heteroskedastic regression. What are the results?

4H13. Radon is a radioactive gas that can cause lung cancer and thus it is something that would be undesirable in a domicile. Unfortunately the presence of a basement may increase the radon levels in a household as radon may enter the household more easily through the ground. We have provided a dataset of the radon levels at homes in Minnesota, in the GitHub repository as well as the county of the home, and the presence of a basement.

1. Run an unpooled regression estimating the effect of basements on radon levels.

2. Create a hierarchical model grouping by county. Justify why this model would be useful for the given the data.

3. Create a non-centered regression. Using plots and diagnostics justify if the non-centered parameterization was needed.

4H14. Generate a synthetic dataset for each of the models below with your own choice of parameters. Then fit two models to each dataset, one model matching the data generating process, and one that does not. See how the diagnostic summaries and plots differ between the two.

For example, we may generate data that follows a linear pattern $x = [1, 2, 3, 4], y = [2, 4, 6, 8]$. Then fit a model of the form $y = bx$ and another of the form $y = bx**2$

(a) Linear Model

(b) Linear model with transformed covariate

(c) Linear model with interaction effect

(d) 4 group model with pooled intercept, and unpooled slope and noise

(e) A Hierarchical Model

4H15. For the hierarchical salad regression model evaluate the posterior geometry for the slope parameter $\beta_{\mu h}$. Then create a version of the model where $\beta_{\mu h}$ is non-centered. Plot the geometry now. Are there any differences? Evaluate the divergences and output as well. Does non-centering help in this case?

4H16. A colleague of yours, who now lives on an unknown planet, ran experiment to test the basic laws of physics. She dropped a ball of a cliff and registers the position for 20 seconds.

The data is available in the Github repository in the file `gravity_measurements.csv` You know that from Newton's Laws of physics if the acceleration is g and the time t then

$$velocity = gt$$
$$position = \frac{1}{2}gt^2$$

(4.12)

Your friend asks you to estimate the following quantities

(a) The gravitational constant of the planet

(b) A characterization of the noise of her measurement device

(c) The velocity of the ball at each point during her measurements

(d) The estimated position of the ball from time 20 to time 30

5

Splines

In this chapter we will discuss splines, which is an extension of concepts introduced into Chapter 3 with the aim of adding more flexibility. In the models introduced in Chapter 3 the relationship between the dependent and independent variables was the same for their entire domain. Splines, in contrast, can split a problem into multiple local solutions, which can all be combined to produce a useful global solution. Let us see how.

5.1 Polynomial Regression

As we already saw in Chapter 3, we can write a linear model as:

$$\mathbb{E}[Y] = \beta_0 + \beta_1 X \tag{5.1}$$

where β_0 is the intercept, β_1 the slope and $\mathbb{E}[Y]$ is the expected value, or mean, of the response (random) variable Y. We can rewrite Equation 5.1 into the following form:

$$\mathbb{E}[Y] = \beta_0 + \beta_1 X + \beta_2 X^2 + \cdots + \beta_m X^m \tag{5.2}$$

This is known as polynomial regression. At first it may seem that Expression 5.2 is representing a multiple linear regression of the covariates $X, X^2 \cdots + X^m$. And in a sense this is right, but the key element to notice and keep in mind is that the covariates X^m are all derived from X by applying successive powers from 1 to m. So in terms of our actual problem we are still fitting a single predictor.

We call m the degree of the polynomial. The linear regressions models from Chapter 3 and Chapter 4 were all polynomials of degree 1. With the one exception of the varying variance example in Section 4.1 where we used $m = 1/2$.

Figure 5.1 shows 3 examples of such polynomial regression using degrees 2, 10, and 15. As we increase the order of the polynomial, we get a more flexible curve.

One problem with polynomials is that they act *globally*, when we apply a polynomial of degree m we are saying that the relationship between the independent and dependent variables is of degree m for the entire dataset. This can be problematic when different regions of our data need different levels of flexibility. This could lead, for example, to curves that are *too flexible* [1]. For example, in the last panel of Figure 5.1 (degree=15), we can see

---

[1] See Runge's phenomenon for details. This can also be seen from Taylor's theorem, polynomials will be useful to approximate a function close to a single given point, but it will not be good over its whole domain. If you got lost try watching this video https://www.youtube.com/watch?v=3d6DsjIBzJ4.

DOI: 10.1201/9781003019169-5

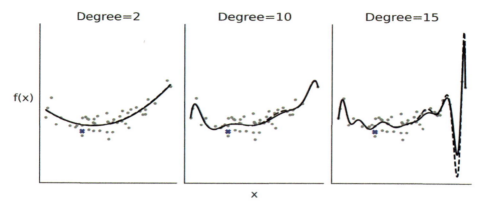

FIGURE 5.1
An example of polynomial regression with degrees 2, 10 and 15. As the degree increases the fit gets more *wiggly*. The dashed lines are the fit when removing the observation indicated with a blue cross. The removal of a data point has a small effect when the degree of polynomial is 2 or 10, but larger when the degree is 15. The fit was calculated using the least squares method.

that the fitted curve presents a *deep valley* followed by a *high peak* towards high values of X, even when there are no data points with such low or high values.

Additionally, as the degree increases the fit becomes more unstable to the removal of points, or equivalently to the addition of future data, in other words as the degree increases the model becomes more prone to overfitting. For example, in Figure 5.1 the black lines represent the fit to the entire data and the dashed lines the fit when we remove one data point, indicated with a cross in the figure. We can see, especially in the last panel, that removing even a single data point changes the model fit with effects even far away from the location of the point.

5.2 Expanding the Feature Space

At a conceptual level we can think of polynomial regression as a recipe for creating new predictors, or in more formal terms to **expanding the feature space**. By performing this expansion we are able to fit a line in the expanded space which gives us a curve on the space of the original data, pretty neat! Nevertheless, feature expansion is not an invitation to statistical anarchy, we can not just apply random transformations to our data and then expect to always get good results. In fact, as we just saw applying polynomials is not problem-free.

To generalize the idea of feature expansion, beyond polynomials we can expand Equation 5.1 into the following form:

$$\mathbb{E}[Y] = \beta_0 + \beta_1 B_1(X_1) + \beta_2 B_2(X_2) + \cdots + \beta_m B_m(X_m) \tag{5.3}$$

where the B_i are arbitrary functions. In this context we call these functions basis functions. A linear combination of them gives us a function f that is what we actually "see" as the fit of the model to the data. In this sense the B_i are an under the hood trick to build a flexible function f.

$$\mathbb{E}[Y] = \sum_i^m \beta_i B_i(X_i) = f(X) \qquad (5.4)$$

There are many choices for the B_i basis functions, we can use polynomials and thus obtain polynomial regression as we just saw, or maybe apply an arbitrary set of functions such as a power of two, a logarithm, or a square root. Such functions may be motivated by the problem at hand, for example, in Section 4.1 we modeled how the length of babies changes with their age by computing the square root of the length, motivated by the fact that human babies, same as other mammals, grow more rapidly in the earlier stages of their life and then the growth tends to level off (similar to how a square root function does).

Another alternative is to use indicator functions like $I(c_i \leq x_k < c_j)$ to break up the original $\boldsymbol{X}$ predictor into (non-overlapping) subsets. And then fit polynomial *locally*, i.e., only inside these subsets. This procedure leads to fitting **piecewise polynomials** [2] as shown in Figure 5.2.

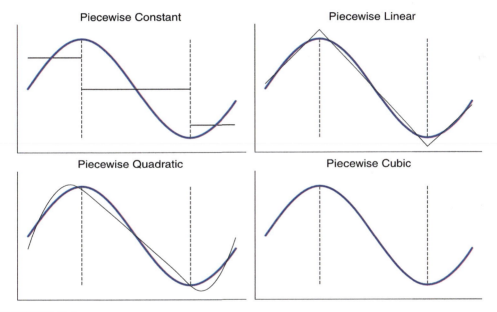

FIGURE 5.2
The blue line is the *true* function we are trying to approximate. The black-solid lines are piecewise polynomials of increasing order (1, 2, 3, and 4). The dashed vertical gray lines are marking the limits of each subdomain on the x-axis.

In the four panels in Figure 5.2 the goal is the same, to approximate the blue function. We proceed by first splitting the function into 3 subdomains, delimited by the gray dashed lines, and then we fit a different function to each subdomain. In the first subpanel (piecewise constant) we fit a constant function. We can think of a constant function as a zero degree polynomial. The aggregated solution, i.e. the 3 segments in black is known as a **step-function**. This may seem to be a rather crude approximation but it may be all that we

---

[2]A piecewise function is a function that is defined using sub-functions, where each sub-function applies to a different interval in the domain.

need. For example, step-functions may be OK if we are trying to find out a discontinuous outcome like the expected mean temperature during morning, afternoon, and night. Or when we are OK about getting a non-smooth approximation even if we think the outcome is smooth [3].

In the second panel (piecewise linear) we do the same as in the first but instead of a constant function we use a linear function, which is a first degree polynomial. Notice that the contiguous linear solutions meet at the dashed lines, this is done on purpose. We could justify this restriction as trying to make the solution as smooth as possible [4].

In the third panel (piecewise quadratic) and fourth panel (piecewise cubic) we use quadratic and cubic piecewise polynomials. As we can see by increasing the degree of the piecewise polynomials we get further and further flexible solutions, which brings better fits but also a higher chance of overfitting.

Because the final fit is a function f constructed from local solutions (the B_i basis functions) we can more easily accommodate the flexibility of the model to the demands of the data at different regions. In this particular case, we can use a simpler function (polynomial with lower degree) to fit the data at different regions, while providing a good overall model fit to the whole domain of the data.

So far we have assumed we have a single predictor X, but the same idea can be extended to more than one predictor $X_0, X_1, \cdots, X_p$. And we can even add an inverse link function ϕ [5] models of this form are known as Generalized Additive Models (GAM): [59, 162].

$$\mathbb{E}[Y] = \phi \left(\sum_i^p f(X_i) \right) \tag{5.5}$$

Recapitulating what we learn in this section, the B_i functions in Equation 5.3 are a clever statistical device that allows us to fit more flexible models. In principle we are free to choose arbitrary B_i functions, and we may do it based on our domain knowledge, as a result of an exploratory data analysis phase, or even by trial and error. As not all transformations will have the same statistical properties, it would be nice to have access to some *default* functions with good general properties over a wider range of datasets. Starting in the next section and for the remainder of this chapter we will restrict the discussion to a family of basis functions known as B-splines [6].

5.3   Introducing Splines

Splines can be seen as an attempt to use the flexibility of polynomials but keeping them under control and thus obtaining a model with overall good statistical properties. To define a spline we need to define knots [7]. The purpose of the knots is to split the domain of the variable X into contiguous intervals. For example, the dashed vertical gray lines in Figure

---

[3] In Chapter 7 we explore how step-functions have a central role in Bayesian Additive Regression Trees.

[4] This can also be justified numerically as this reduces the number of coefficients we need to find to compute a solution.

[5] As usual the identity function is a valid choice.

[6] Other basis functions could be wavelets or Fourier series as we will see in Chapter 6.

[7] Also known as break points, which is arguably a more memorable name, but still knots is widely used in the literature.

5.2 represent knots. For our purposes a spline is a piecewise polynomial constrained to be continuous, that is we enforce two contiguous sub-polynomials to meet at the knots. If the sub-polynomials are of degree n we say the spline is of degree n. Sometimes splines are referred to by their order which would be $n + 1$.

In Figure 5.2 we can see that as we increase the order of the piecewise polynomial the *smoothness* of the resulting function also increases. As we already mentioned the sub-polynomials should meet at the knots. On the first panel it may seem we are cheating as there is a step, also known as a discontinuity, between each line, but this is the best we can do if we use constant values at each interval.

When talking about splines, the sub-polynomials are formally known as basis splines or B-splines for short. Any spline function of a given degree can be constructed as a linear combination of basis splines of that degree. Figure 5.3 shows examples of B-splines of increasing degree from 0 to 3 (top to bottom), the dots at the bottom represent the knots, the blue ones mark the interval at which the highlighted B-spline (in black continuous line) is not zero. All other B-splines are represented with a thinner dashed line for clarity, but all B-splines are equally important. In fact, each subplots in Figure 5.3 is showing all the B-splines as defined by the given knots. In other words B-splines are completely defined by a set of knots and a degree.

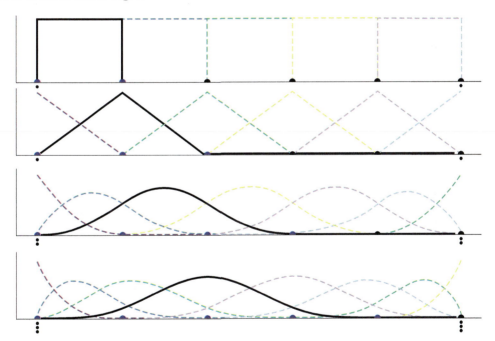

FIGURE 5.3
B-splines of increasing degree, from 0 to 3. On the top subplot we have a step function, on second a triangular function and then increasingly Gaussian-like functions. The *stacked* knots at the boundary (smaller black dots) are added in order to be able to define the splines close to the borders.

From Figure 5.3 we can see that as we increase the degree of the B-spline, the domain of the B-spline spans more and more [8]. Thus, for higher degree spline to make sense we

---
[8]In the limit of infinite degree a B-spline will span the entire real line and not only that, it will converge to a Gaussian https://www.youtube.com/watch/9CS7j5I6a0c.

need to define more knots. Note that in all cases B-splines are restricted to be non-zero only inside a given interval. This property make splines regression more *local* than what we would get from a polynomial regression.

As the number of knots controlling each B-splines grows with the degree, for all degrees larger than 0, we are not able to define a whole B-spline near to the boundaries. This is the reason the B-spline is highlighted in black in Figure 5.3 shifts to the right as we increase the degree. This presents a potential problem, because it leaves us with less B-splines at the boundaries, so our approximation will suffer there. Fortunately, this boundary problem is easy to solve, we just need to add knots at the boundaries (see the small dots in Figure 5.3). So if our knots are (0,1,2,3,4,5) and we want to fit a cubic spline (like in the last subplot of Figure 5.3) we will need to actually use the set of knots (0,0,0,0,1,2,3,4,5,5,5,5). That is, we pad the 0 three times at the beginning and we pad the 5 three times at the end. By doing so we now have the five necessary knots (0,0,0,0,1) to define the first B-spline (see the dashed indigo line that looks like an Exponential distribution in the last subpanel of Figure 5.3). Then we will use the knots 0,0,0,1,2 to define the second B-spline (the one that looks like a Beta distribution), etc. See how the first *complete* B-splines (highlighted in black) is defined by the knots (0,1,2,3,4) which are the knots in blue. Notice that we need to pad the knots at the boundaries as many times as the degree of the spline. That is why we have no extra knots for degree 0 and 6 extra knots for degree 3.

Each single B-spline is not very useful on its own, but a linear combination of all of them allows us to fit complex functions. Thus, in practice fitting splines requires that we choose the order of the B-splines, the number and locations of knots and then find the set of coefficients to weight each B-spline. This is represented in Figure 5.4. We can see the basis functions represented using a different color to help individualize each individual basis function. The knots are represented with black dots at the bottom of each subplot. The second row is more interesting as we can see the same basis functions from the first row scaled by a set of β_i coefficients. The thicker continuous black line represents the spline that is obtained by a weighted sum of the B-splines with the weights given by the β coefficients.

In this example we generated the β_i coefficients by sampling from a Half Normal distribution (Line 17 in Code Block 5.2). Thus, each panel in Figure 5.4 is showing only one realization of a probability distribution over splines. You can easily see this is true by removing the random seed and running Code Block 5.2 a few times, each time you will see a different spline. Additionally, you may also try replacing the Half Normal distribution, with another one like the Normal, Exponential, etc. Figure 5.5 shows four realization of cubic splines.

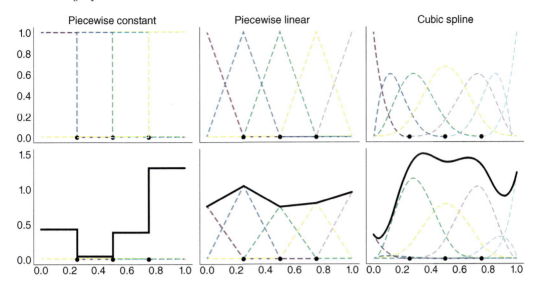

FIGURE 5.4

B-splines defined using Patsy. On the first row we can see splines of increasing order 1 (piecewise constant), 2 (piecewise linear) and 4 (cubic) represented with gray dashed lines. For clarity each basis function is represented with a different color. On the second row we have the basis splines from the first row scaled by a set of coefficients. The thick black line represents the sum of these basis functions. Because the values of the coefficients were randomly chosen we can see each sub-panel in the second row as a random sample from a prior distribution over the *spline space*.

Four is a crowd for splines

Of all possible splines, probably cubic splines are the most commonly used. But why are cubic splines the queen of splines? Figures 5.2 and 5.4 offer some hints. Cubic splines provide us with the lowest order of splines able to generate *smooth enough* curves for most common scenarios, rendering higher order splines less attractive. What do we mean by *smooth enough*? Without going into the mathematical details, we meant that the fitted function does not present sudden changes of slope. One way of doing this is by adding the restriction that two contiguous piecewise polynomials should meet at their common knots. Cubic splines have two additional restrictions, the first and second derivatives are also continuous, meaning that the slope is continuous at the knots and also the slope of the slope [a]. In fact, a spline of degree m will have $m - 1$ derivatives at the knots. Having said all that, splines of lower or higher order can still be useful for some problems, it is just that cubic splines are good defaults.

---

[a]Check https://pclambert.net/interactivegraphs/spline_continuity/spline_continuity for further intuition

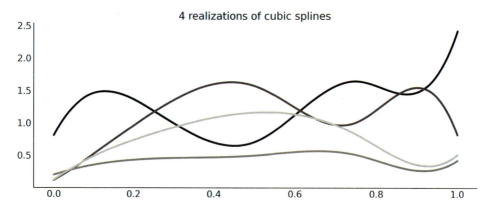

FIGURE 5.5
Four realizations of cubic splines with β_i coefficients sampled from a Half Normal distribution.

5.4   Building the Design Matrix using Patsy

In Figures 5.3 and 5.4 we plot the B-splines, but so far we have omitted how to compute them. The main reason is that computation can be cumbersome and there are already efficient algorithms available in packages like Scipy [9]. Thus, instead of discussing how the B-splines can be computed from scratch we are going to rely on Patsy, a package for describing statistical models, especially linear models, or models that have a linear component, and building design matrices. It is closely inspired by the *formula mini-language* widely used in many packages from the R programming language ecosystem. Just for you to get a taste of the formula language, a linear model with two covariates looks like "y ~ x1 + x2" and if we want to add an interaction we can write "y ~ x1 + x2 + x1:x2". This is a similar syntax as the one shown in Chapter 3 in the box highlighting Bambi. For more details please check the patsy documentation [10].

To define a basis spline design matrix in Patsy we need to pass a string to the `dmatrix` function starting with the *particle* `bs()`, while this particle is a string is parsed by Patsy as a function. And thus it can also take several arguments including the data, an array-like of knots indicating their location and the degree of the spline. In Code Block 5.1 we define 3 design matrices, one with degree 0 (piecewise constant), another with degree 1 (piecewise linear) and finally one with degree 3 (cubic spline).

Code 5.1

```
1  x = np.linspace(0., 1., 500)
2  knots = [0.25, 0.5, 0.75]
3
4  B0 = dmatrix("bs(x, knots=knots, degree=0, include_intercept=True) - 1",
5               {"x": x, "knots":knots})
6  B1 = dmatrix("bs(x, knots=knots, degree=1, include_intercept=True) - 1",
7               {"x": x, "knots":knots})
8  B3 = dmatrix("bs(x, knots=knots, degree=3,include_intercept=True) - 1",
9               {"x": x, "knots":knots})
```

---

[9]If interested you can check https://en.wikipedia.org/wiki/De_Boor's_algorithm.
[10]https://patsy.readthedocs.io

Figure 5.6 represents the 3 design matrices computed with Code Block 5.1. To better grasp what Patsy is doing we also recommend you use Jupyter notebook/lab or your favorite IDE to inspect the objects B0, B1 and B2.

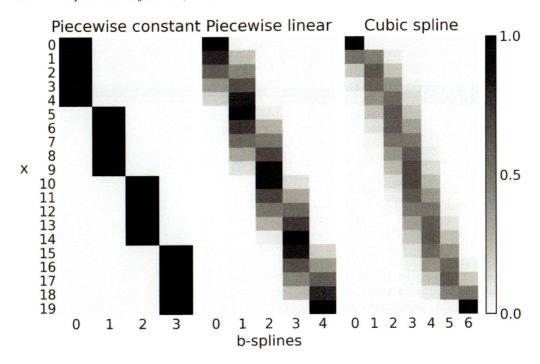

FIGURE 5.6

Design matrices generated with Patsy in Code Block 5.1. The color goes from black (1) to light-gray (0), the number of columns is the number of B-splines and the number of rows the number of datapoints.

The first subplot of Figure 5.6 corresponds to B0, a spline of degree 0. We can see that the design matrix is a matrix with only zeros (light-gray) and ones (black). The first B-spline (column 0) is 1 for the first 5 observations and 0 otherwise, the second B-spline (column 1) is 0 for the first 5 observations, 1 for the second 5 observations and 0 again. And the same pattern is repeated. Compare this with the first subplot (first row) of Figure 5.4, you should see how the design matrix is encoding that plot.

For the second subplot in Figure 5.6 we have the first B-spline going from 1 to 0, the second, third and fourth goes from 0 to 1 and then back from 1 to 0. The fifth B-spline goes from 0 to 1. You should see how this patterns match the line with negative slope, the 3 triangular functions and the line with positive slope in the second subplot (first row) of Figure 5.4.

Finally we can see something similar if we compare how the 7 columns in the third subplot in Figure 5.6 match the 7 curves in the third subplot (first row) of Figure 5.4.

Code Block 5.1 was used to generate the B-splines in Figures 5.4 and 5.6, the only different is that for the former we used x = np.linspace(0., 1., 500), so the curves look smoother and we use x = np.linspace(0., 1., 20) in the later so the matrices are easier to understand.

Code 5.2

```
1  _, axes = plt.subplots(2, 3, sharex=True, sharey="row")
2  for idx, (B, title) in enumerate(zip((B0, B1, B3),
3                                       ("Piecewise constant",
4                                        "Piecewise linear",
5                                        "Cubic spline"))):
6      # plot spline basis functions
7      for i in range(B.shape[1]):
8          axes[0, idx].plot(x, B[:, i],
9                            color=viridish[i], lw=2, ls="--")
10     # we generate some positive random coefficients
11     # there is nothing wrong with negative values
12     β = np.abs(np.random.normal(0, 1, size=B.shape[1]))
13     # plot spline basis functions scaled by its β
14     for i in range(B.shape[1]):
15         axes[1, idx].plot(x, B[:, i]*β[i],
16                           color=viridish[i], lw=2, ls="--")
17     # plot the sum of the basis functions
18     axes[1, idx].plot(x, np.dot(B, β), color="k", lw=3)
19     # plot the knots
20     axes[0, idx].plot(knots, np.zeros_like(knots), "ko")
21     axes[1, idx].plot(knots, np.zeros_like(knots), "ko")
22     axes[0, idx].set_title(title)
```

So far we have explored a couple of examples to gain intuition into what splines are and how to automate their creation with the help of Patsy. We can now move forward into computing the weights. Let us see how we can do that in a Bayesian model with PyMC3.

5.5   Fitting Splines in PyMC3

In this section we are going to use PyMC3 to obtain the values of the regression coefficients β by fitting a set of B-splines to the data.

Modern bike sharing systems allow people in many cities around the globe to rent and return bikes in a completely automated fashion, helping to increase the efficiency of the public transportation and probably making part of the society healthier and even happier. We are going to use a dataset from such a bike sharing system from the University of California Irvine's Machine Learning Repository [11]. For our example we are going to estimate the number of rental bikes rented per hour over a 24 hour period. Let us load and plot the data:

Code 5.3

```
1  data = pd.read_csv("../data/bikes_hour.csv")
2  data.sort_values(by="hour", inplace=True)
3
4  # We standardize the response variable
5  data_cnt_om = data["count"].mean()
6  data_cnt_os = data["count"].std()
```

---

[11]https://archive.ics.uci.edu/ml/datasets/bike+sharing+dataset

```
7  data["count_normalized"] = (data["count"] - data_cnt_om) / data_cnt_os
8  # Remove data, you may later try to refit the model to the whole data
9  data = data[::50]
```

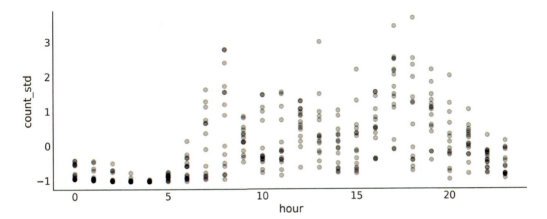

FIGURE 5.7
A visualization of the bikes data. Each point is the normalized number of bikes rented per hour of the day (on the interval [0, 23]). The points are semi-transparent to avoid excessive overlapping of points and thus help see the distribution of the data.

A quick look at Figure 5.7 shows that the relationship between the hour of the day and the number of rental bikes is not going to be very well captured by fitting a single line. So, let us try to use a spline regression to better approximate the nonlinear pattern.

As we already mentioned in order to work with splines we need to define the number and position of the knots. We are going to use 6 knots and use the simplest option to position them, equal spacing between each knot.

Code 5.4

```
1  num_knots = 6
2  knot_list = np.linspace(0, 23, num_knots+2)[1:-1]
```

Notice that in Code Block 5.4 we define 8 knots, but then we remove the first and last knots, ensuring we keep 6 knots which are defined in the *interior* of the data. Whether this is a useful strategy will depends on the data. For example, if the bulk of the data is away from the borders this will be a good idea, also the larger the number of knots the less important their positions.

Now we use Patsy to define and build the design matrix for us

Code 5.5

```
1  B = dmatrix(
2      "bs(cnt, knots=knots, degree=3, include_intercept=True) - 1",
3      {"cnt": data.hour.values, "knots": knot_list[1:-1]})
```

The proposed statistical model is:

$$\begin{aligned}
\tau &\sim \mathcal{HC}(1) \\
\boldsymbol{\beta} &\sim \mathcal{N}(0, \tau) \\
\sigma &\sim \mathcal{HN}(1) \\
Y &\sim \mathcal{N}(\boldsymbol{B}(X)\boldsymbol{\beta}, \sigma)
\end{aligned} \tag{5.6}$$

Our spline regression model is very similar to the linear models from Chapter 3. All the hard-work is done by the design matrix $\boldsymbol{B}$ and its expansion of the feature space. Notice that we are using linear algebra notation to write the multiplications and sums of Equations 5.3 and 5.4 in a shorter form, that is we write $\boldsymbol{\mu} = \boldsymbol{B}\boldsymbol{\beta}$ instead of $\boldsymbol{\mu} = \sum_i^n B_i \boldsymbol{\beta}_i$.

As usual the statistical syntax is translated into PyMC3 in nearly a one-to-one fashion.

Code 5.6

```
1  with pm.Model() as splines:
2      τ = pm.HalfCauchy("τ", 1)
3      β = pm.Normal("β", mu=0, sd=τ, shape=B.shape[1])
4      μ = pm.Deterministic("μ", pm.math.dot(B, β))
5      σ = pm.HalfNormal("σ", 1)
6      c = pm.Normal("c", μ, σ, observed=data["count_normalized"].values)
7      idata_s = pm.sample(1000, return_inferencedata=True)
```

We show in Figure 5.8 the final fitted linear prediction as a solid black line and each weighted B-spline as a dashed line. It is a nice representation as we can see how the B-splines are contributing to the final result.

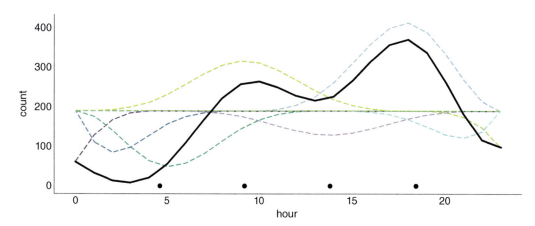

FIGURE 5.8
Bikes data fitted using splines. The B-splines are represented with dashed lines. The sum of them generates the thicker solid black line. The plotted values correspond to mean values from the posterior. The black dots represent the knots. The splines in this figure look very *jagged*, relative to the splines plotted in Figure 5.4. The reason is that we are evaluating the function in fewer points. 24 points here because the data is binned per hour compared to 500 in Figure 5.4.

A more useful plot when we want to display the results of the model is to plot the data with the overlaid splines and its uncertainty as in Figure 5.9. From this figure we can easily see that the number of rental bikes is at the lowest number late at night. There is then an increase, probably as people wake up and go to work. We have a first peak at around hour 10, which levels-off, or perhaps slightly declines, then followed by a second peak as people commute back home at around hour 18, after which there a steady decline.

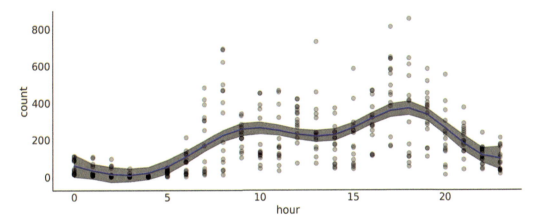

FIGURE 5.9
Bikes data (black dots) fitted using splines. The shaded curve represents the 94% HDI interval (of the mean) and the blue curve represents the mean trend.

In this bike rental example we are dealing with a circular variable, meaning that hour 0 is equal to the hour 24. This may be more or less obvious to us, but it is definitely not obvious to our model. Patsy offers a simple solution to tell our model that the variable is circular. Instead of defining the design matrix using `bs` we can use `cc`, this is a cubic spline that is *circular-aware*. We recommend you check the Patsy documentation for more details and explore using `cc` in the previous model and compare results.

5.6 Choosing Knots and Prior for Splines

One modeling decision we have to make when working with splines is to choose the number and location of the knots. This can be a little bit concerning, given that in general the number of knots and their spacing are not obvious decisions. When faced with this type of choice we can always try to fit more than one model and then use methods such as LOO to help us pick the best model. Table 5.6 shows the results of fitting a model like the one defined in Code Block 5.6 with, 3, 6, 9, 12, and 18 equally distanced knots. We can see that the spline with 12 knots is selected by LOO as the best model.

One interesting observation from Table 5.6, is that the weights are 0.88 for model `m_12k` (the top ranked model) and 0.12 to `m_3k` (the last ranked model). With virtually 0 weight for the rest of the models. As we explained in Section 2.5.6 by default the weights are computed using stacking, which is a method that attempts to combine several models in

	rank	loo	p_loo	d_loo	weight	se	dse	warning	loo_scale
m_12k	0	-377.67	14.21	0.00	0.88	17.86	0.00	False	log
m_18k	1	-379.78	17.56	2.10	0.00	17.89	1.45	False	log
m_9k	2	-380.42	11.43	2.75	0.00	18.12	2.97	False	log
m_6k	3	-389.43	9.41	11.76	0.00	18.16	5.72	False	log
m_3k	4	-400.25	7.17	22.58	0.12	18.01	7.78	False	log

TABLE 5.1
Summary of model comparison using LOO for splines models with different number of knots.

a meta-model in order to minimize the divergence between the meta-model and the *true* generating model. As a result even when models m_6k, m_9k and m_18k have better values of loo, once m_12k is included they do not have much to add and while m_3k is the lowest ranked model, it seems that it still has something new to contribute to the model averaging. Figure 5.10 show the mean fitted spline for all these models.

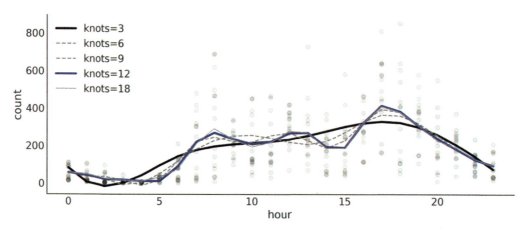

FIGURE 5.10
Mean posterior spline for the model described in Code Block 5.6 with different number of knots (3, 6, 9, 12, 18) . Model m_12k is highlighted in blue as the top ranked model according to LOO. Model m_3k is highlighted in black, while the rest of the models are in grayed-out as they have being assigned a weight of zero (see Table 5.6).

One piece of advice that may help decide the locations of knots is to place them based on quantiles, instead of uniformly. In Code Block 5.4 we could have defined the knot_list using knot_list = np.quantile(data.hour, np.linspace(0, 1, num_knots)). In this way we will be putting more knots where we have more data and less knots where less data. This translates into a more flexible approximation for data-richer portions.

5.6.1 Regularizing Prior for Splines

As choosing too few knots could lead to under-fitting and too many to overfitting, we may want to use a *rather large* number of knots and then choose a regularizing prior. From the definition of splines and Figure 5.4 we can see that the closer the consecutive β coefficients are to each other, the smoother the resulting function will be. Imagine you are dropping two consecutive columns of the design matrix in Figure 5.4, effectively setting those coefficients to 0, the fit will be much less *smooth* as we do not have enough information in the predictor to cover some sub region (recall that splines are *local*). Thus we can achieve smoother fitted regression line by choosing a prior for the β coefficients in such a way that the value of β_{i+1} is correlated with the value of β_i:

$$\beta_i \sim \mathcal{N}(0,1)$$
$$\tau \sim \mathcal{N}(0,1) \tag{5.7}$$
$$\beta \sim \mathcal{N}(\beta_{i-1}, \tau)$$

Using PyMC3 we can write an equivalent version using a Gaussian Random Walk prior distribution:

$$\tau \sim \mathcal{N}(0,1)$$
$$\beta \sim \mathcal{GRW}(\beta, \tau) \tag{5.8}$$

To see the effect of this prior we are going to repeat the analysis of the bike dataset, but this time using `num_knots = 12`. We refit the data using `splines` model and the following model:

Code 5.7

```
1 with pm.Model() as splines_rw:
2     τ = pm.HalfCauchy("τ", 1)
3     β = pm.GaussianRandomWalk("β", mu=0, sigma=τ, shape=B.shape[1])
4     μ = pm.Deterministic("μ", pm.math.dot(B, β))
5     σ = pm.HalfNormal("σ", 1)
6     c = pm.Normal("c", μ, σ, observed=data["count_normalized"].values)
7     trace_splines_rw = pm.sample(1000)
```

On Figure 5.11 we can see that the spline mean function for the model `splines_rw` (black line) is less wiggly than the spline mean function without smoothing prior (gray thick line), although we admit that the difference seems to be rather small.

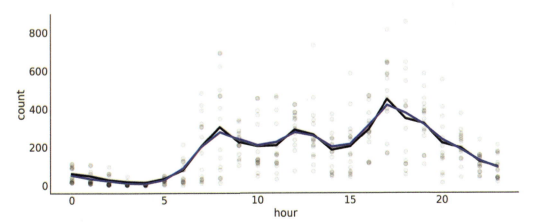

FIGURE 5.11
Bikes data fitted with either a Gaussian prior (black) or a regularizing Gaussian Random Walk Prior (blue). We use 22 knots for both cases. The black line corresponds to the mean spline function computed from `splines` model. The blue line is the mean function for the model `splines_rw`.

5.7   Modeling CO$_2$ Uptake with Splines

For a final example of splines we are going to use data from an experimental study [125, 116]. The experiment consists of measuring the CO$_2$ uptake in 12 different plants under varying conditions. Here we will only explore the effect of the external CO$_2$ concentration, i.e. how the CO$_2$ concentration in the environment affects the consumption of CO$_2$ by different plants. The CO$_2$ uptake was measured at seven CO$_2$ concentrations for each plant, the same seven values for each one of the 12 plants. Let us begin by loading and tidying up the data.

Code 5.8

```
1  plants_CO2 = pd.read_csv("../data/CO2_uptake.csv")
2  plant_names = plants_CO2.Plant.unique()
3
4  # Index the first 7 CO2 measurements per plant
5  CO2_conc = plants_CO2.conc.values[:7]
6
7  # Get full array which are the 7 measurements above repeated 12 times
8  CO2_concs = plants_CO2.conc.values
9  uptake = plants_CO2.uptake.values
10
11 index = range(12)
12 groups = len(index)
```

The first model we are going to fit is one with a single response curve, i.e. assuming the response curve is the same for all the 12 plants. We first define the design matrix, using Patsy, just as we previously did. We set `num_knots=2` because we have 7 observations per plant, so a relatively low number of knots should work fine. In Code Block `CO2_concs` is a list with the values `[95, 175, 250, 350, 500, 675, 1000]` repeated 12 times, one time per plant.

Code 5.9

```
1  num_knots = 3
2  knot_list = np.linspace(CO2_conc[0], CO2_conc[-1], num_knots+2)[1:-1]
3
4  Bg = dmatrix(
5      "bs(conc, knots=knots, degree=3, include_intercept=True) - 1",
6      {"conc": CO2_concs, "knots": knot_list})
```

This problem looks similar to the bike rental problem from previous sections and thus we can start by applying the same model. Using a model that we have already applied in some previous problem or the ones we learned from the literature is a good way to start an analysis. This model-template approach can be viewed as a shortcut to the otherwise longer process of model design [64]. In addition to the obvious advantage of not having to think of a model from scratch, we have other advantages such as having better intuition of how to perform exploratory analysis of the model and then possible routes for making changes into the model either to simplify it or to make it more complex.

Code 5.10

```
1  with pm.Model() as sp_global:
2      τ = pm.HalfCauchy("τ", 1)
3      β = pm.Normal("β", mu=0, sigma=τ, shape=Bg.shape[1])
4      μg = pm.Deterministic("μg", pm.math.dot(Bg, β))
5      σ = pm.HalfNormal("σ", 1)
6      up = pm.Normal("up", μg, σ, observed=uptake)
7      idata_sp_global = pm.sample(2000, return_inferencedata=True)
```

From Figure 5.12 we can clearly see that the model is only providing a good fit for some of the plants. The model is good on average, i.e. if we pool all the species together, but not very good for specific plants.

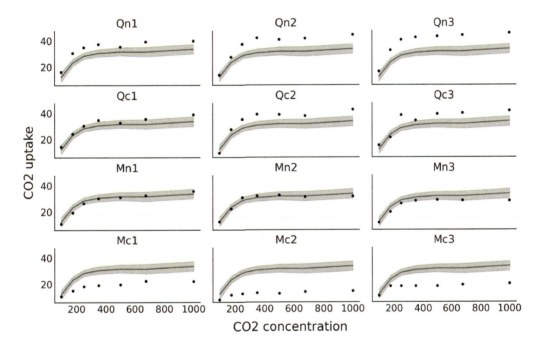

FIGURE 5.12
The black dots represents the CO_2 uptake measured at seven CO_2 concentrations for each one of 12 plants (Qn1, Qn2, Qn3, Qc1, Qc2, Qc3, Mn1, Mn2, Mn3, Mc1, Mc2, Mc3). The black line is the mean spline fit from the model in Code Block 5.10 and the gray shaded curve represents the 94% HDI interval for that fit.

Let us try now with a model with a different response per plant, in order to do this we define the design matrix Bi in Code Block 5.11. To define Bi we use the list CO2_conc = [95, 175, 250, 350, 500, 675, 1000], thus Bi is a 7×7 matrix while Bg is a 84×7 matrix.

Code 5.11

```
1  Bi = dmatrix(
2      "bs(conc, knots=knots, degree=3, include_intercept=True) - 1",
3      {"conc": CO2_conc, "knots": knot_list})
```

Accordingly with the shape of Bi, the parameter β in Code Block 5.12 has now shape shape=(Bi.shape[1], groups)) (instead of shape=(Bg.shape[1]))) and we reshape μi[:,index].T.ravel()

Code 5.12

```
1  with pm.Model() as sp_individual:
2      τ = pm.HalfCauchy("τ", 1)
3      β = pm.Normal("β", mu=0, sigma=τ, shape=(Bi.shape[1], groups))
4      μi = pm.Deterministic("μi", pm.math.dot(Bi, β))
5      σ = pm.HalfNormal("σ", 1)
6      up = pm.Normal("up", μi[:,index].T.ravel(), σ, observed=uptake)
7      idata_sp_individual = pm.sample(2000, return_inferencedata=True)
```

From Figure 5.13 we can now see that we have a much better fit for each one of the 12 plants.

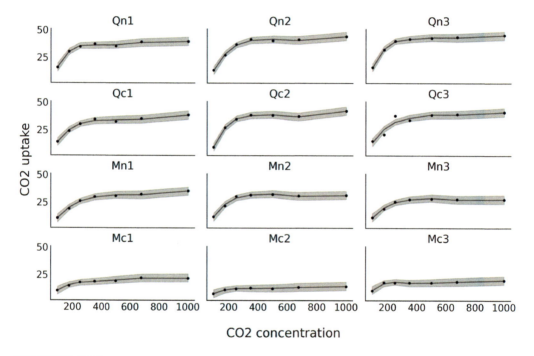

FIGURE 5.13

CO_2 uptake measured at seven CO_2 concentrations for 12 plants. The black line is the mean spline fit from the model in Code Block 5.12 and the gray shaded curve represents the 94% HDI interval for that fit.

We can also mix both previous models [12]. This may be interesting if we want to estimate a global trend for the 12 plants plus individual fits. Model sp_mix in Code Block 5.13 use both previously defined design matrices Bg and Bi.

---

[12]Yes, this is also known as a mixed-effect model, you might recall the related concept we discussed in Chapter 4.

Code 5.13

```
1  with pm.Model() as sp_mix:
2      τ = pm.HalfCauchy("τ", 1)
3      βg = pm.Normal("βg", mu=0, sigma=τ, shape=Bg.shape[1])
4      μg = pm.Deterministic("μg", pm.math.dot(Bg, βg))
5      βi = pm.Normal("βi", mu=0, sigma=τ, shape=(Bi.shape[1], groups))
6      μi = pm.Deterministic("μi", pm.math.dot(Bi, βi))
7      σ = pm.HalfNormal("σ", 1)
8      up = pm.Normal("up", μg+μi[:,index].T.ravel(), σ, observed=uptake)
9      idata_sp_mix = pm.sample(2000, return_inferencedata=True)
```

Figure 5.14 show the fit of model `sp_mix`. One advantage of this model is that we can decompose the individual fit (in blue) into two terms, a global trend, in black, and the deviation of that trend for each plant, in gray. Notice how the global trend, in black, is repeated in each subplot. We can see that the deviations are different not only in the average uptake, i.e. they are not flat straight lines, but they are also different, to various extents, in the shape of their functional responses.

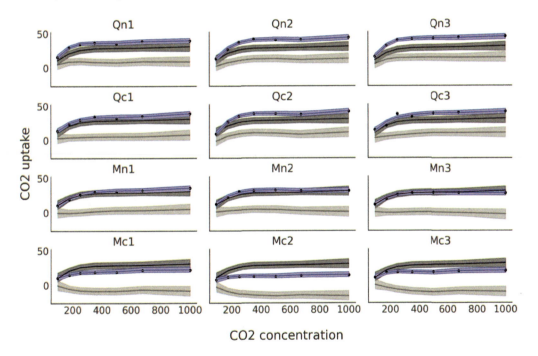

FIGURE 5.14
CO_2 uptake measured at seven CO_2 concentrations for 12 plants. The blue line is the mean spline fit from model in Code Block 5.13 and the gray shaded curve represents the 94% HDI interval for that fit. This fit is decomposed into two terms. In black, and a dark gray band, the global contribution and in gray, and a light gray band, the deviations from that global contribution. The blue line, and blue band, is the sum of the global trend and deviations from it.

Figure 5.15 shows that according to LOO `sp_mix` is a better model than the other two. We can see there is still some uncertainty about this statement as the standard errors for models `sp_mix` and `sp_individual` partially overlap. We can also see that models `sp_mix` and `sp_individual` are penalized harder than `sp_global` (the distance between the empty circle and black circle is shorter for `sp_global`). We note that LOO computation returns warnings about the estimated shape parameter of Pareto distribution being greater than 0.7. For this example we are going to stop here, but for a real analysis, we should pay further attention to these warnings and try to follow some of the actions described in Section 2.5.3

Code 5.14

```
1  cmp = az.compare({"global":idata_sp_global,
2                    "individual":idata_sp_individual,
3                    "mix":idata_sp_mix})
```

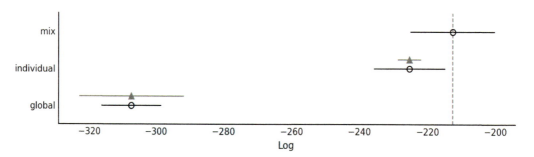

FIGURE 5.15
Model comparison using LOO for the 3 different CO_2 uptake models discussed in this chapter (`sp_global`, `sp_individual`, `sp_mix`). Models are ranked from higher predictive accuracy to lower. The open dots represent the values of LOO, the black dots are the in-sample predictive accuracy. The black segments represent the standard error for the LOO computations. The gray segments, centered at the triangles, represent the standard errors of the difference between the values of LOO for each model and the best ranked model.

5.8   Exercises

5E1.. Splines are quite powerful so its good to know when and where to use them. To reinforce this explain each of the following

(a) The differences between linear regression and splines.

(b) When you may want to use linear regression over splines

(c) Why splines is usually preferred over polynomial regression of high order.

5E2. Redo Figure 5.1 but fitting a polynomial of degree 0 and of degree 1. Does they look similar to any other type of model. Hint: you may want to use the code in the GitHub repository.

5E3. Redo Figure 5.2 but changing the value of one or the two knots. How the position of the knots affects the fit? You will find the code in the GitHub repository.

5E4. Below we provide some data. To each data fit a 0, 1, and 3 degree spline. Plot the fit, including the data and position of the knots. Use `knots = np.linspace(-0.8, 0.8, 4)`. Describe the fit.

    (a) `x = np.linspace(-1, 1., 200)` and `y = np.random.normal(2*x, 0.25)`

    (b) `x = np.linspace(-1, 1., 200)` and `y = np.random.normal(x**2, 0.25)`

    (c) pick a function you like.

5E5. In Code Block 5.5 we used a non-cyclic aware design matrix. Plot this design matrix. Then generate a cyclic design matrix. Plot this one too what is the difference?

5E6. Generate the following design matrices using Patsy.

Code 5.15

```
1  x = np.linspace(0., 1., 20)
2  knots = [0.25, 0.5, 0.75]
3
4  B0 = dmatrix("bs(x, knots=knots, degree=3, include_intercept=False) +1",
5              {"x": x, "knots":knots})
6  B1 = dmatrix("bs(x, knots=knots, degree=3, include_intercept=True) +1",
7              {"x": x, "knots":knots})
8  B2 = dmatrix("bs(x, knots=knots, degree=3, include_intercept=False) -1",
9              {"x": x, "knots":knots})
10 B3 = dmatrix("bs(x, knots=knots, degree=3, include_intercept=True) -1",
11              {"x": x, "knots":knots})
```

    (a) What is the shape of each one of the matrices? Can you justify the values for the shapes?

    (b) Could you explain what the arguments `include_intercept=True/False` and the `+1/-1` do? Try generating figures like 5.3 and 5.6 to help you answer this question

5E7. Refit the bike rental example using the options listed below. Visually compare the results and try to explain the results:

    (a) Code Block 5.4 but do not remove the first and last knots (i.e. without using [1:-1])

    (b) Use quantiles to set the knots instead of spacing them linearly.

    (c) Repeat the previous two points but with less knots

5E8. In the GitHub repository you will find the spectra dataset use it to:

    (a) Fit a cubic spline with knots `np.quantile(X, np.arange(0.1, 1, 0.02))` and a Gaussian prior (like in Code Block 5.6)

    (b) Fit a cubic spline with knots `np.quantile(X, np.arange(0.1, 1, 0.02))` and a Gaussian Random Walk prior (like in Code Block 5.7)

(c) Fit a cubic spline with knots `np.quantile(X, np.arange(0.1, 1, 0.1))` and a Gaussian prior (like in Code Block 5.6)

(d) compare the fits visually and using LOO

5M9. Redo Figure 5.2 extending `x_max` from 6 to 12.

(a) How this change affects the fit?

(b) What are the implications for extrapolation?

(c) add one more knot and make the necessary changes in the code so the fit actually use the 3 knots.

(d) change the position of the third new knot to improve the fit as much as possible.

5M10. For the bike rental example increase the number of knots. What is the effect on the fit? Change the width of the prior and visually evaluate the effect on the fit. What do you think the combination of knot number and prior weights controls?

5M11. Fit the baby regression example from Chapter 4 using splines.

5M12. In Code Block 5.5 we used a non-circular aware design matrix. Since we describe the hours in a day as cyclic, we want to use cyclic splines. However, there is one wrinkle. In the original dataset the hours range from 0 to 23, so using a circular spline patsy would treat 0 and 23 are the same. Still, we want a circular spline regression so perform the following steps.

(a) Duplicate the 0 hour data label it as 24.

(b) Generate a circular design matrix and a non-circular design matrix with this modified dataset. Plot the results and compare.

(c) Refit the bike spline dataset.

(d) Explain what the effect of the circular spine regression was using plots, numerical summaries, and diagnostics.

5M13. For the rent bike example we use a Gaussian as likelihood, this can be seen as a reasonable approximation when the number of counts is large, but still brings some problems, like predicting negative number of rented bikes (for example, at night when the observed number of rented bikes is close to zero). To fix this issue and improve our models we can try with other likelihoods:

(a) use a Poisson likelihood (hint you may need to restrict the β coefficients to be positive, and you can not normalize the data as we did in the example). How the fit differs from the example in the book. is this a better fit? In what sense?

(b) use a NegativeBinomial likelihood, how the fit differs from the previous two? Could you explain the differences (hint, the NegativeBinomial can be considered as a mixture model of Poisson distributions, which often helps to model overdispersed data)

(c) Use LOO to compare the spline model with Poisson and NegativeBinomial likelihoods. Which one has the best predictive performance?

(d) Can you justify the values of `p_loo` and the values of $\hat{\kappa}$?

(e) Use LOO-PIT to compare Gaussian, NegativeBinomial and Poisson models

5M14. Using the model in Code Block 5.6 as a guide and for $X \in [0,1]$, set $\tau \sim$ Laplace$(0,1)$:

(a) Sample and plot realizations from the prior for μ. Use different number and locations for the knots

(b) What is the prior expectation for $\mu(x_i)$ and how does it depend on the knots and X?

(c) What is the prior expectation for the standard deviations of $\mu(x_i)$ and how does it depend on the knots and X?

(d) Repeat the previous points for the prior predictive distribution

(e) Repeat the previous points using a $\mathcal{HC}(1)$

5M15. Fit the following data. Notice that the response variable is binary so you will need to adjust the likelihood accordingly and use a link function.

(a) a logistic regression from a previous chapter. Visually compare the results between both models.

(b) Space Influenza is a disease which affects mostly young and old people, but not middle-age folks. Fortunately, Space Influenza is not a serious concern as it is completely made up. In this dataset we have a record of people that got tested for Space Influenza and whether they are sick (1) or healthy (0) and also their age. Could you have solved this problem using logistic regression?

5M16.

Besides "hour" the bike dataset has other covariates, like "temperature". Fit a splines using both covariates. The simplest way to do this is by defining a separated spline/design matrix for each covariate. Fit a model with a NegativeBinomial likelihood.

(a) Run diagnostics to check the sampling is correct and modify the model and or sample hyperparameters accordingly.

(b) How the rented bikes depend on the hours of the day and how on the temperature?

(c) Generate a model with only the hour covariate to the one with the "hour" and "temperature". Compare both model using LOO, LOO-PIT and posterior predictive checks.

(d) Summarize all your findings

6

Time Series

"It is difficult to make predictions, especially about the future". This is true when dutch politician Karl Kristian Steincke allegedly said this sometime in the 1940s [1], and it is still true today especially if you are working on time series and forecasting problems. There are many applications of time series analysis, from making predictions with forecasting, to understanding what were the underlying latent factors in the historical trend. In this chapter we will discuss some Bayesian approaches to this problem. We will start by considering time series modeling as a regression problem, with the design matrices parsed from the timestamp information. We will then explore the approaches to model temporal correlation using autoregressive components. These models extend into a wider (more general) class of State Space Model and Bayesian Structural Time Series model (BSTS), and we will introduce a specialized inference method in the linear Gaussian cases: Kalman Filter. The remainder of the chapter will give a brief summary of model comparison as well as considerations to be made when choosing prior distributions for time series models.

6.1 An Overview of Time Series Problems

In many real life applications we observe data sequentially in time, generating timestamps along the way each time we make an observation. In addition to the observation itself, the timestamp information can be quite informative when:

- There is a temporal **trend**, for example, regional population, global GDP, annual CO_2 emissions in the US. Usually this is an overall pattern which we intuitively label as "growth" or "decline".

- There is some recurrent pattern correlated to time, called **seasonality** [2]. For example, changes in monthly temperature (higher in the summer and lower in the winter), monthly rainfall amounts (in many regions of the world this is lower in winter and higher during summer), daily coffee consumption in a given office building (higher in the weekdays and lower in the weekends), hourly number of bike rentals(higher in the day than during the night), like we saw in Chapter 5.

- The current data point informs the next data point in some way. In other words where noise or **residuals** are correlated [3]. For example, the daily number of cases resolved at a help desk, stock price, hourly temperature, hourly rainfall amounts.

---

[1] https://quoteinvestigator.com/2013/10/20/no-predict/

[2] There is also a subtlety that not all periodic patterns in the time series should be considered seasonal. A useful distinction to make is between cyclic and seasonal behavior. You can find a nice summary in https://robjhyndman.com/hyndsight/cyclicts/.

[3] This makes the observation not iid and not exchangeable. You can also see in Chapter 4 where we define residuals

It is thus quite natural and useful to consider the decomposition of a time series into:

$$y_t = \text{Trend}_t + \text{Seasonality}_t + \text{Residuals}_t \tag{6.1}$$

Most of the classical time series models are based on this decomposition. In this chapter, we will discuss modeling approaches on time series that display some level of temporal trend and seasonality, and explore methods to capture these regular patterns, as well as the less-regular patterns (e.g., residuals correlated in time).

6.2   Time Series Analysis as a Regression Problem

We will start with modeling a time series with a linear regression model on a widely used demo data set that appears in many tutorials (e.g., PyMC3, TensorFlow Probability) and it was used as an example in the Gaussian Processes for Machine Learning book by Rasmussen and Williams [128]. Atmospheric CO_2 measurements have been taken regularly at the Mauna Loa observatory in Hawaii since the late 1950s at hourly intervals. In many examples the observations are aggregated into monthly average as shown in Figure 6.1. We load the data into Python with Code Block 6.1, and also split the data set into training and testing set. We will fit the model using the training set only, and evaluate the forecast against the testing set.

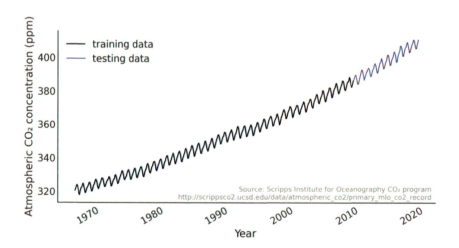

FIGURE 6.1

Monthly CO_2 measurements in Mauna Loa from 1966 January to 2019 February, split into training (shown in black) and testing (shown in blue) set. We can see a strong upward trend and seasonality pattern in the data.

Code 6.1

```
1  co2_by_month = pd.read_csv("../data/monthly_mauna_loa_co2.csv")
2  co2_by_month["date_month"] = pd.to_datetime(co2_by_month["date_month"])
3  co2_by_month["CO2"] = co2_by_month["CO2"].astype(np.float32)
```

```
4  co2_by_month.set_index("date_month", drop=True, inplace=True)
5
6  num_forecast_steps = 12 * 10   # Forecast the final ten years, given previous data
7  co2_by_month_training_data = co2_by_month[:-num_forecast_steps]
8  co2_by_month_testing_data = co2_by_month[-num_forecast_steps:]
```

Here we have a vector of observations of monthly atmospheric CO_2 concentrations y_t with $t = [0, \ldots, 636]$; each element associated with a timestamp. The month of the year could be nicely parsed into a vector of $[1, 2, 3, \ldots, 12, 1, 2, \ldots]$. Recall that for linear regression we can state the likelihood as follows:

$$Y \sim \mathcal{N}(\mathbf{X}\beta, \sigma) \tag{6.2}$$

Considering the seasonality effect, we can use the month of the year predictor directly to index a vector of regression coefficient. Here using Code Block 6.2, we dummy code the predictor into a design matrix with shape = (637, 12). Adding a linear predictor to the design matrix to capture the upward increasing trend we see in the data, we get the design matrix for the time series. You can see a subset of the design matrix in Figure 6.2.

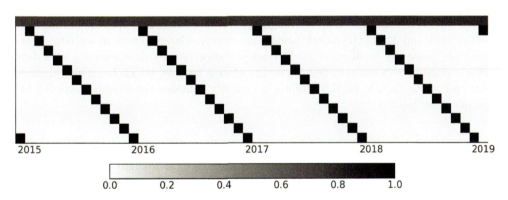

FIGURE 6.2
Design matrix with a linear component and month of the year component for a simple regression model for time series. The design matrix is transposed into *feature* * *timestamps* so it is easier to visualize. In the figure, the first row (index 0) contains continuous values between 0 and 1 representing the time and the linear growth. The rest of the rows (index 1 - 12) are dummy coding of month information. The color coding goes from black for 1 to light gray for 0.

Code 6.2

```
1  trend_all = np.linspace(0., 1., len(co2_by_month))[..., None]
2  trend_all = trend_all.astype(np.float32)
3  trend = trend_all[:-num_forecast_steps, :]
4
5  seasonality_all = pd.get_dummies(
6      co2_by_month.index.month).values.astype(np.float32)
```

```
7  seasonality = seasonality_all[:-num_forecast_steps, :]
8
9  _, ax = plt.subplots(figsize=(10, 4))
10 X_subset = np.concatenate([trend, seasonality], axis=-1)[-50:]
11 ax.imshow(X_subset.T)
```

Parsing timestamps to a design matrix

Treatment of timestamps could be tedious and error prone, especially when time zone is involved. Typical cyclical information we could parse from timestamp are, in order of resolution:

- Second of the hour (1, 2, ..., 60)

- Hour of the day (1, 2, ..., 24)

- Day of the week (Monday, Tuesday, ..., Sunday)

- Day of the month (1, 2, ..., 31)

- Holiday effect (New year's day, Easter holiday, International Workers' Day, Christmas day, etc)

- Month of the year (1, 2, ..., 12)

All of which could be parsed into a design matrix with dummy coding. Effects like day of the week and day of the month usually are closely related to human activities. For example, passenger numbers of public transportation usually show a strong week day effect; consumer spending might be higher after a payday, which is usually around the end of the month. In this chapter we mostly consider timestamps recorded at regular intervals.

We can now write down our first time series model as a regression problem, using `tfd.JointDistributionCoroutine`, using the same `tfd.JointDistributionCoroutine` API and TFP Bayesian modeling methods we introduced in Chapter 3.

Code 6.3

```
1  tfd = tfp.distributions
2  root = tfd.JointDistributionCoroutine.Root
3
4  @tfd.JointDistributionCoroutine
5  def ts_regression_model():
6      intercept = yield root(tfd.Normal(0., 100., name="intercept"))
7      trend_coeff = yield root(tfd.Normal(0., 10., name="trend_coeff"))
8      seasonality_coeff = yield root(
9          tfd.Sample(tfd.Normal(0., 1.),
10                     sample_shape=seasonality.shape[-1],
11                     name="seasonality_coeff"))
12     noise = yield root(tfd.HalfCauchy(loc=0., scale=5., name="noise_sigma"))
13     y_hat = (intercept[..., None] +
14              tf.einsum("ij,...->...i", trend, trend_coeff) +
15              tf.einsum("ij,...j->...i", seasonality, seasonality_coeff))
16     observed = yield tfd.Independent(
```

```
17        tfd.Normal(y_hat, noise[..., None]),
18        reinterpreted_batch_ndims=1,
19        name="observed")
```

As we mentioned in earlier chapters, TFP offers a lower level API compared to PyMC3. While it is more flexible to interact with low level modules and component (e.g., customized composable inference approaches), we usually end up with a bit more boilerplate code, and additional shape handling in the model using `tfp` compared to other PPLs. For example, in Code Block 6.3 we use `einsum` instead of `matmul` with Python Ellipsis so it can handle arbitrary *batch shape* (see Section 10.8.1 for more details).

Running the Code Block 6.3 gives us a regression model `ts_regression_model`. It has similar functionality to `tfd.Distribution` which we can utilize in our Bayesian workflow. To draw prior and prior predictive samples, we can call the `.sample(.)` method (see Code Block 6.4, with the result shown in Figure 6.3).

Code 6.4

```
1  # Draw 100 prior and prior predictive samples
2  prior_samples = ts_regression_model.sample(100)
3  prior_predictive_timeseries = prior_samples.observed
4
5  fig, ax = plt.subplots(figsize=(10, 5))
6  ax.plot(co2_by_month.index[:-num_forecast_steps],
7          tf.transpose(prior_predictive_timeseries), alpha=.5)
8  ax.set_xlabel("Year")
9  fig.autofmt_xdate()
```

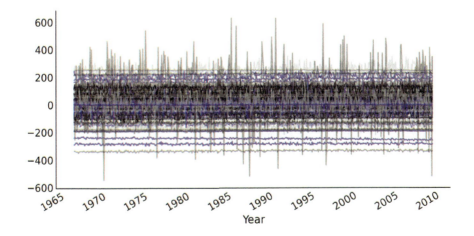

FIGURE 6.3
Prior predictive samples from a simple regression model for modeling the Monthly CO_2 measurements in Mauna Loa time series. Each line plot is one simulated time series. Since we use an uninformative prior the prior prediction has a pretty wide range.

We can now run inference of the regression model and format the result into an `az.InferenceData` object in Code Block 6.5.

Code 6.5

```
1  run_mcmc = tf.function(
2      tfp.experimental.mcmc.windowed_adaptive_nuts,
3      autograph=False, jit_compile=True)
4  mcmc_samples, sampler_stats = run_mcmc(
5      1000, ts_regression_model, n_chains=4, num_adaptation_steps=1000,
6      observed=co2_by_month_training_data["CO2"].values[None, ...])
7
8  regression_idata = az.from_dict(
9      posterior={
10         # TFP mcmc returns (num_samples, num_chains, ...), we swap
11         # the first and second axis below for each RV so the shape
12         # is what ArviZ expects.
13         k:np.swapaxes(v.numpy(), 1, 0)
14         for k, v in mcmc_samples._asdict().items()},
15     sample_stats={
16         k:np.swapaxes(sampler_stats[k], 1, 0)
17         for k in ["target_log_prob", "diverging", "accept_ratio", "n_steps"]}
18 )
```

To draw posterior predictive samples conditioned on the inference result, we can use the `.sample_distributions` method and condition on the posterior samples. In this case, since we would like to also plot the posterior predictive sample for the trend and seasonality components in the time series, while conditioning on both the training and testing data set. To visualize the forecasting ability of the model we construct the posterior predictive distributions in Code Block 6.6, with the result displayed in Figure 6.4 for the trend and seasonality components and in Figure 6.5 for the overall model fit and forecast.

Code 6.6

```
1  # We can draw posterior predictive sample with jd.sample_distributions()
2  # But since we want to also plot the posterior predictive distribution for
3  # each components, conditioned on both training and testing data, we
4  # construct the posterior predictive distribution as below:
5  nchains = regression_idata.posterior.dims["chain"]
6
7  trend_posterior = mcmc_samples.intercept + \
8      tf.einsum("ij,...->i...", trend_all, mcmc_samples.trend_coeff)
9  seasonality_posterior = tf.einsum(
10     "ij,...j->i...", seasonality_all, mcmc_samples.seasonality_coeff)
11
12 y_hat = trend_posterior + seasonality_posterior
13 posterior_predictive_dist = tfd.Normal(y_hat, mcmc_samples.noise_sigma)
14 posterior_predictive_samples = posterior_predictive_dist.sample()
```

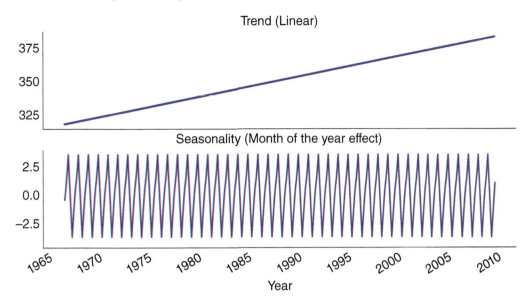

FIGURE 6.4
Posterior predictive samples of the trend component and seasonality component of a regression model for time series.

Looking at the out of sample prediction in Figure 6.5, we notice that:

1. The linear trend does not perform well when we forecast further into the future and gives forecast consistently lower than the actual observed. Specifically the atmospheric CO_2 does not increase linearly with a constant slope over the years [4]

2. The range of uncertainty is almost constant (sometimes also referred to as the forecast cone), where intuitively we expect the uncertainty to increase when we forecast farther into the future.

6.2.1 Design Matrices for Time Series

In the regression model above, a rather simplistic design matrix was used. We can get a better model to capture our knowledge of the observed time series by adding additional information to our design matrix.

Generally, a better trend component is the most important aspect for improving forecast performance: seasonality components are *usually* stationary [5] with easy to estimate parameters. Restated, there is a repeated pattern that forms a kind of a repeated measure. Thus most time series modeling involves designing a latent process that realistically captures the non-stationarity in the trend.

One approach that has been quite successful is using a local linear process for the trend component. Basically, it is a smooth trend that is linear within some range, with an intercept and coefficient that changes, or drifts, slowly over the observed time span. A prime example

---

[4]Which, it is unfortunate for our model and for our planet.

[5]A series is stationary if its characteristic properties such as means and covariances remain invariant across time.

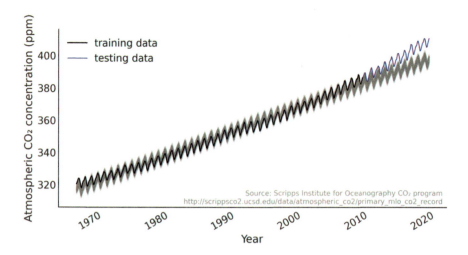

FIGURE 6.5

Posterior predictive samples from a simple regression model for time series in gray, with the actual data plotted in black and blue. While the overall fit is reasonable for the training set (plotted in black), the forecast (out of sample prediction) is poor as the underlying trend is accelerating more than linearly.

of such an application is Facebook Prophet [6], where a semi-smooth step linear function is used to model the trend [147]). By allowing the slope to change at some specific breakpoints, we can generate a trend line that could capture the long-term trend much better than a straight line. This is similar to the idea of indicator functions we discussed in Chapter 5.2. In a time series context we specify this idea mathematically in Equation 6.3

$$g(t) = (k + \mathbf{A}\delta)t + (m + \mathbf{A}\gamma) \tag{6.3}$$

where k is the (global) growth rate, δ is a vector of rate adjustments at each change point, m is the (global) intercept. $\mathbf{A}$ is a matrix with `shape=(n_t, n_s)` with n_s being the number of change points. At time t, $\mathbf{A}$ accumulates the drift effect δ of the slope. γ is set to $-s_j \times \delta_j$ (where s_j is the time location of the n_s change points) to make the trend line continuous. A regularized prior, like Laplace, is usually chosen for δ to express that we don't expect to see sudden or large change in the slope. You can see in Code Block 6.7 for an example of a randomly generated step linear function and its breakdown in Figure 6.6.

---

[6]`https://facebook.github.io/prophet/`

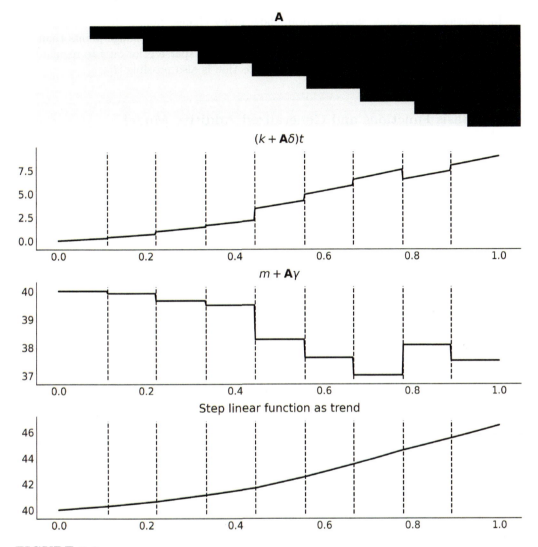

FIGURE 6.6

A step linear function as trend component for a time series model, generated with Code Block 6.7. The first panel is the design matrix **A**, with the same color coding that black for 1 and light gray for 0. The last panel is the resulting function $g(t)$ in Equation 6.3 that we could use as trend in a time series model. The two middle panels are the breakdown of the two components in Equation 6.3. Note how combining the two makes the resulting trend continuous.

Code 6.7

```
1  n_changepoints = 8
2  n_tp = 500
3  t = np.linspace(0, 1, n_tp)
4  s = np.linspace(0, 1, n_changepoints + 2)[1:-1]
5  A = (t[:, None] > s)
6
7  k, m = 2.5, 40
8  delta = np.random.laplace(.1, size=n_changepoints)
9  growth = (k + A @ delta) * t
10 offset = m + A @ (-s * delta)
11 trend = growth + offset
```

In practice, we usually specify a priori how many change points there are so **A** can be generated statically. One common approach is to specify more change points than you believe the time series actually displays, and place a more sparse prior on δ to regulate the posterior towards 0. Automatic change point detection is also possible [2].

6.2.2   Basis Functions and Generalized Additive Model

In our regression model defined in Code Block 6.3, we model the seasonality component with a sparse, index, matrix. An alternative is to use basis functions like B-spline (see Chapter 5), or Fourier basis function as in the Facebook Prophet model. Basis function as a design matrix might provide some nice properties like orthogonality (see Box **Mathematical properties of design matrix**), which makes numerically solving the linear equation more stable [145].

Fourier basis functions are a collection of sine and cosine functions that can be used for approximating arbitrary smooth seasonal effects [77]:

$$s(t) = \sum_{n=1}^{N}\left[a_n\cos\left(\frac{2\pi nt}{P}\right) + b_n\sin\left(\frac{2\pi nt}{P}\right)\right] \tag{6.4}$$

where P is the regular period the time series has (e.g. $P = 365.25$ for yearly data or $P = 7$ for weekly data, when the time variable is scaled in days). We can generate them statically with formulation as shown in Code Block 6.8, and visualize it in Figure 6.7.

Code 6.8

```
1 def gen_fourier_basis(t, p=365.25, n=3):
2     x = 2 * np.pi * (np.arange(n) + 1) * t[:, None] / p
3     return np.concatenate((np.cos(x), np.sin(x)), axis=1)
4
5 n_tp = 500
6 p = 12
7 t_monthly = np.asarray([i % p for i in range(n_tp)])
8 monthly_X = gen_fourier_basis(t_monthly, p=p, n=3)
```

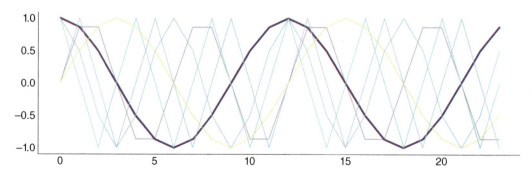

FIGURE 6.7
Fourier basis function with n=3. There are in total 6 predictors, where we highlighted the first one by setting the rest semi-transparent.

Fitting the seasonality using a design matrix generated from Fourier basis function as above requires estimating 2N parameters $\beta = [a_1, b_1, \ldots, a_N, b_N]$.

Regression models like Facebook Prophet are also referred to as a (GAM), as their response variable Y_t depends linearly on unknown smooth basis functions [7]. We also discussed other GAMs previously in Chapter 5.

> **Mathematical properties of design matrix**
>
> Mathematical properties of design matrices are studied quite extensively in the linear least squares problem setting, where we want to solve $min \mid Y - \mathbf{X}\beta \mid^2$ for β. We can often get a sense how stable the solution of β will be, or even possible to get a solution at all, by inspecting the property of matrix $\mathbf{X}^T\mathbf{X}$. One such property is the condition number, which is an indication of whether the solution of β may be prone to large numerical errors. For example, if the design matrix contains columns that are highly correlated (multicollinearity), the conditioned number will be large and the matrix $\mathbf{X}^T\mathbf{X}$ is ill-conditioned. Similar principle also applies in Bayesian modeling. An in-depth exploratory data analysis in your analyses workflow is useful no matter what formal modeling approach you are taking. Basis functions as a design matrix usually are well-conditioned.

A Facebook Prophet-like GAM for the monthly CO_2 measurements is expressed in Code Block 6.9. We assign weakly informative prior to k and m to express our knowledge that monthly measure is trending upward in general. This gives prior predictive samples in a similar range of what is actually being observed (see Figure 6.8).

Code 6.9

```
1  # Generate trend design matrix
2  n_changepoints = 12
3  n_tp = seasonality_all.shape[0]
4  t = np.linspace(0, 1, n_tp, dtype=np.float32)
5  s = np.linspace(0, max(t), n_changepoints + 2, dtype=np.float32)[1: -1]
6  A = (t[:, None] > s).astype(np.float32)
7  # Generate seasonality design matrix
8  # Set n=6 here so that there are 12 columns (same as `seasonality_all`)
9  X_pred = gen_fourier_basis(np.where(seasonality_all)[1],
10                             p=seasonality_all.shape[-1],
11                             n=6)
12 n_pred = X_pred.shape[-1]
13
14 @tfd.JointDistributionCoroutine
15 def gam():
16     beta = yield root(tfd.Sample(
17         tfd.Normal(0., 1.), sample_shape=n_pred, name="beta"))
18     seasonality = tf.einsum("ij,...j->...i", X_pred, beta)
19
20     k = yield root(tfd.HalfNormal(10., name="k"))
21     m = yield root(tfd.Normal(
```

---

[7] A demo of the design matrix used in Facebook Prophet could be found in http://prophet.mbrouns.com from a PyMCon 2020 presentation.

```
22            co2_by_month_training_data["CO2"].mean(), scale=5., name="m"))
23    tau = yield root(tfd.HalfNormal(10., name="tau"))
24    delta = yield tfd.Sample(
25        tfd.Laplace(0., tau), sample_shape=n_changepoints, name="delta")
26
27    growth_rate = k[..., None] + tf.einsum("ij,...j->...i", A, delta)
28    offset = m[..., None] + tf.einsum("ij,...j->...i", A, -s * delta)
29    trend = growth_rate * t + offset
30
31    y_hat = seasonality + trend
32    y_hat = y_hat[..., :co2_by_month_training_data.shape[0]]
33
34    noise_sigma = yield root(tfd.HalfNormal(scale=5., name="noise_sigma"))
35    observed = yield tfd.Independent(
36        tfd.Normal(y_hat, noise_sigma[..., None]),
37        reinterpreted_batch_ndims=1,
38        name="observed")
```

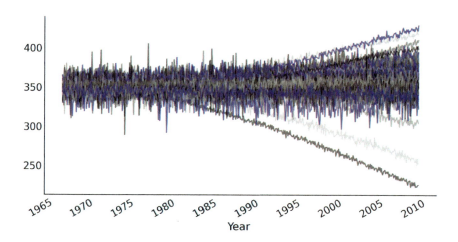

FIGURE 6.8

Prior predictive samples from a Facebook Prophet-like GAM with a weakly informative prior on trend related parameters generated from Code Block 6.9. Each line plot is one simulated time series. The predictive samples are now in a similar range to what actually being observed, particularly when comparing this figure to Figure 6.3.

After inference, we can generate posterior predictive samples. As you can see in Figure 6.9, the forecast performance is better than the simple regression model in Figure 6.5. Note that in Taylor and Letham (2018) [147], the generative process for forecast is not identical to the generative model, as the step linear function is evenly spaced with the change point predetermined. It is recommended that for forecasting, at each time point we first determine whether that time point would be a change point, with a probability proportional to the number of predefined change points divided by the total number of observations, and then generate a new delta from the posterior distribution $\delta_{new} \sim \text{Laplace}(0, \tau)$. Here however, to simplify the generative process we simply use the linear trend from the last period.

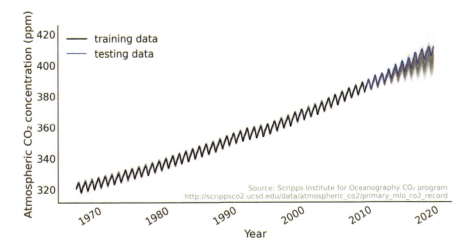

FIGURE 6.9
Posterior predictive samples from a Facebook Prophet-like from Code Block 6.9 in gray, with the actual data plotted in black and blue.

6.3 Autoregressive Models

One characteristic of time series is the sequential dependency of the observations. This usually introduces structured errors that are correlated temporally on previous observation(s) or error(s). A typical example is autoregressive-ness. In an autoregressive model, the distribution of output at time t is parameterized by a linear function of previous observations. Consider a first-order autoregressive model (usually we write that as AR(1) with a Gaussian likelihood:

$$y_t \sim \mathcal{N}(\alpha + \rho y_{t-1}, \sigma) \tag{6.5}$$

The distribution of y_t follows a Normal distribution with the location being a linear function of y_{t-1}. In Python, we can write down such a model with a for loop that explicitly builds out the autoregressive process. For example, in Code Block 6.10 we create an AR(1) process using `tfd.JointDistributionCoroutine` with $\alpha = 0$, and draw random samples from it by conditioned on $\sigma = 1$ and different values of ρ. The result is shown in Figure 6.10.

Code 6.10

```
1   n_t = 200
2
3   @tfd.JointDistributionCoroutine
4   def ar1_with_forloop():
5       sigma = yield root(tfd.HalfNormal(1.))
6       rho = yield root(tfd.Uniform(-1., 1.))
7       x0 = yield tfd.Normal(0., sigma)
8       x = [x0]
9       for i in range(1, n_t):
10          x_i = yield tfd.Normal(x[i-1] * rho, sigma)
11          x.append(x_i)
12
13  nplot = 4
14  fig, axes = plt.subplots(nplot, 1)
15  for ax, rho in zip(axes, np.linspace(-1.01, 1.01, nplot)):
16      test_samples = ar1_with_forloop.sample(value=(1., rho))
17      ar1_samples = tf.stack(test_samples[2:])
18      ax.plot(ar1_samples, alpha=.5, label=r"$\rho$=%.2f" % rho)
19      ax.legend(bbox_to_anchor=(1, 1), loc="upper left",
20              borderaxespad=0., fontsize=10)
```

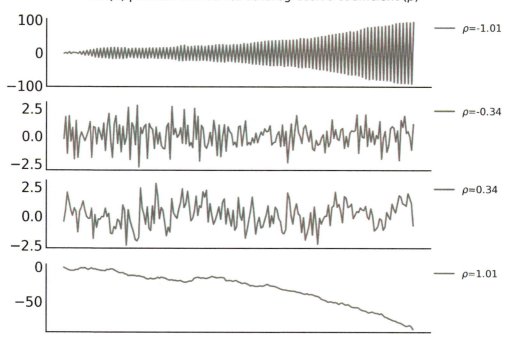

FIGURE 6.10

Random sample of an AR(1) process with $\sigma = 1$ and different ρ. Note that the AR(1) process is not stationary when $| \rho | > 1$.

Using a for-loop to generate the time series random variable is pretty straightforward, but now each time point is a random variable, which makes working with it quite difficult (e.g., it does not scale well with more time points). When possible, we prefer writing models that use vectorized operations. The model above can be rewritten without using for-loop by using the Autoregressive distribution `tfd.Autoregressive` in TFP, which takes a `distribution_fn` that represents Equation 6.5, a function that takes y_{t-1} as input and returns the distribution of y_t. However, the Autoregressive distribution in TFP only retains the end state of the process, the distribution representing the random variable y_t after the initial value y_0 iterates for t steps. To get all the time steps of a AR process, we need to express Equation 6.5 a bit differently using a backshift operator, also called Lag operator) $\mathbf{B}$ that shifts the time series $\mathbf{B}y_t = y_{t-1}$ for all $t > 0$. Re-expressing Equation 6.5 with a backshift operator $\mathbf{B}$ we have $Y \sim \mathcal{N}(\rho \mathbf{B}Y, \sigma)$. Conceptually, you can think of it as evaluating a vectorized likelihood `Normal($\rho$ * y[:-1], $\sigma$).log_prob(y[1:])`. In Code Block 6.11 we construct the same generative AR(1) model for `n_t` steps with the `tfd.Autoregressive` API. Note that we did not construct the backshift operator $\mathbf{B}$ explicitly by just generating the outcome y_{t-1} directly shown in Code Block 6.11, where a Python function `ar1_fun` applies the backshift operation and generates the distribution for the next step.

Code 6.11

```
1  @tfd.JointDistributionCoroutine
2  def ar1_without_forloop():
3      sigma = yield root(tfd.HalfNormal(1.))
4      rho = yield root(tfd.Uniform(-1., 1.))
5
6      def ar1_fun(x):
7          # We apply the backshift operation here
8          x_tm1 = tf.concat([tf.zeros_like(x[..., :1]), x[..., :-1]], axis=-1)
9          loc = x_tm1 * rho[..., None]
10         return tfd.Independent(tfd.Normal(loc=loc, scale=sigma[..., None]),
11                                reinterpreted_batch_ndims=1)
12
13     dist = yield tfd.Autoregressive(
14         distribution_fn=ar1_fun,
15         sample0=tf.zeros([n_t], dtype=rho.dtype),
16         num_steps=n_t)
```

We are now ready to extend the Facebook Prophet -like GAM above with AR(1) process as likelihood. But before we do that let us rewrite the GAM in Code Block 6.9 slightly differently into Code Block 6.12.

Code 6.12

```
1  def gam_trend_seasonality():
2      beta = yield root(tfd.Sample(
3          tfd.Normal(0., 1.), sample_shape=n_pred, name="beta"))
4      seasonality = tf.einsum("ij,...j->...i", X_pred, beta)
5
6      k = yield root(tfd.HalfNormal(10., name="k"))
7      m = yield root(tfd.Normal(
8          co2_by_month_training_data["CO2"].mean(), scale=5., name="m"))
9      tau = yield root(tfd.HalfNormal(10., name="tau"))
10     delta = yield tfd.Sample(
11         tfd.Laplace(0., tau), sample_shape=n_changepoints, name="delta")
```

```
12
13        growth_rate = k[..., None] + tf.einsum("ij,...j->...i", A, delta)
14        offset = m[..., None] + tf.einsum("ij,...j->...i", A, -s * delta)
15        trend = growth_rate * t + offset
16        noise_sigma = yield root(tfd.HalfNormal(scale=5., name="noise_sigma"))
17        return seasonality, trend, noise_sigma
18
19   def generate_gam(training=True):
20
21        @tfd.JointDistributionCoroutine
22        def gam():
23            seasonality, trend, noise_sigma = yield from gam_trend_seasonality()
24            y_hat = seasonality + trend
25            if training:
26                y_hat = y_hat[..., :co2_by_month_training_data.shape[0]]
27
28            # likelihood
29            observed = yield tfd.Independent(
30                tfd.Normal(y_hat, noise_sigma[..., None]),
31                reinterpreted_batch_ndims=1,
32                name="observed"
33            )
34
35        return gam
36
37   gam = generate_gam()
```

Comparing Code Block 6.12 with Code Block 6.9, we see two major differences:

1. We split out the construction of the trend and seasonality components (with their priors) into a separate function, and in the `tfd.JointDistributionCoroutine` model block we use a **yield from** statement so we get the identical `tfd.JointDistributionCoroutine` model in both Code Blocks;

2. We wrap the `tfd.JointDistributionCoroutine` in another Python function so it is easier to condition on both the training and testing set.

Code Block 6.12 is a much more modular approach. We can write down a GAM with an AR(1) likelihood by just changing the likelihood part. This is what we do in Code Block 6.13.

Code 6.13

```
1    def generate_gam_ar_likelihood(training=True):
2
3        @tfd.JointDistributionCoroutine
4        def gam_with_ar_likelihood():
5            seasonality, trend, noise_sigma = yield from gam_trend_seasonality()
6            y_hat = seasonality + trend
7            if training:
8                y_hat = y_hat[..., :co2_by_month_training_data.shape[0]]
9
10           # Likelihood
11           rho = yield root(tfd.Uniform(-1., 1., name="rho"))
```

```
12          def ar_fun(y):
13              loc = tf.concat([tf.zeros_like(y[..., :1]), y[..., :-1]],
14                             axis=-1) * rho[..., None] + y_hat
15              return tfd.Independent(
16                  tfd.Normal(loc=loc, scale=noise_sigma[..., None]),
17                  reinterpreted_batch_ndims=1)
18          observed = yield tfd.Autoregressive(
19              distribution_fn=ar_fun,
20              sample0=tf.zeros_like(y_hat),
21              num_steps=1,
22              name="observed")
23
24      return gam_with_ar_likelihood
25
26  gam_with_ar_likelihood = generate_gam_ar_likelihood()
```

Another way to think about AR(1) model here is as extending our linear regression notion to include an observation dependent column in the design matrix, and setting the element of this column x_i being y_{i-1}. The autoregressive coefficient ρ is then no different to any other regression coefficient, which is just telling us what is the linear contribution of the previous observation to the expectation of the current observation [8]. In this model, we found that the effect is almost negligible by inspecting the posterior distribution of ρ (see Figure 6.11):

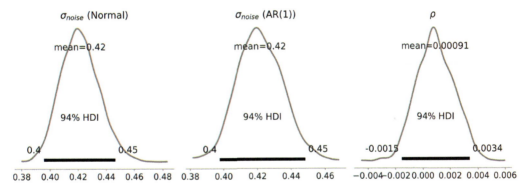

FIGURE 6.11
Posterior distribution of the parameters in the likelihood for the Facebook Prophet -like GAM defined in Code Block 6.13. Leftmost panel is the σ in the model with a Normal likelihood, middle and rightmost panels are σ and ρ in the model with an AR(1) likelihood. Both models return a similar estimation of σ, with the ρ estimated centered around 0.

Instead of using an AR(k) likelihood, we can also include AR in a time series model by adding a latent AR component to the linear prediction. This is the `gam_with_latent_ar` model in Code Block 6.14.

---

[8]That is why is called autoregressive, it applies a linear regression to itself. Hence the similar naming to the autocorrelation diagnostic introduced in Section 2.4.5.

Code 6.14

```
 1  def generate_gam_ar_latent(training=True):
 2
 3      @tfd.JointDistributionCoroutine
 4      def gam_with_latent_ar():
 5          seasonality, trend, noise_sigma = yield from gam_trend_seasonality()
 6
 7          # Latent AR(1)
 8          ar_sigma = yield root(tfd.HalfNormal(.1, name="ar_sigma"))
 9          rho = yield root(tfd.Uniform(-1., 1., name="rho"))
10          def ar_fun(y):
11              loc = tf.concat([tf.zeros_like(y[..., :1]), y[..., :-1]],
12                              axis=-1) * rho[..., None]
13              return tfd.Independent(
14                  tfd.Normal(loc=loc, scale=ar_sigma[..., None]),
15                  reinterpreted_batch_ndims=1)
16          temporal_error = yield tfd.Autoregressive(
17              distribution_fn=ar_fun,
18              sample0=tf.zeros_like(trend),
19              num_steps=trend.shape[-1],
20              name="temporal_error")
21
22          # Linear prediction
23          y_hat = seasonality + trend + temporal_error
24          if training:
25              y_hat = y_hat[..., :co2_by_month_training_data.shape[0]]
26
27          # Likelihood
28          observed = yield tfd.Independent(
29              tfd.Normal(y_hat, noise_sigma[..., None]),
30              reinterpreted_batch_ndims=1,
31              name="observed"
32          )
33
34      return gam_with_latent_ar
35
36  gam_with_latent_ar = generate_gam_ar_latent()
```

With the explicit latent AR process, we are adding a random variable with the same size as the observed data to the model. Since it is now an explicit component added to the linear prediction $\hat{Y}$, we can interpret the AR process to be complementary to, or even part of, the trend component. We can visualize the latent AR component after inference similar to the trend and seasonality components of a time series model (see Figure 6.12).

Another way to interpret the explicit latent AR process is that it captures the temporally correlated *residuals*, so we expect the posterior estimation of the σ_{noise} will be smaller compared to the model without this component. In Figure 6.13 we display the posterior distribution of σ_{noise}, σ_{AR}, and ρ for model `gam_with_latent_ar`. In comparison to model `gam_with_ar_likelihood`, we indeed get a lower estimation of σ_{noise}, with a much higher estimation of ρ.

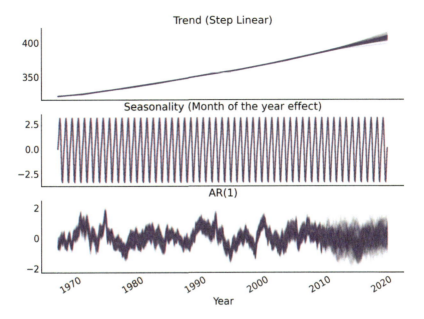

FIGURE 6.12
Posterior predictive samples of the trend, seasonality, and AR(1) components of the GAM based time series model `gam_with_latent_ar` specified in Code Block 6.14.

6.3.1 Latent AR Process and Smoothing

A latent process is quite powerful at capturing the subtle trends in the observed time series. It can even approximate some arbitrary functions. To see that let us consider modeling a toy problem with a time series model that contains a latent (GRW) component, as formulated in Equation 6.6.

$$z_i \sim \mathcal{N}(z_{i-1}, \sigma_z^2) \text{ for } i = 1, \ldots, N$$
$$y_i \sim \mathcal{N}(z_i, \sigma_y^2) \tag{6.6}$$

The GRW here is the same as an AR(1) process with $\rho = 1$. By placing different prior on σ_z and σ_y in Equation 6.6, we can emphasize how much of the variance in the observed data should be accounted for in the GRW, and how much is iid *noise*. We can also compute the ratio $\alpha = \frac{\sigma_y^2}{\sigma_z^2 + \sigma_y^2}$, where α is in the range $[0, 1]$ that can be interpret as the degree of smoothing. Thus we can express the model in Equation 6.6 equivalently as Equation 6.7.

$$z_i \sim \mathcal{N}(z_{i-1}, (1 - \alpha)\sigma^2) \text{ for } i = 1, \ldots, N$$
$$y_i \sim \mathcal{N}(z_i, \alpha\sigma^2) \tag{6.7}$$

Our latent GRW model in Equation 6.7 could be written in TFP in Code Block 6.15. By placing informative prior on α we can control how much "smoothing" we would like to see in the latent GRW (larger α gives smoother approximation). Let us fit the model `smoothing_grw` with some noisy observations simulated from an arbitrary function. The

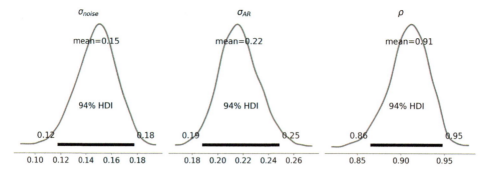

FIGURE 6.13

Posterior distribution of σ_{noise}, σ_{AR}, and ρ of the AR(1) latent component for `gam_with_latent_ar` specified in Code Block 6.14. Note not to be confused with Figure 6.11 where we displays posterior distribution of parameters from 2 different GAMs.

data is shown as black solid dots in Figure 6.14, with the fitted latent Random Walk displayed in the same Figure. As you can see we can approximate the underlying function pretty well.

Code 6.15

```
1  @tfd.JointDistributionCoroutine
2  def smoothing_grw():
3      alpha = yield root(tfd.Beta(5, 1.))
4      variance = yield root(tfd.HalfNormal(10.))
5      sigma0 = tf.sqrt(variance * alpha)
6      sigma1 = tf.sqrt(variance * (1. - alpha))
7      z = yield tfd.Sample(tfd.Normal(0., sigma0), num_steps)
8      observed = yield tfd.Independent(
9          tfd.Normal(tf.math.cumsum(z, axis=-1), sigma1[..., None]))
```

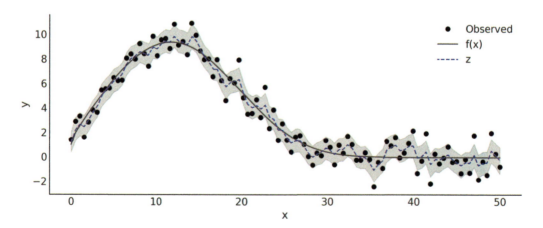

FIGURE 6.14

Simulated observations from $y \sim \text{Normal}(f(x), 1)$ with $f(x) = e^{1+x^{0.5}-e^{\frac{x}{15}}}$, and the inferred latent Gaussian Random Walk. The gray semi-transparent region is the posterior 94% HDI interval of the latent Gaussian Random Walk z, with the posterior mean plot in dash blue line.

There are a few other interesting properties of the AR process, with connection to the Gaussian Process [128]. For example, you might find that the Autoregressive model *alone* is useless to capture the long-term trend. Even though the model seems to fit well the observation, during forecast you will observe the forecast value regress to the mean of the last few time steps very quickly. Same as what you will observe using the Gaussian Process with a constant mean function [9].

An autoregressive component as an additional trend component could place some challenges to model inference. For example, scaling could be an issue as we are adding a random variable with the same shape as the observed time series. We might have an unidentifiable model when both the trend component and the AR process are flexible, as the AR process alone already has the ability to approximate the underlying trend, a smoothed function, of the observed data as we have seen here.

6.3.2   (S)AR(I)MA(X)

Many classical time series models share a similar autoregressive like pattern, where you have some latent parameter at time t that is dependent on the value of itself or another parameter at $t - k$. Two examples of these models are

- Autoregressive conditional heteroscedasticity (ARCH) model, where the scale of the residuals vary over time;

- Moving average (MA) model, which is a linear combination of previous residuals are added to the mean of the series.

Some of these classical time series models could be combined into more complex models, one of such extensions is the Seasonal AutoRegressive Integrated Moving Average with eXogenous regressors model (SARIMAX). While the naming might look intimidating, the basic concept is largely a straightforward combination of the AR and MA model. Extending the AR model with MA we get:

$$y_t = \alpha + \sum_{i=1}^{p} \phi_i y_{t-i} + \sum_{j=1}^{q} \theta_j \epsilon_{t-j} + \epsilon_t \qquad (6.8)$$

$$\epsilon_t \sim \mathcal{N}(0, \sigma^2)$$

where p is the order of the autoregressive model and q is the order of the moving average model. Conventionally, we write models as such being ARMA(p, q). Similarly, for seasonal ARMA we have:

$$y_t = \alpha + \sum_{i=1}^{p} \phi_i y_{t-period-i} + \sum_{j=1}^{q} \theta_j \epsilon_{t-period-j} + \epsilon_t \qquad (6.9)$$

The integrated part of an ARIMA model refers to the summary statistics of a time series: order of integration. Denoted as $I(d)$, a time series is integrated to order d if taking repeated differences d times yields a stationary series. Following Box and Jenkins ([23]), we repeatedly take difference of the observed time series as a preprocessing step to account for the $I(d)$

---

[9]Actually, the AR example in this section *is* a Gaussian Process.

part of an ARIMA(p,d,q) model, and model the resulting differenced series as a stationary process with ARMA(p,q). The operation itself is also quite standard in Python. We can use `numpy.diff` where the first difference computed is `delta_y[i] = y[i] - y[i-1]` along a given axis, and higher differences are calculated by repeating the same operation recursively on the resulting array.

If we have an additional regressor $\mathbf{X}$, in the model above α is replaced with the linear prediction $\mathbf{X}\beta$. We will apply the same differencing operation on $\mathbf{X}$ if $d > 0$. Note that we can have either seasonal (SARIMA) or exogenous regressors (ARIMAX) but not both.

Notation for (S)AR(I)MA(X)

Typically, ARIMA models are denoted as ARIMA(p,d,q), which is to say we have a model containing order p of AR, d degree of I, and order q of MA. For example, ARIMA(1,0,0) is just a AR(1). We denote seasonal ARIMA models as SARIMA$(p, d, q)(P, D, Q)_s$, where s refers to the number of periods in each season, and the uppercase P, Q are the seasonal counter part of the ARIMA model p, d, q. Sometimes seasonal ARIMA are denoted also as SARIMA$(p, d, q)(P, D, Q, s)$. If there are exogenous regressors, we write ARIMAX$(p, d, q)\mathbf{X}[k]$ with $\mathbf{X}[k]$ indicating we have a k columns design matrix $\mathbf{X}$.

As the second example in this chapter, we will use different ARIMA to model the time series of the monthly live births in the United States from 1948 to 1979 [143]. The data is shown in Figure 6.15.

FIGURE 6.15
Monthly live births in the United States (1948-1979). Y-axis shows the number of births in thousands.

We will start with a SARIMA$(1, 1, 1)(1, 1, 1)_{12}$ model. First we load and pre-process the observed time series in Code Block 6.16.

Code 6.16

```
1  us_monthly_birth = pd.read_csv("../data/monthly_birth_usa.csv")
2  us_monthly_birth["date_month"] = pd.to_datetime(us_monthly_birth["date_month"])
3  us_monthly_birth.set_index("date_month", drop=True, inplace=True)
4
5  # y ~ Sarima(1,1,1)(1,1,1)[12]
6  p, d, q = (1, 1, 1)
7  P, D, Q, period = (1, 1, 1, 12)
8  # Time series data: us_monthly_birth.shape = (372,)
9  observed = us_monthly_birth["birth_in_thousands"].values
10 # Integrated to seasonal order $D$
11 for _ in range(D):
12     observed = observed[period:] - observed[:-period]
13 # Integrated to order $d$
14 observed = tf.constant(np.diff(observed, n=d), tf.float32)
```

At time of writing TFP does not have a dedicated implementation of an ARMA distribution. To run inference of our SARIMA model, TFP requires a Python **callable** representing the log posterior density function (up to some constant [94]). In this case, we can archive that by implementing the likelihood function of $SARMA(1,1)(1,1)_{12}$ (since the I part is already dealt with via differencing). We do that in Code Block 6.17 using a `tf.while_loop` to construct the residual time series ϵ_t and evaluated on a Normal distribution [10]. From the programming point of view, the biggest challenge here is to make sure the shape is correct when we index to the time series. To avoid additional control flow to check whether some of the indexes are valid (e.g, we cannot index to $t-1$ and $t-period-1$ when $t=0$), we pad the time series with zeros.

Code 6.17

```
1  def likelihood(mu0, sigma, phi, theta, sphi, stheta):
2      batch_shape = tf.shape(mu0)
3      y_extended = tf.concat(
4          [tf.zeros(tf.concat([[r], batch_shape], axis=0), dtype=mu0.dtype),
5           tf.einsum("...,j->j...",
6                     tf.ones_like(mu0, dtype=observed.dtype),
7                     observed)],
8          axis=0)
9      eps_t = tf.zeros_like(y_extended, dtype=observed.dtype)
10
11     def arma_onestep(t, eps_t):
12         t_shift = t + r
13         # AR
14         y_past = tf.gather(y_extended, t_shift - (np.arange(p) + 1))
15         ar = tf.einsum("...p,p...->...", phi, y_past)
16         # MA
17         eps_past = tf.gather(eps_t, t_shift - (np.arange(q) + 1))
18         ma = tf.einsum("...q,q...->...", theta, eps_past)
19         # Seasonal AR
20         sy_past = tf.gather(y_extended, t_shift - (np.arange(P) + 1) * period)
21         sar = tf.einsum("...p,p...->...", sphi, sy_past)
```

---

[10]The Stan implementation of SARIMA can be found in `https://github.com/asael697/varstan`.

```
22          # Seasonal MA
23          seps_past = tf.gather(eps_t, t_shift - (np.arange(Q) + 1) * period)
24          sma = tf.einsum("...q,q...->...", stheta, seps_past)
25
26          mu_at_t = ar + ma + sar + sma + mu0
27          eps_update = tf.gather(y_extended, t_shift) - mu_at_t
28          epsilon_t_next = tf.tensor_scatter_nd_update(
29              eps_t, [[t_shift]], eps_update[None, ...])
30          return t+1, epsilon_t_next
31
32      t, eps_output_ = tf.while_loop(
33          lambda t, *_: t < observed.shape[-1],
34          arma_onestep,
35          loop_vars=(0, eps_t),
36          maximum_iterations=observed.shape[-1])
37      eps_output = eps_output_[r:]
38      return tf.reduce_sum(
39          tfd.Normal(0, sigma[None, ...]).log_prob(eps_output), axis=0)
```

Adding the prior to the unknown parameters (in this case, `mu0`, `sigma`, `phi`, `theta`, `sphi`, and `stheta`), we can generate the posterior density function for inference. This is shown in Code Block 6.18, with a resulting `target_log_prob_fn` that we sample from in Code Block 6.18 [11].

Code 6.18

```
1  @tfd.JointDistributionCoroutine
2  def sarima_priors():
3      mu0 = yield root(tfd.StudentT(df=6, loc=0, scale=2.5, name='mu0'))
4      sigma = yield root(tfd.HalfStudentT(df=7, loc=0, scale=1., name='sigma'))
5
6      phi = yield root(tfd.Sample(tfd.Normal(0, 0.5), p, name='phi'))
7      theta = yield root(tfd.Sample(tfd.Normal(0, 0.5), q, name='theta'))
8      sphi = yield root(tfd.Sample(tfd.Normal(0, 0.5), P, name='sphi'))
9      stheta = yield root(tfd.Sample(tfd.Normal(0, 0.5), Q, name='stheta'))
10
11 target_log_prob_fn = lambda *x: sarima_priors.log_prob(*x) + likelihood(*x)
```

The preprocessing of the time series to account for the *integrated* part in Code Block 6.16 and the likelihood implementation in Code Block 6.17 could be refactored into a helper Python `Class` that flexibility generate different SARIMA likelihood. For example, Table 6.3.2 shows the model comparison between the SARIMA$(1,1,1)(1,1,1)_{12}$ model from Code Block 6.18 and a similar SARIMA$(0,1,2)(1,1,1)_{12}$ model.

---

[11]For brevity, we omitted the MCMC sampling code here. You can find the details in the accompanying Jupyter Notebook.

	rank	loo	p_loo	d_loo	weight	se	dse
SARIMA$(0,1,2)(1,1,1)_{12}$	0	-1235.60	7.51	0.00	0.5	15.41	0.00
SARIMA$(1,1,1)(1,1,1)_{12}$	1	-1235.97	8.30	0.37	0.5	15.47	6.29

TABLE 6.1
Summary of model comparison using LOO for different SARIMA models. The LOO results here are in log scale.

6.4 State Space Models

In the implementation of the ARMA log-likelihood function above (Code Block 6.17), we iterate through time steps to condition on the observations and construct some latent variables for that time slice. Indeed, unless the models are of a very specific and simple variety (e.g. the Markov dependencies between each two consecutive time steps make it possible to reduce the generative process into vectorized operations), this recursive pattern is a very natural way to express time series models. A powerful, general formulation of this pattern is the State Space model, a discrete-time process where we assume at each time step some latent states X_t evolves from previous step X_{t-1} (a Markov Sequence), and we observed Y_t that is some projection from the latent states X_t to the observable space [12]:

$$
X_0 \sim p(X_0)
$$
$$
\text{for t in 0...T:}
$$
$$
Y_t \sim p^\psi(Y_t \mid X_t)
$$
$$
X_{t+1} \sim p^\theta(X_{t+1} \mid X_t)
$$

(6.10)

where $p(X_0)$ is the prior distribution of the latent states at time step 0, $p^\theta(X_{t+1} \mid X_t)$ is the transition probability distribution parameterized by a vector of parameter θ that describes the system dynamics, and $p^\psi(Y_t \mid X_t)$ being the observation distribution parameterized by ψ that describes the measurement at time t conditioned on the latent states.

---

[12]It might be useful to first consider "space" here being some multi-dimensional Euclidean spaces, so X_t and Y_t is some multi-dimensional array/tensor when we do computations in Python.

Implementation of state space model for efficient computation

There is a harmony between mathematical formulation and computation implementation of a State Space model with API like `tf.while_loop` or `tf.scan`. Unlike using a Python **for** loop or **while** loop, they require compiling the loop body into a function that takes the same structure of tensors as input and outputs. This functional style of implementation is useful to make explicit how the latent states are being transitioned at each time step and how the measurement, from latent state to observed, should be outputted. It is worth noting that implementation of state space model and its associated inference algorithm like Kalman filter also involved design decisions about where to place some of the initial computation. In the formulation above, we place a prior on the initial latent condition, and the first observation is a measure of the initial state directly. However, it is equally valid to make a transition on the latent state at step 0, then make the first observation with modification to the prior distribution the two approaches are equivalent.

There is however a subtle trickiness in dealing with shape when implementing filters for time series problems. The main challenge is where to place the time dimension. An obvious choice is to place it at axis 0, as it becomes nature to do `time_series[t]` with t being some time index. Moreover, loop construction using `tf.scan` or `theano.scan` to loop over a time series automatically places the time dimension on axis 0. However, it conflicts with the batch dimensions, which are usually the leading axis. For example, if we want to vectorize over N batch of k dimension time series, each with T total time stamps, the array will have a shape of `[N, T, ...]` but the output of `tf.scan` will have a shape of `[T, N, ...]`. Currently, it seems unavoidable that modelers need to perform some transpose on a scan output so that it matches the semantic of the batch and time dimension as the input.

Once we have the state space representation of a time series problem, we are in a sequential analysis framework that typically includes tasks like filtering and smoothing:

- Filtering: computing the marginal distribution of the latent state X_k, conditioned on observations up to that time step k: $p(X_k \mid y_{0:k}), k = 0, ..., T$;

  - Prediction: a forecast distribution of the latent state, extending the filtering distribution into the future for n steps: $p(X_k + n \mid y_{0:k}), k = 0, ..., T, n = 1, 2, ...$

- Smoothing: similar to filtering where we try to compute the marginal distribution of the latent state at each time step X_k, but conditioned on all observations: : $p(X_k \mid y_{0:T}), k = 0, ..., T$.

notice how the subscript of $y_{0:...}$ is different in filtering and smoothing: for filtering it is conditioned on $y_{0:k}$ and for smoothing it is conditioned on $y_{0:T}$.

Indeed, there is a strong tradition of considering time series modeling problems from a filtering and smoothing perspective. For example, the way we compute log likelihood of an ARMA process above could be seen as a filtering problem where the observed data is deconstructed into some latent unobserved states.

6.4.1   Linear Gaussian State Space Models and Kalman filter

Perhaps one of the most notable State Space models is Linear Gaussian State Space Model, where we have latent states X_t and the observation model Y_t distributed as (multivariate) Gaussian, with the transition and measurement both being linear functions:

$$
\begin{aligned}
Y_t &= \mathbf{H}_t X_t + \epsilon_t \\
X_t &= \mathbf{F}_t X_{t-1} + \eta_t
\end{aligned}
\tag{6.11}
$$

where $\epsilon_t \sim \mathcal{N}(0, \mathbf{R}_t)$ and $\eta_t \sim \mathcal{N}(0, \mathbf{Q}_t)$ are the noise components. Variables $(\mathbf{H}_t, \mathbf{F}_t)$ are matrices describing the linear transformation (Linear Operators) usually $\mathbf{F}_t$ is a square matrix and $\mathbf{H}_t$ has a lower rank than $\mathbf{F}_t$ that "push-forward" the states from latent space to measurement space. $\mathbf{R}_t, \mathbf{Q}_t$ are covariance matrices (positive semidefinite matrices). You can also find some intuitive examples of transition matrix in Section 11.1.11.

Since ϵ_t and η_t are random variables following Gaussian distribution, the linear function above performs affine transformation of the Gaussian random variables, resulting in X_t and Y_t also distributed as Gaussian. The property of the prior (state at $t-1$) and posterior (state at t) being conjugate make it possible to derive a closed form solution to the Bayesian filtering equations: the Kalman filter (Kalman, 1960). Arguably the most important application of a conjugate Bayesian model, the Kalman filter helped humans land on the moon and is still widely used in many areas.

To gain an intuitive understanding of Kalman filter, we first look at the generative process from time $t-1$ to t of the Linear Gaussian State Space Model:

$$
\begin{aligned}
X_t &\sim p(X_t \mid X_{t-1}) \equiv \mathcal{N}(\mathbf{F}_t X_{t-1}, \mathbf{Q}_t) \\
Y_t &\sim p(Y_t \mid X_t) \equiv \mathcal{N}(\mathbf{H}_t X_t, \mathbf{R}_t)
\end{aligned}
\tag{6.12}
$$

where the conditioned distribution of X_t and Y_t are denoted as $p(.)$ (we use $\equiv$ to indicate that the conditional distribution is a Multivariate Gaussian). Note that X_t only depends on the state from the last time step X_{t-1} but not the past observation(s). This means that the generative process could very well be done by first generating the latent time series X_t for $t = 0...T$ and then project the whole latent time series to the measurement space. In the Bayesian filtering context, Y_t is observed (partly if there is missing data) and thus to be used to update the state X_t, similar to how we update the prior using the observed likelihood in a static model:

$$
\begin{aligned}
X_0 &\sim p(X_0 \mid m_0, \mathbf{P}_0) \equiv \mathcal{N}(m_0, \mathbf{P}_0) \\
X_{t|t-1} &\sim p(X_{t|t-1} \mid Y_{0:t-1}) \equiv \mathcal{N}(m_{t|t-1}, \mathbf{P}_{t|t-1}) \\
X_{t|t} &\sim p(X_{t|t} \mid Y_{0:t}) \equiv \mathcal{N}(m_{t|t}, \mathbf{P}_{t|t}) \\
Y_t &\sim p(Y_t \mid Y_{0:t-1}) \equiv \mathcal{N}(\mathbf{H}_t m_{t|t-1}, \mathbf{S}_t)
\end{aligned}
\tag{6.13}
$$

where m_t and $\mathbf{P}_t$ represent the mean and covariance matrix of the latent state X_t at each time step. $X_{t|t-1}$ is the predicted latent state with associated parameter $m_{t|t-1}$ (predicted mean) and $\mathbf{P}_{t|t-1}$ (predicted covariance), whereas $X_{t|t}$ is the filtered latent state with associated parameter $m_{t|t}$ and $\mathbf{P}_{t|t}$. The subscripts in Equation 6.13 might get confusing, a good high-level view to keep in mind is that from the previous time step we have a filtered state $X_{t-1|t-1}$, which after applying the transition matrix $\mathbf{F}_t$ we get a predicted state $X_{t|t-1}$, and upon incorporating the observation of the current time step we get the filtered state for the next time step $X_{t|t}$.

The parameters of the distributions above in Equation 6.13 are computed using the Kalman filter prediction and update steps:

- Prediction

$$m_{t|t-1} = \mathbf{F}_t m_{t-1|t-1}$$
$$\mathbf{P}_{t|t-1} = \mathbf{F}_t \mathbf{P}_{t-1|t-1} \mathbf{F}_t^T + \mathbf{Q}_t \tag{6.14}$$

- Update

$$z_t = Y_t - \mathbf{H}_t m_{t|t-1}$$
$$\mathbf{S}_t = \mathbf{H}_t \mathbf{P}_{t|t-1} \mathbf{H}_t^T + \mathbf{R}_t$$
$$\mathbf{K}_t = \mathbf{P}_{t|t-1} \mathbf{H}_t^T \mathbf{S}_t^{-1} \tag{6.15}$$
$$m_{t|t} = m_{t|t-1} + \mathbf{K}_t z_t$$
$$\mathbf{P}_{t|t} = \mathbf{P}_{t|t-1} - \mathbf{K}_t \mathbf{S}_t \mathbf{K}_t^T$$

The proof of deriving the Kalman filter equations is an application of the joint multivariate Gaussian distribution. In practice, there are some tricks in implementation to make sure the computation is numerically stable (e.g., avoid inverting matrix $\mathbf{S}_t$, using a Jordan form update in computing $\mathbf{P}_{t|t}$ to ensure the result is a positive definite matrix [157]). In TFP, the linear Gaussian state space model and related Kalman filter is conveniently implemented as a distribution `tfd.LinearGaussianStateSpaceModel`.

One of the practical challenges in using Linear Gaussian State Space Model for time series modeling is expressing the unknown parameters as Gaussian latent state. We will demonstrate with a simple linear growth time series as the first example (see Chapter 3 of Bayesian Filtering and Smoothing [139]):

Code 6.19

```
1  theta0, theta1 = 1.2, 2.6
2  sigma = 0.4
3  num_timesteps = 100
4
5  time_stamp = tf.linspace(0., 1., num_timesteps)[..., None]
6  yhat = theta0 + theta1 * time_stamp
7  y = tfd.Normal(yhat, sigma).sample()
```

You might recognize Code Block 6.19 as a simple linear regression. To solve it as a filtering problem using Kalman filter, we need to assume that the measurement noise σ is known, and the unknown parameters θ_0 and θ_1 follow a Gaussian prior distribution.

In a state space form, we have the latent states:

$$X_t = \left[\begin{array}{c} \theta_0 \\ \theta_1 \end{array} \right] \tag{6.16}$$

Since the latent state does not change over time, the transition operator F_t is an identity matrix with no transition noise. The observation operator describes the "push-forward" from latent to measurement space, which is a matrix form of the linear function [13]:

$$y_t = \theta_0 + \theta_1 * t = \left[\begin{array}{cc} 1, t \end{array} \right] \left[\begin{array}{c} \theta_0 \\ \theta_1 \end{array} \right] \tag{6.17}$$

Expressed with the `tfd.LinearGaussianStateSpaceModel` API, we have:

Code 6.20

```
1  # X_0
2  initial_state_prior = tfd.MultivariateNormalDiag(
3      loc=[0., 0.], scale_diag=[5., 5.])
4  # F_t
5  transition_matrix = lambda _: tf.linalg.LinearOperatorIdentity(2)
6  # eta_t ~ Normal(0, Q_t)
7  transition_noise = lambda _: tfd.MultivariateNormalDiag(
8      loc=[0., 0.], scale_diag=[0., 0.])
9  # H_t
10 H = tf.concat([tf.ones_like(time_stamp), time_stamp], axis=-1)
11 observation_matrix = lambda t: tf.linalg.LinearOperatorFullMatrix(
12     [tf.gather(H, t)])
13 # epsilon_t ~ Normal(0, R_t)
14 observation_noise = lambda _: tfd.MultivariateNormalDiag(
15     loc=[0.], scale_diag=[sigma])
16
17 linear_growth_model = tfd.LinearGaussianStateSpaceModel(
18     num_timesteps=num_timesteps,
19     transition_matrix=transition_matrix,
20     transition_noise=transition_noise,
21     observation_matrix=observation_matrix,
22     observation_noise=observation_noise,
23     initial_state_prior=initial_state_prior)
```

we can apply the Kalman filter to to obtains the posterior distribution of θ_0 and θ_1:

Code 6.21

```
1  # Run the Kalman filter
2  (
3      log_likelihoods,
4      mt_filtered, Pt_filtered,
5      mt_predicted, Pt_predicted,
6      observation_means, observation_cov  # observation_cov is S_t
7  ) = linear_growth_model.forward_filter(y)
```

---

[13]This also gives a nice example of a non-stationary observation matrix **H**.

We can compare the result from the Kalman filter (i.e., iteratively observing each time steps) with the analytic result (i.e., observing the full time series) in Figure 6.16.

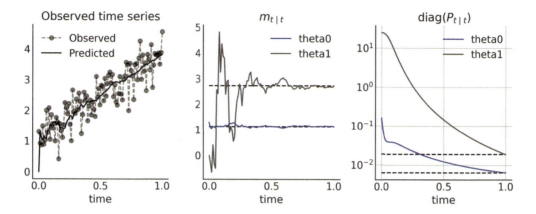

FIGURE 6.16
Linear Growth time series model, inference using a Kalman filter. In the first panel we show the observed data (gray dot connected by dash line) and the one-step prediction from the Kalman filter ($H_t m_{t|t-1}$ in solid black line). The posterior distribution of the latent state X_t after observing each time step is compared with the closed form solution using all data (black solid line) in the middle and rightmost panel.

6.4.2 ARIMA, Expressed as a State Space Model

State space models are a unified methodology that generalized many classical time series models. However, it might not always be obvious how we can express a model in state space format. In this section we will look at how to express a more complex linear Gaussian state space model: ARMA and ARIMA. Recall the ARMA(p,q) Equation 6.8 from above, we have the AR coefficient parameters ϕ_i, the MA coefficient θ_j, and noise parameter σ. It is tempting to use σ to parameterize the observation noise distribution R_t. However, the moving average of the noise from the previous steps in the ARMA(p,q) Equation 6.8 requires us to "record" the current noise. The only solution is to formulate it into the transition noise so it becomes part of the latent state X_t. First, we reformulate ARMA(p,q) Equation 6.8 into:

$$y_t = \sum_{i=1}^{r} \phi_i y_{t-i} + \sum_{i=1}^{r-1} \theta_i \epsilon_{t-i} + \epsilon_t \tag{6.18}$$

where the constant term α from Equation 6.8 is omitted, and $r = max(p, q + 1)$. We pad zeros to coefficient parameters ϕ and θ when needed so that they have the same size r. The component of the state equation for X_t is thus:

$$\mathbf{F}_t = \mathbf{F} = \begin{bmatrix} \phi_1 & 1 & \cdots & 0 \\ \vdots & \vdots & \ddots & \vdots \\ \phi_{r-1} & 0 & \cdots & 1 \\ \phi_r & 0 & \cdots & 0 \end{bmatrix}, \mathbf{A} = \begin{bmatrix} 1 \\ \theta_1 \\ \vdots \\ \theta_{r-1} \end{bmatrix}, \eta'_{t+1} \sim \mathcal{N}(0, \sigma^2), \eta_t = \mathbf{A}\eta'_{t+1} \tag{6.19}$$

With the latent state being:

$$X_t = \begin{bmatrix} y_t \\ \phi_2 y_{t-1} + \cdots + \phi_r y_{t-r+1} + \theta_1 \eta_t' + \cdots + \theta_{r-1} \eta_{t-r+2}' \\ \phi_3 y_{t-1} + \cdots + \phi_r y_{t-r+2} + \theta_2 \eta_t' + \cdots + \theta_{r-1} \eta_{t-r+3}' \\ \vdots \\ \phi_r y_{t-1} + \theta_{r-1} \eta_t' \end{bmatrix} \tag{6.20}$$

The observation operator is thus simply an indexing matrix $\mathbf{H}_t = [1, 0, 0, \dots, 0]$ with the observation equation being $y_t = \mathbf{H}_t X_t$.

For example, an ARMA(2,1) model in state space representation is:

$$\begin{bmatrix} y_{t+1} \\ \phi_2 y_t + \theta_1 \eta_{t+1}' \end{bmatrix} = \begin{bmatrix} \phi_1 & 1 \\ \phi_2 & 0 \end{bmatrix} \begin{bmatrix} y_t \\ \phi_2 y_{t-1} + \theta_1 \eta_t' \end{bmatrix} + \begin{bmatrix} 1 \\ \theta_1 \end{bmatrix} \eta_{t+1}'$$
$$\eta_{t+1}' \sim \mathcal{N}(0, \sigma^2) \tag{6.21}$$

You might notice that the state transition is slightly different than what we defined above, as the transition noise is not drawn from a Multivariate Gaussian distribution. The covariance matrix of η is $\mathbf{Q}_t = \mathbf{A}\sigma^2\mathbf{A}^T$, which in this case results in a singular random variable η. Nonetheless, we can define the model in TFP. For example, in Code Block 6.22 we defines a ARMA(2,1) model with $\phi = [-0.1, 0.5]$, $\theta = -0.25$, and $\sigma = 1.25$, and draw one random time series.

Code 6.22

```
1  num_timesteps = 300
2  phi1 = -.1
3  phi2 = .5
4  theta1 = -.25
5  sigma = 1.25
6
7  # X_0
8  initial_state_prior = tfd.MultivariateNormalDiag(
9      scale_diag=[sigma, sigma])
10 # F_t
11 transition_matrix = lambda _: tf.linalg.LinearOperatorFullMatrix(
12     [[phi1, 1], [phi2, 0]])
13 # eta_t ~ Normal(0, Q_t)
14 R_t = tf.constant([[sigma], [sigma*theta1]])
15 Q_t_tril = tf.concat([R_t, tf.zeros_like(R_t)], axis=-1)
16 transition_noise = lambda _: tfd.MultivariateNormalTriL(
17     scale_tril=Q_t_tril)
18 # H_t
19 observation_matrix = lambda t: tf.linalg.LinearOperatorFullMatrix(
20     [[1., 0.]])
21 # epsilon_t ~ Normal(0, 0)
22 observation_noise = lambda _: tfd.MultivariateNormalDiag(
23     loc=[0.], scale_diag=[0.])
24
25 arma = tfd.LinearGaussianStateSpaceModel(
```

```
26      num_timesteps=num_timesteps,
27      transition_matrix=transition_matrix,
28      transition_noise=transition_noise,
29      observation_matrix=observation_matrix,
30      observation_noise=observation_noise,
31      initial_state_prior=initial_state_prior
32      )
33
34  sim_ts = arma.sample()  # Simulate from the model
```

Adding the appropriate prior and some small rewrite to handle the shape a bit better, we can get a full generative ARMA(2,1) model in Code Block 6.23. Conditioning on the (simulated) data `sim_ts` and running inference are straightforward since we are working with a `tfd.JointDistributionCoroutine` model. Note that the unknown parameters are not part of the latent state X_t, thus instead of a Bayesian filter like Kalman filter, inference is done using standard MCMC method. We show the resulting trace plot of the posterior samples in Figure 6.17.

Code 6.23

```
1   @tfd.JointDistributionCoroutine
2   def arma_lgssm():
3       sigma = yield root(tfd.HalfStudentT(df=7, loc=0, scale=1., name="sigma"))
4       phi = yield root(tfd.Sample(tfd.Normal(0, 0.5), 2, name="phi"))
5       theta = yield root(tfd.Sample(tfd.Normal(0, 0.5), 1, name="theta"))
6       # Prior for initial state
7       init_scale_diag = tf.concat([sigma[..., None], sigma[..., None]], axis=-1)
8       initial_state_prior = tfd.MultivariateNormalDiag(
9           scale_diag=init_scale_diag)
10
11      F_t = tf.concat([phi[..., None],
12                      tf.concat([tf.ones_like(phi[..., 0, None]),
13                                 tf.zeros_like(phi[..., 0, None])],
14                                axis=-1)[..., None]],
15                     axis=-1)
16      transition_matrix = lambda _: tf.linalg.LinearOperatorFullMatrix(F_t)
17
18      transition_scale_tril = tf.concat(
19          [sigma[..., None], theta * sigma[..., None]], axis=-1)[..., None]
20      scale_tril = tf.concat(
21          [transition_scale_tril,
22           tf.zeros_like(transition_scale_tril)],
23          axis=-1)
24      transition_noise = lambda _: tfd.MultivariateNormalTriL(
25          scale_tril=scale_tril)
26
27      observation_matrix = lambda t: tf.linalg.LinearOperatorFullMatrix([[1., 0.]])
28      observation_noise = lambda t: tfd.MultivariateNormalDiag(
29          loc=[0], scale_diag=[0.])
30
31      arma = yield tfd.LinearGaussianStateSpaceModel(
32              num_timesteps=num_timesteps,
33              transition_matrix=transition_matrix,
34              transition_noise=transition_noise,
35              observation_matrix=observation_matrix,
```

```
36              observation_noise=observation_noise,
37              initial_state_prior=initial_state_prior,
38              name="arma")
```

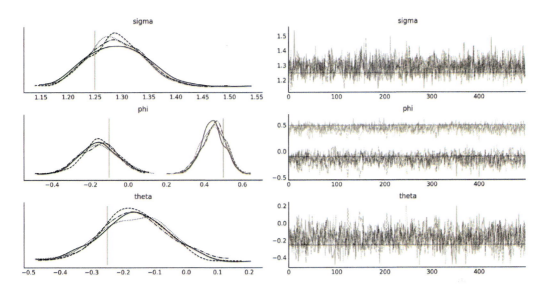

FIGURE 6.17
MCMC sampling result from the ARMA(2,1) model `arma_lgssm` defined in Code Block 6.23, conditioned on the simulated data `sim_ts` generated in Code Block 6.22. The true values of the parameters are plotted as vertical lines in the posterior density plot and horizontal lines in the trace plot.

We can already use this formulation for ARIMA modeling with $d > 0$ by preprocessing the observed time series to account for the integrated part. However, state space model representation gives us an advantage where we can write down the generative process directly and more intuitively without taking the repeated differences d times on the observation in the data preprocessing step.

For example, consider extending the ARMA(2,1) model above with $d = 1$, we have $\Delta y_t = y_t - y_{t-1}$, which means $y_t = y_{t-1} + \Delta y_t$ and we can define observation operator as $\mathbf{H}_t = [1, 1, 0]$, with the latent state X_t and state transition being:

$$
\begin{bmatrix} y_{t-1} + \Delta y_t \\ \phi_1 \Delta y_t + \phi_2 \Delta y_{t-1} + \eta'_{t+1} + \theta_1 \eta'_t \\ \phi_2 \Delta y_t + \theta_1 \eta'_{t+1} \end{bmatrix} = \begin{bmatrix} 1 & 1 & 0 \\ 0 & \phi_1 & 1 \\ 0 & \phi_2 & 0 \end{bmatrix} \begin{bmatrix} y_{t-1} \\ \Delta y_t \\ \phi_2 \Delta y_{t-1} + \theta_1 \eta'_t \end{bmatrix} + \begin{bmatrix} 0 \\ 1 \\ \theta_1 \end{bmatrix} \eta'_{t+1}
$$

$$(6.22)$$

As you can see, while the parameterization results in a larger size latent state vector X_t, the number of parameters stays the same. Moreover, the model is generative in y_t instead of Δy_t. However, challenges may arise when specifying the distribution of the initial state X_0, as the first elements (y_0) are now non-stationary. In practice, we can assign an informative prior around the initial value of the time series after centering (subtracting the mean). More discussion around this topic and an in depth introduction to state space models for time series problems could be found in Durbin and Koopman [51].

6.4.3   Bayesian Structural Time Series

A linear Gaussian state space representation of a time series model has another advantage that it is easily extendable, especially with other linear Gaussian state space models. To combine two models, we follow the same idea of concatenating two normal random variables in the latent space. We generate a block diagonal matrix using the 2 covariance matrix, concatenating the mean on the event axis. In the measurement space the operation is equivalent to summing two normal random variables. More concretely, we have:

$$
\mathbf{F}_t = \begin{bmatrix} \mathbf{F}_{1,t} & 0 \\ 0 & \mathbf{F}_{2,t} \end{bmatrix}, \mathbf{Q}_t = \begin{bmatrix} \mathbf{Q}_{1,t} & 0 \\ 0 & \mathbf{Q}_{2,t} \end{bmatrix}, X_t = \begin{bmatrix} X_{1,t} \\ X_{2,t} \end{bmatrix} \tag{6.23}
$$
$$
\mathbf{H}_t = \begin{bmatrix} \mathbf{H}_{1,t} & \mathbf{H}_{2,t} \end{bmatrix}, \mathbf{R}_t = \mathbf{R}_{1,t} + \mathbf{R}_{2,t}
$$

If we have a time series model $\mathcal{M}$ that is not linear Gaussian. We can also incorporate it into a state space model. To do that, we treat the prediction $\hat{\psi}_t$ from $\mathcal{M}$ at each time step as a static "known" value and add to the observation noise distribution $\epsilon_t \sim N(\hat{\mu}_t + \hat{\psi}_t, R_t)$. Conceptually we can understand it as subtracting the prediction of $\mathcal{M}$ from Y_t and modeling the result, so that the Kalman filter and other linear Gaussian state space model properties still hold.

This *composability* feature makes it easy to build a time series model that is constructed from multiple smaller linear Gaussian state space model components. We can have individual state space representations for the trend, seasonal, and error terms, and combine them into what is usually referred to as a *structural time series* model or dynamic linear model. TFP provides a very convenient way to build Bayesian structural time series with the `tfp.sts` module, along with helper functions to deconstruct the components, make forecasts, inference, and other diagnostics.

For example, we can model the monthly birth data using a structural time series with a local linear trend component and a seasonal component to account for the monthly pattern in Code Block 6.24.

Code 6.24

```
1  def generate_bsts_model(observed=None):
2      """
3      Args:
4          observed: Observed time series, tfp.sts use it to generate prior.
5      """
6      # Trend
7      trend = tfp.sts.LocalLinearTrend(observed_time_series=observed)
8      # Seasonal
9      seasonal = tfp.sts.Seasonal(num_seasons=12, observed_time_series=observed)
10     # Full model
11     return tfp.sts.Sum([trend, seasonal], observed_time_series=observed)
12
13 observed = tf.constant(us_monthly_birth["birth_in_thousands"], dtype=tf.float32)
14 birth_model = generate_bsts_model(observed=observed)
15
16 # Generate the posterior distribution conditioned on the observed
17 target_log_prob_fn = birth_model.joint_log_prob(observed_time_series=observed)
```

We can inspect each component in `birth_model`:

Code 6.25

```
birth_model.components
```

```
[<tensorflow_probability.python.sts.local_linear_trend.LocalLinearTrend at ...>,
 <tensorflow_probability.python.sts.seasonal.Seasonal at ...>]
```

Each of the components is parameterized by some hyperparameters, which are the unknown parameters that we want to do inference on. They are not part of the latent state X_t, but might parameterize the prior that generates X_t. For example, we can check the parameters of the seasonal component:

Code 6.26

```
birth_model.components[1].parameters
```

```
[Parameter(name='drift_scale', prior=<tfp.distributions.LogNormal
 'Seasonal_LogNormal' batch_shape=[] event_shape=[] dtype=float32>,
 bijector=<tensorflow_probability.python.bijectors.chain.Chain object at ...>)]
```

Here the seasonal component of the STS model contains 12 latent states (one for each month), but the component only contains 1 parameter (the hyperparameter that parameterized the latent states). You might have already noticed from examples in the previous session how unknown parameters are treated differently. In the linear growth model, unknown parameters are part of the latent state X_t, in the ARIMA model, the unknown parameters parameterized $\mathbf{F}_t$ and $\mathbf{Q}_t$. For the latter case, we cannot use Kalman filter to infer those parameters. Instead, the latent state is effectively marginalized out but we can nonetheless recover them after inference by running the Kalman filter conditioned on the posterior distribution (represented as Monte Carlo Samples). A conceptual description of the parameterization could be found in the Figure 6.18:

Thus running inference on a structural time series model could conceptually be understood as generating a linear Gaussian state space model from the parameters to be inferred, running the Kalman filter to obtain the data likelihood, and combining with the prior log-likelihood conditioned on the current value of the parameters. Unfortunately, the operation of iterating through each data point is quite computationally costly (even though Kalman filter is already an extremely efficient algorithm), thus fitting structural time series may not scale very well when running long time series.

After running inference on a structural time series model there are some helpful utility functions from **tfp.sts** we can use to make forecast and inspect each inferred component with Code Block 6.27. The result is shown in Figure 6.19.

Code 6.27

```
1  # Using a subset of posterior samples.
2  parameter_samples = [x[-100:, 0, ...] for x in mcmc_samples]
3
4  # Get structual compoenent.
5  component_dists = tfp.sts.decompose_by_component(
6      birth_model,
7      observed_time_series=observed,
8      parameter_samples=parameter_samples)
9
```

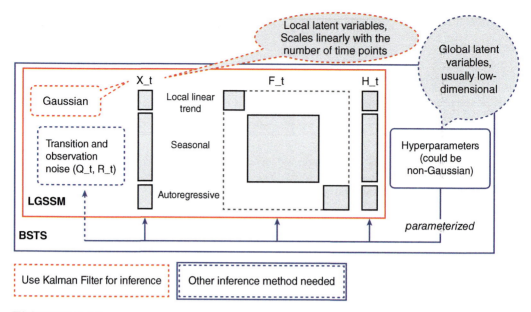

FIGURE 6.18
Relationship between Bayesian Structural Time Series (blue box) and Linear Gaussian State Space Model (red box). The Linear Gaussian State Space Model shown here is an example containing a local linear trend component, a seasonal component, and an Autoregressive component.

```
10  # Get forecast for n_steps.
11  n_steps = 36
12  forecast_dist = tfp.sts.forecast(
13      birth_model,
14      observed_time_series=observed,
15      parameter_samples=parameter_samples,
16      num_steps_forecast=n_steps)
17  birth_dates = us_monthly_birth.index
18  forecast_date = pd.date_range(
19      start=birth_dates[-1] + np.timedelta64(1, "M"),
20      end=birth_dates[-1] + np.timedelta64(1 + n_steps, "M"),
21      freq="M")
22
23  fig, axes = plt.subplots(
24      1 + len(component_dists.keys()), 1, figsize=(10, 9), sharex=True)
25
26  ax = axes[0]
27  ax.plot(us_monthly_birth, lw=1.5, label="observed")
28
29  forecast_mean = np.squeeze(forecast_dist.mean())
30  line = ax.plot(forecast_date, forecast_mean, lw=1.5,
31                 label="forecast mean", color="C4")
32
33  forecast_std = np.squeeze(forecast_dist.stddev())
34  ax.fill_between(forecast_date,
35                  forecast_mean - 2 * forecast_std,
36                  forecast_mean + 2 * forecast_std,
37                  color=line[0].get_color(), alpha=0.2)
```

```
38
39 for ax_, (key, dist) in zip(axes[1:], component_dists.items()):
40     comp_mean, comp_std = np.squeeze(dist.mean()), np.squeeze(dist.stddev())
41     line = ax_.plot(birth_dates, dist.mean(), lw=2.)
42     ax_.fill_between(birth_dates,
43                      comp_mean - 2 * comp_std,
44                      comp_mean + 2 * comp_std,
45                      alpha=0.2)
46     ax_.set_title(key.name[:-1])
```

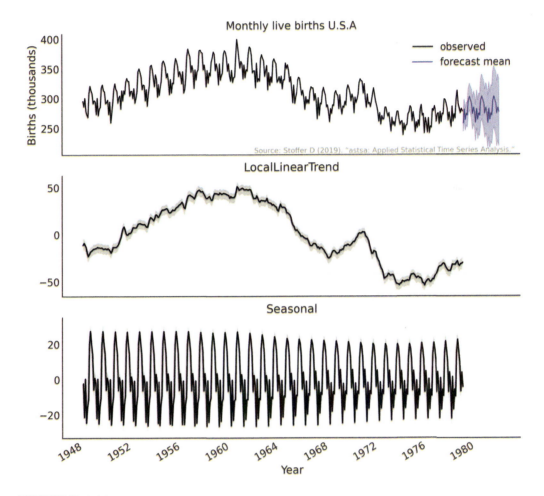

FIGURE 6.19
Inference result and forecast of monthly live births in the United States (1948-1979) using the `tfp.sts` API with Code Block 6.27. Top panel: 36 months forecast; bottom 2 panels: decomposition of the structural time series.

6.5   Other Time Series Models

While structural time series and linear Gaussian state space models are powerful and expressive classes of time series models, they certainly do not cover all our needs. For example, some interesting extensions include nonlinear Gaussian state space models, where the transition function and measurement function are differentiable nonlinear functions. Extended Kalman filter could be used for inference of X_t for these models [73]. There is the Unscented Kalman filter for inference of non-Gaussian nonlinear models [73], and Particle filter as a general filtering approach for state space models [36].

Another class of widely used time series models is the Hidden Markov model, which is a state space model with discrete state space. There are also specialized algorithms for doing inference of these models, for example, the forward-backward algorithm for computing the marginal posterior likelihood, and the Viterbi algorithm for computing the posterior mode.

In addition there are ordinary differential equations (ODE) and stochastic differential equations (SDE) that are continuous time models. In Table 6.5 we divide the space of models by their treatment of stochasticity and time. While we are not going into details of these models, they are well studied subjects with easy to use implementations in the Python computing ecosystem.

	Deterministic dynamics	**Stochastic dynamics**
Discrete time	automata / discretized ODEs	state space models
Continuous time	ODEs	SDEs

TABLE 6.2
Various time series models categorized by treatment of stochasticity and time.

6.6   Model Criticism and Choosing Priors

In the seminal time series book by George E. P. Box et al [23] [14], they outlined five important practical problems for time series modeling:

- Forecasting
- Estimation of Transfer Functions
- Analysis of Effects of Unusual Intervention Events to a System
- Analysis of Multivariate Time Series
- Discrete Control Systems

In practice, most time series problems aim at performing some sort of forecasting (or nowcasting where you try to infer at instantaneous time t some observed quantity that are not yet available due to delay in getting the measurements), which sets up a natural model criticism criteria in time series analysis problems. While we do not have specific treatment around Bayesian decision theory in this chapter, It is worth quoting from West and Harrison [157]:

> Good modeling demands hard thinking, and good forecasting requires an integrated view of the role of forecasting within decision systems.

---

[14]Nothing more puts George E. P. Box's famous quote: "All models are wrong, but some are useful" into perspective, than reading through his seminal book and working on forecasting problems.

In practice, criticism of time series model inference and evaluation of forecasting should be closely integrated with the decision making process, especially how uncertainty should be incorporated into decisions. Nonetheless, forecast performance could be evaluated alone. Usually this is done by collecting new data or keeping some hold out dataset as we did in this Chapter for the CO_2 example, and compare the observation with the forecast using standard metrics. One of a popular choice is Mean Absolute Percentage Error (MAPE), which simply compute:

$$MAPE = \frac{1}{n} \sum_{i=1}^{n} \frac{|\text{forecast}_i - \text{observed}_i|}{\text{observed}_i} \tag{6.24}$$

However, there are some known biases of MAPE, for example, large errors during low value observation periods will significantly impact MAPE. Also, it is difficult to compare MAPE across multiple time series when the range of observation differs greatly.

Cross-validation based model evaluation approaches still apply and are recommended for time series models. However, using LOO for a single time series will be problematic if the goal is to estimate the predictive performance for future time points. Simply leaving out one observation at a time does not respect the temporal structure of the data (or model). For example, if you remove one point t and use the rest of the points for predictions you will be using the points $t_{-1}, t_{-2}, ...$ which may be fine as previous observations (up to some point) inform future ones, but you will be also using points $t_{+1}, t_{+2}, ...$, that is you will be using the future to predict the past. Thus, we can compute LOO, but the interpretation of the number will get will be nonsensical and thus misleading. Instead of leaving one (or some) time points out, we need some form of leave-future-out cross-validation (LFO-CV, see e.g. [29]). As a rough sketch, after initial model inference, to approximate 1-step-ahead predictions we would iterate over the hold out time series or future observations and evaluate on the log predictive density, and refit the model including a specific time point when the Pareto k estimate exceeds some threshold [15]. Thus, LFO-CV does not refer to one particular prediction task but rather to various possible cross validation approaches that all involve some form of prediction of future time points.

6.6.1 Priors for Time Series Models

In Section 6.2.2 we used a regularizing prior, the Laplace prior, for the slope of the step linear function. As we mentioned this is to express our prior knowledge that the change in slope is usually small and close to zero, so that the resulting latent trend is smoother. Another common use of regularizing priors or sparse priors, is for modeling holiday or special days effect. Usually each holiday has its own coefficients, and we want to express a prior that indicates some holidays could have huge effect on the time series, but most holidays are just like any other ordinary day. We can formalize this intuition with a horseshoe prior [33, 120] as shown in Equation 6.25:

$$\begin{aligned} \lambda_t^2 &\sim \mathcal{HC}(1.) \\ \beta_t &\sim \mathcal{N}(0, \lambda_t^2 \tau^2) \end{aligned} \tag{6.25}$$

The global parameter τ in the horseshoe prior pulls the coefficients of the holiday effect globally towards zero. Meanwhile, the heavy tail from the local scales λ_t let some effect break out from the shrinkage. We can accommodate different levels of sparsity by changing the value of τ: the closer τ is to zero the more shrinkage of the holiday effect β_t to tends to zero, whereas with a larger τ we have a more diffuse prior [119] [16]. For example, in Case Study 2 of Riutort-Mayol et al [130] they

---

[15] For a demonstration see `https://mc-stan.org/loo/articles/loo2-lfo.html`
[16] Note that in practice we usually parameterize Equation 6.25 a little bit differently.

included a special day effect for each individual day of a year (366 as the Leap Day is included) and use a horseshoe prior to regularize it.

Another important consideration of prior for time series model is the prior for the observation noise. Most time series data are by nature are non-repeated measures. We simply cannot go back in time and make another observation under the exact condition (i.e., we cannot quantify the **aleatoric** uncertainty). This means our model needs information from the prior to "decide" whether the noise is from measurement or from latent process (i.e., the **epistemic** uncertainty). For example, in a time series model with a latent autoregressive component or a local linear trend model, we can place more informative prior on the observation noise to regulate it towards a smaller value. This will "push" the trend or autoregressive component to overfits the underlying drift pattern and we might have a nicer forecast on the trend (higher forecast accuracy in the short term). The risk is that we are overconfident about the underlying trend, which will likely result in a poor forecast in the long run. In a real world application where time series are most likely non-stationary, we should be ready to adjust the prior accordingly.

6.7   Exercises

6E1. As we explained in Box *Parsing timestamp to design matrix* above, date information could be formatted into a design matrix for regression model to account for the periodic pattern in a time series. Try generating the following design matrix for the year 2021. Hint: use Code Block 6.28 to generate all time stamps for 2021:

Code 6.28

```
datetime_index = pd.date_range(start="2021-01-01", end="2021-12-31", freq='D')
```

- A design matrix for day of the month effect.
- A design matrix for weekday vs weekend effect.
- Company G pay their employee on the 25th of every month, and if the 25th falls on a weekend, the payday is moved up to the Friday before. Try to create a design matrix to encode the pay day of 2021.
- A design matrix for the US Federal holiday effect [17] in 2021. Create the design matrix so that each holiday has their individual coefficient.

6E2. In the previous exercise , the design matrix for holiday effect treat each holiday separately. What if we consider all holiday effects to be the same? What is the shape of the design matrix if we do so? Reason about how does it affects the fit of the regression time series model.

6E3. Fit a linear regression to the "monthly_mauna_loa_co2.csv" dataset:

- A plain regression with an intercept and slope, using linear time as predictor.
- A covariate adjusted regression like the square root predictor in the baby example in Chapter 4 Code Block 4.3.

Explain what these models are missing compared to Code Block 6.3.

---

[17]https://en.wikipedia.org/wiki/Federal_holidays_in_the_United_States#List_of_federal_holidays

6E4. Explain in your own words the difference between regression, autoregressive and state space architectures. In which situation would each be particularly useful.

6M5. Does using basis function as design matrix actually have better condition number than sparse matrix? Compare the condition number of the following design matrix of the same rank using `numpy.linalg.cond`:

- Dummy coded design matrix `seasonality_all` from Code Block 6.2.
- Fourier basis function design matrix `X_pred` from Code Block 6.9.
- An array of the same shape as `seasonality_all` with values drawn from a Normal distribution.
- An array of the same shape as `seasonality_all` with values drawn from a Normal distribution *and* one of the column being identical to another.

6M6. The `gen_fourier_basis` function from 6.8 takes a time index `t` as the first input. There are a few different ways to represent the time index, for example, if we are observing some data monthly from 2019 January for 36 months, we can code the time index in 2 equivalent ways as shown below in Code Block 6.29:

Code 6.29

```
1  nmonths = 36
2  day0 = pd.Timestamp('2019-01-01')
3  time_index = pd.date_range(
4      start=day0, end=day0 + np.timedelta64(nmonths, 'M'),
5      freq='M')
6
7  t0 = np.arange(len(time_index))
8  design_matrix0 = gen_fourier_basis(t0, p=12, n=6)
9  t1 = time_index.month - 1
10 design_matrix1 = gen_fourier_basis(t1, p=12, n=6)
11
12 np.testing.assert_array_almost_equal(design_matrix0, design_matrix1)
```

What if we are observing the data daily? How would you change the Code Block 6.29 to:

- Make `time_index` represent day of the year instead of month of the year.
- Modify the function signature to `gen_fourier_basis` in line 8 and 10 so that the resulting design matrices coded for the month of the year effect.
- How does the new `design_matrix0` and `design_matrix1` differ? How is the differences would impact the model fitting? Hint: validate your reasoning by multiplying them with the same random regression coefficient.

6E7. In Section 6.3 we introduced the backshift operator **B**. You might have already noticed that applying the operation **B** on a time series is the same as performing a matrix multiplication. We can generate a matrix **B** explicitly in Python. Modify Code Block 6.11 to use an explicit **B** constructed in NumPy or TensorFlow.

6E8. The step linear function as defined in Equation 6.3 and Code Block 6.7 rely on a key regression coefficient δ. Rewrite the definition so that it has a similar form compare to other linear regression:

$$g(t) = \mathbf{A}'\delta' \tag{6.26}$$

Find the appropriate expression of design matrix $\mathbf{A}'$ and coefficient δ'.

6E9. As we have seen in past chapters, a great way to understand your data generating process is to write it down. In this exercise we will generate synthetic data which will reinforce the mapping of "real world" ideas to code. Assume we start with a linear trend that is `y = 2x`, `x = np.arange(90)`, and iid noise at each time point draw from a $\mathcal{N}(0, 1)$. Assume that this time series starts on Sunday June 6 2021. Generate 4 synthetic datasets that include:

1. An additive weekend effect where weekends have 2x more volume than weekdays.

2. An additive sinusoidal effect of $\sin(2x)$.

3. An additive AR(1) latent process with autoregressive coefficient of your choice and a noise scale $\sigma = 0.2$.

4. A time series with weekend and sinusoidal effect from (1) and (2), and an AR(1) process on the mean of the time series with the same autoregressive coefficient as in (3)

6E10. Adapt the model in Code Block 6.13 to model the generated time series in **6E9** (4).

6E11. Inspection of the inference result (MCMC trace and diagnostic) of models in this chapter using `ArviZ`. For example, look at:

- Trace plot
- Rank plot
- Summary of posterior sample

Which model contains problematic chains (divergence, low ESS, large $\hat{R}$)? Could you find ways to improve the inference for those models?

6M12. Generate a sinusoidal time series with 200 time points in Python, and fit it with a AR(2) model. Do that in TFP by modifying Code Block 6.11 and in PyMC3 with `pm.AR` API.

6M13. This is an exercise of posterior predictive check for AR models. Generate the prediction distribution at each time step t for the AR2 model in Exercise **6M11**. Note that for each time step t you need to condition on all the observations up to time step $t-1$. Does the one-step-ahead predictive distribution match the observed time series?

6M14. Make forecast for 50 time steps using the AR2 models from Exercise **6M11**. Does the forecast also look like a sinusoidal signal?

6H15. Implement the generative process for the SARIMA$(1, 1, 1)(1, 1, 1)_{12}$ model, and make forecast.

6M16. Implement and inference a $ARIMAX(1, 1, 1)X[4]$ model for the monthly birth dataset in this chapter, with the design matrix generated from a Fourier basis functions with $N = 2$.

6H17. Derive the Kalman filter equations. Hint: first work out the joint distribution of X_t and X_{t-1}, and then follow with the joint distribution of Y_t and X_t. If you are still stuck take at look at Chapter 4 in Särkkä's book [139].

6M18. Inspect the output of `linear_growth_model.forward_filter` by indexing to a given time step:

- Identify the input and output of one Kalman filter step;
- Compute one step of the Kalman filter predict and update step using the input;
- Assert that your computation is the same as the indexed output.

6M19. Study the documentation and implementation of `tfp.sts.Seasonal`, and answer the following questions:

- How many hyperparameters does a seasonal SSM contains?
- How does it parameterized the latent states and what kind of regularization effect does the prior has? Hint: draw connection to the Gaussian Random Walk prior in Chapter 5.

6M20. Study the documentation and implementation of `tfp.sts.LinearRegression` and `tfp.sts.Seasonal`, and reason about the differences of SSM they represent when modeling a day of the week pattern:

- How is the day of the week coefficient represented? Are they part of the latent states?
- How is the model fit different between the two SSMs? Validate your reasoning with simulations.

7

Bayesian Additive Regression Trees

In Chapter 5 we saw how we can approximate a function by summing up a series of (simple) basis functions. We showed how B-splines have some nice properties when used as basis functions. In this chapter we are going to discuss a similar approach, but we are going to use **decision trees** instead of B-splines. Decision trees are another flexible way to represent the piecewise constant functions, or step functions, that we saw in Chapter 5. In particular we will focus on Bayesian Additive Regression Trees (BART). A Bayesian non-parametric model that uses a sum of decision trees to obtain a flexible model [1]. They are often discussed in terms closer to the machine learning verbiage than to the statistical ones [26]. In a sense BART is more of a *fire and forget model* than the carefully hand crafted models we discuss in other chapters.

In the BART literature people generally do not write about basis functions, instead they talk about *learners*, but the overall idea is pretty similar. We use a combination of simple functions, also referred to as learners, to approximate complex functions, with enough regularization so that we can get flexibility without too much model complexity, i.e. without overfitting. Methods that use multiple learners to solve the same problem are known as ensemble methods. In this context, a learner could be any statistical model or data-algorithm you may think of. Ensemble methods are based on the observation that combining multiple *weak learners* is generally a better idea than trying to use a single very *strong learner*. To get good results in terms of accuracy and generalization, it is generally believed that base learners should be as accurate as possible, and also as diverse as possible [165]. The main Bayesian idea used by BARTs is that as decision trees can easily overfit we add a regularizing prior (or shrinkage prior) to make each tree behave as a *weak learner*.

To turn this overall description into something we can better understand and apply, we should first discuss decisions trees. In case you are already familiar with them, feel free to skip the next section.

7.1   Decision Trees

Let us assume we have two variables X_1 and X_2 and we want to use those variables to classify objects into two classes: ● or ▲. To achieve this goal we can use a tree-structure as shown on the left panel of Figure 7.1. A tree is just a collection of nodes, where any two nodes are connected with at most one line or edge. The tree on Figure 7.1 is called binary tree because each node can have at most two children nodes. The nodes without children are known as leaf nodes or terminal nodes. In this example we have two internal, or interior, (nodes represented as rectangles) and 3 terminal nodes (represented as rounded rectangles). Each internal node has a decision rule associated with it. If we follow those decision rules we will eventually reach a single leaf node that will provide us with the answer to our decision problem. For example, if an instance of the variable X_1 is larger than c_1 the decision tree tells us to assign to that instance the class ●. If instead we observe a value of x_{1i}

---

[1]Maybe you have heard about its non-Bayesian cousin: Random Forest [25]

DOI: 10.1201/9781003019169-7

smaller than c_1 and the value of x_{2i} smaller than c_2 then we must assign the class ▲. Algorithmically we can conceptualize a tree as a set of if-else statements that we follow to perform a certain task, like a classification. We can also understand a binary tree from a geometrical perspective as a way to partition the sample space into *blocks*, as depicted on the right panel of Figure 7.1. Each block is defined by axis-perpendicular *splitting* lines, and thus every split of the sample space will be aligned with one of the covariates (or feature) axes.

Mathematically we can say that a g decision tree is completely defined by two sets:

- $\mathcal{T}$ the set of edges and nodes (the squares, rounded squares and the lines joining them in Figure 7.1) together with the decision rules associated with the internal nodes.
- $\mathcal{M} = \{\mu_1, \mu_2, \ldots, \mu_b\}$ denotes a set of parameter values associated with each of the terminal nodes of $\mathcal{T}$.

Then $g(X; \mathcal{T}, \mathcal{M})$ is the function which assigns $\mu_i \in M$ to X. For example, in Figure 7.1 the μ_i values are (●, ● and ▲). And the g function assigns ● to cases with X_1 larger than c_1, ● to X_1 smaller than c_1 and X_2 larger than c_2 and ▲ to X_1 smaller than c_1 and X_2 smaller than c_2.

This abstract definition of a tree as a tuple of two sets $g(\mathcal{T}, \mathcal{M})$, will become very useful in a moment when we discuss priors over trees.

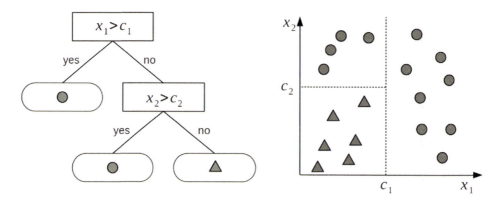

FIGURE 7.1
A binary tree (left) and the corresponding partition space (right). The internal nodes of the tree are those having children. They have a link to a node below them. Internal nodes have splitting rules associated with them. Terminal nodes, or leaves, are those without children and they contain the values to return, in this example ● or ▲. A decision tree generates a partition of the sample space into blocks delimited by axis-perpendicular splitting lines. This means that every split of the sample space will be aligned with one of the covariate axes.

While Figure 7.1 shows how to use a decision tree for a classification problem, where $\mathcal{M}_j$ contains classes or label-values, we can also use trees for regression. In such cases instead of associating a terminal node with a class label, we can associate it with a real number like the mean of the data points inside a block. Figure 7.2 shows such a case for a regression with only one covariate. On the left we see a binary tree similar to the one from Figure 7.1, with the main difference that instead of returning a class value at each leaf node, the binary tree in Figure 7.2 returns a real valued number. Compare the tree to the sinusoidal like data on the right, in particular noting how instead of a continuous function approximation the data been split into three blocks, and the average is approximating each one of those blocks.

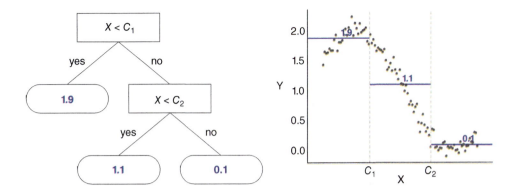

FIGURE 7.2
A binary tree (left) and the corresponding partition space (right). The internal nodes of the tree are those having children (they have a link to a node below them), internal nodes have splitting rules associated with them. Terminal nodes (or leafs) are those without children and they contain the values to return (in this example 1.1, 1.9 and 0.1). We can see how a tree is a way to represent piecewise function, like the ones discussed in Chapter 5.

Regression trees are not limited to returning the mean of the data points inside a block, there are alternatives. For example, it is possible to associate the leaf nodes with the median of the data points, or we can fit a linear regression to the data points of each block, or even more complex functions. Nevertheless, the mean is probably the most common choice for regression trees.

It is important to notice that the output of a regression tree is not a smooth function but a piecewise step-function. This does not mean regression trees are necessarily a bad choice to fit smooth functions. In principle we can approximate any continuous function with a step function and in practice this approximation could be good enough.

One appealing feature of decision trees is its interpretability, you can literally read the tree and follow the steps needed to solve a certain problem. And thus you can transparently understand what the method is doing, why it is performing the way it is, and why some classes may not be properly classified, or why some data is poorly approximated. Additionally it is also easy to explain the result to a non-technical audience with simple terms.

Unfortunately the flexibility of decision trees means that they could easily overfit as you can always find a complex enough tree that has one partition per data point. See Figure 7.3 for an overly complex solution to a classification problem. This is also easy to see for yourself by grabbing a piece of paper, drawing a few data points, and then creating a partition that isolates each of them individually. While doing this exercise you may also notice that in fact there is more than one tree that can fit the data equally well.

One interesting property of trees arises when we think about them in terms of main effects and interactions as we did for linear models (see Chapter 4). Notice that the term $\mathbb{E}(Y \mid X)$ equals to the sum of all the leaf node parameters μ_{ij}, thus:

- When a tree depends on a single variable (like Figure 7.2) each such μ_{ij} represents a main effect
- When a tree depends on more than one variable (like Figure 7.1) each such μ_{ij} represents an interaction effect. Notice for example how returning a triangle requires the interaction of X_1 and X_2 as the condition of the child node ($X_2 > c_2$) is predicated on the condition of the parent node ($X_1 > c_1$).

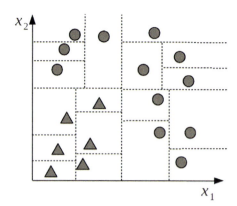

FIGURE 7.3
An overly complex partition of the sample space. Each data point is assigned to a separate block. We say this is an *overcomplex* partition because we can explain and predict the data at the same level of accuracy using a much simpler partition like the one used in Figure 7.1 The most simple partition is most likely to generalize than the more complex one, i.e. it is most likely to predict, and explain new data. .

As the size of the trees is variable we can use trees to model interaction effects of varying orders. As a tree gets deeper the chance for more variables to entry the tree increases and then also the potential to represent higher order interactions. Additionally, because we use an ensemble of trees we can build virtually any combination of main and interaction effects.

7.1.1   Ensembles of Decision Trees

Considering that over-complex trees will likely not be very good at predicting new data, it is common to introduce devices to reduce the complexity of decision trees and get a fit that better adapts to the complexity of the data at hand. One such solution relies on fitting an ensemble of trees where each individual tree is regularized to be shallow. As a result each tree individually is only capable of explaining a small portion of the data. It is only by combining many such trees that we are able to provide a proper answer. This is data-science incarnation of the motto "for the union makes us strong". This ensemble strategy is followed both by Bayesian methods like BARTs and non-Bayesian methods like random forests. In general ensemble models leads to lower generalization error while maintaining the ability to flexibly fit a given dataset.

Using ensembles also helps to alleviate the *step-ness* because the output is a combination of trees and while this is still a step function it is one with more steps and thus a somehow smoother approximation. This is true as long as we ensure that trees are diverse enough.

One downside of using ensembles of trees is that we lose the interpretability of a single decision tree. Now to obtain an answer we can not just follow a single tree but many, which generally obfuscates any simple interpretation. We have traded interpretability for flexibility and generalization.

7.2   The BART Model

If we assume that the B_i functions in equation 5.3 are decision trees we can write:

$$\mathbb{E}[Y] = \phi\left(\sum_{j=0}^{m} g_j(\boldsymbol{X}; \mathcal{T}_j, \mathcal{M}_j), \theta\right) \tag{7.1}$$

Where each g_j is a tree of the form $g(\boldsymbol{X}; \mathcal{T}_j, \mathcal{M}_j)$, where $\mathcal{T}_j$ represents the structure of a binary tree, i.e. the set of internal nodes and their associated decision rules and a set of terminal nodes. While $\mathcal{M}_j = \{\mu_{1,j}, \mu_{2,j}, \cdots, \mu_{b,j}\}$ represents the values at the b_j terminal nodes, ϕ represents an arbitrary probability distribution that will be used as the likelihood in our model and θ other parameters from ϕ not modeled as a sum of trees.

For example we could set ϕ as a Gaussian and then we will have:

$$Y = \mathcal{N}\left(\mu = \sum_{j=0}^{m} g_j(\boldsymbol{X}; \mathcal{T}_j, \mathcal{M}_j), \sigma\right) \tag{7.2}$$

Or we can do as we did for Generalized Linear Models in Chapter 3 and try other distributions. For example if ϕ is a Poisson distribution we get

$$Y = \text{Pois}\left(\lambda = \sum_{j}^{m} g_j(\boldsymbol{X}; \mathcal{T}_j, \mathcal{M}_j)\right) \tag{7.3}$$

Or maybe ϕ is the Student's t-distribution, then:

$$Y = \text{T}\left(\mu = \sum_{j}^{m} g_j(\boldsymbol{X}; \mathcal{T}_j, \mathcal{M}_j), \sigma, \nu\right) \tag{7.4}$$

As usual to fully specify a BART model we need to choose priors. We are already familiar to prior specifications for σ for the Gaussian likelihood or over σ and ν for the Student's t-distribution so now we will focus on those priors particular to the BART model.

7.3   Priors for BART

The original BART paper [35], and most subsequent modifications and implementations rely on conjugate priors. The BART implementation in PyMC3 does not use conjugate priors and also deviates in other ways. Instead of discussing the differences we will focus on the PyMC3 implementation, which is the one we are going to use for the examples.

7.3.1   Prior Independence

In order to simplify the specification of the prior we assume that the structure of the tree $\mathcal{T}_j$ and the leaf values $\mathcal{M}_j$ are independent. Additionally these priors are independent from the rest of the parameters, θ in Equation 7.1. By assuming independence we are allowed to split the prior specification into parts. Otherwise we should devise a way to specify a single prior over the space of trees [2].

7.3.2   Prior for the Tree Structure $\mathcal{T}_j$

The prior for the tree structure $\mathcal{T}_j$ is specified by three aspects:

- The probability that a node at depth $d = (0, 1, 2, \dots)$ is non-terminal, given by α^d. α it is recommended to be $\in [0, 0.5)$ [134] [3]
- The distribution over the splitting variable. That is which covariate is included in the tree (X_i in Figure 7.1). Most commonly this is Uniform over the available covariates.
- The distribution over the splitting rule. That is, once we choose a splitting variable which value we use to make a decision (c_i in Figure 7.1). This is usually Uniform over the available values.

7.3.3   Prior for the Leaf Values μ_{ij} and Number of Trees m

By default PyMC3 does not set a prior value for the leaf values, instead at each iteration of the sampling algorithm it returns the mean of the residuals.

Regarding the number of trees in the ensemble m. This is also generally predefined by the user. In practice it has been observed that good results are generally achieved by setting the values of $m = 200$ or even as low as $m = 10$. Additionally it has been observed that inference could be very robust to the exact value of m. So a general rule of thumb is to try a few values of m and perform cross-validation to pick the most adequate value for a particular problem [4].

7.4   Fitting Bayesian Additive Regression Trees

So far we have discussed how decision trees can be used to encode piecewise functions that we can use to model regression or classification problems. We have also discussed how we can specify priors for decision trees. We are now going to discuss how to efficiently sample trees in order to find the posterior distribution over trees for a given dataset. There are many strategies to do this and the details are too specific for this book. For that reason we are going to only describe the main elements.

To fit BART models we cannot use gradient-based samplers like Hamiltonian MonteCarlo because the space of trees is discrete and thus not *gradient-friendly*. For that reason researchers have

---

[2]for alternatives see [6, 136]

[3]Node depth is defined as distance from the root. Thus, the root itself has depth 0, its first child node has depth 1, etc.

[4]In principle we can go fully Bayesian and estimate the number of tree m from the data, but there are reports showing this is not always the best approach. More research is likely needed in this area.

developed MCMC and Sequential Monte Carlo (SMC) variations tailored to trees. The BART sampler implemented in PyMC3 works in a sequential and iterative fashion. Briefly, we start with a single tree and we fit it to the Y response variable, then the residual R is computed as $R = Y - g_0(\boldsymbol{X}; \mathcal{T}_0, \mathcal{M}_0)$. The second tree is fitted to R, not to Y. We then update the residual R by considering the sum of the trees we have fitted so far, thus $R - g_1(\boldsymbol{X}; \mathcal{T}_0, \mathcal{M}_0) + g_0(\boldsymbol{X}; \mathcal{T}_1, \mathcal{M}_1)$ and we keep doing this until we fit m trees.

This procedure will lead to a single sample of the posterior distribution, one with m trees. Notice that this first iteration can easily lead to suboptimal trees, the main reasons are: the first fitted trees will have a tendency to be more complex than necessary, trees can get stuck in local minimum and finally the fitting of later trees is affected by the previous trees. All these effects will tend to vanish as we keep sampling because the sampling method will revisit previously fitted trees several times and give them the opportunity to re-adapt to the updated residuals. In fact, a common observation when fitting BART models is that trees tend to be deeper during the first rounds and then they *collapse* into shallower trees.

In the literature, specific BART models are generally tailored to specific samplers as they rely on conjugacy, thus a BART model with a Gaussian likelihood is different than a one with a Poisson one. PyMC3 uses a sampler based on the Particle Gibbs sampler [93] that is specifically tailored to work with trees. PyMC3 will automatically assign this sampler to a `pm.BART` distribution and if other random variables are present in the model, PyMC3 will assign other samplers like NUTS to those variables.

7.5   BART Bikes

Let us see how BART fits the bikes dataset which we previously studied in 5. The model will be:

$$
\begin{aligned}
\mu &\sim \text{BART}(m = 50) \\
\sigma &\sim \mathcal{HN}(1) \\
Y &\sim \mathcal{N}(\mu, \sigma)
\end{aligned}
\tag{7.5}
$$

Building a BART model in PyMC3 is very similar to building other kind of models, one difference is that specifying the random variable `pm.BART` needs to know both the independent and dependent variables. The main reason is that the sampling method used to fit the BART models proposes a new tree in terms of the residuals, as explained in the previous section.

Having made all these clarifications the model in PyMC3 looks as follows:

Code 7.1

```
1  with pm.Model() as bart_g:
2      σ = pm.HalfNormal("σ", Y.std())
3      μ = pm.BART("μ", X, Y, m=50)
4      y = pm.Normal("y", μ, σ, observed=Y)
5      idata_bart_g = pm.sample(2000, return_inferencedata=True)
```

Before showcasing the end result of fitted model we are going to explore the intermediate steps a little bit. This will give us more intuition on how BART works. Figure 7.4 shows trees sampled from the posterior computed from the model in Code Block 7.1. On the top we have three individual trees, out of the m=50 trees. The actual value returned by the tree are the solid dots, with the lines being a visual aid connecting them. The range of the data (the number of rented bikes per hour) is approximately in the range 0-800 bikes rented per hour. So even when the figures omit the data, we can see that the fit is rather crude and these piecewise functions are mostly flat in the scale of the data. This is expected from our discussion of the trees being *weak learners*. Given that we used a Gaussian likelihood, negative count values are allowed by the model.

On the bottom panel we have samples from the posterior, each one is a sum over m trees.

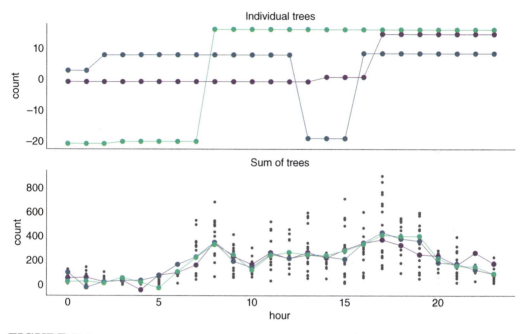

FIGURE 7.4
Posterior tree realizations. Top panel, three individuals trees sampled from the posterior. Bottom panel, three posterior samples, each one is a sum over m trees. Actual BART sampled values are represented by circles while the dashed lines are a visual aid. Small dots (only in bottom panel) represent the observed number of rented bikes.

Figure 7.5 shows the result of fitting BART to the bike dataset (number of rented bikes vs hour of the day). The figure provides a similar fit compared to Figure 5.9, created using splines. The more clear difference is the more jagged aspect of the BART's fit compared to the one obtained using splines. This is not to say there are not other differences like the width of the HDI.

The literature around BART tends to highlight its ability to, generally, provide competitive answers without tuning [5]. For example, compared with fitting splines we do not need to worry about manually setting the knots or choose a prior to regularize knots. Of course someone may argue that for some problems being able to adjust the knots could be beneficial for the problem at hand, and that is fine.

[5]The same literature generally shows that using cross-validation to tune the number of trees and/or the prior over the depth of the tree can be further beneficial.

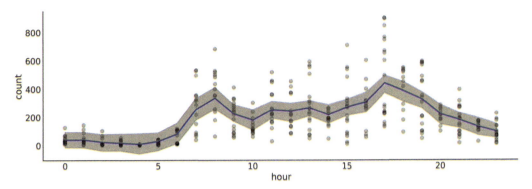

FIGURE 7.5
Bikes data (black dots) fitted using BARTs (specifically `bart_model`). The shaded curve represents the 94% HDI interval (of the mean) and the blue curve represents the mean trend. Compare with Figure 5.9.

7.6 Generalized BART Models

The PyMC3 implementation of BART attempts to make it easy to use different likelihoods [6] similar to how the Generalized Linear Model does as we saw in Chapter 3. Let us see how to use a Bernoulli likelihood with BART. For this example we are going to use a dataset of the Space Influenza disease, which affect mostly young and old people, but not middle-age folks. Fortunately, Space Influenza is not a serious concern as it is completely made up. In this dataset we have a record of people that got tested for Space Influenza and whether they are sick (1) or healthy (0) and also their age. Using the BART model with Gaussian likelihood from Code Block 7.1 as reference we see that differences are small:

Code 7.2

```
1  with pm.Model() as model:
2      μ = pm.BART("μ", X, Y, m=50,
3                  inv_link="logistic")
4      y = pm.Bernoulli("y", p=μ, observed=Y)
5      trace = pm.sample(2000, return_inferencedata=True)
```

First we no longer need to define the σ parameter as the Bernoulli distribution has a single parameter **p**. For the definition of BART itself we have one new argument, `inv_link`, this is the inverse link function, which we need to restrict the values of μ to the interval $[0, 1]$. For this purpose we instruct PyMC3 to use the logistic function, as we did in Chapter 3 for logistic regression).

Figure 7.6 shows a comparison of the model in Code Block 7.2 with 4 values for m, namely (2, 10, 20, 50) using LOO. And Figure 7.7 shows the data plus the fitted function and HDI 94% bands. We can see that according to LOO $m = 10$ and $m = 20$ provides good fits. This is in qualitative agreement with a visual inspection, as $m = 2$ is a clear underfit (the value of the ELPD is low but the difference between the in-sample and out-of-sample ELPD is not that large) and $m = 50$ seems to be overfitting (the value of the ELPD is low and the difference between the in-sample and out-of-sample ELPD is large).

---

[6] Other implementations are less flexible or require adjustments under the hood to make this work.

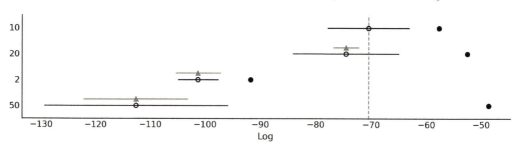

FIGURE 7.6
LOO comparison of the model in Code Block 7.2 with m values (2, 10, 20, 50). According to LOO, $m = 10$ provides the best fit.

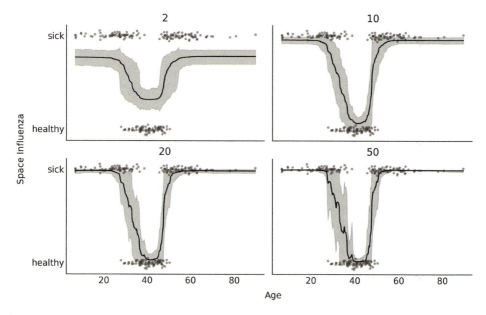

FIGURE 7.7
BART fit to the Space Influenza dataset with 4 values for m (2, 10, 20, 50). In line with LOO, the model with m is underfitting and with the one with $m = 50$ is overfitting.

So far we have discussed regressions with a single covariate, we do this for simplicity. However it is possible to fit datasets with more covariates. This is trivial from the implementation perspective in PyMC3, we just need to pass an X 2-d array containing more than 1 covariate. But it raises some interesting statistical questions, like how to easily interpret a BART model with many covariates or how to find out how much each covariate is contributing to the outcome. In the next sections we will show how this is done.

7.7 Interpretability of BARTs

Individual decision trees are generally easy to interpret, but this is no longer true when we add a bunch of trees together. One may think that the reason is that by adding trees we get some weird unrecognizable or difficult to characterize object, but actually the sum of trees is just another tree. The difficulty to interpret this *assembled* tree is that for a complex problem the decision rules will be hard to grasp. This is like playing a song on piano, playing individual notes is fairly easy, but playing a combination of notes in a musical-pleasant way is both what makes for the richness of sound and complexity in individual interpretation.

We may still get some useful information by directly inspecting a sum of trees (see Section 7.8 variable selection), but not as transparent or useful as with a simpler individual tree. Thus to help us interpret results from BART models we generally rely on model diagnostics tools [104, 105], e.g. tools also used for multivariate linear regression and other non-parametric methods. We will discuss two related tools below: **Partial Dependence Plots** (PDP) [54] and **Individual Conditional Expectation** (ICE) plots [68].

7.7.1   Partial Dependence Plots

A very common method that appears in the BART literature is the so called Partial Dependence Plot (PDP) [54] (see Figure 7.8). A PDP shows how the value of the predicted variable changes when we change a covariate while averaging over the marginal distribution of the rest of the covariates. That is, we compute and then plot:

$$\tilde{Y}_{\boldsymbol{X}_i} = \mathbb{E}_{\boldsymbol{X}_{-i}}[\tilde{Y}(\boldsymbol{X}_i, \boldsymbol{X}_{-i})] \approx \frac{1}{n} \sum_{j=1}^{n} \tilde{Y}(\boldsymbol{X}_i, \boldsymbol{X}_{-ij}) \tag{7.6}$$

where $\tilde{Y}_{\boldsymbol{X}_i}$ is the value of the predicted variable as a function of $\boldsymbol{X}_i$ while all the variables except i ($\boldsymbol{X}_{-i}$) have been marginalized. In general X_i will be a subset of 1 or 2 variables, the reason being that plotting in higher dimensions is generally difficult.

As shown in Equation 7.6 the expectation can be approximated numerically by averaging over the predicted values conditioned on the observed $\boldsymbol{X}_{-i}$. Notice however, this implies that some of the combinations in $\boldsymbol{X}_i, \boldsymbol{X}_{-ij}$ might not correspond to actual observed combinations. Moreover it might even be the case that some of the combinations are not possible to observe. This is similar to what we already discussed regarding counterfactuals plots introduced in Chapter 3. In fact partial dependence plots are one kind of counterfactual device.

Figure 7.8 shows a PDP after fitting a BART model to synthetic data: $Y \sim \mathcal{N}(0,1)$ $X_0 \sim \mathcal{N}(Y, 0.1)$ and $X_1 \sim \mathcal{N}(Y, 0.2)$ $X_2 \sim \mathcal{N}(0,1)$. We can see that both X_0 and X_1 show a linear relation with Y, as expected from the generation process of the synthetic data. We can also see that the effect of X_0 on Y is stronger compared to X_1, as the slope is steeper for X_0. Because the data is sparser at the tails of the covariate (they are Gaussian distributed), these regions show higher uncertainty, which is desired. Finally, the contribution from X_2 is virtually negligible along the entire range of the variable X_2.

Let now go back to the bikes dataset. This time we will model the number of rented bikes (the predicted variable) with four covariates; the hour of the day, the temperature, the humidity and the wind speed. Figure 7.9 shows the partial dependence plot after fitting the model. We can see that the partial dependence plot for the hour of the day looks pretty similar to Figure 7.5, the one we obtained by fitting this variable in the absence of others. As the temperature increases the number of rented bikes increase too, but at some point this trend levels off. Using our external domain knowledge we could conjecture this pattern is reasonable as people are not too motivated to bike when the temperature is too low, but riding a bike at temperatures that are *too high* is also a little bit less appealing. The humidity shows a flat trend followed by a negative contribution, again we can imagine why a higher humidity reduces people's motivation to ride a bike. The wind

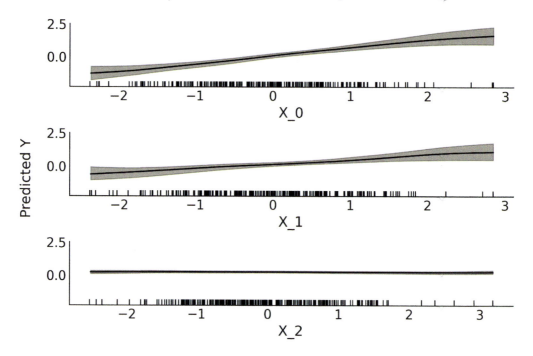

FIGURE 7.8
Partial dependence plot. Partial contribution to Y from each variable X_i while marginalizing the contributions from the rest of the variables (X_{-i}). The gray bands represent the HDI 94%. Both the mean and HDI bands has been smoothed (see `plot_ppd` function). The rugplot, the black bars at the bottom of each subplot, shows the observed values for each covariate.

speed shows an even flatter contribution, but still we see an effect, as it seems that less people are prone to rent a bike under windier conditions.

One assumption when computing partial dependence plots is that variables X_i and X_{-i} are uncorrelated, and thus we perform the average across the marginals. In most real problem this is hardly the case, and then partial dependence plot can hide relationships in the data. Nevertheless if the dependence between the subset of chosen variables is not too strong then partial dependence plots can be useful summaries [54].

Computational cost of partial dependence

Computing partial dependence plots is computationally demanding. Because at each point that we want to evaluate the variable X_i we need to compute n predictions (with n being the sample size). And for BART to obtain a prediction $\tilde{Y}$ we need to first sum over m trees to get a point-estimate of Y and then we also average over the entire posterior distribution of sum of trees to get credible interval. This ends up requiring quite a bit of computation! If needed, one way to reduce computations is to evaluate X_i at p points with $p << n$. We could choose p equally spaced points or maybe at some quantiles. Alternative we can achieve a dramatic speed-up if instead of marginalize over X_{-ij} we fix them at their mean value. Of course this means we will be losing information and it may happen that the mean value is not actually very representative of the underlying distribution. Another option, specially useful for large datasets, is to subsample X_{-ij}.

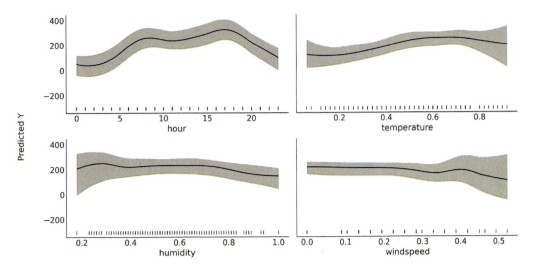

FIGURE 7.9
Partial dependence plot. Partial contribution to the number of rented bikes from the variables, hour, temperature, humidity and windspeed while marginalizing the contributions from the rest of the variables (X_{-i}). The gray bands represent the HDI 94%. Both the mean and HDI bands have been smoothed (see `plot_ppd` function). The rugplot, the black bars at the bottom of each subplot, shows the observed values for each covariate.

7.7.2 Individual Conditional Expectation

Individual Conditional Expectation (ICE) plots are closely related to PDPs. The difference is that instead of plotting the target covariates' average partial effect on the predicted response, we plot the n estimated conditional expectation curves. That is, each curve in an ICE plot reflects the partial predicted response as a function of covariate X_i for a fixed value of X_{-ij}. See Figure 7.10 for an example. If we average all the gray curves at each X_{ij} value we get the blue curve, which is the same curve that we should have obtained if we have computed the mean partial dependence in Figure 7.9.

Individual conditional expectation plots are best suited to problems where variable have strong interactions, when this is not the case partial dependence plots and individual conditional expectations plots convey the same information. Figure 7.11 shows an example where the partial dependence plots hides a relationship in the data, but an individual conditional expectation plot is able to show it better. The plot was generated by fitting a BART model to the synthetic data: $Y = 0.2X_0 - 5X_1 + 10X_1 \mathbb{1}_{X_2 \geq 0} + \epsilon$ where $X \sim \mathcal{U}(-1, 1)$ $\epsilon \sim \mathcal{N}(0, 0.5)$. Notice how the value of X_1 depends on the value of X_2.

In the first panel of Figure 7.11 we plot X_1 versus Y. Given that there is an interaction effect that the value of Y can linearly increase or decrease with X_1 conditional on the values of the X_2 variable, the plot displays the *X-shaped* pattern. The middle panel shows a partial dependence plot, we can see that according to this plot the relationship is flat, which is true *on average* but hides the interaction effect. On the contrary the last panel, an individual conditional expectation plot helps to uncover this relationship. The reason is that each gray curve represents one value of $X_{0,2}$ [7]. The blue curve is the average of the gray curves and while is not exactly the same as the partial dependence mean curve it shows the same information [8].

---

[7]This notation means the variables (X_0, X_2), that is, excluding X_1

[8]The mean of the ICE curves and the mean partial dependence curve are slightly different. This is due to internal details on how these plots were made including the order in which we average over the

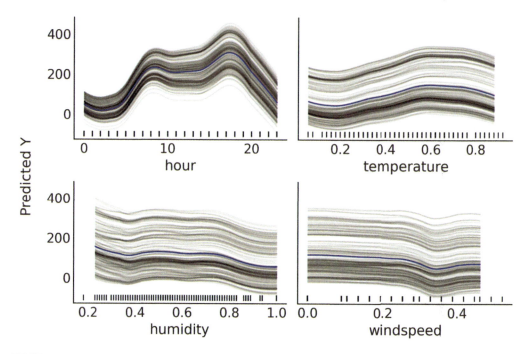

FIGURE 7.10
Individual conditional expectation plot. Partial contribution to the number of rented bikes from the variables; hour, temperature, humidity and wind speed while fixing the rest (X_{-i}) at one observed value. The blue curve corresponds to the average of the gray curves. All curves have been smoothed (see `plot_ice` function). The rugplot, the black bars at the bottom of each subplot, shows the observed values for each covariate.

7.8   Variable Selection

When fitting regressions with more than one predictor it is often of interest to learn which predictors are most important. Under some scenarios we may be genuinely interested in better understanding how different variables contribute to generate a particular output. For example, which dietary and environmental factors contribute to colon cancer. In other instances collecting a dataset with many covariates may be unaffordable financially, take too long, or be too complicated logistically. For example, in medical research measuring a lot of variable from a human can be expensive, time consuming or annoying (or even risky for the patient). Hence we can afford to measure a lot of variables in a pilot study, but to scale such analysis to a larger population we may need to reduce the number of variables. In such cases we want to keep the smallest (cheapest, more convenient to obtain) set of variables that still provide a reasonable high predictive power. BART models offer a very simple, and almost computational-free, heuristic to estimate variable importance. It keeps track of how many times a covariate is used as a splitting variable. For example, in Figure 7.1 we have two splitting nodes one includes variable X_1 and the other X_2, so based on this tree both variables are equally important. If instead we would have count X_1 twice and X_2 once. We would

---

posterior samples or over the observations. What really matter is the general features, for instance in this case that both curves are essentially flat. Also, to speed up computation we evaluate X_1 over 10 equally separated points for partial dependence plots and we subsample $X_{0,2}$ for computing the individual conditional expectation plot

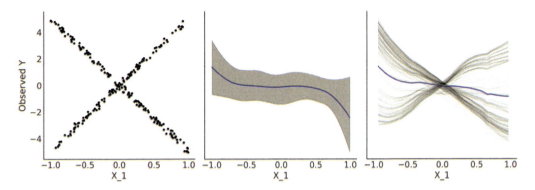

FIGURE 7.11
Partial dependence plot vs individual conditional expectation plot. First panel, scatter plot between X_1 and Y, middle panel partial dependence plot, last panel individual conditional expectation plot.

say that X_1 is twice as important as X_2. For BART models the variable importance is computed by averaging over the m trees and over all posterior samples. Note that using this simple heuristic we can only report the importance in relative fashion, as there is not simple way to say this variable is important and this another one not important.

To further ease interpretation we can report the values normalized so each value is in the interval $[0, 1]$ and the total importance is 1. It is tempting to interpret these numbers as posterior probabilities, but we should keep in mind that this is just a simple heuristic without a very strong theoretical support, or to put it in more nuanced terms, it is not yet well understood [97].

Figure 7.12 shows the relative variable importance for 3 different datasets from known generative processes.

- $Y \sim \mathcal{N}(0, 1)$ $X_0 \sim \mathcal{N}(Y, 0.1)$ and $X_1 \sim \mathcal{N}(Y, 0.2)$ $\boldsymbol{X}_{2:9} \sim \mathcal{N}(0, 1)$. Only the first 2 independent variables are unrelated to the predictor, and the first is more related than the second.

- $Y = 10\sin(\pi X_0 X_1) + 20(X_2 - 0.5)^2 + 10X_3 + 5X_4 + \epsilon$ Where $\epsilon \sim \mathcal{N}(0, 1)$ and $\boldsymbol{X}_{0:9} \sim \mathcal{U}(0, 1)$ This is usually called the Friedman's five dimensional test function [54]. Notice that while the first five random variables are related to Y (to different extend) the last 5 are not.

- $\boldsymbol{X}_{0:9} \sim \mathcal{N}(0, 1)$ and $Y \sim \mathcal{N}(0, 1)$. All variables are unrelated to the response variable.

One thing we can see from Figure 7.12 is the effect of increasing the number of trees m. In general, as we increase m, the distribution of the relative importance tends to become *flatter*. This is a well known observation with an intuitive explanation. As we increase the value of m we demand less predictive power from each tree, this implies that less relevant features have a higher chance to be part of a given tree. On the contrary, if we decrease the value of m we demand more from each single tree and this induces a more stringent *competition* between variables to be part of the trees, as a consequence only the *really important* variables will be included in the final trees.

Plots like Figure 7.12 can be used to help separate the more important variables from the less important ones [35, 31]. This can be done by looking at what happens when we move from low values of m to higher ones. If the relative importance decreases the variable is *more important* and if the variable importance increases then the variable is *less important*. For example, in the first panel it is clear that for different values of m the first two variables are much more important than the rest. And something similar can be concluded from the second panel for the first 5 variables. On the last panel all variables are equally (un)important.

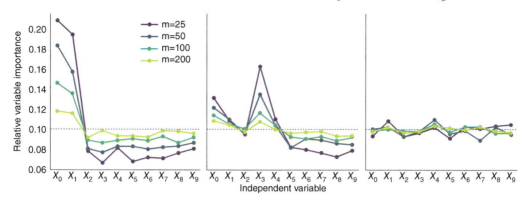

FIGURE 7.12

Relative variable importance. Left panel, the first 2 input variables contribute to the predictor variable and the rest are noise. Middle panel, the first 5 variable are related to the output variable. Finally on the right panel the 10 input variables are completely unrelated to the predictor variable. The black dashed line represents the value of the variable importance if all variables were equally important.

This way to assess variable importance can be useful, but also tricky. Under some circumstances it can help to have confidence intervals for the variable importance and not just point estimates. We can do this by running BART many times, with the same parameters and data. Nevertheless, the lack of a clear threshold separating the important from the unimportant variables can be seen as problematic. Some alternative methods have been proposed [31, 20]. One of such methods can be summarized as follow:

1. Fit a model many times (around 50) using a small value of m, like 25 [9]. Record the root mean squared error.

2. Eliminate the least informative variable across all 50 runs.

3. Repeat 1 and 2, each time with one less variable in the model. Stop once you reach a given number of covariates in the model (not necessarily 1).

4. Finally, select the model with the lowest average root mean square error.

According to Carlson [31] this procedure seems to almost always return the same result as just creating a figure like Figure 7.12. Nevertheless one can argue that is more automatic (with all the pros and cons of automatic decisions). Also nothing prevents us for doing the automatic procedure and then using the plot as a visual check.

Let us move to the rent bike example with the four covariates: hour, temperature, humidity and windspeed. From Figure 7.13 we can see that hour and temperature are more relevant to predict the number of rented bikes than humidity or windspeed. We can also see that the order of the variable importance qualitatively agrees with the results from partial dependence plots (Figure 7.9) and individual conditional expectation plots (Figure 7.10).

---

[9]The original proposal suggests 10, but our experience with the BART implementation in PyMC3 is that values of m below 20 or 25 could be problematic.

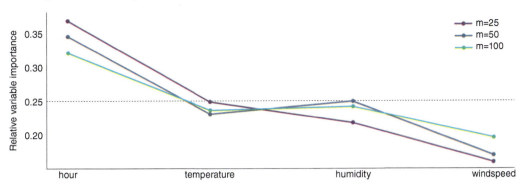

FIGURE 7.13

Relative variable importance from fitted BARTs with different number of trees. Hour is the most important covariate followed by the temperature. The humidity and windspeed appear as less relevant covariates.

7.9 Priors for BART in PyMC3

Compared to other models in this book, BARTs are the most *blackboxsy*. We are not able to set whatever priors we want to generate a BART model. We instead control predefined priors through a few parameters. PyMC3 allows to control priors for BARTS with 3 arguments:

- The number of trees m
- The depth of the trees α
- The distribution over the split variables.

We saw the effect of changing the number of trees, which has been shown to provide robust predictions for values in the interval 50-200. Also there are many examples showing that using cross-validation to determine this number can be beneficial. We also saw that by scanning m for relative low values like in the range 25-100 we can evaluate the variable importance. We did not bother to change the default value of $\alpha = 0.25$ as this change seems to have even less impact, although research is still needed to better understand this prior [134]. As with m cross-validation can also be used to tune it for better efficiency. Finally PyMC3 provides the option to pass a vector of weights so different variables have different prior probabilities of being selected, this can be useful when the user has evidence that some variables may be more important than others, otherwise it is better to just keep it Uniform. More sophisticated Dirichlet-based priors have been proposed [10] to achieve this goal and to allow for better inference when inducing sparsity is desired. This is useful in cases where we have a lot of covariates, but only a few are likely to contribute and we do not know beforehand which ones are the most relevant. This is a common case, for example, in genetic research where measuring the activity of hundreds or more genes is relatively easy but how they are related is not only not known but the goal of the research.

Most BART implementations have been done in the context of individual packages, in some cases even oriented to particular sub-disciplines. They are typically not part of probabilistic programming languages, and thus users are not expected to tweak BART models too much. So even when it could be possible to put a prior directly over the number of trees, this is not generally how

---

[10]This is likely to be added in the future versions of PyMC3.

it is done in practice. Instead the BART literature praises the good performance of BART with default parameters while recognizing that cross-validation can be used to get some extra juice. The BART implementation in PyMC3 slightly departure from this tradition, and allows for some extra flexibility, but is still very limited, compared to how we use other primitives like Gaussian or Poisson distribution, or even non-parametric distributions like Gaussian Processes. We envision that this may change in the not so far future, partly because of our interest in exploring more flexible implementations of BART that could allow users to build flexible and problem-tailored models as is usually the case with probabilistic programming languages.

7.10   Exercises

7E1. Explain each of the following

    (a) How is BART different from linear regression and splines.

    (b) When you may want to use linear regression over BART?

    (c) When you may want to use splines over BART?

7E2. Draw at least two more trees that could be used to explain the data in Figure 7.1.

7E3. Draw a tree with one more internal node than the one in Figure 7.1 that explains the data equally well.

7E4. Draw a decision tree of what you decide to wear each morning. Label the leaf nodes and the root nodes.

7E5. What are the priors required for BART? Explain what is the role of priors for BART models and how is this similar and how is this different from the role of priors in the models we have discussed in previous chapters.

7E6. In your own words explain why it can be the case that multiple small trees can fit patterns better than one single large tree. What is the difference in the two approaches? What are the tradeoffs?

7E7. Below we provide some data. To each data fit a BART model with m=50. Plot the fit, including the data. Describe the fit.

    (a) `x = np.linspace(-1, 1., 200)` and `y = np.random.normal(2*x, 0.25)`

    (b) `x = np.linspace(-1, 1., 200)` and `y = np.random.normal(x**2, 0.25)`

    (c) pick a function you like

    (d) compare the results with the exercise **5E4.** from Chapter 5

7E8. Compute the PDPs For the dataset used to generate Figure 7.12. Compare the information you get from the variable importance measure and the PDPs.

7M9. For the rental bike example we use a Gaussian as likelihood, this can be seen as a reasonable approximation when the number of counts is large, but still brings some problems, like predicting negative number of rented bikes (for example, at night when the observed number of rented bikes is close to zero). To fix this issue and improve our models we can try with other likelihoods:

    (a) use a Poisson likelihood (hint you will need to use an inverse link function, check `pm.Bart` docstring). How the fit differs from the example in the book. Is this a better fit? In what sense?

(b) use a NegativeBinomial likelihood, how the fit differs from the previous two? Could you explain the result.

(c) how this result is different from the one in Chapter 5? Could you explain the difference?

7M10. Use BART to redo the first penguin classification examples we performed in Section 3.4.2 (i.e. use "bill_length_mm" as covariate and the species "Adelie" and "Chistrap" as the response). Try different values of m like, 4, 10, 20 and 50 and pick a suitable value as we did in the book. Visually compare the results with the fit in Figure 3.19. Which model do you think performs the best?

7M11. Use BART to redo the penguin classification we performed in Section 3.4.2. Set m=50 and use the covariates "bill_length_mm", "bill_depth_mm", "flipper_length_mm" and "body_mass_g".

Use Partial Dependence Plots and Individual Conditional Expectation. To find out how the different covariates contribute the probability of identifying "Adelie", and "Chinstrap" species.

Refit the model but this time using only 3 covariates "bill_depth_m", "flipper_length_mm", and "body_mass_g". How results differ from using the four covariates? Justify.

7M12. Use BART to redo the penguin classification we performed in Section 3.4.2. Build a model with the covariates "bill_length_mm", "bill_depth_mm", "flipper_length_mm", and "body_mass_g" and assess their relative variable importance. Compare the results with the PDPs from the previous exercise.

8

Approximate Bayesian Computation

In this chapter we discuss Approximate Bayesian Computation (ABC). The "approximate" in ABC refers to the lack of explicit likelihood, but not to the use of numerical methods to approximate the posterior, such as Markov chain Monte Carlo or Variational Inference. Another common, and more explicit name, for ABC methods is likelihood-free methods, although some authors mark a difference between these terms others use them interchangeably.

ABC methods may be useful when we do not have an explicit expression for the likelihood, but we have a parameterized *simulator* capable of generating synthetic data. The simulator has one or more unknown parameters and we want to know which set of parameters generates synthetic data *close enough* to the observed data. To this extent we will compute a posterior distribution of those parameters.

ABC methods are becoming increasingly common in the biological sciences, in particular in sub-fields like systems biology, epidemiology, ecology and population genetics [146]. But they are also used in other domains as they provide a flexible way to solve many practical problems. This diversity is also reflected in the Python packages available for ABC [52, 96, 85]. Nevertheless, the extra layer of approximation comes with its own set of difficulties. Mainly defining what *close enough* means in the absence of a likelihood and then being able to actually compute an approximated posterior.

We will discuss these challenges in this chapter from a general perspective. We highly recommend readers interested into applying ABC methods to their own problems to complement this chapter with examples from their own domain knowledge.

8.1 Life Beyond Likelihood

From Bayes theorem (Equation 1.1), to compute a posterior we need two basic ingredients, a prior and a likelihood. However, for particular problems, we may find that we can not express the likelihood in closed-form, or it is prohibitively costly to compute it. This seems to be a dead end for our Bayesian enthusiasm. But that is not necessarily the case as long as we are able to somehow generate synthetic data. This generator of synthetic data is generally referred to as a *simulator*. From the perspective of the ABC method the simulator is a black-box, we feed parameter values at one side and get simulated data from the other. The complication we add however, is uncertainty about which inputs are good enough to generate synthetic data similar to the observed data.

The basic notion common to all ABC methods is to replace the likelihood by a δ function that computes a distance or more generally some form of discrepancy between the observed data Y and the synthetic data $\hat{Y}$ generated by a parameterized simulator Sim.

$$\hat{Y} \sim Sim(\theta) \tag{8.1}$$

$$p(\theta \mid Y) \underset{\sim}{\propto} \delta(Y, \hat{Y} \mid \epsilon) \, p(\boldsymbol{\theta}) \tag{8.2}$$

DOI: 10.1201/9781003019169-8

We aim at using a function δ to obtain a *practically good enough* approximation to the *true* likelihood:

$$\lim_{\epsilon \to 0} \delta(Y, \hat{Y} \mid \epsilon) = p(Y \mid \boldsymbol{\theta}) \qquad (8.3)$$

We introduce a tolerance parameter ϵ because the chance of generating a synthetic data-set $\hat{Y}$ being equal to the observed data Y is virtually null for most problems [1]. The larger the value of ϵ the more tolerant we are about how close Y and $\hat{Y}$ has to be in order to consider them as *close enough*. In general and for a given problem, a larger value of ϵ implies a more crude approximation to the posterior, we will see examples of this later.

In practice, as we increase the sample size (or dimensionality) of the data it becomes harder and harder to find a small enough values for the distance function δ [2]. A naive solution is to increase the value of ϵ, but this means increasing the error of our approximation. A better solution could be to instead use one or more summary statistics S and compute the distance between the data summaries instead of between the simulated and real datasets.

$$\delta\left(S(Y), S(\hat{Y}) \mid \epsilon\right) \qquad (8.4)$$

We must be aware that using a summary statistic introduces an additional source of error to the ABC approximation, unless the summary statistics are sufficient with respect to the model parameters θ. Unfortunately, this is not always possible. Nevertheless non-sufficient summary statistics can still be very useful in practice and they are often used by practitioners.

In this chapter we will explore a few different distances and summary statistics focusing on some proven methods. But know that ABC handles so many different types of simulated data, in so many distinct fields, that it may be hard to generalize. Moreover the literature is advancing very quickly so we will focus on building the necessary knowledge, skills and tools, so you find it easier to generalize to new problems as the ABC methods continues to evolve.

Sufficient statistics

A statistic is sufficient with respect to a model parameter if no other statistic computed from the same sample provides any additional information about that sample. In other words, that statistics is *sufficient* to summarize your samples without losing information. For example, given a sample of independent values from a normal distribution with expected value μ and known finite variance the sample mean is a **sufficient statistic** for μ. Notice that the mean says nothing about the dispersion, thus it is only sufficient with respect to the parameter μ. It is known that for iid data the only distributions with a sufficient statistic with dimension equal to the dimension of θ are the distributions from the Exponential family [42, 87, 123, 4]. For other distribution, the dimension of the sufficient statistic increases with the sample size.

---

[1] It can work for discrete variables, especially if they take only a few possible values.

[2] This is another manifestation of the curse of dimensionality. See Chapter 11 Section 11.8 for a full explanation.

8.2 Approximating the Approximated Posterior

The most basic method to perform Approximate Bayesian Computation is probably rejection sampling. We will describe it using Figure 8.1 together with the high level step by step description of the algorithm as follows.

1. Sample a value of θ from the prior distribution.
2. Pass that value to the simulator and generate synthetic data.
3. If the synthetic data is at a *distance* δ closer than ϵ save the proposed θ, otherwise reject it.
4. Repeat until having the desired number of samples.

The major drawback of the ABC-rejection sampler is that if the prior distribution is too different from the posterior distribution we will spend most of the time proposing values that will be rejected. A better idea is to propose from a distribution closer to the actual posterior. Generally we do not know enough about the posterior to do this by hand, but we can achieve it using a Sequential Monte Carlo (SMC) method. This is a general sampler method, like the MCMC methods we have been using in the book. SMC can be adapted to perform ABC and then it is called SMC-ABC. If you want to learn more about the detail of the SMC method you can read Section 11.9, but to understand this chapter you just need to know that SMC proceeds by increasing the value of a auxiliary parameter β in s successive stages $\{\beta_0 = 0 < \beta_1 < ... < \beta_s = 1\}$. This is done in such a way that we start sampling from the prior ($\beta = 0$) until we reach the posterior ($\beta = 1$). Thus, we can think of β as a parameter that *gradually turns the likelihood on*. The intermediate values of β are automatically computed by SMC. The more informative the data with respect to the prior and/or the more complex the geometry of the posterior the more intermediate steps SMC will take. Figure 8.2 shows an hypothetical sequence of intermediate distributions from the prior in light grey to the posterior in blue.

8.3 Fitting a Gaussian the ABC-way

Let us warm up with a simple example, the estimation of the mean and standard deviation from Gaussian distributed data with mean 0 and standard deviation 1. For this problem we can fit the model:

$$
\begin{aligned}
\mu &\sim \mathcal{N}(0, 1) \\
\sigma &\sim \mathcal{HN}(1) \\
s &\sim \mathcal{N}(\mu, \sigma)
\end{aligned}
\tag{8.5}
$$

The straightforward way to write this model in PyMC3 is shown in Code Block 8.1.

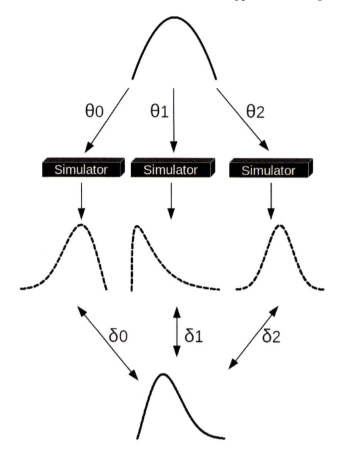

FIGURE 8.1

One step of an ABC-rejection sampler. We sample a set of θ values from the prior distribution (at the top). Each value is passed to the simulator, which generates synthetic datasets (dashed distributions), we compare the synthetic data with the observed one (the distribution at the bottom). In this example only θ_1 was able to generate a synthetic dataset close enough to the observed data, thus θ_0 and θ_2 were rejected. Notice that if we were using a summary statistics, instead of the entire dataset we should compute the summary statistics of the synthetic and observed data after step 2 and before step 3.

Code 8.1

```
1  with pm.Model() as gauss:
2      μ = pm.Normal("μ", mu=0, sigma=1)
3      σ = pm.HalfNormal("σ", sigma=1)
4      s = pm.Normal("s", μ, σ, observed=data)
5      trace_g = pm.sample()
```

The equivalent model using SMC-ABC is shown in Code Block 8.2.

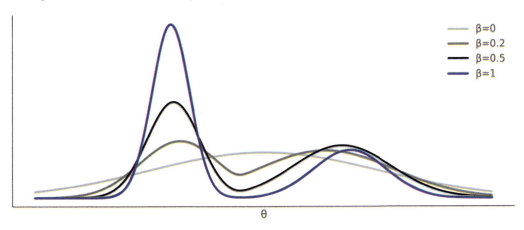

FIGURE 8.2
Hypothetical sequence of tempered posteriors explored by an SMC sampler, from the prior ($\beta = 0$), light gray, to the actual posterior ($\beta = 1$), blue. Low β values at the beginning helps the sampler to not get stuck in a single maximum.

Code 8.2

```
1  with pm.Model() as gauss:
2      μ = pm.Normal("μ", mu=0, sigma=1)
3      σ = pm.HalfNormal("σ", sigma=1)
4      s = pm.Simulator("s", normal_simulator, params=[μ, σ],
5                          distance="gaussian",
6                          sum_stat="sort",
7                          epsilon=1,
8                          observed=data)
9      trace_g = pm.sample_smc(kernel="ABC")
```

We can see there are two important differences between Code Block 8.1 and Code Block 8.2:

- The use of the `pm.Simulator` *distribution*
- The use of `pm.sample_smc(kernel="ABC")` instead of `pm.sample()`.

By using `pm.Simulator` we are telling PyMC3 that we are not going to use a closed form expression for the likelihood, and instead we are going to define a pseudo-likelihood. We need to pass a Python function that generates synthetic data, in this example the function `normal_simulator`, together with its parameters. Code Block 8.3 shows the definition of this function for a sample size of 1000 and unknown parameters μ and σ.

Code 8.3

```
1  def normal_simulator(μ, σ):
2      return np.random.normal(μ, σ, 1000)
```

We may also need to pass other, optional, arguments to `pm.Simulator` including the distance function `distance`, the summary statistics `sum_stat` and the value of the tolerance parameter ϵ `epsilon`. We will discuss these arguments in detail later. We also pass the observed data to the simulator distribution as with a regular likelihood.

By using `pm.sample_smc(kernel="ABC")`[3] we are telling PyMC3 to look for a `pm.Simulator` in the model and use it to define a pseudo-likelihood, the rest of the sampling process is the same as the one described for the SMC algorithm. Other samplers will fail to run when `pm.Simulator` is present.

The final ingredient is the `normal_simulator` function. In principle we can use whatever Python function we want, in fact we can even wrap non-Python code, like Fortran or C code. That is where the flexibility of ABC methods reside. In this example our simulator is just a wrapper around a NumPy random generator function.

As with other samplers it is recommended that we run more than one chain so we can diagnose if the sampler failed to work properly, PyMC3 will try to do this automatically. Figure 8.3 shows the result of running Code Block 8.2 with two chains. We can see that we were able to recover the true parameters and that the sampler is not showing any evident sampling issue.

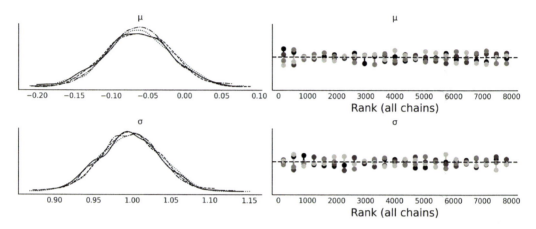

FIGURE 8.3

As expected $\mu \approx 0$ and $\sigma \approx 1$, both chains agree about the posterior as reflected by the KDEs and also by the rank plots. Notice that each of these 2 chains was obtained by running 2000 parallel SMC-chains/particles as described in the SMC algorithm.

8.4   Choosing the Distance Function, ϵ and the Summary Statistics

Defining a useful distance, summary statistic and ϵ is problem dependent. This means that we should expect some trial and error before getting good results, especially when jumping into a new problem. As usual thinking first about good options helps to reduce the number of choices. But we should embrace running experiments too as they are always helpful to better understand the problem and to make a more informed decision about these hyperparameters. In the following sections we will discuss a few general guidelines.

---

[3]The default SMC `kernel` is `"metropolis"`. See Section 11.9 for details.

8.4.1 Choosing the Distance

We run Code Block 8.2 with the default distance function `distance="gaussian"`, which is defined as:

$$\sum_i -\frac{||X_{oi} - X_{si}||^2}{2\epsilon_i^2} \tag{8.6}$$

Where X_o is the observed data, X_s is the simulated data and ϵ its scaling parameter. We call 8.6 *Gaussian* because it is the Gaussian kernel[4] in log scale. We use the log scale to compute pseudo-likelihood as we did with actual likelihoods (and priors)[5]. $||X_{oi} - X_{si}||^2$ is the Euclidean distance (also known as L2 norm) and hence we can also describe Equation 8.6 as a weighted Euclidean distance. This is a very popular choice in the literature. Other popular options are the L1 norm (the sum of absolute differences), called Laplace distance in PyMC3, the L∞ norm (the maximum absolute value of the differences) or the Mahalanobis distance: $\sqrt{(xo - xs)^T \Sigma (xo - xs)}$, where Σ is a covariance matrix.

Distances such as Gaussian, Laplace, etc can be applied to the whole data or, as we already mentioned, to summary statistics. There are also some distance functions that have been introduced specifically to avoid the need of summary statistics and still provide good results [117, 83, 13]. We are going to discuss two of them, the Wasserstein distances and the KL divergence.

In Code Block 8.2 we use `sum_stat="sort"` [6], this tells PyMC3 to sort the data before computing Equation 8.6. Doing this is equivalent to computing the 1D 2-Wasserstein distance and if we do the same but we use the L1 norm we get the 1D 1-Wasserstein distance. It is possible to define Wasserstein distances for dimensions larger than 1 [13].

Sorting the data before computing the distance makes the comparison between distributions much more fair. To see this imagine we have two samples that are exactly equal, but out of pure luck one is ordered from low to high and the other from high to low. In such a case if we apply a metric like Equation 8.6 we would conclude both samples are very dissimilar, even when they are the same sample. But if we sort first, we will conclude they are the same. This is a very extreme scenario but it helps clarify the intuition behind sorting the data. One more thing, if we sort the data we are assuming we only care about the distribution and not the order of the data, otherwise sorting will destroy the structure in the data. This could happen, for example, with a time series, see Chapter 6.

Another distance introduced to avoid the need to define a summary statistic is the use of the KL divergence (see Section 11.3). The KL divergence is approximated using the following expression [117, 83]:

$$\frac{d}{n} \sum \left(-\frac{\log(\frac{\nu_d}{\rho_d})}{\epsilon} \right) + \log \left(\frac{n}{n-1} \right) \tag{8.7}$$

Where d is the dimension of the dataset (number of variables or features), n is the number of observed datapoints. ν_d contains the 1-nearest neighbor distances of the observed to simulated data and ρ_d the 2-nearest neighbor distances of the observed data to itself (notice that if you compare a dataset with itself the 1-nearest neighbor distances will always be zero). As this method involves 2n operations of nearest neighbor search, it is generally implemented using k-d trees [12].

---

[4]Is similar to the Gaussian distribution but without the normalization term $\frac{1}{\sigma\sqrt{2\pi}}$.

[5]This is something PyMC3 does, other packages could be different

[6]Even when PyMC3 uses `sum_stat="sort"` as summary statistic, sorting is not a true summary as we are still using the whole data

8.4.2   Choosing ϵ

In many ABC methods the ϵ parameter works as a hard-threshold, θ values generating samples with distance larger than ϵ are rejected. Additionally ϵ can be a list of decreasing values that the user has to set or the algorithm adaptive finds [7].

In PyMC3, ϵ is the scale of the distance function, like in Equation 8.6, so it does not work as a hard-threshold. We can set ϵ according to our needs. We can choose a scalar value (which is equivalent to setting ϵ_i equal for all i). This is useful when evaluating the distance over the data instead of using summary statistics. In this case a reasonably educated guess could be the empirical standard deviation of the data. If we instead use a summary statistic then we can set ϵ to a list of values. This is usually necessary as each summary statistic may have a different scale. If the scales are too different then the contribution of each summary statistic will be uneven, it may even occur that a single summary statistic dominates the computed distances. A popular choice for ϵ in those cases is the empirical standard deviation of the ith summary statistic under the prior predictive distribution, or the median absolute deviation, as this is more robust to outliers. A problem with using the prior predictive distribution is that it can be way broader than the posterior predictive distribution. Thus to find a useful value of ϵ we may want to take these educated guesses previously mentioned as upper bound and then from those values try also a few lower values. Then we could choose a final value of ϵ based on several factors including the computational cost, the needed level of precision/error and the efficiency of the sampler. In general the lower the value of ϵ the better the approximation. Figure 8.4 shows a forest plot for μ and σ for several values of ϵ and also for the "NUTS" sampler (using a normal likelihood instead of a simulator).

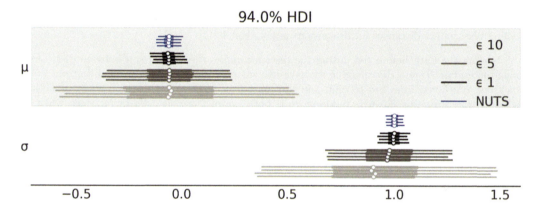

FIGURE 8.4
Forest plot for μ and σ, obtained using NUTS or ABC with increasing values of ϵ, 1, 5, and 10.

Decreasing the value of ϵ has a limit, a too low value will make the sampler very inefficient, signaling that we are aiming at an accuracy level that does not make too much sense. Figure 8.5 shows how the SMC sampler fails to converge when the model from Code Block 8.2 is sampled with a value of `epsilon=0.1`. As we can see the sampler fails spectacularly.

To help us decide on a good value for ϵ we can get help from the model criticism tools we have been using for non-ABC methods, like Bayesian p-values and posterior predictive checks as exemplified in Figures 8.6, 8.7, and 8.8. Figure 8.6 includes the value $\epsilon = 0.1$. We do that here to show what poorly calibrated models look like. But in practice if we obtain a rank plot like the one in Figure 8.5 we should stop right there with the analysis of the computed posterior and

---

[7]In a similar fashion as the β parameters in the description of the SMC/SMC-ABC algorithm explained before

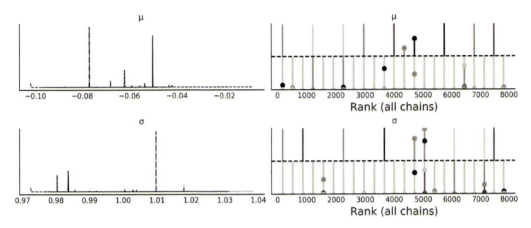

FIGURE 8.5
KDE and rank plot for model `trace_g_001`, failure of convergence could indicate that the value $\epsilon = 0.1$ is too low for this problem.

reinspect the model definition. Additionally, for ABC methods, we should also inspect the value of the hyperparameter ϵ, the summary statistics we have chosen or the distance function.

8.4.3 Choosing Summary Statistics

The choice of summary statistics is arguably more difficult and will have a larger effect than the choice of the distance function. For that reason a lot of research has been focused on the subject from the use of distance that does not require summary statistics [83, 13] to strategies for choosing summary statistics [144].

A good summary statistic provides a balance between low dimension and informativeness. When we do not have a sufficient summary statistic it is tempting to overcompensate by adding a lot of summary statistics. The intuition is that the more information the better. However, increasing the number of summary statistics can actually reduce the quality of the approximated posterior [144]. One explanation for this is that we move from computing distances over data to distances over summaries to reduce the dimensionality, by increasing the number of summaries statistics we are defeating that purpose.

In some fields like population genetics, where ABC methods are very common, people have developed a large collection of useful summary statistics [10, 9, 127]. In general it is a good idea to check the literature from the applied field you are working on to see what others are doing, as chances are high they have already tried and tested many alternatives.

When in doubt we can follow the same recommendations from the previous section to evaluate the model fit, i.e rank plots, Bayesian p-values, posterior predictive checks, etc and try alternatives if necessary (see Figures 8.5, 8.6, 8.7, and 8.8).

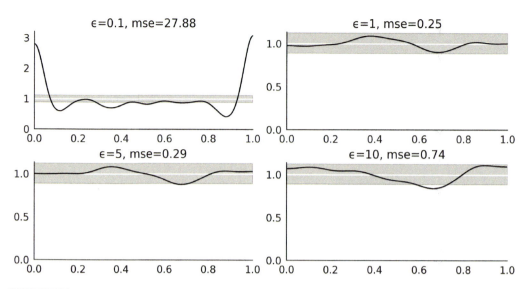

FIGURE 8.6

Distribution of marginal Bayesian p-values for increasing values of ϵ. For a well calibrated model we should expect a Uniform distribution. We can see that for $\epsilon = 0.1$ the calibration is terrible, this is not surprising as this value of ϵ is too. For all the other values of ϵ the distribution looks much more Uniform and the level of uniformity decreases as ϵ increases. The se values are the (scaled) squared differences between the expected Uniform distribution and the computed KDEs.

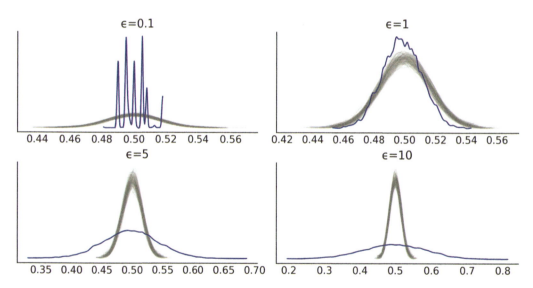

FIGURE 8.7

Bayesian p-values for increasing values of epsilon. The blue curve is the observed distribution and the gray curves the expected ones. For a well calibrated model we should expect a distribution concentrated around 0.5. We can see that for $\epsilon = 0.1$ the calibration is terrible, this is not surprising as this value of ϵ is too low. We can see that $\epsilon = 1$ provides the best results.

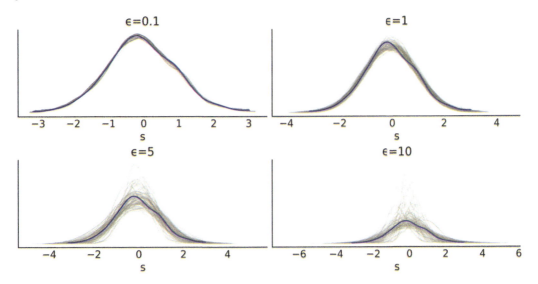

FIGURE 8.8
Posterior predictive checks for increasing values of ϵ. The blue curve is the observed distribution and the gray curves the expected ones. Surprisingly from $\epsilon = 0.1$ we get what seems to be a good adjustment, even when we know that the samples from that posterior are not trustworthy, this is a very simple example and we got the right answer out of pure luck. This is an example of *a too good to be true fit*. These are the worst! If we only consider models with posterior samples that look reasonable (i.e. not $\epsilon = 0.1$), we can see that $\epsilon = 1$ provides the best results.

8.5   g-and-k Distribution

Carbon monoxide (CO) is a colorless, odorless gas that can be harmful, even fatal, when inhaled in large amounts. This gas is generated when something is burned, especially in situations when oxygen levels are low. CO together with other gases like Nitrogen Dioxide (NO_2) are usually monitored in many cities around the world to assess the level of air pollution and the quality of air. In a city the main sources of CO are cars, and other vehicles or machinery that work by burning fossil fuels. Figure 8.9 shows a histogram of the daily CO levels measured by one station in the city of Buenos Aires from 2010 to 2018. As we can see the data seems to be slightly right skewed. Additionally the data present a few observations with very high values. The bottom panel omits 8 observations between 3 and 30.

To fit this data we are going to introduce the univariate g-and-k distribution. This is a 4 parameter distribution able to describe data with high skewness and/or kurtosis [151, 129]. Its density function in unavailable in closed form and the g-and-k distribution are defined through its quantile function, i.e. the inverse of the cumulative distribution function:

$$a + b\ \left(1 + c \tanh\left[\frac{gz(x)}{2}\right]\right)\left(1 + z(x)^2\right)^k z(x) \tag{8.8}$$

where z is the inverse of the standard normal cumulative distribution function and $x \in (0, 1)$.

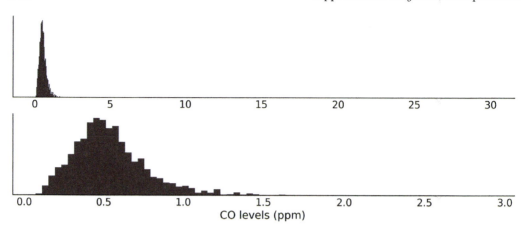

FIGURE 8.9

Histogram of CO levels. The top panel shows the entire data and the bottom one omits values larger than 3.

The parameters a, b, g and k are the location, scale, skewness and kurtosis parameters respectively. If g and k are 0, we recover the Gaussian distribution with mean a and standard deviation b. $g > 0$ gives positive (right) skewness and $g < 0$ gives negative (left) skewness. The parameter $k \geqslant 0$ gives longer tails than the normal and $k < 0$ gives shorter tails than the normal. a and g can take any real value. It is common to restrict b to be positive and $k \geqslant -0.5$ or sometimes $k \geqslant 0$ i.e. tails as heavy or heavier than those from a Gaussian distribution. Additionally it is common to fix $c = 0.8$. With all these restrictions we are guaranteed to get a strictly increasing quantile function [129] which is a hallmark of well-defined continuous distribution functions.

Code Block 8.4 defines a g-and-k quantile distribution. We have omitted the calculation of the cdf and pdf because they are a little bit more involved, but most importantly because we are not going to use them for our examples [8]. While the probability density function of the g-and-k distribution can be evaluated numerically [129, 126], simulating from the g-and-k model using the inversion method is more straightforward and fast [49, 126]. To implement the inversion method we sample $x \sim \mathcal{U}(0, 1)$ and replace in Equation 8.8. Code Block 8.4 shows how to do this in Python and Figure 8.10 shows examples of g-and-k distributions.

Code 8.4

```python
class g_and_k_quantile:
    def __init__(self):
        self.quantile_normal = stats.norm(0, 1).ppf

    def ppf(self, x, a, b, g, k):
        z = self.quantile_normal(x)
        return a + b * (1 + 0.8 * np.tanh(g*z/2)) * ((1 + z**2)**k) * z

    def rvs(self, samples, a, b, g, k):
        x = np.random.normal(0, 1, samples)
        return ppf(self, x, a, b, g, k)
```

To fit a g-and-k distribution using SMC-ABC, we can use the Gaussian distance and

---

[8]In Prangle [126] you will find a description of an R package with a lot of functions to work with g-and-k distributions.

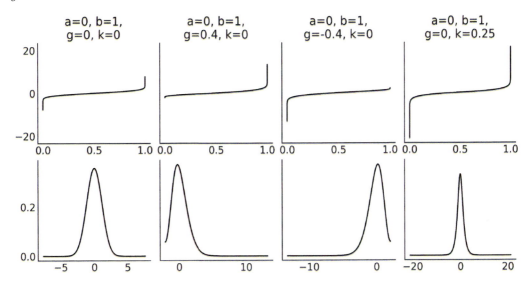

FIGURE 8.10
The first row shows the quantile function, also known as the inverse of the cumulative distribution function. You feed it with a quantile value and it returns the value of the variable that represents that quantile. For example, if you have $P(X <= x_q) = q$, you pass q to the quantile function and you get x_q. The second row shows the (approximated) pdf. For this example the pdf has been computed using a kernel density estimation from the random samples generated with Code Block 8.4.

`sum_stat="sort"` as we did for the Gaussian example. Alternative, we can also think of a summary statistic tailored for this problem. As we know, the parameters a, b, g and k are associated with location, scale, skewness and kurtosis respectively. Thus, we can think of a summary statistic based on robust estimates for these quantities [49]:

$$
\begin{aligned}
sa &= e4 \\
sb &= e6 - e2 \\
sg &= (e6 + e2 - 2 * e4)/sb \\
sk &= (e7 - e5 + e3 - e1)/sb
\end{aligned}
\tag{8.9}
$$

where $e1$ to $e7$ are octiles, i.e. the quantiles that divide a sample into eight subsets.

If we pay attention we can see that sa is the median and sb the interquartile range, which are robust estimators of location and dispersion. Even when sg and sk may look a little bit more obscure, they are also robust estimators of skewness [22] and kurtosis [107], respectively. Let us make this more clear. For a symmetric distribution $e6-e4$ and $e2-e4$ will have the same magnitude but opposite signs so in such a case sg will be zero, and for skewed distributions either $e6 - e4$ will be larger than $e2 - e4$ or vice versa. The two terms in the numerator of sk increase when the mass in the neighbourhood of $e6$ and $e2$ decreases, i.e. when we *move* mass from the central part of the distribution to the tails. The denominator in both sg and sk acts as a normalization factor.

With this idea in mind we can use Python to create a summary statistic for our problem as specified in the following code block.

Code 8.5

```
1  def octo_summary(x):
2      e1, e2, e3, e4, e5, e6, e7 = np.quantile(
3          x, [.125, .25, .375, .5, .625, .75, .875])
4      sa = e4
5      sb = e6 - e2
6      sg = (e6 + e2 - 2*e4)/sb
7      sk = (e7 - e5 + e3 - e1)/sb
8      return np.array([sa, sb, sg, sk])
```

Now we need to define a simulator, we can just wrap the `rvs` method from the `g_and_k_quantile()` function previously defined in Code Block 8.4.

Code 8.6

```
1  gk = g_and_k_quantile()
2  def gk_simulator(a, b, g, k):
3      return gk.rvs(len(bsas_co), a, b, g, k)
```

Having defined the summary statistic and the simulator and having imported the data, we can define our model. For this example we use weakly informative priors based on the fact that all the parameters are restricted to be positive. CO levels can not take negative values so a is positive and g is also expected to be 0 or positive as most common levels are expected to be "low", with some measurement taking larger values. We also have reasons to assume that the parameters are most likely to be below 1.

Code 8.7

```
1  with pm.Model() as gkm:
2      a = pm.HalfNormal("a", sigma=1)
3      b = pm.HalfNormal("b", sigma=1)
4      g = pm.HalfNormal("g", sigma=1)
5      k = pm.HalfNormal("k", sigma=1)
6
7      s = pm.Simulator("s", gk_simulator,
8      params=[a, b, g, k],
9                        sum_stat=octo_summary,
10                       epsilon=0.1,
11                       observed=bsas_co)
12
13     trace_gk = pm.sample_smc(kernel="ABC", parallel=True)
```

Figure 8.11 shows a pair plot of the fitted `gkm` model.

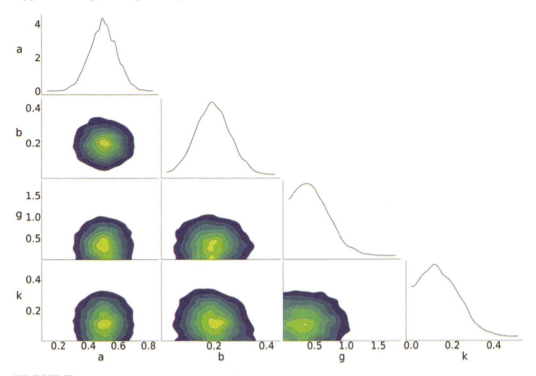

FIGURE 8.11
The distribution is slightly skewed and with some degree of kurtosis as expected from the few CO levels with values one or two orders of magnitude larger than the bulk of CO values. We can see that b and k are (slightly) correlated. This is expected, as the density in the tail (kurtosis) increases, the dispersion increases, but the g-and-k distribution can keep b small if k increases. It is like k is *absorbing* part of the dispersion, similar to what we observed with the scale and the ν parameter in a Student's t-distribution.

8.6 Approximating Moving Averages

The moving-average (MA) model is a common approach for modeling univariate time series (see Chapter 6). The MA(q) model specifies that the output variable depends linearly on the current and q previous past values of a stochastic term λ. q is known as the order of the MA model.

$$y_t = \mu + \lambda_t + \theta_1 \lambda_{t-1} + \cdots + \theta_q \lambda_{t-q} \tag{8.10}$$

where λ are white Gaussian noise error terms [9].

We are going to use a toy-model taken from Marin et al [98]. For this example we are going to use the MA(2) model with mean value 0 (i.e. $\mu = 0$), thus our model looks like:

$$y_t = \lambda_t + \theta_1 \lambda_{t-1} + \theta_2 \lambda_{t-2} \tag{8.11}$$

---

[9]In the literature is common to use ε to denote these terms, but we want to avoid confusion with the ϵ parameter in the SMC-ABC sampler

Code Block 8.8 shows a Python simulator for this model and in Figure 8.12 we can see two realizations from that simulator for the values $\theta1 = 0.6, \theta2 = 0.2$.

Code 8.8

```
1  def moving_average_2(θ1, θ2, n_obs=200):
2      λ = np.random.normal(0, 1, n_obs+2)
3      y = λ[2:] + θ1*λ[1:-1] + θ2*λ[:-2]
4      return y
```

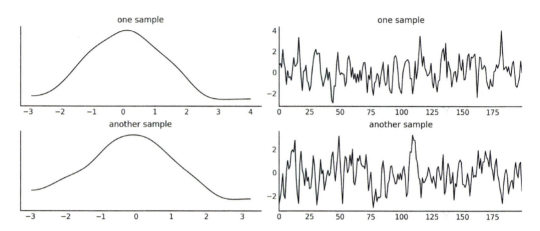

FIGURE 8.12

Two realizations of a MA(2) model, one with $\theta1 = 0.6, \theta2 = 0.2$. On the left column the kernel density estimation on the right column the time series.

In principle we could try to fit a MA(q) model using any distance function and/or summary statistic we want. Instead, we can use some properties of the MA(q) model as a guide. One property that is often of interest in MA(q) models is their autocorrelation. Theory establishes that for a MA(q) model the lags larger than q will be zero, so for a MA(2) seems to be reasonable to use as summary statistics the autocorrelation function for lag 1 and lag 2. Additionally, and just to avoid computing the variance of the data, we will use the auto-covariance function instead of the auto-correlation function.

Code 8.9

```
1  def autocov(x, n=2):
2      return np.array([np.mean(x[i:] * x[:-i]) for i in range(1, n+1)])
```

Additionally MA(q) models are non-identifiable unless we introduce a few restrictions. For a MA(1) model, we need to restrict $-1 < \theta_1 < 1$. For MA(2) we have $-2 < \theta_1 < 2$, $\theta_1 + \theta_2 > -1$ and $\theta_1 - \theta_2 < 1$, this implies that we need to sample from a triangle as shown in Figure 8.14.

Combining the custom summary statistics and the identifiable restrictions we have that the ABC model is specified as in Code Block 8.10.

Code 8.10

```python
with pm.Model() as m_ma2:
    θ1 = pm.Uniform("θ1", -2, 2)
    θ2 = pm.Uniform("θ2", -1, 1)
    p1 = pm.Potential("p1", pm.math.switch(θ1+θ2 > -1, 0, -np.inf))
    p2 = pm.Potential("p2", pm.math.switch(θ1-θ2 < 1, 0, -np.inf))

    y = pm.Simulator("y", moving_average_2,
                     params=[θ1, θ2],
                     sum_stat=autocov,
                     epsilon=0.1,
                     observed=y_obs)

    trace_ma2 = pm.sample_smc(3000, kernel="ABC")
```

A `pm.Potential` is a way to incorporate arbitrary terms to a (pseudo)-likelihood, without adding new variables to the model. It is specially useful to introduce restrictions, like in this example. In Code Block 8.10 we sum 0 to the likelihood if the first argument in `pm.math.switch` is true or $-\infty$ otherwise.

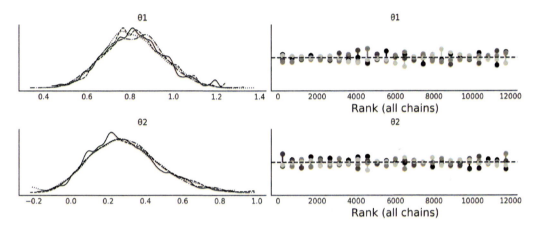

FIGURE 8.13
ABC trace plot for the MA(2) model. As expected the true parameters are recovered and the rank plots look satisfactorily flat.

8.7 Model Comparison in the ABC Context

ABC methods are frequently used for model choice. While many methods have been proposed [144, 8], here we will discuss two approaches; Bayes factors, including a comparison with LOO, and random forest [127].

As with parameter inference, the choice of summaries is of crucial importance for model comparison. If we evaluate two or more models using their predictions, we can not favour one model

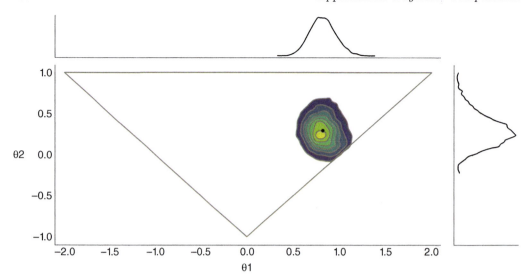

FIGURE 8.14
ABC posterior for the MA(2) model as defined in Code Block 8.10. In the center subplot the joint posterior and in the margins the marginal distributions for $\theta 1$ and $\theta 2$. The gray triangle represents the prior distribution. The mean is indicated with a black dot.

over the other if they all make roughly the same predictions. The same reasoning can be applied to model choice under ABC with summary statistics. If we use the mean as the summary statistic, but models predict the same mean, then this summary statistic will not be sufficient to discriminate between models. We should take more time to think about what makes models different.

8.7.1   Marginal Likelihood and LOO

One common quantity used to perform model comparison for ABC methods is the marginal likelihood. Generally such comparison takes the form of a ratio of marginal likelihoods, which is known as Bayes factors. If the value of a Bayes factor is larger than 1, the model in the numerator is preferred over the one in the denominator and vice versa. In the appendix Section 11.7.2 we discuss more details about Bayes factors, including their caveats. One such caveat is that the marginal likelihood is generally difficult to compute. Fortunately, SMC methods and by extension SMC-ABC methods are able to compute the marginal likelihood as a byproduct of sampling. PyMC3's SMC computes and saves the log marginal likelihood in the trace. We can access its value by doing `trace.report.log_marginal_likelihood`. As this value is in a log scale, to compute a Bayes factor we can do:

Code 8.11

```
1  ml1 = trace_1.report.log_marginal_likelihood
2  ml2 = trace_2.report.log_marginal_likelihood
3  np.exp(ml1 - ml2)
```

When using summary statistics the marginal likelihood computed from ABC methods cannot be generally trusted to discriminate between competing models [131], unless the summary statistics are sufficient for model comparison. This is worrisome as, outside a few formal examples or particular models, there is no general guide to ensure sufficiency across models [131]. This is not a problem if we use all the data i.e. we do not rely on summary statistics [10]. This resembles our discussion (see Section 11.7.2) about how computing the marginal likelihood is generally a much more difficult problem that computing the posterior. Even if we manage to find a summary statistic that is good enough to compute a posterior, that is not a guarantee it will be also useful for model comparison.

To better understand how the marginal likelihood behaves in the context of ABC methods we will now analyze a short experiment. We also include LOO, as we consider LOO an overall better metric than the marginal likelihood and thus Bayes factors.

The basic setup of our experiment is to compare the values of the log marginal likelihood and the values computed using LOO for models with an explicit likelihood against values from ABC models using a simulator with and without summary statistics. The results are shown in Figures 8.15 models in 8.1 and 8.2. The values of the marginal (pseudo)likelihood are computed as by products of SMC and the values of LOO using `az.loo()`. Notice that LOO is properly defined on the pointwise log-likelihood values, but in ABC we only have access to the pointwise log-*pseudo*likelihood values.

From Figure 8.15 we can see that in general both LOO and the log marginal likelihood behave similarly. From the first column we see that `model_1` is consistently chosen as better than `model_0` (here higher is better). The difference between models (the slopes) is larger for the log marginal likelihood than for LOO, this can be explained as the computation of the marginal likelihood explicitly takes the prior into account while LOO only does it indirectly through the posterior (see Section 11.7.2 for details). Even when the values of LOO and the marginal likelihood vary across samples they do it in a consistent way. We can see this from the slopes of the lines connecting `model_0` and `model_1`. While the slopes of the lines are not exactly the same, they are very similar. This is the ideal behavior of a model selection method. We can reach similar conclusions if we compare `model_1` and `model_2`. With the additional consideration that both models are basically indistinguishable for LOO, while the marginal likelihood reflects a larger difference. Once again the reason is that LOO is computed just from the posterior while the marginal likelihood directly takes the prior into account.

The second column shows what happens when we move into the ABC realm. We still get `model_1` as a better choice, but now the dispersion of `model_0` is much larger than the one from `model_1` or `model_2`. Additionally we now get lines crossing each other. Taken together, both observations seems to indicate that we still can use LOO or the log marginal likelihood to select the best model, but the values of the relative weights, like the ones computed by `az.compare()` or the Bayes factors will have larger variability.

The third column shows what happens when we use the mean as summary statistic. Now model `model_0` and `model_1` seems to be on par and `model_2` looks like a bad choice. It is almost like the specular image of the previous column. This shows that when using an ABC method with summary statistics the log marginal likelihood and LOO can fail to provide a reasonable answer.

The fourth column shows what happens when we use the standard deviation in addition to the mean as summary statistic. We see than we can qualitatively recover the behavior observed when using ABC with the entire dataset (second column).

---

[10] Good moment to remember that `sum_stat="sort"` is not actually a summary statistic as we are using the entire dataset

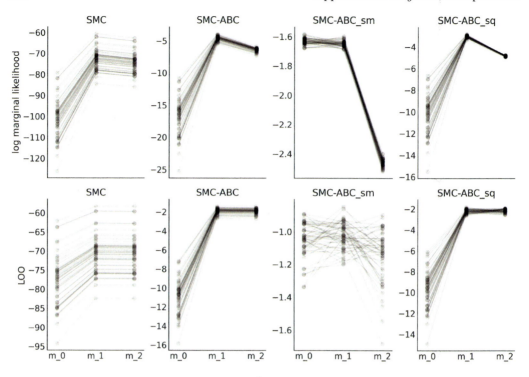

FIGURE 8.15
Model m_0 is similar as the model described in Equation 8.5 but with $\sigma \sim \mathcal{HN}(0.1)$. model_1 the same as Equation 8.5. model_2 is the same as Equation 8.5 but with $\sigma \sim \mathcal{HN}(10)$. The first row corresponds to values of the log marginal likelihood and the second row to values computed using LOO. Sequential Monte Carlo SMC, SMC-ABC with the entire dataset SMC-ABC, SMC-ABC using the mean as summary statistic SMC-ABC_sm and finally SMC-ABC using the mean and standard deviation SMC-ABC_sq. We run 50 experiments each one with sample size 50.

> **On the scale of the pseudolikelihood**
>
> Notice how the scale on the y-axes is different, especially across columns. The reason is two-fold, first when using ABC we are approximating the likelihood with a kernel function scaled by ϵ, second when using a summary statistic we are decreasing the size of the data. Notice also that this size will keep constant if we increase the sample size for summary statistics like the mean or quantiles, i.e. the mean is a single number irrespective if we compute it from 10 or 1000 observations.

Figure 8.16 can help us to understand what we just discussed from Figure 8.15. We recommend you analyze both figures together by yourself. For the moment we will focus on two observations. First, when performing SMC-ABC_sm we have a sufficient statistics for the mean but nothing to say about the dispersion of the data, thus the posterior uncertainty of both parameters a and σ is essentially controlled by the prior. See how the estimates from model_0 and model_1 are very similar for μ and the uncertainty from model_2 is ridiculously large. Second, and regarding the parameter σ the uncertainty is very small for model_0, wider that it should be for model_1 and ridiculously large for model_2. Taken all together we can see why the log marginal likelihood and LOO indicate that model_0 and model_1 are on par but model_2 is very different. Basically, SMC-ABC_sm is failing to provide a good fit! Once we see this is no longer surprising that the log marginal likelihood and LOO computed from SMC-ABC_sm contradicts what is observed when we use SMC or SMC-ABC. If we use the mean and the standard deviation SMC-ABC_sq as summary statistics we partially recover the behavior of using the whole data-set SMC-ABC.

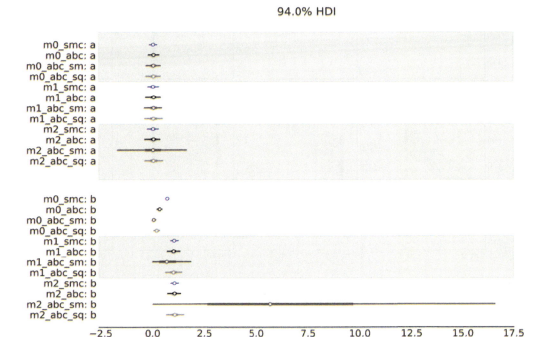

FIGURE 8.16
Model m_0 is similar as the model described in Equation 8.5 but with $\sigma \sim \mathcal{HN}(0.1)$. model_1 the same as Equation 8.5. model_2 is the same as Equation 8.5 but with $\sigma \sim \mathcal{HN}(10)$. The first row contains the values of the marginal likelihood and the second the values of LOO. The column represents different methods of computing these values. Sequential Monte Carlo SMC, SMC-ABC with the entire dataset SMC-ABC, SMC-ABC using the mean as summary statistic SMC-ABC_sm and finally SMC-ABC using the mean and standard deviation SMC-ABC_sq. We run 50 experiments each one with sample size 50.

Figures 8.17 and 8.18 shows a similar analysis but model_0 is a geometric model and model_1 is a Poisson model. The data follows a shifted Poisson distribution $\mu \sim 1 + \text{Pois}(2.5)$. We leave the analysis of these figures as an exercise for the readers.

In the ABC literature it is common to use Bayes factors in an attempt to assign relative probabilities to models. We understand this can be perceived as valuable in certain fields. So we want to warn those practitioners about the potential problems of this practice under the ABC framework, especially because it is much more common to use summary statistics than not. Model comparison can still be useful, mainly if a more exploratory approach is adopted together with model criticism performed before model comparison to improve or discard clearly misspecified models. This is the general approach we have adopted in this book for non-ABC methods so we consider natural to extend it into the ABC framework as well. In this book we also favor LOO over the marginal likelihood, while research about the benefits and drawbacks of LOO for ABC methods are currently lacking, we consider LOO to be potentially useful for ABC methods too. Stay tuned for future news!

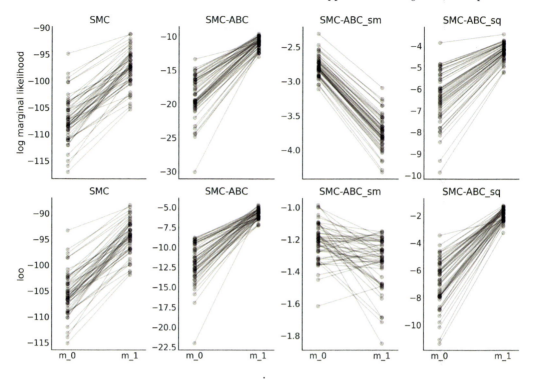

FIGURE 8.17

Model `m_0` is a geometric distribution with prior $p \sim \mathcal{U}(0,1)$ and `model_1` is a Poisson distribution with prior $\mu \sim \mathcal{E}(1)$. The data follows a shifted Poisson distribution $\mu \sim 1 + \text{Pois}(2.5)$. Sequential Monte Carlo `SMC`, SMC-ABC with the entire dataset `SMC-ABC`, SMC-ABC using the mean as summary statistic `SMC-ABC_sm` and finally SMC-ABC using the mean and standard deviation `SMC-ABC_sq`. We run 50 experiments each one with sample size 50.

Model criticism and model comparison

While some amount of misspecification is always expected, and model comparison can help to better understand models and their misspecification. Model comparison should be done only after we have shown the models provide a reasonable fit to the data. It does not make too much sense to compare models that are clearly a bad fit.

8.7.2 Model Choice via Random Forest

The caveats we discussed in the previous section has motivated the research of new methods for model choice under the ABC framework. One such alternative method reframes the model selection problem as random forest classification problem [127] [11]. A random forest is a method for classification and regression based on the combination of many decision trees and it is closely related to BARTs from Chapter 7.

---

[11]Other classifiers could have been chosen, but the authors decided to use a random forest.

The main idea of this method is that the most probable model can be obtained by constructing a random forest classifier from simulations from the prior or posterior predictive distributions. In the original paper authors use the prior predictive distribution but mention that for more advanced ABC method other distributions can be used too. Here we will use the posterior predictive distribution. The simulations are ordered in a reference table (see Table 8.1), where each row is a sample from the posterior predictive distribution and each column is one out of n summary statistics. We use this reference table to train the classifier, the task is to correctly classify the models given the values of the summary statistics. It is important to note that the summary statistics used for model choice does not need to be the same used to compute the posterior. In fact it is recommended to include many summary statistics. Once the classifier is trained we feed it with the same n summary statistics we used in the reference table, but this time applied to our observed data. The predicted model by the classifier will be our best model.

Additionally, we can also compute an approximated posterior probability for the *best* model, relative to the rest of the models. Once again, this can be done using a random forest, but this time we use a regression, with the misclassification error rate as response variable and the summary statistics in the reference table as independent variables [127].

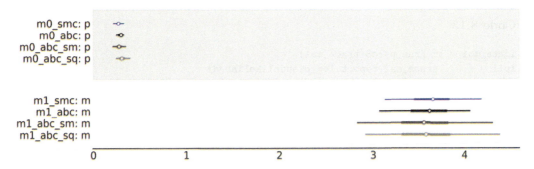

FIGURE 8.18
`model_0` a geometric model/simulator with prior $p \sim \mathcal{U}(0,1)$ `model_1` A Poisson model/simulator with prior $p \sim \mathrm{Expo}(1)$. The firs row contains the values of the marginal likelihood and the second the values of LOO. The column represents different methods of computing these values. Sequential Monte Carlo `SMC`, SMC-ABC with the entire dataset `SMC-ABC`, SMC-ABC using the mean as summary statistic `SMC-ABC_sq` and finally SMC-ABC using quartiles `SMC-ABC_sq`. We run 50 experiments each one with sample size 50.

Model	S^0	S^1	...	S^n
0			...	
0			...	
...	...	...	...	...
1			...	
1			...	
...	...	...	...	...
m			...	

TABLE 8.1
For each model up to m models we compute samples from the posterior (or prior) predictive distribution. Then we apply up to n summary statistics to those samples. In the ABC literature this is known as a reference table and it is the *training dataset* we use to train a random forest model.

8.7.3 Model Choice for MA Model

Let us go back to the moving average example, this time we will focus on the following question. Is a MA(1) or MA(2) a better choice? To answer this question we will use LOO (based on the pointwise pseudo-likelihood values) and random forest. The MA(1) models looks like this

Code 8.12

```
1  with pm.Model() as m_ma1:
2      θ1 = pm.Uniform("θ1", -1, 1)
3      y = pm.Simulator("y", moving_average_1,
4                      params=[θ1], sum_stat=autocov, epsilon=0.1, observed=y_obs)
5      trace_ma1 = pm.sample_smc(2000, kernel="ABC")
```

In order to compare ABC-models using LOO. We cannot directly use the function `az.compare`. We first to need to create an `InferenceData` object with a `log_likelihood` group as detailed in Code Block 8.13 [12]. The result of this comparison is summarized in Table 8.7.3. As expected, we can see that the MA(2) model is preferred.

Code 8.13

```
1  idata_ma1 = az.from_pymc3(trace_ma1)
2  lpll = {"s": trace_ma2.report.log_pseudolikelihood}
3  idata_ma1.log_likelihood = az.data.base.dict_to_dataset(lpll)
4
5  idata_ma2 = az.from_pymc3(trace_ma2)
6  lpll = {"s": trace_ma2.report.log_pseudolikelihood}
7  idata_ma2.log_likelihood = az.data.base.dict_to_dataset(lpll)
8
9  az.compare({"m_ma1":idata_ma1, "m_ma2":idata_ma2})
```

	rank	loo	p_loo	d_loo	weight	se	dse	warning	loo_scale
model_ma2	0	-2.22	1.52	0.00	1.0	0.08	0.00	True	log
model_ma1	1	-3.53	2.04	1.31	0.0	1.50	1.43	True	log

To use the random forest method we can use the `select_model` function included in the accompanying code for this book. To make this function work we need to pass a list of tuples with the PyMC3's model names and traces, a list of summary statistics, and the observed data. Here as summary statistics we will use the first six auto-correlations. We choose these particular summary statistics for two reasons, first to show that we can use a set of summary statistics different from the one used to fit the data and second two show that we can mix useful summary statistics (the first two auto-correlations), with not very useful ones (the rest). Remember that theory says that for a MA(q) processes there are at most q auto-correlations. For complex problems, like those from population genetics it is not uncommon to use several hundreds or even tens of thousands of summary statistics [38].

---

[12]In future versions of PyMC `pm.sample_smc` will return and InferenceData object with the proper groups.

Code 8.14

```
1  from functools import partial
2  select_model([(m_ma1, trace_ma1), (m_ma2, trace_ma2)],
3               statistics=[partial(autocov, n=6)],
4               n_samples=5000,
5               observations=y_obs
```

`select_model` returns the index of the best model (starting from 0) and the estimated posterior probability for that model. For our example we get model 0 with a probability of 0.68. It is a little bit reassuring that, at least for this example, both LOO and the random forest method agree on model choice and even their relative weight.

8.8 Choosing Priors for ABC

Not having a closed form likelihood makes it more difficult to get good models and thus ABC methods are in general more brittle than other approximations. Consequently we should be extra careful about modeling choices, including prior elicitation, and more thorough about model evaluation than when we have an explicit likelihood. These are the costs we pay for approximating the likelihood.

A more careful prior elicitation can be much more rewarding with ABC methods than with other approaches. If we lose information by approximating the likelihood we can maybe partially compensate that loss by using a more informative prior. Additionally, better priors will generally save us from wasting computational resources and time. For ABC rejection methods, where we use the prior as the sampling distribution, this is more or less evident. But it is also the case for SMC methods, specifically if the simulator are sensitive to the input parameter. For example, when using ABC to inference a ordinary differential equation, some parameter combination could be numerical challenging to simulate, resulting in extremely slow simulation. Another problem of using vague prior arise during the weighted sampling in SMC and SMC-ABC, as almost all but few samples from the prior would have extremely small weights when evaluated on the tempered posteriors. This leads to the SMC particles to become singular after just a few steps (as only few samples with large weight are selected). This phenomenon is called weight collapse, a well known issue for particle methods [17]. Good priors can help to reduce the computational cost and thus to some extent allow us to fit more complex models when we are using SMC and SMC-ABC. Beyond the general advice of more informative prior and what we have already discussed elsewhere in the book about prior elicitation/evaluation, we do not have further recommendation specific for ABC methods.

8.9   Exercises

8E1. In your words explain how ABC is approximate? What object or quantity is approximated and how.

8E2. In the context of ABC, what is the problem that SMC is trying to solve compared to rejection sampling?

8E3. Write a Python function to compute the Gaussian kernel as in Equation 8.6, but without the summation. Generate two random samples of size 100 from the same distribution. Use the implemented function to compute the distances between those two random samples. You will get two distributions each of size 100. Show the differences using a KDE plot, the mean and the standard deviation.

8E4. What do you expect to the results to be in terms of accuracy and convergence of the sampler if in model `gauss` model from Code Block 8.2 we would have used `sum_stat="identity"`. Justify.

8E5. Refit the `gauss` model from Code Block 8.2 using `sum_stat="identity"`. Evaluate the results using:

   (a) Trace Plot
   (b) Rank Plot
   (c) $\hat{R}$
   (d) The mean and HDI for the parameters μ and σ.

   Compare the results with those from the example in the book (i.e. using `sum_stat="sort"`).

8E6. Refit the `gauss` model from Code Block 8.2 using quintiles as summary statistics.

   (a) How the results compare with the example in the book?
   (b) Try other values for `epsilon`. Is 1 a good choice?

8E7. Use the `g_and_k_quantile` class to generate a sample (n=500) from a g-and-k distribution with parameters a=0,b=1,g=0.4,k=0. Then use the `gkm` model to fit it using 3 different values of ϵ (0.05, 0.1, 0.5). Which value of ϵ do you think is the best for this problem? Use diagnostics tools to help you answer this question.

8E8. Use the sample from the previous exercise and the `gkm` model. Fit the using the summary statistics `octo_summary`, the `octile-vector` (i.e. the quantiles 0.125, 0.25, 0.375, 0.5, 0.625, 0.75, 0.875) and `sum_stat="sorted"`. Compare the results with the known parameter values, which option provides higher accuracy and lower uncertainty?

8M9. In the GitHub repository you will find a dataset of the distribution of citations of scientific papers. Use SMC-ABC to fit a g-and-k distribution to this dataset. Perform all the necessary steps to find a suitable value for `"epsilon"` and ensuring the model converge and results provides a suitable fit.

8M10. The Lotka-Volterra is well-know biological model describing how the number of individuals of two species change when there is a predator-prey interaction [112]. Basically, as the population of prey increase there is more food for the predator which leads to an increase in the predator population. But a large number of predators produce a decline in the number of pray which in turn produce a decline in the predator as food becomes scarce. Under certain conditions this leads to an stable cyclic pattern for both populations. In the GitHub repository you will find a Lotka-Volterra simulator with unknown parameters and the data set `Lotka-Volterra_00`. Assume the unknown parameters are positive. Use a SMC-ABC model to find the posterior distribution of the parameters.

8H11. Following with the Lotka-Volterra example. The dataset `Lotka-Volterra_01` includes data for a predator prey with the twist that at some point a disease suddenly decimate the prey population. Expand the model to allow for a "switchpoint", i.e. a point that marks two different predator-prey dynamics (and hence two different set of parameters).

8H12. This exercise is based in the sock problem formulated by Rasmus Bååth. The problem goes like this. We get 11 socks out of the laundry and to our surprise we find that they are all unique, that is we can not pair them. What is the total number of socks that we laundry? Let assume that the laundry contains both paired and unpaired socks, we do not have more than two socks of the same kind. That is we either have 1 or 2 socks of each kind.

Assume the number of socks follows a $NB(30, 4.5)$. And that the proportion of unpaired socks follows a $Beta(15, 2)$

Generate a simulator suitable for this problem and create a SMC-ABC model to compute the posterior distribution of the number of socks, the proportion of unpaired socks, and the number of pairs.

9

End to End Bayesian Workflows

Some restaurants offer a style of dining called menu *dégustation*, or in English a tasting menu. In this dining style, the guest is provided a curated series of dishes, typically starting with *amuse bouche*, then progressing through courses that could vary from soups, salads, proteins, and finally dessert. To create this experience a recipe book alone will do nothing. A chef is responsible for using good judgement to determine selecting specific recipes, preparing each one, and structuring the courses as a whole to create an impactful experience for the guest all with impeccable quality and presentation.

This same idea holds true for Bayesian analysis. A book of math and code alone will do nothing. A statistician haphazardly applying techniques will not get far either. Successful statisticians must be able to identify the desired outcome, determine the techniques needed, and work through a series of steps to achieve that outcome.

9.1 Workflows, Contexts, and Questions

Generically all cooking recipes follow a similar structure: ingredients are selected, processed through one or more methods, and then finally assembled. How it is done specifically depends on the diner. If they want a sandwich the ingredients include tomatoes and bread, and a knife for processing. If they want tomato soup, tomatoes are still needed but now a stove is also needed for processing. Considering the surroundings is relevant as well. If the meal is being prepared at a picnic and there is no stove, making soup, from scratch, is not possible.

At a high level performing Bayesian analysis shares some similarities with a cooking recipe, but the resemblance is only superficial. The Bayesian data analysis process is generally very iterative, with the steps performed in a nonlinear fashion. Moreover, the exact necessary steps needed to obtain good results are more difficult to anticipate. This process is called Bayesian workflow[64] and a simplified version of it is shown in Figure 9.1. The Bayesian workflow includes the three steps of model building: inference, model checking/improvement, and model comparison. In this context the purpose of model comparison is not necessarily restricted to pick the *best* model, but more importantly to better understand the models. A Bayesian workflow, and not just Bayesian inference, is important for several reasons. Bayesian computation can be challenging and generally requires exploration and iteration over alternative models in order to achieve inference that we can trust. Even more, for complex problems we typically do not know ahead of time what models we want to fit and even if so, we would still want to understand the fitted model and its relation to the data. Some commons elements to all Bayesian analyses, that are reflected in Figure 9.1, are the need of data and some prior (or domain) knowledge, some technique used to process the data, and an audience typically wanting a report of some kind with the conclusion of what we learn.

The most influential factor in the specific techniques used is what we will refer to as the *driving question*. This is the question that is of value to our colleagues and stakeholders, that we are

DOI: 10.1201/9781003019169-9

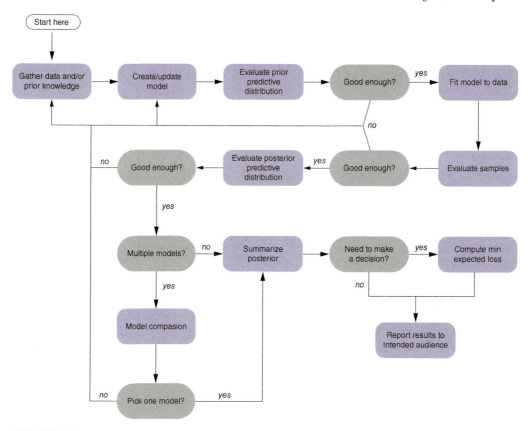

FIGURE 9.1

A high level generic Bayesian workflow showing the main steps involved. The workflow has many junctures requiring decisions, and some steps may be omitted entirely. It is the responsibility of the practitioner to make this determination in each situation. For example, "pick a model" could mean choosing a single model, averaging some of all of them, or even presenting all the models and discussing their strength and shortcomings. Also notice that all the "evaluate" steps can be used for model comparison. We can compare models based on their posterior predictive distributions or pick a model with good convergence diagnostics or the one with the prior predictive distribution closer to our domain knowledge. Finally, we must notice that sometimes we, unfortunately, will need to give up. Even if we are not entirely happy with some model it may be the best model we can achieve given the available resources. A more detailed version of the Bayesian workflow can be see in a paper aptly titled Bayesian Workflow by Gelman et al [64] and the article Towards a Principled Bayesian Workflow by Betancourt [16]

trying to answer with our analysis, and is worth the time and effort to try to find an answer. It is important to differentiate this question from any others. During our analysis we will run into many other questions, such as data questions, modeling questions, inference questions, which answer "How should we conduct our analysis"; but should not be confused with driving question, which is "why we are conducting our analysis".

So before starting any statistical analysis, the first and foremost task is to clearly define the questions you are trying to answer. The simple reason is that the driving question affects every downstream choice in a Bayesian workflow. This will help us determine, what data you should collect, what tools are needed, if a model is appropriate, what model is appropriate, how to formulate models, how to choose priors, what to expect from the posterior, how to pick between models, what the results are indicating, how to summarize results, what conclusion to communicate. The answers to each of these affect whether the analysis will be useful to your audience or will just collect digital dust in a hard drive. And equally as important how much time and effort is worthwhile in pursuit of the answer.

All too often data practitioners, given an idea of a question, decide it needs an answer and instantly reach for the most complex and nuanced statistical tools, spending little to no time understanding the need. Consider the equivalent situation if we were a chef. They hear someone is hungry so they prepare a \$10,000 dish of caviar only to learn a simple bowl of cereal would have sufficed. Yet there have been actual instances where Data Scientists generate \$10,000 cloud computing bills on big GPU machines using neural networks when a linear regression may have been sufficient. Do not be the Data Scientist and statistician that immediately reaches for Bayesian Methods, Neural Networks, Distributed Computing Clusters, or other complex tools before truly understanding the need.

9.1.1 Applied Example: Airlines Flight Delays Problem

For most sections in this chapter each example will build upon the previous section, which we will start with here. Let us imagine we work at the Madison Wisconsin airport, in the United States, as a statistician. Delays in flight arrivals are leading to frustrations and our mathematical skills can help quantify the situation. We first recognize there are multiple individuals involved, a traveler who has to decide when to arrive at an airport, an accountant working for the airport, or the CEO of the airport who has to manage the whole operation.

Each of these folks has different concerns, which leads to different questions, some of which could be:

1. What is the chance my flight departure is going to get delayed?
2. What is the chance my flight arrival is going to get delayed?
3. How many flight arrivals were delayed last week?
4. How much do flight delays cost the airport?
5. Given two business choices which one should I make?
6. What correlates with flight departure delays?
7. What is causing flight departure delays?

Each of these questions, while all related, are subtly different. The traveler is concerned with the delay of their particular flight, but the airport accountant and executives care about the delays across all flights. The accountant is not worried about the time duration of flight delays, but is interested in the cost of those delays for financial records. The executive is less concerned about history, and more concerned about what strategic decision to make given future flight delays.

At this point you as the reader might be asking, I came here to learn Bayesian Modeling, when are we getting to that? Before we get there consider this case. If the driving question is *"How many plane arrivals were late last week?"* do we need a Bayesian model? The unsatisfying answer is no, inference is not needed, just basic counting. Do not assume that Bayesian statistics is needed for every problem. Strongly consider whether summary statistics such as simple counts, means, and plots, will be enough to answer the driving question.

Now, suppose the airport CEO comes to you, the airport statistician, with a dilemma. For each arrival the airport must keep staff on standby to guide the airplane landing and a gate available to unload passengers. This means when airplanes arrive late, staff and airport infrastructure are left idle waiting for the arrival and ultimately money wasted on unused resources. Because of this the airport and airlines have an agreement that for each minute late the airline will pay the airport 300 dollars a minute. The airlines however have now asked this agreement be changed. They propose all delays under 10 minutes to cost a flat rate of 1000 dollars, a delay between 10 minutes and 100 minutes to cost 5000 dollars, and a delay over 100 minutes to cost 30,000 dollars. Your CEO suspects the airlines are proposing this structure to save themselves money. The airport CEO asks you to use your data abilities to answer the question, "Should we accept the new late fee structure or keep the old one?". The airline CEO mentions how expensive this decision could be if it was made incorrectly and asks you to prepare a report regarding the potential financial affects. As experienced statistician you decide to quantify the underlying distribution of delays and use decision analysis to aid with the infrastructure investment choice. We believe an integrated End to End Bayesian analysis will provide a more complete understanding of future outcomes. You are able to justify the cost and complexity of model development as the financial risk of making a poor decision far outweights the time and cost to make a Bayesian model. If you are not sure how we reached this conclusion do not worry, we will walk through the thought process step by step in subsequent sections. We come back to this flight delay problem in the sub-sections with title start with *Applied Example*.

9.2 Getting Data

Cooking a good dish is impossible for a chef without ingredients and challenging with poor quality ingredients. Likewise inference is impossible without data. challenging with poor quality data, and the best statisticians dedicate a fair amount of time understanding the nuance and detail of their information. Unfortunately there is no one size fits all strategy for what data is available or how to collect it for every driving question. Considerations span topics from required precision needed, to cost, to ethics, to speed of collection. There are however, some broad categories of data collection that we can consider, each with its pros and cons.

9.2.1 Sample Surveys

In American history there is this folk idea of "asking for your neighbors for a cup of sugar", convenient for the times when you run out. For statistician the equivalent is Sample surveys, also known as polling. The typical motivation of polling is to estimate a population parameter, Y, using a finite number of observations. Sample surveys also can include covariates, for example age, gender, nationality, to find correlations. Various methodologies for sampling exist, such as random sampling, stratified sampling, and cluster sampling. Different methods make tradeoffs between cost, ignorability and other factors.

9.2.2 Experimental Design

A very popular dining concept these days is farm to table. For a chef this can be appealing as they are free from the constraints of what is typically available, and can instead acquire a much broader range of ingredients while maintaining control over every aspect. For statisticians the equivalent process is called experimental design. In experiments statisticians are able to decide what they want to study, then design the data generating process that will help them best understand their topic of interest. Typically this involves a "treatment" where the experimenter can change part of the process, or in other words vary a covariate, to see the effect on y_{obs}. The typical example is pharmaceutical drug trials, where the effectiveness of new drugs is tested withholding the drug from one group and giving the drug to another group. Examples of treatment patterns in experimental design include randomization, blocking, and factorial design. Examples of data collection methodologies include topics such as double blind studies, where neither the subject nor the data collector know which treatment was applied. Experimental design is typically the best choice to identify causality, but running experiments typically comes at a high cost.

9.2.3 Observational Studies

Farming your own ingredients can be expensive, so a cheaper alternative could be foraging for ingredients are growing by themselves. The statistician's version of this is observational studies. In observational studies the statistician has little to no control over the treatments or the data collection. This makes inference challenging as the available data may not be adequate to achieve the goals of the analysis effort. The benefit however is that, especially in modern times, observational studies are occurring all the time. For example when studying the use of public transportation during inclement weather, it is not feasible to randomize rain or no rain, but the effect can be estimated by recording the weather for the day with other measurements like ticket sales of the day. Like experimental design, observational studies can be used to determine causality, but much more care must be taken to ensure data collection is ignorable (you will see a definition shortly below) and that the model does not exclude any hidden effects.

9.2.4 Missing Data

All data collection is susceptible to missing data. Folks may fail to respond to a poll, an experimenter could forget to write things down, or in observational studies a day's logs could be deleted accidentally. Missing data is not always a binary condition either, it could also mean part of the data is missing. For example, failing to record digits after a decimal points leading e.g. missing precision.

To account for this we can extend our formulation of Bayes' theorem to account for missingness by adding a terms as shown in Equation 9.1[59]. In this formulation I is the inclusion vector that denotes which data points are missing or included, and ϕ represents the parameters of the distribution inclusion vector.

$$
\begin{aligned}
Y_{obs} &= (i, j) : I_{ij} = 1 \\
Y_{mis} &= (i, j) : I_{ij} = 0 \\
p(\boldsymbol{\theta}, \boldsymbol{\phi} \mid Y_{obs}, I) &\propto p(Y_{obs}, I \mid \boldsymbol{\theta}, \boldsymbol{\phi}) p(\boldsymbol{\theta}, \boldsymbol{\phi})
\end{aligned}
\tag{9.1}
$$

Even if missing data is not explicitly modeled it is prudent to remain aware that your observed data is biased just due to the fact that it has been observed! When collecting data be sure not only pay attention to what is present, but consider what may not be present.

9.2.5 Applied Example: Collecting Airline Flight Delays Data

Working at the airport you have access to many datasets, from current temperature, to revenue from the restaurants and shops, to airport hours, number of gates, to data regarding the flight.

Recalling our driving question, "Based on the late arrivals of airplanes, which late fee structure would we prefer?". We need a dataset the quantifies that notion of lateness. If the late fee structures had been binary, for example, 100 dollars for each late arrival, then a boolean True/False would have sufficed. In this case both the current late fee structure and previous late fee structure require minute level data on arrival delays.

You realize that as a small airport, Madison has never had a flight arrival from far off destinations such as London Gatwick Airport, or Singapore Changi Airport, a big gap in your observed dataset. You ask your CEO about this and she mentions this agreement will only apply to flights coming from Minneapolis and Detroit airports. With all this information you feel comfortable that you understand the data you will need to model the relevant flight delays.

From knowledge of the "data generating process" you know that weather and airline companies have an effect on flight delays. However you decide not to include these in your analysis for three reasons. Your boss is not asking why flights are delayed, obviating the need for an analysis of covariates. You independently assume that historical weather and airline company behavior will remain consistent, meaning you will not need to perform any counterfactual adjustments for expected future scenarios. And lastly you know your boss is under a short deadline so you specifically designed a simple model that can be completed relatively quickly.

With all that your data needs have narrowed down to minute level dataset of flight arrival delays. In this situation using the prior history of observational data is the clear choice above experimental designs or surveys. The United States Bureau of Transportation Statistics keeps detailed logs of flight data which includes delays information. The information is kept to the minute precision which is adequate for our analysis, and given how regulated airline travel is we expect the data to be reliable. With our data in hand we can move to our first dedicated Bayesian task.

9.3 Making a Model and Probably More Than One

With our question and data firmly in hand we are ready to start constructing our model. Remember model building is iterative and your first model will likely be wrong in some way. While this may seem concerning, it actually can be freeing, as we can start from good fundamentals and then use the feedback we get from our computational tools to iterate to a model that answers our driving question.

9.3.1 Questions to Ask Before Building a Bayesian Model

In the construction of a Bayesian model a natural place to start is the Bayes Formula. We could use the original formulation but instead we suggest using Formula 9.1 and thinking through each parameter individually

- $p(Y)$: (Likelihood) What distribution describes the observed data given X?
- $p(X)$: (Covariates) What is the structure of the latent data generating process?
- $p(I)$: (Ignorability) Do we need to model the data collection process?
- $p(\theta)$: (Priors) Before seeing any data what is a reasonable set of parameters?

Additionally since we are computational Bayesians we must also answer another set of questions

- Can I express my model in a Probabilistic Programming framework?
- Can we estimate the posterior distributions in a reasonable amount of time?
- Does the posterior computation show any deficiencies?

All of these questions do not need to be answered immediately and nearly everyone gets them wrong when initially building a new model. While the ultimate goal of the final model is to answer the driving question, this is not typically the goal of the first model. The goal of the first model is to express the simplest reasonable and computable model. We then use this simple model to inform our understanding, tweak the model, and rerun as shown in Figure 9.1. We do this using numerous tools, diagnostics, and visualizations that we have seen through out this book.

Types of Statistical Models

If we refer to D. R. Cox [41] there are two general ways to think about building statistical models, a model based approach where "The parameters of interest are intended to capture important and interpretable features of that generating process, separated from the accidental features of the particular data. Or a design based approach where "sampling existing populations and of experimental design there is a different approach in which the probability calculations are based on the randomization used by the investigator in the planning phases of the investigation". The fundamentals of Bayes formula has no opinion on which approach is used and Bayesian methods can be used in both approaches. Our airline example is a model based approach, whereas the experimental model at the end of the chapter is a design based approach. For example, it can be argued that most frequentist based analyses follow the design based approach. This does not make them right or wrong, just different approaches for different situations.

9.3.2 Applied Example: Picking Flight Delay Likelihoods

For our flight delay dilemma we decide to start the modeling journey by picking a likelihood for the observed flight delays. We take a moment to collect our detail our existing domain knowledge. In our dataset, delays can be negative or positive valued. Positive valued means flight is late, negative valued means flight is early. We could make choice here to only model delays and ignore all early arrivals. However, we will choose to model all arrivals so we can build a generative model for all flight arrivals. This may come in handy for the decision analysis we will be doing later.

Our driving question does not pose any questions about correlation or causation, so we will model the observed distribution without any covariates for simplicity. This way we can just focus on likelihood and priors. Adding covariates may help modeling the observed distribution even if they are of no individual interest themselves, but we do not want to get ahead of ourselves. Let us plot the observed data to get a sense of its distribution using Code Block 9.1, the result is shown in Figure 9.2.

Code 9.1

```
1 df = pd.read_csv("../data/948363589_T_ONTIME_MARKETING.zip",
2 fig, ax = plt.subplots(figsize=(10,4))
3
4 msn_arrivals = df[(df["DEST"] == "MSN") & df["ORIGIN"]
5                 .isin(["MSP", "DTW"])]["ARR_DELAY"]
6
7 az.plot_kde(msn_arrivals.values, ax=ax)
8 ax.set_yticks([])
9 ax.set_xlabel("Minutes late")
```

Thinking through likelihood we have a couple of choices. We could model this as a discrete categorical distribution, where every possible minute is assigned a probability. But this might pose some challenges: from a statistical perspective we need to pick the number of buckets. While there

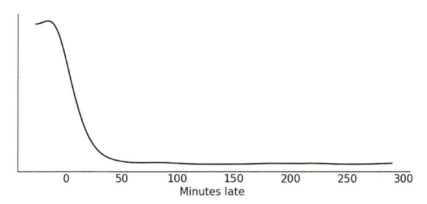

FIGURE 9.2

Kernel density estimate plot for the observed arrival delay data. Note a couple of interesting features. The bulk of all flight arrivals is between -20 and 40 and in this region there is a general bell shaped pattern. However, there is a long tail of large values indicating that while relatively few flights are late, some of them can be really late in arriving to the Madison airport.

are non-parametric techniques that allow the number of buckets to vary, this now means we also have to create a model that can estimate bucket number, on top of estimating each probability for each bucket.

From domain expertise we know each minute is not quite independent of each other. If many planes are 5 minutes late, it makes intuitive sense that many planes will also be 4 minutes late or 6 minutes late. Because of this a continuous distribution seems more natural. We would like to model both early and late arrivals so distribution must have support over negative and positive numbers. Combining statistical and domain knowledge we know that most planes are on time, and that flights usually arrive a little early or a little late, but if they are late they can be really late.

Exhausting our domain expertise we can now plot the data, checking for both consistency with our domain expertise and for further clues to help form our model. From Figure 9.2, we have a few reasonable choices of likelihood distributions: Normal, Skew-Normal, and Gumbel distribution. A plain Normal is symmetrical which is inconsistent with the skewness of the distribution, but it is an intuitive distribution that could be used for baseline comparison. The Skew-Normal as the name suggests has an additional parameter α controlling the skewness of the distribution. And lastly the Gumbel distribution is specifically designed to describe the maximum value of a set of values. If we imagine that an airplane delay is caused from the maximum value of luggage loading, passenger loading, and other latent factors the idea of this distribution fits with the reality of flight arrival processes.

As airline processes are tightly regulated we do not feel that we need to model missing data at this time. Additionally we choose to ignore covariates to simplify our Bayesian workflow. It is generally advised to start with a simple model, and let the full Bayesian workflow inform your decisions to add complexity as needed, versus starting with a complex model that becomes more challenging to debug in later steps. Typically we would pick one likelihood and work all the way through the Bayesian workflow before trying another. But to avoid backtracking this example we will continue through two in parallel. For now we will move forward with the Normal and Gumbel likelihood in Code Block 9.2, leaving the Skew-Normal likelihood model as an exercise for the reader.

Code 9.2

```
1  with pm.Model() as normal_model:
2      normal_alpha = ...
3      normal_sd = ...
4
5      normal_delay = pm.Normal("delays", mu=mu, sigma=sd,
6                               observed=delays_obs)
7
8  with pm.Model() as gumbel_model:
9      gumbel_beta = ...
10     gumbel_mu = ...
11
12     gumbel_delays = pm.Gumbel("delays", mu=mu, beta=beta,
13                               observed=delays_obs)
```

For now all the priors have the placeholder Ellipsis operator (...). Picking priors will be the topic of the next section.

9.4   Choosing Priors and Predictive Priors

Now that we have settled on likelihoods we need to pick priors. Similar to before there are some general questions that help guide the choice of prior.

1. Does the prior make sense in the context of math?
2. Does the prior make sense in the context of the domain?
3. Can our inference engine produce a posterior with the chosen prior?

We have covered the priors extensively in previous sections. In Section 1.4 we showed multiple principled options for prior selected, such as Jeffrey's prior or weakly informative priors. In Section 2.2 we showed how to evaluate choices of priors computationally as well. As a quick refresher, prior choice should be justified in context with likelihood, model goal such as whether that is parameter estimation or prediction. And we can also use prior distributions to codify our prior domain knowledge about the data generating process. We may also use priors as a tool to focus the inference process, to avoid spending time and computation exploring parameter spaces that are "clearly wrong", at least as we would expect using our domain expertise.

In a workflow, sampling and plotting the prior and prior predictive distribution gives us two key pieces of information. The first is that we can express our model in our PPL of choice, and the second is an understanding of the characteristics of our model choice, and the sensitivity to our priors. If our model fails in prior predictive sampling, or we realize we do not understand our model's response in the absence of data we may need to repeat previous steps before moving forward. Luckily with PPLs we can change the parameterization of our priors, or the structure of our model, to understand its effects and ultimately the informativeness of the chosen specification.

There should be no illusion that the prior distribution or likelihood distributions are preordained, What is printed in this book is the result of numerous trials and tweaking to find parameters that provided a sensible prior predictive distribution. When writing your own models expect that you should also iterate on the priors and likelihood before moving onto the next step, inference.

9.4.1 Applied Example: Picking Priors for Flight Delays Model

Before making any specific numerical choices we take stock of our domain knowledge about flight arrivals. Airline flight arrivals can be early or late (negative or positive respectively) but exhibit some bounds. For example, it seems unlikely that a flight would arrive more than 3 hours late, but also unlikely it will be more than 3 hours early. Let us specify a parameterization and plot the prior predictive to ensure consistency with our domain knowledge, shown in Code Block 9.3.

Code 9.3

```
1  with pm.Model() as normal_model:
2      normal_sd = pm.HalfStudentT("sd",sigma=60, nu=5)
3      normal_mu = pm.Normal("mu", 0, 30)
4
5      normal_delay = pm.Normal("delays",mu=normal_mu,
6                              sigma=normal_sd, observed=msn_arrivals)
7      normal_prior_predictive = pm.sample_prior_predictive()
8
9  with pm.Model() as gumbel_model:
10     gumbel_beta = pm.HalfStudentT("beta", sigma=60, nu=5)
11     gumbel_mu = pm.Normal("mu", 0, 40)
12
13     gumbel_delays = pm.Gumbel("delays",
14                             mu=gumbel_mu,
15                             beta=gumbel_beta,
16                             observed=msn_arrivals)
17     gumbel_prior_predictive = pm.sample_prior_predictive()
```

With no errors in our prior predictive simulation reported from the PPL and with reasonable prior predictive distributions in Figure 9.3 we decide our choice of priors are sufficient to continue to our next steps.

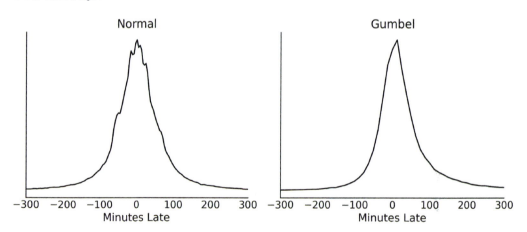

FIGURE 9.3

Prior predictive distributions for each of the models. Prior to conditioning on data both distributions look reasonable for our domain problem and similar to each other.

9.5   Inference and Inference Diagnostics

Dear reader, we hope that you have not skipped straight to this section. Inference is the "most fun" part where everything comes together and the computer gives us "the answer". But inference without a good understanding of the question, data, and model (including priors) could be useless, and misleading. In a Bayesian workflow inference builds upon the previous steps. A common mistake is to attempt to fix divergences by first tweaking sampler parameters, or running extra long chains, when really it is the choice of priors or likelihood that is the root cause of the issue. The folk theorem of statistical computing says: "when you have computational problems, often there is a problem with your model"[61].

That being said we have a strong prior that if you made it this far you are a diligent reader and understand all our choices thus far so let us dive into inference.

9.5.1   Applied Example: Running Inference on Flight Delays Models

We choose to use the default HMC sampler in PyMC3 to sample from the posterior distribution.

Let us run our samplers and evaluate our MCMC chains using the typical diagnostics. Our first indication of sampling challenges would be divergences during MCMC sampling. With this data and model none were raised. If some were raised however, this would indicate that further exploration should be done such as the steps we performed in Section 4.6.1.

Code 9.4

```
1  with normal_model:
2      normal_delay_trace = pm.sample(random_seed=0, chains=2)
3  az.plot_rank(normal_delay_trace)
4
5  with gumbel_model:
6      gumbel_delay_trace = pm.sample(chains=2)
7  az.plot_rank(gumbel_delay_trace)
```

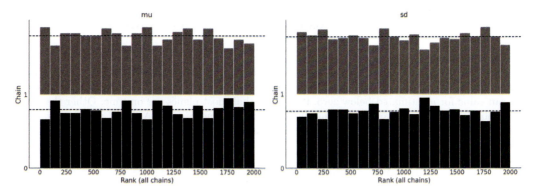

FIGURE 9.4
Rank plot of the posterior samples from the model with Normal likelihood.

For both models the rank plots, shown in Figures 9.4 and 9.5, look fairly uniform across all ranks, which indicates little bias across chains. Due to the lack of challenges in this example it

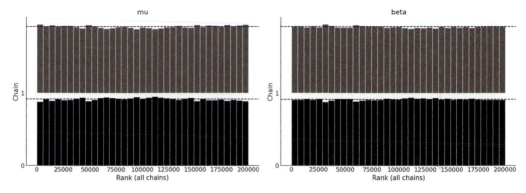

FIGURE 9.5
Rank plot of the posterior samples from the model with Gumbel likelihood.

seems that inference is as easy as "pushing a button and getting results". However, it was easy because we had already spent time up front understanding the data, thinking about good model architectures, and setting good priors. In the exercises you will be asked to deliberately make "bad" choices and then run inference to see what occurs during sampling.

Satisfied with the posterior samples generated from NUTS sampler we will move onto our next step, generating posterior predictive samples of estimated delays.

9.6   Posterior Plots

As we have discussed posterior plots are primarily used to visualize the posterior distribution. Sometimes a posterior plot is the end goal of an analysis, see Section 9.11 for an example. In some other cases direct inspection of the posterior distribution is of very little interest. This is the case for our airline example which we elaborate on further below.

9.6.1   Applied Example: Posterior of Flight Delays Models

After ensuring there are no inference errors in our model we quickly check the posterior plots of the Normal and Gumbel models in Figures 9.6 and 9.7. At a glance they look well formed, with no unexpected aberrations. In both distributions, from a domain perspective it is reasonable to see the mean value for μ estimated below zero, indicating that most planes are on time. Other than those two observations the parameters themselves are not very meaningful. After all your boss needs to make a decision of whether to stay with the current fee structure or accept the airlines proposal for a new one. Given that a decision is the goal of our analysis, after a quick sanity check we continue with the workflow.

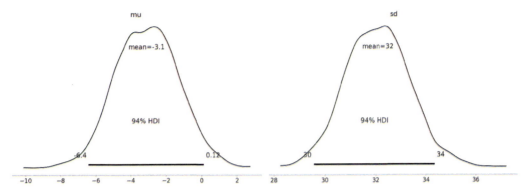

FIGURE 9.6

Posterior plot for Normal model. Both distributions looks reasonably formed and there are no divergences adding more evidence that our sampler has reasonably estimated the parameters.

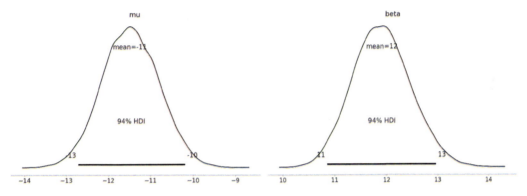

FIGURE 9.7

Posterior plot for Gumbel model parameters. Similar to Figure 9.6 these estimates look well formed and give us confidence in our parameter estimates.

9.7 Evaluating Posterior Predictive Distributions

As shown in the workflow in Figure 9.1, a Bayesian analysis does not concludes once the posterior estimates are obtained. We can take many additional steps, like for example generating posterior predictive distributions if any of the following are desired.

- We want to use posterior predictive checks to evaluate our model calibration.
- We want to obtain predictions or perform counterfactual analyses
- We want to be able to communicate our results in the units of the observed data, and not in term of the parameters of our model.

We specified the mathematical definition for a posterior predictive distribution in Equation 1.8. Using modern PPLs sampling from the posterior predictive distribution is easy as adding a couple lines of code shown in Code Block 9.5.

9.7.1 Applied Example: Posterior Predictive Distributions of Flight Delays

In our airline example we have been asked to help make a decision based on unseen future flight delays. To do that we will need estimates of the distribution of future flight delays. Currently however, we have two models and need to pick between the two. We can use posterior predictive checks to evaluate the fit against the observed data visually as well as using test statistics to compare certain specific features.

Let us generate posterior predictive samples for our Normal likelihood model shown in Code Block 9.5.

Code 9.5

```
1  with normal_model:
2      normal_delay_trace = pm.sample(random_seed=0)
3      normal_ppc = pm.sample_posterior_predictive(normal_delay_trace)
4      normal_data = az.from_pymc3(trace=normal_delay_trace,
5                          posterior_predictive=normal_ppc)
```

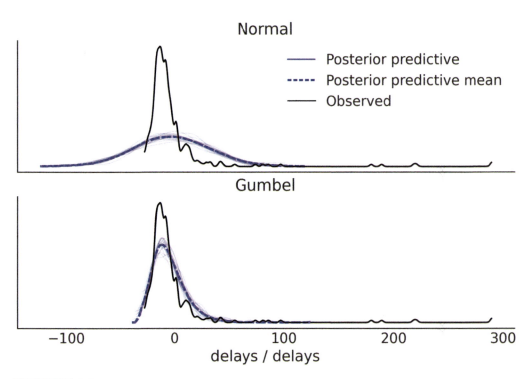

FIGURE 9.8
Posterior predictive checks for Normal and Gumbel models. The Normal model does not capture the long tail well and also return more predictions below the bound of the observed data. The Gumbel model fit is better but there is still quite a bit of mismatch for values below 0 and the tail.

From Figure 9.8 we can see that the Normal model is failing to capture the distribution of arrival times. Moving onto the Gumbel model we can see that the posterior predictive samples seem to do a poor job at predicting flights that arrive early, but a better job at simulating flights that arrive late. We can run posterior predictive checks using two test statistics to confirm. The first is to check the proportion of flights arriving late, and the second is to check the median of flight delays (in minutes) between the posterior predictive distribution and the observed data. Figure 9.9 shows that the Gumbel model does a better job of fitting the median of flight delays than the Normal model, but does a poor job of fitting the proportion of on time arrivals. The Gumbel model also does a better job of fitting the median of flight delays.

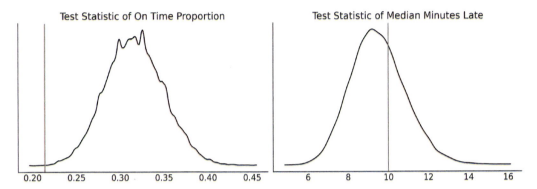

FIGURE 9.9
Posterior predictive checks with test statistics for Gumbel model. On the left we see the estimated distribution of on time proportion compared to the observed proportion. On the right is the test statistic of median minutes late. It seems the Gumbel model is better at estimating how late a flight will be versus what proportion of flights will be late.

9.8 Model Comparison

So far we have used posterior predictive checks to evaluate each model independently. That type of evaluation is useful to understand each model individually. When we have multiple models however, it begs the question how models perform relative to each other. Model comparison can further help us understand in what regions one model may be performing well, where another is struggling, or which data points are particularly challenging to fit.

9.8.1 Applied Example: Model Comparison with LOO of Flight Delays

For our flight delay model we have two candidate models. From our previous visual posterior predictive check it seemed clear that the Normal likelihood did not tend to fit the skewed distribution of flight delays well, particularly compared to the Gumbel distribution. We can verify this observation using the comparison method in ArviZ:

Code 9.6

```
1  compare_dict = {"normal": normal_data,"gumbel": gumbel_data}
2  comp = az.compare(compare_dict, ic="loo")
3  comp
```

Table 9.1, generated with Code Block 9.6, shows the model ranked by their ELPD. It should be no surprise that the Gumbel model does much better job modeling the observed data.

	rank	loo	p_loo	d_loo	weight	se	dse	warning	loo_scale
gumbel	0	-1410.39	5.85324	0	1	67.4823	0	False	log
normal	1	-1654.16	21.8291	243.767	1.07773e-81	46.1046	27.5559	True	log

TABLE 9.1
Summary of model comparison for the `gumbel` and `normal` models.

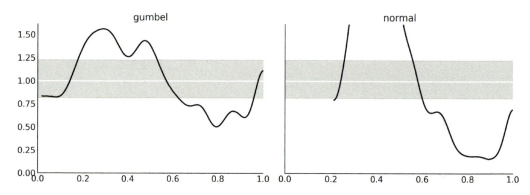

FIGURE 9.10
Model calibration using LOO-PIT. We can see that both models have problems at capturing the same portion of the data. The models are underestimating the largest observations (largest delays) and over estimating earlier arrivals. These observations are in line with Figure 9.8. Even when both models show problems the Gumbel model has smaller deviations from the expected Uniform distribution.

From Table 9.1 we can see that the Normal model is giving a value of `p_loo` way higher than the number of parameters in the model, showing the model is missespecified. Also we are getting a warning indicating that we have at least one high value of $\hat{\kappa}$. From Figure 9.11 (bottom right panel) we can see that the offending observation is the datapoint 157. We can also see (Figure 9.11 top panel) that the Normal model is having a hard time at capturing this observation together with observations 158 and 164. Inspection of the data reveals that these 3 observations are the ones with the largest delays.

We can also generate a visual check with 9.7which results in Figure 9.12. We see that even when considering the uncertainty in LOO the Gumbel model is better representation of the data than the Normal model.

Code 9.7

```
az.plot_compare(comp)
```

From our previous comparison of the posterior predictive check, and our direct LOO comparison, we can make the informed choice to proceed only with the Gumbel model. This does not imply our Normal model was useless, in fact quite the opposite. Developing multiple models helps build confidence in our selection of one, or a subset of models. It also does not mean that the Gumbel model is the true or even the best possible model, in fact we have evidence of it shortcomings. Thus, there still room for improvement if we explore different likelihoods, collect more data, or make some other modification. What is important at this step is we are sufficiently convinced that the Gumbel model is the most "adequate" model from all the reasonable models we have evaluated.

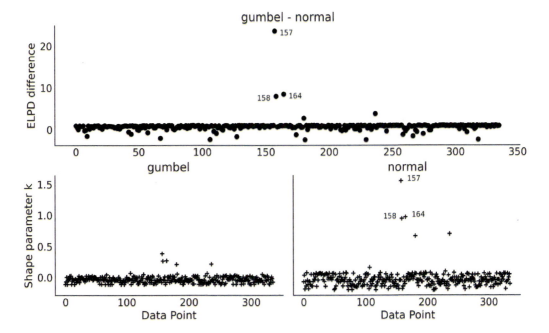

FIGURE 9.11
Top panel ELPD difference between the Gumbel and Normal model. The 3 observations with the largest deviation are annotated (157, 158 and 164). Bottom panels, plots for the $\hat{\kappa}$ values from the Pareto smooth importance sampling. Observations 157, 158 and 164 has values larger than 0.7

9.9 Reward Functions and Decisions

Throughout this book we have seen how converting a set of quantities in one space to another allows us to make calculations simpler or shifts our mode of thinking. For example, in the last section we used the posterior predictive sampling to move from parameter space to observed quantity space. Reward functions, also sometimes referred to as cost, loss, or utility functions, are yet another transformation from observed quantity space to the reward derived from an outcome (or the decision space). Recall the bike example in Section 7.5 we have the posterior estimates of the count of bikes rented in each hour (see e.g. Figure 7.5). If we were instead interested in revenue per day we could use a reward function to calculate the revenue per rental and sum the total counts, effectively converting counts to revenue. Another example is to estimate a person's level of happiness if they are rained on, versus if they are dry. If we have a model and an estimate of whether it will rain or not (based on weather data), and we have a function that maps how wet or dry a person's clothes is to a happiness value, we can map our weather estimate to an expected happiness estimate.

Where reward functions become particularly useful is in the presence of a decision. By being able to estimate all future outcomes, and map those outcomes to expected reward, you are able to make the choice that is likely to yield the maximum reward. An intuitive example is deciding to pack an umbrella in the morning. Carrying an umbrella is annoying, which can be considered a negative reward, but being wet from rain is a worse outcome. The choice of whether you pack an umbrella depends on how likely it is to rain.

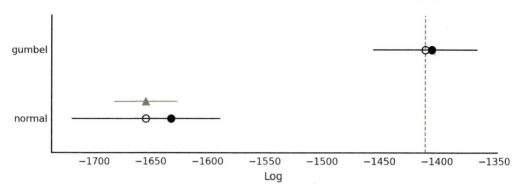

FIGURE 9.12
Model comparison using LOO of the two flight delay models from Code Block 9.7. We confirm our notion that the Gumbel data is better at estimating the observed distribution than the Normal model.

We can extend this example a bit more to expose a key idea. Let us say you want to build a model that helps individuals in your family decide when to pack an umbrella. You build a Bayesian model that will estimate the probability it will rain, this is the inference portion. However, after you build the model you learn your brother hates carrying an umbrella so much he will never carry one unless it is already raining, whereas your mother dislikes being wet so much she will preemptively carry an umbrella even if there is not a cloud in the sky. In this case the quantity under estimation, the probability it is going to rain, is exactly the same, but because the reward differs, the action taken is different. More specifically, the Bayesian portion of the model is consistent, but the difference in reward yields a different action.

Neither rewards nor actions need to be binary, both can be continuous. A classic example in supply chain is the newsvendor model [1], in which a newsvendor must decide how many newspapers to buy each morning when demand is uncertain. If they buy too little they risk losing sales, if they buy too many they lose money on unsold inventory.

Because Bayesian statistics provide full distributions we are able to provide better estimates of future reward than methods that provide point estimates [2]. Intuitively we can get a sense of this when we consider that Bayes' theorem includes features such as tail risk, whereas point estimates will not.

With a generative Bayesian model, particularly a computational one, it becomes possible to convert a posterior distribution of model parameters of parameters, to a posterior predictive distributions in the domain of observed units, to a distributional estimate of reward (in financial units), to a point estimate of most likely outcome. Using this framework we can then test the outcomes of various possible decisions.

9.9.1 Applied Example: Making Decisions Based on Flight Delays Modeling Result

Recall that delays are quite costly to the airport. In preparation for a flight arrival the airport must ready the gate, have staff on hand to direct the airplane when it lands, and with a finite amount of capacity, late flights arrivals ultimately mean less flight arrivals. We also recall the late flight penalty structure. For every minute late a flight is, the airline must pay the airport a fee of 300 dollars. We can convert this statement into a reward function in Code Block 9.8.

---

[1]https://en.wikipedia.org/wiki/Newsvendor_model
[2]www.ee.columbia.edu/~vittorio/BayesProof.pdf

Code 9.8

```
1  def current_revenue(delay):
2      if delay >= 0:
3          return 300 * delay
4      return np.nan
```

Now given any individual late flight we can calculate the revenue we will receive from the flight delay. Since we have a model can produce a posterior predictive distribution of delays we can convert this into an estimate of expected revenue as shown in Code Block 9.9, which provides both an array of revenue for each late flight, and the average estimate.

Code 9.9

```
1  def revenue_calculator(posterior_pred, revenue_func):
2      revenue_per_flight = revenue_func(posterior_pred)
3      average_revenue = np.nanmean(revenue_per_flight)
4      return revenue_per_flight, average_revenue
5
6  revenue_per_flight, average_revenue = revenue_calculator(posterior_pred,
7  current_revenue)
8  average_revenue
```

```
3930.88
```

From the posterior predictive distribution and the current late fee structure we expect each late flight to provide 3930 dollars of revenue on average. We can also plot the distribution of late flight revenue per flight in Figure 9.13.

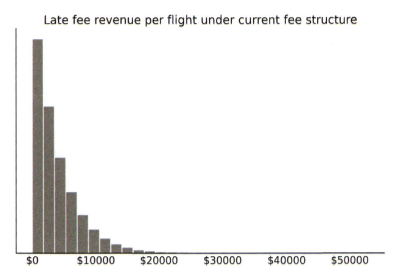

FIGURE 9.13
Expected late flight revenue from current late fee structure calculated using reward function and posterior predictive distribution. There are very few very late flights hence the seemingly empty right portion of the plot.

Recalling the cost structure proposed by the airline, If a flight is between 0 and 10 minutes late, the fee is 1,000 dollars. if the flight is between 10 and 300 minutes late the fee is 5,000 dollars, and if more than 100 minutes late the fee is 30,000 dollars. Assuming that the cost structure has no effect on the on time or late arrival of planes, you are able to estimate the revenue under the new proposal by writing a new cost function and reusing the previously calculated posterior predictive distribution.

Code 9.10

```
 1  @np.vectorize
 2  def proposed_revenue(delay):
 3      """Calculate proposed revenue for each delay """
 4      if delay >= 100:
 5          return 30000
 6      elif delay >= 10:
 7          return 5000
 8      elif delay >= 0:
 9          return 1000
10      else:
11          return np.nan
12  revenue_per_flight_proposed, average_revenue_proposed = \
13      revenue_calculator(posterior_pred, proposed_revenue)
```

```
2921.97
```

In the new cost structure you estimate that on average the airport will make 2921.97 dollars per late flight, which is less than the current penalty pricing structure. We again can plot the distribution of estimated late flight revenue in Figure 9.14.

9.10 Sharing the Results With a Particular Audience

One of the most important steps in the Bayesian workflow is to communicate your results to others. Throwing numbers and graphs on paper, or on screens, does nothing. The conclusion portion of inference only matters when it changes or informs a decision, whether indirectly or directly. This will require some preparation, the amount of effort required should not be underestimated. In some situations this step takes more time than all the previous one combined. There is no specific formulation here, what needs to be done depends heavily on the specific situation and audience, but we will cover the concepts in a high level to survey the landscape.

9.10.1 Reproducibility of Analysis Workflow

Reproducibility of an analysis workflow is the notion that another individual or group is able to go through all the steps and achieve the same, or similar conclusions that were previously reported. Reproducibility allows people, including yourself, to understand what work was performed, what assumptions were made, and why that led to a result. If reproducibility is neglected then it will be challenging or impossible to understand the reasoning behind a conclusion, or extend the result at a future date. Often times the outcome is at best wasted resources recreating the same workflow

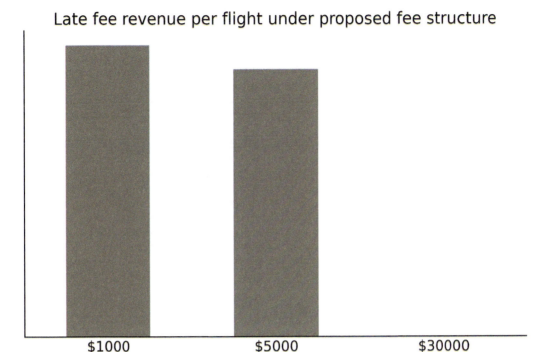

FIGURE 9.14
Expected late flight revenue calculated using proposed reward function and posterior predictive distribution. Note that the posterior predictive distribution is exactly the same as in Figure 9.13. It is simply the change in reward function which makes this plot differ.

steps and at worst invalidation of the original conclusion and possibly also loss of reputation. The ideal of reproducibility is complete reproducibility which means the conclusion can be recreated automatically "from scratch". We instead will focus on analysis reproducibility, which means given a conclusion, all the steps from the raw data through the Bayesian workflow, to the final result are reproducible. Analysis reproducibility is comprised of four main pillars which we will detail in turn

- Management of the source data
- Modeling and analysis code
- Compute environment specification
- Documentation

When performing an analysis it is important to note or preserve the raw data that serves as the basis for the analysis. This is why you will tend to see the same datasets, such as Palmer Penguins, Radon, and Eight Schools, over and over again. The data is well understood and commonly available which make it a simple reference for those looking to share methods. The specific methods in which specific data is tagged, recognized, stored, and accessed will differ per situation, size, organization, as well as ethical and legality but is important to note this. Some examples are including the data in code version control or referencing a link to a dataset stored on a server.

The next is the modeling and analysis code, such as all the code seen throughout this book. Ideally this code would be versioned with a version control system, such as git, and stored in an accessible location, such as an open source repository. We want to highlight that version control is useful even if you are a solo practitioner and not working in a group. Using version control will allow you to jump between versions of your code, it enables you to test ideas easily, with less risk of knowledge loss or losing results. This helps tremendously with increasing iteration speed between steps in the workflow and comparing results.

In computational statistics a key portion of any result is the computer itself. While the mechanics of computation are largely unchanging, the libraries that are used for computation change rapidly. As we have seen, modern Bayesian methods rely at least on a PPL but that is just the tip of the iceberg. The operating system version as well as the hundreds of other software libraries that are used in conjunction all play a part in providing a result. When environments cannot be replicated one outcome is code that was working, now throws exceptions or errors and fails. This outcome, while frustrating, is at least helpful in that the failure state is obvious. An even more dangerous but subtle issue is that the code still runs but the results are different. This can occur because the library may change, or the algorithm itself. For example, TFP may change the number of tuning samples or PyMC3 may refactor the sampler between one version and the next. No matter what the reason, even if the data and analysis code is the same, the two alone are insufficient to fully computationally reproduce an analysis without the full specification of the compute environment. A common way to specify an environment is through an explicit list of dependencies, commonly seen in Python packages as *requirements.txt* or *environment.yml* files. Another way is through compute environment virtualization, such as virtual machines or containerization.

Seeding pseudo random number generator

One challenge in creating reproducible Bayesian workflow is the stochastic-ness in the pseudo random number generator being used in the algorithm. In general, your workflow should be robust that changing the seed to the pseudo random number generator does not change your conclusion, but there are situations where you might want to fix the seed to get fully reproducible results. This is tricky as fixing the seed alone does not mean you will always get completely reproducible results, as the actual pseudo random number generator used in different operating systems could be different. If your inference algorithm and conclusion is sensitive to the choice of seeds, it is usually a red flag of your workflow.

With the data, code, and compute environment, the computer is able to reproduce only a portion of the analysis. The last pillar, documentation, is for the human to understand the analysis as well. As we have seen through this book there are many choices that statistical practitioners need to make throughout the modeling process, from choices of priors, to filtering data, to model architecture. Over time it is quite easy to forget why a certain choice was made which is why so many tools exist solely to help the humans behind the keyboard. The simplest is code documentation which is comments within the code. Another popular method for applied scientists is the notebook format that mixes code blocks, with documentation blocks containing text, code, and images. The Jupyter notebooks used with this book are an example. For Bayesian practitioners dedicated tools such as ArviZ exist to help make analysis reproducible as well.

At this point it is worth restating the primary beneficiary in reproducibility is yourself. Few things are worse than being asked to extend an analysis, or discovering a bug, only to realize your code will not run anymore. The secondary beneficiaries are your peers. Their ability to reproduce your work is the most immersive way to share your workflow and results. In short reproducible analyses both helps you and others build confidence in your prior results, and also helps future efforts extend the work.

9.10.2 Understanding the Audience

It is important to understand who your audience is and how to communicate with them, both in terms of content and the way of delivery. As you get to your final set of results you end up with many ideas, visualizations, and results generated along the way, which were necessary to achieve the result, but not of any interest otherwise. Recalling our cooking analogy, a diner wants to be served a dish, but does not want the dirty pans and food waste that was generated during the process alongside it. The same idea holds with statistical analysis. Take a moment to consider:

- What does your audience want and not want?
- In what ways can you deliver it?
- How long do they have to consume it?

It takes concerted effort and thought to distill your results to the most digestible version. This means reviewing the original questions and motivation for the analysis, who wanted the results and why they wanted it. It also means considering the background and aptitude of the audience. For example, a more statistical audience may prefer to see details about models and assumptions. A more domain-oriented audience may still be interested in the assumptions in the model but mostly in the context of the domain problem.

Think through presentation format, is it verbal or visual? If it is visual will it be static, such as this book, or a pdf or paper, or in a potentially dynamic format, like a webpage or video? And consider the timing as well, does your audience have a couple moments to hear the highlights, or is there a dedicated time slot solely focused on going through the details? Answers to all these questions will inform what you share, but also how you share it

Numerical Summaries

Numerical summaries, as the name implies, are numbers that summarize your results. In this book we have seen many, from means and medians which summarize the position of a distribution, to variance or HDI which summarize the dispersion, or PDFs which summarize probability. For example Table 3.2, which summarized penguin mass. Numerical summaries confer a great advantage as they compress a great deal of information into a small representation, can be easily remembered, easily compared, and presented in many formats. They are particularly effective in verbal conversations as no other aides are required to disseminate them. In business conversations reward functions, as discussed in Section 9.9, can capture the full uncertainty of your analysis into a single number and can also be framed in the most universal business language, money.

Unfortunately numerical summaries may obscure the nuances of distributions and can be misunderstood. Many people when hearing a mean value tend to overly expect that value, even though in reality the probability of the mean outcome may be rare. To aid with this sharing a set of numerical summaries at once can help the audience understand various aspects of a distribution, for example a maximumlLikelihood to get a sense of the mode and HDI to get a sense of dispersion. However, sharing too many numerical summaries becomes harmful. It is both difficult to a recite table of numbers and hard for your audience to retain all the information if many numbers are shared at once.

9.10.3 Static Visual Aids

There is an adage that says a picture is worth a 1000 words. This is particularly true with Bayesian statistics where posterior plots convey a level of detail that is not as easily described with words. ArviZ comes prepackaged with many of the common visualizations such as posterior plots. However, we also suggest making bespoke graphics as well. Examples in this text include posterior estimates such as Figure 7.5 which shows both the observed data, mean trend, and uncertainty for all hours a day. Static visual aids are like numerical summaries, they are also fairly easily shared these days. With the widespread use of laptops and phones, as well as internet connected devices, sharing a picture has become easier than before. However, the downside is they do require paper or a screen to share, and need to be either prepped or quickly found in the event they are needed. Another risk is they can communicate too much to your audience, who sometimes might just want the mean or maximum likelihood value.

Animation

Anyone who has seen the difference between a picture and film, even a silent film, understands how powerful motion can be in communication. Often times ideas that are are very easily understood when animated than in other formats [3], such as MCMC sampling [4]. Animations can now be generated in many visualization packages, including Matplotlib, which ArviZ utilizes for animated Posterior Predictive Checks. Notable examples of animation used in uncertainty communication are the New York Times Election Needle [5], which used a shaking needle gauge to highlight . Another election example is Matthew Kay's Presidential Plinko [6]. Both of these visualizations used motion to show the estimated outcome of various United States election results and how it was generated. Most importantly both used animation give a sense of the uncertainty, from the shaking needle in the New York Times visualization, or the randomness of the plinko drops in Matthey Kay's example.

Animations are able to display many images to show a changing state, and therefore convey a sense of motion, progression, and iteration. As with static images, widespread use of digital screens means they can be viewed more easily, but they require more time from the viewer who has to pause and watch the full animation. They also require more work from a developer, as they are more challenging to generate and share than a simple picture.

Interactive Aids

Interactive aids give the viewers control over what is being displayed. In both static visualization and animations the audience is being told a story they have no control over. Interactive aids flip the script, the user is able to create their own story. A simple example may include a slider that changes what is being displayed, such as limits of the axes or the opacity of data points. It may also include a tooltip which shows the user a value at a particular point. The user may also be able to control the computation. For example in our posterior predictive predictions of penguins which picked the mean flipper length and plotted the results of Figure 3.11. Different people may be interested in the posterior predictive distribution at a different value hence the interactivity. Examples include visualizations of various MCMC techniques [7] where allowing the user to select different samplers, distributions, and parameters allows the user to make the specific comparisons they would like.

Similar to static plots and animations many software libraries support animation for instance, Matplotlib or Bokeh, another Python visualization library which is explicitly designed for this type of interaction. The downside of interactivity is that they typically require a live computing environment and software deployment of some sort. It is not as easy as sharing a static image or a video.

---

[3]See https://bost.ocks.org/mike/algorithms/
[4]See https://elevanth.org/blog/2017/11/28/build-a-better-markov-chain/
[5]See https://www.nytimes.com/interactive/2020/11/03/us/elections/forecast-president.html
[6]See http://presidential-plinko.com/
[7]https://chi-feng.github.io/mcmc-demo/app.html

9.10.4   Reproducible Computing Environments

Thinking back to reproducibility above, the gold standard of sharing results is a fully reproducible computation environment that contains everything needed to replicate your result. This historically was a high hurdle, it took time and expertise, to setup a local computation environment on one's own device, but is becoming much easier through virtualization technologies like containerization. These days the computation environment and code can be packaged and easily distributed over the internet. With projects like Binder, make it literally one click for a colleague to gain access to a bespoke environment in their browser, no local install needed. Most people will only want the results, not all the raw ingredients per say. But in the situations where someone absolutely needs to run the code, for example a tutorial or an in depth review, being able to share a live environment easily is quite helpful.

9.10.5   Applied Example: Presenting the Flight Delay Model and Conclusions

Confident with your rigor in model building, inference run, and cost function correctness you now need to communicate the results to other in your organization, both to justify your analysis approach to your data peers and to aid your boss's decision between the current fee structure, and the proposed fee structure. You realize you have two different groups of audiences and prepare content differently for each one.

Before approaching your boss you need to complete a peer review with your peers. As your peers are statistically and computation savvy you provide them the Jupyter Notebook of your analysis that mixes narration, code, and results. This notebook includes all the previous models, assumptions, and plots, that you used to come to the recommendation for your boss. Since the notebook has all the details and is reproducible your colleagues are able to confidently assess your work is correct. Some of your colleagues ask if they can run the model with different priors to check for prior sensitivity. You provide the Dockerfile[8], which fully specifies the environment. With that they are able to run the Jupyter notebook and recreate portions of your workflow.

Focusing now on your initial task of informing your boss you start thinking through strategies of how to communicate to her. You know that you have at most 30 minutes and it will be in her office. You will have your laptop to show visual aids but you know your boss also needs to be able to communicate this idea to her peers in situations where she will not have visual aids. You also know your boss might want to test different fee structures to understand where she can safely negotiate. In other words she wants to see the effect of different reward functions. You set up a simple notebook that takes the reward function as an input and produces the revenue histogram and table. You set a meeting with your boss and quickly explain "I spent some time using past late flight delays to create a model of what future flights delays could look like. Using the model I estimate in the current fee structure we will make 3930 dollars per late flight on average, in the airline's proposed fee structure we will make 2921 dollars per late flight on average". You show your boss the bottom plot Figure 9.8, explaining this is the distribution of late flights both expected and modeled, and Figure 9.13 showing the revenue that is projected to be generated in the future. You then show your boss Table 9.2 showing the expected revenue under the new paradigm. You chose a table over a figure because the proportion of flights in the 100+ minute lateness category was not evident in a plot. You use the table to explain that there are so few flights that are likely to be over 100 minutes late, that from a revenue perspective that category is negligible in your simulations. You recommend that your boss either reject the proposal, or that she negotiates a higher late fees for delays that lie within the 0 to 100 minute categories. Your boss then asks if you can test a couple different fee structures of her choosing so she can see the effect. With your boss's

---

[8]Docker is one method to create fully reproducible environments that has become quite popular

Late Fee	Revenue
$1000	52%
$5000	47%
$30000	.03%

TABLE 9.2
Percentages of expected revenue from each fee category. There are so few late flights in the $30000 fee category that it is essentially negligible

understanding the goal of inference has been achieved, your boss has all the information needed to make an informed decision in her negotiation.

9.11 Experimental Example: Comparing Between Two Groups

For our second applied example will show the use of Bayesian statistics in a more experimental setting where the difference between two groups is of interest. Before addressing the statistics we will explain the motivation.

When mechanical engineers are designing products, a primary consideration is the properties of the material that will be used. After all, no one wants their airplane to fall apart midflight. Mechanical engineers have reference books of weight, strength, and stiffness for materials such as ceramics, metals, woods which have existed for eons. More recently plastics and fiber reinforced composites have become available and more commonly used. Fiber reinforced composites are often made from a combination of plastic and woven cloth which gives them unique properties.

To quantify the strength properties of materials a physical test mechanical engineers run a procedure called a tensile test, where a specimen of material is held in two clamps and a tensile test machine pulls on the specimen until it breaks. Many data points and physical characteristics can be estimated from this one test. In this experiment the focus was on ultimate strength, or in other words, the maximum load before total material failure. As part of a research project [9] one of the authors manufactured 2 sets, of 8 samples each, that were identical in every way except for the weave of the reinforcing fibers. In one the fibers were flat on top of each other referred to as unidirectional weave. In the other the fibers were woven together into an interlocking pattern referred to as a bidirectional weave.

A series of tensile tests were run independently on each sample and the results were recorded in pound-force [10]. Customary to mechanical engineering the force is divided by area to quantify force per unit area, in this case pound force per square inch. For example, the first bidirectional specimen failed at 3774 lbf (1532 kg) at a cross section area of .504 inches (12.8mm) by .057 inches (1.27), yielding an ultimate strength of 131.393 ksi (kilopound per square inch). For reference this means a coupon with a cross sectional area of 1/3 a USB A connector is theoretically capable of lifting the weight of a small car [11].

In the original experiment a frequentist hypothesis test was performed which concluded in the rejection the null hypothesis that the ultimate tensile were equivalent. This type of statistical test however, could not characterize either the distribution of ultimate strengths for each material

---

[9] Much gratitude to Dr. Mehrdad Haghi and Dr. Winny Dong for funding and facilitating this research

[10] A recordings of the tests are available https://www.youtube.com/watch?v=u_XDUWgzs_Y

[11] This is in an ideal situation. Factors other than ultimate strength can limit the true load bearing capacity in real world situations.

Bidirectional Ultimate Strength (ksi)	Unidirectional Ultimate Strength (ksi)
131.394	127.839
125.503	132.76
112.323	133.662
116.288	136.401
122.13	138.242
107.711	138.507
129.246	138.988
124.756	139.441

independently or the magnitude of difference in strengths. While this represents an interesting research result, it yields a non-useful practical result, as engineers who intend to choose one material over another in a practical setting need to know *how* much "better" one material is than another, not just that there is a significant result. While additional statistical tests could be performed to answer these questions, in this text we will focus on how we can answer all these questions using a single Bayesian model well as extend the results further.

Let us define a model for the unidirectional specimens in Code Block 9.11. The prior parameters have already been assessed using domain knowledge. In this case the prior knowledge comes from the reported strength properties of other composite specimens of similar type. This is a great case where the knowledge from other experimental data and empirical evidence can help reduce the amount of data needed to reach conclusions. Something especially important when each data point requires a great deal of time and cost to obtain, like in this experiment.

Code 9.11

```
1  with pm.Model() as unidirectional_model:
2      sd = pm.HalfStudentT("sd_uni", 20)
3      mu = pm.Normal("mu_uni", 120, 30)
4
5      uni_ksi = pm.Normal("uni_ksi", mu=mu, sigma=sd,
6                          observed=unidirectional)
7
8      uni_trace = pm.sample(draws=5000)
```

We plot the posterior results in 9.15. As seen many times with the Bayesian modeling approach we get distribution estimates for both the mean ultimate strength and the standard deviation parameters, which is very helpful in understanding how reliable this particular material is.

Code 9.12

```
az.plot_posterior(uni_data)
```

Our research question however, was about the differences in the ultimate strength between unidirectional and bidirectional composites. While we could run another model for the bidirectional specimens and compare estimates, a more convenient option would be to compare both in a single model., We can leverage John Kruschke's model framework as defined in "Bayesian estimation supersedes the t-test" [89] to obtain this "one and done" comparison as shown in Code Block 9.13.

Code 9.13

```
1  μ_m = 120
2  μ_s = 30
3
```

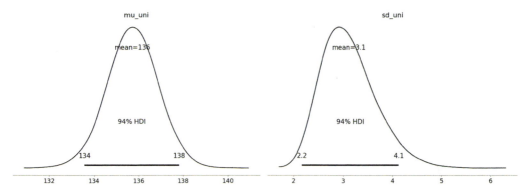

FIGURE 9.15
Posterior Plot of all parameters with 94% HDI and point statistic

```
4  σ_low = 1
5  σ_high = 100
6
7  with pm.Model() as model:
8      uni_mean = pm.Normal("uni_mean", mu=μ_m, sigma=μ_s)
9      bi_mean = pm.Normal("bi_mean", mu=μ_m, sigma=μ_s)
10
11     uni_std = pm.Uniform("uni_std", lower=σ_low, upper=σ_high)
12     bi_std = pm.Uniform("bi_std", lower=σ_low, upper=σ_high)
13
14     ν = pm.Exponential("ν_minus_one", 1/29.) + 1
15
16     λ1 = uni_std**-2
17     λ2 = bi_std**-2
18
19     group1 = pm.StudentT("uni", nu=ν, mu=uni_mean, lam=λ1,
20         observed=unidirectional)
21     group2 = pm.StudentT("bi", nu=ν, mu=bi_mean, lam=λ2,
22         observed=bidirectional)
23
24     diff_of_means = pm.Deterministic("difference of means",
25                                   uni_mean - bi_mean)
26     diff_of_stds = pm.Deterministic("difference of stds",
27                                   uni_std - bi_std)
28     pooled_std = ((uni_std**2 + bi_std**2) / 2)**0.5
29     effect_size = pm.Deterministic("effect size",
30                                   diff_of_means / pooled_std)
31
32     t_trace = pm.sample(draws=10000)
33
34  compare_data = az.from_pymc3(t_trace)
```

After fitting the model we can visualize the difference in means using a Forest Plot in Figure 9.16, there does not seem to be much overlap between the mean of two types of samples, suggesting their ultimate strength is indeed different, with the unidirectional being stronger and perhaps even being a little bit more reliable.

Code 9.14

```
az.plot_forest(t_trace, var_names=["uni_mean","bi_mean"])
```

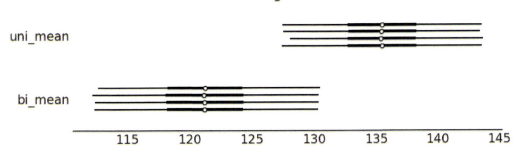

FIGURE 9.16
Forest plot of the means of each group. The 94% HDI is separated indicating a difference in the means.

There is an additional benefit to both Kruschke's formulation, and a trick in our PPL. We can have the model automatically calculate the difference directly, in this case one of them being posterior distribution of the difference of means.

Code 9.15

```
1 az.plot_posterior(trace,
2                    var_names=["difference of means","effectsize"],
3                    hdi=.95, ref_val=0);
```

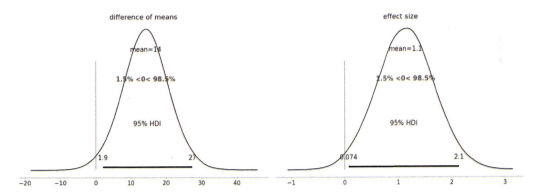

FIGURE 9.17
Posterior Plot of difference of means and effect size including reference value at 0. In both the plots a value of 0 seems is relatively unlikely indicating there is both an effect and a difference.

We can compare the numerical summaries for each parameter as well.

Code 9.16

```
az.summary(t_trace, kind="stats")
```

	mean	sd	hpd_3%	hpd_97%
uni_mean	135.816	1.912	132.247	139.341
bi_mean	121.307	3.777	114.108	128.431
uni_std	4.801	1.859	2.161	8.133
bi_std	9.953	3.452	4.715	16.369
ν_minus_one	33.196	30.085	0.005	87.806
difference of means	14.508	4.227	6.556	22.517
difference of stds	-5.152	3.904	-13.145	1.550
effect size	1.964	0.727	0.615	3.346

From these numerical summary and posterior plot we can be more sure there is a difference in the mean strength of the two composites which helps when making a selection between the two material types. We also have obtained the specific estimated values of strength, with their dispersion, helping an engineer understand where and how the material can be used, safely, in real world applications. It is quite convenient that one model can help us reach multiple conclusions.

9.12   Exercises

9E1. What kind of data collection scheme would be most appropriate for these situations scenarios. Justify your choices by asking questions such as "How important is it that the information is reliable?" or "Can we collect the data in a reason time?" Explain how you would collect the data

  (a) A medical trial for for a new drug treatment for cancer patients

  (b) An estimate of the most popular ice cream flavors for a local newspaper article

  (c) An estimate of which parts needed for a factory have the longest delivery lead times

9E2. What kind likelihood is suited for these types of data? Justify your choice. What other information would be useful to pick a likelihood?

  (a) Count of customers that visit a shop each day

  (b) Proportion of parts that fail in a high volume manufacturing line

  (c) Weekly revenue of a restaurant

9E3. For our airline model provide a justification, or lack thereof, for each of these priors of the mean of a Gumbel likelihood, using your domain knowledge and a prior predictive check. Do these seem reasonable to use in a model? Why or why not?

  (a) $\mathcal{U}(-200, 200)$

  (b) $\mathcal{N}(10, .01)$

  (c) $(Pois)(20)$

9E4. For each of the priors in the exercise above perform an inference run using the Gumbel model in Code Block 9.3

    (a) Are any errors raised by the sampler?

    (b) For the completed inference run generate post sampling diagnostics such as autocorrelation plots. What are the results? Would you consider the run to be a successful inference run?

9E5. For our airline delays model we initially included arrivals from the MSP and DTW airports. We are now asked to include another arrival airport, ORD, into the analysis. Which steps of the Bayesian Workflow do we need to reconsider? Why is that the case? What if instead we are asked to include SNA? What steps would we need to reconsider?

9E6. In Chapter 6 we forecasted the CO_2 concentration. Using the figures and models in the chapter what conclusions can we reach about CO_2? Communicate your understanding of projected CO_2 levels, including an explanation of the uncertainty, in the following ways. Be sure to include specific numbers. You may need to run the examples to obtain them. Justify which model you chose and why

    (a) A 1 minute verbal explanation without visual aid to data scientist colleague

    (b) A 3 slide presentation for an non-statistician executive.

    (c) Use a Jupyter notebook for a software engineering colleague who wants to productionize the model as well.

    (d) Write a half page document for a general internet audience. Be sure to include at least one figure.

9E7. As the airport statistician your boss asks you to rerun the fee revenue analysis with a different cost function than the one specified in Code Block 9.8. She asks that any minute delay that is even costs 1.5 dollars per minute of delay, any that minute delay that is odd costs 1 dollar a minute of delay. What will the average revenue per late flight be the airport be with this fee model?

9M8. Read the workflow article and paper from Betancourt[16] and Gelman[64]. From each list a step which is the same? Which steps are different? Explain why these examples workflows may be different. Do all practitioners follow the same workflow? Why would they differ if not?

9M9. In our bike rental model from Code Block 5.6 we used splines to estimate bike rentals per hour. The bike rental company wants to know how much money they will make from rentals. Assume each rental costs 3 dollars. Now assume that the rental company is proposing that from the hours of 0 to 5 bike rentals are reduced to 1.5 dollars, but it is projected rentals will increase 20% due to the reduced cost. What is the expected revenue per hour?

    Write a reward function specifically to estimate both situations above.

    (a) What is the mean projected revenue per day? What would be reasonable upper and lower estimates?

    (b) Does the estimated mean and revenue seem reasonable? Note any issues you see and explain you may fix them? (Don't actually make any changes)

    (c) Now assume that the rental company is proposing that from the hours of 0 to 5 bike rentals are reduced to 1.5 dollars, but it is projected rentals will increase 20% due to the reduced cost. What is the expected revenue per day?

9M10. For the airline delay model replace the likelihood in Code Block 9.3 with a Skew Normal likelihood. Prior to refitting explain why this likelihood is, or is not, a reasonable choice for the airline flight delay problem. After refitting make the same assessment. In particular justify if the Skew Normal is "better" than the Gumbel model for the airline delays problem.

9H11. Clark and Westerberg[37] ran an experiment with their students to see if coin flips can be biased through tosser skill. The data from this experiment is in the repository under `CoinFlips.csv`. Fit a model that estimates the proportion of coin tosses that will come up heads from each student.

    (a) Generate 5000 posterior predictive samples for each student. What is the expected distribution of heads for each student?

    (b) From the posterior predictive samples which student is the worst at biasing coin towards heads?

    (c) The bet is changed to 1.5 dollars for you if heads comes up, and 1 dollar of tails comes up. Assuming the students don't change their behavior, which student do you play against and what is your expected earnings?

9H12. Make an interactive plot of the posterior airline flights using Jupyter Notebook and Bokeh. You will need to install Bokeh into your environment and using external documentation as needed.

    (a) Compare this to the static Matplotlib in terms of understanding the plotted values, and in terms of story telling.

    (b) Craft a 1 minute explanation posterior for general audience that isn't familiar statistics using Matplotlib static visualization.

    (c) Craft a 1 minute explanation to the same audience using the Bokeh plot, incorporating the additional interactivity allowed by Bokeh.

10

Probabilistic Programming Languages

In Chapter 1 Section 1.1, we used cars as analogy to understand applied Bayesian concepts. We will revisit this analogy but this time to understand Probabilistic Programming Languages. If we treat a car as a system, their purpose is to move people or cargo to a chosen destination with wheels connected to a power source. This whole system is presented to users with an interface, typically a steering wheel and pedals. Like all physical objects cars have to obey the laws of physics, but within those bounds human designers have a multitude of components to choose from. Cars can have big engines, or small tires, 1 seat or 8 seats. The end result however, is informed by the specific purpose. Some cars are designed to go fast with a single person around a racetrack, such as Formula 1 cars. Others are designed for family life like carrying families and groceries home from the store. No matter what the purpose, someone needs to pick the components, for the right car, for the right purpose.

The story of Probabilistic Programming Languages (PPL) is similar. The purpose of PPLs is help Bayesian practitioners build generative models to solve problem at hand, for example, perform inference of a Bayesian model through estimating the posterior distribution with MCMC. The power source for computational Bayesians is, well, a computer which are bound by computer science fundamentals. Within those bounds however, PPL designers can choose different components and interfaces, with the specifics being determined by anticipated user need and preference. In this chapter we will focus our discussion on what the components of PPLs are, and different design choices that can be made within those components. This knowledge will help you as Bayesian practitioner when you need to pick a PPL when starting a project or debug that arises during your statistical workflow. This understanding ultimately will lead to better experience for you, the modern Bayesian practitioner.

10.1   A Systems Engineering Perspective of a PPL

Wikipedia defines systems engineering as "an interdisciplinary field of engineering and engineering management that focuses on how to design, integrate, and manage complex systems over their life cycles". PPLs are by this definition a complex system. PPLs span across computational backends, algorithms, and base languages. As the definition also states the integration of components is a key part of systems engineering, which is true of PPLs as well. A choice of computational backend can have an effect on the interface, or the choice of base language can limit the available inference algorithms. In some PPLs the user can make component selections themselves. For example, Stan users can choose their base language between R, Python, or the command line interface among others, whereas PyMC3 users cannot change base languages, they must use Python.

In addition to the PPL itself there is the consideration of the organization and manner in which it will be used. A PhD student using a PPL in a research lab has different needs than an engineer working in a corporation. This is also relevant to the lifecycle of a PPL. Researchers may only need a model once or twice in a short period to write a paper, whereas an engineer in a corporation may maintain and run the model over the course of years.

DOI: 10.1201/9781003019169-10   293

In a PPL the two necessary components are: an application programming interface for the user to define the model [1], and algorithms to performs inference and manage the computation. Other components exist but largely to improve the system in some fashion, such as computational speed or ease of use. Regardless of the choice components, when a system is designed well the day to day user need not be aware of the complexity, just as most drivers are able to use cars without understanding the details of each part. In the ideal case a PPL the user should just feel as though things work just the way they want them. This is the challenge PPL designers must meet.

In the remaining of the chapter, we will give some overview of some general components of a PPL, with examples of design choice from different PPLs. We are not aiming to provide an exhaustive descriptions of all PPLs [2], and we are also not trying to convince you to develop a PPL [3]. Rather, by understanding the implementation consideration, we hope that you will gain a better understanding of how to write more performative Bayesian models, and to diagnose computation bottlenecks and errors when they occur.

10.1.1   Example: Rainier

Consider the development of Rainier [4], a PPL written in Scala developed at Stripe. Stripe is a payments processing company that handles finances for many thousands of partner business. In Stripe, they need to estimate the distribution of risk associated with each partnered business, ideally with a PPL that is able to support many parallel inferences (one per each business partner) and easy to deploy in Stripe's compute cluster. As Stripe's compute clusters included a Java run time environment, they choose Scala as it can be compiled to Java bytecode. Rainier. In this case PyMC3 and Stan were considered as well, but due to either the restriction of Python use (PyMC3), or the requirement for a C++ compiler (Stan), creating a PPL for their particular use case was the best choice.

Most users will not need to develop their own PPL but we present this case study to highlight how considerations of both the environment in which you are using the code, and the functionality of the available PPLs can help inform a decision for a smoother experience as a computational Bayesian.

10.2   Posterior Computation

Inference is defined as a conclusion reached on the basis of evidence and reasoning and the posterior computational methodology is the engine that gets us to the conclusion. The posterior computation method can largely be thought of as two parts, the computation algorithm, and the software and hardware that makes the calculation, often referred to as the computational backend. When either designing or selecting a PPL, the available posterior computation methods ends up being a key decision that informs many factors of the workflow, from the speed of inference, hardware needed,

---

[1] With the prerequisite that basic ingredients like APIs to specify probability distribution and random variables, basic numerical transformations are already implemented.

[2] Even Wikipedia only contains a partial list https://en.wikipedia.org/wiki/Probabilistic_programming#List_of_probabilistic_programming_languages.

[3] *An Introduction to Probabilistic Programming* by van de Meent et al [102] is a good starting point if you are interested in both PPL development and usage.

[4] https://github.com/stripe/rainier. A more in-depth reflection of the development of Rainer is described in a podcast https://www.learnbayesstats.com/episode/22-eliciting-priors-and-doing-bayesian-inference-at-scale-with-avi-bryant

complexity of PPL, and breadth of applicability. There are numerous algorithms to compute the posterior [5], from exact computations when using conjugate models, to numerical approximations like grid search to Hamiltonian Monte Carlo (HMC), to model approximation like Laplace approximation and variational inference (covered in more detail in Section 11.9.5). When selecting an inference algorithms both the PPL designer and the user need to make a series of choices. For the PPL designer the algorithms have different levels of implementation complexity. For example, conjugate methods are quite easy to implement, as there exists analytical formulas that can be written in a couple lines of code, whereas MCMC samplers are more complex, typically requiring a PPL designer to write much more code than an analytical solution. Another tradeoff in computational complexity, conjugate methods do not require much computation power and can return a posterior in sub millisecond on all modern hardware, even a cell phone. By comparison, HMC is slow and require a system that can compute gradients, such as the one we will present in Section 10.2.1. This limits HMC computation to relatively powerful computers, sometimes with specialized hardware.

The user faces a similar dilemma, more advanced posterior computation methods are more general and require less mathematical expertise, but require more knowledge to assess and ensure correct fit. We have seen this throughout this book, where visual and numerical diagnostics are necessary to ensure our MCMC samplers have converged to an *estimate* of the posterior. Conjugate models do not need any convergence diagnostics due to the fact they calculate the posterior *exactly*, every time if the right mathematics are used.

For all these reasons there is no universal recommendation for an inference algorithm that suits every situation. At time of writing MCMC methods, especially adaptive Dynamic Hamiltonian Monte Carlo, are the most flexible, but not useful in all situations. As a user it is worthwhile understanding the availability and tradeoffs of each algorithm to be able to make an assessment for each situation.

10.2.1 Getting the Gradient

An incredibly useful piece of information in computational mathematics is the gradient. Also known as the slope, or the derivative for one dimensional functions, it indicates how fast a function output value is changing at any point in its domain. By utilizing the gradient many algorithms are developed to more efficiently achieve their goal. With inference algorithms we have seen this difference when comparing the Metropolis Hasting algorithm, which does not need a gradient when sampling, to Hamiltonian Monte Carlo, which does use the gradient and usually returns high quality samples faster [6].

Just as Markov chain Monte Carlo was originally developed in the sub field of statistical mechanics before computational Bayesians adopted it, most of the gradient evaluation libraries were originally developed as part of "Deep Learning" libraries mostly intended for backpropagation computation to train Neural Networks. These include Theano, TensorFlow and PyTorch. Bayesians however, learned to use them as computational backends for Bayesian Inference. An example of computational gradient evaluation using JAX [24], a dedicated autograd library, shown in Code Block 10.1. In this Code Block the gradient of x^2 is computed at a value of 4. We can solve this analytically with the rule rx^{r-1}, and we can then calculate $2 * 4 = 8$. However, with autograd libraries users do not need to think about closed form solutions. All that is needed is an expression of the function itself and the computer can automatically calculate the gradient, as implied by "auto" in autograd.

---

[5] See Section 11.9 for a discussion of some of more prevalent posterior computation methods.

[6] In terms of effective samples per second.

Code 10.1

```
1  from jax import grad
2
3  simple_grad = grad(lambda x: x**2)
4  print(simple_grad(4.0))
```

```
8.0
```

Methods such us Adaptive Dynamic Hamiltonian Monte Carlo or Variational Inference use gradients to estimate posterior distributions. Being able to obtain gradient easily becomes even more important when we realize that in posterior computation the gradient typically gets computed thousands of times. We show one such calculation in Code Block 10.2 using JAX for a small "hand built" model.

Code 10.2

```
1  from jax import grad
2  from jax.scipy.stats import norm
3
4  def model(test_point, observed):
5      z_pdf = norm.logpdf(test_point, loc=0, scale=5)
6      x_pdf = norm.logpdf(observed, loc=test_point, scale=1)
7      logpdf = z_pdf + x_pdf
8      return logpdf
9
10 model_grad = grad(model)
11
12 observed, test_point = 5.0, 2.5
13 logp_val = model(test_point, observed)
14 grad = model_grad(test_point, observed)
15 print(f"log_p_val: {logp_val}")
16 print(f"grad: {grad}")
```

```
log_p_val: -6.697315216064453
grad: 2.4000000953674316
```

For comparison we can make the same calculation using a PyMC3 model and computing the gradient using Theano in Code Block 10.3.

Code 10.3

```
1  with pm.Model() as model:
2      z = pm.Normal("z", 0., 5.)
3      x = pm.Normal("x", mu=z, sd=1., observed=observed)
4
5  func = model.logp_dlogp_function()
6  func.set_extra_values({})
7  print(func(np.array([test_point])))
```

```
[array(-6.69731498), array([2.4])]
```

From the output we can see the PyMC3 model returns the same logp and gradient as the JAX model.

10.2.2 Example: Near Real Time Inference

As a hypothetical example consider a statistician at a credit card company that is concerned with detecting credit card fraud quickly so it can disable cards before the thief can make more transactions. A secondary system classifies transactions as fraudulent or legitimate but the company wants to ensure it does not block cards with a low number of events and wants to be able to set priors for different customers to control the sensitivity. It is decided that the users accounts will be disabled when mean of the posterior distribution is above a probability threshold of 50%. In this near real time scenario inference needs to be performed in less than a second so fraudulent activity can be detected before the transaction clears. The statistician recognizes that this can be analytically expressed using a conjugate model which she then writes in Equation 10.1, where the α and β parameters, representing the prior of fraud and non-fraud transactions directly. As transactions are observed they are used fairly directly compute the posterior parameters.

$$
\begin{aligned}
\alpha_{post} &= \alpha_{prior} + fraud\_observations \\
\beta_{post} &= \beta_{prior} + non\_fraud\_observations \\
p(\theta \mid y) &= Beta(\alpha_{post}, \beta_{post}) \\
\mathbb{E}[p(\theta \mid y)] &= \frac{\alpha_{post}}{\alpha_{post} + \beta_{post}}
\end{aligned}
\tag{10.1}
$$

She can then fairly trivially express these calculations in Python as shown in Code Block 10.4. No external libraries needed either, making this function quite easy to deploy.

Code 10.4

```
1  def fraud_detector(obs_fraud, obs_non_fraud, fraud_prior=8, non_fraud_prior=6):
2      """Conjugate beta binomial model for fraud detection"""
3      expectation = (fraud_prior+observed_fraud) / (
4          fraud_prior+observed_fraud+non_fraud_prior+obs_non_fraud)
5
6      if expectation > .5:
7          return {"suspend_card":True}
8
9  %timeit fraud_detector(2, 0)
```

```
152 ns ± 0.969 ns per loop (mean ± std. dev. of 7 runs, 100 loops each)
```

To meet the sensitivity and probability computation time requirements of less than one second a conjugate prior is selected, and the model posterior is calculated in Code Block 10.4. The calculations took about 152 ns, in contrast an MCMC sampler will take around 2 seconds on the same machine which is over 6 orders of magnitude. It is unlikely that any MCMC sampler would meet the time requirement needed from this system, making a conjugate prior the clear choice.

Hardware and Sampling Speed

From a hardware perspective, there are three ways to increase MCMC sampling speed. The first is typically the clock speed of the processing unit, often measured in hertz, or Gigahertz for modern computers. This is the speed at which the instructions are executed, so generally speaking a 4 Gigahertz computer can execute twice as many instructions in a second than a 2 Gigahertz computer. In MCMC sampling the clock speed will correlate with the number of samples that can be taken in a timespan for a single chain. The other is parallelization across multiple cores in a processing unit. In MCMC sampling each chains can be sampled in parallel on computers with multiple cores. This coincidentally is convenient as many convergence metrics use multiple chains. On a modern desktop computer anywhere from 2 to 16 cores are typically available. The last method is specialized hardware such as the Graphics Processing Units (GPUs) and Tensor Processing Units (TPUs). If paired with the correct software and algorithms these are able to both sample each chain more quickly, but also sample more chains in parallel.

10.3 Application Programming Interfaces

Application Programming Interfaces (API) "define interactions between multiple software intermediaries". In the Bayesian case the most narrow definition is the interactions between the user and the method to compute the posterior. At its most broad it can include multiple steps in the Bayesian workflow, such as specifying a random variable with a distribution, linking different random variables to create the model, prior and posterior predictive checks, plotting, or any task. The API is typically first part, and sometimes the only part, a PPL practitioner interactions with and typically is where the practitioner spends the most amount of time. API design is both a science and an art and designers must balance multiple concerns.

On the science side PPLs must be able to interface with a computer and provide the necessary elements to control the computation methods. Many PPLs are defined with base languages and typically need to follow the fixed computational constraints of the base language as well as the computational backend. In our conjugate inference example in Section 10.2.2, only a 4 parameters and one line of code were needed to obtain an exact result. Contrast this with MCMC examples that had various inputs such as number of draws, acceptance rate, number of tuning steps and more. The complexity of MCMC, while mostly hidden, still surfaced additional complexity in the API.

> **So many APIs, so many interfaces**
>
> In a modern Bayesian workflow there is not just the PPL API but APIs of all the supporting packages in the workflow. In this book we have also used the Numpy, Matplotlib, Scipy, Pandas and ArviZ APIs across examples, not to mention the Python API itself. In the Python ecosystem. These choices of packages, and the APIs they bring, are also subject to personal choice. A practitioner may choose to use Bokeh as a replacement to Matplotlib for plotting, or xarray in addition to pandas, and in doing so the user will need to learn those APIs as well.
>
> In addition to just APIs there are many code writing interfaces to write Bayesian models, or just code in general. Code can be written in the text editors, notebook, Integrated Development Environments (IDEs), or the command line directly.
>
> The use of these tools, both the supporting packages and the coding interface, is not mutually exclusive. For someone new to computational statistics this can be a lot to take in. When starting out we suggest using a simple text editor and a few supporting packages to allow for your focus to be on the code and model, before moving onto more complex interfaces such as notebooks or Integrated Development Environments. We provide more guidance regarding this topic in Section 11.10.5.

On the art side API is the interface for human users. This interface is one of the most important parts of the PPL. Some users tend to have strong, albeit subjective views, about design choices. Users want the simplest, most flexible, readable, and easy to write API, objectives which, for the poor PPL designer, are both ill defined and opposed with each other. One choice a PPL designer can make is to mirror style and functionality of the base language. For example, there is a notion of "Pythonic" programs which are follow in a certain style [7]. This notion of pythonic API is what informs the PyMC3 API, the goal is to explicitly have users feel like they are writing their models in Python. In contrast Stan models are written in a domain specific language informed by other PPLs such as BUGS[66] and languages such as C++[32]. The Stan language includes notable API primitives such as curly braces and uses a block syntax as shown in Code Block 10.5. Writing a Stan model distinctly *does not* feel like writing Python, but this is not a knock against the API. It is just a different choice from a design standpoint and a different experience for the user.

10.3.1   Example: Stan and Slicstan

Depending on the use case, user might prefer different level of abstraction in terms model specification, independent of any other PPL component. Stan and Slicstan using from Gorinova etal [69] which is specifically dedicated to studying and proposing Stan APIs. In Code Block 10.5 we show the, original, Stan model syntax. In the Stan syntax various pieces of a Bayesian model are indicated by blocks declarations. These names correspond with the various sections of the workflow, such as specifying the model and parameters, data transformations, prior and posterior predictive sampling, with corresponding names such as parameters, model, transformed parameters, and generated quantities.

Code 10.5

```
1  parameters {
2      real y_std;
3      real x_std;
4  }
5  transformed parameters {
```

---

[7]The Zen of Python detai the philosophy behind this idea of pythonic designhttps://www.python.org/dev/peps/pep-0020/

```
6    real y = 3 * y_std;
7    real x = exp(y/2) * x_std;
8  }
9  model {
10     y_std ~ normal(0, 1);
11     x_std ~ normal(0, 1);
12 }
```

An alternative syntax for Stan models is Slicstan[69], the same model of which is shown in Code Block 10.6. Slicstan provides a compositional interface to Stan, letting users define functions which can be named and reused, and does away with the block syntax. These features mean Slicstan programs can be expressed in less code than standard Stan models. While not always the most important metric less code means less code that the Bayesian modeler needs to write, and less code that a model reviewer needs to read. Also, like Python, composable functions allow the user to define an idea once and reuse it many times, such as `my_normal` in the Slicstan snippet.

Code 10.6

```
1  real my_normal(real m, real s) {
2  real std ~ normal(0, 1);
3      return s * std + m;
4  }
5  real y = my_normal(0, 3);
6  real x = my_normal(0, exp(y/2));
```

For the original Stan syntax, it has the benefit of familiarity (for those who already use it) and documentation. The familiarity may come from Stan's choice to model itself after BUGS ensuring that users who have prior experience with that language, will be comfortable transitioning to the Stan syntax. It also is familiar for people who have been using Stan for numerous years. Since it was released 2012, there have now been multiple years for users to get familiar with the language, publish examples, and write models. For new users the block model forces organization so when writing a Stan program they will end up being more consistent.

Note both Stan and Slicstan use the same codebase under the API layer the difference in API is solely for the benefit of the user. In this case which API is "better" is a choice for each user. We should note this case study is only a shallow discussion of the Stan API. For full details we suggest reading the full paper, which formalizes both sets of syntax and shows the level of detail goes into API design.

10.3.2   Example: PyMC3 and PyMC4

Our second API is a case study of an API design change that was required because of a computational backend change, in this case from Theano in PyMC3 to TensorFlow in PyMC4 a PPL that was initially intended to replace PyMC3 [86]. In the design of PyMC4 the designers of the language desired to keep the syntax *as close as possible* to the PyMC3 syntax. While the inference algorithms remained the same, the fundamental way in which TensorFlow and Python works meant the PyMC4 API forced into a particular design due to the change in computational backend. Consider the Eight Schools model [137] implemented in PyMC3 syntax in Code Block 10.7 and the now, defunct [8] PyMC4 syntax in Code Block 10.8.

---

[8]https://pymc-devs.medium.com/the-future-of-pymc3-or-theano-is-dead-long-live-theano-d8005f8a0e9b. contains more details about the decision and future road map of PyMC3

Code 10.7

```
1  with pm.Model() as eight_schools_pymc3:
2      mu = pm.Normal("mu", 0, 5)
3      tau = pm.HalfCauchy("tau", 5)
4      theta = pm.Normal("theta", mu=mu, sigma=tau, shape=8)
5      obs = pm.Normal("obs", mu=theta, sigma=sigma, observed=y)
```

Code 10.8

```
1  @pm.model
2  def eight_schools_pymc4():
3      mu = yield pm.Normal("mu", 1, 5)
4      tau = yield pm.HalfNormal("tau", 5)
5      theta = yield pm.Normal("theta", loc=mu, scale=sigma, batch_stack=8)
6
7      obs = yield pm4.Normal("obs", loc=theta, scale=sigma, observed=y)
8      return obs
```

The differences in PyMC4 is the decorator `@pm.model`, the declaration of a Python function, the use of generators indicated by **yield**, and differing argument names. You may have noticed that the **yield** is the same that you have seen in the TensorFlow Probability code. In both PPLs **yield** statement was a necessary part of the API due to the choice coroutine. These APIs changes were not desired however, as users would have to learn a new syntax, all existing PyMC3 code would have to be rewritten to use PyMC4, and all existing PyMC3 documentation would become obsolete. This is an example where the API is informed not by user preference, but by the choice computational backend used to calculate the posterior. In the end the feedback from users to keep the PyMC3 API unchanged was one of the reasons to terminate PyMC4 development.

10.4   PPL Driven Transformations

In this book we saw many mathematical transformations that allowed us to define a variety of models, easily and with great flexibility such as GLMs. Or we saw transformations that allowed us to make results more interpretable such as centering. In this section we will specifically discuss transformations that are driven more specifically by PPL. They are sometimes a bit implicit and we will discuss two examples in this section.

10.4.1   Log Probabilities

One of the most common transformations is the log probability transform. To understand why let us go through an example where we calculate an arbitrary likelihood. Assume we observe two independent outcomes y_0 and y_1, their joint probability is:

$$p(y_0, y_1 \mid \boldsymbol{\theta}) = p(y_0 \mid \boldsymbol{\theta})p(y_1 \mid \boldsymbol{\theta}) \tag{10.2}$$

To give a specific situation let us say we observed the value 2 twice and we decide to use a Normal distribution as a likelihood in our model. We can specify our model by expanding Equation 10.2 into:.

$$\mathcal{N}(2, 2 \mid \mu = 0, \sigma = 1) = \mathcal{N}(2 \mid 0, 1)\mathcal{N}(2 \mid 0, 1) \tag{10.3}$$

Being computational statisticians we can now calculate this value with a little bit of code.

Code 10.9

```
1  observed = np.repeat(2, 2)
2  pdf = stats.norm(0, 1).pdf(observed)
3  np.prod(pdf, axis=0)
```

```
0.0029150244650281948
```

With two observations we get 20 decimals of precision for joint probability density in Code Block 10.9 with no issues, but now let us assume we see a total of 1000 observations, all of the same value of 2. We can repeat our calculation in Code Block 10.10. This time however, we have an issue, Python reports a joint probability density of 0.0, which cannot be true.

Code 10.10

```
1  observed = np.repeat(2, 1000)
2  pdf = stats.norm(0, 1).pdf(observed)
3  np.prod(pdf, axis=0)
```

```
0.0
```

What we are seeing is an example of *floating point precision* error in computers. Due to the fundamental way computers store numbers in memory and evaluate calculations, only a limited amount of precision is possible. In Python this error in precision is often hidden from the user [9], although in certain cases the user is exposed to the lack of precision, as shown in Code Block 10.11

Code 10.11

```
1.2 - 1
```

```
0.19999999999999996
```

With relatively "large" numbers the small error in the far decimal place matter little. However, in Bayesian modeling we often are working with very small float point numbers, and even worse we multiply them together many times making them smaller yet. To mitigate this problem PPLs perform a log transformation of probability often abbreviated to *logp*. Thus expression 10.2 turns into:

$$\log(p(y_0, y_1 \mid \boldsymbol{\theta})) = \log(p(y_0 \mid \boldsymbol{\theta})) + \log(p(y_1 \mid \boldsymbol{\theta})) \tag{10.4}$$

This has two effects, it makes small numbers relatively large, and due to the product rule of logarithms, changes the multiplication into a sum. Using the same example but performing the calculation in log space, we see a more numerically stable result in Code Block 10.12.

Code 10.12

```
1  logpdf = stats.norm(0, 1).logpdf(observed)
2
3  # Compute individual logpdf two ways for one observation, as well as total
4  np.log(pdf[0]), logpdf[0], logpdf.sum()
```

```
(-2.9189385332046727, -2.9189385332046727, -2918.9385332046736)
```

---

[9] https://docs.Python.org/3/tutorial/floatingpoint.html

10.4.2 Random Variables and Distributions Transformations

Random variables that distributed as a bounded distributions, like the Uniform distribution that is specified with a fixed interval $[a, b]$, present a challenge for gradient evaluation and samplers based on them. Sudden changes in geometry make it difficult to sample the distribution at the neighborhood of those sudden changes. Imagine rolling a ball down a set of stairs or a cliff, rather than a smooth surface. It is easier to estimate the trajectory of the ball over a smooth surface rather than the discontinuous surface. Thus, another useful set of transformations in PPLs [10] are transformations that turn bounded random variables, such as those distributed as Uniform, Beta, Halfnormal, etc, into unbounded random variables that span entire real line from $(-\infty, \infty)$. These transformations however, need to be done with care as we must now correct for the volume changes in our transformed distributions. To do so we need to compute the Jacobians of the transformation and accumulate the calculated log probabilities, explained in further detail in Section 11.1.9.

PPLs usually transform bounded random variables into unbounded random variables and perform inference in the unbounded space, and then transform back the values to the original bounded space, all can happen without user input. Thus users do not need to interact with these transformations if they do not want to. For a concrete example both the forward and backward transform for the Uniform random variable are shown in Equation 10.5 and computed in Code Block 10.13. In this transformation the lower and upper bound a and b are mapped to $-\infty$ and ∞ respectively, and the values in between are "stretched" to values in between accordingly.

$$
\begin{aligned}
x_t &= \log(x - a) - \log(b - x) \\
x &= a + \frac{1}{1 + e^{-x_t}}(b - a)
\end{aligned}
\tag{10.5}
$$

Code 10.13

```
1 lower, upper = -1, 2
2 domain = np.linspace(lower, upper, 5)
3 transform = np.log(domain - lower) - np.log(upper - domain)
4 print(f"Original domain: {domain}")
5 print(f"Transformed domain: {transform}")
```

```
Original domain:[-1.    -0.25  0.5   1.25  2.  ]
Transformed domain: [-inf -1.09861229, 0., 1.09861229, inf]
```

The automatic transform can be seen by adding a Uniform random variable to a PyMC3 model and inspecting the variable and the underlying distribution in the model object, as shown in Code Block 10.14.

Code 10.14

```
1 with pm.Model() as model:
2     x = pm.Uniform("x", -1., 2.)
3
4 model.vars
```

```
([x_interval__ ~ TransformedDistribution])
```

Seeing this transform we can also then query the model to check the transformed logp values

---

[10]https://mc-stan.org/docs/2_25/reference-manual/variable-transforms-chapter.html

in Code Block 10.15. Note how with the transformed distribution we can sample outside of the interval $(-1, 2)$ (the boundaries of the un-transformed Uniform) and still obtain a finite logp value. Also note the logp returned from the `logp_nojac` method, and how the value is the same for the values of -2 and 1, and how when we call `logp` the Jacobian adjustment is made automatically.

Code 10.15

```
1  print(model.logp({"x_interval__":-2}),
2        model.logp_nojac({"x_interval__":-2}))
3  print(model.logp({"x_interval__":1}),
4        model.logp_nojac({"x_interval__":1}))
```

```
-2.2538560220859454 -1.0986122886681098
-1.6265233750364456 -1.0986122886681098
```

Log transformation of the probabilities and unbounding of random variables are transformations that PPLs usually apply without most users knowing, but they both have a practical effect on the performance and usability of the PPL across a wide variety of models.

There are other more explicit transformations users can perform directly on the distribution itself to construct new distribution. User can then create random variables distributed as these new distributions in a model. For example, the bijectors module [47] in TFP can be used to transform a base distribution into more complicated distributions. Code Block 10.16 demonstrates how to construct a $LogNormal(0,1)$ distribution by transforming the base distribution $\mathcal{N}(0,1)$ [11]. This expressive API design even allows users to define complicated transformation using trainable bijectors (e.g., a neural network [114]) like `tfb.MaskedAutoregressiveFlow`.

Code 10.16

```
1  tfb = tfp.bijectors
2
3  lognormal0 = tfd.LogNormal(0., 1.)
4  lognormal1 = tfd.TransformedDistribution(tfd.Normal(0., 1.), tfb.Exp())
5  x = lognormal0.sample(100)
6
7  np.testing.assert_array_equal(lognormal0.log_prob(x), lognormal1.log_prob(x))
```

Whether explicitly used, or implicitly applied, we note that these transformations of random variables and distributions are not a strictly required components of PPLs, but certainly are included in nearly every modern PPL in some fashion. For example, they can be incredibly helpful in getting good inference results efficiently, as shown in the next example.

10.4.3   Example: Sampling Comparison between Bounded and Unbounded Random Variables

Here we create a small example to demonstrate the differences between sampling from transformed and un-transformed random variable. Data is simulated from a Normal distribution with a very small standard deviation and model is specified in Code Block 10.17.

---

[11]In fact, this is how `tfd.LogNormal` is implemented in TFP, with some additional overwrite of class method to make computation more stable.

Code 10.17

```
1  y_observed = stats.norm(0, .01).rvs(20)
2
3  with pm.Model() as model_transform:
4      sd = pm.HalfNormal("sd", 5)
5      y = pm.Normal("y", mu=0, sigma=sd, observed=y_observed)
6      trace_transform = pm.sample(chains=1, draws=100000)
7
8  print(model_transform.vars)
9  print(f"Diverging: {trace_transform.get_sampler_stats('diverging').sum()}")
```

```
[sd_log__ ~ TransformedDistribution()]
Diverging: 0
```

We can inspect free variables and after sampling we can count the number of divergences. From the code output from Code Block 10.17 we can verify the bounded HalfNormal **sd** variable has been transformed, and in subsequent sampling there are no divergences.

For a counterexample, let us specify the same model in Code Block 10.18 but in this case the HalfNormal prior distribution explicitly was not transformed. This is reflected both in the model API, as well as when inspecting the models free variables. Subsequent sampling sampling reports 423 divergences.

Code 10.18

```
1  with pm.Model() as model_no_transform:
2      sd = pm.HalfNormal("sd", 5, transform=None)
3      y = pm.Normal("y", mu=0, sigma=sd, observed=y_observed)
4      trace_no_transform = pm.sample(chains=1, draws=100000)
5
6  print(model_no_transform.vars)
7  print(f"Diverging: {trace_no_transform.get_sampler_stats('diverging').sum()}")
```

```
[sd ~ HalfNormal(sigma=10.0)]
Diverging: 423
```

In the absence of automatic transforms the user would need to spend some time assessing why the divergences are occurring, and either know that a transformation is needed from prior experience or come to this conclusion through debugging and research, all efforts that take time away from building the model and performing inference.

10.5   Operation Graphs and Automatic Reparameterization

One manipulation that some PPLs perform is reparameterizing models, by first creating an *operation graph* and then subsequently optimizing that graph. To illustrate what this means let us define a computation:

$$x = 3$$
$$y = 1 \tag{10.6}$$
$$x * (y/x) + 0$$

Humans, with basic algebra knowledge, will quickly see that the x terms cancel leaving the addition $y + 0$, which has no effect, leading to an answer of 1. We can also perform this calculation in pure Python and get the same answer which is great, but what is not great is the wasted computation. Pure Python, and libraries like numpy, just see these operations as *computational steps* and will faithfully perform each step of the stated equation, first dividing y by x, then multiplying that result by x, then adding 0.

In contrast libraries like Theano work differently. They first construct a *symbolic* representation of the computation as shown in Code Block 10.19.

Code 10.19

```
x = theano.tensor.vector("x")
y = theano.tensor.vector("y")
out = x*(y/x) + 0
theano.printing.debugprint(out)
```

```
Elemwise{add,no_inplace} [id A] ''
 |Elemwise{mul,no_inplace} [id B] ''
 | |x [id C]
 | |Elemwise{true_div,no_inplace} [id D] ''
 |   |y [id E]
 |   |x [id C]
 |InplaceDimShuffle{x} [id F] ''
   |TensorConstant{0} [id G]
```

> **What is Aesara?**
>
> As you have seen Theano is the workhorse of PyMC3 models in terms of graph representation, gradient calculation, and much more. However, Theano was deprecated in 2017 by the original authors. Since then PyMC developers have been maintaining Theano to support of PyMC3. In 2020 the PyMC developers decided to move from maintaining Theano to improving it. In doing so the PyMC developers forked Theano and named the fork Aesara [a]. With a focused effort led by Brandon Willard the legacy portions of the code base have been drastically modernized. Additionally Aesara includes expanded functionality particularly for Bayesian use cases. These include adding new backends (JAX and Numba) for accelerated numerical computation and better support modern compute hardware such GPU and TPU. With greater control and coordination over more of the PPL components between the PyMC3 and Aesara the PyMC developers are looking to continuously foster a better PPL experience for developers, statisticians, and users.
>
> ---
> [a]In Greek mythology Aesara is the daughter of Theano, hence the fitting name.

In the output of Code Block 10.19, working inside out, we see on Line 4 the first operation is the division of x and y, then the multiplication x, then finally the addition of 0 represented in a computation graph. This same graph is shown visually in Figure 10.1. At this point no actual numeric calculations have taken place, but a sequence of operations, albeit an unoptimized one, has been generated.

We can now optimize this graph using Theano, by passing this computation graph to `theano.function` in Code Block 10.20. In the output nearly all the operations have disappeared, as Theano has recognized that both multiplication and division of x cancels out, and that the addition of 0 has no effect on the final outcome. The optimized operation graph is shown in Figure 10.2.

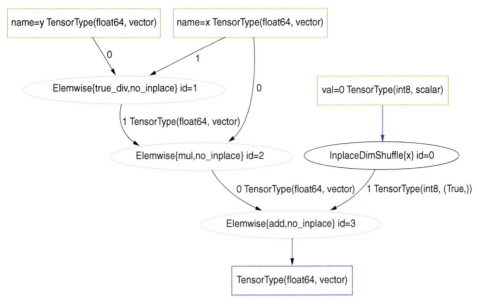

FIGURE 10.1
Unoptimized Theano operation graph of Equation 10.6 as declared in Code Block 10.19.

Code 10.20

```
1 fgraph = theano.function([x,y], [out])
2 theano.printing.debugprint(fgraph)
```

```
DeepCopyOp [id A] 'y'   0
 |y [id B]
```

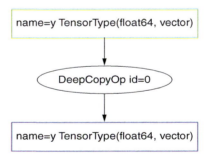

FIGURE 10.2
Optimized Theano operation graph of Equation 10.6 after optimization in 10.20.

Theano can then calculate the answer when the optimized function is called with the numerical inputs as shown in Code Block 10.21.

Code 10.21

```
fgraph([1],[3])
```

```
[array([3.])]
```

To perform the algebraic simplication, your computer did not become sentient and rederive the rules of algebra from scratch. Theano is able to perform these optimizations thanks to a code optimizer [12] that inspects the operation graph stated through the Theano API by a user, scans the graph for algebraic patterns, and simplifies computation and give users the desired result.

Bayesian models are just a special case of both mathematics and computation. In Bayesian computation typically desired output is the logp of the model. Before optimization the first step is a symbolic representation of the operations graph, an example of which is shown in Code Block 10.22 where a one line PyMC3 model is turned into multi line computation graph at the operation level.

Code 10.22

```
1  with pm.Model() as model_normal:
2      x = pm.Normal("x", 0., 1.)
3
4  theano.printing.debugprint(aesara_normal.logpt)
```

```
Sum{acc_dtype=float64} [id A] '__logp'
 |MakeVector{dtype='float64'} [id B] ''
   |Sum{acc_dtype=float64} [id C] ''
     |Sum{acc_dtype=float64} [id D] '__logp_x'
       |Elemwise{switch,no_inplace} [id E] ''
         |Elemwise{mul,no_inplace} [id F] ''
         | |TensorConstant{1} [id G]
         | |Elemwise{mul,no_inplace} [id H] ''
         |   |TensorConstant{1} [id I]
         |   |Elemwise{gt,no_inplace} [id J] ''
         |     |TensorConstant{1.0} [id K]
         |     |TensorConstant{0} [id L]
         |Elemwise{true_div,no_inplace} [id M] ''
         | |Elemwise{add,no_inplace} [id N] ''
         | | |Elemwise{mul,no_inplace} [id O] ''
         | | | |Elemwise{neg,no_inplace} [id P] ''
         | | | | |TensorConstant{1.0} [id Q]
         | | | |Elemwise{pow,no_inplace} [id R] ''
         | | |   |Elemwise{sub,no_inplace} [id S] ''
         | | |   | |x ~ Normal(mu=0.0, sigma=1.0) [id T]
         | | |   | |TensorConstant{0.0} [id U]
         | | |   |TensorConstant{2} [id V]
         | | |Elemwise{log,no_inplace} [id W] ''
         | |   |Elemwise{true_div,no_inplace} [id X] ''
         | |     |Elemwise{true_div,no_inplace} [id Y] ''
         | |     | |TensorConstant{1.0} [id Q]
         | |     | |TensorConstant{3.141592653589793} [id Z]
         | |     |TensorConstant{2.0} [id BA]
         | |TensorConstant{2.0} [id BB]
         |TensorConstant{-inf} [id BC]
```

Just like algebraic optimization this graph can then be optimized in ways that benefit the Bayesian user[160]. Recall the discussion in Section 4.6.1, certain models benefit from non-centered

---

[12]https://theano-pymc.readthedocs.io/en/latest/optimizations.html?highlight=o1# optimizations

parameterizations, as this helps eliminate challenging geometry such as Neal's funnel. Without automatic optimization the user must be aware of the geometrical challenge to the sampler and make the adjust themselves. In the future, libraries such as symbolic-pymc [13] will be able to make this reparameterization automatic, just as we say the automatic transformation of log probability and bounded distributions above. With this upcoming tool PPL users can further focus on the model and let the PPL "worry" about the computational optimizations.

10.6   Effect handling

Effect handlers [84] are an abstraction in programming languages that gives different interpretations, or side effects, to the standard behavior of statements in a program. A common example is exception handling in Python with **try** and **except**. When some specific error is raised in the code block under **try** statement, we can perform different processing in the **except** block and resume computation. For Bayesian models there are two primary effects we want the random variable to have, draw a value (sample) from its distribution, or condition the value to some user input. Other use cases of effect handlers are transforming bounded random variables and automatic reparameterization as we mentioned above.

Effect handlers are not a required component of PPLs but rather a design choice that strongly influences the API and the "feel" of using the PPL. Harkening back to our car analogy this is similar to a power steering system in a car. It is not required, it is usually hidden from the driver under the hood but it definitely changes the driving experience. As effect handlers are typically "hidden" they are more easily explained through example rather than theory.

10.6.1   Example: Effect Handling in TFP and Numpyro

In the rest of this section we will see how effect handling works in TensorFlow Probability and NumPyro. Briefly NumPyro is another PPL based on Jax. Specifically, we will compare the high level API between **tfd.JointDistributionCoroutine** and model written with NumPyro primitives, which both represent Bayesian model with a Python function in a similar way. Also, we will be using the JAX substrate of TFP, so that both API share the same base language and numerical computation backend. Again consider the model in Equation 10.7, in Code Block 10.23 we import the libraries and write the model:

Code 10.23

```
1  import jax
2  import numpyro
3  from tensorflow_probability.substrates import jax as tfp_jax
4
5  tfp_dist = tfp_jax.distributions
6  numpyro_dist = numpyro.distributions
7
8  root = tfp_dist.JointDistributionCoroutine.Root
9  def tfp_model():
10     x = yield root(tfp_dist.Normal(loc=1.0, scale=2.0, name="x"))
11     z = yield root(tfp_dist.HalfNormal(scale=1., name="z"))
12     y = yield tfp_dist.Normal(loc=x, scale=z, name="y")
```

---

[13]https://github.com/pymc-devs/symbolic-pymc

```
13
14 def numpyro_model():
15     x = numpyro.sample("x", numpyro_dist.Normal(loc=1.0, scale=2.0))
16     z = numpyro.sample("z", numpyro_dist.HalfNormal(scale=1.0))
17     y = numpyro.sample("y", numpyro_dist.Normal(loc=x, scale=z))
```

From a glance, `tfp_model` and `numpyro_model` looks similar, both are Python functions with no input argument and return statement (note NumPyro model can have inputs and return statements), both need to indicate which statement should be considered as random variable (TFP with `yield`, NumPyro with `numpyro.sample` primitives). Moreover, the default behavior of both `tfp_model` and `numpyro_model` is ambiguous, they do not really do anything [14] until you give it specific instruction. For example, in Code Block 10.24 we draw prior samples from both models, and evaluate the log probability on the same prior samples (that returned by the TFP model).

Code 10.24

```
1  sample_key = jax.random.PRNGKey(52346)
2
3  # Draw samples
4  jd = tfp_dist.JointDistributionCoroutine(tfp_model)
5  tfp_sample = jd.sample(1, seed=sample_key)
6
7  predictive = numpyro.infer.Predictive(numpyro_model, num_samples=1)
8  numpyro_sample = predictive(sample_key)
9
10 # Evaluate log prob
11 log_likelihood_tfp = jd.log_prob(tfp_sample)
12 log_likelihood_numpyro = numpyro.infer.util.log_density(
13     numpyro_model, [], {},
14     # Samples returning from JointDistributionCoroutine is a
15     # Namedtuple like Python object, we convert it to a dictionary
16     # so that numpyro can recognize it.
17     params=tfp_sample._asdict())
18
19 # Validate that we get the same log prob
20 np.testing.assert_allclose(log_likelihood_tfp, log_likelihood_numpyro[0])
```

We can also condition some random variable to user input value in our model, for example, in Code Block 10.25 we condition `z = .01` and then sample from the model.

Code 10.25

```
1  # Condition z to .01 in TFP and sample
2  jd.sample(z=.01, seed=sample_key)
3
4  # Condition z to .01 in NumPyro and sample
5  predictive = numpyro.infer.Predictive(
6      numpyro_model, num_samples=1, params={"z": np.asarray(.01)})
7  predictive(sample_key)
```

---

[14]The default behavior of a Pyro model is to sample from the distribution, but not in NumPyro.

From user perspective effect handling mostly happens behind the scenes when high level APIs are used. In TFP a `tfd.JointDistribution` encapsulate the effect handlers inside of a single object, and change the behavior of a function within that object when the input arguments are different. For NumPyro the effect handling is a bit more explicit and flexible. A set of effect handlers are implemented in `numpyro.handlers`, which powers the high level APIs we just used to generate prior samples and compute model log probability. This is shown again in Code Block 10.26, where we conditioned random variable $z = .01$, draw a sample from x, and construct conditional distribution $p(y \mid x, z)$ and sample from it.

Code 10.26

```
1  # Conditioned z to .01 in TFP and construct conditional distributions
2  dist, value = jd.sample_distributions(z=.01, seed=sample_key)
3  assert dist.y.loc == value.x
4  assert dist.y.scale == value.z
5
6  # Conditioned z to .01 in NumPyro and construct conditional distributions
7  model = numpyro.handlers.substitute(numpyro_model, data={"z": .01})
8  with numpyro.handlers.seed(rng_seed=sample_key):
9      # Under the seed context, the default behavior of a NumPyro model is the
10     # same as in Pyro: drawing prior sample.
11     model_trace = numpyro.handlers.trace(numpyro_model).get_trace()
12  assert model_trace["y"]["fn"].loc == model_trace["x"]["value"]
13  assert model_trace["y"]["fn"].scale == model_trace["z"]["value"]
```

The Python assertion in Code Block 10.26 is to validate that the conditional distribution is indeed correct. Compare to the `jd.sample_distributions(.)` call, You could see the explicit effect handling in NumPyro with `numpyro.handlers.substitute` that returns a conditioned model, `numpyro.handlers.seed` to set the random seed (a JAX requirement for drawing random samples), and `numpyro.handlers.trace` to trace the function execution. More information of the effect handling in NumPyro and Pyro could be found in their official documentation [15].

10.7 Base Language, Code Ecosystem, Modularity and Everything Else

When serious car enthusiasts pick a car, the availability of different components that can be mixed and match can be an informative factor in which car is ultimately purchased. These owners may choose to make aesthetic changes to fit their preference such as a new hood for a different look, or they may choose to perform an engine swap, which substantially changes the performance of the vehicle. Regardless most car owners would prefer to have more choices and flexibility in how they can modify their vehicle then less, even if they do not choose to modify their vehicle at all.

In this same way PPL users are not only concerned about the PPL itself, but also what related code bases and packages exist in that particular ecosystem, as well as the modularity of the PPL itself. In this book we have used Python as the base language, and PyMC3 and TensorFlow Probability as our PPLs. With them however, we have also used Matplotlib for plotting, NumPy for numerical operations, Pandas and xarray for data manipulation, and ArviZ for exploratory analysis of Bayesian models. Colloquially these are all part of the PyData stack. However, there are other base languages such as R with their own ecosystem of packages. This ecosystem has similar set of

---

[15]https://pyro.ai/examples/effect_handlers.html

tools under the tidyverse moniker, as well as specific Bayesian packages aptly named loo, posterior, bayesplot among others. Luckily Stan users are able to change base languages relatively easily, as the model is defined in the Stan language and there is a choice of interfaces available such as pystan, rstan, cmdstan and others. PyMC3 users are relegated to Python. However, with Theano there is modularity in the computational backend that can be used, from the Theano native backend, to the newer JAX backend. Along with all the above there is a laundry list of other points that matter, non-uniformly, to PPL users including.

- Ease of development in production environments
- Ease of installation in development environment
- Developer speed
- Computational speed
- Availability of papers, blog posts, lectures
- Documentation
- Useful error messages
- The community
- What colleagues recommend
- Upcoming features

Just having choices is not enough however, to use a PPL a user must be able to install and understand how to use them. The availability of work that references the PPL tends to indicate how widely accepted it is and provide confidence that it is indeed useful. Users are not keen to invest time into a PPL that will no longer be maintained. And ultimately as humans, even data informed Bayesian users, the recommendation of a respected colleagues and other presence of a large user base, are all influential factors in evaluating PPL, as much as the technical capabilities in many circumstances.

10.8   Designing a PPL

In this section we will switch our perspective from a PPL overview as a user and to one of a PPL designer. Now that we identified the big components let us design a hypothetical PPL to see how components fit together and also how they sometimes do not fit as easily as you would hope! The choices we will make are for illustrative purposes but frame how the system comes together, and also how a PPL designer thinks when putting together a PPL.

First we choose a base language with a numerical computing backend. Since this book focuses on Python let us use NumPy. Ideally, we also have a set of commonly used mathematical functions implemented for us already. For example, the central piece for implementing a PPL is a set of (log)probability mass or density function, and some pseudo random number generators. Luckily, those are readily available via `scipy.stats`. Let us put these together in Code Block 10.27 with a simple demonstration of drawing some samples from a $\mathcal{N}(1, 2)$ distribution and evaluate their log probability:

Code 10.27

```
1  import numpy as np
2  from scipy import stats
3
```

```
4  # Draw 2 samples from a Normal(1., 2.) distribution
5  x = stats.norm.rvs(loc=1.0, scale=2.0, size=2, random_state=1234)
6  # Evaluate the log probability of the samples
7  logp = stats.norm.logpdf(x, loc=1.0, scale=2.0)
```

where `stats.norm` is a Python class in the `scipy.stats` module [16] which contains methods and statistical functions associated with *the family of* Normal distributions. Alternatively, we can initialize a Normal distribution with fixed parameters as shown in Code Block 10.28.

Code 10.28

```
1  random_variable_x = stats.norm(loc=1.0, scale=2.0)
2
3  x = random_variable_x.rvs(size=2, random_state=1234)
4  logp = random_variable_x.logpdf(x)
```

Both Code Block 10.27 and 10.28 return exactly the same output `x` and `logp` as we also supplied the same `random_state`. The differences here is that Code Block 10.28 we have a "frozen" random variable [17] `random_variable_x` that could be considered as the SciPy representation of $x \sim \mathcal{N}(1, 2)$. Unfortunately, this object does work well when we try to use it naively when writing a full Bayesian models. Consider the model $x \sim \mathcal{N}(1, 2), y \sim \mathcal{N}(x, 0.1)$. Writing it in Code Block 10.29 raises an exception because `scipy.stats.norm` is expecting the input to be a NumPy array [18].

Code 10.29

```
1  x = stats.norm(loc=1.0, scale=2.0)
2  y = stats.norm(loc=x, scale=0.1)
3  y.rvs()
```

```
...
TypeError: unsupported operand type(s) for +: 'float' and 'rv_frozen'
```

From this it becomes evident how tricky it is to design an API, what seems intuitive for the user may not be possible with the underlying packages, In our case to write a PPL in Python we need to make a series of API design choices and other decision to make Code Block 10.29 work. Specifically we want:

1. A representation of random variables that could be used to initialize another random variable;

2. To be able to condition the random variable on some specific values (e.g., the observed data);

3. The graphical model, generated by a collection of random variables, to behave in a consistent and predictable way.

Getting Item 1 to work is actually pretty straightforward with a Python class that could be recognized by NumPy as an array. We do this in Code Block 10.30 and use the implementation to specific the model in Equation 10.7.

$$
\begin{aligned}
x &\sim \mathcal{N}(1, 2) \\
z &\sim \mathcal{HN}(1) \\
y &\sim \mathcal{N}(x, z)
\end{aligned}
\tag{10.7}
$$

---

[16] https://docs.scipy.org/doc/scipy/reference/stats.html
[17] We will go into more details about random variable in Chapter 11.
[18] To be more precise, a Python object with a `__array__` method.

Code 10.30

```
1  class RandomVariable:
2      def __init__(self, distribution):
3          self.distribution = distribution
4
5      def __array__(self):
6          return np.asarray(self.distribution.rvs())
7
8  x = RandomVariable(stats.norm(loc=1.0, scale=2.0))
9  z = RandomVariable(stats.halfnorm(loc=0., scale=1.))
10 y = RandomVariable(stats.norm(loc=x, scale=z))
11
12 for i in range(5):
13     print(np.asarray(y))
```

```
3.7362186279475353
0.5877468494932253
4.916129854385227
1.7421638350544257
2.074813968631388
```

A more precise description for the Python class we wrote in Code Block 10.30 is a stochastic array. As you see from the Code Block output, instantiation of this object, like `np.asarray(y)`, always gives us a different array. Adding a method to conditioned the random variable to some value, with a `log_prob` method, we have in Code Block 10.31 a toy implementation of a more functional `RandomVariable`:

Code 10.31

```
1  class RandomVariable:
2      def __init__(self, distribution, value=None):
3          self.distribution = distribution
4          self.set_value(value)
5
6      def __repr__(self):
7          return f"{self.__class__.__name__}(value={self.__array__()})"
8
9      def __array__(self, dtype=None):
10         if self.value is None:
11             return np.asarray(self.distribution.rvs(), dtype=dtype)
12         return self.value
13
14     def set_value(self, value=None):
15         self.value = value
16
17     def log_prob(self, value=None):
18         if value is not None:
19             self.set_value(value)
20         return self.distribution.logpdf(np.array(self))
21
22 x = RandomVariable(stats.norm(loc=1.0, scale=2.0))
23 z = RandomVariable(stats.halfnorm(loc=0., scale=1.))
24 y = RandomVariable(stats.norm(loc=x, scale=z))
```

We can look at the value of y with or without conditioning the value of its dependencies in Code Block 10.32, and the output seems to match the expected behavior. In Code Block below note how y is much closer to x if we set z to a small value.

Code 10.32

```
 1 for i in range(3):
 2     print(y)
 3
 4 print(f"  Set x=5 and z=0.1")
 5 x.set_value(np.asarray(5))
 6 z.set_value(np.asarray(0.05))
 7 for i in range(3):
 8     print(y)
 9
10 print(f"  Reset z")
11 z.set_value(None)
12 for i in range(3):
13     print(y)
```

```
RandomVariable(value=5.044294197842362)
RandomVariable(value=4.907595148778454)
RandomVariable(value=6.374656988711546)
  Set x=5 and z=0.1
RandomVariable(value=4.973898547458924)
RandomVariable(value=4.959593974224869)
RandomVariable(value=5.003811456458226)
  Reset z
RandomVariable(value=6.421473681641824)
RandomVariable(value=4.942894375257069)
RandomVariable(value=4.996621204780431)
```

Moreover, we can evaluate the unnormalized log probability density of the random variable. For example, in Code Block 10.33 we generate the posterior distribution for x and z when we observe y = 5.0.

Code 10.33

```
 1 # Observed y = 5.
 2 y.set_value(np.array(5.))
 3
 4 posterior_density = lambda xval, zval: x.log_prob(xval) + z.log_prob(zval) + \
 5                 y.log_prob()
 6 posterior_density(np.array(0.), np.array(1.))
```

```
-15.881815599614018
```

We can validate it with an explicit implementation of the posterior density function, as shown in Code Block 10.34:

Code 10.34

```
 1 def log_prob(xval, zval, yval=5):
 2     x_dist = stats.norm(loc=1.0, scale=2.0)
 3     z_dist = stats.halfnorm(loc=0., scale=1.)
 4     y_dist = stats.norm(loc=xval, scale=zval)
```

```
5        return x_dist.logpdf(xval) + z_dist.logpdf(zval) + y_dist.logpdf(yval)
6
7   log_prob(0, 1)
```

```
-15.881815599614018
```

At this point, it seems we have fulfilled the requirements of Item 1 and Item 2 , but Item 3 is the most challenging [19]. For example, in a Bayesian workflow we want to draw prior and prior predictive sample from a model. While our `RandomVariable` draws a random sample according to its prior, when it is not conditioned on some value, it does not record the values of its parents (in a graphical model sense). We need additional graph utilities assign to `RandomVariable` so that the Python object aware of its parents and children (i.e., its Markov blanket), and propagates the change accordingly if we draw a new sample or conditioned on some specific value [20]. For example, PyMC3 uses Theano to represent the graphical model and keep track of the dependencies (see Section 10.5 above) and Edward [21] uses TensorFlow v1 [22] to achieve that.

Spectrum of Probabilistic Modelling Libraries

One aspect of PPLs that is worth mentioning is universality. A universal PPL is a PPL that is **Turing-complete**. Since the PPLs used in this book are an extension of a general-purpose base language, they could all be considered Turing-complete. However, research and implementation dedicated to universal PPLs usually focus on areas slightly different from what we discussed here. For example, an area of focus in a universal PPL is to express dynamic models, where the model contains complex control flow that dependent on random variable [161]. As a result, the number of random variables or the shape of a random variable could change during the execution of a dynamic probabilistic model. A good example of universal PPLs is Anglican [148]. Dynamic models might be valid or possible to write down, but there might not be an efficient and robust method to inference them. In this book, we discuss mainly PPLs focusing on static models (and their inference), with a slight sacrifice and neglect of universality. On the other end of the spectrum of universality, there are great software libraries that focus on some specific probabilistic models and their specialized inference [a], which could be better suited for user's applications and use cases.

---

[a]For example, `https://github.com/jmschrei/pomegranate` for Bayesian Network.

Another approach is to treat model in a more encapsulated way and write the model as a Python function. Code Block 10.34 gave an example implementation of the joint log probability density function of the model in Equation 10.7, but for prior samples we need to again rewrite it a bit, shown in Code Block 10.35:

Code 10.35

```
1   def prior_sample():
2       x = stats.norm(loc=1.0, scale=2.0).rvs()
3       z = stats.halfnorm(loc=0., scale=1.).rvs()
4       y = stats.norm(loc=x, scale=z).rvs()
5       return x, z, y
```

---

[19]Getting the shape right, minimizing unwanted side effects, to name a few.

[20]The graphical representation of a Bayesian Model is a central concept in PPL, but in many cases they are implicit.

[21]`https://github.com/blei-lab/edward`

[22]The API of TensorFlow changed significantly between v1 and the current version (v2).

With effect handling and function tracing [23] in Python, we can actually combine `log_prob` from Code Block 10.34 and `sample` from Code Block 10.35 into a single Python function the user just need to write once. The PPL will then change the behavior of how the function is executed depending on the context (whether we are trying to obtain prior samples or evaluate the log probability). This approach of writing a Bayesian model as function and apply effect handler has gained significant popularity in recent years with Pyro [18] (and NumPyro [118]), Edward2 [149] [106], and JointDistribution in TensorFlow Probability [122] [24] [25].

10.8.1   Shape Handling in PPLs

Something that all PPLs must deal with, and subsquently PPL designers must think about, is shapes. One of the common requests for help and frustrations that PPL designers hear from Bayesian modeler and practitioner are about *shape errors*. They are misspecification of the intended flow of array computation, which can cause issues like broadcasting errors. In this section we will give some examples to highly some subtleties of shape handling in PPLs.

Consider the prior predictive sample function defined in Code Block 10.35 for the model in Equation 10.7, executing the function draws a single sample from the prior and prior predictive distribution, it is certainly quite inefficient if we want to draw a large among of iid samples from it. Distribution in `scipy.stats` has a `size` keyword argument to allow us to draw iid samples easily, with a small modification in Code Block 10.36 we have:

Code 10.36

```
1  def prior_sample(size):
2      x = stats.norm(loc=1.0, scale=2.0).rvs(size=size)
3      z = stats.halfnorm(loc=0., scale=1.).rvs(size=size)
4      y = stats.norm(loc=x, scale=z).rvs()
5      return x, z, y
6
7  print([x.shape for x in prior_sample(size=(2))])
8  print([x.shape for x in prior_sample(size=(2, 3, 5))])
```

```
[(2,), (2,), (2,)]
[(2, 3, 5), (2, 3, 5), (2, 3, 5)]
```

As you can see, the function can handle arbitrary sample shape by adding `size` keyword argument when calling the random method `rvs`. Note however, for random variable y, we do not supply the `size` keyword argument as the sample shape is already implied from its parents.

Consider another example in Code Block 10.37 for a linear regression model, we implemented `lm_prior_sample0` to draw one set of prior samples, and `lm_prior_sample` to draw a batch of prior samples.

---

[23]See the Python documentation for a complete explanation `https://docs.python.org/3/library/trace.html`

[24]Also see mcx `https://github.com/rlouf/mcx` that use Python AST to do function rewrite; and oryx `https://www.tensorflow.org/probability/oryx` that make use of the JAX tracing for function transformation

[25]If you are interested in more details about PPL development in Python, take a look at this PyData Talk: `https://www.youtube.com/watch?v=WHoS1ETYFrw`

Code 10.37

```
1  n_row, n_feature = 1000, 5
2  X = np.random.randn(n_row, n_feature)
3
4  def lm_prior_sample0():
5      intercept = stats.norm(loc=0, scale=10.0).rvs()
6      beta = stats.norm(loc=np.zeros(n_feature), scale=10.0).rvs()
7      sigma = stats.halfnorm(loc=0., scale=1.).rvs()
8      y_hat = X @ beta + intercept
9      y = stats.norm(loc=y_hat, scale=sigma).rvs()
10     return intercept, beta, sigma, y
11
12 def lm_prior_sample(size=10):
13     if isinstance(size, int):
14         size = (size,)
15     else:
16         size = tuple(size)
17     intercept = stats.norm(loc=0, scale=10.0).rvs(size=size)
18     beta = stats.norm(loc=np.zeros(n_feature), scale=10.0).rvs(
19         size=size + (n_feature,))
20     sigma = stats.halfnorm(loc=0., scale=1.).rvs(size=size)
21     y_hat = np.squeeze(X @ beta[..., None]) + intercept[..., None]
22     y = stats.norm(loc=y_hat, scale=sigma[..., None]).rvs()
23     return intercept, beta, sigma, y
```

Comparing the two functions above, we see that to make the prior sample function to handle arbitrary sample shape, we need to make a few changes in `lm_prior_sample`:

- Supply `size` keyword argument to the sample call of root random variables only;
- Supply `size + (n_feature,)` keyword argument to the sample call of `beta` due to API limitations, which is a length `n_feature` vector of regression coefficient. We need to additionally make sure `size` is a tuple in the function so that it could be combined with the original shape of `beta`;
- Shape handling by appending a dimension to `beta`, `intercept`, and `sigma`, and squeezing of the matrix multiplication result so that they are broadcast-able.

As you can see, there is a lot of rooms for error and flexibility of how you might go about to implementing a "shape-safe" prior sample function. The complexity does not stop here, shape issues also pop up when computing model log probability and during inference (e.g., how non-scalar sampler MCMC kernel parameters broadcast to model parameters). There are convenience function transformations that vectorize your Python function such as `numpy.vectorize` or `jax.vmap` in JAX, but they are often not a silver bullet solution to fixing the all issues. For example, it requires additional user input if the vectorization is across multiple axes.

An example of a well defined shape handling logic is the shape semantic in TensorFlow Probability [47] [26], which conceptually partitions a Tensor's shape into three groups:

- *Sample shape* that describes iid draws from the distribution.
- *Batch shape* that describes independent, not identically distributed draws. Usually it is a set of (different) parameterizations to the same distribution.
- *Event shape* that describes the shape of a single draw (event space) from the distribution. For example, samples from multivariate distributions have non-scalar event shape.

---

[26]See also https://www.tensorflow.org/probability/examples/TensorFlow_Distributions_Tutorial

Explicit batch shape is a powerful concept in TFP, which can be considered roughly along the line of *independent copy of the same thing that I would like to "parallelly" evaluate over.* For example, different chains from a MCMC trace, a batch of observation in mini-batch training, etc. For example, applying the shape semantic to the prior sample function in Code Block 10.37, we have a `beta` distributed as a `n_feature` batch of $\mathcal{N}(0, 10)$ distribution. Note that while it is fine for the purpose of prior sampling, to be more precise we actually want the Event shape being `n_feature` instead of the batch shape. In that case the shape is correct for both forward random sampling and inverse log-probability computation. In NumPy it could be done by defining and sampling from a `stats.multivariate_normal` instead.

When a user defines a TFP distribution, they can inspect the batch shape and the event shape to make sure it is working as intended. It is especially useful when writing a Bayesian model using `tfd.JointDistribution`. For example, we rewrite the regression model in Code Block 10.37 into Code Block 10.38 using `tfd.JointDistributionSequential`:

Code 10.38

```
jd = tfd.JointDistributionSequential([
    tfd.Normal(0, 10),
    tfd.Sample(tfd.Normal(0, 10), n_feature),
    tfd.HalfNormal(1),
    lambda sigma, beta, intercept: tfd.Independent(
        tfd.Normal(
            loc=tf.einsum("ij,...j->...i", X, beta) + intercept[..., None],
            scale=sigma[..., None]),
        reinterpreted_batch_ndims=1,
        name="y")
])

print(jd)

n_sample = [3, 2]
for log_prob_part in jd.log_prob_parts(jd.sample(n_sample)):
    assert log_prob_part.shape == n_sample
```

```
tfp.distributions.JointDistributionSequential 'JointDistributionSequential'
batch_shape=[[], [], [], []]
event_shape=[[], [5], [], [1000]]
dtype=[float32, float32, float32, float32]
```

A key thing to look for when ensuring the model is specified correctly is that `batch_shape` are consistent across arrays. In our example they are since they are all empty. Another helpful way to check that output is a structure of Tensor with the same shape `k` when calling `jd.log_prob_parts(jd.sample(k))` (line 15-17 in Code Block 10.38). This will make sure the computation of the model log probability (e.g., for posterior inference) is correct. You can find a nice summary and visual demonstration of the shape semantic in TFP in a blog post by Eric J. Ma (*Reasoning about Shapes and Probability Distributions*) [27].

---

[27]See https://ericmjl.github.io/blog/2019/5/29/reasoning-about-shapes-and-probability-distributions/. Luciano Paz also wrote an excellent introduction on shape handling in PPLs in *PyMC3 shape handling* https://lucianopaz.github.io/2019/08/19/pymc3-shape-handling/

10.9   Takeaways for the Applied Bayesian Practitioner

We want to stress to the reader that the goal of this chapter is *not* to make you a proficient PPL designer but more so an informed PPL user. As a user, particularly if you are just starting out, it can be difficult to understand which PPL to choose and why. When you first learn about a PPL, it is good to keep in mind the basic components we listed in this chapter. For example, what primitives parameterize a distribution, how to evaluate the log-probability of some value, or what primitives define a random variables and how to link different random variables to construct a graphical model (the effect handling) etc.

There are many considerations when picking PPL aside from the PPL itself. Given everything we have discussed in this chapter so far its very easy to get lost trying to optimize over each component to "pick the best one". Its also very easy for experienced practitioners to argue about why one PPL is better than another ad nauseum. Our advice is to pick the PPL that you feel most comfortable starting with and learn what is needed in your situation from applied experience.

However, over time you will get a sense of what you need from a PPL and more importantly what you do not. We suggest trying out a couple of PPLs, in addition to the ones presented in this book, to get a sense of what will work for you. As a user you have the most to gain from actually *using* the PPL.

Like Bayesian modeling when you explore the distribution of possibilities the collection of data becomes more informative than any single point. With the knowledge of how PPLs are constructed from this chapter, and personal experience through "taking some for a spin" we hope you will be finding the one that works best for you.

10.10   Exercises

10E1. Find a PPLs that utilizes another base language other than Python. Determine what differences are between PyMC3 or TFP. Specifically note a difference between the API and the computational backend.

10E2. In this book we primarily use the PyData ecosystem. R is another popular programming language with a similar ecosystem. Find the R equivalents for

- Matplotlib
- The ArviZ LOO function
- Bayesian visualization

10E3. What are other transformations that we have used on data and models throughout this book? What effect did they have? Hint: Refer to Chapter 3

10E4. Draw a block diagram of a PPL[28]. Label each component and explain what it does in your own words. There is no one right answer for this question.

10E5. Explain what batch shape, event shape, and sample shape are in your own words. In particular be sure to detail why its helpful to have each concept in a PPL.

---

[28]https://en.wikipedia.org/wiki/Block_diagram

10E6. Find the Eight Schools NumPyro example online. Compare this to the TFP example, in particular noting the difference in primitives and syntax. What is similar? What is different?

10E7. Specify the following computation in Theano

$$\sin(\frac{1}{2}\pi x) + \exp(\log(x)) + \frac{(x-2)^2}{(x^2 - 4x + 4)} \tag{10.8}$$

Generate the unoptimized computational graph. How many lines are printed. Use the `theano.function` method to run the optimizer. What is different about the optimized graph? Run a calculation using the optimized Theano function where $x = 1$. What is the output value?

10M8. Create a model with following distributions using PyMC3.

- Gamma(alpha=1, beta=1)
- Binomial(p=5,12)
- TruncatedNormal(mu=2, sd=1, lower=1)

Verify which distributions are automatically transformed from bounded to unbounded distributions. Plot samples from the priors for both the bounded priors and their paired transforms if one exists. What differences can you note?

10H9. BlackJAX is a library of samplers for JAX. Generate a random sample of from $(N)(0, 10)$ of size 20. Use the HMC sampler in JAX to recover the parameters of the data generating distribution. The BlackJAX documentation and Appendix 11.9.3 will be helpful.

10H10. Implement the linear penguins model defined in Code Block 3.13 in NumPyro. After verifying the result are roughly the same as TFP and PyMC3, what differences do you see from the TFP and PyMC3 syntax? What similarities do you see? Be sure not just compare models, but compare the entire workflow.

10H11. We have explained reparameterization in previous chapter, for example, center and non-center parameterization for linear model in Chapter 4 Section 4.6.1. One of the use case for effect handling is to perform automatic reparameterization [70]. Try to write a effect handler in NumPyro to perform automatic non-centering of a random variable in a model. Hint: NumPyro already provides this functionality with `numpyro.handlers.reparam`.

11

Appendiceal Topics

This chapter is different from the rest because it is not about any specific topic. Instead it is a collection of different topics that provide support for the rest of the book by complementing topics discussed in other chapters. These topics are here for readers who are interested in going deeper into each of the methods and theory. In terms of writing style it will be a little bit more theoretical and abstract than other chapters.

11.1   Probability Background

The Spanish word azahar (the flower of certain critics) and azar (randomness) are not similar out of pure luck. They both come from the Arabic language [1]. From ancient times, and even today, certain games of chance use a bone that it has two flat sides. This bone is similar to a coin or a two-side die. To make it easier to identify one side from the other, at least one side has a distinctive mark, for example, ancient Arabs commonly used a flower. With the passage of time Spanish adopted the term azahar for certain flowers and azar to mean randomness. One of the motivation to the development of probability theory can be track back to understanding games of chance and probably trying to make an small fortune in the process. So let us start this brief introduction to some of the central concepts in probability theory[2] imagining a 6-sided die. Each time we roll the die it is only possible to obtain an integer from 1 to 6 without preference of one over another. Using Python we can program a die like this in the following way:

Code 11.1

```
1  def die():
2      outcomes = [1, 2, 3, 4, 5, 6]
3      return np.random.choice(outcomes)
```

Suppose we suspect that the die is biased. What could we do to evaluate this possibility? A scientific way to answer this question is to collect data and analyze it. Using Python we can simulate the data collection as in Code Block 11.2.

---

[1] Most of the territory of what we now call Spain and Portugal was part of Al-Andalus and Arabic state, this had a tremendous influence in the Spanish/Portuguese culture, including food, music, language and also in the genetic makeup.

[2] For those who are interested in delving further into the subject, we recommend reading the book Introduction to Probability by Joseph K. Blitzstein and Jessica Hwang [21].

DOI: 10.1201/9781003019169-11   323

Code 11.2

```python
def experiment(N=10):
    sample = [die() for i in range(N)]

    for i in range(1, 7):
        print(f"{i}: {sample.count(i)/N:.2g}")

experiment()
```

```
1: 0
2: 0.1
3: 0.4
4: 0.1
5: 0.4
6: 0
```

The numbers in the first column are the possible outcomes. Those in the second column correspond to the frequency with which each number appears. Frequency is the number of times each of the possible outcomes appears divided by N, the total number of times we roll the die.

There are at least two things to take note of in this example. First if we execute `experiment()` several times, we will see that we obtain a different result each time. This is precisely the reason for using dice in games of chance, every time we roll them we get a number that we cannot predict. Second, if we roll the same die many times, the ability to predict each single outcome does not improve. Nevertheless, data collection and analysis can actually help us to estimate the *list of frequencies* for the outcomes, in fact the ability improves as the value of N increases. Run the experiment for N=10000 times you will see that the frequencies obtained are approximately 0.17 and it turns out that $0.17 \approx \frac{1}{6}$ which is what we would expect if each number on the die had the same chance.

These two observations are not restricted to dice and games of chance. If we weigh ourselves every day we would obtain different values, since our weight is related to the amount of food we eat, the water we drink, how many times we went to the bathroom, the precision of the scale, the clothes we wear and many other factors. Therefore, a single measurement may not be *representative* of our weight. Of course it could be that the variations are small and we do not consider them important, but we are getting ahead of ourselves. At this point what matters is that the data measurement and/or collection is accompanied by uncertainty. Statistics is basically the field concerned with how to deal with uncertainty in practical problems and Probability theory is one of the theoretical pillars of statistics. Probability theory help us formalize discussion like the one we just had and extend them beyond dice. This is so we can better ask and answer questions related to expected outcomes, such as what happens when we increase the number of experiments, what event has higher chance than another, etc.

11.1.1   Probability

Probability is the mathematical device that allow us to quantify uncertainty in a principled way. Like other mathematical objects and theories, they can be justified entirely from a pure mathematical perspective. Nevertheless, from a practical point of view we can justify them as *naturally* arising from performing experiments, collecting observational data and even when doing computational simulations. For simplicity we will talk about experiments, knowing we are using this term in a very broad sense. To think about probabilities we can think in terms of mathematical sets. The **sample space** $\mathcal{X}$ is the set of all possible events from an **experiment**. An **event** A is a subset of

$\mathcal{X}$. We say A happens when we perform an experiment and we get A as the outcome. For a typical 6 face die we can write:

$$\mathcal{X} = \{1, 2, 3, 4, 5, 6\} \tag{11.1}$$

We may define the event A as any subset of $\mathcal{X}$, for example, getting an even number, $A = \{2, 4, 6\}$. We can associate probabilities to events. If we want to indicate the probability of the event A we write $P(A = \{2, 4, 6\})$ or to be more concise $P(A)$. The probability function P takes an event A which is a subset of $\mathcal{X}$ as input and returns $P(A)$. Probabilities, like $P(A)$, can take any number in the interval 0 to 1 (including both extremes), using interval notation we write this is as $[0, 1]$, the brackets meaning inclusive bounds. If the event never happens then the probability of that event is 0, for example $P(A = -1) = 0$, if the event always happens then it has probability 1, for example $P(A = \{1, 2, 3, 4, 5, 6\}) = 1$. We say events are disjoint if they can not happen together, for example, if the event A_1 represent odds numbers and A_2 even numbers, then the probability of rolling a die an getting both A_1 and A_2 is 0. If the event $A_1, A_2, \cdots A_n$ are disjoint, meaning they can not happen at the same time, then $\sum_i^n P(A_i) = 1$. Continuing with the example of A_1 representing odd numbers and A_2 even numbers, then the probability of rolling a die and getting either A_1 or A_2 is 1. Any function that satisfies these properties is a valid probability function. We can think of probability as a positive, conserved quantity that is allocated across the possible events [3].

As we just saw, probabilities have a clear mathematical definition. How we interpret probabilities is a different story with different schools of thought. As Bayesian we tend to interpret probabilities as degrees of uncertainty. For example, for a fair die, the probability of getting an odd number when rolling a die is 0.5, meaning we are half-sure we will get an odd number. Alternatively we can interpret this number as saying if we roll a die infinite times, half the time we will get odd numbers and half the time even numbers. This is the frequentist interpretation which is also a useful way of thinking about probabilities. If you do not want to roll the die infinite times you can just roll it a large number of times and say that you will approximately get odds half of the time. This is in fact what we did in Code Block 11.2. Finally, we notice that for a fair die we expect the probability of getting any single number to be $\frac{1}{6}$, but for a non-fair die this probability may be different. The equiprobability of the outcomes is just a special case.

If probabilities reflect uncertainty, then is *natural* to ask what is the probability that the mass of Mars is 6.39×10^{23} kg, or the probability of rain on May 1 in Helsinki, or the probability that capitalism gets replaced by a different socio-economical system in the next 3 decades. We say this definition of probability is epistemic, since it is not about a property of the *real world* (whatever that is) but a property about our knowledge about that world. We collect data and analyze it, because we think that we can update our internal knowledge state based on external information.

We notice that what can happen in the *real world* is determined by all the details of the experiments, even those we do not control or are not aware of. On the contrary the sample space is a mathematical object that we define either implicitly or explicitly. For example, by defining the sample space of our die as in Equation 11.1 we are ruling out the possibility of the die landing on an edge, which is actually possible when rolling dice in a non-flat surface. Elements from the sample space may be excluded on purpose, for example, we may have designed the experiment in such a way that we roll the die until we get one integer from $\{1, 2, 3, 4, 5, 6\}$. Or by omission, like in a survey we may ask people about their gender, but if we only include female or male as options in the possible response, we may force people to choose between two non-adequate answers or completely miss their answers as they may not feel interested in responding to the rest of the survey. We must be aware that the platonic world of ideas which includes all mathematical concepts

---

[3] From this definition John K. Kruschke wonderfully states that Bayesian inference is reallocation of credibility (probability) across possibilities [88].

is different from the *real world*, in statistical modeling we constantly switch back and forth between these two worlds.

11.1.2   Conditional Probability

Given two events A and B with $P(B) > 0$, the probability of A given B, which we write as $P(A \mid B)$ is defined as :

$$P(A \mid B) = \frac{P(A, B)}{P(B)} \tag{11.2}$$

$P(A, B)$ is the probability that the events A and B occur, it is also usually written as $P(A \cap B)$ (the symbol $\cap$ indicates intersection of sets), the probability of the intersection of the events A and B.

$P(A \mid B)$ it is known as conditional probability, and it is the probability that event A occurs, conditioned by the fact that we know (or assume, imagine, hypothesize, etc) that B has occurred. For example, the probability that a sidewalk is wet is different from the probability that such a sidewalk is wet given that it is raining.

A conditional probability can be viewed as the reduction or restriction of the sample space. Figure 11.1 shows how we went from having the events A and B in the sample space $\mathcal{X}$, on the left, to having B as the sample space and a subset of A, the one being compatible with B. When we say *that B has occurred* we are not necessarily talking about something in the past, it is just a more colloquial way of saying, *once we have conditioned on B* or *once we have restricted the sample space to agree with the evidence B*.

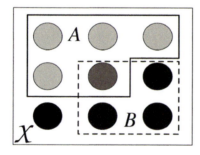 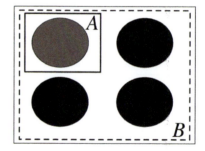

FIGURE 11.1

Conditioning is redefining the sample space. On the left we see the sample $\mathcal{X}$, each circle represent a possible outcome. We have two events, A and B. On the right we have represented $P(A \mid B)$, once we know B we can rule out all events not in B. This figure was adapted from Introduction to Probability [21].

The concept of conditional probability is at the heart of statistics and is central to thinking about how we should update our knowledge of an event in the light of new data. All probabilities are conditional, with respect to some assumption or model. Even when we do not express it explicitly, there are no probabilities without context.

11.1.3 Probability Distribution

Instead of calculating the probability of obtaining the number 5 when rolling a die, we may be more interested in finding out the *list of probabilities* for all numbers on a die. Once this list is computed we can display it or use it to compute other quantities like the probability of getting the number 5, or the probability of getting a number equal or larger than 5. The formal name of this *list* is **probability distribution**.

Using Code Block 11.2 we obtained an empirical probability distribution of a die, that is, a distribution calculated from data. But there are also theoretical distributions, which are central in statistics among other reasons because they allow the construction of probabilistic models.

Theoretical probability distributions have precise mathematical formulas, similar to how circles have a precise mathematical definition. A circle is the geometric space of points on a plane that are equidistant from another point called the center. Given the parameter radius, a circle is perfectly defined [4]. We could say that there is not a single circumference, but a family of circumferences where each member differs from the rest only by the value of the parameter radius, since once this parameter is also defined, the circumference is defined.

Similarly, probability distributions come in families, whose members are perfectly defined by one or more parameters. It is common to write the parameter names with letters of the Greek alphabet, although this is not always the case. Figure 11.2 is an example of such families of distributions, that we may use to represent a loaded die. We can see how this probability distribution is controlled by two parameters α and β. If we change them the *shape* of the distribution changes, we can make it flat or concentrated towards one side, push most of the mass the extremes, or concentrated the mass in the middle. As the radius of the circumference is restricted to be positive, the parameters of distributions also have restrictions, in fact α and β must both be positive.

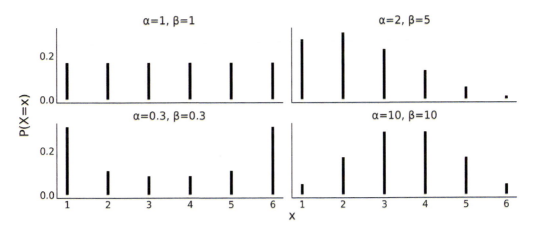

FIGURE 11.2
Four members of a family of discrete distributions with parameters α and β. The height of the bars represents the probability of each x value. The values of x not drawn have probability 0 as they are out of the support of the distribution.

---

[4] If we need to locate the circumference relative to other objects in the plane, we would also need the coordinates of the center, but let us omit that detail for now.

11.1.4   Discrete Random Variables and Distributions

A random variable is a function that maps the sample space into the real numbers $\mathbb{R}$. Continuing with the die example if the events of interest were the number of the die, the mapping is very simple, we associate ⊡ with the number 1, ⊡ with 2, etc. With two dice we could have an S random variable as the sum of the outcomes of both dice. Thus the domain of the random variable S is $\{2, 3, 4, 5, 6, 7, 8, 9, 10, 11, 12\}$, and if both dice are fair then their probability distribution is depicted in Figure 11.3.

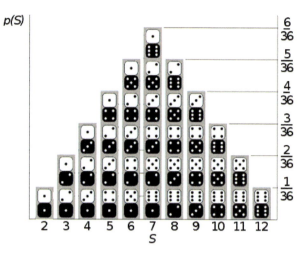

FIGURE 11.3

If the sample space is the set of possible numbers rolled on two dice, and the random variable of interest is the sum S of the numbers on the two dice, then S is a discrete random variable whose distribution is described in this figure with the probability of each outcome represented as the height of the columns. This figure has been adapted from `https://commons.wikimedia.org/wiki/File:Dice_Distribution_(bar).svg`

We could also define another random variable C with sample space $\{\text{red}, \text{green}, \text{blue}\}$. We could map the sample space to $\mathbb{R}$ in the following way:

$$C(\text{red}) = 0$$
$$C(\text{green}) = 1$$
$$C(\text{blue}) = 2$$

This encoding is useful, because performing math with numbers is easier than with strings regardless of whether we are using analog computation on "pen and paper" or digital computation with a computer.

As we said a random variable is a function, and given that the mapping between the sample space and $\mathbb{R}$ is deterministic it is not immediately clear where the randomness in a random variable comes from. We say a variable is random in the sense that if we perform an experiment, i.e. we *ask* the variable for a value like we did in Code Block 11.1 and 11.2 we will get a different number each time without the succession of outcomes following a deterministic pattern. For example, if we ask for the value of random variable C 3 times in a row we may get red, red, blue or maybe blue, green, blue, etc.

A random variable X is said to be discrete if there is a finite list of values $a_1, a_2, \ldots, a_n$ or an infinite list of values $a_1, a_2, \ldots$ such that the total probability is $\sum_j P(X = a_j) = 1$. If X is a discrete random variable then a finite or countably infinite set of values x such that $P(X = x) > 0$ is called the *support* of X.

As we said before we can think of a probability distribution as a list associating a probability with each event. Additionally a random variable has a probability distribution associated to it. In the particular case of discrete random variables the probability distribution is also called a Probability Mass Function (PMF). It is important to note that the PMF is a function that returns probabilities. The PMF of X is the function $P(X = x)$ for $x \in \mathbb{R}$. For a PMF to be valid, it must be non-negative and sum to 1, i.e. all its values should be non-negative and the sum over all its domain should be 1.

It is important to remark that the term *random* in random variable does not implies that any value is allowed, only those in the sample space. For example, we can not get the value orange from C, nor the value 13 from S. Another common source of confusion is that the term random implies equal probability, but that is not true, the probability of each event is given by the PMF, for example, we may have $P(C = \text{red}) = \frac{1}{2}, P(C = \text{green}) = \frac{1}{4}, P(C = \text{blue}) = \frac{1}{4}$. The equiprobability is just a special case.

We can also define a discrete random variable using a cumulative distribution function (CDF). The CDF of a random variable X is the function F_X given by $F_X(x) = P(X \leq x)$. For a CDF to be valid, it must be monotonically increasing [5], right-continuous [6], converge to 0 as x approaches to $-\infty$, and converge to 1 as x approaches ∞.

In principle, nothing prevents us from defining our own probability distribution. But there are many already defined distributions that are so commonly used, they have their own names. It is a good idea to become familiar with them as they appear quite often. If you check the models defined in this book you will see that most of them use combinations of predefined probability distributions and only a few examples used custom defined distribution. For example, in Section 8.6 Code Block 8.10 we used a Uniform distribution and two potentials to define a 2D triangular distribution.

Figures 11.4, 11.5, and 11.6, are example of some common discrete distribution represented with their PMF and CDF. On the left we have the PMFs, the height of the bars represents the probability of each x. On the right we have the CDF, here the *jump* between two horizontal lines at a value of x represents the probability of x. The figure also includes the values of the mean and standard deviation of the distributions, is important to remark that these values are properties of the distributions, like the length of a circumference, and not something that we compute from a finite sample (see Section 11.1.8 for details).

Another way to describe random variables is to use stories. A story for X describes an experiment that could give rise to a random variable with the same distribution as X. Stories are not formal devices, but they are useful anyway. Stories have helped humans to make sense of their surrounding for millennia and they continue to be useful today, even in statistics. In the book Introduction to Probability [21] Joseph K. Blitzstein and Jessica Hwang make extensive use of this device. They even use story proofs extensively, these are similar to mathematical proof but they can be more intuitive. Stories are also very useful devices to create statistical models, you can think about how the data may have been generated, and then try to write that down in statistical notation and/or code. We do this, for example, in Chapter 9 with our flight delay example.

Discrete Uniform Distribution

This distribution assigns equal probability to a finite set of consecutive integers from interval a to b inclusive. Its PMF is:

$$P(X = x) = \frac{1}{b - a + 1} = \frac{1}{n} \tag{11.3}$$

---

[5] Increase or remain constant but never decrease.

[6] Loosely speaking, a right-continuous function has no jump when the limit point is approached from the right.

for values of x in the interval $[a, b]$, otherwise $P(X = x) = 0$, where $n = b - a + 1$ is the total number values that x can take.

We can use this distribution to model, for example, a fair die. Code Block 11.3 shows how we can use Scipy to define a distribution and then compute useful quantities such as the PMF, CDF, and moments (see Section 11.1.8).

Code 11.3

```
1  a = 1
2  b = 6
3  rv = stats.randint(a, b+1)
4  x = np.arange(1, b+1)
5
6  x_pmf = rv.pmf(x)   # evaluate the pmf at the x values
7  x_cdf = rv.cdf(x)   # evaluate the cdf at the x values
8  mean, variance = rv.stats(moments="mv")
```

Using Code Block 11.3 plus a few lines of Matplotlib we generate Figure 11.4. On the left panel we have the PMF where the height of each point indicates the probability of each event, we use points and dotted lines to highlight that the distribution is discrete. On the right we have the CDF, the height of the jump at each value of x indicates the probability of that value.

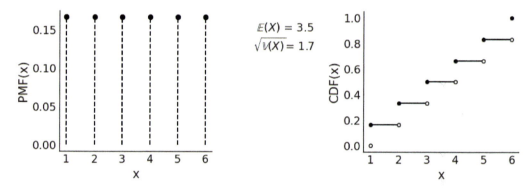

FIGURE 11.4
Discrete Uniform with parameters (1, 6). On the left the PMF. The height of the lines represents the probabilities for each value of x. On the right the CDF. The height of the jump at each value of x represent its probability. Values outside of the support of the distribution are not represented. The filled dots represent the inclusion of the CDF value at a particular x value, the open dots reflect the exclusion.

In this specific example the discrete Uniform distribution is defined on the interval $[1, 6]$. Therefore, all values less than 1 and greater than 6 have probability 0. Being a Uniform distribution, all the points have the same height and that height is $\frac{1}{6}$. There are two parameters of the Uniform discrete distribution, the lower limit a and upper limit b.

As we already mentioned in this chapter if we change the parameters of a distribution the *particular shape* of the distribution will change (try for example, replacing `stats.randint(1, 7)` in Code Block 11.3 with `stats.randint(1, 4)`). That is why we usually talk about family of distributions, each member of that family is a distribution with a particular and valid combination of parameters. Equation 11.3 defines the family of discrete Uniform distributions as long as $a < b$ and both a and b are integers.

When using probability distributions to create statistical applied models it is common to link the parameters with quantities that make physical sense. For example, in a 6 sided die it makes sense that $a = 1$ and $b = 6$. In probability we generally know the values of these parameters while in statistics we generally do not know these values and we use data to infer them.

Binomial Distribution

A Bernoulli trial is an experiment with only two possible outcomes yes/no (success/failure, happy/sad, ill/healthy, etc). Suppose we perform n independent [7] Bernoulli trials, each with the same success probability p and let us call X the number of success. Then the distribution of X is called the Binomial distribution with parameters n and p, where n is a positive integer and $p \in [0, 1]$. Using statistical notation we can write $X \sim Bin(n, p)$ to mean that X has the Binomial distribution with parameters n and p, with the PMF being:

$$P(X = x) = \frac{n!}{x!(n - x)!} p^x (1 - p)^{n-x} \tag{11.4}$$

The term $p^x(1 - p)^{n-x}$ counts the number of x success in n trials. This term only considers the total number of success but not the precise sequence, for example, $(0, 1)$ is the same as $(1, 0)$, as both have one success in two trials. The first term is known as Binomial Coefficient and computes all the possible combinations of x elements taken from a set of n elements.

The Binomial PMFs are often written omitting the values that return 0, that is the values outside of the support. Nevertheless it is important to be sure what the support of a random variable is in order to avoid mistakes. A good practice is to check that PMFs are valid, and this is essential if we are proposing a new PMFs instead of using one off the *shelf*.

When $n = 1$ the Binomial distribution is also known as the Bernoulli distribution. Many distributions are special cases of other distributions or can be obtained somehow from other distributions.

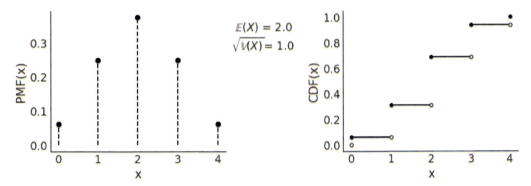

FIGURE 11.5
$Bin(n = 4, p = 0.5)$ On the left the PMF. The height of the lines represents the probabilities for each value of x. On the right the CDF. The height of the jump at each value of x represent its probability. Values outside of the support of the distribution are not represented.

Poisson Distribution

This distribution expresses the probability that x events happen during a fixed time interval (or space interval) if these events occur with an average rate μ and independently from each other. It

---

[7]The result of one outcome does not affect the others.

is generally used when there are a large number of trials, each with a small probability of success. For example

- Radioactive decay, the number of atoms in a given material is huge, the actual number that undergo nuclear fission is low compared to the total number of atoms.

- The daily number of car accidents in a city. Even when we may consider this number to be high relative to what we would prefer, it is low in the sense that every maneuver that the driver performs, including turns, stopping at lights, and parking, is an independent trial where an accident could occur.

The PMF of a Poisson is defined as:

$$P(X = x) = \frac{\mu^x e^{-\mu}}{x!}, x = 0, 1, 2, \ldots \tag{11.5}$$

Notice that the support of this PMF are all the natural numbers, which is an infinite set. So we have to be careful with our *list* of probabilities analogy, as summing an infinite series can be tricky. In fact Equation 11.5 is a valid PMF because of the Taylor series $\sum_0^\infty \frac{\mu^x}{x!} = e^\mu$

Both the mean and variance of the Poisson distribution are defined by μ. As μ increases, the Poisson distribution approximates to a Normal distribution, although the latter is continuous and the Poisson is discrete. The Poisson distribution is also closely related to the Binomial distribution. A Binomial distribution can be approximated with a Poisson, when $n >> p$ [8], that is, when the probability of success (p) is low compared with the number o trials (n) then $\text{Pois}(\mu = np) \approx \text{Bin}(n, p)$. For this reason the Poisson distribution is also known as *the law of small numbers* or the *law of rare events*. As we previously mentioned this does not mean that μ has to be small, but instead that p is low with respect to n.

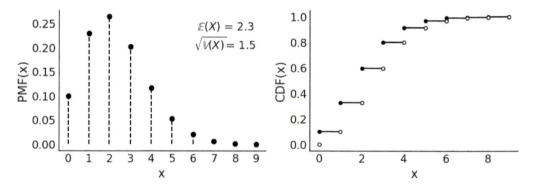

FIGURE 11.6
Pois(2.3) On the left the PMF. The height of the lines represents the probabilities for each value of x. On the right the CDF. The height of the jump at each value of x represent its probability. Values outside of the support of the distribution are not represented.

11.1.5   Continuous Random Variables and Distributions

So far we have seen discrete random variables. There is another type of random variable that is widely used called continuous random variables, whose support takes values in $\mathbb{R}$. The most

---

[8]Or more precisely if we take the limit of the $\text{Bin}(n, p)$ distribution as $n \to \infty$ and $p \to 0$ with np fixed we get a Poisson distribution.

important difference between discrete and continuous random variables is that the latter can take on any x value in an interval, although the probability of any x value is exactly 0. Introduced this way you may think that these are the most useless probability distributions ever. But that is not the case, the actual problem is that our analogy of treating a probability distribution as a finite list is a very limited analogy and it fails badly with continuous random variables [9].

In Figures 11.4, 11.5, and 11.6, to represent PMFs (discrete variables), we used the height of the lines to represent the probability of each event. If we add the heights we always get 1, that is, the total sum of the probabilities. In a continuous distribution we do not have *lines* but rather we have a continuous curve, the height of that curve is not a probability but a **probability density** and instead of of a PMF we use a Probability Density Function (PDF). One important difference is that height of PDF(x) can be larger than 1, as is not the probability value but a probability density. To obtain a probability from a PDF instead we must integrate over some interval:

$$P(a < X < b) = \int_a^b pdf(x)dx \tag{11.6}$$

Thus, we can say that the area below the curve of the PDF (and not the height as in the PMF) gives us a probability, the total area under the curve, i.e. evaluated over the entire support of the PDF, must integrate to 1. Notice that if we want to find out how much more likely the value x_1 is compared to x_2 we can just compute $\frac{pdf(x_1)}{pdf(x_2)}$.

In many texts, including this one, it is common to use the symbol p to talk about the *pmf* or *pdf*. This is done in favour of generality and hoping to avoid being very rigorous with the notation which can be an actual burden when the difference can be more or less clear from the context.

For a discrete random variable, the CDF jumps at every point in the support, and is flat everywhere else. Working with the CDF of a discrete random variable is awkward because of this jumpiness. Its derivative is almost useless since it is undefined at the jumps and 0 everywhere else. This is a problem for gradient-based sampling methods like Hamiltonian Monte Carlo (Section 11.9). On the contrary for continuous random variables, the CDF is often very convenient to work with, and its derivative is precisely the probability density function (PDF) that we have discussed before.

Figure 11.7 summarize the relationship between the CDF, PDF and PMF. The transformations between discrete CDF and PMF on one side and continuous CDF and PMF on the other are well defined and thus we used arrows with solid lines. Instead the transformations between discrete and continuous variables are more about numerical approximation than well defined mathematical operations. To approximately get from a discrete to a continuous distribution we use a smoothing method. One form of smoothing is to use a continuous distribution instead of a discrete one. To go from continuous to discrete we can discretize or bin the continuous outcomes. For example, a Poisson distribution with a large value of μ looks approximately Gaussian [10], while still being discrete. For those cases using a scenarios using a Poisson or a Gaussian maybe be interchangeable from a practical point of view. Using ArviZ you can use `az.plot_kde` with discrete data to approximate a continuous functions, how nice the results of this operation look depends on many factors. As we already said it may look good for a Poisson distribution with a relatively large value of μ. When calling `az.plot_bpv(.)` for a discrete variable, ArviZ will smooth it, using an interpolation method, because the probability integral transform only works for continuous variables.

---

[9] A proper discussion that avoids non-sensical statements would require a discussion of measure theory. But we will side-step this requirement.

[10] You can use check this statement yourself with the help of SciPy.

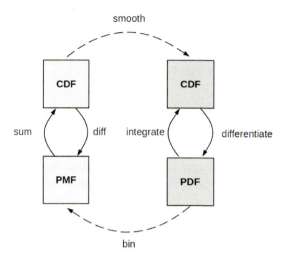

FIGURE 11.7
Relationship between the CDF, PDF and PMF. Adapted from the book Think Stats [48].

As we did with the discrete random variables, now we will see a few example of continuous random variables with their PDF and CDF.

Continuous Uniform Distribution

A continuous random variable is said to have a Uniform distribution on the interval (a, b) if its PDF is:

$$p(x \mid a, b) = \begin{cases} \frac{1}{b-a} & if\, a \leq x \leq b \\ 0 & \text{otherwise} \end{cases} \tag{11.7}$$

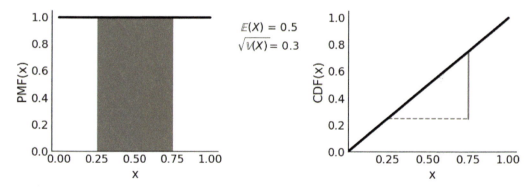

FIGURE 11.8
$\mathcal{U}(0, 1)$ On the left the PDF, the black line represents the probability density, the gray shaded area represents the probability $P(0.25 < X < 0.75) = 0.5$. On the right the CDF, the height of the gray continuous segment represents $P(0.25 < X < 0.75) = 0.5$. Values outside of the support of the distribution are not represented.

The most commonly used Uniform distribution in statistics is $\mathcal{U}(0, 1)$ also known as the standard Uniform. The PDF and CDF for the standard Uniform are very simple: $p(x) = 1$ and $F_{(x)} =$

x respectively, Figure 11.8 represents both of them, this figure also indicated how to compute probabilities from the PDF and CDF.

Gaussian or Normal Distribution

This is perhaps the best known distribution [11]. On the one hand, because many phenomena can be described approximately using this distribution (thanks to central limit theorem, see Subsection 11.1.10 below). On the other hand, because it has certain mathematical properties that make it easier to work with it analytically.

The Gaussian distribution is defined by two parameters, the mean μ and the standard deviation σ as shown in Equation 11.8. A Gaussian distribution with $\mu = 0$ and $\sigma = 1$ is known as the **standard Gaussian distribution**.

$$p(x \mid \mu, \sigma) = \frac{1}{\sigma\sqrt{2\pi}} e^{-\frac{(x-\mu)^2}{2\sigma^2}} \tag{11.8}$$

On the left panel of Figure 11.9 we have the PDF, and on the right we have the CDF. Both the PDF and CDF are represented for the invertal [-4, 4], but notice that the support of the Gaussian distribution is the entire real line.

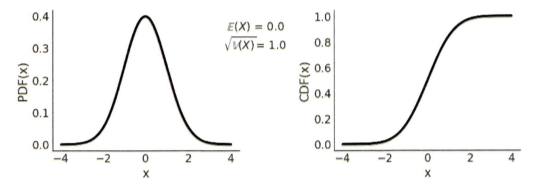

FIGURE 11.9
Representation of $\mathcal{N}(0, 1)$, on the left the PDF, on the right the CDF. The support of the Gaussian distribution is the entire real line.

Student's t-distribution

Historically this distribution arose to estimate the mean of a normally distributed population when the sample size is small [12]. In Bayesian statistics, a common use case is to generate models that are robust against aberrant data as we discussed in Section 4.4.

$$p(x \mid \nu, \mu, \sigma) = \frac{\Gamma(\frac{\nu+1}{2})}{\Gamma(\frac{\nu}{2})\sqrt{\pi\nu}\sigma} \left(1 + \frac{1}{\nu}\left(\frac{x-\mu}{\sigma}\right)^2\right)^{-\frac{\nu+1}{2}} \tag{11.9}$$

---

[11] Not only on planet Earth, but even on other planets judging by the Gaussian-shaped UFOs we have observed (just kidding, this is of course a joke, just as ufology).

[12] This distribution was discovered by William Gosset while trying to improve the methods of quality control in a brewery. Employees of that company were allow to publish scientific papers as long as they did not use the word beer, the company name, and their own surname. Thus Gosset publish under the name Student.

where Γ is the gamma function [13] and ν is commonly called degrees of freedom. We also like the name degree of normality, since as ν increases, the distribution approaches a Gaussian. In the extreme case of $\lim_{\nu \to \infty}$ the distribution is exactly equal to a Gaussian distribution with the same mean and standard deviation equal to σ.

When $\nu = 1$ we get the Cauchy distribution [14]. Which is similar to a Gaussian but with tails decreasing very slowly, so slowly that this distribution does not have a defined mean or variance. That is, it is possible to calculate a mean from a data set, but if the data came from a Cauchy distribution, the spread around the mean will be high and this spread will not decrease as the sample size increases. The reason for this strange behavior is that distributions, like the Cauchy, are dominated by the tail behavior of the distribution, contrary to what happens with, for example, the Gaussian distribution.

For this distribution σ is not the standard deviation, which as already said could be undefined, σ is the scale. As ν increases the scale converges to the standard deviation of a Gaussian distribution.

On the left panel of Figure 11.10 we have the PDF, and on the right we have the CDF. Compare with Figure 11.9, a standard normal and see how the tails are heavier for the Student T distribution with parameter $\mathcal{T}(\nu = 4, \mu = 0, \sigma = 1)$

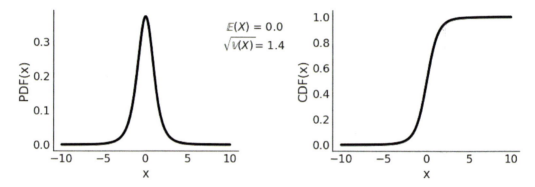

FIGURE 11.10
$\mathcal{T}(\nu = 4, \mu = 0, \sigma = 1)$ On the left the PDF, on the right the CDF. The support of the Students T distribution is the entire real line.

Beta Distribution

The Beta distribution is defined in the interval $[0, 1]$. It can be used to model the behavior of random variables limited to a finite interval, for example, modeling proportions or percentages.

$$p(x \mid \alpha, \beta) = \frac{\Gamma(\alpha + \beta)}{\Gamma(\alpha)\Gamma(\beta)} x^{\alpha - 1}(1 - x)^{\beta - 1} \tag{11.10}$$

The first term is a normalization constant that ensures that the PDF integrates to 1. Γ is the Gamma function. When $\alpha = 1$ and $\beta = 1$ the Beta distribution reduces to the standard Uniform distribution. In Figure 11.11 we show a Beta($\alpha = 5, \beta = 2$) distribution.

If we want to express the Beta distribution as a function of the mean and the dispersion around the mean, we can do it in the following way. $\alpha = \mu\kappa$, $\beta = (1 - \mu)\kappa$ where μ the mean and κ a parameter called concentration as κ increases the dispersion decreases. Also note that $\kappa = \alpha + \beta$.

---

[13]https://en.wikipedia.org/wiki/Gamma_function
[14]ν can take values below 1.

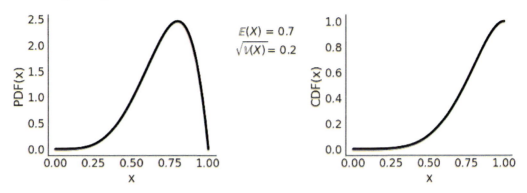

FIGURE 11.11

Beta($\alpha = 5, \beta = 2$) On the left the PDF, on the right the CDF. The support of the Beta distribution is on the interval $[0, 1]$.

11.1.6   Joint, Conditional and Marginal Distributions

Let us assume we have two random variables X and Y with the same PMF Bin($1, 0.5$). Are they dependent or independent? If X represent heads in on coin toss and Y heads in another coin toss then they are independent. But if they represent heads and tails, respectively, on the same coin toss, then they are dependent. Thus even when individual (formally known as univariate) PMFs/PDFs fully characterize individual random variables, they do not have information about how the individual random variables are related to other random variables. To answer that question we need to know the **joint** distribution, also known as multivariate distributions. If we consider that $p(X)$ provides all the information about the probability of finding X on the real line, in a similar way $p(X, Y)$, the joint distribution of X and Y, provides all the information about the probability of finding the tuple (X, Y) on the plane. Joint distributions allow us to describe the behavior of multiple random variables that arise from the same experiment, for example, the posterior distribution is the joint distribution of all parameters in the model after we have conditioned the model on observed data.

The joint PMF is given by

$$p_{X,Y}(x, y) = P(X = x, Y = y) \tag{11.11}$$

The definition for n discrete random variable is similar, we just need to include n terms. Similarly to univariate PMFs valid joint PMFs must be nonnegative and sum to 1, where the sum is taken over all possible values.

$$\sum_x \sum_y P(X = x, Y = y) = 1 \tag{11.12}$$

In a similar way the joint CDF of X and Y is

$$F_{X,Y}(x, y) = P(X \leq x, Y \leq y) \tag{11.13}$$

Given the joint distribution of X and Y, we can get the distribution of X by summing over all the possible values of Y:

$$P(X = x) = \sum_y P(X = x, Y = y) \tag{11.14}$$

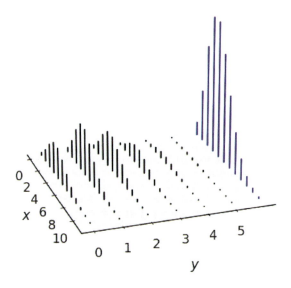

FIGURE 11.12
The black lines represent the joint distribution of x and y. The blue lines in the marginal distribution of x are obtained by adding the heights of the lines along the y-axis for every value of x.

In previous section we called $P(X = x)$ the PMF of X, or just the distribution of X, when working with joint distributions we often call it the **marginal** distribution of X. We do this to emphasize we are talking about the *individual* X, without any reference to Y. By summing over all the possible values of Y we *get rid of* Y. Formally this process is known as **marginalizing out** Y. To obtain the PMF of Y we can proceed in a similar fashion, but summing over all possible values of X instead. In the case of a joint distribution of more than 2 variables we just need to sum over all *the other* variables. Figure 11.12 illustrates this.

Given the joint distribution it is straightforward to get the marginals. But going from the marginals to the joint distribution is not generally possible unless we make further assumptions. In Figure 11.12 we can see that there is just one way to add heights of the bars along the y-axis or x-axis, but to do the inverse we must *split* bars and there are infinite ways of making this split.

We already introduced conditional distributions in Section 11.1.2, and in Figure 11.1 we show that conditioning is redefining the sample space. Figure 11.13 demonstrates conditioning in the context of a joint distribution of X and Y. To condition on $Y = y$ we take the joint distribution at the $Y = y$ value and forget about the rest. i.e. those for which $Y \neq y$, this is similar as indexing a 2d array and picking a single column or row. The *remaining* values of X, those in bold in Figure 11.13 needs to sum 1 to be a valid PMF, and thus we re-normalize by dividing by $P(Y = y)$

We define continuous joint CDFs as in Equation 11.13 the same as with discrete variables and the joint PDFs as the derivative of the CDFs with respect to x and y. We require valid joint PDFs to be nonnegative and integrate to 1. For continuous variables we can marginalize variables out in a similar fashion we did for discrete ones, with the difference that instead of a sum we need to compute an integral.

$$pdf_X(x) = \int pdf_{X,Y}(x,y)dy \qquad (11.15)$$

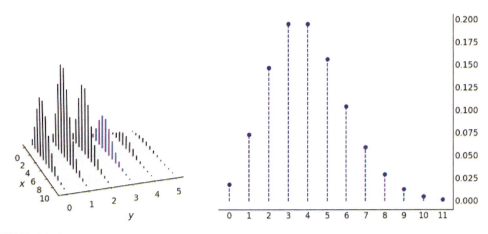

FIGURE 11.13
On the left the joint distribution of x and y. The blue lines represent the conditional distribution $p(x \ midy = 3)$. On the right we plot the same conditional distribution separately. Notice that there are as many conditional PMF of x as values of y and vice versa. We are just highlighting one possibility.

Figure 11.15 show another example of a a join distribution with its marginals distribution. This is also a clear example that going from the joint to the marginals is straightforward, as there is a unique way of doing it, but the inverse is not possible unless we introduce further assumptions. Joint distributions can also be a hybrid of discrete and continuous distributions. Figure 11.16 shows an example.

11.1.7 Probability Integral Transform (PIT)

The probability integral transform (PIT), also known as the universality of the Uniform distribution, states that given a random variable X with a continuous distribution with cumulative distribution F_X, we can compute a random variable Y with standard Uniform distribution as:

$$Y = F_X(X) \tag{11.16}$$

We can see this is true as follows, by the definition of the CDF of Y

$$F_Y(y) = P(Y \leq y) \tag{11.17}$$

Replacing Equation 11.16 in the previous one

$$P(F_X(X) \leq y) \tag{11.18}$$

Taking the inverse of F_X to both sides of the inequality

$$P(X \leq F_X^{-1}(y)) \tag{11.19}$$

By the definition of CDF

$$F_X(F_X^{-1}(y)) \tag{11.20}$$

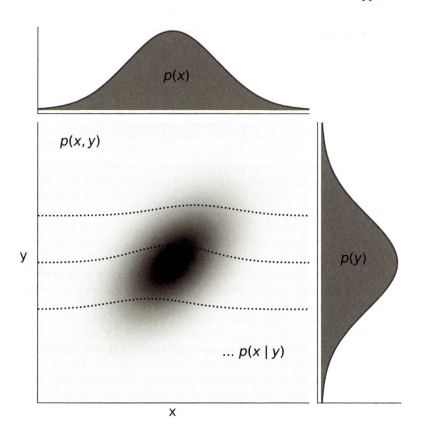

FIGURE 11.14

At the center of the figure we have the joint probability $p(x, y)$ represented with a gray scale, darker for higher probability density. At the top and right *margins* we have the marginal distributions $p(x)$ and $p(y)$ respectively. The dashed lines represents the conditional probability $p(x \mid y)$ for 3 different values of y. We can think of these as (renormalized) slices of the joint $p(x, y)$ at a given value of y.

Simplifying, we get the CDF of a standard Uniform distribution $\mathcal{U}(0, 1)$.

$$F_Y(y) = y \tag{11.21}$$

If we do not know the CDF F_X but we have samples from X we can approximate it with the empirical CDF. Figure 11.17 shows example of this property generated with Code Block 11.4

Code 11.4

```
1  xs = (np.linspace(0, 20, 200), np.linspace(0, 1, 200), np.linspace(-4, 4, 200))
2  dists = (stats.expon(scale=5), stats.beta(0.5, 0.5), stats.norm(0, 1))
3
4
5  _, ax = plt.subplots(3, 3)
6
7  for idx, (dist, x) in enumerate(zip(dists, xs)):
8      draws = dist.rvs(100000)
```

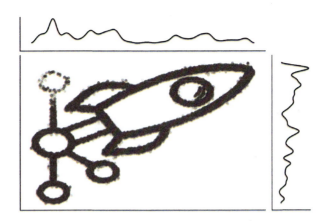

FIGURE 11.15
The PyMC3 logo as a sample from a joint distribution with its marginals. This figure was created with imcmc https://github.com/ColCarroll/imcmc a library for turning 2D images into probability distributions and then sampling from them to create images and gifs.

```
9     data = dist.cdf(draws)
10    # PDF original distribution
11    ax[idx, 0].plot(x, dist.pdf(x))
12    # Empirical CDF
13    ax[idx, 1].plot(np.sort(data), np.linspace(0, 1, len(data)))
14    # Kernel Density Estimation
15    az.plot_kde(data, ax=ax[idx, 2])
```

The probability integral transform is used as part of tests to evaluate if a given dataset can be modeled as arising from a specified distribution (or probabilistic model). In this book we have seen PIT used behind both visual test `az.plot_loo_pit()` and `az.plot_pbv(kind="u_values")`.

PIT can also be used to sample from distributions. If the random variable X is distributed as $\mathcal{U}(0, 1)$, then $Y = F^{-1}(X)$ has the distribution F. Thus to obtain samples from a distribution we just need (pseudo)random number generator like `np.random.rand()` and the inverse CDF of the distribution of interest. This may not be the most efficient method, but its generality and simplicity are difficult to beat.

11.1.8 Expectations

The expectation is a single number summarizing the center of mass of a distribution. For example, if X is a discrete random variable, then we can compute its expectation as:

$$\mathbb{E}(X) = \sum_x x P(X = x) \tag{11.22}$$

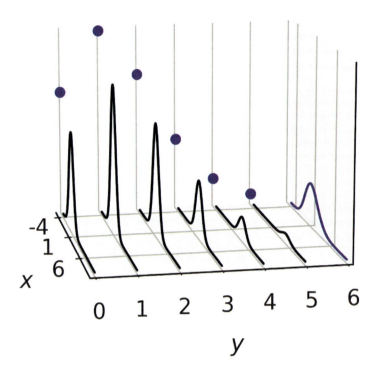

FIGURE 11.16
A hybrid joint distribution in black. The marginals are represented in blue, with X being distributed as a Gaussian and Y as a Poisson. It is easy to see how for each value of Y we have a (Gaussian) conditional distribution.

As is often the case in statistics we want to also measure the spread, or dispersion, of a distribution, for example, to represent uncertainty around a point estimate like the mean. We can do this with the variance, which itself is also an expectation:

$$\mathbb{V}(X) = \mathbb{E}(X - \mathbb{E}X)^2 = \mathbb{E}(X^2) - (\mathbb{E}X)^2 \tag{11.23}$$

The variance often appears *naturally* in many computations, but to report results it is often more useful to take the square root of the variance, called the standard deviation, as this will be in the same units as the random variable.

Figures 11.4, 11.5, 11.6, 11.8, 11.9, 11.10, and 11.11 show the expectation and the standard deviations for different distributions. Notice that these are not values computed from samples but properties of theoretical mathematical objects.

Expectation is linear, meaning that:

$$\mathbb{E}(cX) = c\mathbb{E}(X) \tag{11.24}$$

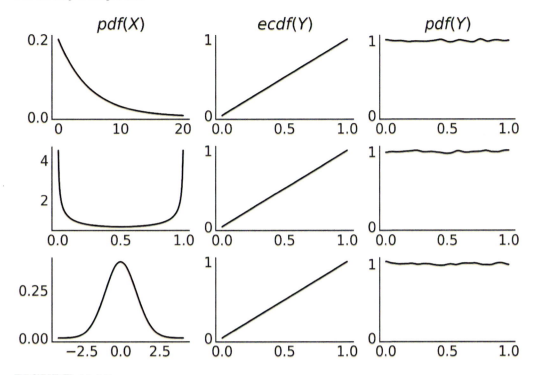

FIGURE 11.17
On the first column we have the PDF of 3 different distributions. To generate the plots in the middle column, we take 100000 draws from the corresponding PDF compute the CDF for those draws. We can see these are the CDF for the Uniform distribution. The last column is similar to the middle one, except that instead of plotting the empirical CDF we use a a kernel density estimator to approximate the PDF, which we can see that is approximately Uniform. The figure was generated with Code Block 11.4.

where c is a constant and

$$\mathbb{E}(X + Y) = \mathbb{E}(X) + \mathbb{E}(Y) \tag{11.25}$$

which are true even in the case that X and Y are dependent. Instead, the variance is not linear:

$$\mathbb{V}(cX) = c^2 \mathbb{V}(X) \tag{11.26}$$

and in general:

$$\mathbb{V}(X + Y) \neq \mathbb{V}(X) + \mathbb{V}(Y) \tag{11.27}$$

except, for example, when X and Y are independent.

We denote the nth moment of a random variable X is $\mathbb{E}(X^n)$, thus the expected value and the variance are also known as the first and second moments of a distribution. The third moment, the skew, tells us about the asymmetry of a distribution. The skewness of a random variable X with mean μ and variance σ^2 is the third (standardized moment) of X:

$$\text{skew}(X) = \mathbb{E}\left(\frac{X - \mu}{\sigma}\right)^3 \tag{11.28}$$

The reason to compute the skew as a standardized quantity, i.e. to subtract the mean and divide by the standard deviation is to make the skew independent of the localization and scale of X, this is reasonable as we already have that information from the mean and variance and also it will make the skweness independent of the units of X, so it becomes easier to compare skewness.

For example, a Beta$(2, 2)$ has a 0 skew while for Beta$(2, 5)$ the skew is positive and for Beta$(5, 2)$ negative. For unimodal distributions, a positive skew generally means that the right tail is longer, and the opposite for a negative skew. This is not always the case, the reason is that a 0 skew means that the *total mass* at the tails on both sides is balanced. So we can also balance the mass by having one long thin tail an another short and fat tail.

The fourth moment, known as kurtosis, tells us about the behavior of the tails or the *extreme values* [159]. It is defined as

$$\text{Kurtosis}(X) = \mathbb{E}\left(\frac{X - \mu}{\sigma}\right)^4 - 3 \tag{11.29}$$

The reason to subtract 3 is to make the Gaussian have 0 kurtosis, as it is often the case that kurtosis is discussed in comparison with the Gaussian distribution, but sometimes it is often computed without the -3, so when in doubt ask, or read, for the exact definition used in a particular case. By examining the definition of kurtosis in Equation 11.29 we can see that we are essentially computing the expected value of the standardized data raised to the fourth power. Thus any standardized values less than 1 contribute virtually nothing to the kurtosis. Instead the only values that has something to contribute are the *extreme* values.

As we increase increase the value of ν in a Student t distribution the kurtosis decreases (it is zero for a Gaussain distribution) and the kurtosis increases as we decrease ν. The kurtosis is only defined when $\nu > 4$, in fact for the Student T distribution the nth moment is only defined for $\nu > n$.

The stats module of SciPy offers a method `stats(moments)` to compute the moments of distributions as you can see in Code Block 11.3 where it is used to obtain the mean and variance. We notice that all we have discussed in this section is about computing expectation and moments from probability distributions and not from samples, thus we are talking about properties of theoretical distributions. Of course in practice we usually want to estimate the moments of a distribution from data and for that reason statisticians have studies estimators, for example, the sample mean and the sample median are estimators of $\mathbb{E}(X)$.

11.1.9   Transformations

If we have a random variable X and we apply a function g to it we obtain another random variable $Y = g(X)$. After doing so we may ask, given that we know the distribution of X how can we find out the distribution of Y. One easy way of doing it, is by sampling from X applying the transformation and then plotting the results. But of course there are formals ways of doing it. One such way is applying the **change of variables** technique.

If X is a continuous random variable and $Y = g(X)$, where g is a differentiable and strictly increasing or decreasing function, the PDF of Y is:

$$p_Y(y) = p_X(x)\left|\frac{dx}{dy}\right| \tag{11.30}$$

We can see this is true as follows. Let g be strictly increasing, then the CDF of Y is:

$$
\begin{aligned}
F_Y(y) &= P(Y \leq y) \\
&= P(g(X) \leq y) \\
&= P(X \leq g^{-1}(y)) \\
&= F_X(g^{-1}(y)) \\
&= F_X(x)
\end{aligned}
\tag{11.31}
$$

and then by the chain rule, the PDF of Y can be computed from the PDF of X as:

$$
p_Y(y) = p_X(x)\frac{dx}{dy}
\tag{11.32}
$$

The proof for g strictly decreasing is similar but we end up with a minus sign on the right hand term and thus the reason we compute the absolute value in Equation 11.30.

For multivariate random variables (i.e in higher dimensions) instead of the derivative we need to compute the Jacobian determinant, and thus it is common to refer the term $\left|\frac{dx}{dy}\right|$ as the Jacobian even in the one dimensional case. The absolute value of the Jacobian determinant at a point p gives us the factor by which a function g expands or shrinks volumes near p. This interpretation of the Jacobian is also applicable to probability densities. If the transformation g is not linear then the affected probability distribution will shrink in some regions and expand in others. Thus we need to properly take into account these deformations when computing Y from the known PDF of X. Slightly rewriting Equation 11.30 like below also helps:

$$
p_Y(y)dy = p_X(x)dx
\tag{11.33}
$$

As we can now see that the probability of finding Y in a tiny interval $p_Y(y)dy$ is equal to the probability of finding X in a tiny interval $p_X(x)dx$. So the Jacobian is telling us how we remap probabilities in the space associated to X with those associated with Y.

11.1.10 Limits

The two best known and most widely used theorems in probability are the law of large numbers and the central limit theorem. They both tell us what happens to the sample mean as the sample size increases. They can both be understood in the context of repeated experiments, where the outcome of the experiment could be viewed as a sample from some underlying distribution.

The Law of Large Numbers

The law of large number tells us that the sample mean of an iid random variable converges, as the number of samples increase, to the expected value of the random variable. This is not true for some distributions such as the Cauchy distribution (which has no mean or finite variance).

The law of large numbers is often misunderstood, leading to the gambler's fallacy. An example of this paradox is believing that it is smart to bet in the lottery on a number that has not appeared for a long time. The erroneous reasoning here is that if a particular number has not appeared for a while then there is must be some kind of force that increases the probability of that number in the next draws. A force that re-establish the equiprobability of the numbers and the *natural order of the universe*.

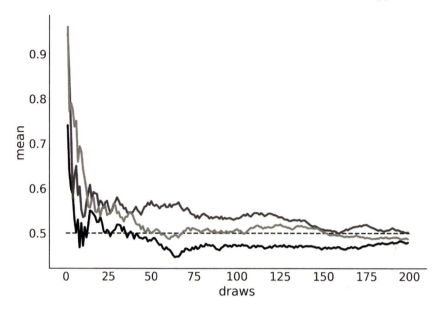

FIGURE 11.18

Running values from a $\mathcal{U}(0,1)$ distribution. The dashed line at 0.5 represent the expected value. As the number of draws increases, the empirical mean approaches the expected value. Each line represents a different sample.

The Central Limit Theorem

The central limit theorem states that if we sample n values independently from an arbitrary distribution the mean $\bar{X}$ of those values will distribute approximately as a Gaussian as $n \to \infty$:

$$\bar{X}_n \dot{\sim} \mathcal{N}\left(\mu, \frac{\sigma^2}{n}\right) \tag{11.34}$$

where μ and σ^2 are the mean and variance of the arbitrary distribution.

For the central limit theorem to be fulfilled, the following assumptions must be met:

- The values are sampled independently
- Each value come from the same distribution
- The mean and standard deviation of the distribution must be finite

Criteria 1 and 2 can be relaxed *quite a bit* and we will still get roughly a Gaussian, but there is no way to escape from Criterion 3. For distributions such as the Cauchy distribution, which do not have a defined mean or variance, this theorem does not apply. The average of N values from a Cauchy distribution do not follow a Gaussian but a Cauchy distribution.

The central limit theorem explains the prevalence of the Gaussian distribution in nature. Many of the phenomena we study can be explained as fluctuations around a mean, or as the result of the sum of many different factors.

Figure 11.19 shows the central limit theorem in action for 3 different distributions, Pois(2.3), $\mathcal{U}(0,1)$, Beta(1, 10), as n increases.

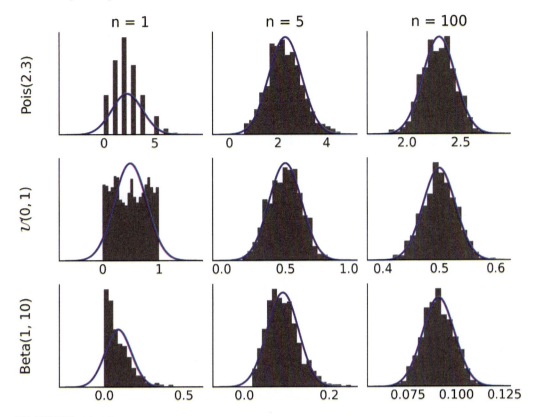

FIGURE 11.19

Histograms of the distributions indicated on the left margin. Each histogram is based on 1000 simulated values of $\bar{X}_n$. As we increase n the distribution of $\bar{X}_n$ approach a Normal distribution. The black curve corresponds to a Gaussian distribution according to the central limit theorem.

11.1.11 Markov Chains

A Markov Chain is a sequence of random variables $X_0, X_1, \ldots$ for which the future state is conditionally independent from all past ones given the current state. In other words, knowing the current state is enough to know the probabilities for all future states. This is known as the Markov property and we can write it as:

$$P(X_{n+1} = j \mid X_n = i, X_{n-1} = i_{n-1}, \ldots, X_0 = i_0) = P(X_{n+1} = j \mid X_n = i) \qquad (11.35)$$

A rather effective way to visualize Markov Chains is imagining you or some object moving in space [15]. The analogy is easier to grasp if the space is finite, for example, moving a piece in a square board like checkers or a salesperson visiting different cities. Given this scenarios you can ask questions like, how likely is to visit one state (specific squares in the board, cities, etc)? Or maybe more interesting if we keep moving from state to state how much time will we spend at each state in the long-run?

Figure 11.20 shows four examples of Markov Chains, the first one show a classical example, an oversimplified weather model, where the states are rainy or sunny, the second example shows

---

[15]See, for example, https://www.youtube.com/watch?v=i5oND7rHtFs

a deterministic die. The last two example are more abstract as we have not assigned any concrete representation to them.

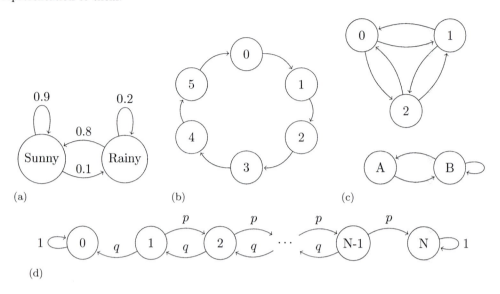

(a)   (b)   (c)

(d)

FIGURE 11.20
Markov Chains examples. (a) An oversimplified weather model, representing the probability of a rainy or sunny day, the arrows indicate the transition between states, the arrows are annotated with their corresponding transition probabilities. (b) An example of periodic Markov Chain. (c) An example of a disjoint chain. The states 1, 2, and 3 are disjoint from states A and B. If we start at the state 1, 2, or 3 we will never reach state A or B and vice versa. Transition probabilities are omitted in this example. (d) A Markov chain representing the gambler's ruin problem, two gamblers, A and B, start with i and $N - i$ units of money respectively. At any given money they bet 1 unit, gambler A has probability p of and probability $q = 1 - p$ of losing. If X_n is the total money of gambler A at time n. Then $X_0, X_1, \ldots$ is a Markov chain as the one represented.

A convenient way to study Markov Chains is to collect the probabilities of moving between states in one step in a transition matrix $\mathbf{T} = (t_{ij})$. For example, the transition matrix of example A in Figure 11.20 is

$$
\begin{array}{c}
 \\
\text{sunny} \\
\text{rainy}
\end{array}
\begin{array}{cc}
\text{sunny} & \text{rainy} \\
\left(\begin{array}{cc}
0.9 & 0.1 \\
0.8 & 0.2
\end{array} \right)
\end{array}
$$

and, for example, the transition matrix of example B in Figure 11.20 is

$$
\begin{array}{c}
 \\
0 \\
1 \\
2 \\
3 \\
4 \\
5
\end{array}
\begin{array}{cccccc}
0 & 1 & 2 & 3 & 4 & 5 \\
\left(\begin{array}{cccccc}
0 & 1 & 0 & 0 & 0 & 0 \\
0 & 0 & 1 & 0 & 0 & 0 \\
0 & 0 & 0 & 1 & 0 & 0 \\
0 & 0 & 0 & 0 & 1 & 0 \\
0 & 0 & 0 & 0 & 0 & 1 \\
1 & 0 & 0 & 0 & 0 & 0
\end{array} \right)
\end{array}
$$

The ith row of the transition matrix represents the conditional probability distribution of moving from state X_n to the state X_{n+1}. That is, $p(X_{n+1} \mid X_n = i)$. For example, if we are at state *sunny* we can move to *sunny* (i.e. stay at the same state) with probability 0.9 and move to state *rainy* with probability 0.1. Notice how the total probability of moving from *sunny* to somewhere is 1, as expected for a PMF.

Because of the Markov property we can compute the probability of n consecutive steps by taking the nth power of $\mathbf{T}$.

We can also specify the starting point of the Markov chain, i.e. the initial conditions $s_i = P(X_0 = i)$ and let $\mathbf{s} = (s_1, \ldots, s_M)$. With this information we can compute the marginal PMF of X_n as $\mathbf{s}\mathbf{T}^n$.

When studying Markov chains it makes sense to define properties of individual states and also properties on the entire chain. For example, if a chain returns to a state over and over again we call that state recurrent. Instead a transient state is one that the chain will eventually leave forever, in example (d) in Figure 11.20 all states other than 0 or N are transient. Also, we can call a chain irreducible if it is possible to get from any state to any other state in a finite number of steps example (c) in Figure 11.20 is not irreducible, as states 1,2 and 3 are disconnected from states A and B.

Understanding the long-term behavior of Markov chains is of interest. In fact, they were introduced by Andrey Markov with the purpose of demonstrating that the law of large numbers can be applied also to non-independent random variables. The previously mentioned concepts of recurrence and transience are important for understanding this long-term run behavior. If we have a chain with transient and recurrent states, the chain may spend time in the transient states, but it will eventually spend all the eternity in the recurrent states. A natural question we can ask is how much time the chain is going to be at each state. The answer is provided by finding the **stationary distribution** of the chain.

For a finite Markov chain, the stationary distribution $\mathbf{s}$ is a PMF such that $\mathbf{s}\mathbf{T} = \mathbf{s}$ [16]. That is a distribution that is not changed by the transition matrix $\mathbf{T}$. Notice that this does not mean the chain is not moving anymore, it means that the chain moves in such a way that the time it will spend at each state is the one defined by $\mathbf{s}$. Maybe a physical analogy could helps here. Imagine we have a glass not completely filled with water at a given temperature. If we seal it with a cover, the water molecules will evaporate into the air as moisture. Interestingly it is also the case that the water molecules in the air will move to the liquid water. Initially more molecules might be going one way or another, but at a given point the system will find a dynamic equilibrium, with the same amount of water molecules moving to the air from the liquid water, as the number of water molecules moving from the liquid water to the air. In physics/chemistry this is called a steady-state, locally things are moving, but globally nothing changes [17]. Steady state is also an alternative name to stationary distribution.

Interestingly, under various conditions, the stationary distribution of a finite Markov chain exists and is unique, and the PMF of X_n converges to $\mathbf{s}$ as $n \to \infty$. Example (d) in Figure 11.20 does not have a unique stationary distribution. We notice that once this chain reaches the states 0 or N, meaning gambler A or B lost all the money, the chain stays in that state forever, so both $s_0 = (1, 0, \ldots, 0)$ and $s_N = (0, 0, \ldots, 1)$ are both stationary distributions. On the contrary example B in Figure 11.20 has a unique stationary distribution which is $s = (1/6, 1/6, 1/6, 1/6, 1/6, 1/6)$, event thought the transition is deterministic.

If a PMF $\mathbf{s}$ satisfies the reversibility condition (also known as detailed balance), that is $s_i t_{ij} = s_j t_{ji}$ for all i and j, we have the guarantee that $\mathbf{s}$ is a stationary distribution of the Markov chain

---

[16] For those familiar with eigenvectors and eigenvalues this should ring a bell.

[17] Another analogy comes from politics, when politicians/government changes but pressing issues like inequality or climate change are not properly addressed.

with transition matrix $\mathbf{T} = t_{ij}$. Such Markov chains are called reversible. In Section 11.9 we will use this property to show why Metropolis-Hastings is guaranteed to, asymptotically, work.

Markov chains satisfy a central limit theorem which is similar to Equation 11.34 except that instead of dividing by n we need to divide by the effective sample size (ESS). In Section 2.4.1 we discussed how to estimate the effective sample size from a Markov Chain and how to use it to diagnose the quality of the chain. The square root of $\frac{\sigma^2}{\text{ESS}}$ is the Monte Carlo standard error (MCSE) that we also discussed in Section 2.4.3.

11.2   Entropy

In the *Zentralfriedhof*, Vienna, we can find the grave of Ludwig Boltzmann. His tombstone has the legend $S = k \log W$, which is a beautiful way of saying that the second law of thermodynamics is a consequence of the laws of probability. With this equation Boltzmann contributed to the development of one of the pillars of modern physics, statistical mechanics. Statistical mechanics describes how macroscopic observations such as temperature are related to the microscopic world of molecules. Imagine a glass with water, what we perceive with our senses is basically the average behavior of a huge number water molecules inside that glass [18]. At a given temperature there is a given number of arrangements of the water molecules compatible with that temperature (Figure 11.21). As we decrease the temperature we will find that less and less arrangements are possible until we find a single one. We have just reached 0 Kelvin, the lowest possible temperature in the universe! If we move into the other direction we will find that molecules can be found in more and more arrangements.

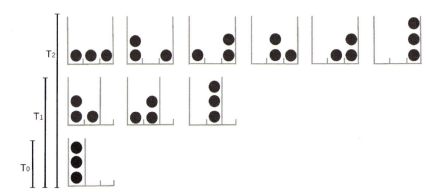

FIGURE 11.21
The number of possible arrangements particles can take is related to the temperature of the system. Here we represent discrete system of 3 equivalent particles, the number of possible arrangements is represented by the available cells (gray high lines). increasing the temperature is equivalent to increasing the number of available cells. At $T = 0$ only one arrangement is possible, as the temperature increase the particles can occupy more and more states.

We can analyze this mental experiment in terms of uncertainty. If we know a system is at 0 Kelvin we know the system can only be in a single possible arrangement, our certainty is

---

[18]To be precise we should include the molecules of glass and the molecules in the air, and... but let just focus on the water.

absolute [19], as we increase the temperature the number of possible arrangements will increase and then it will become more and more difficult to say, "Hey look! Water molecules are in this particular arrangement at this particular time!" Thus our uncertainty about the microscopic state will increase. We will still be able to characterize the system by averages such the temperature, volume, etc, but at the microscopic level the certainty about particular arrangements will decrease. Thus, we can think of entropy as a way of measuring uncertainty.

The concept of entropy is not only valid for molecules. It could also be applies to arrangements of pixels, characters in a text, musical notes, socks, bubbles in a sourdough bread and more. The reason that entropy is so flexible is because it quantifies the arrangements of objects - it is a property of the underlying distributions. The larger the entropy of a distribution the less informative that distribution will be and the more evenly it will assign probabilities to its events. Getting an answer of "42" is more certain than "42 ± 5", which again more certain than "any real number". Entropy can translate this qualitative observation into numbers.

The concept of entropy applies to continue and discrete distributions, but it is easier to think about it using discrete states and we will see some example in the rest of this section. But keep in mind the same concepts apply to the continuous cases.

For a probability distribution p with n possible different events which each possible event i having probability p_i, the entropy is defined as:

$$H(p) = -\mathbb{E}[\log p] = -\sum_i^n p_i \log p_i \tag{11.36}$$

Equation 11.36 is just a different way of writing the entropy engraved on Boltzmann's tombstone. We annotate entropy using H instead of S and set $k = 1$. Notice that the multiplicity W from Boltzmann's version is the total number of ways in which different outcomes can possibly occur:

$$W = \frac{N!}{n_1! n_2! \cdots n_t!} \tag{11.37}$$

You can think of this as rolling a t-sided die N times, where n_i is the number of times we obtain side i. As N is large we can use Stirling's approximation $x! \approx \left(\frac{x}{e}\right)^x$.

$$W = \frac{N^N}{n_1^{n_1} n_2^{n_2} \cdots n_t^{n_t}} e^{(n_1 n_2 \cdots n_t - N)} \tag{11.38}$$

noticing that $p_i = \frac{n_i}{N}$ we can write:

$$W = \frac{1}{p_1^{n_1} p_2^{n_2} \cdots p_t^{n_t}} \tag{11.39}$$

And finally by taking the logarithm we obtain

$$\log W = -\sum_i^n p_i \log p_i \tag{11.40}$$

which is exactly the definition of entropy.

---

[19] Do not let that Heisenberg guy and his uncertainty principle spoil the party

We will now show how to compute entropy in Python using Code Block 11.5, with the result shown in Figure 11.22.

Code 11.5

```
1  x = range(0, 26)
2  q_pmf = stats.binom(10, 0.75).pmf(x)
3  qu_pmf = stats.randint(0, np.max(np.nonzero(q_pmf))+1).pmf(x)
4  r_pmf = (q_pmf + np.roll(q_pmf, 12)) / 2
5  ru_pmf = stats.randint(0, np.max(np.nonzero(r_pmf))+1).pmf(x)
6  s_pmf = (q_pmf + np.roll(q_pmf, 15)) / 2
7  su_pmf = (qu_pmf + np.roll(qu_pmf, 15)) / 2
8
9  _, ax = plt.subplots(3, 2, figsize=(12, 5), sharex=True, sharey=True,
10                       constrained_layout=True)
11 ax = np.ravel(ax)
12
13 zipped = zip([q_pmf, qu_pmf, r_pmf, ru_pmf, s_pmf, su_pmf],
14              ["q", "qu", "r", "ru", "s", "su"])
15 for idx, (dist, label) in enumerate(zipped):
16     ax[idx].vlines(x, 0, dist, label=f"H = {stats.entropy(dist):.2f}")
17     ax[idx].set_title(label)
18     ax[idx].legend(loc=1, handlelength=0)
```

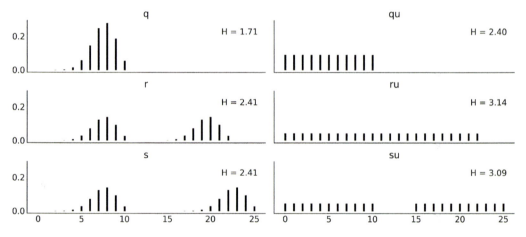

FIGURE 11.22
Discrete distributions defined in Code Block 11.5 and their entropy values H.

Figure 11.22 shows six distributions, one per subplot with its corresponding entropy. There are a lot of things moving on in this figure, so before diving in be sure to set aside an adequate amount of time (this maybe a good time to check your e-mails before going on). The most peaked, or least spread distribution is q, and this is the distribution with the lowest value of entropy among the six plotted distributions. $q \sim \text{binom}(n = 10, p = 0.75)$, and thus there are 11 possible events. qu is a Uniform distribution with also 11 possible events. We can see that the entropy of qu is larger than q, in fact we can compute the entropy for binomial distributions with $n = 10$ and different values of p and we will see that none of them have larger entropy than qu. We will need to increase n ≈ 3 times to find *the first* binomial distribution with larger entropy than qu. Let us move to the next row. We generate distribution r by taking q and *shifting* it to the right and then normalizing (to ensure the sum of all probabilities is 1). As r is more spread than q its entropy is larger. ru is the Uniform distribution with the same number of possible events as r (22), notice we are including as possible values those *in the valley between both peaks*. Once again the entropy of the *Uniform* version is the one with the largest entropy. So far entropy seems to be proportional to the variance of a distribution, but before jumping to conclusions let us check the last two distributions in Figure 11.22. s is essentially the same as r but with a more extensive *valley between both peaks* and as we can see the entropy remains the same. The reason is basically that entropy does not care about those events in the *valley* with probability zero, it only cares about possible events. su is constructed by replacing the two peaks in s with qu (and normalizing). We can see that su has lower entropy than ru even when it looks more spread, after a more careful inspection we can see that su spread the total probability between fewer events (22) than ru (with 23 events), and thus it makes totally sense for it to have lower entropy.

11.3 Kullback-Leibler Divergence

It is common in statistics to use one probability distribution q to represent another one p, we generally do this when we do not know p but can approximate it with q. Or maybe p is complex and we want to find a simpler or more convenient distribution q. In such cases we may ask how much information are we losing by using q to represent p, or equivalently how much extra uncertainty are we introducing. Intuitively, we want a quantity that becomes zero only when q is equal to p and be a positive value otherwise. Following the definition of entropy in Equation 11.36, we can achieve this by computing the expected value of the difference between $\log(p)$ and $\log(q)$. This is known as the Kullback-Leibler (KL) divergence:

$$\mathbb{KL}(p \parallel q) = \mathbb{E}_p[\log p - \log q] \tag{11.41}$$

Thus the $\mathbb{KL}(p \parallel q)$ give us the average difference in log probabilities when using q to approximate p. Because the events appears to us according to p we need to compute the expectation with respect to p. For discrete distributions we have:

$$\mathbb{KL}(p \parallel q) = \sum_i^n p_i(\log p_i - \log q_i) \tag{11.42}$$

Using logarithmic properties we can write this into probably the most common way to represent KL divergence:

$$\mathbb{KL}(p \parallel q) = \sum_i^n p_i \log \frac{p_i}{q_i} \tag{11.43}$$

We can also arrange the term and write the $\mathbb{KL}(p \parallel q)$ as:

$$\mathbb{KL}(p \parallel q) = -\sum_i^n p_i(\log q_i - \log p_i) \tag{11.44}$$

and when we expand the above rearrangement we find that:

$$\mathbb{KL}(p \parallel q) = \overbrace{-\sum_i^n p_i \log q_i}^{H(p,q)} - \overbrace{\left(-\sum_i^n p_i \log p_i\right)}^{H(p)} \tag{11.45}$$

As we already saw in previous section, $H(p)$ is the entropy of p. $H(p, q) = -\mathbb{E}_p[\log q]$ is like the entropy of q but evaluated according to the values of p.

Reordering above we obtain:

$$H(p, q) = H(p) + D_{\mathrm{KL}}(p \parallel q) \tag{11.46}$$

This shows that the KL divergences can be effectively interpreted as the extra entropy with respect to $H(p)$, when using q to represent p.

To gain a little bit of intuition we are going to compute a few values for the KL divergence and plot them., We are going to use the same distributions as in Figure 11.22.

Code 11.6

```
1  dists = [q_pmf, qu_pmf, r_pmf, ru_pmf, s_pmf, su_pmf]
2  names = ["q", "qu", "r", "ru", "s", "su"]
3
4  fig, ax = plt.subplots()
5  KL_matrix = np.zeros((6, 6))
6  for i, dist_i in enumerate(dists):
7      for j, dist_j in enumerate(dists):
8          KL_matrix[i, j] = stats.entropy(dist_i, dist_j)
9
10 im = ax.imshow(KL_matrix, cmap="cet_gray")
```

The result of Code Block 11.6 is shown in Figure 11.23. There are two features of Figure 11.23 that immediately pop out. First, the figure is not symmetric, the reason is that $\mathbb{KL}(p \parallel q)$ is not necessarily the same as $\mathbb{KL}(q \parallel p)$. Second, we have many white cells. They represent ∞ values. The definition of the KL divergence uses the following conventions [40]:

$$0 \log \frac{0}{0} = 0, \quad 0 \log \frac{0}{q(\boldsymbol{x})} = 0, \quad p(\boldsymbol{x}) \log \frac{p(\boldsymbol{x})}{0} = \infty \tag{11.47}$$

We can motivate the use of a log-score in computing expected log pointwise predictive density (introduced in Chapter 2 Equation 2.5) based on the KL divergence. Let us assume we have k models posteriors $\{q_{M_1}, q_{M_2}, \cdots q_{M_k}\}$, let further assume we know the *true* model M_0 then we can compute:

$$\mathbb{KL}(p_{M_0} \parallel q_{M_1}) = \mathbb{E}[\log p_{M_0}] - \mathbb{E}[\log q_{M_1}]$$
$$\mathbb{KL}(p_{M_0} \parallel q_{M_2}) = \mathbb{E}[\log p_{M_0}] - \mathbb{E}[\log q_{M_2}]$$
$$\cdots \tag{11.48}$$
$$\mathbb{KL}(p_{M_0} \parallel q_{M_k}) = \mathbb{E}[\log p_{M_0}] - \mathbb{E}[\log q_{M_k}]$$

This may seems a futile exercise as in real life we do not know the true model M_0. The trick is to realize that as p_{M_0} is the same for all comparisons, thus building a ranking based on the KL-divergence is equivalent to doing one based on the log-score.

11.4   Information Criterion

An information criterion is a measure of the predictive accuracy of a statistical model. It takes into account how well the model fits the data and penalizes the complexity of the model. There

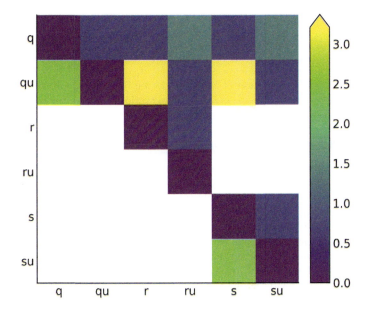

FIGURE 11.23
KL divergence for all the pairwise combinations of the distributions q, qu, r, ru, s, and su shown in Figure 11.22, the white color is used to represent infinity values.

are many different information criterion based on how they compute these two terms. The most famous family member, especially for non-Bayesians, is the Akaike Information Criterion (AIC) [3]. It is defined as the sum of two terms. The $\log p(y_i \mid \hat{\theta}_{mle})$ measures how well the model fits the data and the penalization term p_{AIC} to account for the fact that we use the same data to fit the model and to evaluate the model.

$$AIC = -2 \sum_{i}^{n} \log p(y_i \mid \hat{\theta}_{mle}) + 2p_{AIC} \tag{11.49}$$

where $\hat{\theta}_{mle}$ is the maximum-likelihood estimation of $\boldsymbol{\theta}$ and p_{AIC} is just the number of parameters in the model.

AIC is quite popular in non-Bayesian settings, but is not well equipped to deal with the generality of Bayesian models. It does not use the full posterior distribution, thus discarding potentially useful information. On average, AIC will behave worse and worse as we move from flat prior into weakly-informative or informative priors, and/or if we add more structure into our model, like with hierarchical models. AIC assumes that the posterior can be well represented (at least asymptotically) by a Gaussian distribution, but this is not true for a number of models, including hierarchical models, mixture models, neural networks, etc. In summary we want to use some better alternatives.

The Widely applicable Information Crieria (WAIC [20]) [156] can be regarded as a fully Bayesian extension of AIC. It also contains two terms, roughly with the same interpretation as the Akaike criterion. The most important difference is that the terms are computed using the full posterior distribution.

---

[20] Generally pronounced as W-A-I-C, even when something like wæɪk is less of a mouthful

$$WAIC = \sum_i^n \log \left(\frac{1}{s} \sum_j^S p(y_i \mid \boldsymbol{\theta}^j) \right) - \sum_i^n \left(\mathop{\mathbb{V}}_j^s \log p(Y_i \mid \boldsymbol{\theta}^j) \right) \tag{11.50}$$

The first term in Equation 11.50 is just the log-likelihood as in AIC but evaluated pointwise, i.e, at each i observed data-point over the n observations. We are taking into account the uncertainty in the posterior by taking the average over the s samples from the posterior. This first term is a practical way to compute the theoretical expected log pointwise predictive density (ELPD) as defined in Equation 2.4 and its approximation in Equation 2.5.

The second term might look a little bit weird, as is the variance over the s posterior samples (per observation). Intuitively, we can see that for each observation the variance will be low if the log-likelihood across the posterior distribution is similar and it will be larger if the log-likelihood varies more for different samples from the posterior distribution. The more observations we find to be sensitive to the *details* of the posterior the larger the penalization will be. We can also see this from another equivalent perspective; A more flexible model is one that can effectively accommodate more datasets. For example, a model that included straight but also upward curves is more flexible than one that only allows straight lines; and thus the log-likelihood of those observation evaluated across the posterior on the later model will have, on average, a higher variance. If the more flexible model is not able to compensate this penalization with a higher estimated ELPD then the simpler model will we ranked as a better choice. Thus the variance term in Equation 11.50 prevents overfitting by penalizing an overly complex model and it can be loosely interpreted as the effective number of parameters as in AIC.

Neither AIC nor WAIC are attempting to measure whether the model is *true*, they are only a relative measure to compare alternative models. From a Bayesian perspective the prior is part of the model, but WAIC is evaluated over the posterior, and the prior effect is only indirectly taken into account by the way it affects the resulting posterior. There are other information criteria like BIC and WBIC that attempts to answer that question and can be seen as approximations to the Marginal Likelihood, but we do not discuss them in this book.

11.5   LOO in Depth

As discussed in Section 2.5.1 in this book we use the term LOO to refer to a particular method to approximate Leave-One-Out Cross-Validation (LOO-CV) known as Pareto Smooth Importance Sampling Leave Once Out Cross Validation (PSIS-LOO-CV). In this section we are going to discuss a few details of this method.

LOO is an alternative to WAIC, in fact it can be shown that asymptotically they converge to the same numerical value [156, 153]. Nevertheless, LOO presents two importance advantages for practitioners. It is more robust in finite samples settings, and it provides useful diagnostics during computation [153, 57].

Under LOO-CV the expected log pointwise predictive density for a new dataset is:

$$\text{ELPD}_{\text{LOO-CV}} = \sum_{i=1}^n \log \int p(y_i \mid \boldsymbol{\theta}) \, p(\boldsymbol{\theta} \mid y_{-i}) d\boldsymbol{\theta} \tag{2.6}$$

where y_{-i} represents the dataset excluding the i observation.

Given that in practice we do not know the value of $\boldsymbol{\theta}$ we can approximate Equation 2.6 using s samples from the posterior:

$$\sum_i^n \log \left(\frac{1}{s} \sum_j^s p(y_i \mid \boldsymbol{\theta}_{-i}^j) \right) \tag{11.51}$$

Notice that this term looks similar to the first term in Equation 11.50, except we are computing n posteriors removing one observation each time. For this reason, and contrary to WAIC, we do not need to add a penalization term. Computing $\text{ELPD}_{\text{LOO-CV}}$ in 11.51 is very costly as we need to compute n posteriors. Fortunately if the n observations are conditionally independent we can approximate Equation 11.51 with Equation 11.52 [65, 153]:

$$\text{ELPD}_{\text{psis-loo}} = \sum_i^n \log \sum_j^s w_i^j p(y_i \mid \boldsymbol{\theta}^j) \tag{11.52}$$

where w is a vector of normalized weights.

To compute w we used importance sampling, this is a technique for estimating properties of a particular distribution f of interest, given that we only have samples from a different distribution g. Using importance sampling makes sense when sampling from g is easier than sampling from f. If we have a set of samples from the random variable X and we are able to evaluate g and f pointwise, we can compute the importance weights as:

$$w_i = \frac{f(x_i)}{g(x_i)} \tag{11.53}$$

Computationally, it goes as follow:

- Draw N samples x_i from g
- Calculate the probability of each sample $g(x_i)$
- Evaluate f over the N samples $f(x_i)$
- Calculate the importance weights $w_i = \frac{f(x_i)}{g(x_i)}$
- Return N samples from g with weights w, (x_i, w_i), that could be plug into some estimator

Figure 11.24 shows an example of approximating the same target distribution (dashed line) by using two different proposal distributions. On the first row the proposal is wider than the target distribution. On the second row the proposal is narrower than the target distribution. As we can see the approximation is better in the first case. This is a general feature of importance sampling.

Going back to LOO, the distribution that we have computed is the posterior distribution. In order to evaluate the model we want samples from the leave-one-out posterior distribution, thus the importance weights we want to compute are:

$$w_i^j = \frac{p(\theta^j \mid y_{-i})}{p(\theta^j \mid y)} \propto \frac{1}{p(y_i \mid \theta^j)} \tag{11.54}$$

Notice that this proportionality is great news, because it allows us to compute w almost for free. However, the posterior is likely to have thinner tails than the leave-one-out distributions, which as we saw in Figure 11.24 can result in poor estimation. Mathematically the problem is that the importance weights can have high or even infinite variance. In order to keep the variance in

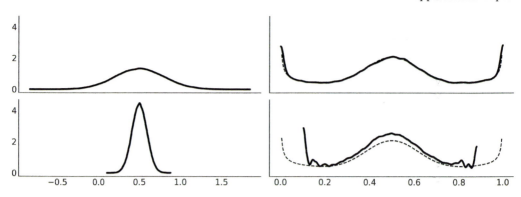

FIGURE 11.24
Importance sampling. On the left we have KDEs of samples from the proposal distributions
g, on the right the dashed line represents the target distribution and the continuous line
the approximated distribution after re-weighting the samples from the proposal distribution
with the weights computed as in Equation 11.53.

check, LOO applies a smoothing procedure that involves replacing the largest importance weights
with values from an estimated Pareto distribution. This help to make LOO much more robust
[153]. Moreover, the estimated $\hat{\kappa}$ parameter of the Pareto distribution can be used to detect highly
influential observations, i.e. observations that have a large effect on the predictive distribution
when they are left out. In general, higher values of $\hat{\kappa}$ can indicate problems with the data or model,
especially when $\hat{\kappa} > 0.7$ [154, 57].

11.6   Jeffreys' Prior Derivation

In this section we will show how to find the Jeffreys' prior for the binomial likelihood, first for the
number of successes parameter θ, and then for the odds parameter κ, where $\kappa = \frac{\theta}{1-\theta}$.

Recall from Chapter 1, for the one-dimensional case JP for θ is defined as:

$$p(\theta) \propto \sqrt{I(\theta)} \tag{1.18}$$

where $I(\theta)$ is the Fisher information:

$$I(\theta) = -\mathbb{E}_{\mathbb{Y}}\left[\frac{d^2}{d\theta^2} \log p(Y \mid \theta)\right] \tag{1.19}$$

11.6.1   Jeffreys' Prior for the Binomial Likelihood in Terms of θ

Binomial likelihood could be expressed as:

$$p(Y \mid \theta) \propto \theta^y (1-\theta)^{n-y} \tag{11.55}$$

where y is the number of successes, n the total number of trials, and thus $n - y$ is the numbers
of failures. We write is as a proportionality as the Binomial coefficient in the likelihood does not
depend on θ.

To compute the Fisher information we need to take the logarithm of the likelihood:

$$\ell = \log(p(Y \mid \theta)) \propto y \log(\theta) + (n - y) \log(1 - \theta) \tag{11.56}$$

And then compute the second derivative:

$$\frac{d\ell}{d\theta} = \frac{y}{\theta} - \frac{n - y}{1 - \theta}$$
$$\frac{d^2\ell}{d\theta^2} = -\frac{y}{\theta^2} - \frac{n - y}{(1 - \theta)^2} \tag{11.57}$$

The Fisher information is the expected value of the second derivative of the likelihood, then:

$$I(\theta) = -\mathbb{E}_Y \left[-\frac{y}{\theta^2} + \frac{n - y}{(1 - \theta)^2} \right] \tag{11.58}$$

As $\mathbb{E}[y] = n\theta$, we can write:

$$I(\theta) = \frac{n\theta}{\theta^2} - \frac{n - n\theta}{(1 - \theta)^2} \tag{11.59}$$

which we can rewrite as:

$$I(\theta) = \frac{n}{\theta} - \frac{n(1 - \theta)}{(1 - \theta)^2} = \frac{n}{\theta} - \frac{n}{(1 - \theta)} \tag{11.60}$$

We can express these fractions in terms of a common denominator,

$$I(\theta) = n \left[\frac{1 - \theta}{\theta(1 - \theta)} - \frac{\theta}{\theta(1 - \theta)} \right] \tag{11.61}$$

By regrouping:

$$I(\theta) = n \frac{1}{\theta(1 - \theta)} \tag{11.62}$$

If we omit n then we can write:

$$I(\theta) \propto \frac{1}{\theta(1 - \theta)} = \theta^{-1}(1 - \theta)^{-1} \tag{11.63}$$

Finally, we need to take the square root of the Fisher information in Equation 11.63, which resulting the Jeffreys' prior for θ of Binomial likelihood as follow:

$$p(\theta) \propto \theta^{-0.5}(1 - \theta)^{-0.5} \tag{11.64}$$

11.6.2   Jeffreys' Prior for the Binomial Likelihood in Terms of κ

Let us now see how to obtain the Jeffreys' prior for the Binomial likelihood in terms the odds κ. We begin by replacing $\theta = \frac{\kappa}{\kappa+1}$ in expression 11.55:

$$p(Y \mid \kappa) \propto \left(\frac{\kappa}{\kappa + 1} \right)^y \left(1 - \frac{\kappa}{\kappa + 1} \right)^{n-y} \tag{11.65}$$

Which can also be written as:

$$p(Y \mid \kappa) \propto \kappa^y (\kappa + 1)^{-y} (\kappa + 1)^{-n+y} \tag{11.66}$$

and further simplified into:

$$p(Y \mid \kappa) \propto \kappa^y (\kappa + 1)^{-n} \tag{11.67}$$

Now we need to take the logarithm:

$$\ell = \log(p(Y \mid \kappa)) \propto y \log \kappa - n \log (\kappa + 1) \tag{11.68}$$

we then compute the second derivative:

$$\frac{d\ell}{d\kappa} = \frac{y}{\kappa} - \frac{n}{\kappa + 1}$$
$$\frac{d^2\ell}{d\kappa^2} = -\frac{y}{\kappa^2} + \frac{n}{(\kappa + 1)^2} \tag{11.69}$$

The Fisher information is the expected value of the second derivative of the likelihood, then:

$$I(\kappa) = -\mathbb{E}_Y \left[-\frac{y}{\kappa^2} + \frac{n}{(\kappa + 1)^2} \right] \tag{11.70}$$

As $\mathbb{E}[y] = n\theta = n\frac{\kappa}{\kappa+1}$, we can write:

$$I(\kappa) = \frac{n}{\kappa(\kappa + 1)} - \frac{n}{(\kappa + 1)^2} \tag{11.71}$$

We can express these fractions in terms of a common denominator,

$$I(\kappa) = \frac{n(\kappa + 1)}{\kappa(\kappa + 1)^2} - \frac{n\kappa}{\kappa(\kappa + 1)^2} \tag{11.72}$$

Then we combine into a single fraction

$$I(\kappa) = \frac{n(\kappa + 1) - n\kappa}{\kappa(\kappa + 1)^2} \tag{11.73}$$

We then distribute n over $(\kappa + 1)$ and we simplify:

$$I(\kappa) = \frac{n}{\kappa(\kappa + 1)^2} \tag{11.74}$$

Finally, by taking the square root, we get the Jeffreys' prior for the Binomial likelihood when parameterized by the odds:

$$p(\kappa) \propto \kappa^{-0.5}(1 + \kappa)^{-1} \tag{11.75}$$

11.6.3 Jeffreys' Posterior for the Binomial Likelihood

To obtain the Jeffrey's posterior when the likelihood is parameterized in terms of θ we can combine Equation 11.55 with Equation 11.64

$$p(\theta \mid Y) \propto \theta^y (1-\theta)^{n-y} \theta^{-0.5} (1-\theta)^{-0.5} = \theta^{y-0.5} (1-\theta)^{n-y-0.5} \tag{11.76}$$

Similarly, the Jeffreys' posterior when the likelihood is parameterized in terms of κ we can combine 11.67 with 11.75

$$p(\kappa \mid Y) \propto \kappa^y (\kappa+1)^{-n} \kappa^{-0.5} (1+\kappa)^{-1} = \kappa^{(y-0.5)} (\kappa+1)^{(-n-1)}) \tag{11.77}$$

11.7 Marginal Likelihood

For some models, such as those using conjugate priors, the marginal likelihood is analytically tractable. For the rest, numerically computing this integral is notoriously difficult, since this involves a high-dimensional integration over a usually complicated and highly variable function [55]. In this section we will try to gain intuition into why this is generally a hard task.

Numerically, and in low dimensions, we can compute the marginal likelihood by evaluating the product of the prior and the likelihood, over a grid and then applying the trapezoid rule, or some other similar method. As we will see in Section 11.8 using grids does not scale well with dimension, as the number of required grid points increase rapidly as we increase the number of variables in our model. Thus grid-based methods becomes impractical for problems with more than a few variables. Monte Carlo integration can also be problematic, at least in the most naive implementations (see Section 11.8). For that reason many dedicated methods have been proposed to compute the marginal likelihood [55]. Here we will only discuss one of them. Our main concern is not learning how to compute the marginal likelihood in practice, but instead to illustrate why is hard to do it.

11.7.1 The Harmonic Mean Estimator

A rather infamous estimator of the marginal likelihood is the harmonic mean estimator [110]. A very appealing feature of this estimator is that it only requires s samples from the posterior:

$$p(Y) \approx \left(\frac{1}{s} \sum_{i=1}^{s} \frac{1}{p(Y \mid \theta_i)} \right)^{-1} \tag{11.78}$$

We can see that we are averaging the inverse of the likelihood over samples taken from the posterior, then computing the inverse of the result. In principle, this is a valid Monte Carlo estimator of the following expectation:

$$\mathbb{E}\left[\frac{1}{p(Y \mid \theta)} \right] = \int_{\Theta} \frac{1}{p(Y \mid \theta)} p(\theta \mid Y) d\theta \tag{11.79}$$

Notice that Equation 11.79 is a particular instance of Equation 1.5 which may seems to indicate we are doing something right by being very Bayesian.

If we expand the posterior term we can write:

$$\mathbb{E}\left[\frac{1}{p(Y \mid \boldsymbol{\theta})}\right] = \int_{\boldsymbol{\Theta}} \frac{1}{p(Y \mid \boldsymbol{\theta})} \frac{p(Y \mid \boldsymbol{\theta})p(\theta)}{p(Y)} d\boldsymbol{\theta} \tag{11.80}$$

which we can simplify into:

$$\mathbb{E}\left[\frac{1}{p(Y \mid \boldsymbol{\theta})}\right] = \frac{1}{p(Y)} \underbrace{\int_{\boldsymbol{\Theta}} p(\boldsymbol{\theta}) d\boldsymbol{\theta}}_{=1} = \frac{1}{p(Y)} \tag{11.81}$$

We are assuming the prior is proper, and thus its integral should be 1. We can see that Equation 11.78 is in fact an approximation of the marginal likelihood.

Unfortunately the good news does not last too long. The number of samples s needed to feed into Equation 11.78 in order to get close to the right answer is generally very large, to the point that the harmonic mean estimator is not very useful in practice [110, 55]. Intuitively we can see that the sum will be dominated by samples with very low likelihood. Even worse, the harmonic mean estimator can have infinite variance. Infinite variance means that even if we increase s we will not get a better answer, thus sometimes even a huge amount of samples could still be insufficient. The other problem with the harmonic mean estimator is that it is rather insensitive to changes in the prior. But even the exact marginal likelihood is in fact very sensitive to changes in the prior distribution (as we will show later, see Figure 11.26). These two problems will be exacerbated when the likelihood turns to be much more concentrated with respect to the prior, or when the likelihood and prior concentrate into different regions of the parameter space.

By using samples from a more peaked posterior, with respect to the prior, we will be missing all the regions from the prior that have low posterior density. In a sketchy way we can think of Bayesian Inference as using data to update the prior into a posterior. Prior and posterior will only be similar if the data is not very informative.

Figure 11.25 shows a heatmap with the relative error of computing the harmonic mean estimator compared to the analytical value. We can see than even for a simple 1D problem like the Beta-Binomial model the harmonic estimator can fail spectacularly.

As we will see in Section 11.8 when we increase the dimensionality of our models the posterior concentrates more an more into a thin hyper-shell. Getting samples from outside this thin shell is irrelevant to compute a good posterior approximation. On the contrary when computing the marginal likelihood obtaining samples just from this thin shell is not enough. Instead, we need to take samples over the entire prior distribution and this can be a really hard task to do in a proper way.

There are a few computational methods better suited to compute marginal likelihood, but even those are not bullet-proof. In Chapter 8 we discuss the Sequential Monte Carlo (SMC) method mainly for the purpose of doing Approximate Bayesian Computation, but this method can also compute the marginal likelihood. The main reason why it works is because SMC uses a series of intermediate distributions to represent the transition from the prior to the posterior distributions. Having these *bridging* distribution alleviates the problem of sampling from a wide prior and evaluating in a much more concentrated posterior.

11.7.2   Marginal Likelihood and Model Comparison

When performing inference the marginal likelihood is generally regarded as a normalization constant and often could be omitted or canceled out during computation. Instead, the marginal

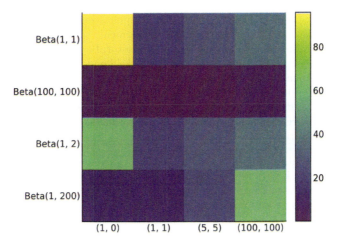

FIGURE 11.25
Heatmap showing the relative error when using the harmonic mean estimator to approximate the marginal likelihood of a Beta-Binomial model. Rows corresponds to different prior distributions. Each column is a different observed scenario, with the number in parentheses corresponding to the number of success and failures.

likelihood is often seen as crucial during model comparison [74, 109, 140]. To better understand why let us write Bayes' theorem in a way that explicitly shows that our inferences are model dependent:

$$p(\boldsymbol{\theta} \mid Y, M) = \frac{p(Y \mid \boldsymbol{\theta}, M)\, p(\boldsymbol{\theta} \mid M)}{p(Y \mid M)} \qquad (11.82)$$

where Y represents the data and $\boldsymbol{\theta}$ represents the parameters in model M.

If we have a set of k models and our main objective is to choose only one of them, we can choose the one with the largest value of the marginal likelihood $p(Y \mid M)$. Choosing the model with the largest marginal likelihood is perfectly justified from Bayes theorem under the assumption of a discrete Uniform prior distribution for the k models under comparison.

$$p(M \mid Y) \propto p(Y \mid M)\, p(M) \qquad (11.83)$$

If all models have the same a priori probability then computing $p(Y \mid M)$ is equivalent to computing $p(M \mid Y)$. Notice that we are talking about the prior probability we assign to models $p(M)$ and not about the priors we assign to parameters for each model $p(\theta \mid M)$.

As the value of $p(Y \mid M_k)$ does not tell us anything by-itself, in practice people usually compute the ratio of two marginal likelihoods. This ratio is called Bayes factor:

$$BF = \frac{p(Y \mid M_0)}{p(Y \mid M_1)} \qquad (11.84)$$

Values of $BF > 1$ indicates that model M_0 it is better at explaining the data when compared with model M_1. In practice it is common to use rules of thumb indicating when a BF is small, large, not that large, etc [21].

---

[21] We do not like these rules of thumb, but you can check, for example, here https://en.wikipedia.org/wiki/Bayes_factor#Interpretation

Bayes factor is appealing because it is a direct application of Bayes' theorem as we can see from Equation 11.83, but this is also true for the harmonic mean estimator (see Section 11.7.1) and that does not automatically makes it a good estimator. Bayes factor is also appealing because, contrary to the likelihood of a model, the marginal likelihood does not necessarily increases with the complexity of the model. The intuitive reason is that the larger the number of parameters the more *spread out* the prior will be with respect to the likelihood. Or in other words a more *spread out* prior is one that admits more datasets, as plausible, than a more concentrated one. This will be reflected in the marginal likelihood as we will get a smaller value with a wider prior than with a more concentrated prior.

Besides the computational problem, the marginal likelihood has a feature that it is usually considered as a bug. It is *very sensitive* to the choice of priors. By *very sensitive* we mean changes that while irrelevant for inference, have a practical effect in the value of the marginal likelihood. To exemplify this, assume we have the model:

$$\mu \sim \mathcal{N}(0, \sigma_0)$$
$$Y \sim \mathcal{N}(\mu, \sigma_1) \tag{11.85}$$

The marginal log-likelihood for this model is can be computed analytically as follows:

Code 11.7

```
1 σ_0 = 1
2 σ_1 = 1
3 y = np.array([0])
4 stats.norm.logpdf(loc=0, scale=(σ_0**2 + σ_1**2)**0.5, x=y).sum()
```

```
-1.2655121234846454
```

If you change the value of the prior parameter σ_0 to 2.5 instead of 1, the marginal likelihood will be about 2 times smaller and by changing it to 10 it will be about 7 times smaller. You can use a PPL to compute the posterior for this model and see for yourself how influential is the change of the prior in the posterior. Additionally you can check Figure 11.26 in the next section.

11.7.3 Bayes Factor vs WAIC and LOO

In this book we do not use Bayes factors to compare model, we prefer instead the use of LOO. So it maybe useful to better understand how BFs are related to these other estimators. If we omit the details we can say that:

- WAIC is the posterior-averaged log-likelihood
- LOO is the posterior-averaged log-likelihood
- The marginal likelihood is the prior-averaged (log)likelihood [22].

Let us discuss how this helps to understand the similarities and differences between these three quantities. All of them use a log-score as a measure of fitness with different computation. WAIC use a penalization term computed from the posterior variance. While both LOO and marginal likelihood avoids needing to use an explicit penalization term. LOO achieves this by approximating a leave-one-out cross-validation procedure. That is, it approximates using a dataset to fit the data and a different dataset to evaluate its fit. The penalization in marginal likelihood comes from

---

[22] In practice it is very common to actually compute the marginal likelihood in log-scale for computational stability. In such a case a Bayes factor becomes a difference of two log marginal likelihoods

averaging over the entire prior, with the spread of the prior (relatively) to the likelihood working as built-in penalizer. The penalization used in the marginal likelihood it seems to be somehow similar to the penalization in WAIC, although WAIC uses the variance of the posterior and so is close to the penalization in cross validation. Because, as previously discussed, a more spread prior admits more datasets as plausible than a more concentrated one, computing marginal likelihood is like implicitly averaging over all the datasets admitted by the prior.

An alternative, and equivalent, way to conceptualize the marginal likelihood is to notice that it is the prior predictive distribution evaluated at a particular dataset Y. Thus, it is telling us how likely the data is under our model. And the model includes the prior and the likelihood.

For WAIC and LOO the role of the prior is indirect. The prior affects the value of WAIC and LOO only by its effect on the posterior. The more informative the data with respect to the prior, or in other words the greater the difference between prior and posterior, the less sensitive will be WAIC and LOO to the details of the prior. Instead, marginal likelihood use priors directly as we need to average the likelihood over the prior. Conceptually we can say that Bayes factors are focused on identifying the best model (and the prior is part of the model) while WAIC and LOO are focused on which (fitted) model and parameter will give the best predictions. Figure 11.26 shows 3 posteriors for the model defined in Equation 11.85, for $\sigma_0 = 1$, $\sigma_0 = 10$ and $\sigma_0 = 100$. As we can see, the posteriors are very close to each other, especially the last two. We can see that the values of WAIC and LOO only slightly change for the different posteriors, while the log marginal likelihood is sensitive to the choice of the prior. The posterior and log marginal likelihoods were computed analytically, WAIC and LOO were computed from samples from the posterior (for details see the accompanying code).

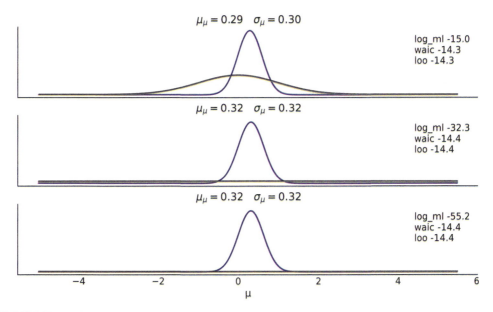

FIGURE 11.26
Prior (gray line) and posterior (blue line) for the model in Equation 11.85. WAIC and LOO reflect that the posterior distributions are almost identical, while the marginal likelihood reflects that the prior are different.

The above discussion helps to explain why Bayes factors are widely used in some fields and disliked in others. When priors are closer to reflecting some underlying *true* model, the sensitivity of the marginal likelihood to the prior specification is less worrisome. When priors are mainly used for their regularizing properties and when possible to provide some background knowledge, that sensitivity could be seen as problematic.

As a result, we think WAIC, and especially LOO, has more practical value, as their computation is generally more robust, and without the need to use special inference methods. And in the case of LOO, we also have good diagnostics.

11.8   Moving out of Flatland

In Flatland: A Romance of Many Dimensions by Edwin Abbott [1] it tells the story of a square living in flatland, a two dimensional world inhabited by n-side polygons and where status is defined by the number of sides; with women being simple line-segments, and priests insisting they are circles even when then are just high-order polygons. The novel, first published in 1984, works equally well as social satire about the difficulties to understand ideas beyond our common experience.

As it happens to Square in flatland we are now going to evidence the weirdness of higher-dimensional spaces.

Suppose we want to estimate the value of π. A simple procedure to do this is as follows. Inscribe a circle into a square, generate N points uniformly lying in that square and then count the proportion that fall inside the circle. Technically this is a Monte Carlo integration as we are calculating the value of a definite integral by using a (pseudo)random number generator.

The area of the circle and square are proportional to the number of points inside the circle and the total points. If the square has side $2R$, it area will be $(2R)^2$ and the circle inscribe it inside of the square will have area πR^2. The we have that:

$$\frac{\text{inside}}{N} \propto \frac{\pi R^2}{(2R)^2} \tag{11.86}$$

By simplifying and rearranging we get that we can approximate π as:

$$\hat{\pi} = 4\frac{\text{Count}_{inside}}{N} \tag{11.87}$$

We can implement this in a few lines of Python code as in Code Block 11.8 and the simulated points with the estimated value of π and the error of the approximation is shown in Figure 11.27.

Code 11.8

```
1  N = 10000
2  x, y = np.random.uniform(-1, 1, size=(2, N))
3  inside = (x**2 + y**2) <= 1
4  pi = inside.sum()*4/N
5  error = abs((pi - np.pi) / pi) * 100
```

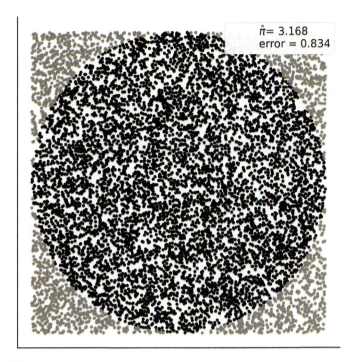

$\hat{\pi}= 3.168$
error = 0.834

FIGURE 11.27
Estimating π using Monte Carlo samples, legend shows the estimation and percentage error.

As the draws are iid, we can apply the central limit theorem here and then we know the error is reduced at a rate $\frac{1}{\sqrt{N}}$), meaning that for each additional decimal place of accuracy we want we will need to increase the number of draws N by a factor of 100.

What we have just done is an example of a Monte Carlo method [23], basically any method that uses (pseudo)random samples to compute something. And technically what we have done is a Monte Carlo integration as we are calculating the value of a definite integral (an area) by using samples. Monte Carlo methods are everywhere in statistics.

In Bayesian statistics we need to compute integrals to obtain posteriors or compute expectations from it. You may suggest that we can use a variation of this idea to compute quantities more interesting than π. It turns out that this method will generally not work very well as we increase the dimensionality of the problem. In Code Block 11.9 we count the number of points inside a circle when sampled from a square as we did before but from dimension 2 to 15. The result is in Figure 11.28, weirdly, we see that as we increase the dimension of the problem and even when the hypersphere is *touching* the walls of the hypercube, the proportion of points inside drops rapidly. In a sense in higher dimensions all the volume of the hypercube is at the corners [24].

Code 11.9

```
1  total = 100000
2
3  dims = []
4  prop = []
5  for d in range(2, 15):
```

---

[23] The names derived from a famous casino with that name in the Principality of Monaco.

[24] This video shows a closely related example in a very calm and clear way https://www.youtube.com/watch?v=zwAD6dRSVyI

```
6    x = np.random.random(size=(d, total))
7    inside = ((x * x).sum(axis=0) < 1).sum()
8    dims.append(d)
9    prop.append(inside / total)
```

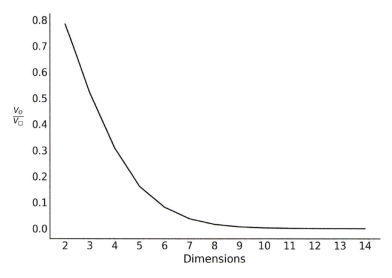

FIGURE 11.28

As we increase the dimensions the chance of getting a point inside an hypersphere inscribed into a hyper-cube goes to zero. This shows that in higher dimensions, almost all of the volume of an hypercube is in its corners.

Let us see another examples using Multivariate Gaussian. Figure 11.29 shows that as we increase the dimensionality of a Gaussian, most of the mass of that Gaussian is located further and further away from the mode. In fact, most of the mass is around an *annulus* at radius $\sqrt{d}$ from the mode, in other words as we increase the dimensionality of the Gaussian the mode becomes less and less typical. In higher dimensions the mode, which is also the mean, is actually an outlier. The reason is that it is very unusual for any given point to be average in all dimensions!

We can also see this from another perspective. The mode is always the point with highest density, even if in high dimensional space. The key insight is noting that it is unique (like the point from flatland!). If we move away from the mode we will find points that are individually less likely but there are a lot of them. As we saw in Section 11.1.5 a probability is computed as the integral of the density over a volume (actually an interval in the one dimensional case), so to find out where all the mass of a distribution is we have to balance both the density and their volume. As we increase the dimension of the Gaussian we will be most likely to pick a point from an *annulus* that excludes the mode. The region of the space containing most of the mass of a probability distribution is known as the typical set. In Bayesian statistics we care about it, because if we are going to approximate a high dimensional posterior with samples it suffices that the samples come from the typical set.

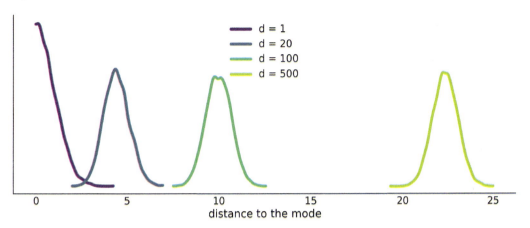

FIGURE 11.29
As we increase the dimension of a Gaussian most of the mass is distributed farther and farther away from the mode of that Gaussian.

11.9 Inference Methods

There a a myriad of methods to compute the posterior. If we exclude the exact analytical solutions we already discussed in Chapter 1 when we discussed conjugate priors, we can classify inference methods into 3 large groups:

1. Deterministic integration methods, that we have not yet seen in the book, but we will do next

2. Simulations methods, also introduced in Chapter 1 and the methods of choice through out the entire book and finally

3. Approximation methods, for example, the ABC method discussed in Chapter 8, in the case that the likelihood function does not have a closed form expression.

While some methods could be combinations of these categories, we still think it is useful as to order the plethora of available methods.

For a good chronological tour of Bayesian computation methods over the past two and a half centuries, with an special emphasis on those that transformed Bayesian inference we recommend you read Computing Bayes: Bayesian Computation from 1763 to the 21st Century [99]

11.9.1 Grid Method

The grid method is a simple brute-force approach. We want to know the value of posterior distribution over its domain to be able to use it (finding the maximum, computing expectation, etc). Even if you are not able to compute the whole posterior, you may be able to evaluate the prior and the likelihood density function point-wise; this is a pretty common scenario, if not the most common one. For a single parameter model, the grid approximation is:

- Find a reasonable interval for the parameter (the prior should give some hints).
- Define a grid of points (generally equidistant) on that interval.

- For each point in the grid, multiply the likelihood and the prior. Optionally, we may normalize the computed values so the posterior sum to 1 by dividing the result at each point by the sum of all points

Code Block 11.10 computes the posterior the Beta-Binomial model:

Code 11.10

```
1  def posterior_grid(ngrid=10, α=1, β=1, heads=6, trials=9):
2      grid = np.linspace(0, 1, ngrid)
3      prior = stats.beta(α, β).pdf(grid)
4      likelihood = stats.binom.pmf(heads, trials, grid)
5      posterior = likelihood * prior
6      posterior /= posterior.sum()
7      return posterior
```

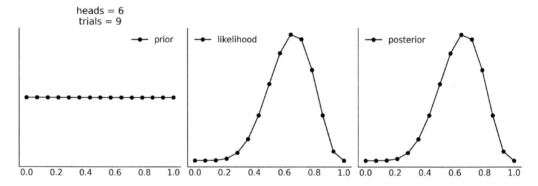

FIGURE 11.30
By evaluating the prior and the likelihood pointwise over a grid we can approximate the posterior.

We can get a better approximation by increasing the number of points of the grid. In fact if we use infinite number of points we will get the exact posterior, at the cost of needing infinite computing resources. The biggest caveat of the grid approach is that this method scales poorly with the number of parameters as explained in Section 11.8.

11.9.2   Metropolis-Hastings

We introduced Metropolis-Hastings algorithm [103, 78, 135] very early in Section 1.2 and show a simple Python implementation in Code Clock 1.3. We will now provide more detail about why this method works. We will do it using the language of Markov Chains introduced in Section 11.1.11.

The Metropolis-Hastings algorithm is a general method that allow us to start with any irreducible Markov chain on the state space of interest and then modify it into a new Markov chain that has the stationary distribution that we really care. In other words we take samples from an easy to sample distribution like a Multivariate Normal and we turn those samples into samples from our target distribution. The way we modify the original chain is by being selective, we only accept some of the samples and reject the others. As we saw in Chapter 1. The probability of accepting a new proposal is:

$$p_a(x_{i+1} \mid x_i) = \min\left(1, \frac{p(x_{i+1})\, q(x_i \mid x_{i+1})}{p(x_i)\, q(x_{i+1} \mid x_i)}\right) \qquad (1.9)$$

Let us rewrite this in a shorter form, for easier manipulation.

$$a_{ij} = \min\left(1, \frac{p_j q_{ji}}{p_i q_{ij}}\right) \tag{11.88}$$

That is we propose with probability q_{ij} (read the subscript ij as from i to j) and accepts the proposal with probability a_{ij}. One of the nice feature of this method is that we do not need to know the normalizing constant of the distribution we want to sample, as it will be cancelled out when we compute $\frac{p_j}{p_i}$. This is very important because in may many problems, including Bayesian inference, computing that normalization constant (the marginal likelihood) is very difficult.

We will now show that the Metropolis-Hastings chain is reversible with stationary distribution p as we mentioned in Section 11.1.11. We need to proof that the detailed balance condition i.e. the reversibility condition holds, that is:

Let $\mathbf{T}$ be the transition matrix, we just need to show that $p_i t_{ij} = p_j t_{ji}$ for all i and j, this is trivial when $i = j$ so we assume that $i \neq j$, we can write:

$$t_{ij} = q_{ij} a_{ij} \tag{11.89}$$

Meaning that the probability to transition from i to j is the probability of proposing the move times the probability of accepting it. Let us first see the case where the probability of acceptance is less that 1, this happens when $p_j q_{ji} \leq p_i q_{ij}$, then we have that

$$a_{ij} = \frac{p_j q_{ji}}{p_i q_{ij}} \tag{11.90}$$

and also

$$a_{ji} = 1 \tag{11.91}$$

Using Equation 11.89, we have

$$p_i t_{ij} = p_i q_{ij} a_{ij} \tag{11.92}$$

replacing a_{ij} in Equation 11.90

$$p_i t_{ij} = p_i q_{ij} \frac{p_j q_{ji}}{p_i q_{ij}} \tag{11.93}$$

simplifying above we get:

$$p_i t_{ij} = p_j q_{ji} \tag{11.94}$$

Because $a_{ji} = 1$ we can include it without changing the validity of the equation.

$$p_i t_{ij} = p_j q_{ji} a_{ji} \tag{11.95}$$

which finally we get that

$$p_i t_{ij} = p_j t_{ji} \tag{11.96}$$

By symmetry when $p_j q_{ji} > p_i q_{ij}$ we will arrive at the same result. As the reversibility condition holds, p is the stationary distribution of our Markov chain with transition matrix $\mathbf{T}$.

The above proof gives us the theoretical confidence that we can use Metropolis-Hastings to sample from virtually any distribution we want. We can also see that while this is a very general result, it does not help us to choose a proposal distribution. In practice the proposal distribution is very important as the efficiency of the method depends heavily on this choice. In general it is observed that if the proposal makes large jumps the probability of acceptance is very low, and the method spend most of the time rejecting new states and thus stuck in one place. On the contrary if the proposal takes too small jumps the acceptance rate is high but the exploration is poor, as the new states are in a small neighborhood of the old state. A good proposal distribution is one that generates new putative states far away from the old state with high acceptance rate. This is generally difficult to do if we do not know the geometry of the posterior distribution, but that is precisely what we want to find out. In practice useful Metropolis-Hastings methods are those that are adaptive [76, 5, 132, 141]. For example, we can use a Multivariate Gaussian distribution as proposal distribution. During tuning we can compute the empirical covariance from the posterior samples and use it as the covariance matrix of the proposal distribution. We can also scale the covariance matrix so that the average acceptance rate approach a predefined acceptance rate [62, 133, 11]. In fact there is evidence that under certain circumstances and when the dimensionality of the posterior increases the optimal acceptance rate converges to the magic number 0.234 [62]. In practice it seems that an acceptance rate around 0.234 or a little bit higher gives more or less the same performance but the general validity and useful of this result has also been disputed [142, 124].

In the next section we will discuss a clever way to generate proposals that help to correct most of the problems with basic Metropolis-Hastings.

11.9.3   Hamiltonian Monte Carlo

Hamiltonian Monte Carlo (HMC) [25] [50, 27, 14] is a type of MCMC method that makes use of gradients to generate new proposed states. The gradients of the log-probability of the posterior evaluated at some state provides information of the geometry of the posterior density function. HMC attempts to avoid the random walk behavior typical of Metropolis-Hastings by using the gradient to propose new positions far from the current one with high acceptance probability. This allows HMC to better scale to higher dimensions and in principle more complex geometries, than alternatives.

In simple terms, a Hamiltonian is a description of the total energy of a physical system. We can decompose the total energy into two terms, the kinetic and the potential energy. For a real system like rolling a ball down a hill, the potential energy is given by the position of the ball. The higher the ball the higher the potential energy. The kinetic energy is given by the velocity of the ball, or more correctly by its momentum (which takes into account both the velocity and the mass of the object). We will assume the total energy preserves, meaning that if the system gains kinetic energy then is because it has lost the same amount of potential energy. We can write the Hamiltonian of such a systems as:

$$H(\mathbf{q}, \mathbf{p}) = K(\mathbf{p}, \mathbf{q}) + V(\mathbf{q}) \tag{11.97}$$

where $K(\mathbf{p}, \mathbf{q})$ is called the kinetic energy, and $V(\mathbf{q})$ is the potential energy. The probability of finding the ball at a particular position with a particular momentum is then given by:

$$p(\mathbf{q}, \mathbf{p}) = e^{-H(\mathbf{q}, \mathbf{p})} \tag{11.98}$$

---

[25]The name Hybrid Monte Carlo is also used because is was originally conceived as a hybrid method combining molecular mechanics, a widely-used simulation technique for molecular systems, and Metropolis-Hastings.

To simulate such a systems we need to solve the so called Hamiltonian equations:

$$\frac{d\mathbf{q}}{dt} = \frac{\partial H}{\partial \mathbf{p}} = \frac{\partial K}{\partial \mathbf{p}} + \frac{\partial V}{\partial \mathbf{p}} \tag{11.99}$$

$$\frac{d\mathbf{p}}{dt} = -\frac{\partial H}{\partial \mathbf{q}} = -\frac{\partial K}{\partial \mathbf{q}} - \frac{\partial V}{\partial \mathbf{q}} \tag{11.100}$$

Note that $\frac{\partial V}{\partial \mathbf{p}} = \mathbf{0}$.

Because we are not interested in modeling an idealized ball rolling down an idealized hill, but to model an idealized particle along the posterior distribution, we need to make a few adjustments. First the potential energy is given by the probability density we are trying to sample from $p(\mathbf{q})$. For the momentum we are just going to invoke an auxiliary variable. That is, a made up variable that will help us. If we choose $p(\mathbf{p} \mid \mathbf{q})$ then we can write:

$$p(\mathbf{q}, \mathbf{p}) = p(\mathbf{p}|\mathbf{q})p(\mathbf{q}) \tag{11.101}$$

This ensures us that we can recover our target distribution by marginalize out the momentum. By introducing the auxiliary variable, we can keep working with the physical analogy, and later remove the auxiliary variable and go back to our problem, sampling the posterior. If we replace Equation 11.101 in Equation 11.98 we got:

$$H(\mathbf{q}, \mathbf{p}) = \overbrace{- \log p(\mathbf{p} \mid \mathbf{q})}^{K(\mathbf{p},\mathbf{q})} \overbrace{- \log p(\mathbf{q})}^{+V(\mathbf{q})} \tag{11.102}$$

As explained previously, the potential energy $V(\mathbf{q})$ is given by the $p(\mathbf{q})$ the density function of the target posterior distribution, and we are free to choose the kinetic energy. If we choose it to be Gaussian, and drop the normalization constant, we have:

$$K(\mathbf{p}, \mathbf{q}) = \frac{1}{2}\mathbf{p}^T M^{-1}\mathbf{p} + \log |M| \tag{11.103}$$

where M is the **precision matrix** that parameterized the Gaussian distribution (also referred to as the mass matrix in Hamiltonian Monte Carlo literature). And if we choose $M = I$, i.e. the identity matrix which is $n \times n$ square matrix with ones on the main diagonal and zeros elsewhere, we have:

$$K(\mathbf{p}, \mathbf{q}) = \frac{1}{2}\mathbf{p}^T \mathbf{p} \tag{11.104}$$

This makes calculations easier as now

$$\frac{\partial K}{\partial \mathbf{p}} = \mathbf{p} \tag{11.105}$$

and

$$\frac{\partial K}{\partial \mathbf{q}} = \mathbf{0} \tag{11.106}$$

We can then simplify Hamilton's equations to:

$$\frac{d\mathbf{q}}{dt} = \mathbf{p} \tag{11.107}$$

$$\frac{d\mathbf{p}}{dt} = -\frac{\partial V}{\partial \mathbf{q}} \tag{11.108}$$

Summarizing,the HMC algorithm is then:

1. Sample a $\mathbf{p} \sim \mathcal{N}(0, I)$

2. Simulate $\mathbf{q}_t$ and $\mathbf{p}_t$ for some amount of time T

3. $\mathbf{q}_T$ is our new proposed state

4. Use the Metropolis acceptance criterion to accept or reject $\mathbf{q}_T$.

Why we still need to use the Metropolis acceptance criterion? Intuitively because we can think of HMC as a Metropolis-Hasting algorithm with a better proposal distribution. But there is also a very good numerical justification, because this steps corrects for errors introduced by the numerical simulation of the Hamiltonian equations.

To compute the Hamiltonian equations we have to compute a trajectory of the particle, i.e. all the intermediate points between one state and the next. In practice this involves computing a series of small *integration* steps using an integrator method. The most popular one is the leapfrog integrator. Leapfrog integration is equivalent to updating positions q_t momentum q_t at interleaved time points, staggered in such a way that they *leapfrog* over each other.

Code Block 11.11 shows a leapfrog integrator implemented in Python [26]. The arguments are: q and p the initial position and momentum respectively. dVdq is a Python function that returns the gradient of the position of some target density function at position q $\frac{\partial V}{\partial \mathbf{q}}$. We used JAX [24] auto-differentiation ability to generate this function. `path_len` indicates how long to integrate for and `step_size` how large each integration step should be. As a result we obtain a new position and momentum as output of the function `leapfrog`.

Code 11.11

```
1  def leapfrog(q, p, dVdq, path_len, step_size):
2      p -= step_size * dVdq(q) / 2  # half step
3      for _ in range(int(path_len / step_size) - 1):
4          q += step_size * p  # whole step
5          p -= step_size * dVdq(q)  # whole step
6      q += step_size * p  # whole step
7      p -= step_size * dVdq(q) / 2  # half step
8
9      return q, -p  # momentum flip at end
```

Note that in function `leapfrog` we flip the sign of the output momentum. This is the simplest way to achieve a reversible Metropolis-Hastings proposal, as it augment the numerical integration with a negative step.

We have now all the ingredients to implement a HMC method in Python, as in Code Block 11.12. Like our previous Metropolis-Hasting example in Code Block 1.3 this is not meant to be use for serious model inference but instead a simple example to demonstrate the method. The arguments are `n_samples` the number of samples to return, `negative_log_prob` the negative log probability to sample from, `initial_position` the initial position to start sampling, `path_len`, `step_size`, as a result we obtain sample from the target distribution.

---

[26]Code copied from our good friend Colin Carroll's blogpost on HMC https://colindcarroll.com/2019/04/11/hamiltonian-monte-carlo-from-scratch/

Code 11.12

```
1  def hamiltonian_monte_carlo(
2      n_samples, negative_log_prob, initial_position,
3      path_len, step_size):
4      # autograd magic
5      dVdq = jax.grad(negative_log_prob)
6
7      # collect all our samples in a list
8      samples = [initial_position]
9
10     # Keep a single object for momentum resampling
11     momentum = stats.norm(0, 1)
12     # If initial_position is a 10d vector and n_samples is 100, we want
13     # 100 x 10 momentum draws. We can do this in one call to momentum.rvs, and
14     # iterate over rows
15     size = (n_samples,) + initial_position.shape[:1]
16     for p0 in momentum.rvs(size=size):
17         # Integrate over our path to get a new position and momentum
18         q_new, p_new = leapfrog(
19             samples[-1], p0, dVdq, path_len=path_len, step_size=step_size,
20         )
21
22         # Check Metropolis acceptance criterion
23         start_log_p = negative_log_prob(samples[-1]) - np.sum(momentum.logpdf(p0))
24         new_log_p = negative_log_prob(q_new) - np.sum(momentum.logpdf(p_new))
25         if np.log(np.random.rand()) < start_log_p - new_log_p:
26             samples.append(q_new)
27         else:
28             samples.append(np.copy(samples[-1]))
29
30     return np.array(samples[1:])
```

Figure 11.31 shows 3 different trajectories around the same 2D normal distribution. For practical sampling we do not want the trajectories to be circular, because they will arrive at the same position that we started at. Instead we want to move as far as possible from our starting point, for example, by avoiding U-turns in the trajectory, and hence the name of one of the most popular dynamic HMC method No U-Turn Sampling (NUTS).

We show another example in Figure 11.32, which contains 3 different trajectory around the same Neal's funnel, a common geometry arising in (centered) hierarchical models as we showed in 4.6.1. This is an example of a trajectory failing to properly simulate following the correct distribution, we call such trajectories divergent trajectories, or simply divergences. They are useful diagnostics as explained in Section 2.4.7. Usually, Symplectic integrators like leapfrog integrator are highly accurate even for long trajectories, as they tend to be tolerant of small errors and *oscillate* around the correct trajectory. Moreover, these small errors can be corrected exactly by applying the metropolis criteria to accept or reject the Hamiltonian proposal. However, there is an importance exception to this ability to generate small, easy to fix errors: when the exact trajectories lie on regions of high curvature, the numerical trajectories generated by symplectic integrators can diverge, generating trajectory that rapidly get off towards the boundaries of the distribution we are trying to explore.

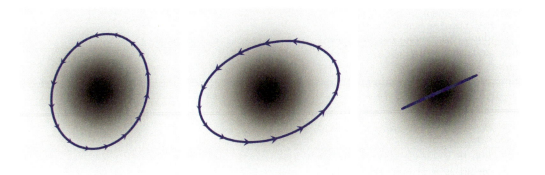

FIGURE 11.31

Three HMC trajectories *around* a 2D multivariate normal. The momentum is indicated by the size and direction of the arrows, with small arrows indicating small kinetic energy. All these trajectories are computed in such a way that they end at their starting position, which completing an elliptical trajectory.

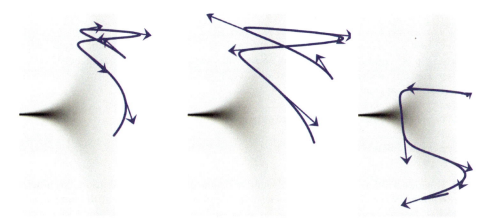

FIGURE 11.32

Three HMC trajectories *around* a 2D Neal's funnel. This kind geometry turns up in centered hierarchical models. We can see that all these trajectories when wrong. We call this kind these divergences and we can used as diagnostics of the HMC samplers.

Both Figures 11.31 and 11.32 highlight the fact that an efficient HMC method requires proper tuning of its hyperparameters. HMC has three hyparameters:

- the time discretization (step size of the leapfrog)
- the integration time (number of leapfrog steps)
- the precision matrix M that parameterized the kinetic energy

For example, if the step size is too large, the leapfrog integrator will be inaccurate and too many proposals will be rejected. However, if it is too small we will waste computation resources. If the number of steps is too small, the simulated trajectory at each iteration will be too short and sampling will fall back to random walk. But if it is too large the trajectory might runs in circles and we again waste computation resources. If the estimated covariance (inverse of the precision matrix) is too different from the posterior covariance, the proposal momentum will be suboptimal and the movement in the position space will be too large or too small in some dimension.

Adaptive dynamics Hamiltonian Monte Carlo methods, like those used by default in PyMC3, Stan and other PPLs can adapt these hyperparameters automatically during the warm-up or tuning phase. The step size can be learning automatically by adjusting it to match a predefined acceptance-rate target. For example, in PyMC3 you set the argument `target_accept` [27] The precision matrix M or its inverse can be estimated from the samples during warm-up phase and the number of steps can be dynamically adapted at each MCMC step using the NUTS algorithm [80]. In order to avoid too long trajectory that could go near the initialization point, NUTS extends the trajectory backward and forwards until a U-turn criterion is met. Additionally, NUTS applies a multinomial sampling to choose from all the generated points from the trajectory, as this provides a better criteria for efficient exploration of the target distribution (sampling from the trajectory could be done with fixed integration time HMC as well).

11.9.4 Sequential Monte Carlo

Sequential Monte Carlo is a family of Monte Carlo methods also known as particle filters. It has wide application to Bayesian inference for static models and dynamic models such as sequential time series inference and signal processing [44, 34, 108, 36]. There are many variations and implementation under the same or similar name, with different application. Thus you might at times find the literature a bit confusing. We will give a brief description of the SMC/SMC-ABC method as implemented in PyMC3 and TFP. For a detailed discussion of SMC methods under a unified framework we recommend the book An Introduction to Sequential Monte Carlo [36].

First note that we can write the posterior in the following way:

$$p(\boldsymbol{\theta} \mid Y)_\beta \propto p(Y \mid \boldsymbol{\theta})^\beta \, p(\boldsymbol{\theta}) \qquad (11.109)$$

When $\beta = 0$ we see that $p(\boldsymbol{\theta} \mid Y)_\beta$ is the prior and when $\beta = 1$ we see that $p(\boldsymbol{\theta} \mid Y)_\beta$ is the *true* posterior [28].

SMC proceeds by increasing the value of β in s successive stages $\{\beta_0 = 0 < \beta_1 < ... < \beta_s = 1\}$. Why is this a good idea? There are two related ways to justify it. First, the stepping stones analogy. Instead of directly trying to sample from the posterior we begin by sampling from the prior, which is generally easier to do. Then we add some intermediate distributions until we reach the posterior (see Figure 8.2). Second is the temperature analogy. The β parameters is analogue to the inverse temperature of a physical system, as we decrease its value (increase the temperature) the system is able to access to more states, and as we decrease its value (decrease the temperature) the system "freezes" into the posterior [29]. Figure 8.2 shows an hypothetical sequence of tempered posteriors. The use of the temperature (or its inverse) as an auxiliary parameter is known as tempering, the term annealing is also common [30].

The SMC method, as implemented in PyMC3 and TFP, can be summarized as follows:

1. Initialize β at zero.
2. Generate N samples s_β from the tempered posterior.

---

[27]This value is in the interval $[0, 1]$, and by default this value is 0.8. See Section 2.4.7.

[28]We mean true purely from a mathematical point of view, without any reference to how adequate is such posterior to any particular practical problem.

[29]See Section 11.2 for more details on this analogy with physical system.

[30]These terms are borrowed from metallurgy in particular describing specific processes where alloyed metal is heated and cooled to obtain a particular molecular structure.

3. Increase β in order to keep the effective sample size [31] at a predefined value.

4. Compute a set of N importance weights W. The weights are computed according to the new and old tempered posterior.

5. Obtain s_w by resampling s_β according to W.

6. Run N MCMC chains for k steps, starting each one from a different sample in s_w and retaining only the samples in the last step.

7. Repeat from step 3 until $\beta = 1$

The resampling step works by removing samples with a low probability and replacing them with samples with a higher probability. This step decreases the diversity of the samples. Then, the MCMC step perturbs the samples, hopefully increasing the diversity and therefore helping SMC to explore the parameter space. Any valid MCMC transition kernel could be used in SMC, and depending on your problem you might find some perform better than others. For example, with ABC methods we generally need to rely on gradient-free methods such as Random Walk Metropolis-Hasting as the simulators are generally not differentiable.

The efficiency of the tempered method depends heavily on the intermediate values of β. The smaller the difference between two successive values of β, the closer the two successive tempered posteriors will be, and thus the easier the transition from one stage to the next. But if the steps are too small, we will need many intermediate stages, and beyond some point this will waste a lot of computational resources without really improving the accuracy of the results. Another important factor is the efficiency of the MCMC transitional kernel that adds diversity to the samples. To help improve the efficiency of the transition, PyMC3 and TFP uses the samples from the previous stage to tune the proposal distribution of the current stage and also the number of steps taken by the MCMC, with the number of steps being the same across all chains.

11.9.5   Variational Inference

While we do not use variational inference in this book, it is a useful approach to know about. Compared to MCMC, VI tends to be easier to scale to large data and is faster to run computationally, but with less theoretical guarantees of convergence [164].

As we previously mentioned in Section 11.3, we can use one distribution to approximate another and then use the Kullback-Leibler (KL) divergence to measure how good the approximation is. Turns out we can use this approach to do Bayesian inference as well! Such approach is called variational inference (VI) [19]. The goal of VI is to approximate the target probability density, in our case the posterior distribution $p(\boldsymbol{\theta} \mid Y)$, with a surrogate distribution $q(\boldsymbol{\theta})$. In practice we usually choose $q(\boldsymbol{\theta})$ to be of simpler form than $p(\boldsymbol{\theta} \mid Y)$, and we find the member of that family of distributions, which is the closest to the target in the KL divergence sense, using optimization. With small rewrite to Equation 11.41, we have:

$$\mathbb{KL}(q(\boldsymbol{\theta}) \parallel p(\boldsymbol{\theta} \mid Y)) = \mathbb{E}_q[\log q(\boldsymbol{\theta}) - \log p(\boldsymbol{\theta} \mid Y)] \tag{11.110}$$

However, this objective is hard to compute because it requires the marginal likelihood of $p(Y)$. To see that let us expand Equation 11.110:

$$\begin{aligned}\mathbb{KL}(q(\boldsymbol{\theta}) \parallel p(\boldsymbol{\theta} \mid Y)) &= \mathbb{E}[\log q(\boldsymbol{\theta})] - \mathbb{E}[\log p(\boldsymbol{\theta} \mid Y)] \\ &= \mathbb{E}[\log q(\boldsymbol{\theta})] - \mathbb{E}[\log p(\boldsymbol{\theta}, Y)] + \log p(Y)\end{aligned} \tag{11.111}$$

---

[31]This effective sample size is computed from the importance weights which is different from the ESS we have been computing to diagnosing MCMC samplers, that is computed from the autocorrelation of the samples.

Luckily, since $\log p(Y)$ is a constant with respect to $q(\boldsymbol{\theta})$, we can omit it during optimization. Thus, in practice, we maximize the evidence lower bound (ELBO) as shown in Equation 11.112, which is equivalent to minimizing the KL divergence:

$$\text{ELBO}(q) = \mathbb{E}[\log p(\boldsymbol{\theta}, Y)] - \mathbb{E}[\log q(\boldsymbol{\theta})] \qquad (11.112)$$

The last piece of the puzzle is to figure out how to compute the expectation in Equation 11.112. Instead of solving an expensive integration, we compute the average using Monte Carlo samples drawn from the surrogate distribution $q(\boldsymbol{\theta})$ and plug them into 11.112.

The performance of VI depends on many factors. One of them being the family of surrogate distributions we choose from. For example, a more expressive surrogate distribution helps capture more complex, nonlinear dependencies among components of the target posterior distribution, and thus usually gives better result (see Figure 11.33). Automatically choosing a good surrogate family distribution and efficiently optimizing it is currently an active research area. Code Block 11.13 shows a simple example of using VI in TFP, with two different types of surrogate posterior distributions. The result is shown in Figure 11.33.

Code 11.13

```
1  tfpe = tfp.experimental
2  # An arbitrary density function as target
3  target_logprob = lambda x, y: -(1.-x)**2 - 1.5*(y - x**2)**2
4
5  # Set up two different surrogate posterior distribution
6  event_shape = [(), ()]   # theta is 2 scalar
7  mean_field_surrogate_posterior = tfpe.vi.build_affine_surrogate_posterior(
8      event_shape=event_shape, operators="diag")
9  full_rank_surrogate_posterior = tfpe.vi.build_affine_surrogate_posterior(
10     event_shape=event_shape, operators="tril")
11
12 # Optimization
13 losses = []
14 posterior_samples = []
15 for approx in [mean_field_surrogate_posterior, full_rank_surrogate_posterior]:
16     loss = tfp.vi.fit_surrogate_posterior(
17         target_logprob, approx, num_steps=100, optimizer=tf.optimizers.Adam(0.1),
18         sample_size=5)
19     losses.append(loss)
20     # approx is a tfp distribution, we can sample from it after training
21     posterior_samples.append(approx.sample(10000))
```

11.10 Programming References

Part of computational Bayes is well, the computer and the software tools now available. Using these tools help modern Bayesian practitioner share models, reduce mistakes, and speed up the model building and inference process. To have the computer work for us we need to program it but often this is easier said than done. To use them effectively still requires thought and understanding. In this last section we will provide some high level guidance for the major concepts.

Mean-field Approximation   Full-rank Approximation

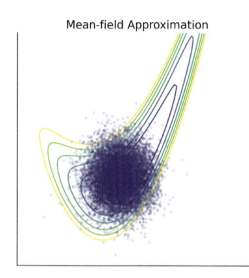 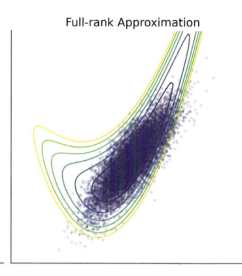

FIGURE 11.33
Using variational inference to approximate a target density function. The target density is
a 2D banana shaped function plotted using contour lines. Two types of surrogate posterior
distributions are used for the approximation: on the left panel a mean-field Gaussian (one
univariate Gaussian for each dimension with trainable location and scale) and on the right
panel a full-rank Gaussian (a 2D multivariate Gaussian with trainable mean and covariance
matrix) [90]. Samples from the approximation after optimization are plotted as dots overlay
on top of the true density. Comparing the two, you can see that while both approximations does not fully capture the shape of the target density, full-rank Gaussian is a better
approximation thanks to its more complex structure.

11.10.1   Which Programming Language?

There are many programming languages. We primarily used Python, but other popular languages
such as Julia, R, C/C++ exist with specialized application for Bayesian computation as well. So
which programming language should you use? There is no universal right or wrong answer here.
Instead you should always consider the complete ecosystem. In this book we use Python because
packages like ArviZ, Matplotlib, and Pandas to make data processing and displaying easy. This is
not exclusive to Python. For a Bayesian specifically consider the PPLs available in that particular
language, because if none exists then you might want to reconsider your programming language
of choice. Also consider the community you want to work with and what language they use. One
of the authors of this book lives in Southern California, so knowing English, and a bit of Spanish
makes a lot of sense, because with those two he could communicate in common situations. It is the
same with programming languages, if you future lab group uses R then learning R is a good idea.

Computational purists may exclaim that some languages are faster than others computationally.
This of course is true but we advise not getting too wrapped up in the discussion of "which is the
fastest ppl". In real life scenarios different models take different amount of time to run. Additionally
there is "human time" which is the time for one to iterate and come up with a model, and "model
run time" which is the time it takes for the computer to return a useful result. These are not
the same and in different situations one is more important than the other. This is all to say, do
not worry too much about picking the "right" up front language, if you learn one effectively the
concepts will transfer to another.

11.10.2   Version Control

Version control is not necessary but is absolutely recommended and will incur great benefits if utilized. When working alone, version control lets you iterate through model designs without worry about losing your code or making changes or experiment that breaks your model. This by itself lets you iterate quicker and with more confidence, as well as the ability to switch back and forth between different model definitions. When working with others, version control enables collaboration and code sharing, that would be challenging or impossible to perform without the snapshotting or comparison features that version control systems allows. There are many different version control systems (Mercurial, SVN, Perforce) but git is currently the most popular. Version control is not typically tied to a particular programming language.

11.10.3   Dependency Management and Package Repositories

Nearly all code relies on other code to run (it is turtles all the way down). PPLs in particular rely on a lot of different libraries to run. We strongly suggest familiarizing yourself with a requirements management tool that helps you see, list, and freeze the packages your analysis relies on. Additionally package repositories are where these requirement packages are fetched from. These are typically specific to the language, for example, one requirements management tool in Python is pip, and a popular cloud repository is pypi. In Scala sbt is one tool that helps with dependencies and Maven is a popular package repository. All mature languages will have this tooling, but you must make the conscious choice to use them.

11.10.4   Environment Management

All code executes in an environment. Most people forget this until their code suddenly stops working, or does not work on another computer. Environment management is the set of tools used to create a reproducible computation environment. This is of particular importance to Bayesian Modelers who deal with enough randomness in their models, and do not want the computer to add an additional layer of variability. Unfortunately Environment Management is also one of the most confusing portions of programming. In general there are two rough types of environment control, language specific and language agnostic. In Python virtualenv is a python specific environment manager, whereas containerization and virtualization are language agnostic. We have no specific suggestion here as the choice depends largely on your comfort with these tool, and also where you plan to run the code. We do absolutely recommend making a deliberate choice here though, as it makes sure you have reproducible results.

11.10.5   Text Editor vs Integrated Development Environment vs Notebook

When writing code, you must well, write it somewhere. For data minded folks there are typically three interfaces for this.

The first and simplest is a text editor. The most basic text editors allow you to, surprise, edit text and save it. With these editors you can write a python program, save it, and then run it. Typically text editors are very "light weight" and do not include much extra functionality besides basic things like find and replace. Think of text editors like a bicycle. They are simple, their interface is basically a handlebar and some pedals, and they will get you from here to there but its mostly on you to do the work.

Integrated Development Environments (IDE) by comparison the modern airplanes. They have an insane amount of functionality, a lot buttons, and a lot of automation. IDEs let you edit text at their core, but as the name suggests they integrate many other aspects of development as well. For example, functionality for running code, unit-testing, linting code, version control, code version comparison, and much much more. IDEs are typically most useful when writing a lot of complicated code that spans many modules.

While we would love to provide a simple definition of a text editor vs IDE, the line these days is very blurry. Our suggestion is start more on the text editor side and move to IDEs once familiar with how code works. Otherwise it will be hard for you to tell what the IDE is doing for you "under the hood".

Notebooks are an entirely different interface. Notebooks are special in they mix code, output, and documentation, as well as allowing nonlinear code execution. For this book the majority of the code, and figures, are presented in Jupyter Notebook files. We also provide links to Google Colab which a cloud notebook environment. Notebooks are typically best used for exploratory data analysis, and explanatory type situations, such as this book. They are not so well suited for running production code.

Our suggestion for notebooks is similar to IDEs. If new to statistical computing start with a text editor first. Once you have a strong handle of how to run code from individual files, then move to notebook environments, either a cloud hosted Google colab, or Binder instance, or a local Jupyter Notebook

11.10.6   The Specific Tools Used for this Book

Here is what we used for this book. This does not mean these are the only tools you can use, these are just the ones we used.

- **Programming Language**: Python
- **Probabilistic Programming Languages**: PyMC3, TensorFlow Probability. Stan and Numpyro are displayed briefly as well.
- **Version control**: git
- **Dependency Management**: pip and conda
- **Package repository**: pypi, conda-forge
- **Environment Management**: conda
- **General Documentation**: LaTeX (for book writing), Markdown (for code package), Jupyter Notebooks

Glossary

Autocorrelation: Autocorrelation is the correlation of a signal with a lagged copy of itself. Conceptually, you can think of it as how similar observations are as a function of the time lag between them. Large autocorrelation is a concern in MCMC samples as it reduces the effective sample size.

Aleatoric Uncertainty: Aleatoric uncertainty is related to the notion that there are some quantities that affect a measurement or observation that are intrinsically unknowable or random. For example, even if we were able to exactly replicate condition such as direction, altitude and force when shooting an arrow with a bow. The arrow will still not hit the same point, because there are other conditions that we do not control like fluctuations of the atmosphere or vibrations of the arrow shaft, that are random.

Bayesian Inference: Bayesian Inference is a particular form of statistical inference based on combining probability distributions in order to obtain other probability distributions. In other words is the formulation and computation of conditional probability or probability densities, $p(\boldsymbol{\theta} \mid \boldsymbol{Y}) \propto p(\boldsymbol{Y} \mid \boldsymbol{\theta})p(\boldsymbol{\theta})$.

Bayesian workflow: Designing a good enough model for a given problem requires significant statistical and domain knowledge expertise. Such design is typically carried out through an iterative process called Bayesian workflow. This process includes the three steps of model building [64]: inference, model checking/improvement, and model comparison. In this context the purpose of model comparison is not necessarily restricted to pick the *best* model, but more importantly to better understand the models.

Causal inference: or Observational causal inference. The procedures and tools used to estimate the impact of a treatment (or intervention) in some system without testing the intervention. That is from observational data instead of experimental data.

Covariance Matrix and Precision Matrix: The covariance matrix is a square matrix that contains the covariance between each pair of elements of a collection of random variable. The diagonal of the covariance matrix is the variance of the random variable. The precision matrix is the matrix inverse of the covariance matrix.

Design Matrix: In the context of regression analysis a design matrix is a matrix of values of the explanatory variables. Each row represents an individual object, with the successive columns corresponding to the variables and their specific values for that observation. It can contain indicator variables (ones and zeros) indicating group membership, or it can contain continuous values.

Decision tree: A decision tree is a flowchart-like structure in which each internal node represents a "test" on an attribute (e.g. whether a coin flip comes up heads or tails), each branch represents the outcome of the test, and each leaf node represents a class label (decision taken after computing all attributes). The paths from root to leaf represent classification rules. The values at the leaf nodes can be continuous if the tree is used for regression.

dse: The standard error of component-wise differences of `elpd_loo` between two models. This error is smaller than the standard error (`se` in `az.compare`) for individual models. The reason being that generally some observations are as easy/hard to predict for all models and thus this introduce correlations.

d_loo: The difference in elpd_loo) for two models. If more than two models are compared, the difference is computed relative to the model with highest elpd_loo).

Epistimic Uncertainty: Epistemic uncertainty is related to the lack of knowledge of the states of a system by some observer. It is related to the knowledge that we could have in principle but not in practice and not about the intrinsic unknowable quantity of nature (contrast with aleatory uncertainty). For example, we may be uncertain of the weight of an item because we do not have an scale at hand, so we estimate the weight by lifting it, or we may have one scale but with a precision limited to the kilogram. We could also have epistemic uncertainty if we design an experiment or perform a computation ignoring factors. For example, to estimate how much time we will have to drive to another city, we may omit the time spent at tolls, or we may assume excellent weather or road conditions etc. In other words epistemic uncertainty is about ignorance and in opposition to aleatoric, uncertainty, we can in principle reduce it by obtaining more information.

Statistic A statistic (not plural) or sample statistic is any quantity computed from a sample. Sample statistics are computed for several reasons including estimating a population (or data generating process) parameter, describing a sample, or evaluating a hypothesis. The sample mean (also known as empirical mean) is a statistic, the sample variance (or empirical variance) is another example. When a statistic is used to estimate a population (or data generating process) parameter, the statistic is called an estimator. Thus, the sample mean can be an estimator and the posterior mean can be another estimator.

ELPD: Expected Log-pointwise Predictive Density (or expected log pointwise predictive probabilities for discrete model). This quantity is generally estimated by cross-validation or using methods such as WAIC (elpd_waic) or LOO (elpd_loo). As probability densities can be smaller or larger than 1, the ELPD can be negative or positive for continuous variables and non-negative for discrete variables.

Exchangeability: A sequence of Random variables is exchangeable if their joint probability distribution does not change when the positions in the sequence is altered. Exchangeable random variables are not necessarily iid, but iid are exchangeable.

Exploratory Analysis of Bayesian Models: The collection of tasks necessary to perform a successful Bayesian data analysis that are not the inference itself. This includes. Diagnosing the quality of the inference results obtained using numerical methods. Model criticism, including evaluations of both model assumptions and model predictions. Comparison of models, including model selection or model averaging. Preparation of the results for a particular audience.

Hamiltonian Monte Carlo Hamiltonian Monte Carlo (HMC) is a Markov chain Monte Carlo (MCMC) method that uses the gradient to efficiently explore a probability distribution function. In Bayesian statistics this is most commonly used to obtain samples from the posterior distribution. HMC methods are instances of the Metropolis–Hastings algorithm, where the proposed new points are computed from a Hamiltonian, this allows the methods to proposed new states to be far from the current one with high acceptance probability. The evolution of the system is simulated using a time-reversible and volume-preserving numerical integrator (most commonly the leapfrog integrator). The efficiency of the HMC method is highly dependant on certain hyperparameters of the method. Thus, the most useful methods in Bayesian statistics are adaptive dynamics versions of HMC that can adjust those hyperparameters automatically during the warm-up or tuning phase.

Heteroscedasticity: A sequence of random variables is heteroscedastic if its random variables do not have the same variance, i.e. if they are not homoscedastic. This is also known as heterogeneity of variance.

Homoscedasticity: A sequence of random variables is homoscedastic if all its random variables have the same finite variance. This is also known as homogeneity of variance. The complementary notion is called heteroscedasticity.

iid: Independent and identically distributed. A collection of random variables is independent and identically distributed if each random variable has the same probability distribution as the others and all are mutually independent. If a collection of random variables is iid it is also exchangeable, but the converse is not necessarily true.

Individual Conditional Expectation ICE: An ICE shows the dependence between the response variable and a covariate of interest. This is done for each sample separately with one line per sample. This contrast to PDPs where the average effect of the covariate is represented.

Inference: Colloquially, inference is reaching a conclusion based on evidence and reasoning. In this book refer to inference we generally mean about Bayesian Inference, which has a more restricted and precise definition. Bayesian Inference is the process of conditioning models to the available data and obtaining posterior distributions. Thus, in order to reach a conclusion based on evidence and reasoning, we need to perform more steps that mere Bayesian inference. Hence the importance of discussing Bayesian analysis in terms of exploratory analysis of Bayesian models or more generally in term of Bayesian workflows.

Imputation: Replacing missing data values through a method of choice. Common methods may include most common occurrence or interpolation based on other (present) observed data.

KDE: Kernel Density Estimation. A non-parametric method to estimate the probability density function of a random variable from a finite set of samples. We often use the term KDE to talk about the estimated density and not the method.

LOO: Short for Pareto smoothed importance sampling leave one out cross-validation (PSIS-LOO-CV). In the literature "LOO" may be restricted to leave one out cross-validation.

Maximum a Posteriori (MAP) An estimator of an unknown quantity, that equals the mode of the posterior distribution. The MAP estimator requires optimization of the posterior, unlike the posterior mean which requires integration. If the priors are flat, or in the limit of infinite sample size, the MAP estimator is equivalent to the Maximum Likelihood estimator.

Odds A measure of the likelihood of a particular outcome. They are calculated as the ratio of the number of events that produce that outcome to the number that do not. Odds are commonly used in gambling.

Overfitting: A model overfits when produces predictions too closely to the dataset used for fitting the model failing to fit new datasets. In terms of the number of parameters an overfitted model contains more parameters than can be justified by the data.[2] An arbitrary over-complex model will fit not only the data but also the noise, leading to poor predictions.

Partial Dependence Plots PDP: A PDP shows the dependence between the response variable and a set of covariates of interest, this is done by marginalizing over the values of all other covariates. Intuitively, we can interpret the partial dependence as the expected value of the response variable as function of the covariates of interest.

Pareto k estimates $\hat{k}$: A diagnostic for Pareto smoothed importance sampling (PSIS), which is used by LOO. The Pareto k diagnostic estimates how far an individual leave-one-out observation is from the full distribution. If leaving out an observation changes the posterior too much then importance sampling is not able to give reliable estimates. If $\hat{\kappa} < 0.5$, then the corresponding component of `elpd_loo` is estimated with high accuracy. If $0.5 < \hat{\kappa} < 0.7$ the accuracy is lower, but still useful in practice. If $\hat{\kappa} > 0.7$, then importance sampling is not able to provide a useful estimate for that observation. The $\hat{\kappa}$ values are also useful as a measure of influence of an observation. Highly influential observations have high $\hat{\kappa}$ values. Very high $\hat{\kappa}$ values often indicate model misspecification, outliers, or mistakes in the data processing.

Point estimate A single value, generally but not necessarily in parameter space, used as a summary of *best estimate* of an unknown quantity. A point estimate can be contrasted with an interval estimate like highest density intervals, which provides a range or interval of values describing the unknown quantity. We can also contrast a point estimate with distributional estimates, like the posterior distribution or its marginals.

p_loo: The difference between `elpd_loo:` and the non-cross-validated log posterior predictive density. It describes how much more difficult it is to predict future data than the observed data. Asymptotically under certain regularity conditions, **p_loo** can be interpreted as the effective number of parameters. In well behaving cases **p_loo** should be lower than the number of parameters in the model and smaller than the number observations in the data. If not, this is an indication that the model has very weak predictive capability and may thus indicate a severe model misspecification. See high Pareto k diagnostic values.

Probabilistic Programming Language: A programming syntax composed of primitives that allows one to define Bayesian models and perform inference automatically. Typically a Probabilistic Programming Language also includes functionality to generate prior or posterior predictive samples or even to analysis result from inference.

Prior predictive distribution: The expected distribution of the data according to the model (prior and likelihood). That is, the data the model is expecting to see before seeing any data. See Equation 1.7. The prior predictive distribution can be used for prior elicitation, as it is generally easier to think in terms of the observed data, than to think in terms of model parameters.

Posterior predictive distribution: This is the distribution of (future) data according to the posterior, which in turn is a consequence of the model (prior and likelihood) and observed data. In other words, these are the model's predictions. See Equation 1.8. Besides generating predictions, the posterior predictive distribution can be used to asses the model fit, by comparing it with the observed data.

Residuals: The difference between an observed value and the estimated value of the quantity of interest. If a model assumes that the variance is finite and the same for all residuals, we say we have homoscedasticity. If instead the variance can change, we say we have heteroscedasticity.

Sufficient statistics: A statistic is sufficient with respect to a model parameter if no other statistic computed from the same sample provides any additional information about that sample. In other words, that statistic is *sufficient* to summarize your samples without losing information. For example, given a sample of independent values from a normal distribution with expected value μ and known finite variance the sample mean is sufficient statistics for μ. Notice that the mean says nothing about the dispersion, thus it is only sufficient with respect to the parameter μ. It is known that for iid data the only distributions with a sufficient statistic with dimension equal to the dimension of θ are the distributions from the exponential family. For other distribution, the dimension of the sufficient statistic increases with the sample size.

Synthetic data: Also known as fake data it refers to data generated from a model instead of being gathered from experimentation or observation. Samples from the posterior/prior predictive distributions are examples of synthetic data.

Timestamp: A timestamp is an encoded information to identify when a certain event happens. Usually a timestamp is written in the format of date and time of day, with more accurate fraction of a second when necessary.

Turing-complete In colloquial usage, is used to mean that any real-world general-purpose computer or computer language can approximately simulate the computational aspects of any other real-world general-purpose computer or computer language.

Bibliography

[1] E.A. Abbott and R. Jann. *Flatland: A Romance of Many Dimensions*. Oxford World's Classics. OUP Oxford, 2008. ISBN: 9780199537501.

[2] Ryan Prescott Adams and David JC MacKay. "Bayesian online changepoint detection". In: *arXiv preprint arXiv:0710.3742* (2007).

[3] Hirotogu Akaike. "Information theory and an extension of the maximum likelihood principle". In: *Selected papers of hirotugu akaike*. Springer, 1998, pp. 199–213.

[4] Erling Bernhard Andersen. "Sufficiency and exponential families for discrete sample spaces". In: *Journal of the American Statistical Association* 65.331 (1970), pp. 1248–1255.

[5] Christophe Andrieu and Johannes Thoms. "A tutorial on adaptive MCMC". In: *Statistics and computing* 18.4 (2008), pp. 343–373.

[6] Matej Balog and Yee Whye Teh. "The Mondrian process for machine learning". In: *arXiv preprint arXiv:1507.05181* (2015).

[7] Douglas Bates et al. "Fitting linear mixed-effects models using lme4". In: *arXiv preprint arXiv:1406.5823* (2014).

[8] Mark A. Beaumont. "Approximate Bayesian Computation". In: *Annual review of statistics and its application* 6 (2019), pp. 379–403.

[9] Mark A. Beaumont. "Approximate Bayesian computation in evolution and ecology". In: *Annual review of ecology, evolution, and systematics* 41 (2010), pp. 379–406.

[10] Mark A. Beaumont, Wenyang Zhang, and David J Balding. "Approximate Bayesian computation in population genetics". In: *Genetics* 162.4 (2002), pp. 2025–2035.

[11] Mylene Bedard. "Optimal acceptance rates for Metropolis algorithms: Moving beyond 0.234". In: *Stochastic Processes and their Applications* 118.12 (2008), pp. 2198–2222.

[12] Jon Louis Bentley. "Multidimensional binary search trees used for associative searching". In: *Communications of the ACM* 18.9 (1975), pp. 509–517.

[13] Espen Bernton et al. "Approximate Bayesian computation with the Wasserstein distance". In: *Journal of the Royal Statistical Society: Series B (Statistical Methodology)* 81.2 (2019), pp. 235–269.

[14] Michael Betancourt. "A conceptual introduction to Hamiltonian Monte Carlo". In: *arXiv preprint arXiv:1701.02434* (2017).

[15] Michael Betancourt. *Hierarchical Modeling*. https://betanalpha.github.io/assets/case_studies/hierarchical_modeling.html. Nov. 2020.

[16] Michael Betancourt. *Towards A Principled Bayesian Workflow*. https://betanalpha.github.io/assets/case_studies/principled_bayesian_workflow.html. Apr. 2020.

[17] Peter Bickel, Bo Li, Thomas Bengtsson, et al. "Sharp failure rates for the bootstrap particle filter in high dimensions". In: *Pushing the limits of contemporary statistics: Contributions in honor of Jayanta K. Ghosh*. Institute of Mathematical Statistics, 2008, pp. 318–329.

[18] Eli Bingham et al. "Pyro: Deep universal probabilistic programming". In: *The Journal of Machine Learning Research* 20.1 (2019), pp. 973–978.

[19] David M. Blei, Alp Kucukelbir, and Jon D. McAuliffe. "Variational inference: A review for statisticians". In: *Journal of the American statistical Association* 112.518 (2017), pp. 859–877.

[20] Justin Bleich et al. "Variable selection for BART: an application to gene regulation". In: *The Annals of Applied Statistics* (2014), pp. 1750–1781.

[21] J.K. Blitzstein and J. Hwang. *Introduction to Probability, Second Edition*. Chapman & Hall/CRC Texts in Statistical Science. CRC Press, 2019. ISBN: 9780429766732.

[22] A.L. Bowley. *Elements of Statistics*. Elements of Statistics v. 2. P.S. King, 1920.

[23] G.E.P. Box, G.M. Jenkins, and G.C. Reinsel. *Time Series Analysis: Forecasting and Control*. Wiley Series in Probability and Statistics. Wiley, 2008. ISBN: 9780470272848.

[24] James Bradbury et al. *JAX: composable transformations of Python+NumPy programs*. Version 0.2.5. 2018. URL: `http://github.com/google/jax`.

[25] Leo Breiman. "Random forests". In: *Machine learning* 45.1 (2001), pp. 5–32.

[26] Leo Breiman. "Statistical modeling: The two cultures (with comments and a rejoinder by the author)". In: *Statistical science* 16.3 (2001), pp. 199–231.

[27] S. Brooks et al. *Handbook of Markov Chain Monte Carlo*. Chapman & Hall/CRC Handbooks of Modern Statistical Methods. CRC Press, 2011. ISBN: 9781420079425.

[28] Paul-Christian Bürkner. "brms: An R package for Bayesian multilevel models using Stan". In: *Journal of statistical software* 80.1 (2017), pp. 1–28.

[29] Paul-Christian Bürkner, Jonah Gabry, and Aki Vehtari. "Approximate leave-future-out cross-validation for Bayesian time series models". In: *Journal of Statistical Computation and Simulation* 90.14 (2020), pp. 2499–2523.

[30] Tomás Capretto et al. "Bambi: a simple interface for fitting bayesian linear models in Python". In: *arXiv preprint arXiv:2012.10754* (2020).

[31] Colin J. Carlson. "embarcadero: Species distribution modelling with Bayesian additive regression trees in R". In: *Methods in Ecology and Evolution* 11.7 (2020), pp. 850–858.

[32] Bob Carpenter et al. "Stan: A probabilistic programming language". In: *Journal of statistical software* 76.1 (2017), pp. 1–32.

[33] Carlos M. Carvalho, Nicholas G. Polson, and James G. Scott. "The horseshoe estimator for sparse signals". In: *Biometrika* 97.2 (2010), pp. 465–480.

[34] Jianye Ching and Yi-Chu Chen. "Transitional Markov chain Monte Carlo method for Bayesian model updating, model class selection, and model averaging". In: *Journal of engineering mechanics* 133.7 (2007), pp. 816–832.

[35] Hugh A. Chipman, Edward I. George, and Robert E. McCulloch. "BART: Bayesian additive regression trees". In: *The Annals of Applied Statistics* 4.1 (2010), pp. 266–298.

[36] N. Chopin and O. Papaspiliopoulos. *An Introduction to Sequential Monte Carlo*. Springer Series in Statistics. Springer International Publishing, 2020. ISBN: 9783030478445.

[37] Matthew P.A. Clark and Brian D. Westerberg. "How random is the toss of a coin?" In: *Cmaj* 181.12 (2009), E306–E308.

[38] François-David Collin et al. "Bringing ABC inference to the machine learning realm: AbcRanger, an optimized random forests library for ABC". In: *JOBIM 2020*. Vol. 2020. 2020.

[39] Wikipedia contributors. *Conceptual model — Wikipedia, The Free Encyclopedia*. Page Version ID: 952394363. URL: https://en.wikipedia.org/w/index.php?title=Conceptual_model&oldid=952394363.

[40] T.M. Cover and J.A. Thomas. *Elements of Information Theory*. Wiley, 2012. ISBN: 9781118585771.

[41] D.R. COX. *Principles of statistical inference*. English. Cambridge University Press, 2006, p. 178. ISBN: 978-0521685672.

[42] Georges Darmois. "Sur les lois de probabilitéa estimation exhaustive". In: *CR Acad. Sci. Paris* 260.1265 (1935), p. 85.

[43] C. Davidson-Pilon. *Bayesian Methods for Hackers: Probabilistic Programming and Bayesian Inference*. Addison-Wesley Data & Analytics Series. Pearson Education, 2015. ISBN: 9780133902921.

[44] Pierre Del Moral, Arnaud Doucet, and Ajay Jasra. "Sequential monte carlo samplers". In: *Journal of the Royal Statistical Society: Series B (Statistical Methodology)* 68.3 (2006), pp. 411–436.

[45] David Deming. "Do extraordinary claims require extraordinary evidence?" In: *Philosophia* 44.4 (2016), pp. 1319–1331.

[46] Persi Diaconis. "Theories of Data Analysis: From Magical Thinking Through Classical Statistics". In: *Exploring Data Tables, Trends, and Shapes*. John Wiley & Sons, Ltd, 2006. Chap. 1, pp. 1–36. ISBN: 9781118150702.

[47] Joshua V. Dillon et al. "Tensorflow distributions". In: *arXiv preprint arXiv:1711.10604* (2017).

[48] Allen B. Downey. *Think Stats: Exploratory Data Analysis*. O'Reilly Media; 2014.

[49] Christopher C. Drovandi and Anthony N. Pettitt. "Likelihood-free Bayesian estimation of multivariate quantile distributions". In: *Computational Statistics & Data Analysis* 55.9 (2011), pp. 2541–2556.

[50] Simon Duane et al. "Hybrid monte carlo". In: *Physics letters B* 195.2 (1987), pp. 216–222.

[51] James Durbin and Siem Jan Koopman. *Time series analysis by state space methods*. Oxford university press, 2012.

[52] Ritabrata Dutta et al. "ABCpy: A user-friendly, extensible, and parallel library for approximate Bayesian computation". In: *Proceedings of the platform for advanced scientific computing conference*. 2017, pp. 1–9.

[53] J. Fox. *Applied Regression Analysis and Generalized Linear Models*. SAGE Publications, 2015. ISBN: 9781483321318.

[54] Jerome H. Friedman. "Greedy function approximation: a gradient boosting machine". In: *Annals of statistics* (2001), pp. 1189–1232.

[55] Nial Friel and Jason Wyse. "Estimating the evidence–a review". In: *Statistica Neerlandica* 66.3 (2012), pp. 288–308.

[56] Jonah Gabry and Ben Goodrich. *Estimating Generalized (Non-)Linear Models with Group-Specific Terms with rstanarm*. June 2020. URL: https://mc-stan.org/rstanarm/articles/glmer.html.

[57] Jonah Gabry et al. "Visualization in Bayesian workflow". In: *Journal of the Royal Statistical Society: Series A (Statistics in Society)* 182.2 (2019), pp. 389–402.

[58] A. Gelman, J. Hill, and A. Vehtari. *Regression and Other Stories*. Analytical Methods for Social Research. Cambridge University Press, 2020. ISBN: 9781107023987.

[59] A. Gelman et al. *Bayesian Data Analysis, Third Edition*. Chapman & Hall/CRC Texts in Statistical Science. Taylor & Francis, 2013. ISBN: 9781439840955.

[60] Andrew Gelman. "Analysis of variance—why it is more important than ever". In: *The annals of statistics* 33.1 (2005), pp. 1–53.

[61] Andrew Gelman. *The Folk Theorem of Statistical Computing*. https://statmodeling.stat.columbia.edu/2008/05/13/the_folk_theore/. May 2008.

[62] Andrew Gelman, Walter R Gilks, and Gareth O Roberts. "Weak convergence and optimal scaling of random walk Metropolis algorithms". In: *The annals of applied probability* 7.1 (1997), pp. 110–120.

[63] Andrew Gelman, Daniel Simpson, and Michael Betancourt. "The prior can often only be understood in the context of the likelihood". In: *Entropy* 19.10 (2017), p. 555.

[64] Andrew Gelman et al. "Bayesian workflow". In: *arXiv preprint arXiv:2011.01808* (2020).

[65] W.R. Gilks, S. Richardson, and D. Spiegelhalter. *Markov Chain Monte Carlo in Practice*. Chapman & Hall/CRC Interdisciplinary Statistics. CRC Press, 1995. ISBN: 9781482214970.

[66] Wally R. Gilks, Andrew Thomas, and David J Spiegelhalter. "A language and program for complex Bayesian modelling". In: *Journal of the Royal Statistical Society: Series D (The Statistician)* 43.1 (1994), pp. 169–177.

[67] Tilmann Gneiting and Adrian E Raftery. "Strictly proper scoring rules, prediction, and estimation". In: *Journal of the American statistical Association* 102.477 (2007), pp. 359–378.

[68] Alex Goldstein et al. "Peeking inside the black box: Visualizing statistical learning with plots of individual conditional expectation". In: *journal of Computational and Graphical Statistics* 24.1 (2015), pp. 44–65.

[69] Maria I. Gorinova, Andrew D. Gordon, and Charles Sutton. "Probabilistic programming with densities in SlicStan: efficient, flexible, and deterministic". In: *Proceedings of the ACM on Programming Languages* 3.POPL (2019), pp. 1–30.

[70] Maria Gorinova, Dave Moore, and Matthew Hoffman. "Automatic reparameterisation of probabilistic programs". In: *International Conference on Machine Learning*. PMLR. 2020, pp. 3648–3657.

[71] Kristen B. Gorman, Tony D. Williams, and William R. Fraser. "Ecological sexual dimorphism and environmental variability within a community of Antarctic penguins (genus Pygoscelis)". In: *PloS one* 9.3 (2014), e90081.

[72] Brian Greenhill, Michael D. Ward, and Audrey Sacks. "The separation plot: A new visual method for evaluating the fit of binary models". In: *American Journal of Political Science* 55.4 (2011), pp. 991–1002.

[73] Mohinder S. Grewal and Angus P. Andrews. *Kalman filtering: Theory and Practice with MATLAB*. John Wiley & Sons, 2014.

[74] Quentin F. Gronau et al. "A tutorial on bridge sampling". In: *Journal of mathematical psychology* 81 (2017), pp. 80–97.

[75] Frank E. Grubbs. "Procedures for detecting outlying observations in samples". In: *Technometrics* 11.1 (1969), pp. 1–21.

[76] Heikki Haario, Eero Saksman, and Johanna Tamminen. "An adaptive Metropolis algorithm". In: *Bernoulli* (2001), pp. 223–242.

[77] Andrew C. Harvey and Neil Shephard. "Structural time series models". In: *Handbook of Statistics,(edited by GS Maddala, CR Rao and HD Vinod)* 11 (1993), pp. 261–302.

[78] WK HASTINGS. "Monte Carlo sampling methods using Markov chains and their applications". In: *Biometrika* 57.1 (1970), pp. 97–109.

[79] Jennifer A. Hoeting et al. "Bayesian model averaging: a tutorial (with comments by M. Clyde, David Draper and EI George, and a rejoinder by the authors". In: *Statistical science* 14.4 (1999), pp. 382–417.

[80] Matthew D. Hoffman and Andrew Gelman. "The No-U-Turn Sampler: Adaptively Setting Path Lengths in Hamiltonian Monte Carlo". In: *Journal of Machine Learning Research* 15.47 (2014), pp. 1593–1623.

[81] Allison Marie Horst, Alison Presmanes Hill, and Kristen B Gorman. *palmerpenguins: Palmer Archipelago (Antarctica) penguin data*. R package version 0.1.0. 2020. DOI: 10.5281/zenodo.3960218. URL: https://allisonhorst.github.io/palmerpenguins/.

[82] Stephan Hoyer and Joe Hamman. "xarray: ND labeled arrays and datasets in Python". In: *Journal of Open Research Software* 5.1 (2017).

[83] Bai Jiang. "Approximate Bayesian computation with Kullback-Leibler divergence as data discrepancy". In: *International conference on artificial intelligence and statistics*. PMLR. 2018, pp. 1711–1721.

[84] Ohad Kammar, Sam Lindley, and Nicolas Oury. "Handlers in action". In: *ACM SIGPLAN Notices* 48.9 (2013), pp. 145–158.

[85] Emmanuel Klinger, Dennis Rickert, and Jan Hasenauer. "pyABC: distributed, likelihood-free inference". In: *Bioinformatics* 34.20 (2018), pp. 3591–3593.

[86] Max Kochurov et al. *PyMC4: Exploiting Coroutines for Implementing a Probabilistic Programming Framework*. Program Transformations for ML Workshop at NeurIPS. 2019. URL: https://openreview.net/forum?id=rkgzj5Za8H.

[87] Bernard Osgood Koopman. "On distributions admitting a sufficient statistic". In: *Transactions of the American Mathematical society* 39.3 (1936), pp. 399–409.

[88] J.K. Kruschke. *Doing Bayesian Data Analysis: A Tutorial with R, JAGS, and Stan*. Academic Press. Academic Press, 2015. ISBN: 9780124058880.

[89] John K. Kruschke. "Bayesian estimation supersedes the t test." In: *Journal of Experimental Psychology: General* 142.2 (2013), p. 573.

[90] Alp Kucukelbir et al. "Automatic differentiation variational inference". In: *The Journal of Machine Learning Research* 18.1 (2017), pp. 430–474.

[91] Ravin Kumar et al. "ArviZ a unified library for exploratory analysis of Bayesian models in Python". In: *Journal of Open Source Software* 4.33 (2019), p. 1143.

[92]   Daniel Lakens et al. "Justify your alpha". In: *Nature Human Behaviour* 2.3 (2018), pp. 168–171.

[93]   Balaji Lakshminarayanan, Daniel Roy, and Yee Whye Teh. "Particle Gibbs for Bayesian additive regression trees". In: *Artificial Intelligence and Statistics*. PMLR. 2015, pp. 553–561.

[94]   Junpeng Lao et al. "tfp.mcmc: Modern Markov chain Monte Carlo tools built for modern hardware". In: *arXiv preprint arXiv:2002.01184* (2020).

[95]   Nathan P. Lemoine. "Moving beyond noninformative priors: why and how to choose weakly informative priors in Bayesian analyses". In: *Oikos* 128.7 (2019), pp. 912–928.

[96]   Jarno Lintusaari et al. "Elfi: Engine for likelihood-free inference". In: *Journal of Machine Learning Research* 19.16 (2018), pp. 1–7.

[97]   Yi Liu, Veronika Ročková, and Yuexi Wang. "Variable selection with ABC Bayesian forests". In: *Journal of the Royal Statistical Society: Series B (Statistical Methodology)* (2019).

[98]   Jean-Michel Marin et al. "Approximate Bayesian computational methods". In: *Statistics and Computing* 22.6 (2012), pp. 1167–1180.

[99]   Gael M. Martin, David T. Frazier, and Christian P. Robert. "Computing Bayes: Bayesian computation from 1763 to the 21st century". In: *arXiv preprint arXiv:2004.06425* (2020).

[100]   O. Martin. *Bayesian Analysis with Python: Introduction to Statistical Modeling and Probabilistic Programming Using PyMC3 and ArviZ, 2nd Edition*. Packt Publishing, 2018. ISBN: 9781789341652.

[101]   R. McElreath. *Statistical Rethinking: A Bayesian Course with Examples in R and Stan*. Chapman & Hall/CRC Texts in Statistical Science. CRC Press, 2020. ISBN: 9781482253481.

[102]   Jan-Willem van de Meent et al. "An introduction to probabilistic programming". In: *arXiv preprint arXiv:1809.10756* (2018).

[103]   Nicholas Metropolis et al. "Equation of state calculations by fast computing machines". In: *The journal of chemical physics* 21.6 (1953), pp. 1087–1092.

[104]   C. Molnar. *Interpretable Machine Learning*. Lulu.com, 2020. ISBN: 9780244768522.

[105]   Christoph Molnar, Giuseppe Casalicchio, and Bernd Bischl. "Interpretable machine learning–a brief history, state-of-the-art and challenges". In: *Joint European Conference on Machine Learning and Knowledge Discovery in Databases*. Springer. 2020, pp. 417–431.

[106]   Dave Moore and Maria I Gorinova. "Effect handling for composable program transformations in edward2". In: *arXiv preprint arXiv:1811.06150* (2018).

[107]   JJA Moors. "A quantile alternative for kurtosis". In: *Journal of the Royal Statistical Society: Series D (The Statistician)* 37.1 (1988), pp. 25–32.

[108]   Christian A. Naesseth, Fredrik Lindsten, and Thomas B. Schön. "Elements of sequential monte carlo". In: *arXiv preprint arXiv:1903.04797* (2019).

[109]   Danielle Navarro. "A personal essay on Bayes factors". In: (2020).

[110]   Radford M. Neal. "Contribution to the discussion of "Approximate Bayesian inference with the weighted likelihood bootstrap" by Michael A. Newton and Adrian E. Raftery". In: *Journal of the Royal Statistical Society. Series B (Methodological)* 56 (1994), pp. 41–42.

[111] Radford M. Neal. "Slice sampling". In: *The annals of statistics* 31.3 (2003), pp. 705–767.

[112] S.P. Otto and T. Day. *A Biologist's Guide to Mathematical Modeling in Ecology and Evolution.* Princeton University Press, 2011. ISBN: 9781400840915.

[113] Topi Paananen et al. "Implicitly adaptive importance sampling". In: *Statistics and Computing* 31.2 (2021), pp. 1–19.

[114] George Papamakarios et al. "Normalizing flows for probabilistic modeling and inference". In: *arXiv preprint arXiv:1912.02762* (2019).

[115] Omiros Papaspiliopoulos, Gareth O. Roberts, and Martin Sköld. "A general framework for the parametrization of hierarchical models". In: *Statistical Science* (2007), pp. 59–73.

[116] Eric J. Pedersen et al. "Hierarchical generalized additive models in ecology: an introduction with mgcv". In: *PeerJ* 7 (2019), e6876.

[117] Fernando Pérez-Cruz. "Kullback-Leibler divergence estimation of continuous distributions". In: *2008 IEEE international symposium on information theory.* IEEE. 2008, pp. 1666–1670.

[118] Du Phan, Neeraj Pradhan, and Martin Jankowiak. "Composable effects for flexible and accelerated probabilistic programming in NumPyro". In: *arXiv preprint arXiv:1912.11554* (2019).

[119] Juho Piironen and Aki Vehtari. "On the hyperprior choice for the global shrinkage parameter in the horseshoe prior". In: *Artificial Intelligence and Statistics.* PMLR. 2017, pp. 905–913.

[120] Juho Piironen, Aki Vehtari, et al. "Sparsity information and regularization in the horseshoe and other shrinkage priors". In: *Electronic Journal of Statistics* 11.2 (2017), pp. 5018–5051.

[121] Jose Pinheiro et al. *nlme: Linear and Nonlinear Mixed Effects Models.* R package version 3.1-151. 2020. URL: https://CRAN.R-project.org/package=nlme.

[122] Dan Piponi, Dave Moore, and Joshua V Dillon. "Joint distributions for tensorflow probability". In: *arXiv preprint arXiv:2001.11819* (2020).

[123] Edwin James George Pitman. "Sufficient statistics and intrinsic accuracy". In: *Mathematical Proceedings of the cambridge Philosophical society.* Vol. 32. 4. Cambridge University Press. 1936, pp. 567–579.

[124] Christopher C.J. Potter and Robert H. Swendsen. "0.234: The myth of a universal acceptance ratio for Monte Carlo simulations". In: *Physics Procedia* 68 (2015), pp. 120–124.

[125] Catherine Potvin, Martin J. Lechowicz, and Serge Tardif. "The statistical analysis of ecophysiological response curves obtained from experiments involving repeated measures". In: *Ecology* 71.4 (1990), pp. 1389–1400.

[126] Dennis Prangle. "gk: An R package for the g-and-k and generalised g-and-h distributions". In: *arXiv preprint arXiv:1706.06889* (2017).

[127] Pierre Pudlo et al. "Reliable ABC model choice via random forests". In: *Bioinformatics* 32.6 (2016), pp. 859–866.

[128] Carl Edward Rasmussen and Christopher K.I. Williams. *Gaussian Processes for Machine Learning.* English. Cambridge, Mass: The MIT Press, 2005. ISBN: 978-0-262-18253-9.

[129]   Glen D. Rayner and Helen L. MacGillivray. "Numerical maximum likelihood estimation for the g-and-k and generalized g-and-h distributions". In: *Statistics and Computing* 12.1 (2002), pp. 57–75.

[130]   Gabriel Riutort-Mayol et al. "Practical Hilbert space approximate Bayesian Gaussian processes for probabilistic programming". In: *arXiv preprint arXiv:2004.11408* (2020).

[131]   Christian P. Robert et al. "Lack of confidence in approximate Bayesian computation model choice". In: *Proceedings of the National Academy of Sciences* 108.37 (2011), pp. 15112–15117.

[132]   Gareth O. Roberts and Jeffrey S. Rosenthal. "Examples of adaptive MCMC". In: *Journal of computational and graphical statistics* 18.2 (2009), pp. 349–367.

[133]   Gareth O. Roberts and Jeffrey S. Rosenthal. "Optimal scaling for various Metropolis-Hastings algorithms". In: *Statistical science* 16.4 (2001), pp. 351–367.

[134]   Veronika Ročková and Enakshi Saha. "On theory for BART". In: *The 22nd International Conference on Artificial Intelligence and Statistics*. PMLR. 2019, pp. 2839–2848.

[135]   Marshall N. Rosenbluth. "Genesis of the Monte Carlo algorithm for statistical mechanics". In: *AIP Conference Proceedings*. Vol. 690. 1. American Institute of Physics. 2003, pp. 22–30.

[136]   Daniel M. Roy and Yee Whye Teh. "The Mondrian process". In: *Proceedings of the 21st International Conference on Neural Information Processing Systems*. 2008, pp. 1377–1384.

[137]   Donald B. Rubin. "Estimation in parallel randomized experiments". In: *Journal of Educational Statistics* 6.4 (1981), pp. 377–401.

[138]   John Salvatier, Thomas V. Wiecki, and Christopher Fonnesbeck. "Probabilistic programming in Python using PyMC3". In: *PeerJ Computer Science* 2 (2016), e55.

[139]   S. Särkkä. *Bayesian Filtering and Smoothing*. Bayesian Filtering and Smoothing. Cambridge University Press, 2013. ISBN: 9781107030657.

[140]   Daniel J. Schad et al. "Workflow techniques for the robust use of bayes factors". In: *arXiv preprint arXiv:2103.08744* (2021).

[141]   Dino Sejdinovic et al. "Kernel adaptive metropolis-hastings". In: *International conference on machine learning*. PMLR. 2014, pp. 1665–1673.

[142]   Chris Sherlock. "Optimal scaling of the random walk Metropolis: general criteria for the 0.234 acceptance rule". In: *Journal of Applied Probability* 50.1 (2013), pp. 1–15.

[143]   R. Shumway and D. Stoffer. *Time Series: A Data Analysis Approach Using R*. Chapman & Hall/CRC Texts in Statistical Science. CRC Press, 2019. ISBN: 9781000001563.

[144]   S.A. Sisson, Y. Fan, and M. Beaumont. *Handbook of Approximate Bayesian Computation*. Chapman & Hall/CRC Handbooks of Modern Statistical Methods. CRC Press, 2018. ISBN: 9781439881514.

[145]   G. Strang. *Introduction to Linear Algebra*. Wellesley-Cambridge Press, 2009. ISBN: 9780980232714.

[146]   Mikael Sunnåker et al. "Approximate bayesian computation". In: *PLoS computational biology* 9.1 (2013), e1002803.

[147] Sean J. Taylor and Benjamin Letham. "Forecasting at scale". In: *The American Statistician* 72.1 (2018), pp. 37–45.

[148] David Tolpin et al. "Design and implementation of probabilistic programming language anglican". In: *Proceedings of the 28th Symposium on the Implementation and Application of Functional programming Languages.* 2016, pp. 1–12.

[149] Dustin Tran et al. "Simple, distributed, and accelerated probabilistic programming". In: *arXiv preprint arXiv:1811.02091* (2018).

[150] John W. Tukey. *Exploratory Data Analysis.* Addison-Wesley, 1977.

[151] John W. Tukey. "Modern Techniques in Data Analysis". In: *proceesings of the Sponsored Regional Research Conference.* SF-Sponsored Regional Research Conference. Southern Massachusetts University, North Dartmouth, 1977.

[152] Aki. Vehtari and Jonah. Gabry. *LOO glossary.* en. https://mc-stan.org/loo/reference/loo-glossary.html. (Visited on 05/20/2021).

[153] Aki Vehtari, Andrew Gelman, and Jonah Gabry. "Practical Bayesian model evaluation using leave-one-out cross-validation and WAIC". In: *Statistics and computing* 27.5 (2017), pp. 1413–1432.

[154] Aki Vehtari et al. "Pareto smoothed importance sampling". In: *arXiv preprint arXiv:1507.02646* (2021).

[155] Aki Vehtari et al. "Rank-Normalization, Folding, and Localization: An Improved $\widehat{R}$ for Assessing Convergence of MCMC". In: *Bayesian Analysis* (2021), pp. 1–38. DOI: 10.1214/20-BA1221. URL: https://doi.org/10.1214/20-BA1221.

[156] Sumio Watanabe and Manfred Opper. "Asymptotic equivalence of Bayes cross validation and widely applicable information criterion in singular learning theory." In: *Journal of machine learning research* 11.12 (2010).

[157] M. West and J. Harrison. *Bayesian Forecasting and Dynamic Models.* Springer Series in Statistics. Springer New York, 2013. ISBN: 9781475793659.

[158] P. Westfall and K.S.S. Henning. *Understanding Advanced Statistical Methods.* Chapman & Hall/CRC Texts in Statistical Science. Taylor & Francis, 2013. ISBN: 9781466512108.

[159] Peter H. Westfall. "Kurtosis as peakedness, 1905–2014. RIP". In: *The American Statistician* 68.3 (2014), pp. 191–195.

[160] Brandon T. Willard. "miniKanren as a Tool for Symbolic Computation in Python". In: *arXiv preprint arXiv:2005.11644* (2020).

[161] Frank Wood, Jan Willem Meent, and Vikash Mansinghka. "A new approach to probabilistic programming inference". In: *Artificial Intelligence and Statistics.* PMLR. 2014, pp. 1024–1032.

[162] S.N. Wood. *Generalized Additive Models: An Introduction with R, Second Edition.* Chapman & Hall/CRC Texts in Statistical Science. CRC Press, 2017. ISBN: 9781498728379.

[163] Yuling Yao et al. "Using stacking to average Bayesian predictive distributions (with discussion)". In: *Bayesian Analysis* 13.3 (2018), pp. 917–1007.

[164] Yuling Yao et al. "Yes, but did it work?: Evaluating variational inference". In: *International Conference on Machine Learning.* PMLR. 2018, pp. 5581–5590.

[165] Z.H. Zhou. *Ensemble Methods: Foundations and Algorithms.* Chapman & Hall/CRC data mining and knowledge discovery series. CRC Press, 2012. ISBN: 9781439830055.

Index

AIC, 60, 354
Approximate Bayesian Computation (ABC), 233
autocorrelation, 41
autoregressive model, 181

basis function, 146, 150, 178, 213
Bayes factor, 364
Bayes' theorem, 3, 4, 363
Bayesian Additive Regression Trees (BART), 213
Bayesian inference, 1, 3, 369
Bayesian modeling, 1
Bayesian models, 2
Bayesian p-value, 36, 240, 242
Bayesian t-test, 67
Bayesian workflow, 2, 32, 48, 67, 75, 173, 261, 262, 298
Beta distribution, 15, 336
Binomial distribution, 15, 331

central limit theorem, 346, 350, 367
classification, 92, 213, 221
condition number, 179
conditional distribution, 337
conditional probability, 326
conjugate priors, 15, 195, 217, 295, 297, 361
constant effect, 125
convergence diagnostics, 40, 240, 298
cross-validation, 53, 139, 207, 218, 229

decision trees, 213
design matrix, 152, 175
discrete Uniform distribution, 329
divergences, 48, 134, 135, 305

effective sample size (ESS), 41, 295, 350, 378
empirical probability, 327
entropy, 20, 350
epistemic, 325
expected log pointwise predictive density (ELPD), 52, 221, 356
expected value, 5, 67, 341, 345, 367
exploratory analysis of Bayesian models, 31

fixed effect, 125

g-and-k distribution, 243

Gaussian Random Walk, 187
generalized additive models, 179
generalized linear models, 90

Hamiltonian Monte Carlo (HMC), 372
hierarchical models, 126
highest density interval (HDI), 9
horseshoe prior, 208

improper prior, 19
individual conditional expectation plot (ICE), 225
information criterion, 354
interaction, 112, 215
irreducible, 349

Jeffreys' prior, 18, 358
joint distribution, 337

kernel density estimator (KDE), 10
knot, 148
Kullback-Leibler divergence, 353

likelihood function, 3
linear models, 67, 107
linear regression, 77
link function, 91, 148, 221
log odds, 98
logistic regression, 33, 91, 221
LOO, 53, 97, 139, 207, 221, 250, 275, 356, 364
LOO-PIT, 59, 275
loss functions, 277

marginal distribution, 48, 223, 337
marginal likelihood, 361
Markov chain Monte Carlo, 6, 40, 41, 43, 51, 293, 295, 298, 372, 378
Markov chains, 347
maximum entropy, 20
Metropolis-Hastings, 7, 370
mixed effects, 119
model averaging, 60
Monte Carlo standard error (MCSE), 43, 350
multilevel models, 119
multiple linear regression, 85

Neal's funnel, 131, 309, 375

nonlinear regression, 145, 213
non-parametric model, 213
Normal distribution, 335

objective prior, 18
outliers, 114
overfitting, 25, 52, 87, 146, 215, 354

p_loo, 54, 58, 275
Pareto shape parameter, 57, 164, 275
partial dependence plot (PDP), 223
partial pooling, 126
Poisson distribution, 331
polynomial regression, 145
pooling, 119
posterior distribution, 3, 14, 337
posterior predictive distribution, 6, 14, 35, 36, 52, 54, 59, 71, 75, 81, 83, 109, 139, 174, 180, 187, 240, 255, 273, 274, 281
prior distribution, 14
prior predictive distribution, 5, 14, 32, 74, 93, 173, 180, 240, 255, 269, 270, 317, 365
probabilistic programming languages, 10, 51, 67, 71–73, 293
probability, 324
probability density function, 333
probability distribution, 327
probability integral transform (PIT), 339
probability mass function, 329

quantile function, 243

$\hat{R}$, 43, 70
random effect, 125
random variable, 328, 332
rank plot, 46, 70, 72, 238, 241, 249, 271, 272
regularization, 23, 213
reparameterization, 18, 50, 131, 305
residuals, 169
reward functions, 277
robust regression, 114

separation plot, 97
Sequential Monte Carlo (SMC), 219, 235, 377
shrinkage, 23, 207, 213
splines, 145
stacking, 61, 157
state space model, 193
Student's t-distribution, 114, 335
sufficient statistics, 234
summary statistics, 238

the law of large numbers, 345
time series, 169
trace plots, 45, 201
transformation centering, 83

Uniform distribution, 334
universal inference engines, 6, 10, 131, 369

variable selection, 226
Variational inference, 378
varying effect, 125

WAIC, 60, 354, 364
weakly informative priors, 23